CONTENTS

INTRODUCTION

In the fall of 2006, our father, Arthur Schlesinger, Jr., approached us—his two oldest sons—about editing for publication his private journals. We were both surprised by his request, for he had never asked us to collaborate on any of his literary and historical projects before, and touched that he trusted us to review some of the most important recorded moments in his life. Certainly, we thought, he might have more ideally chosen an experienced historian or scholar for this work. And frankly, we wondered whether we, as his sons, could bring a useful independent sensibility to the editing process and judiciously appraise his journal entries in an appropriate manner. Apart from these initial misgivings, we had also never seen his diaries, had no idea what condition they were in, and possessed little sense of their contents.

Our father's agent, Andrew Wylie, had initially come upon our father's journals in an authorized inspection of his office one day earlier in 2006, when he found them all bunched together on a shelf above a small icebox. They amounted to more than 6,000 pages in entirety and comprised almost half a century of his activities, from 1952 to 2000. We first saw the journals in November 2006, in Mr. Wylie's office, where we found them piled on a number of large tables in dozens of file-folders, each containing a year's worth of his reminiscences in clean typewritten form. (It turns out that our father's intrepid secretary for years, Gretchen Stewart, had carefully transcribed them through the decades.) What we were seeing was a jewel box of memoirs.

After a quick look, we were riveted. A few perusals of the documents gave us fresh knowledge of our father's life that we had not been privy to before, as well as the pleasure of reading a superior diarist with a masterful style. His journals were full of rich, witty and revelatory observations about the famous events and larger-than-life personalities in American life for nearly five decades. We decided then and there to do the project.

From the start, our father's publisher, The Penguin Press, had made the decision to publish the journals in a one-volume, abridged edition for the occasion of what would be our father's ninetieth birthday, on October 15, 2007. This gave us approximately three months to reduce the 6,000 pages to a more manageable 1,000, thereby extracting only the most illuminating and widely heralded episodes our father described. We split the burden of editorial oversight, passing the thousands of pages back and forth between us in New York and Cambridge, together making the occasionally agonizing decisions over what to include and what to leave behind. Our two intrepid Penguin Press editors, Scott Moyers and his deputy, Laura Stickney, contributed further suggestions and emendations.

Though the notion of cutting three quarters of our father's extraordinary journals was daunting, the narrative magic of the book helped resolve many selection problems for us. We were ineluctably drawn to the unique series of transfixing, amusing, provocative, sardonic, moving and revealing encounters that he had with the foremost progressive (and occasionally conservative) figures of his time. It is not an exaggeration to say that his broad circle of friends—both men and women—

virtually dominated the political, social, artistic and literary landscape of the post–World War II era.

Our father's journals are not necessarily personal recountings of his lifetime pilgrimage, along the lines of, say, the diaries of Edmund Wilson. While he did write about his family and his two wives, his mind was always most keenly focused on the events of the day. This was likely due to his penchant as a historian for concentrating on what he considered the crucial details of his time—but surely, too, it was also due to his proper New England upbringing which frowned upon writing much about intimacy. In any case, we think it is fair to say that he was primarily trying in these journals to give recognition to the most notable happenings in his own American lifetime as he saw them—what a collection of stories, anecdotes and tales he was able to recount.

Of course, the journal entries always reflect his particular mood at the time he was writing. At any given hour, his voice might be full of indignation, pleasure, shock, fun, anger or happiness. This is the way of a diarist. Inevitably, the candor of some of these reflections may strike friends and acquaintances as indiscreet. For example, our father occasionally quotes intemperate or rash remarks made by his associates about others—remarks they may later regret. Also, he often changed his mind about his associates. That is unavoidable in such annals. Most important, in our father's mind, was always to be truthful to history and, for the most part, he was singularly balanced in his judgments.

It is astonishing to remember that our father wrote some thirteen books during the period of these recollections—even while logging these diaries, teaching at Harvard, helping out on political campaigns, engaging in topical debates, participating in the Kennedy Administration, serving as a university professor at the City University of New York, leading a crowded social life and meeting crushing obligations of every kind. Over the course of the years covered in these journals, he authored the following tomes: *The Crisis of the Old Order* (1957); *The Coming of the New Deal* (1958); *The Politics of Upheaval* (1960); *Kennedy or Nixon: Does It Make Any Difference?* (1960); *The Politics of Hope* (1963); *A Thousand*

Days (1965); *The Bitter Heritage* (1966); *The Crisis of Confidence* (1969); *The Imperial Presidency* (1973); *Robert Kennedy and His Times* (1978); *The Cycles of American History* (1986); *The Disuniting of America* (1991); and *A Life in the 20th Century* (2000).

His diaries offer a somewhat different sense of the rhythms of American life over this half century than his books. They provide a vibrant and almost panoramic view of his country through the voices of the giants he both admired and occasionally disdained. As the United States alternatively went off- and on-track through this turbulent period, our father's idée fixe was, from the start, to count the passage of time in America via the quadrennial Democratic presidential conventions which he almost always attended, lovingly commented upon, and sometimes personally influenced. For him, these conclaves marked the great moments of possible change in the country, but also signaled the time when everyday citizens had a chance to vent their feelings and take action in a democratic way. Of course, for him, these were also terrifically entertaining and exhilarating affairs.

Just as fascinating for our father, as these journals attest, were the political campaigns that followed the conventions. Like an anthropologist picking through the scattered debris of an ancient site, our father observed these races carefully and assessed their building blocks, their strategic imperatives and their often messy internal structures. He analyzed the strengths and weaknesses of the contestants. Beginning with his days on the stump with Adlai Stevenson, he frequently took part directly in these crusades, getting an adrenaline rush from campaign work—authoring speeches, advising on policies, advancing strategies, delivering addresses, winging around the country with the candidates. As a historian who had written about the presidencies of Andrew Jackson, Franklin Roosevelt and John Kennedy, he knew quite well the ins and outs of political warfare in America. But he learned something new and vital for his own scholarly uses from every new cause in which he participated or advised.

What these ventures also did was to introduce him to a remarkable lot of men and women who directly influenced his life: Adlai Stevenson;

Averell and Pamela Harriman; John Kenneth Galbraith; Hubert Humphrey; John, Robert and Edward Kennedy; Robert McNamara; Katherine Graham; George Kennan; Jackie Onassis; Ted Sorensen; Lyndon Johnson; George McGovern; Walter Mondale; Henry Kissinger; Bill and Hillary Clinton; and the list goes on. There were also foreign leaders and intellectuals he became acquainted with through these circles, ranging from Romulo Betancourt, one-time president of Venezuela, to German leader Willy Brandt, to former British prime ministers Edward Heath and Margaret Thatcher, to the philosopher Isaiah Berlin, and others. And there were the mesmerizing political writers of the period, such as Walter Lippmann, Joseph Alsop, Rowland Evans, James Wechsler, Richard Rovere—and their sundry brethren—whom he also got to know.

But his omnivorous interests drew him beyond the political battle lines into other arenas. His almost voluptuous eyes and soul led him to rove widely and far afield. He adored American movies and did film reviews for various publications. He became close friends with such vibrant movie personalities as Lauren Bacall, Rex Harrison, Angie Dickinson, Marlene Dietrich and Douglas Fairbanks Jr. He relished the theater, especially Broadway musicals. He spent many evenings with composers and lyricists like Leonard Bernstein, Alan Jay Lerner, and Betty Comden and Adolph Green. He became a cohort to a slew of writers across a wide spectrum of the literary scene, including the likes of Norman Mailer, Carlos Fuentes, William Styron, Edna O'Brien, Edwin O'Connor, Joan Didion, Edmund Wilson, Saul Bellow, Mary McCarthy, Lillian Hellman and Philip Roth—an endless parade of talented artisans. The importance of these friendships—and the way they so deeply enhanced his life—are all documented in these journals.

Our father died of a heart attack on February 28, 2007, while dining in a New York restaurant, just as we were finishing up our labors on his diaries. His death came as a shock to us, because, despite his infirmities—including the onset of Parkinson's disease, which had rendered his speech almost unintelligible—his mind remained as sharp as ever. He could still turn out an occasional wicked and penetrating op-ed piece when the spirit seized him. And he was very helpful to us when we consulted with him, from time to time, in the months before his death, on what he wanted to keep or excise from his accounts. However, there was astonishingly little he wished to take out. As he once said, "What the hell, you have to call them as you see them." Our consolation in the end was that he lived his life as he wanted to, to the fullest, until the very last moments—and that he gave us the treasure of these journals, reminding us once again how remarkable his time on earth really was.

—*Andrew Schlesinger and Stephen Schlesinger*

1952

✦

March 29
Washington

Joe Rauh offered me his ticket for the Jefferson-Jackson Day dinner. It turned out that George Ball had given his ticket to Libby Donahue; so I suggested we go together. I borrowed a black tie from Phil Graham and put on a white shirt, trusting that with a dark blue suit on I would look properly dressed in the half-light. Making our way to our table, we became entangled in one of the head table lines. In quick succession came the three nicest men in public life—Wilson Wyatt, Adlai Stevenson, Averell Harriman. Averell suggested that we go out for a drink afterward.

The speaking was indifferent. The Armory was too vast for people to feel much involvement in what was going on. [Sam] Rayburn gave a speech with a nice human quality. [Alben] Barkley was loud and vigorous.

The meeting warmed up a bit when President [Truman] began. It was a good, fighting campaign speech, I thought; nothing new, but lively, and delivered with humor and composure. Libby, bored, whispered to me toward the end, "This is the most utterly meaningless speech I have ever heard." At that moment, the President announced that he would not be a candidate for reelection, would not seek the nomination. The audience was stunned and confused. Some people reacted automatically by applause (as Adlai said in the car later, "They applauded with really macabre enthusiasm"); others shouted "No." I found myself shouting "No" with vigor; then I wondered why the hell I was shouting "No," since this is what I had been hoping would happen for months. Still the shouts of "No" seemed the least due to the President for a noble and courageous renunciation. He hurriedly finished the speech and disappeared, leaving the audience still stunned. Half the people did not seem to know what had happened.

We went out to meet Averell. He said that he had asked Adlai to accompany us. Adlai, in the meantime, was surrounded by a screaming mob of newspapermen, photographers, radio people, etc. This went on for 15 or 20 minutes. Finally we pulled him out and got into Averell's car. Adlai told me that he was completely astonished by the President's decision.

The bar [at the Metropolitan Club] was closed; but we went upstairs to talk. Adlai, looking very tired, tending to bury his head in his hands, was obviously appalled at the great abyss opening up before him. He kept saying that he didn't want to be a candidate. Running against Taft was one thing; but he wasn't certain that Eisenhower would ruin the country. Averell at this point became very eloquent. Eisenhower's nomination, he said, would eliminate foreign policy as an issue, but this would make domestic policy all the more important. Averell went on to say how much a successful foreign policy depended on a successful domestic policy, and how unreliable an Eisenhower administration would be. Adlai simply groaned. Finally Averell said, "For the sake of the party and of the nation, Adlai, you've just got to run. There isn't anybody else." Adlai groaned, looked as if he were going to cry, put his head in his hands, and finally said, half humorously, half agonizedly, "This will probably shock you all; but at the moment I don't give a god damn what happens to the party or to the country." Averell, who was not shocked, correctly ascribed these sentiments to fatigue, confusion, an impending cold; and we shortly afterward dispersed.

July 21 [Chicago Democratic convention]

We heard Adlai's enormously effective speech of welcome to the convention (really a speech of keynote, nomination and acceptance rolled into one) and Paul Douglas's noble if heavy speech on the Korean War. Adlai's speech even made a dent on the strongly anti-Adlai atmosphere of the Harriman headquarters.

July 22

This morning at 7:45 I was awakened by a phone call from Averell. "Have you had a chance to see that fellow yet?" I said no. Averell said that he wanted to give me the picture—in general that he was convinced that he (Averell) had "great underlying strength," that "if Adlai were still a liberal," he should join with the other liberal forces to support Averell, and that there was real danger, in case of a deadlock, of "the Boss's" deciding to run; "that's what a lot of people have been working for." Jim Loeb and FDR Jr. had tried to see Adlai, but he would not see them. "You're the only contact I have." The conversation went on for about ten minutes. Averell seemed calm, resolute, hopeful, not too bitter at Adlai.

At 3:15 I finally made contact with Adlai and talked for about half an hour. It was a long, meandering conversation, revolving around the following points.

1. He kept wondering whether he should make a Sherman statement [a categorical rejection of candidacy as made by William Tecumseh Sherman]. FDR Jr. had apparently suggested it. Adlai's reactions were that it would help [Estes] Kefauver more than it would Harriman; and that it would terminate his own political career. After all, Sherman was 68 years old when he issued the

statement, and he did not have much of a political future. "I do hope to continue to be able to do things for my state and party."

2. He said he had instructed his alternate to vote for Averell; but the reports that came to him of Averell's political strength were very discouraging. If Averell were nominated, he said, the party would take a terrible beating. Kefauver would do better. He felt that Averell had been misinformed about his political strength.

3. He sounded a bit resentful of the reports of Averell's irritation with him. "I've done everything I could for Averell," he said, then added, "short of coming out for him."

4. He sketched very clearly his own design as to how he hoped things would work out. He did not want the nomination, he said, and, if he had to take it, he hoped it would come only because the available candidates all recognized that none of them could win. Having mutually exhausted each other, he hoped they would all come to him and ask him to run. Instead, he said, it now looked as if he might get the nomination with the ill-will and abuse of the other candidates. I said that he must understand that the irritation on the part of the other candidates was only natural, but that it need not harden into a permanent grudge, and that I hoped he would call Averell as soon as the nomination looked certain.

5. He seemed very much opposed to doing anything which might drive the South out of the party. Averell, he said, was a "disunity" candidate; the party needed a "unity" candidate against Eisenhower. The southern governors had told him at Houston that Harriman was as bad as Truman; that if they had to have this kind of president, they would rather have the real thing. It is clear that on this issue Adlai belongs with those who see no great moral point involved in pushing the South around on these issues.

My overall impression was that Adlai would reluctantly run.

July 23

Averell came in dog-tired from talks with delegates, etc, and I had a tête-à-tête dinner with him. He seemed, on the whole, to be in excellent condition, if weary, though his prospects by this time had come to seem fairly hopeless. At one point, I said, "Win or lose, you have done a fine job, and it was all worth the effort." "Don't say, 'win or lose' " he said, "I am not deceiving myself about my chances. I know they are small. But I think there is enough chance to justify my carrying on the fight."

July 24

While waiting in the Harriman dug-out, we saw Kefauver give an effective TV interview, protesting the boss-ridden convention, denouncing the phony draft of Adlai Stevenson, and calling on all his listeners to deluge their delegates in Chicago with wires and phone calls telling them to vote for Kefauver. He seemed to have the smell of victory in his nostrils. This confirmed my feeling that there was no hope in the Kefauver discussions, and it accelerated my growing and now urgent conviction that Harriman should have a meeting with Stevenson.

Averell listened, then asked John Carroll and John Kenney their opinions. As we discussed it, Hubert Humphrey arrived for a general strategy discussion. This proceeded for a few minutes when Averell beckoned me out of the room, and asked me to set up an appointment with Adlai as quickly as possible.

July 25

I hurriedly showered and shaved and, with no time for breakfast, jumped into a cab and went out to 1448 North Lake Shore Drive and to an apartment on the 17th floor, currently occupied by the Iveses, Adlai's sister and brother-in-law. Averell and John Kenney were there.

[Adlai] seemed calm, cheerful and business-like.

Adlai declared that he definitely did not countenance any of the pressure moves on his behalf. He had not sought the nomination; he did not want it; if he had to take it, he wanted only a genuine draft. Yet he had no doubt that Arvey's people, after assuring him they would not do anything to advance his cause, went out and employed all kinds of pressures. As he talked, he made it clear that he had little use for Arvey, and that he was eager to do what could be done to improve his relations with the liberals.

There was some discussion of the vice presidency. Adlai mentioned the names of Kefauver, [John] Sparkman, Mike Monroney and Barkley. The Vice President, he said, had to be thought of from two angles; first, how useful he would be before the election—how much strength he would bring to the ticket; and then how useful he would be after the election—how effectively he would serve the President as liaison with Congress. Adlai thought that Kefauver would add the most immediate strength but might be a pain-in-the-neck after election ("I don't know why it is," Adlai said; "Kefauver has never done anything to me, yet somehow I just instinctively don't like that fellow"). Sparkman and Monroney, he thought, would be excellent vice presidents but would create political problems. Toward the end, I threw in the name of FDR Jr. Adlai's reaction was interested, though somewhat fearful about southern reactions. (It later occurred to me that a Stevenson-Roosevelt ticket would be impossible, since both ends of the ticket would be divorced men.)

I think our one mistake in the conversation was not to lay more emphasis on the [adverse] consequences of a southerner on the second spot in the ticket. We did not do so because all of us more or less agreed that Sparkman was the best person among those whose names were being considered. Adlai kept showing special solicitude for the southern situation, he said more than once that he understood that Texas, Virginia, South Carolina and Florida might flop over into the Republican camp, and that it was important to win them back. When I pointed out that their total electoral votes were equal to a couple of northern industrial states, the point seemed to register intellectually rather than emotionally.

Stevenson was clearly much worried (as well he might be) over his relationship with Truman, whom I think he regards as a kind of Old Man of the Sea, clinging to his shoulders while he tried to run a campaign of his own. He repeated several times his desire to dissociate himself from Truman and his administration until Averell finally pointed out that Truman was a very popular man who would be an invaluable asset in the campaign.

The [meeting] was conducted on the assumption of Stevenson's nomination. Averell said about his own position substantially that he had not given up, that if he had been able to arrange the right kind of deal with Kefauver he would certainly have done so, that he had no immediate intention of withdrawal, but that he preferred Adlai to any other candidate next to himself and would, if necessary, use his strength to support Adlai against Barkley or Kefauver.

We left the apartment, ran a barrage of reporters and cameramen and went straight down to the Amphitheatre, arriving shortly after noon as the polling [for the presidential nomination was] about to commence. I spent the afternoon, alternating between the convention, the corridors and the Harriman dug-out, while the vote droned on. The completion of the first ballot showed Kefauver in a slight lead. As the second ballet went on, Stevenson seemed to be gaining some, but so did Kefauver; and there was considerable apprehension expressed over whether things were proceeding according to schedule.

Marian [Cannon, Arthur M. Schlesinger, Jr.'s first wife] and I had dinner at the Stockyards Inn with the Alsops, Suzanne Roosevelt, Prich [Edward F. Prichard, Jr.], Joe Rauh and the Claiborne Pells. After dinner we returned to the Amphitheatre for the last act. Averell [had now withdrawn], followed by [Governor] Paul Dever's declaration for Stevenson, [making] it clear enough how things were going.

[Stevenson's] nomination brought great cheers and excitement. Unfortunately it was followed by what seemed hours of singing before the President made his appearance. The crowd went wild when Harry finally came in—the brisk, relaxed, jaunty little man. His speech, unhappily, was tired and cliché-ridden, and delivered without his usual verve. But he—and we—got through it; and then he introduced Adlai.

The Stevenson speech was an extraordinary performance—a brilliant literary document, complex and carefully wrought in its composition, bearing the imprint of a highly individual, complicated, sensitive and distinguished personality. It had too much business in it about how he had not wanted the job and was not up to it; but it also had wonderful passages of political polemic; and it was suffused throughout with a sense of the immensity and impenetrability of the crisis of our time. He delivered the speech with great polish and dignity. The crowd listened with fervent attention, applauded frequently and gave him a great ovation at the end. I found myself both impressed and troubled by the speech. It was like watching an acrobat accomplishing dazzling and dangerous leaps on the high wires; he always made the next ring, but each new try was nerve-wracking. I also could not help thinking about Jim Rowe's remark that he was planning a book about the Stevenson administration to be called "Hamlet in the White House." But, whatever else Stevenson is, he is an original personality in our public life; he is the start of something new.

July 26

I was awakened around 9:15 by a call from Averell who was trying to get in touch with Adlai. I gave him various phone numbers and street addresses; and he invited us over to breakfast. We got there about 10. Averell was in good, urbane, cheerful form. He had some of the same misgivings about the speech that I had—and also about the whole shape of Adlai's campaign. The only hope of winning in November, he said, was to go to the people and fight on the issues of the New Deal and Fair Deal; he knew it because he had spoken all around the country in the last two months, and these were the issues to which people responded. Averell fears that Adlai will attempt the kind of campaign that Walter Lippmann talks about in his column. If he does, he will lose; if the people want an Eisenhower, they will take the real thing.

August 8

On Monday, July 28, Harriman called to say that he had talked to Stevenson about my working on the compaign, and that Stevenson wanted to know how to get hold of me. On Tuesday Adlai called, and I said that I would stop at Springfield before leaving the Middle West. On Wednesday, Marian, the children and I got into the car and started driving, going along the beautiful gorge of the Mississippi, cutting across Iowa (Dubuque to Davenport) and arriving at Springfield Thursday evening. I spent all day Friday and half of Saturday there, leaving for Cambridge Saturday afternoon.

Adlai seemed in good shape, though a trifle overwhelmed by the multiplicity of problems suddenly descending on him. He looked well, was relaxed, made wry jokes, seemed reasonably belligerent, regarded the fact that he is not much known through the country as his main handicap and seemed determined to remedy this as quickly as possible.

The headquarters seemed suffused with a fear of "identification"— "identification" with the Truman administration, with labor, with ADA, with the liberals—indeed, with almost any group apparently except the South. There seemed to me an unreasonable concern with smoothing ruffled southern feelings—a tendency to bear with and explain away southern contrariness, while becoming quickly impatient with labor and the liberals.

Marian and the kids arrived in mid-afternoon. On the way to the garden I walked past the Governor's office window holding the hands of Chrissie and Andy. Adlai, who was conferring with [Paul] Douglas, waved at us; then apparently told his secretary to tell the housekeeper that he wanted us all for dinner. So we all dined in the garden that night—Mrs. Ives, the kids and I at one table; Adlai and Marian at the other. Stephen and Kathy were wordless with excitement. When they came to say good-bye, we were in Adlai's office. He took Kathy and Stephen over to a facsimile of Lincoln's autograph [and an] autobiography and read them the portions dealing with his schooling. It could not have been nicer.

My general reaction on leaving Springfield was that Adlai was probably even more conservative than I had thought, perhaps, indeed, at this stage, the most conservative Democratic candidate since John W. Davis. His campaign seems currently oriented toward two groups:

1) The high-minded Republicans, who provided the margin of victory in Illinois and who—the Stevenson people seem to think—can be won away in quantity from Ike; and,
2) The southerners, for whom solicitude is fairly constant. For both these groups one can emphasize the issues of foreign policy and, to some degree, of civil liberties. But economic and social reform clearly must be muted.

The logic of this campaign is thus to softpedal the issues which really appeal to labor, the liberals and the minorities. To gain the South, in short, and a few dissident Republicans, there is a great risk of losing the industrial North. The assumption, of course, is that labor and the Negroes will have no other place to go. But they can always stay home—and they well may.

I left Springfield thinking that I would be lucky if I could get the candidate to mention the New Deal in the course of his campaign. Yet, on reflection, I probably overstated the gravity of the problem. Adlai Stevenson still seems to me a man who will rise to the necessities of any crisis. He is the one man in politics today who strikes an authentically new and fresh note. Eisenhower utters the clichés of the right, Harriman the clichés of the left (with which I agree, but which are clichés nonetheless); all the other candidates are equally uninteresting and sterile. Stevenson promises the possibility of adjourning the tired old debates, moving beyond them and ushering us into the post-Roosevelt era, toward which we are groping.

August 11
[Springfield, Illinois]

In the morning Carl McGowan and I had a session with Adlai on the speech schedule. This included some discussion about the Labor Day address in Detroit. He wants to say that labor has duties as well as privileges, etc., and he wants to warn labor against trying to take over the Democratic party.

There is a kind of Calvinism in Adlai. He has a natural and honorable dislike of the kind of speech which seeks to buy votes by making promises. But he recoils from this with a political puritanism which regards any popular political position (at least on the liberal side) as somehow immoral. He flinches from civil rights *because* it will be construed as a bid for Negro votes. Thus his whole desire is to lecture the veterans at the American Legion, to lecture the workers in Detroit, etc. When I noted this, he said, "Well, I would rather lecture them than try to win their votes by promising them material benefits."

As I say, this is an honorable position. But it would be more honorable if he were as austere in his attitude toward special interests on the right as he is toward special interests on the left.

I spent most of the day working on Adlai's Thursday speech. I had dinner with Scotty Reston. We spent two or three hours trying to sort out the varied and perplexing reactions to Adlai. Scotty thinks that Adlai and Ike are not unlike in some respects—both are good but not great men. He will vote for Ike in order to spare the country four more years of Yalta, Hiss, McCarthy, etc. (This position distresses me far less than it would have a few weeks ago. If we are going to have a Republican President it might as well be on the Republican ticket.)

August 12
[In Springfield, Illinois, the speech-writing team convened.]

My heart sank as the discussion proceeded; even Wilson [Wyatt] seemed to be endorsing awfully conservative positions. I finally decided that the purposes of this campaign were so remote from my beliefs that I had better confine myself to a technical role in the campaign and stay out of policy discussions. So I kept quiet for a time until finally we began to consider the question of the dangers of centralization and the revitalization of local government. This roused my Hamiltonian instincts, and I launched into an eloquent defense of the role of a purposeful central government in promoting our national life. Somewhat to my surprise, Clayton [Fritchey] vigorously supported me. We finally got the others (Wilson coming around first) to agree that there should be no implication that the revitalization of state and local government would materially reduce the size, cost or power of the present federal government. This would make it clear that the statement would not contribute to the vulgar clamor against the allegedly swollen and power-hungry bureaucracy.

I am not sure that I am right in my differences with Stevenson. It may be that this line is the future, and that I am an increasingly obsolescent New Dealer. But I cannot escape the conclusion that his conception of a responsible and sober business community is likely to stand up less well than the New Deal picture of a confused, selfish and irresponsible business community.

September 4

Yesterday morning I flew with the Governor's party to Denver and thence to Los Angeles. The stopover at Denver was long enough to permit me to drive into town in one of the lesser cars in the motorcade. The crowds were practically non-existent. Nonetheless, I must confess that I get a great kick out of the political spectacle—the review of speeches in the plane, the arrival, the newspapermen, the local dignitaries and so on—all great fun.

The trip was uneventful until the Governor came on Scotty Reston's story in the Wednesday *New York Times* supplying detailed information about the speech-writing group. This made him quite mad for a few minutes.

I think he feels really very sensitive to any suggestion that he does not write his own speeches. He spent most of the trip reworking the main Denver draft. As Carl and I made suggestions for certain cuts, the Governor protested plaintively about how his own best phrases were always cut out. Actually, of course, most of the speech was his.

September 10
[San Francisco to Los Angeles train trip]

I got up at 6:15 today, breakfasted with Ben Heineman, and went to the station along with Ben, Dick Rovere and Scotty Reston. This began a day of whistle-stopping large crowds, sunshine, corny pontifical introductions, wisecracks and seriousness from Adlai, the introduction of Borden [Stevenson] and John Fell to the audiences, and so on. I greatly enjoyed it—and so did the Governor, I think, though it wore him down a bit, and he affected a new horror at each new stop. I was particularly delighted by his proposal for a deal with the Republicans—"if they stop telling lies about us, we will stop telling the truth about them." He told me that he had used it in 1948—but that he had heard it years before, and that it was an old gag in Illinois. New to me!

September 12
[Springfield, Illinois]

The Governor asked me to come to the Executive Mansion for dinner. Very pleasant. The Wyatts, Bill Blair, and the boys. After dinner, we immediately got down to business about the next trip. Carl, Dave Bell, Ken Galbraith, Jack Fischer and Sid Hyman joined us.

The Governor first read a very friendly letter from the President of September 10th. Truman said, among other things, that this was becoming "one of the dirtiest campaigns I have ever been in" but told the Governor that he should not mind. The letter was addressed by the way, "Dear Governor."

Adlai then described his conception of the political problem. The liberal and the progressive record, he said, had been made on the western trip, now is the time to get back to the middle of the road. "We haven't said a damn thing about cost of government, efficiency, economy, anti-socialism, anti–concentration of power in Washington. The impression is that we are moving more and more to the left, that I am becoming the captive of the special interest groups [*sic*—interesting revelation of where he thinks the special interest groups lie]. Now I want some good hard licks on the conservative side, fiscal responsibility against waste and extravagance. I don't want to be euchered out of that position. We mustn't let them preempt the position of fiscal responsibility."

These themes were repeated and developed at length. The thing he most wants to talk about, he says, is government economy, though he conceded that cost of living (inflation) should probably have priority.

September 18
[Springfield, Illinois]

I lunched with Wilson Wyatt today. He was in a fairly gloomy state. This morning he had gone to the airport to see the Governor off. Along the way he suggested some course of action to him. The Governor demurred, saying, "You know I didn't want this job. I didn't want to be nominated." This is in part, of course, a manner of speaking for the Governor. Yet every once in a while he acts as if he were doing his entourage and even the country a favor by running.

In the evening Wilson held a strategy meeting. We were all pretty gloomy—a gloom accentuated by Wilson's reading of secret and rather depressing figures from Elmo Roper. These figures show, by the way, that the Governor's best chance is to turn left. We were all impressed by Averell Harriman's analysis—that the thinking minority had been convinced, but that we had made very little inroad on the unthinking majority. The Governor has persuaded people; he has not excited them.

October 12

Last Tuesday (the 7th) we left for Michigan. Our first stop was Saginaw, a city apparently populated largely by juvenile delinquents. All the way into town, little monsters chanted "I like Ike." The schools had been let out—a hideous error—and the hall where the speech was given was crowded with children. They set up an "I like Ike" howl when Adlai first entered and continued it at intervals throughout the speech. Scotty Reston said that it was the most ill-mannered crowd that he had ever seen.

The Governor was annoyed by all this, but concealed it pretty well on the platform. When he got back to the plane, he said gloomily, "Shaw was right, 'Youth is too wonderful a thing to waste on children.'"

October 16

On Tuesday the Governor left for his last western trip. The reports from the trip increased our optimism. We are developing a technique of alternating high spiritual speeches (Salt Lake City, Los Angeles fireside) with rousing political speeches (San Francisco, Los Angeles rally); and the result is pretty effective. The Governor himself is still reluctant to be a demagogue—still reluctant to make broad and easy promises, or to flay the foe too hard—but he is coming along. Probably his own sense of timing on these matters is far better than ours anyway.

October 24
[The final campaign train trip]

I did not arise for the Niagara Falls whistle-stop at 7:15. But I did get up in time to hear the Rochester speech at 9:30—the one I had written desperately from midnight to 2:30 the night before. We had discovered at the last minute that the 24th was United Nations Day; we also wanted to meet more directly the increasingly vehement Republican exploitation of the Korean issue; so on the basis of material sent along by Dr. Frank Graham, I composed a sharp speech on the UN and Korea. It proved a great success—so much so that the newspapermen immediately demanded texts and made it their lead for the day.

October 25

I got up in time for the Hyde Park [New York] stop at 8 A.M. It was a beautiful, brilliantly sunny fall day, brisk and bracing. I have never seen the Hudson look so blue. The train stopped at the Hyde Park station, where Mrs. Roosevelt, Franklin and Sue [Roosevelt] and the Morgenthaus met us—also Dick and Eleanor Rovere. The Governor went off to Val-Kill for breakfast, while the Roveres took Carl and Jody McGowan and me to see the Library and the house. We finally found Herman Kahn who gave us an excellent swift tour.

Then to Poughkeepsie, where the Governor spoke from the balcony of the Nelson House to a disappointingly small and apathetic crowd. I had written a speech in which I tried to define his relationship to FDR and the New Deal. He had not made many changes in it, and it did represent an attempt to set forth a little of the Stevenson philosophy. It had read pretty well to me the night before; but it was certainly a flop in the morning. The Poughkeepsie audience evidently did not give a damn about Roosevelt. This was one of the few disappointing receptions we had on the trip.

Thence to Massachusetts. The first stop was Pittsfield, where Paul Dever, Jack Kennedy and a collection of Massachusetts politicians, volunteers, etc., all got on. We got to Boston about six. Marian, Kathy, Stephen and mother met me. I had not seen the kids since Labor Day, and they were a welcome sight. I promptly went home. Later we dined at Locke-Ober with Joe Alsop, Jack Kennedy, one of his pretty sisters, John Miller (London *Times*) and two or three other people.

October 28
[Stopover in New York City]

I spent all Tuesday working away at the [Biltmore] hotel, while Marian went motercading into New Jersey. The big problem was the Madison Square Garden speech. This speech raised a tough and typical question: should it be beamed to the local audience, which wanted a fighting rally speech? or to the great television audience, which would presumably want something more serious and statesmanlike? On the basis of a draft by Jimmy Wechsler, I had written a very good pour-it-on speech. Bill Wirtz had written a more serious and substantial speech.

After considerable discussion, it was decided to combine the Wechsler-Schlesinger and Wirtz drafts, striking on the whole a thoughtful rather than a pour-it-on note.

Marian and I dined at Marietta Tree's, where we got into more or less violent arguments with the Alsop brothers over their now announced decision to vote for Eisenhower. I bet Stewart $25 that Stevenson would be elected. After dinner we went over to the Garden. We arrived by 9 o'clock; Adlai was not to go on until 10:30, but the Garden was already hopelessly crowded, and it was impossible even to get near it. All our elaborate badges and passes seemed to avail us not, until one of the cops recognized David Niven, who was one of our party, and we were waved on in.

I have never seen a more exciting rally atmosphere than Madison Square Garden that night. The crowd was tense, excited, hushed with expectancy. A number of speakers were warming it up. Harriman, for example, gave an excellent short speech and got a tremendous rising ovation.

The Garden was crawling with Hollywood and Broadway talent. (Lauren Bacall hailed me excitedly at one point and beckoned me over. I went. She said, her voice quivering with feeling, "Arthur, did you read Walter Lippmann's column this morning?") An act presenting the Republican platform in terms of doubletalk was particularly successful. At 10:30 the Governor came on. The excitement was by now overwhelming, and the ovation tremendous. The speech itself was unfortunately something of a flop so far as the immediate audience was concerned.

Afterward we went back to the Trees' for a good and long party. Marie Harriman raked Joe Alsop fore-and-aft for his apostasy. Averell seemed cheerful; Wilson Wyatt was in good form; so too were the Sherwoods; Marietta, lovely as ever; etc.

November 1
[Final stop in Chicago]

We stayed at the Conrad Hilton in Chicago. I went in to see the Governor before the speech to say good-bye; he was going on to Springfield that night, and I was returning to Cambridge the next day to vote. He was in a good mood, just out of the shower, clad only in shorts, filled with a wry but definite confidence. "Of course, I'm going to win," he said, "I knew it all the time. That is why I was reluctant to run. . . . I figure that I will get about 366 votes. I don't see how I can lose." (I should add parenthetically that Carl and Wilson were equally confident. I guessed 325 for the pool. The only man to seem really gloomy about things had been [Jake] Arvey when we left Chicago on the 21st.)

The Governor chatted on. "But I have been giving some thought," he said, "to what I should say if I happen to lose. I thought that I would use the old story Abraham Lincoln used to tell—the one about the boy who stubbed his toe in the dark, who said that he was too old to cry but he couldn't laugh because it hurt too much."

I assured him he would not have to tell the story.

The Chicago speech was a fantastic success. The Governor even finished on time. The whole atmosphere was electric with confidence. Lauren Bacall and Humphrey Bogart gave me a lift into town. We all went to a party given by Oscar Chapman at the Palmer House. (What a beautiful—and delightful—girl Lauren Bacall is!—even more attractive in the flesh than on the screen.)

November 3

I took the plane back to Cambridge [on Sunday]. I was still completely certain that we would win. I ran into Max Lerner when I changed planes in New York. He seemed unhappy and apprehensive—the first voice of pessimism I had encountered since Jake Arvey. When I got back to Cambridge that night, Marian was very worried about Massachusetts. Conversation the next day with several people persuaded me that we would probably lose Massachusetts. But I still considered this only a local phenomenon—McCarthyism, the Irish Catholic defection, etc.

Monday night, McCarthy erupted again. Then the Democrats had their concluding half hour, ending up with a rather sad little speech by Stevenson, cut off, as usual, before he had reached the climax. This was followed by an hour of unparalleled vulgarity and cynicism on behalf of Eisenhower and Nixon.

November 5

Tuesday night was sad. I knew as soon as I heard the results from Connecticut (about 8 P.M.) that we had lost. I received a flurry of phone calls in the course of the evening—from Tufts in Springfield, from Chet Kerr in New Haven, from Kay Graham and Evangeline Bruce in Washington, from Bill Wirtz and Ben Heineman in Springfield. Melancholy settled more heavily on all of us as the evening moved on. After [Paul] Fitzpatrick conceded New York and [Jake] Arvey Illinois, it was only a question of time before the Governor would speak.

November 26

Just a few words in conclusion. I suspect that I have given a more jaundiced picture of Stevenson than I actually feel. That is partly because at the beginning, one tends to overestimate Stevenson's articulateness and see it as expression rather than as ejaculation. He verbalizes all the time and, like FDR, for a variety of reasons. The important thing should be, not what he says, but what he does. Every time things came to an issue of policy, he made the correct decision.

Also I now believe that on a number of things he was right and I was wrong. For example, I came very much to overestimate (as did Carl and Wilson also) the power of the prosperity/depression issue. It seems clear now that this issue appealed only to those who had personal memories of the Great Depression—which meant, on the whole, people in their forties and older. This issue meant very little to younger people, for whom Social Security and collective bargaining and economic opportunity were as secure and unalterable parts of the landscape as the trees and bushes. Adlai was right in saying that we should not run against Hoover. We were wrong in insisting that he should—at least, to the extent that we relied on it. One consequence was to weaken our appeal to the young.

Still, one consolation about being beaten 56 to 0 is that there is no point in wondering whether you would have done better if you had had a different left tackle—or a different quarterback. We made mistakes, all right, but none of them would have altered the outcome if done differently.

What we confronted this time was an upsurge of natural forces. Our number was up—and very little we could have done would have altered the outcome. But we did lay down a clear record. And the Governor did establish himself as a great national leader—gallant and honorable and dedicated. In retrospect, he seems to me more than ever the voice of the liberal future—the one creative hope in our politics. I shall always be proud to have served him in this campaign.

December 29

I saw the President today at 9:45. As I went in, I marvelled once again at the ease and informality of the American system. Dave Lloyd took me across the street from his office at Old State, past a couple of doors, and there I was in the outer office; then, two seconds later, I was in with the President.

Harry S. Truman was very cheerful, scrubbed and natty. He talked most of the time in a generally philosophical mood about the beating he had been taking from the press and about his confidence that history would vindicate him and his administration. When I came in, he quoted a set of figures on the national income, gross national product, employment, etc., and said, "Well, this is the ruined and collapsing state in which I am leaving the country."

He was much concerned about the state of civil liberties. He said that he had feared post-war hysteria—it had always come after other wars, the Citizen Genet episode, and the KKK after the Civil War and the Palmer raids after the First World War—but that he had hoped he might be able to avoid it this time.

He felt that one of the great lies was the current attack on politicians. He feels that, as soon as he learned of any wrongdoing in his administration, he moved immediately to remedy it. "The professional politician," he said, "is the straightest-shooting man in the country. I don't mean the city machine type; but the man who makes a career of elective politics. The biggest crooks in the country are the businessmen. You know," he continued, with feeling, "they'll do anything—absolutely anything—for a dollar."

I said that I thought that the Republicans through smear and slander would try to put the Democratic party out of business in the next four years. He smiled and said, "Well, they may try, but they won't succeed. The Democratic party was here before any of them were, and it will be around long after they have been forgotten."

He described his attempt to impress Eisenhower with the magnitude and gravity of the presidential job. "I called in [Dean] Acheson and [Robert] Lovett and [John] Snyder and Harriman and had them all brief him. He just sat there, his face cold and hard." I asked whether he thought Eisenhower had gotten the point. HST shook his head and said, "No, I don't think he got it." What had happened to Eisenhower? did we all in the past just miscalculate the kind of man he was? HST said, "Yes, I guess that's what we did."

He spoke affably of Stevenson except to say that he was oversuspicious of the professional politicians.

I noticed that he still speaks of FDR as "the President." He made several references to "the coalition of reactionary Republicans and anti–civil rights Democrats."

1953

September 12–14
Democratic Party conference

I arrived in Chicago Saturday evening, September 12. After registering at the Congress, I went over to the Conrad Hilton and located some
newspapermen. One of them gave me the number of AES's suite. I
phoned up, got Bill Blair and then went up. Adlai was there, having just
returned from dinner with HST. He said that they had had a long talk
together, and that HST had kept urging him to take over the active
leadership of the party. AES evidently kept protesting his lack of qualifications; HST finally said, "Well, if a knucklehead like me can be a successful President, I guess you can do it all right." HST made it clear that
he was altogether in Adlai's corner.

1954

❖

March 8
[Boston]

President Truman came to town today to address a fund-raising lunch for the Truman Library. I had fifteen minutes to talk with him in the morning in his suite at the Sheraton-Plaza.

We talked considerably about McCarthy. He then began to muse about the incidence of periods of hysteria in American history. He told me (as he has before) that he had completed a "monograph" on this subject. As he figures it, the periodicity is about 8–10 years: thus, from the Alien and Sedition Acts to the trial of Aaron Burr; the Know-Nothing and anti-abolitionist sentiment of the fifties; Reconstruction through the election of 1876; from A. Mitchell Palmer to the campaign of 1928. So he guesses that it will take McCarthyism 8–10 years to burn itself out—which means anywhere from 1956 to 1960 before it is over. But he affirmed, both touchingly and impressively, his faith in the decency of the American people and their capacity to recover from these binges of fear and panic.

HST looked very well—trim, natty and cheerful as usual.

September 10
Libertyville, Illinois

Adlai met me at the station. He looked fine, and was as warm and easy as ever. He was delighted at Averell's fortune in New York, while at the same time somewhat baffled over the political calculations involved, and quite respectful and even admiring about Franklin [Roosevelt Jr.]. He is optimistic about Humphrey and [Guy] Gillette.

He outlined his position in the following terms. He will not seek the nomination in '56. He definitely will not enter primaries. If he is drafted, he will accept; but realistically he concedes that he will not be drafted twice. What he would really like to do in 1956 is to run for Governor of Illinois, or be Secretary of State. In the meantime, he does not want to be constrained by the Democratic party line; he would like to feel free to speak out his conscience as he sees it; and he thinks that this role would not only suit him better but would, in the long run, be smarter politics. "My present position," he said, "is morally repugnant, emotionally unbearable and intellectually inconsistent."

1955

October 16
[Cambridge]

Cold, rainy afternoon. AES [Adlai E. Stevenson] arrived about 2:30; around 4:15 went to the MacLeishes'; left about 5:30.

1. AES seemed philosophical about HST [Harry S. Truman]. Could not understand why HST should consider him superior to politicians, in view of the fact that he was the third generation of a family of fairly successful politicians; but presumes that HST does not consider him sufficiently an orthodox Fair Dealer and does not like his campaigning style.

His last face-to-face talk with HST was in Chicago in July. At that point HST reiterated his support and strongly advised AES to announce on Labor Day. AES then told him that he could not do that, that he felt he had no claim on the nomination, that he could only announce after there was some display of sentiment for him in the party.

Just before HST came East, AES called him to ask whether he was going through Chicago. HST replied that he was going through St. Louis this time. AES commented that he was worried about the Harriman problem; hoped that nothing would happen which might divide the party and weaken its chances in the election. HST: "Don't worry about that. That's why I'm going to Albany. I want to fix things up." AES's comment: "He fixed things up all right."

Since Albany HST has told both Acheson and [Tom] Finletter that AES remains his number one choice. AES seems to doubt this, though I commented that I now believed that HST was just giving WAH [W. Averell Harriman] a run for his money and perhaps hoping to stimulate AES into a more militant stance.

2. On WAH: AES says that he is not much worried about the political effect of Averell's candidacy, but is troubled and a bit hurt by the manner of it. He now thinks that WAH planned this from the start and deliberately deceived him about it. He is uncertain what he should do about it; is disinclined to make an open fight at this point. Obviously the Harriman problem concerns him more than anything else at this moment.

3. On [Estes] Kefauver: he spoke with admiration of EK's well-organized campaign—the postcards; telegrams; the letter of congratulations from Moscow received by a Wisconsin Democrat on the birth of a child; etc. But he also rather fears that EK will try to strike a bargain for the vice presidency. While AES admires his legislative record, he feels that EK would be hopeless as Vice President; that he could not effectively serve as a liaison between the White House and the Hill, because he is so hated on the Hill. Apparently Johnson and Rayburn emphasized this to AES, saying that EK was the most-hated man to serve in Congress for many years.

Johnson's candidate for Vice President is Humphrey. AES feels that Humphrey would be much better from the viewpoint of discharging the congressional function.

4. AES's present plan is to announce late in Oct. or early in Nov.

5. AES made very emphatically his point that the political problem, as he saw it, was to meet the great "spiritual hunger" and unrest of our time—a hunger and unrest signaled in the popular response to any

number of stimuli, from Joe McCarthy to Billy Graham. How to convert this anxiety into political issues?

November 5–6
Chicago
Meeting to formulate Stevenson 1956
campaign strategy

We met Saturday evening around six at Bill Blair's a house. Stevenson and [Roger] Tubby, coming up from Bloomington, joined us about nine. The meeting broke up a little after midnight and resumed at ten the next morning. It then continued until about one, at which time we adjourned for drinks and Lauren Bacall.

AES himself was in good form. At times he was responsive to the argument for statemanship, at times not. "You know what I would really like to do?" he said at one point. "What I'd really like to do is to attack the adminstration from A to Z—go down the line, taking up every item in the book: the lies they have told to the people, the raid on the natural resources, the packing of regulatory commissions, the smear and slander, and all the rest. I'd like to call them on every point. I'm tired of this statesmanlike stuff." Bill Wirtz intervened: "You might like to do it. But you would hate to have done it."

AES said, "I think it is time to change my methods. My speeches must be more simple, vivid, concrete. In the past they have been too abstract and philosophical. I've always tried to cover too much. Now I must work hard to get specific instances and examples which will carry over to people and mean something to them."

He described his recent talk with HST. Truman said, "Do you want to know what the issue of the campaign is?" He went to the window and pointed at a passerby. "The issue is, who's looking after that guy? The people down in Washington aren't looking after him. They're looking after themselves. What we have to tell the country is that we Democrats intend to look after the ordinary guy."

1956

February 26

I spent the evening with AES at young Adlai's. We talked mostly about the civil rights and Middle Eastern problems.

On civil rights, he kept saying that the basic fact was the difficulty of the adjustment; that it was raising false hopes to suggest that people's minds and hearts could be changed by coercion; that the Negro leaders were defeating their own purposes when they put on pressure; that the only Negro hope was to reduce tension and let the moderate-minded southerners assume local leadership and work out the problems of adjustment in a gradualist way.

I pointed out to all this that the Negroes had never gotten anywhere except through putting on pressure, and they knew it; also that, if he proposed to be a voice of moderation, he must be a two-way voice—i.e., not only explaining to the North why its demands were aggravating problems in the South, but also explain to the South why its resistance seemed shameful to the North and to most of the free world. I said that he expected the Negroes to be more reasonable than he expected the southerners to be, and that this seemed to me unfair. He replied that of course it was unfair; it was like expecting business to behave badly and labor to behave intelligently; but life was unfair.

I do not know what impact, if any, I had; but it was a satisfactory conversation in the sense that I felt perfectly free to say everything I had on my mind. I think that he conceded that his appeal to the Negroes for moderation could succeed only if he first laid the basis by demonstrating a convincing emotional concern over their problems; I think he conceded too that his past statements had explained the South to the North much more than they had explained the North to the South. But I have a feeling that his basic convictions in this area are very deeply rooted.

April 8

On Sunday Bill Blair drove the Finletters, Marietta and me out early to Libertyville, Illinois. At one point AES called TKF [Thomas K. Finletter] and me into an upstairs room for a talk.

In connection with New York, we made the point that he must give a liberal speech or not come to New York. This got us into the civil rights question. AES now made an impassioned speech about how his role was that of the conciliator, that this was a role requiring far more courage than pro–civil rights demagoguery, and that making remarks which provoked the South would only delay the eventual achievement of the objective. What did we think, he asked, of the idea of a year moratorium on all further agitation, legal action, etc., in the civil rights field?

Tom and I both came away deeply disheartened. It seems evident that he does not feel any strong moral issue in the civil rights fight; that he identifies instinctively with the problems of the southern white rather than with the sufferings of the southern Negro; that he feels it to be easy to be what he calls a demagogue on the issue; and that any strong positions he might take will be against his convictions.

August 16
Democratic National Convention, Chicago

[After breakfast] I went up to the Blackstone suite (of AES) to see what had happened to the nominating speeches. I found the usual condition of chaos. Though the nominations were to begin in a couple of hours, some of the seconders had not even received copies of their speeches.

Bill Wirtz informed me that the Governor had rejected the various redrafts of his speech, including the last Schlesinger-Wirtz draft, and had gone back to his own first draft. There seemed nothing for me to do there, so I headed out to the amphitheater for the nominations, picking up Marietta on the way. We arrived in the midst of the Stevenson demonstration. Other nominations and demonstrations then took place. As usual, great fun.

It was evident from the first that AES would sweep through without difficulty.

August 17

I went out to the convention just in time for the beginning of the vice-presidential fight. This was the most exciting thing I have ever seen at a convention. I was strongly for Kennedy until the moment of climax in the second ballot when Albert Gore [Sr.] announced that Tennessee was shifting to Kefauver. Then I was suddenly seized by an unexpected onrush of emotion and found myself shouting wildly for Kefauver. On reflection, this seemed to me right. Jack, who made himself a national political figure in this convention, will have many more chances. Estes has earned this chance, if anyone has; and we are fielding our strongest possible ticket.

HST began the evening proceedings with an excellent speech, a model of its sort. Then Estes gave a typically third-rate speech; and then Adlai came on. His appearance produced a tumultuous ovation, prolonged for half an hour as HST, Kefauver, Harriman and other Democratic dignitaries joined him on the platform. Stevenson never looked more forceful, and his voice, when he began to speak, was sure and confident. Here seemed the moment to cap the convention by giving the emotional surge of the last 24 hours a fitting expression. Instead there came a diffuse mass of words. After a few moments, the sense of excitement was trickling away.

I was much upset by the speech, which had not benefited at all from the work done on it or the criticisms levelled against it. Ball, Finletter and McGowan had held a meeting that afternoon to go over the final draft. They had made many criticisms; but, when Wirtz carried them to Stevenson, they were nearly all ignored. Where McGowan, in moments of stress in 1952, would simply cross things out that AES liked and thus make sure that they would not appear in the speech draft, Wirtz gave up this fight. He is not temperamentally tough enough, and he has the weary feeling, "Well, it's his speech; I guess he has the right to say what he wants."

Nearly everyone was vastly disappointed. Phil Graham said, "You know, I thought that the Democrats had a real chance to win until Adlai began to speak." Bill Fulbright thought it was the worst speech he had ever heard AES give. Al Friendly said that in intellectual content it was indistinguishable from an Eisenhower speech. Averell Harriman was contemptuous. One felt that the image of the new Stevenson, this grim, masterful figure, had suddenly disappeared, and in its place appeared the old Stevenson, the literary critic, the man obsessed with words and with portentous generalization.

October 9

September was a great success. The Governor seized the ball and ran with it most of the month. His aggressive, hard-hitting speeches displayed him in a new role—as a fighting, masterful leader; they commanded the newspapers, caught the public imagination (to a degree anyway) and put the Republicans on the defensive. Eisenhower, who had intended a quiet campaign, had to expand his speaking schedule;

and on issue after issue the Republicans found themselves being outma-
neuvered and outwitted.

The Governor, however, began to exhibit symptoms of unhappiness
in the middle of the month. The first crisis came with the Harrisburg
telecast on September 13. There were two schools of thought on this.
Jim Finnegan and Clayton Fritchey wanted a slashing attack on the
President as an instrument of the big interests. Jane Dick wanted a
high-level "affirmative" speech which would refrain from excessive attack. The Governor inclined toward the second approach. In the end,
Bill Wirtz attempted a draft which sought to do both. The text was not
bad, but whatever merit there was in it was dissipated in the delivery.

One trouble is the Governor's own split between his desire to win
and his desire to live up to the noble image of himself which exists in the
minds of such people as Barbara Ward and Eugenie Anderson. When
they tell him he should take the high road and educate the people about
the issues of destruction and survival, he then begins to feel ashamed of
his attacks on the Republicans as the party of the big interests.

October 16

My last note, as I recall, dealt with AES's emerging revolt against the
Populist emphasis of the campaign. It is not that he disagrees with the
argument that the fight against single-interest government is the major
part of the campaign. It is partly that the constant reiteration of this
somewhat bores him, and even more that he feels increasingly frustrated by the fact that he cannot adequately discuss what interests him
more than anything else (and what he considers more important than
anything else)—foreign policy and peace.

When the matter was discussed on the train after the Pittsburgh
speech, I joined with Finnegan and Blair in sharp opposition to the
Governor's desire to shift to foreign policy. In the next week, however, I
found my views gradually changing for several reasons. One reason was
that, as the Governor became more frustrated in his desire to speak
about foreign policy, he began to fight his speeches more and more till at

times he almost seemed to sabotage his own effects—stepping on applause lines, uttering strong lines without conviction, diluting them in delivery, etc. I began to feel that he had to get foreign policy out of his system, and that he could do it with least harm this week. After a few days of foreign policy, we could tell whether it worked or not; and AES, having done his duty to statesmanship, would perhaps be readier to revert to Populism in the last two weeks of the campaign.

But I found myself changing for another and more serious reason. I began to feel that something new had to be added to the campaign—that we had pushed Populism about as far as we could go for the moment, that we had laid a good basis and could keep it going in the minor speeches, and that we badly needed some new element to revive interest in the campaign. I felt too that perhaps the Eisenhower strategy had been wiser than I had at first thought. Inviting battle on our strongest ground—domestic policy—he was in effect invading our strongest ground and trying to seize—or at least to confuse—our strongest issue. This suggested that a counteroffensive on peace might equally confuse their strongest issue. Moreover, it was necessary to fill out the image of AES by having him display competence in the peace field.

Having reached these conclusions about October 10, I went to Chicago on the 13th to confer with AES and others on their return from the Coast. They returned in a state of euphoria about the H-bomb issue which had apparently raised the roof wherever it was mentioned. AES ventured the thought that this might be the make-or-break issue—that somehow all the other issues we had been trying to make against the Eisenhower administration were coming to focus in this issue (the fearfulness, the lack of imagination, the complacency, the rigidity). The H-bomb, in other words, might become the great symbolic issue. My own feeling is that it will work better in areas with strong religious and pacifist leanings (California, Middle West) than it will in the urban and sophisticated East, but we shall see.*

---

* Adlai Stevenson lost the election to Dwight Eisenhower on November 6, 1956.

1957

March 30–31
Washington, D.C.

I saw Lyndon Johnson from about 12:10 to about 1:45 on Saturday [March 30]. The meeting took place at his request.

George Reedy took me into Johnson's office. He was sitting there with Jim Rowe. After a few moments, Reedy and Rowe left. Johnson then talked without interruption for almost an hour and a half. He is an affable figure, medium sized, lined, weather-beaten face, looking somewhat tense and tired. His flow of talk was incessant, almost compulsive. The language was vivid and picturesque but unforced. One got the sense of a man who exists almost completely in the realm of tactics, a virtuoso in senatorial operation; yet with a nostalgic identification of himself as a liberal and a desire, other things being equal, to be on the liberal side. While plainly intelligent, he seemed little concerned with the merits of issues. On questions of parliamentary manipulation and of the

personalities of his colleagues, he seemed enormously astute and perceptive. I found him both more attractive, more subtle and more formidable
than I expected.

He began by saying that he was a sick man with no political future
of his own. His main desire, he said, was to live. He had no interest at
all in the presidential nomination. He did not even mean to run again
for the Senate. He planned only to serve out his present term. Being
entirely disinterested, he wanted only to do the best he could for his
party and his nation in the three, or two, or one year remaining to him.
(One almost heard violins in the background. Yet he may well have
been perfectly sincere.)

He then poured out his stream-of-consciousness on the problems of
leadership in the Senate. He described the problems of keeping the conservative southerners (he called them "the Confederates") and the liberal northeners in the same harness; he analyzed a number of insoluble
parliamentary situations which he had mastered through his own brilliance and perseverance; he gave a generally fascinating account of the
role which timing, persuasion, parliamentary knowledge, etc., have in
getting bills through.

In the course of this discourse, he said, "I want you to know the kind
of material I have to work with." He then ran down the list of 48 Democratic senators, pausing to make a thumbnail sketch of each. It was a
brilliant performance, with full assessment of their strength and weakness, their prejudices, their openness to persuasion, their capacity for
teamwork, etc. When he came to [Dennis] Chavez, whose trouble is al-
coholism, Johnson imitated Chavez drunk—very funny. He rated
[Mike] Mansfield very high, though felt him a little too shy and unag-
gressive; also [Richard] Neuberger ("a man with real Rooseveltian qualities") and Humphrey (or, as he called him, Umphrey). He called
[Joseph] Clark "excellent." He put [Sam] Ervin and [John] Stennis high
among the conservatives. He felt that [Paul] Douglas was too "tempera-
mental." No use at all for Kefauver. He told how he kept [Herman] Tal-
madge off Judiciary and was concentrating his energies on helping the
tenant farmer. He seemed surprisingly sympathetic toward [Wayne]

Morse; highly favorable about Kennedy, but no special excitement. Very down on [Frank] Lausche.

I made the point that the responsibility of leadership in the Senate is not only to get bills passed but to build public issues and to educate the electorate in the decisions they must confront. He replied, "How do you go about building issues? In one case after another, I've tried to build issues, and it just hasn't gone over." I brought up the minimum wage situation in the last session, when the Democrats sneaked a bill through so quickly that the country didn't know what was happening, and Ike was later able to claim credit for the $1 minimum wage when, in fact, he had opposed it. Johnson said that this was the only way the $1 minimum wage could have been got through—if it had been held for extended debate, it would have split the Democratic party and probably would have mobilized the southern conservatives against it. "But a number of times I deliberately held the Senate in debate for several days or a couple of weeks. Take the Gore bill on atomic energy; or the revision of the Social Security Act—permanent disability, and retirement age for women. I prolonged the debate on these as long as possible. I made them as dramatic as possible. I thought I had real issues. But they meant nothing in the campaign. What can you do if the press muffles every attempt you make to project an issue?" I did not have an answer to this.

"He seemed quite annoyed that the organized liberals do not regard him as one of their own. Look at ADA [Americans for Democratic Action]," he said. "ADA regards Cliff Case as a good liberal, worthy of ADA support. They regard me as a southern reactionary. But have you ever compared my record with Cliff Case's?" I said, No, I hadn't, whereupon he opened his drawer and pulled out a comparison of his voting record with those of Case, [Frederick] Payne, [Margaret] Smith and [Leverett] Saltonstall on fifteen issues. On each one, he had voted for the liberal side and Case for the conservative side. "And yet they look on me as some kind of southern bigot."

He went on to say that doubtless this showed undue sensitivity to liberal criticism. "But what a sad day it will be for the Democratic party when its Senate leader isn't sensitive to liberal criticism."

Johnson obviously regards the liberal Republicans with contempt. He said that the only Republicans who mattered in the Senate were [William] Knowland and [Styles] Bridges.

On civil rights, he said that he greatly feared a sectional split in the party. "I've never said or done anything in my life to aggravate the sectional feeling." The Negroes in Texas voted for him, he said, because of his fairness to them when he was NYA administrator. Maybe, he said sadly, the northerners won't be satisfied until they split off and try a party of their own. But they won't get very far, he said, for several reasons—among them the fact that the southerners were much better politicians. I said that in most northern states, the Democratic party had to take a strong liberal line—a Morse-Harriman-Clark-Williams line—if it was going to get anywhere at all. He said glumly, "I guess you are right."

1959

March 29
Independence, Missouri
[Meeting of the Board of Directors of the Truman Library]

HST, as usual, talked a good deal of American history, overflowing with facts and opinions, a good many of them wrong, yet conveying a sense that he regarded all past figures more or less as contemporaries. He thinks every great President has been followed by mediocre Presidents and claims to include Adams, Madison, Van Buren and himself in the list of mediocrities; makes an exception for Andrew Johnson.

On Modern Art, he was, as usual, at his worst. He told how one evening at Mary Lasker's he looked hard and attentively at a Picasso on her wall until she came up and asked him what he thought about it. HST then said, "Mary, there is just one thing wrong with it; you've hung it upside down."

"I can't understand these modern fellows. I went to a chapel in Southern France decorated by—what's that fellow's name?—Matisse.

I've never seen such a thing on my life. There was the Virgin with a couple of big tits spilling out over her dress. I walked through it and never said a thing. . . . Then one day I went to lunch with Picasso. A short, jolly man, bald, I liked him a lot. He had a picture of a goat, and there was the real goat wandering around the yard. I said to him, Do you mean to say that you took this beautiful goat and turned it into this monstrosity and can say to me that they look alike? He turned on his heel and walked away. The Boss [Truman's wife] was never so mad at me in her life."

Straight out of *The Innocents Abroad*!

July 19

Jack Kennedy called up around noon and asked us to come to dinner at Hyannis Port this evening. Marian could not go, so I went alone. The Kennedy place was less grand than I had imagined. I expected miles of ocean frontage with no alien houses in view; but it is a cluster of Kennedy houses, all large and comfortable but not palatial, in the midst of a settled community.

Jackie Kennedy was the only other person present; and we all drank and talked from about 8 to 12:30. I only brought two cigars, one of which Jack took, having (typically) no cigars in the house. Jackie wanted for a moment to go and see *A Nun's Story*, which was being screened in a projection room in one of the other houses; but, though somewhat encouraged by Jack to go, finally stayed the evening out with us. She was lovely but seemed excessively flighty on politics, asking with wide-eyed naiveté questions like: "Jack, why don't you just tell them that you won't go into any of those old primaries?" Jack was in a benign frame of mind and did not blink; but clearly such remarks could, in another context, be irritating. This is all the more so since Jackie, on other subjects, is intelligent and articulate. She was reading Proust when I arrived; she talked very well about Nicolas Nabokov, Joe Alsop and other personalities; and one feels that out of some perversity she pretends an ignorance about politics larger even than life.

As for Jack, he gave his usual sense of seeming candor. I write "seeming" without meaning to imply doubts; so far as I could tell, he was exceedingly open; and this was, indeed, the freest, as well as the longest, talk I have ever had with him. As usual, he was impersonal in his remarks, quite prepared to see the views and interests of others. He showed more animation and humor than usual and, indeed, was rather funny in some of his assessments of people and situations.

He seems fairly optimistic about his presidential chances. He thinks that Humphrey can't win, that Johnson will take care of [Stuart] Symington, and that he will go into Los Angeles with a large delegate lead. He is pretty optimistic about the East (for example, he thinks he will get New Jersey after the first ballot) but plainly feels that he needs some dramatic primary victories to maintain his momentum. He seems to regard Stevenson as the next most likely person to get the nomination.

Jack was well aware of the dangers of division—especially between Hubert and himself—as a consequence of primary contests. He says that Gene McCarthy apologized to him for his remark at the press conference launching Hubert's campaign (when asked how it was to be financed, McCarthy said in effect, Well, if I wanted to be mean, I would say that his father isn't paying for it); but he expects more and more of this as the Humphrey people get more and more desperate. He says that he likes and admires Hubert, as well as Rowe, Rauh and Loeb (though he rather fears that Rowe may try to swing the Humphrey strength to Lyndon, if Hubert should collapse). I told him that Joe Rauh had told me that he would go to Kennedy if Hubert collapsed, and Jack seemed very pleased. He would like Hubert to come on the ticket with him for VP; if Hubert were reluctant, because of the senatorial contest, Jack would like Orville Freeman. And he obviously regards Stevenson as inevitable for Secretary of State.

We had considerable talk about [Joe] McCarthy. Kennedy said he felt that it would be a good idea to admit frankly that he had been wrong in not taking a more forthright position. I said that he was paying the price of having written a book called *Profiles in Courage*. He replied ruefully, "Yes, but I didn't have any chapter in it about myself."

I think he genuinely thinks he was wrong about it; but says he was constrained for a long time because Bobby had joined the committee staff—over Jack's opposition, he says. He also said that his father and Joe were great friends and that his father would defend Joe as a person to this day.

He spoke of Eisenhower throughout with dislike and contempt. "I could understand it if he golfed all the time with old Army friends; but no man is less loyal to old friends than Eisenhower. He is a terribly cold man. All his golfing pals are rich men he has met since 1945." Eisenhower's remarks about [Charles] Bohlen seemed to him typical; as did his willingness to drop Nixon in 1956. "He won't stand by anybody. He is terribly cold and terribly vain. In fact, he is a shit."

I asked him about Addison's disease. He said that after the war the fevers associated with malaria produced a malfunctioning of the adrenal glands; that this had cleared up; and that he was now perfectly OK. He pointed out that he had none of the symptoms of Addison's disease—yellowed skin, black spots in mouth, unusual vulnerability to infection. "No one who has Addison's disease ought to run for President; but I do not have it and have never had it." I asked him whether, for example, he took cortisone for his adrenal deficiency. He said that the deficiency was over and that he took nothing.

December 27

With Adlai Stevenson in Libertyville [Illinois]. After the others (Wirtz, McGowan, J. B. Martin) left, AES said, "I have something I want to discuss with you. I am greatly troubled over the general misunderstanding about my attitude toward the nomination. People seem to think that I am engaged in a subtle plot of some sort to get the nomination. No one seems to understand that I really don't want it. I think I ought to issue some sort of clarifying statement before I leave for Latin America."

"What would you say in such a statement?"

"I'd like to say that I am not seeking the nomination, that I am not working for it, that I wish others would stop working for me, that I *don't want* the nomination. The question is whether I should go beyond this." He paused. "The question is whether I should add that, if the convention wants me, I could not, of course, decline the nomination."

I said that I doubted whether such a statement would clarify very much; that it only expressed what most people thought was his position already.

He said that he hoped that such a statement might reduce the impression of his coyness by making clear that he really didn't want the nomination.

I said that the statement he described would only magnify the impression of coyness; that there was no point in issuing any statement at all unless it said something new.

1960

January 2

Jack Kennedy asked the Galbraiths and ourselves to dine with him at Locke-Ober following his telecast with Mrs. Roosevelt. Earlier in the day he had announced his candidacy in a press conference in Washington. At dinner he was, as usual, spirited and charming, but he also conveyed an intangible feeling of depression. I had the sense that he feels himself increasingly hemmed in as a result of a circumstance over which he has no control—his religion; and he inevitably tends toward gloom and irritation when he considers how this circumstance may deny him what he thinks his talents and efforts have earned.

I asked him what he considered the main sources of his own appeal. He said obviously there were no great differences between himself and Humphrey on issues, that it came down to a question of personality and image. "Hubert is too hot for the present mood of the people. He gets people too excited, too worked up. What they want today is a more boring, monotonous personality, like me."

Jack plainly has no doubt about his capacity to beat Nixon and can hardly wait to take him on.

January 9
[Washington, D.C.]

I came at 5 o'clock in the afternoon (Saturday) to his magnificent new leader's office where he sits opposite a large oil painting of himself. He was sipping a Scotch and soda and offered me a drink, promptly brought by his pretty secretary. Then he launched into the usual monologue.

He said he had recently been in a number of states, and didn't think the Democrats could carry any. In Texas, he said, Nixon could beat any Democratic candidate except Johnson. In the main, he thought the election had been lost already.

Why? Because of [Joseph] Clark and [William] Proxmire and their success in conveying the picture of the Democratic party as a divided party with a militant wing of "wasters, spenders and wild men."

"The country doesn't want this. The country wants to be comfortable. It doesn't want to be stirred up. It doesn't like spending. Have a revolution, all right, but don't say anything about it until you are entrenched in office. That's the way Roosevelt did it."

He defended his leadership strategy. "Congress is not the action arm of government, and the things we can do are limited. We can't impose policy on the executive. We sought the best and did the possible."

He did not seem much interested in foreign policy or much impressed by my contention that Eisenhower's trips were responsible for the recovery of the Republican party at the polls. He seemed to attach great importance to local issues. (I had the impression that he was confusing running for Congress—which depends to a great degree on local issues—with running for the presidency, which requires a clearcut national party image.)

I said something about his candidacy. He brushed it off, implying that he hadn't yet made up his mind. At one point he said, "I would support

Stevenson with enthusiasm. I would support Humphrey with enthusiasm. [Pause] I would support Kennedy. I would support Symington."

January 23

Washington: Jefferson-Jackson Day dinner. I went down to the Congressional Hotel to attend the ADA board meeting in the morning. At the hotel I ran into Hubert Humphrey, who asked me whether I would go over to his office and take a look at his speech for the dinner. He didn't like it much, nor did I, when I looked at it—too crude and direct in its attack on Nixon. I then sat down at the typewriter and rewrote it in a form which he used in the evening with minor changes.

On returning from the Congressional to the Sheraton Park, I encountered Averell Harriman who was wandering in a lonely way around the lobbies. He was staying at the Mayflower and consequently had changed into his dinner clothes, though it was only about 4:30. He came up to my room, and we talked for three quarters of an hour. He seemed measured though a little forlorn. He said that Johnson had been wooing him with barely concealed remarks about the State Department, but he (WAH) did not seem much impressed. He obviously prefers Humphrey and has given him some money, but does not think much of his chances. He spoke in a rather friendly way about Kennedy.

Humphrey stole the show in the evening, with Kennedy a close second. Johnson was a flop; his attack on the Eisenhower administration for not balancing the budget fell with a conspicuous thud.

March 25–27
Detroit
Midwest Conference

When we got to the hotel, I ran into Jack Kennedy returning with [John] Bailey. Bailey signalled me to come with them to his suite, which I did. The suite was virtually deserted—in Boston, it would have been filled with meaningless politicians milling around and trying to cadge free drinks. Two men from *Time* and one from the *Wall Street Journal* were waiting when we arrived: Ted Sorensen soon appeared. But that was about all.

Jack seemed tired but was obviously in good spirits. His lack of pretense was refreshing; for example, he kept answering ringing phones himself, and, when a message was required he sat down and wrote it out. He was quite funny on [Senator] Wayne Morse who had been very affable toward him earlier in the evening. Half the time, he said, Morse clapped him on the shoulder and congratulated him; the other half, he denounced him as a traitor to liberalism and an enemy of the working class. It all reminded him, said Kennedy, of *City Lights* and the millionaire who, when drunk, loaded Charlie Chaplin with gifts and insisted that he spend the night but, when sober, couldn't recognize him and threw him out of the house. Soon after I arrived, Kennedy asked me to come into his bedroom for a private talk. After we finished, we came out and chatted with the press, Jack occasionally retiring to woo the people from Kansas or W Va. This went on till about 2. I must say that I adore sitting around hotel rooms with politicians and newspapermen exchanging gossip over drinks.

May 14

Jack Kennedy called this morning. He was lunching on the road in Maryland; his talk was punctuated with bites and swallows.

His chief concern was with Stevenson. He does not see why Stevenson won't help him—if Stevenson is still a candidate, then "he can get somewhere only over my dead body," so he might as well try to assure Kennedy's support by helping him; if he isn't a candidate, then why stay out?

Jack's calculation is that he needs about 80–100 votes. He thinks that Stevenson can provide what is needed in California and Pennsylvania and can be helpful with Colorado and Minnesota. "He is the essential ingredient in my combination. I don't want to have to go hat-in-hand to all those southerners, but I'll have to do that if I can't get the votes from the North." He said that he had learned a lot in West Virginia—that he had carried the Negro wards just because [Senator Robert] Byrd had helped Humphrey; "this proved to me that it's absolutely fatal to have southern support. I want to be nominated by the liberals. I don't want to go screwing around with all those southern bastards."

May 15

I talked with AES in Libertyville this morning. He said that Blair had been pressuring him, "as he has for the past year," to come out for Kennedy. AES went on to say that he felt to come out now would be inconsistent with the past positions he has taken and with his whole personal style. "It would look as if I were jumping on the bandwagon. Everyone would say, 'There's the deal we told you about.' It would look as if I were angling for a job. I can't do this sort of thing."

I asked him whether he might not consider helping Kennedy before the convention. He said, "On the basis of present alternatives, I would be quite prepared to do it in terms calculated to preserve as much party harmony as possible. To come out now and kick Lyndon and Stuart in the face and demean my own position of neutrality and aloofness would be an error."

AES said that pressures for a Stevenson draft continue to mount— 11 telegrams so far this morning. People called and said that Kennedy's youth and religion were too much of a burden—the only answer was a Stevenson-Kennedy ticket. When they asked whether they could work for this, AES would reply, he said, "Not so far as I'm concerned. If you do anything about this, you must do it on your own." (He didn't sound as if he were discouraging them too hard.)

May 22

Jack Kennedy called me late Sunday afternoon to report on his convesation with AES in Libertyville Saturday morning. He said that it had been wholly pleasant, but that obviously AES did not intend to do anything for the moment. Jack said that he was not much impressed by AES's account of why he did not wish to act; but supposed this to be because he did not wish to disclose his real reason—that, if he said nothing, there might still be a possibility that he would emerge out of the scramble as the candidate.

Jack's particular fear was that AES had been "snowed" by Johnson—that Lyndon on Monday had told him that, if he stayed aloof, he would be Lyndon's second choice (next to himself), that anything might happen, and that therefore he should do nothing to sew the nomination up for Jack. Speaking with a certain detached bitterness, Jack said: "I told him that Lyndon was a chronic liar; that he has been making all sorts of assurances to me for years and has lived up to none of them." Adlai emphasized to Jack the importance of party harmony and his remaining on good terms with Lyndon. Jack made clear that he regards party harmony as no problem at all: "Everyone will come around the day after the convention; and anyone who doesn't come around will be left out and won't matter."

His general attitude was rueful but philosophical. "I guess there's nothing I can do except go out and collect as many votes as possible and hope that Stevenson will decide to come along."

May 29

Phone call from AES. He began by saying that he was sorry that Kennedy felt "regretful" over their conversation. (This was taking a word from my letter out of context and making too much of it; I quickly replied that he was regretful only over AES's reluctance to endorse him forthwith but was wholly philosophical about the conversation in general.) AES said that he obviously made a "dire mistake" in mentioning Johnson; this provoked the only flash of temper on Kennedy's part. "Obviously the feeling between the two of them is savage." AES said again how fiercely Johnson had spoken against Kennedy when they met in Washington. AES said, "I suppose I made a mistake bringing Johnson up; but I thought that, if I were to serve under Kennedy, it might be helpful if I could keep a personal in with Johnson. If I double-cross Johnson now, it would mean that he had no personal relations with anyone in the new adminstration." (The phrase "double-cross" was interesting: does this mean that AES has assured LBJ that he won't endorse Kennedy? Or did he just use the word loosely?)

June 16
Berlin

Let me recapitulate the confused and disturbing events of the past week. On June 5, AES spent the night. Two days later, Charles Cleveland of the *Chicago Sun-Times* wrote a story that Galbraith, Rauh, [Henry Steele] Commager and I were coming out for Kennedy; Tom Winship, who had been holding the story for a few days, came out with the same thing in the *Globe* the next day. Commager is generally blamed for the leak. But, for the historical record, I am bound to confess that Cleveland called me and extracted from me enough to be able to put the right questions to Commager. In any case, leaks were inevitable; Jock Saltonstall had been calling up people around the country asking them if they would go along with a pro-Kennedy statement to be signed by this group.

In the meantime, the US-USSR Summit exploded, with the consequent resurgence of interest in AES. The sudden outburst of Stevenson activity made me wonder whether I should sign the Saltonstall letter. But there was as yet no agreed-upon draft; and I was fairly certain that the whole thing would hang fire until I was safely off to Berlin. Because nothing seemed imminent, I did not discuss the matter with AES when he stayed with us; my intention was either to get off to Berlin without signing, or to tell AES well in advance that I intended to sign. I did urge AES again to consider coming out for K. but said nothing about my own plans. It couldn't have been worse for AES to read it all in the *Chicago Daily News* 48 hours after he stayed with us in Cambridge. I felt sick about it; and still feel guilty and sad.

Once the story broke, I issued a statement saying, that AES was best qualified but that, since he was not a candidate, I was for Kennedy.

I have come, I think, to the private conclusion that I would rather have Kennedy as President. Stevenson is a much richer, more thoughtful, more creative person; but he has been away from power too long; he gives me an odd sense of unreality. Probably he would snap back soon enough; but I felt in Barbados and in Cambridge this strange feeling that he had been away from things too long. I find it hard to define this feeling—a certain frivolity, distractedness, overinterest in words and phrases? I don't know; but K. in contrast gives a sense of cool, measured, intelligent concern with action and power. I feel that his administration would be less encumbered than S.'s with commitments to past ideas or sentimentalities; that he would be more radical; and that, though he is less creative personally, he might be more so politically. But I cannot mention this feeling to anyone.

At any rate, I felt terribly all week (still feel so). My greatest affection is for AES; my greatest debt is to him; if he were a declared candidate, I would of course, despite all misgivings, be for him. I wrote him a letter trying to set forth my position. He replied a few days later, rather casually, I thought; a little cool and hurt? I fear so. I would have been in his place.

On Sunday, June 12, Ken, Marian and I went down to Hyannis Port to spend the day with the Kennedys. We arrived about noon on a hot, overcast day. Jack and Jackie were playing croquet on the lawn with a couple of friends. They stopped, and we had daiquiris on the terrace. Then Jack took Ken and me for a ride in his power launch. Then lunch; we drove back to Cambridge around 4.

Conversation was discursive but covered a good deal. Ken and I could discover no issue on which we disagreed with K. His views everywhere were cool, judicious and practical. He regards Johnson as his main opponent now. We commented on the discrepancy between his standing in Washington and outside. K. went into an historical excursus, comparing J. to Peel and others who were omnipotent in Parliament but had no popularity in the country. He was quite amusing on J.'s personality, describing him as a "riverboat gambler."

He displayed most emotion when talking about Addison's disease. Apparently his situation is one of adrenal depletion; In pure Addison's disease, the adrenal gland doesn't function at all. He denied once again that he took regular medication. In certain times of fatigue or stress, he said, he would take medication which would bring his adrenal functioning back to normal. He denied any special susceptibility to infections; and pointed to his primary record as evidence of his health and energy.

July 9

I go on to L.A. this evening with considerable trepidation and in considerable bafflement. The San Francisco papers have been building up the picture of a strong Stevenson movement, and predicting a Kennedy-Stevenson showdown at the convention. On the other hand, today's *New York Times*, which I have just bought at the airport, discounts the Stevenson movement. If AES has any chance, I would feel happier in Los Angeles if I were working for him, or at least I think I would; I think I would feel happier with myself. The ties of loyalty, of affection, of personal admiration bind me to him. Yet it may be that Kennedy, with his cool, sharp mind and his Rooseveltian political genius, would be the better President. Still, I feel guilty and unhappy over appearing to abandon AES (especially now that his candidacy has much more active support than it did when I said I would come out for Kennedy). Politics requires a toughness in human relations which in this case I find hard to achieve.

July 13
Los Angeles—Democratic convention

At 10:30 A.M. Hubert called the Minnesota caucus to order. Kennedy and the other candidates had addressed it the day before. Now Stevenson had agreed to come—an indication of how far he is being pushed into active candidacy. When Adlai entered the door of the room, the crowd went wild. It was obvious enough where Minnesota's heart lay. Then Adlai gave a speech. It was polished, graceful, courtly, charming, rather noncommittal; but so characteristically Stevensonian that I found myself weeping in the corner. But, deeply as the speech moved me, it also reinforced my sense that, if nominated, he would be beaten in the election. When he moved into the substantive part of his speech, he rehearsed the series of foreign policy errors of the Eisenhower administration, beginning with the pledge of 1953 to unleash Chiang Kai-shek. I have been trying to persuade him for years that no one cares anything any more about what Eisenhower did or didn't do in 1953 but to no avail; and I could see a campaign stretching ahead in which Stevenson gave passionate and rather waspish historical lectures about which no one gave a damn.

I went to the Furniture Mart to participate in a panel discussion before the Young Democrats. The star of the occasion was Mrs. Roosevelt, who had already arrived, greeted me pleasantly and (the old pro) explained to me privately, as she has already been telling delegations publicly, that I was the reason she was here—that the statement that we thought Stevenson was the best man but were for Kennedy had provoked her into trying to make the best man the candidate.

Later the convention hall was filling up. Mrs. Roosevelt arrived, producing an ovation, and word went around that AES was coming on to the floor at 6 o'clock. The appearance of a candidate on the floor is generally regarded as a breach of etiquette; it got Kefauver into trouble when he did it in 1952. I suppose that the Stevenson people urged it on him in the belief that it couldn't make his position any worse and might detonate a major demonstration; and I suppose that he agreed to do it on the ground that he wasn't a candidate. At any rate he appeared. The result was the first massive outburst of honest emotion in the convention. The galleries went mad, of course, but even on the floor there was pandemonium. Eventually Stevenson was invited to the rostrum. If he had spoken two or three sober sentences at this point, he might almost have made himself a serious candidate. But he chose instead to make a feeble joke which he had made earlier in the day at the Minnesota caucus

("After going back and forth through the Biltmore today, I know who's going to be the nominee of this convention—the last man to survive") and which all too typically cast himself as a helpless, buffeted man at the mercy of events. I had the sinking feeling, as I had in the morning, that he would be cruelly beaten if nominated. After his joke, the demonstration quieted down almost instantly. As Leonard Lyons said to me later in the evening, "He let all the air out with that one bad joke."

Around 8:30 we went off to Romanoff's for Gore Vidal's party. As he had described it to me yesterday, he said, "I have always wanted to give a party where at some point I could say—Carmine de Sapio, meet Christopher Isherwood." This was indeed such a party—everyone from Max Lerner to Gina Lollobrigida. I had a pleasant talk with Jack Lemmon—very small, quick; mobile features. I told him that I had much preferred *Some Like It Hot* to *The Apartment*. He made the statesmanlike remark that many people had and went on to say how wonderful he thought Billy Wilder was. I also had an agreeable talk with Charlton Heston, who may be described as the serious-type Hollywood star, filled with speculations about Castro and quotes from Walter Lippmann—not pretentious, though, and very likeable. I liked Shelley Winters and met a number of pretty younger girls—Hope Lange, Diana Lynn, etc. Lollobrigida was a disappointment.

July 14

I got up in time for Bobby Kennedy's 8:30 staff meeting. Here he ran through the states in order to get the rock-bottom Kennedy tally. Once again, I was impressed with the sharpness of his direction of the campaign. He insisted practically on the name, address and telephone number of every half-vote. "I don't want generalities or guesses," he would say. "There's no point in our fooling ourselves. I want the cold facts. I want to hear only the votes we are guaranteed to get on the first ballot." The result showed about 740 votes—21 short of a majority. However, Bob thought that, if Jack had 720 votes by Washington, enough votes would shift thereafter to put Kennedy over.

I then went off to breakfast with Ed Morgan and Dick Neustadt. I discovered that both of them had gone to Kennedy. Much speculation about the Vice President: Hubert has presumably eliminated himself by going for Stevenson. Scoop Jackson is supposedly Kennedy's personal favorite, but the political pressure is reportedly for Symington. Everyone dismisses Johnson as impossible; it may have to be offered to him, they say, but he wouldn't accept it (I have an uneasy feeling he might).

In due course the balloting began. Everything went as scheduled. By Washington Kennedy had about 720 votes; and, as Bobby had forecast, the rush to him began and quickly put him over. He was nominated by Wyoming. I did not feel that the convention was overcome with helpless enthusiasm, but there was considerable cheering, and people seemed fairly happy.

I went up to the Kennedy headquarters. There I saw Bobby Kennedy and began to urge on him the importance of doing something to conciliate the Stevenson people and bring them into the campaign. He listened patiently for a while, then came over to me, put his hand on my knee and said, "Arthur, human nature requires that you allow us 48 hours. Adlai has given us a rough time over the last three days. In 48 hours, I will do anything you want, but right now I don't want to hear anything about the Stevensonians. You have to allow for human nature."

I arrived at Stevenson's at about 3:20. The Governor, visibly shaken, came out and said that Phil Graham had just called him to say that Kennedy had chosen Lyndon Johnson for the vice presidential nomination!

Later, as I began to circulate around the Sports Arena, I ran into Phil and Kay Graham. Noting my angry mien and flashing eye, Phil drew me into a back room at the CBS booth and tried to explain to me why the Johnson nomination was logical and right. I was impressed without being convinced; but by the time I began to wander on the floor, I was calmer than I had been when I entered the auditorium. I first ran into Harriman who told me that he thought this was a fine ticket and anticipated no trouble in New York.

After a couple of hours, the opposition to Johnson, which for a moment had been sharp and widespread, began to simmer down.

Everybody was there—the Bruces, Blair Clark, Clayton Fritchey, Mary Chewning, the Barry Binghams, Pat Brown (who said that the Johnson nomination would cost the ticket 100,000 votes in California but hastily added that it might bring in another 100,000 which might not otherwise have voted Democratic), the Harrimans, etc., etc. Evangeline, who had practically cut me at the convention on Wednesday, was much friendlier; but Stevensonism dies hard. We left about two—Bill Walton, Ed Morgan, Clayton, Marian and I (Stephen had gone home earlier), with Randolph Churchill in hot pursuit. There were no taxis, and Randolph caught up with us as we waited on Wilshire Boulevard. He then explained at length how much he hated Joe Kennedy (for good reason too). I finally went in to phone for a cab. Suddenly Bill Walton charged into the hotel and called for me to come out. I came out in time to see Marian disappearing down Wilshire Boulevard in an open car. I naturally inquired as to what this was all about and was told that Sarge Shriver, very drunk, had come along Wilshire Boulevard, stopped, invited Marian into the car and sped away. In a few moments he was back. He then took us into Los Angeles, leaving Randolph Churchill on the curb, pleading with someone to come and have a drink with him.

I rather like Sarge Shriver, but this incident somewhat increased my sense of discomfort over the new dispensation.

July 15

We went to the Beverly Hilton for dinner with the Grahams; we were joined by Lally and Stephen as they made their way back from the rally. Phil told me the whole story as he knew it of the Johnson nomination. On Tuesday he and Joe Alsop said to each other that it was essential to put Johnson on the ticket. Joe then said, "Why don't we go and talk to Jack about it?" So they went around to the Kennedy suite and, after a few moments, were ushered in. At this point, improbably enough, Joe was struck dumb and whispered to Phil, "You do the talking." Phil said that they had come to urge Jack to put Lyndon on the ticket. Jack said, "That is right and I mean to do it."

Jack seems to have kept this resolution to himself for the next day or so. The meeting convened after his own nomination evidently included no serious consideration of Johnson. Early Thursday morning Kennedy called Lyndon. He spoke for a moment to Lady Bird and said he wanted to discuss the vice presidency with her husband. But when he called on Lyndon around 10:30, he said nothing about the question of Lyndon's going on the ticket. In the meantime, Lyndon had been discussing with Rayburn, Phil and others whether or not, if the offer were made, he should accept. Rayburn and Lady Bird were at first dubious. Phil argued that Lyndon should do it in the national interest. After a time Lyndon agreed and told Phil that he could pass the word on to Jack that he would take it.

There followed a long interlude of suspense. Bobby came down to see Rayburn, but he talked about the chairmanship of the National Committee as well as the vice presidency. Lyndon declined to see Bobby at this time on the ground that he should deal directly with his principal. For a considerable period, there was no direct word from Jack. Phil called the Kennedy people to check on what had happened; and finally, after 3 o'clock, Jack called Johnson and asked him to go on the ticket. In the meantime, Bobby had been discovering that the choice of Johnson would stir considerable opposition in the north. He now reappeared in the Johnson suite and told Rayburn that Johnson would face a floor fight and, for Jack's sake, should withdraw. It was then that Rayburn probably said that, if there was opposition on the floor, Johnson would fight and win—a statement which, taken out of context, gave rise to Jack Knight's story that Johnson forced himself on the ticket by threatening to run anyway. Bobby persisted in his argument and was invited inside to continue it with Johnson. Phil meanwhile got Jack on the phone and said that his brother wanted Lyndon to withdraw. Jack said calmly to tell Bobby that it was too late; he had already released his statement. Bobby then went on the phone to hear this directly, after which he slammed down the receiver.

Why did Jack go for Johnson? Basically, I think he believed that Johnson would add the most strength to the ticket. In addition, he knew it would greatly simplify his life during the special session and (if elected) the next four years, if he had Johnson under his eye as vice president rather than running a competing administration as majority leader. It was a case of grasping the nettle, and it was another evidence of the impressively cold and tough way Jack is going about his affairs.

After reflection, I am reconciled to the Johnson nomination and believe that it may come to be seen as a master stroke. The great drawback is the blurring of the liberal image. But this may be overcome if Johnson puts through a strong radical program in the special session; and in any case Jack will have to move slightly to the left during the campaign to make up for having Johnson on the ticket. I now think that on balance, from the viewpoint both of winning the election and of governing the country, the Johnson decision was brave and wise.

As is no doubt evident from these notes, my admiration for Kennedy's strength and ability has increased during this convention; my affection for him and personal confidence in him have declined. It was inevitable that he should best Stevenson. But I feel that as a consequence of Kennedy's victory and Stevenson's defeat something I greatly value has gone out of national politics.

It all became clear to me when I went over to Stevenson's Sheraton West suite on Friday morning and found Finletter, Doyle, Monroney, Bell, Carroll, Blair, Wirtz, Minow and the others. These—along with absent Stevensonians like Herbert Lehman, Eugene McCarthy, Wilson Wyatt, Dore Shary—are the nicest people in the Democratic party and the ones for whom I have the greatest regard and with whom I feel the greatest rapport. Yet as I saw them there together, I suddenly saw one great reason for Stevenson's failure. The Stevenson crowd consisted almost entirely of such nice people. It had too much the aspect of a private club made up of intimate friends who prefer each other's company to anything else. When one thinks of them, one thinks of tranquil Sunday afternoons at Libertyville or gay parties at Marietta's. Nothing could be more fun. But the Stevenson movement was not tough enough or serious enough or professional enough. It lacked the basic instinct for power necessary for success in a hard world.

One great difference between Stevenson and Kennedy is the amateur vs. the professional. There is no "we happy few" nonsense about the Kennedy camp. And this is part of a more decisive difference—the difference in their attitude toward power. The thought of power induces in Stevenson doubt, reluctance, even guilt. He is obsessively concerned with the awesome responsibilities of the presidential office. Possessing the genuine modesty of a profoundly civilized man, he is hesitant about imposing his own views on others. Feeling (or claiming to feel) inadequacy in the face of high office (for which no one is adequate), at the same time he recognizes that he has seemed on occasion to work almost willfully toward his own defeat. Lauren Bacall once argued persuasively to me that he had a political death wish. I have never believed that Stevenson is essentially indecisive in the sense that he would balk for a moment at executive necessities. I am sure that he would have ordered American troops into South Korea quite as swiftly as Harry Truman. Yet the exercise of power does present a problem for him. Kennedy, on the other hand, is like FDR. The thought of power neither rattles nor discomposes him. He takes power in his stride. He had absolute assurance about his own capacity to do the job, and he has a sure instinct about how to get what he wants. In Jack Kennedy the will to victory and the will to command are both plain and visible.

I have no regrets about having backed Kennedy. I think that Adlai Stevenson would have made a great President, but I do not think he could have made it against Nixon. Yet I find myself feeling much cooler about Kennedy at the end of the convention than at the beginning. I believe him to be a liberal, but committed by a sense of history rather than consecrated by inner conviction. I also believe him to be a devious and, if necessary, ruthless man. I rather think, for example, that Ken and I were in a sense had by him; that he sought our support when he considered it useful before the convention to have liberal Democratic names behind him, but that, if he thinks our names would cause the slightest trouble when he starts appealing to Republicans, he will drop us without a second thought. I am not even sure that he has at any time seriously intended to make Stevenson his Secretary of State—not that he has anyone else in view for the job, but that in his own mind he has always reserved the decision till after the election, while leaving contrary impressions in the minds of others.

I do not dispute—indeed, I have recognized—the inevitability of Kennedy. But I feel that my own pleasure in national politics is coming to an end. Nothing again will ever be as agreeable as those days with Stevenson. If I go into the Kennedy campaign, it will be into something quite different; and I don't really much care whether I get into it or not. And, while understanding why Kennedy had to win and Stevenson had to lose in this convention, one must understand at the same time what Stevenson accomplished in the last eight years. Under his leadership a revolution took place in the Democratic party. Almost single-handedly, he wrought a transformation in the party's ideas and style and sense of purpose. Thus no one in Los Angeles sounded like Harry Truman; all the contenders, even Johnson, were speaking in the spirit and often in the idiom of Stevenson, and none more so than Kennedy. Under Truman the essence of the Democratic appeal was to promise benefits; under Kennedy it is to demand sacrifices; what conclusive evidence of the Stevensonian triumph! Kennedy is the heir and executor of the Stevenson revolution—whether either Jack or Adlai realize this fact. In the long perspective of history, as I said on Tuesday, Stevenson must go down as the true victor in the convention.

But I cannot find it in me to blame Kennedy for being as he is. Indeed, I fear he may have learned too well the lesson of the last part of *The Coming of the New Deal.* He has commented to me several times in the past how illuminating he found my discussion of FDR's executive methods. I am quite sure now that Kennedy has most of FDR's lesser qualities. Whether he has FDR's greater qualities is the problem for the future.

August 6

Last Tuesday night (the 2nd) Jack Kennedy called up, in person, and invited us for lunch on Saturday, the 6th. This was my first communication with him since the convention.

We drove down from Cambridge on a beautiful summer day, sunny, clear and quiet. Everyone else decided to go to the Cape too, and we ran into hopeless traffic. We had been invited for 11:45; but it soon became evident that we could not make it. Finally we abandoned the central road and made better time on the back roads, finally arriving about 40 minutes late. It made no difference, however, because Hyannis Port had suffered an invasion of the Foreign Nationalities Branch of the Democratic National Committee, mostly bearing dolls in native costumes intended for Caroline Kennedy. Soapy Williams and Tom Quimby were there; also Norman Mailer, waiting for an interview with Jack. Jackie greeted us warmly and offered us drinks. Jack appeared, apologized for the delay and said that we should be prepared to go with them on the boat at 1.

We embarked shortly after 1—Jack, Jackie, Lee (Jackie's sister) and her husband Prince Radziwill, Marian and me. Jack seemed much more relaxed than he has been recently. We brought along several hand-cases of empty coke and tonic bottles; these were to be targets for rifle-shooting. After we got out an appropriate distance, the boat stopped, and Jack tossed the bottles overboard. Several of them sank straight away. Others floated for a moment, and Jack and Radziwill shot at them. Jack is plainly an excellent shot. All this was carried out agreeably with much banter and laughter. Then we drank Bloody Marys, swam from the boat and finally settled down for an excellent lunch. After lunch, cigars and conversation. Finally, shortly before 5, we returned to port.

I do not think I have ever seen Jack in better form. He was warm, funny, quick, intelligent and spontaneous. Even Marian, a Stevenson girl to the end, came away wholly impressed and reconciled. Indeed, the whole affair reminded me in a curious way of an afternoon with

Stevenson—the same spacious, tranquil country house; the same upper class ease of manners; the same sense of children and dogs about; the same humor; the frank conversation about a wide variety of subjects; the same quick transition from the serious to the frivolous. Since Radziwill's interest in American politics is limited, I was able to talk freely with Jack most of the time. He talked about everything without constraint. Let me summarize his remarks in various categories.

Nixon. He said that, after the Hawaiian trip, he felt much better about Nixon—i.e., that Nixon was human and would make mistakes (Jack had pounced that morning on Nixon's apparent willingness to invite support from Jack Hall of the Bridges union). He was rather irritated by a piece written by Eric Sevareid in the morning *Globe*—a brilliant piece arguing that Kennedy and Nixon were peas from the same pod. Jack said that this was the fashionable cliché of the campaign and he was getting tired of it. He said that he thought that Nixon and Johnson were rather alike, while he and Stevenson were rather alike. The distinction, I take it, was between totally absorbed professional politicians on the one hand, and those who took politics at a gentleman-intellectual's distance on the other. Also he kept saying about Nixon that he had "no taste." And he said, rather revealingly, "Nixon is about as far advanced as I was ten years ago."

Foreign policy. I urged him to consider giving a major speech which would take off from Castro on the theory that this would give him a chance to contrast his approach to foreign policy with that of Nixon's. He seemed interested in this and appeared fully to recognize the limitations on US action against the Castro regime. "We can't do anything except through the OAS," he said, "and most of the members of the OAS don't want to do anything at all. Our best hope is to stop the spread of Castro's influence by helping genuine democracy elsewhere in the continent." I had been a little worried that his friendship with Earl Smith, the former ambassador to Cuba, might have inhibited him; but he said, "You know Earl Smith once said to me that the American Ambassador is the second most important man in Cuba. What a hell of a note that is! Naturally those conditions couldn't last."

He had lunched the day before in NYC with Luce and the editors of *Time* and *Life*. Luce had asked him to sum up in a sentence how his foreign policy would differ from Nixon's. Jack said that he had declined to do this and instead had insisted on discussing the matter area by area. He asked me how I would have answered Luce. I said that I would have said that the real spirit and effectiveness of foreign policy depended on the character of the community from which it proceeded; that the US had had impact on the world only under liberal administrations at home; and that the first necessity in recovering world leadership was a revival in our own nation. He agreed enthusiastically with this and cited a statement by Nixon to the effect that he was conservative at home, liberal abroad—this, he said, we should shoot at.

Domestic policy. Jack said that he rather liked Luce. "He is like a cricket, always chirping away. After all, he made a lot of money through his own individual enterprise so naturally he thinks that individual enterprise can do anything. I don't mind people like that. They have earned the right to talk that way. After all, that's the atmosphere in which I grew up. My father's that way. But what I can't stand are all the people around Luce who agree with everything he has to say." He imitated Luce saying to Hedley Donovan, "Well, Hedley, what's your view on all this?" and Hedley's hasty agreement with whatever Luce had just said.

He said that everyone was excited about Galbraith and regarded him as a great radical. "Actually," Jack said, "he is a conservative." He then said to me, "You had better watch out for yourself. In 1952 everyone was mad at you. Now people seem to like you. Everyone is mellow about you. You must be slipping."

General attitude. Jack seems still to be reading a great deal. He had read a good part of *The Liberal Hour*. He spoke with appreciation and enjoyment of Murray Kempton's stories from Hyannis Port in the *New York Post*. He had read the *Time* cover story on Che Guevara (which I had not) and had read Dick Rovere's convention pieces in the *New Yorker*. Norman Mailer had been there in the morning when we arrived; Jack quoted a sentence from a Mailer story for a paper in

Provincetown in which Mailer said that he had thought Stevenson's speech on the Friday night much better than Kennedy's; Jack added to me, "You wrote Stevenson's speech, didn't you?"

I was struck by the sense that both he and especially Jackie seem to have about the importance of preserving their private identities; they talked of the Nixons and the Johnsons as people wholly committed to politics, so that their private faces had given way completely to their public faces, "as if they were on television all the time." Jackie, trying to have a friendly and candid exchange with Lady Bird, said, "And what have you been doing since the convention?" expecting her to reply, "Oh, God, I've been resting up after that madhouse," or something of the sort. Lady Bird said, "I've been writing letters to all those good people who sent congratulations to Lyndon and me." Jackie was impressed by the notebook in which Lady Bird entered the names and telephone numbers of people in the expectation that Lyndon might need them.

August 30

Last weekend, I went out to Marshall, Virginia, and spent the night with the Grahams. Phil is very enthusiastic about Jack. He said that he had the impression about Jack that he was concerned about Adlai's position on Berlin—e.g., that Adlai seemed to think that the UN should take over. (Archie Cox, over the phone today, in trying to distinguish between K's and S's views on foreign policy, said, "Of course Stevenson thinks much more can be done in the way of building bridges to the Communists; Kennedy is rather pessimistic about all that.")

Before going to the Grahams, I spent an hour or so in confidential talk with Cox. He was concerned and perplexed by the Sorensen situation. Every speech submitted by the Cox group had been discarded by Sorensen and replaced by one of his own. Archie had asked Ted over to meet the group. Ted came, went through a big-shot telephoning act, wheeled around in his chair, and said: "Jack Kennedy is very hard to write for. No one has been able to do it except for me. If you fellows can't do it, we'll have to let you go." Archie had reached the point of frustration where he had called Mrs. Lincoln to make a date to see Jack. He said that Bill Attwood and others were on the verge of leaving.

I can't really pronounce on the merits of the Sorensen-Cox situation. Sorensen is obviously far more skilled at writing political speeches. On the other hand Sorensen can't hope to write everything for the rest of the campaign. He seems to me another Bill Wirtz with more literary skill but with far less personal generosity or self-discipline.

I lunched today (Tuesday, 30 Aug) with Henry Kissinger. He had gone to see Nelson Rockefeller last week in Seal Harbor to explain to him why he couldn't help him in the fall campaign; Henry says he will do nothing which might aid Nixon. He said that Rockefeller appeared low and sunk—that he had been quite disappointed at the lack of response in Chicago. I asked about the Nixon-Rockefeller talks. Henry said that Nixon had come armed with polls to argue NR into accepting the vice presidential nomination. Nixon had offered him (a) dictation of the platform, (b) complete control over foreign policy, (c) New York state patronage if he would run on the ticket, but NR turned everything down. As Henry says, pronouncing the word in two syllables, "He loathes Nixon."

Kissinger said to me at lunch, "We need someone who will bring about a big jump—not just an improvement of existing tendencies, but a shift into a new atmosphere, a new world. If all Kennedy does is to argue that he can manipulate the status quo better than Nixon, he is lost."

August 31

Phil Graham called this afternoon to report on his meeting last night with JFK. Also present: Kay, and Lyndon Johnson! During cocktails, they talked mainly about the southern situation. As they went into dinner, Phil said, "Now we've talked about one part of your coalition. Let's talk a little while about the other and more important part—the northern liberals." Our hero said, "The trouble with the northern liberals is that they want their arses kissed all the time. I'm perfectly willing to kiss Mrs. Roosevelt's arse; in fact I rather enjoyed it. But I can't spend all my time doing it." He seemed at first quite impatient about the liberal situation. But Phil pointed out to him that he hadn't been drafted for the job and that he must expect to be prepared to do things himself to get people moving. K wearily agreed. Obviously he has been spending a good deal of his time since the convention buttering people up and is getting tired of it.

October 16

I have been remiss in not keeping a more faithful account of the progress of the campaign. When I returned from my first visit to California on September 20, I felt a kind of subdued pessimism about the campaign. It seemed that the Stevenson Democrats were gradually swinging into line; but Jack's campaign as a whole did not seem to be getting off the ground.

Things began to improve, though, during the week of the 26th. The first debate took place on the night of the 26th. Marian saw it with Jackie at Hyannis Port. I left the press conference for my book KENNEDY OR NIXON to catch a plane to Boston in the hope of taking a chartered plane to Hyannis Port. But, through stupidity, I went to the wrong airport; and, by the time I reached Boston, Hyannis was fogged in. So I caught the show at 109 Irving Street. Kennedy had only to hold his own to win, since ending up equal would have deflated the "experience" argument. But he did much better than that, of course. The result was to give his campaign a vital stimulus.

By the time I went back to San Francisco on October 1, I could already detect the change in the atmosphere. Things were moving faster than they had two weeks before. The liberals were showing more enthusiasm and commitment. One had a sense of tremendous Kennedy gains. I flew from San Francisco to Washington on October 3 and had a long talk with Archie Cox the next morning. This was a little discouraging. I had hoped that the Sorensen-Cox problem would solve itself as the campaign went along and demonstrated that there was enough for both of them to do. But Sorensen, with his bloc of Dick Goodwin and

Mike Feldman (all members of Jack's senatorial staff), have managed to maintain a stranglehold on the speech situation. We had some talk about my own situation, as I did also with John Bartlow Martin. I had offered to do anything Jack wanted, including joining him on tour. Sorensen had wired back that he would like me to do major speech drafts (Warm Springs and the Al Smith Memorial Dinner were specified), but it was evident that he wished them done at a distance. My first impulse was to say that speeches could not be written in a vacuum, especially at this late stage in a campaign, and that I had better apply myself to other things, such as speaking myself or helping Stevenson. But both Martin and Cox urged me not to do this. They independently recommended that I go along with Ted's request on the theory that, as demands and fatigue caught up with them, they would need more outside help, and that I would be the logical person to join them. John mentioned that there had been some discussion, however, of the bad publicity which might result from my appearance in view of Nixon's line about the Dem party of Jefferson and Jackson degenerating into the Dem Party of Schlesinger, Galbraith and Bowles.

On Sunday the 9th I received a call from Jackie Kennedy (who seems to have become my channel of communication with the candidate) saying that, before departing on the leg of his campaign, Jack had asked her to call me and ask me to come to NY, with Ken, to aid in debate preparation this week. I was going to NY anyway on the 10th to appear on the Jack Paar show and said that I would be of course glad to stay over, though I would like to go to Joe Alsop's 50th birthday celebration in Washington on the evening of the 11th.

The Paar show. Marian and I stayed at the Finletters; and the next morning Jackie called to ask whether I could lunch with Jack that day. So I went to the duplex apartment on the top floors of the Carlyle for lunch. The view was superb—34 stories high, and splendid vistas up and down the island. Jack greeted me with his usual affability and started talking about the debates. He said that it was impossible to debate with Nixon—he would never address himself to issues but always went into little speeches; and his opponent had to spend so much time correcting

N's misrepresentation of his position that there was little time left to develop a case of his own. Moreover, he felt that the Republicans had been playing dirty. Thus the studio had been cooled to almost 60 degrees when he arrived (this was in Washington on the 7th); and, when he tried out his position, he discovered that four lights were shining in his eyes as against one shining on Nixon. "When I saw all these things, I decided that NBC had chosen its candidate." After the broadcast, Jack said, he had gone over to shake hands with Nixon. They had a moment or so of totally inconsequential talk. While they were chatting, a photographer came by and started to take a picture. As soon as Nixon saw this, without altering the subject of conversation or his tone of voice, he started waving his finger in Jack's face to give the photographic impression that he was telling off Kennedy as he had told off Khrushchev. Jack told this with a mixture of contempt and incredulity. "The man is a shit—a total shit." We talked a bit about my own situation. Jack said that this had to be looked at coolly. He would like me along—might need me, since his own people were getting tired and running out of ideas—but there would be certain publicity reactions which had to be taken into account. He feared that my joining the group would be played up as "Kennedy's team is collapsing and Stevenson's ace speech writer is coming in to take over." Jack felt this might be especially unfortunate at a time when he was taking a Stevensonian position on Quemoy and Matsu. "Think it over till Thursday," he said, "and we can talk about it then."

Jackie, Lee and Radziwill joined us for lunch. I mentioned the formation of the Committee of Arts, Letters and Sciences for Kennedy and asked whether he could briefly attend a launching press conference on Thursday. He said he could and suggested that Ken and I meet him there and then go on for lunch and a pre-debate session.

Jack seemed totally relaxed and was very friendly. About three he had to go down to the Biltmore to make some TV shorts with Humphrey. He asked me to come along with him, which I did, and we had some more conversation there. I finally left to go back to the Carlyle (where I also was staying) and work on a draft for AES for the 18th.

That evening I flew to Washington for the Alsop party given by the Grahams at Mrs. Meyer's. It was great fun. One thing that struck me particularly was the extent to which the senior commentators—not only Joe but Lippmann, Reston and Phil himself—are emotionally engaged in this campaign. They cannot stand the thought of a Nixon victory, and they have a confidence in Jack which none of them really had in AES. Dean Acheson said to me, however, that he considered both of them school kids, bright sophomores, and couldn't see how anything either of them had said or done qualified them for the presidency. Emmett Hughes was there. I asked him whether we were on the same side at last; he said, "Of course," and talked quite unguardedly about his preference for Kennedy and his fears about Nixon.

Ken and I met for breakfast on the morning of the 13th (Thursday) and spent most of the morning working out some new ideas to present to Jack (who had said to me on Tuesday that he was getting tired of everything he had been saying, feared that he was getting repetitious and boring, and wanted something new). At noon we attended the Arts, Letters and Sciences press conference (staged by Jock Saltonstall; attended by a group ranging from Bette Davis to Van Wyck Brooks). Jack arrived a little late, shook hands all around, said a few words and then, after an impromptu press conference, took Ken, Ted and me back to the 34th floor for luncheon.

He was notably more tired and harrassed than he had been on Tuesday. I had the impression that he was a little nervous about the Q–M issue. For a couple of hours we ran through possible questions for the evening debate; and most of our consideration revolved around the offshore islands. We had very little talk about anything else. As he left, he said to me, "I think we had better delay any decision about you. For the next week or so, perhaps you had better do any speaking you have to do on your own."

I must add a brief story about Robert Frost. I called to ask him to join the cultural committee for Jack. He replied that he couldn't do this— that he liked Jack, admired him, had sent for his absentee ballot, expected to vote for him; but that he had never signed something with a lot of people in his life, hated the idea of "ganging up" about things, and felt that any such action would be contrary to the whole point of his poetry and his life. He said, "My father was a rabid Democrat. I regard myself as a Democrat too—a gold-standard, Grover Cleveland Democrat. My first political memory is shouting for Cleveland in 1884. I hope to vote for Kennedy. But I don't want to commit myself. I want to listen to every speech in the campaign knowing that it still might change my mind. So I sympathize with you but I'm sorry and I can't do it."

As I left JFK on Thursday, I handed him a copy of a draft for the Alfred E. Smith dinner, a project of Cardinal Spellman's attended by eminent Catholics. I explained that on reading over the draft I was afraid that it was too Catholic. Kennedy said, "You and Ted keep writing Catholic speeches. I guess I am the only Protestant around here."

I should add a word about the Stevenson situation. I see I have omitted mention of the Liberal Party banquet on September 14. Both JFK and AES asked me to do their speeches that night, and I could not resist the thought of doing both, so I did, a fact I have carefully kept secret from everybody (especially the two principals). I dropped in to see Adlai at the Savoy Hilton Wednesday afternoon. He was cordial, but an indefinite strain of some sort remains, and I did not get the feeling that he was particularly glad to see me or that he wanted me to stay. His speech was a great success in the evening, but so was Kennedy's. I can well see how the situation was galling for Adlai. To be a featured performer on an occasion where in 1952 and 1956 he was the star must be difficult; and, on top of all that, there is a general mortification of his position—helping the cause of a much younger man who declines to say anything about Adlai's remaining ambition and instead seems to keep him dangling. After the banquet, we went to Roger Stevens's apartment. Adlai appeared; he was brilliant but preoccupied and almost, it seemed to me, on the verge of tears. This overstates it, but there was a sad, shining quality about his eyes which affected me a good deal.

October 20–November 8

I had a couple of talks with Kennedy (by phone) on the 20th. He had spoken Wednesday night (the 19th) at Cardinal Spellman's Al Smith dinner. He was ironically entertained by the fact that this high Catholic audience had applauded Nixon a good deal more than it had applauded him. "It all goes to show," he said, "that, when the chips are down, money counts more than faith." I asked him how he felt things were going in general. He said that he thought he had everything made except the religious issue; this would remain the great uncertainty.

We talked a little about the Cuban issue. He said, as he had before, that action against the Castro regime must be multilateral and in concert with the other American republics. After hearing these reasonable and moderate views, I was considerably surprised to read in the evening papers a jingoistic Kennedy statement on Cuba, promising support to the fighters for freedom. (I later learned from Jack that Dick Goodwin had put this statement out without clearing with him.)

Jack was also considerably exercised over the report that *Life* intended to publish a pro-Nixon article by Billy Graham. Endorsement by a popular preacher, coming about the same time as Reformation Sunday, seemed calculated to stir the religious issue. Kennedy had called Luce and made this point to him. Luce was at first not disposed to withdraw the article. He finally agreed that a comparable piece should be run on Kennedy, suggesting Eugene McCarthy or Jack's prep school headmaster as possible authors. Both these suggestions left Jack cold. The choice of McCarthy would emphasize the Catholic issue; moreover, McCarthy detests Kennedy. And who would care about the views of the headmaster of Choate? Jack accordingly asked me about Lippmann and Niebuhr. I said I doubted whether Lippmann would do it, with which he agreed, and said I would explore the Niebuhr possibility. I called Reinhold the next day, and he said he would be glad to do a "case for Kennedy" piece. In the meantime, Luce had communicated his own developing misgivings to Graham, who decided to spend the weekend in prayer to determine whether or not he should leave the article in.

Eventually prayer told him to cease and desist; so, early the next week, he withdrew the piece and substituted for it a plea to virtuous citizens to be sure and go to the polls. So Niebuhr never had to write his piece.

Late Sunday afternoon I left for Chicago. When I presented my ticket at the United Air Lines ticket counter, I was told that Senator Kennedy had been trying to call me from Madison, Wisconsin. I promptly called him. He had read Scotty Reston's column in that day's *Times* describing his Cuban statement of the 20th as his first major blunder of the campaign. Jack was afraid of continued bad reactions from Reston, and from Lippmann too, and wanted me to clarify his meaning to them—i.e., explain to them that by support he meant moral and psychological support, not political or military support, and to assure them that he was committed to working within the framework of the OAS.

When I called from Chicago that night, I was unable to reach Reston, who had disappeared on to the Nixon train. I reached Lippmann the next day. He was not particularly impressed by the explanation, said that he thought the Kennedy people had been trying to play the issue both ways and deserved to be called on it, but added that he planned a column which, while criticizing Kennedy, would criticize Lodge's behavior during the Hungarian crisis of 1956 much more.

Walter's analysis is quite correct. The Kennedy people, wanting to be sure of the suburban Catholics, decided that anti-Castroism was a major means of doing so. They consequently planned to be harder than Nixon on Castro. Kennedy's "soft" position on Quemoy-Matsu confirmed their intention of being "hard" on Cuba. At the same time, they supposed that their quiet affirmations in support of multilateral action would provide the escape-hatch in case anyone challenged them after the election. They deserved to be condemned for this tactic. My impression is that the Reston and Lippmann columns had a thoroughly healthy effect on the candidate and a very chastening effect on Goodwin, who, up to that time, was prepared to say anything which would win the election regardless of its post-election consequences.

On Wednesday I went to New York where I spoke at a Citizens' rally. The next day I went around with Kennedy on the first lap of his

New York tour. I heard him speak in the garment district and again at an outdoor Liberal Party rally. His earnestness, his intensity, his confidence were all impressive; and so too was the electric enthusiasm he produced in the crowds.

On Wednesday, November 2, I flew to Providence where I joined the Kennedy party for the last day of the campaign. It was a beautiful day and great fun. We went to Springfield, Hartford, Burlington, Vermont, Manchester, New Hampshire, and then on to Boston. I saw Jack only once to speak to. As we crossed from Massachusetts into Connecticut in an interval of motorcade, everything stopped while the Massachusetts pols got out and the Connecticut pols got in. We all got out of the press bus to watch. After the exchange had been completed, I started on my way back when I heard my name being called. I looked around, could see no one but Pierre Salinger and started to respond to him when I saw that he had not seen me. I started to continue on my way when I heard my name being called again. So I turned again and saw, beyond Salinger, the candidate himself, getting out of his car and making his way toward me through a cordon of policemen. He greeted me with the utmost cordiality, asked how things were going and made his way back to his car.

The campaign concluded with an uproaring rally in the Boston Garden. It was, as Mary McGrory later wrote, the young prince come home. Jack's speech was pretty much the same one he has given for the last week; but he gave it with his usual charm and power, and it was all impressive and exciting. Later that night Tom Braden (who was staying with us) remarked that he had recently seen the tape of Jack's debate with the Houston ministers. What had impressed him most, he said, was not the brilliance of Jack's performance but the difference between the intelligent but still young and anxious figure of September and the supremely powerful and confident leader of November. Mrs. Roosevelt said somewhat the same thing at Diane Michaelis's on the 12th. She said that, like Franklin, Jack seemed to gain strength in the course of the campaign—that the great leaders drew vitality and power from their crowds—and that Jack was the first man she had seen since Franklin to have that quality.

I was sorry, of course, not to have taken a greater part in the campaign. I love the drama of campaigning—the airplanes and motorcades, the hotel rooms and telephone calls and speech crises, the policy conferences and the tense decisions and the constant air of excitement and anxiety and passion and fatigue. I missed it all terribly. But Jack obviously did not much need the kind of thing I am good at. He wisely decided to concentrate on a single theme and to hammer that theme home until everyone in America understood it—understood his sense of the decline of our national power and influence and his determination to arrest and reverse this course. He did this with such brilliant success that, even in time of apparent prosperity and apparent peace, and even as a Catholic, he was able to command a majority (though such a slim majority) of the voters. It was a great campaign, and I think he will make a great President.*

November 21

Averell has returned to my life. I have gotten several amiable telephone calls from him in the last few days. One of them described the message he has received from Khrushchev. Averell had asked NSK to speak with equal harshness of both candidates lest his intervention help Nixon. NSK now replied by calling Averell's attention to the fact that he had taken care to be as critical of Kennedy as of Nixon, though he added that his words about Kennedy were less sharp than his words about Nixon. His further language suggested that he regarded Jack's election as wiping the slate clean and wished to resume further discussions.

I should add that I encountered in Washington, to my dismay, a powerful movement to put some Republicans, particularly Douglas Dillon, in the cabinet. Phil Graham, with whom Galbraith and I dined on the 16th, was euphorically insistent on Dillon as Secretary of the Treasury—to such an extent that Phil and I had our first serious wrangle in years,

---

* John F. Kennedy defeated Richard Nixon on November 8, 1960.

and I left for the airport in a state of extreme irritation. (Phil charmingly called up the next day to apologize.) Joe Alsop is equally impassioned about Dillon and far more violent against Stevenson and Bowles.

I hope that Jack will resist these pressures, though obviously the narrowness of his margin complicates things for him. If he must have a conservative in the cabinet, let him be placed in Defense and not in Treasury or State. The gold crisis makes Treasury especially critical, since the orthodox answer would be to reduce public spending and increase the interest rate, and the crisis would therefore reinforce all Dillon's natural inclinations. Kennedy needs as Secretary of State a man who will defend the dollar but who believes it can be done without jettisoning the New Frontier. We shall see.

December 1

On my way through Washington to Winston-Salem yesterday, I called Bill Walton to check the atmosphere around JFK. The newspaper speculation was concentrated increasingly on a collection of rather respectable and conservative names for the Cabinet, and I wanted to find out whether this was based on anything beyond reporters interviewing each other. Bill (who had spent Thanksgiving with the Kennedys) was quite reassuring, and said that he was not worried. He added that he thought Joe was throwing his influence against such Establishment characters as McCloy. Bill went on to say that he thought I should stop in and see JFK. I demurred but eventually decided I could at least tell Evelyn Lincoln I was passing through. She wanted to make an appointment right away but I told her to talk to Jack first. Then she called me in Winston-Salem to tell me to come to Jack's Senate office at noon the next day.

I reached Jack's office shortly before noon. Scoop Jackson was holding a TV press conference squarely in front of the door, but in due course I got in. After a few moments, Jack appeared. He greeted me with his usual cordiality. We talked for a moment or two. Then, after an interval, we went down to the car and to Georgetown. When we arrived, he asked me to come into the house and have a drink. I did and we chatted for a time, with Caroline, an enchanting little girl, dashing in and out carrying a football. (The Kennedys apparently believe in breaking them in early.) In due course Bob Lovett came in for lunch. I finished my drink and soon took my leave.

I said that the liberals were concerned about having a spokesman in the Cabinet and that, with Williams out of the picture, this left Freeman as the main candidate. Jack said, "Yes, I know, the liberals want visual reassurance just like everybody else. But they shouldn't worry. What matters is the program. We are going down the line on the program." Then he said: "I don't know what to do about Orville. There is only Labor left." I said, "What about Attorney General!" Jack reacted a little sharply to this and said, "Oh, I don't think Orville is qualified for that by temperament or by interest. And besides we couldn't put a man in there who ran so far behind the ticket as Orville did. He'd be too vulnerable politically." He went on to say that he was thinking of Arthur Goldberg for Labor, though this would make the Building Trades unhappy. I started to say something about Freeman's labor troubles, meaning his troubles with business over his seizure of a packing house, but Jack interpreted this as meaning troubles with the labor movement and said. "Those fellows are as bad as businessmen. They always have some petty objection." I had assumed from his remark that Labor was all that was left: that Udall is definite for Interior. I started to say something about Agriculture, and he started to comment on it, but then this part of the conversation was somehow derailed.

Then he said, "State, Treasury and Defense are giving me the most trouble. I'd like to have some new faces here, but all I get are the same old names. It's discouraging. But I suppose that it will take a little while to develop new talent." I made my usual pitch about the Treasury. He said, "Have you a candidate?" I said, "I suppose Dick Bolling is out because he won't reassure the business community. If we must have a businessman, I am in favor of Bill Youngman." I later said, "What about Averell?" Jack said something to the general effect that he was too old hat.

I then challenged the idea of appointing Dillon, saying that it seemed too bad to give a big Cabinet post to a man who had been only a subcabinet official in the defeated government and who had contributed generously to Nixon. Jack said, "Oh, I can't care about those things. All I want to know is: Is he able? and will he go along with the program?"

He asked me about Dick Bissell, whom I praised lavishly, though I neglected to find out what he had Dick in mind for. He asked me what I thought about David Bruce. I said that I had known him for a long time and that Evangeline was a great friend of mine (at which he smiled). I said that David was able and high-minded, that he would have the confidence of the Department and would surround himself with able people, but that he wouldn't bring great personal imagination or initiative to the job. I said that he wouldn't have too many ideas of his own. Jack said a little sourly, "Well, Chester Bowles has enough ideas for everybody." I said that David would be OK as Secretary if Jack wanted to supply the drive and vision himself: otherwise he would make a fine Ambassador to Rome. Jack said quickly, "Well, he will either get one or the other."

Later, at his house, he talked favorably about Fulbright. Again, his influence on the Hill seemed a paramount consideration. I said, "Wouldn't he alienate the Negroes and the Jews?" Jack said, "I don't care about the Jews [in this connection]. Actually Bill is in a position to help them more than anyone else precisely because of the stands he has taken." Jack then repeated his remark about Bill's weight in the Senate. I judge from all this that Bill is currently ahead for State.

Then Jack said, "Have you seen Adlai? I understand that Adlai doesn't want to do the UN job. Why is that?" I started to explain that Adlai felt he had done his UN stint, and that he wanted to help form policy rather than just be on the receiving end. Jack broke in and said, "The UN is different now. I think this job has great possibilities." Then he said, "I have another thought. What about Adlai for Attorney General?" I was taken a back for a minute. Jack continued, "I'd like Stevenson for Attorney General and Paul Freund for Solicitor General." I said, "It's certainly a new idea, and maybe a good one." As I left, he said, "I suppose that Bill Blair is the man to call about this, isn't he? I think I'll call him tonight."

At one point I said that I hoped he had Mac Bundy under consideration for something. He said that he was thinking about him as Undersecretary of State for Administration—the Loy Henderson job. He then said that he wanted to make Ken Galbraith Ambassador to India. I heartily seconded this remembering that Ken a few weeks back had expressed his desire for New Delhi. When I reported this conversation to Ken later, however, there was a moment of hurt silence; evidently he had interpreted Kennedy's note to him ("I have a proposition to put to you which I hope very much you will accept") as referring to the Senate. Ken said that his enthusiasm for New Delhi had faded after his mind became fixed on the Senate.

Then Jack said, "How about you? Wouldn't you like to be an Ambassador?" I said that I didn't think so. He said, "I think an ambassadorship would be a great job. I'd like to be one myself. Are you sure you wouldn't want one?" I repeated that I didn't think so.

At one point I asked him if he was enjoying all this. He said, "Yes. There are problems and irritations. But, on the whole, I like it all very much."

My broad impression is that he is much more on the defensive than he seemed at Hyannis Port—much more impressed, for example, by the need to appoint people who will get along with a conservative Congress. Hence the bypassing of Williams and Freeman: hence the upgrading of Fulbright: hence (perhaps) the desire to export Galbraith and Schlesinger. At one point he said, "We'll have to go along with this for a year or so. Then I would like to bring in some new people." He paused and added, "I suppose it may be hard to get rid of these people once they are in." His present idea, I would judge, is an administration of conservative men and liberal measures. This is partly rationalized by the argument that, especially with a liberal Congress, conservative-appearing men can win more support for liberal measures than all-outers. Of course there is something to this argument.

December 11

On my way back from Montana, I stopped off in New York and lunched at Marietta's with Bill Blair, the Wechslers and the Backers. Bill reported on Adlai's talk with Jack. Jack apparently told Adlai that he had become too "controversial" for appointment as Secretary of State; had taken too many public positions on things; that it was necessary to have someone with a blanker record and fewer established enemies. Adlai said that he could not accept the UN job until he knew who the Secretary of State would be. Jack made it clear that he would guarantee as President any of Adlai's conditions and specifications about the job. Adlai said that he had worked in government and knew that his immediate superior had to be someone with whom he had a relationship of mutual confidence. Jack seemed rather irritated that his presidential guarantee was not enough.

Adlai was later told by Walter Lippmann that Mac Bundy was going to be Secretary of State. Adlai says that he will not serve under Mac because Mac voted against him twice and only became a Democrat this fall.

Bill felt (as I do) that AES made a mistake in not accepting straightaway (or declining)—that his temporizing only reinforces the public image of indecision and only irritates JFK. Jimmy Wechsler felt that the delay was necessary for Adlai's dignity; otherwise he might be seeming to show undue alacrity at the thought of a job, any job.

Elizabeth Farmer told me this evening that, at five this afternoon, it looked as if it would be Rusk in State, with Bowles and Bundy as Undersecretaries. (Ken, by the way, told me that Jack had called him on the 7th and talked seriously about Mac as Secretary.) I asked why Rusk had finally emerged. Elizabeth said, "He was the lowest common denominator." Apparently Harris Wofford succeeded in stirring the Negroes and Jews up so effectively that the uproar killed Fulbright, who was apparently Jack's first choice.

1961

February 2

As I reach the end of my second full day at the White House, I shall make an effort to recapitulate the series of events which brought me here.

Last December, when I had lunch in Washington with Bob Kennedy, he suggested to me the possibility of coming to the White House as some sort of roving reporter and trouble-shooter. The proposed assignment could not have appealed to me more, and I said that I would of course be delighted to come. He said that he would bring this up with Jack and that I would probably hear from JFK after the first of the year.

After Christmas, JFK told Ken that I was under consideration for the Gordon Gray job—i.e., the National Security Council man at the White House. He seems to have thought seriously of this for a few minutes; but eventually, when Dean Rusk and McGeorge [Mac] Bundy could not work out a mutually satisfactory arrangement, JFK very sensibly picked Mac to do the National Security Council job. The next thing

I heard was the suggestion that I become Assistant Secretary of State for Cultural Affairs. This idea I quickly knocked down. Then Fred Holborn informed me that, when JFK made his visit to Cambridge for the Board of Overseers meeting on January 9, he wondered whether he could use 109 Irving Street [Schlesinger's address at the time] in the afternoon for his appointments, including one with me.

This was an exciting day for the Schlesingers. Secret service men vetted the house; Harvard and Cambridge police surrounded it; and around 2 P.M. a small crowd of curiosity seekers and fans began to collect. It was a cold day, but many of them stayed through the afternoon, watching JFK's arrival at about 2:20 and his departure shortly after 5. By the latter hour there must have been about 300 people in attendance.

JFK conducted his business in the living room. I was with him from about 2:30 to 3:30, when the tax task force, headed by Stanley Surrey, took over. There followed appointments with Abe Chayes, Mac Bundy and Julius Stratton and Jerry Wiesner.

Our talk ranged over a number of issues. The question of scientific appointments was much on his mind: Atomic Energy Commission, Science Advisor, NASA. At this point Mac came up with the idea of Glenn Seaborg for Atomic Energy Commission and, after talking it over with JFK, called Seaborg from our house.*

February 6

I settled down in an office in the East Wing of the White House and tried to find out what I was supposed to do. I had the impression that JFK was equally baffled, and he had somewhat more weighty matters on his mind. McGeorge Bundy was most helpful in this sterile period, as was Fred Holborn. The others at the White House went about their business.

---

* Schlesinger was appointed Special Assistant to the President following JFK's visit to Cambridge.

JFK decided to have a personal representative accompany [George McGovern] the Food For Peace mission and underline his concern about general Latin American problems. Because he had been told of the disaffection of the Latin American intellectual community, the choice fell on me. I guess he decided that this would dramatize as effectively as anything the shift from the Old to the New Frontier. My first reaction to the proposal that I should go was that it sounded like a WPA project. But on consideration it seemed to present opportunities; and in any case I had no real choice but to go (though JFK put it up to me in a manner which would have permitted me to decline).

What Latin America needs above all is revolution—not proletarian or peasant revolution, but middle-class revolution. Mexico, Brazil and Argentina have achieved semi-revolutions. The other countries (how rashly I generalize) remain under the control of the landholding oligarchy. This oligarchy constitutes the chief barrier to the middle-class revolution and, by thwarting the middle-class revolution, may well bring about the proletarian revolution.

The gap between the U.S. and the rest of the hemisphere is widening—i.e., our living standards are rising faster than theirs.

February 20
Rio de Janeiro

At 5:30 we went with Ambassador [John M.] Cabot to pay a call on Carlos Lacerda, one time fiery editor, now governor of the state which includes Rio. We found him in his gubernatorial palace, a splendid example of Portuguese baroque. We talked most of the time about the *favellas* of Rio. The first *favella* apparently arose around the turn of the century on the Hill of Favella—hence, of course, the name. They began to appear in quantity only after the Second World War. Some of the land occupied by *favella*s is public land; in other cases, it is unused land held by private owners, in which case the owner rarely or never dares challenge the *favella*. They get electric light when someone puts a tap on a power line and then sells electric power to the *favella* dwellers. Their favorite form of organization is the samba club. They take dancing seriously and spend disproportionate amounts of money on their carnival costumes. Both politicans and Communists try to exploit the samba organizations for their own purposes. Lacerda, like the Archbishop, emphasized the importance of rural reform in order to hold more of these people on the land. As he pointed out, life in the *favella*, however appalling it seemed, is considerably more attractive than life in a stagnant rural village.

Once one becomes sensitized to the existence of *favella*s, one begins to see them everywhere. The result is to give a sinister undertone to the quality of life in this lively and lovely city. Color and gaiety pervade; then one suddenly sees the gray, creeping invasion of the *favella*, trickling down hillsides, rising out of railroad yards, appearing wherever there is open space. When we went to the Copacabana beach in the morning, we saw from a slight distance the *favella* we had visited on Friday; it is only a couple of blocks from the beach and thus in the midst of the most desirable part of Rio. No doubt all this has value as a reminder of morality; the *favella* in Rio is certainly a constant symbol of the skull beneath the skin.

February 24
La Paz, Bolivia

At 5 o'clock, we went over to see the Bolivian President. In due course we were ushered into the presidential presence. [Victor] Paz Estenssoro turned out to be an agreeable, intelligent, harassed man.

The exchange of remarks was entirely between Paz and myself. He had begun by saying that he knew my books and had long looked forward to meeting me. I now took the opportunity to say that I was an old friend of the Bolivian Revolution and that I had been one of the few people in Washington to urge an early recognition of the Villarrel government in 1943. I then said that JFK would be interested in his views of the problems and prospects of democracy in the hemisphere.

He began by an intelligent presentation of the case for revolution. The great need, he said, was to incorporate the poor people both into the money economy and into the political society. But too much of Latin America was in a quasi-feudal state, with the poor, and especially the Indians, under the domination of a landed oligarchy convinced it was ruling by divine right. The longer these people resist change, he said, the more violent the revolution will be when it comes. He mentioned Peru and Ecuador as especially near the point of social explosion.

I said that I looked on this analysis with much sympathy, and so did many Americans. I was not, I said, a member of the Republican party; but even the recent Republican administration had been a friend of the Bolivian Revolution and had provided the margin of financial support which had saved that revolution from economic disaster. He interjected his agreement with this point and his gratitude for the timely assistance.

I went on the say that the United States, itself a child of revolution, accepted the necessity of social change in Latin America. If revolution meant healthy social change, the American people would be all for it. But if revolution meant the establishment of dictatorship, the repression of freedom and the entry of alien forces into the hemisphere, then the American people would be against revolution.

I added that the problem of social revolution in Latin America implied a two-front battle. It was not only necessary to protect the integrity of the revolution from the oligarchy of the right; it was also necessary to protect it from the conspiracy and sabotage of the left.

The Cuban Revolution [I pointed out] may have begun as a national revolution, but it has now been clearly seized by forces from outside the hemisphere intent on destroying free institutions and establishing a Communist state. What could the hemisphere do with this focus of infection? He answered without hesitation, "Castro must be eliminated." I asked him how he thought this could be done. He said that first the economic screws must be tightened against him. Then an educational campaign should be undertaken to acquaint the hemisphere with the true character of the Castro regime. Thus no one in Bolivia would be impressed by the argument that the Cuban Revolution had violated the property rights of American business. But they are impressed by a comparison between the Cuban and Bolivian methods of land reform—a comparison which concludes by pointing out that, where the Bolivian system puts land into the hands of the peasants, the Cuban system puts the land into the hands of Fidel Castro.

It was now nearly 7 o'clock, and I felt it was time to stop. In parting I said that I welcomed his distinction between the Cuban and Bolivian ways and counted on his government to keep that distinction as clearcut in the future as it had been in the past. He said that we need not worry; that if Bolivia could get the assistance to surmount its economic difficulties, he could deal with his local Communist problem.

I gather that this was a typical Paz performance which [Carl W.] Strom and [Herb] Thompson had heard before. His words are excellent, but his actions belie his words.

March 16

On the night of the 15th we went to a party at the White House. This was given for the Radziwills. There were about 80 guests, Lester Lanin's band, and we stayed till nearly three in the morning. It was really a tremendous success. The President had a Pinchot girl [Mary and Tony] on each side during dinner and afterward. Jackie couldn't have looked prettier. [George] Smathers, [John] Cooper and Symington were the senators present. Pierre Salinger was the only other representative of the White House staff.

Late this afternoon Robert Triffin and I went out to pay our respects to Jean Monnet at the Westchester. I asked him what he thought of the New Frontier. He said, "The thing I note is that the discussion is recommencing. You cannot have serious government without collective consideration. I have missed that in Washington recently. Now I feel it is starting again." We talked about the modern world in general. "Instability is the source of progress," Monnet said. "The one thing I realized early in life was that things change, and that whoever tried to ignore or evade the fundamental fact was doomed." He spoke very interestingly about [Charles] de Gaulle. "The great thing about de Gaulle," he said "is his precise and persistant concern with the figure he will cut in history. Whenever he considers a decision, he wonders how it will look in the history books thirty years from now. So, against all his natural instincts, he had abandoned the French Empire."

March 19

I worked steadily on the Cuban White Paper on Friday and Saturday. My effort is to contrive a document which will make some impression on people who were initially pro-Castro and who feel that U.S. motives in opposing Castro are anti-revolutionary rather than pro-freedom. Hence great emphasis on Castro as the man who betrayed the Cuban Revolution.

March 23

In the course of Thursday and Friday I cleared the Cuban White Paper with State (Rusk, [Adolf] Berle and [Thomas] Mann), CIA (Tracy Barnes) and USIA (United States Information Agency) (Ed Murrow and staff). Oddly enough, both State and CIA seemed quite pleased and had only factual suggestions. The USIA people, on the other hand, were plainly unhappy about it. It seemed essentially too racy and liberal a document. They didn't want me to attack the Batista regime, for example, on the ground that such an attack would raise the question why we supported that regime. I pointed out that "we" had changed since January, and it was not necessary for Kennedy to identify himself with all the errors of the Eisenhower policy, and that no one in Latin America would dream of blaming Kennedy for Eisenhower's support of [Fulgencio] Batista.

March 28

Late in the afternoon I saw the President about the Cuba piece. He was surprisingly generous in his comment. He then made a few specific criticisms, almost all well taken. Where I had written of the initial Castro programs that they were impressive in conception "if not in execution," he wondered whether this last phrase was not "snide" and suggested its omission. As usual, he was temperate, quick and effective. As we finished, I said, "What do you think about this damned invasion?" He said wryly, "I think about it as little as possible." We agreed that the critical point—and the weak part of the case for action—lay in the theory of an immediate local response to a landing.

April 5

The newspaper reaction on Tuesday [to my Cuban White Paper] was favorable, though the *Times* played up the call to Castro to sever his Communist connections, a very marginal part of the argument, rather than the main thrust—the affirmation of our faith in social progress and our rejection of the Castro revolution, not as revolutionary, but as Communist.

In the late afternoon on Tuesday we held the penultimate Cuba meeting. This was in a small conference room beside Dean Rusk's office in the State Department. We went through the usual business, with CIA demonstrations, mild disclaimers by various people present about what they thought. Bill Fulbright, who had not appeared before, denounced the operation as excessive (in terms of the threat of our security) and hazardous (in terms of our international relations and our treaty commitments). It was an excellent old-American speech, honorable, sensible and strong. It moved me and perhaps the President, but not most of the others. McNamara said he favored the operation.

At 3:30 today I met with Phil Bonsal, Berle and Miro Cardona, the Cuban Revolutionary Council chairman. Miro is an affable Cuban in his late fifties, bald, flushed, with the inordinately heavy horn-rimmed

glasses beloved by the Latinos. The point of the meeting was to persuade Miro to give the Cuban Revolutionary program more social and
economic content. As I said at one point, "It is foolish if the Cuban Revolutionary Council turns out to be to the right of the New Frontier." We
pointed out that the existing program was filled with appeals to the foreign investor, the private bankers, the dispossessed property owner, but
had very little to say to the worker or the farmer. He agreed with all this
and said only that we must understand the situation in Miami: when he
gives a speech about social justice and economic progress, half the audience goes away thinking that he is a Communist.

April 7

Thursday morning opened with the usual Cuba meeting. We seem
now destined to go ahead on a quasi-minimum basis—a large-scale in-
fliltration (hopefully) rather than an invasion.

In the meantime, more and more details about the Cuban operation
are appearing in the papers. On Thursday morning Gil Harrison sent
over a piece (pseudonymous) entitled "Our Men in Miami." It was a careful and substantially accurate account of CIA activites in Miami. Reading
the piece confronted me with a predictable moral struggle. Obviously
publication of this article in a responsible magazine would cause great
trouble. On the other hand, should one intervene in such matters of editorial judgment? I resolved the struggle by handing the article to the President, who soon sent me word that he hoped it could be stopped. So I called
Gil, who accepted the suggestion promptly and without questions—a
gentlemanly and patriotic act, which made me feel rather unhappy.

This morning Dick Goodwin and I met for breakfast to see whether
it would be worth making one more try to reverse the decision.
But Bundy and [Walt] Rostow joined us and discouraged our efforts.
Obviously I must work now to minimize the political and diplomatic
damage.

At the end of the afternoon, I went to see the President. It is apparent that he has made his decision and is not likely now to reverse it. He

feels he has pared down the operation from an invasion to a mass infiltration. "If we have to get rid of those 800 men, it is much better to dump them in Cuba than in the United States." I remarked that the political and diplomatic contingency planning was much less advanced than the operational planning. He agreed with vigor.

April 12

On Saturday morning, the 8th, I went to see Rusk. I expressed misgivings about the Cuban operation. Rusk seemed to share these misgivings. He said that he had been wanting for some time to write up a balance sheet on the project, that he planned to do so over the weekend, and that he would try and talk to the President about it on Monday.

I then took a plane to New York. I went immediately to the office of the U.S. Delegation to the UN. Adlai E. Stevenson made clear that he wholly disapproves of the project, objects to the fact that he was given no opportunity to comment on it, and believes it will cause infinite trouble. However, he is substantially the good soldier about it and is prepared to try and make the best possible U.S. case.

Tuesday was spent largely in worry over how to deal with press conference questions on Cuba. In the evening we went to Bobby Kennedy's for a large Irish birthday party for Ethel. It was a messy, disordered, chaotic party, always trembling on the verge of total disintegration, but somehow held together by the raucous high spirits of the company. After dinner there were skits—Ethel taking off, Bobby going to work, etc. In certain respects it was a terrible party, but it was also tremendous fun. One can imagine no greater contrast than with the party the President gave at the White House a month ago. That was chic, decorous, urbane; this was raffish, confused, loud—Brockton rather than Hobe Sound.

I went to our last Cuba meeting today. The President again emphasized the importance of transforming this as much as possible into a Cuban operation. He inquired rather sharply whether the Revolutionary Council understood that U.S. recognition would have to await the establishment of a secure position in Cuba and that in no case would there be overt U.S. intervention. Berle and I are supposed to put this over to Cardona tomorrow.

April 16

On Saturday the pace of action began to mount in Cuba, and the long-awaited Cuban appeal to the UN produced an emergency session of the Security Council. Rusk, Berle, Bundy, Bissell and I were discussing the next step with the President, when Mac brought down the house—and especially JFK—by saying, as we were all engaged in what JFK calls "Scarlet Pimpernel" discussions, "Mr. President, do you realize that you are surrounded by five ex-professors?"

April 18

The pace began to quicken in Cuba over the weekend. On Saturday, fliers landed in Florida after attacks on Cuban air fields and claimed to be defectors. Through an unfortunate misunderstanding, Stevenson in New York was permitted by the State Department to testify to this effect in his UN speech Saturday afternoon. They were *not* defectors. This, plus the impression given Stevenson by the CIA that no action was imminent, made him unhappy and suspicious over the turn of events. The President, who probably had misgivings of this own, responded to this mood and called off an air strike scheduled for Monday morning. This meant that the landings at the Bay of Pigs had to take place under the guns of what remained of the Cuban Air Force. In particular, the Cuban T-33s [Lockheed jets] turned out to be far more effective than any of us had been led to suppose. This created havoc on Monday and Tuesday. In addition, Castro's tanks reached the beachhead sooner than had been expected. And the landings failed to set off mass uprisings behind the line. By Tuesday evening, it looked to be all over. It was a grim and sad two days. Many fine men have been killed or lost; and one cannot resist the belief that this was an ill-considered and mistaken expedition.

I had seen Scotty Reston Monday afternoon. At the end of the afternoon I reported this to the President, who decided that it might be a good idea to have Scotty in for luncheon on Tuesday.

JFK was in superb form at lunch. Scotty went away starry-eyed (as did I). We talked a little about Cuba, though without going into operational detail. The President made it clear that he felt he had been given poor advice by the CIA. "I probably made a mistake in keeping Allen Dulles on," he said. "It's not that Dulles is not a man of great ability. He is. But I have never worked with him and therefore I can't estimate his meaning when he tells me things. We will have to do something about the CIA. I must have someone there with whom I can be in complete and intimate contact—someone from whom I know I will be getting the exact pitch." He added, "I made a mistake in putting Bobby in the Justice Department. He is wasted there. Byron White could do that job perfectly well. Bobby should be in the CIA." (In my view, the President is dead right.) He spoke about all this in excellent humor. "Dulles," he said, "is a legendary figure, and it's hard to operate with legendary figures. . . . It is a hell of way to learn things, but I have learned one thing from this business—that is, that we will have to deal with the CIA. McNamara has dealt with Defense; Rusk has done a lot with State; but no one has dealt with the CIA."

Given the faltering of the Cuban adventure, the next question is whether we should accept defeat or enlarge our support of the rebels. Stewart Alsop, with whom I had a drink at the Metropolitan Club before the lunch, had argued that defeat would cause irreparable harm; that we had no choice but to intervene, if necessary, to avert disaster. But the President had already made his mind up on this. He felt that defeat in Cuba would obviously be a setback; but that it would be an incident, not a disaster. The test had always been whether the Cuban people would back up a revolt against Castro. If they wouldn't, we could not impose a new regime on them. But would not U.S. prestige suffer if we let the rebellion flicker out? "What is prestige?" said the President. "Is it the shadow of power or the substance of power? We are going to work on the substance of power. No doubt we will be kicked in the ass for the next couple of weeks, but that won't affect the main business."

After the luncheon, I joined Mac [Bundy] and Ken O'Donnell in the President's office. Ken, who has penetrating good sense on practically everything, suggested the general line: the Cuban insurgents should say that they achieved their basic objectives—supply and reinforcement— and vanish into the hills. The President was still playing around with the idea of evacuating the patriots from the beaches; but Mac feared that this would provide evidence of U.S. intervention without bringing us any gains. I was glad to see that Mac accepted the situation and did not favor the commitment of U.S. forces. In an interlude, we discussed the CIA situation. Mac felt that Dulles had more misgivings about the project than he had ever expressed to the President, and that he had not done so out of loyalty to Bissell. As for Bissell, Mac simply said that he personally would not be able to accept Dick's estimates of a situation like this again. Mac did not feel that the cancellation of the air strike had fundamentally changed the situation; it would not have altered the immense Castro advantage on the ground. His conclusion is that Castro is far better organized and more formidable than we had supposed. (For example, the insurgents appear to have run out of pilots, despite the months of training.)

All in all, a gloomy day. If this thing must fail, it is just as well that it fails quickly. But I cannot banish from my mind the picture of these brave men, pathetically underequipped, dying on Cuban beaches before Soviet tanks.

April 21

At 1:00 A.M. in the morning of Wednesday the 19th, just as I had gone to bed, I was awakened by a call from the White House. It was Mac Bundy. He said, "I am in the President's office, and he would like to have you come down here as soon as possible." I dressed and drove down to the White House.

In the President's office were Kennedy, Johnson, Rusk, McNamara and [Army chief of staff Lyman L.] Lemnitzer, all resplendent in white tie and tails (the Congressional ball was going on in the White House), plus Bundy and Rostow. They were gloomily reading dispatches from Cuba. Mac said to me, "We have no news, but we fear that things are going badly. In any case, the Revolutionary Council is very upset. Some of its members are threatening extreme action. The President wants Berle to go down and talk with them. If he can't get Berle, he wants you."

The President was concerned and sharp in his comment. It was increasingly clear, even with a breakdown of communications, that things were going badly on the beachhead—though no one knew how badly. There was talk of a concealed U.S. air strike for the next morning. The strike, it was argued, would nullify Castro's T-33's, and enable the exiles' B-26's to deal with Castro's tanks. This was discussed in a desultory and rather distraught way. Finally Berle arrived. The President described the state of mind of the Revolutionary Council. "One member is threatening suicide. Others want to be put on the beachhead. All are furious with the CIA. They do not know how dismal things are. You must go down and talk to them." Berle said, "Yes." He added wryly, "I can think of happier missions."

The meeting broke up about 2:00. The President said to me, "You ought to go with Berle." I said that I would have to go back to Georgetown and pack a bag. I did so, and in a short time Berle picked me up. We drove to the MATS depot at the National Airport. A plane was awaiting us; we climbed aboard, and in a few moments were heading south. Two berths had been made up for us. But Adolf rightly thought we should discuss our strategy for the morrow. After discussing various aspects of the problem, we climbed into our respective berths around 3:30.

At 7:00 we were awakened with words that we were approaching Miami. We got up for a dreary MATS breakfast. We started driving through mile after mile of hot, vulgar, sterile Miami landscape. Eventually we approached an abandoned government air field at Opa-locka.

We nerved ourselves for the Cuban Revolutionary Council. We drove another two minutes and disembarked a few yards from a nondescript house deep in the encampment. The house was patrolled by young American G.I.'s, their revolvers conspicuous in their holsters. We entered the house. It was about 8:15 A.M. A radio was playing in the background. As we stumbled on to the sunporch, a young man lying asleep on a cot stirred uneasily and got up; it was (I later discovered) Manuel Ray.

Our arrival brought the house to life. In a few moments we were all seated around a table. There were six members of the Revolutionary Council, all in khaki fatigues: Miro Cardona (with a son on the beachhead); Ray; Antonio Varona (with a son, two brothers and two nephews); Carlos Hevia; Justo Carillo; and Antonio Maseo (with a son). The famous [Frank] Bender of the CIA, with two other CIA people, joined us and helped interpret.

Miro Cardona opened the recital. He looked ten years older than he had seemed in New York just a short week before, when he and Berle and John Plank and I had lunched at the Century. Miro talked with impressive earnestness. It was, he said, a life-and-death struggle. It was not too late to turn the tide. Yesterday they had talked with Colonel Baker. He had given them assurances of support.

Miro expressed profound and urgent concern over the situation produced by the landings. The only excuse the Revolutionary Council could offer to the people of Cuba, he said, was to be permitted to go to Cuba and to die with the men on the beach. There is no alternative to this, he said. It is this—he said with tremendous gravity—which I request, this which I beg.

Miro was followed by Varona. Where Miro was earnest and grave, Varona was intense, florid and declamatory. His manner was both more truculent and more rhetorical than Miro's. For five minutes he seemed to say nothing. Then there began to emerge from his resonant periods a bitter indictment of the CIA. There had been, he said, no consultation with the Revolutionary Council; there had been no coordination with resistance groups behind the lines; all there had been was a landing of 1,400 men in the worst possible place in Cuba.

What was the situation now? Evacuation was impossible. The only possible course was the dispatch of U.S. Marines. If this were not done, then the U.S. would be in the position of having been defeated by Fidel Castro. After all, Varona said, the U.S. could not escape responsibility for this enterprise. The troops might be Cuban; but the training, the command, the timing, the decision to invade—all were American. The U.S. could never deny its primary role in the whole operation.

The continuation of the struggle, Varona said, required first of all U.S. planes at the field of battle—planes from U.S. bases, whether Key West, Guantanamo or a carrier. Complete control of the air was necessary to the success of the operation. Unless this were immediately achieved, no Cuban would ever trust the U.S. again.

Castro, Varona said, has Soviet planes, Soviet tanks, Soviet technicians. Why cannot the U.S. do as much for its friends? Does not the U.S. understand that its whole future in Latin America depends on whether it meets the challenge of Castro in Cuba?

The next speaker was Manuel Ray. He was quiet, direct, non-rhetorical and exceedingly impressive. His group, he said, had argued that the proper strategy was internal insurrection, not external invasion. He had tried in vain to interest the CIA in this strategy. "We could get no support for our proposal. There were guerrillas in the Escambray, but they only received help when it could no longer be used. There had never been any serious attempt to support internal uprisings."

Instead the CIA had staked everything on the strategy of external invasion. Miro, after talking with the CIA, had set forth this strategy to the Revolutionary Council. We did not like it, Ray said; but, if that is what the leading nation of the free world wanted, we saw no alternative to going along with it. We did not wish to do anything which would help the Communists. For this reason, contrary to our convictions, we accepted the second strategy.

We were told that the landings would be followed up by all necessary support. We were even told that 10–15,000 men would be available. But nothing was done to bring our people into the operation.

It was now past 10:00, and Berle and I retired for consultation. Our first thought was to ship them all to Nicaragua. But we returned to the hangar and called Washington to get the latest reports. We were quickly told that the operation was substantially over. The only signal from the beach was a wail of S-O-S's. The CIA desk said that there appeared to be no hope; the time had passed even to consider the possibility of evacuation.

Our hearts sank as we heard this report. We walked out for a moment in the bright sun. What could be done? How to break the news that the CIA has shattered their hopes and sent their sons to death or captivity? How to do so and at the same time dissuade them from calling a press conference, telling all they knew and issuing public denunciations of the CIA and the Kennedy administration? I said to Adolf, "Can't we do something to bring the President into it?" Adolf said, "We must take them to Washington and have the President see them." I immediately called the White House, and Mrs. Lincoln put me through to the President's office. Dean Rusk answered the phone, and I told him the situation. He agreed that the Council should be brought to Washington, though he seemed a little uncertain whether the President should see them.

I put another call in to the President with the idea of explaining to him why we thought he should see the group personally. When I reached him, he said that he wanted us to bring them to the White House as soon as we arrived.

We arrived in Washington late in the afternoon. We went immediately to the White House. The Revolutionary Council assembled in the Cabinet Room, while Berle and I went in to see the President. We briefed him quickly on the problem.

In a few minutes the group filed in. They sat down on the two couches facing each other in front of the fireplace. The President drew up his rocking chair. In a quiet but plainly impressive way, he expressed his regret over the events of the last 48 hours. He explained why he had decided against American intervention and also explained why he had supposed that the operation had a chance of success on its own.

News from the front was still scanty, so the President said that he would get in touch with them in the morning.

April 21

There was another Presidential breakfast Friday morning to prepare for the President's press conference [on Cuba]. Dean Rusk, Pierre Salinger, Mac, Ted and Dick Goodwin were there. The President said rather emphatically, "There is only one person in the clear [in Cuba]— that's Bill Fulbright. And he probably would have been converted if he had attended more of the meetings. If he had received the same treatment we received [here a dash of the hand]—discontent in Cuba, morale of the free Cubans, rainy season, Russian MIG's and destroyers, impregnable beachhead, easy escape into the Escambray, what elso to do with these people—it might have moved him down the road, too."

Mac Bundy reminded him that I, too, had been opposed to the expedition. "Oh sure," he said. "Arthur wrote me a memorandum that will look pretty good when he gets around to writing his book on my administration—only he better not publish that memorandum while I'm still alive!" This was said in one of those typical flashes of high sardonic humor. He added, "And I know what the book will be called— *Kennedy: The Only Years*."

Later in the day I went around to the President's office to say good-bye before leaving for Italy. The Vice President was sitting by his desk, but he invited me in. We talked about the CIA. I said that the most effective way to re-establish world confidence in the Kennedy administration would be a quick and visible reorganization of the CIA. He said he agreed. He could not understand, he said, how Dulles and Bissell could be so wrong. Dulles had sat in this very office and said that he was much more confident about the Cuban operation than he had ever been about Guatemala.

How does one add all this up?

Kennedy [had] asked whether feasible plans could be drawn up *on the basis of no U.S. military intervention.* The CIA drew up plans, and Lemnitzer and [Admiral Arleigh] Burke pronounced them feasible. Obviously, with an invading force of 1200 against a defending force of 200,000, an invasion could not succeed unless (a) it was backed by U.S. armed forces—now excluded—or (b) it was accompanied by mass defections from the militia and mass uprisings behind the line. The CIA testified that these would take place if the bridgehead could be established, and the Army and Navy endorsed the CIA's contention that a bridgehead could be secured and stabilized without too much trouble. Since the Cubans wanted desperately to go back, and the U.S. Government was under no obligation to protect Castro from the Revolutionary Council, the President decided to go ahead on what he regarded as, not an invasion, but a mass infiltration.

The calculations were mistaken. The question of stabilizing a bridgehead involves technical military issues, about which I had no judgment. But the question of the likelihood of defections and insurrections is a political matter. I always thought that the CIA was wrong on this and that landings would set off very little in the way of interior reaction. But the person who should have raised these points with vigor and who should have told the President to cancel the whole thing was the Secretary of State. I would regard his failure as almost the most reprehensible of all.

Rusk had plenty of private misgivings. He stated some in one or two of the meetings. But he never, to my knowledge, opposed the operation, never argued against it, never told the President to call it off. On April 8th, I went to him to urge him to do something. He said he planned to see the President about it but had not yet had time to draw up a balance sheet. With Rusk going along with the operation, with Dulles advocating it, with McNamara and Lemnitzer endorsing it, the President would have had to overrule all his senior advisers in order to call it off. He nearly did so. Next time I am sure he will.

April 22
Bologna, Italy

I arrived in Bologna today from Washington via New York and Rome. It is evident that the Cuban affair has done us immense damage. Everybody had been so delighted by Kennedy; all sides had nearly accepted the theory that the New Frontier meant new policies for the U.S. Now Kennedy is revealed as if no more than a continuation of the Eisenhower-Dulles past. JFK's triumph up to this point had been to establish an impression of U.S. foreign policy as mature, controlled and, above all, *intelligent*. No one I have met here can understand why anyone in Washington should have supposed that a thousand Cuban exiles could overthrow an entrenched and popular revolutionary government. We not only look like imperialists; we look like ineffectual imperialists, which is worse; and we look like stupid, ineffectual imperialists, which is worst of all. Allen Dulles and Dick Bissell brought down in a day what Kennedy had been laboring patiently and successfully to build up in three months.

May 7

I returned from Europe on May 2, arriving in Washington early in the morning of May 3. I saw the President late that afternoon. He seemed, as usual, cool and composed. We talked again about Cuba. He commented ruefully on the advice he had received. "If it hadn't been for Cuba," he said, "we might be about to intervene in Laos now." He waved a sheaf of cables from Lemnitzer apparently urging such intervention. "I might have taken this man's advice seriously," the President said.

He was much impressed by the great discrepancy between the European and American reactions. He pointed out the extreme popularity of the Cuban adventure in the United States; "if I had gone further, they would have liked me even more." (At this point Evelyn Lincoln [Kennedy's secretary] came into the office with an advance on the new

Gallup poll, showing Kennedy at an unprecedented 82 percent of approval. Kennedy tossed it aside and said, "It's just like Eisenhower. The worse I do, the more popular I get.")

June 7

Within the administration, the Cuban affair has produced, it seems to me, a profound prejudice against the taking of risks anywhere. Because this bold initiative flopped, there is now a general predisposition against boldness in all fields. I surmise a rather profound shock to the President's own self-confidence. Beneath his total control, he saw from the moment things began to go wrong the whole proportions of the catastrophe. He is wholly honest with himself, I think, and he has not spared himself when it comes to post-mortems. Bill Walton says that Jackie told him that JFK had been deeply upset after Cuba.

June 18

I saw little of the President this week. My impression when I did see him was that his back was causing him definite trouble. He could concentrate with his usual effectiveness on whatever the matter was at hand; but the customary wit and relaxation were lacking. Ken Galbraith, who has been here all week, had the same impression.

Ken told me that he had urged on both the President and Bobby one indispensable requirement for the new head of the CIA—that he must be a man whose first loyalty is to the President and not to the organization and who could in consequence be counted upon to protect the interests of the President rather than to advance the special interests of the CIA. Unfortunately there are no obvious candidates. Apparently the President said to Ken, "What about Arthur?" This is, of course, a wild idea. It would cause consternation on the Hill. More to the point, the new director of the CIA should be someone prepared to do the job for years, which I would not be prepared to do. I imagine that the President was joking.

The week ended in a burst of frivolity. On Friday night, we dined at the Grahams' and went to the Mellons' for a fantastic ball (Eliza Lloyd's coming-out party). Everything was done with immense style—a special pavilion erected for dancing; forty minutes of fireworks; tents around the house for visiting boys, all gaily decorated and lit and giving the impression of the night before Agincourt; two bands (Emil Coleman and Count Basie); and an infinitude of champagne, whiskey, food, girls and everything one could want. I had a particularly nice time with Babe Paley. The author of *The Affluent Society* and the author of *The Crisis of the Old Order* had a splendid time helping spend the ill-gotten gains of Andrew Mellon.

On Saturday Bobby and Ethel Kennedy gave another great party to celebrate their 11th anniversary. This had Lester Lanin playing by the swimming pool, with tables set up on the lawn and a general atmosphere of Kennedy high spirits. In the later stages of the evening, Teddy Kennedy emerged as the dominant figure, singing, plunging fully dressed into the swimming pool and demonstrating in general that the Kennedy vitality is far from extinct in the lower reaches of the family. Judy Garland, Kay Thompson and Ethel sang; there was wild dancing, in which I took an enthusiastic but inexpert part; and around four in the morning, as things began to grow increasingly uninhibited, with more and more people being pushed into the pool, I decided that the better part of valor would be to go home. As Teddy emerged from the pool, a huge dripping mass in a now hopelessly rumpled dinner jacket, Ben Bradlee said, "It's just like a horror movie." It was all great fun—a perfect expression of the rowdier aspects of the New Frontier.

July 22

My main occupation this week was the proposed test ban. I rewrote the Ed Murrow memorandum to Chester Bowles setting forth a test ban strategy. On Thursday afternoon Mac, Ted Sorensen and I discussed it with the President. The President made repeatedly clear his lack of enthusiasm over the resumption of tests. He is obviously unconvinced that the military gains will make up for the political losses; and the whole idea of testing seems to leave him cold. At one point I said that [British prime minister Harold] Macmillan was opposed to the resumption of nuclear tests. He looked up wryly and said, "It cannot be said that I'm hot for it myself." His immediate desire is to do everything possible to emphasize the American dedication to the test ban treaty. The trouble is the rising pressure at home for immediate resumption. A good deal of this comes from the Joint Committee on Atomic Energy, and it is hard to deal with because, as JFK put it, "Those fellows think that they invented the bomb themselves and look on everyone else as Johnny-come-latelies and amateurs."

July 28

I missed the presidential plane back to Washington on Monday morning, the 24th—perhaps providential, since the detour to Boston and the trip to Washington on Northeast permitted me finally to read the long and documented State Department account of the test ban negotiations. Having done this, I was able on Monday afternoon to start work on the test ban White Paper.

On Tuesday night the President delivered his speech on Berlin.* The newspapers oddly concentrated on the military build-up and in the main ignored the most significant part of the speech—that is, the invitation to negotiation.

---

* JFK affirmed the United States' commitment to defend West Berlin from Soviet or East German encroachment, but made clear he sought a diplomatic solution to this crisis. "In short," he said, "while we are ready to defend our interests, we shall also be ready to search for peace."

Scotty Reston on Thursday told me that his wife Sally was genuinely upset over the speech. One of their boys is reaching the end of his military service and now may be held in the Army for an indefinite future period. I must confess that, with Stephen now of draft age, I can no longer look at these problems as serenely as I once did.

The speech does signal, I believe, an important change of direction in Washington. Up until rather recently, "negotiation" has been almost a dirty word, virtually synonymous with appeasement. Now that the military measures are out of the way, everyone concedes that we are entering a phase in which diplomatic and political considerations are important. This feeling is reinforced by mounting evidence from Europe that even the West Germans are looking for a diplomatic resolution of the crisis. For two weeks, the President has been trying in every way to stimulate the State Department to start preparing negotiating positions. However (at least according to Mac), very little progress has been made, presumably for the usual reasons—Rusk's passivity and lack of leadership.

Henry Kissinger came by on Friday morning and told me that he had a great feeling of being excluded by Mac. He said that, though the President had asked him to come down full time, Mac had strongly urged him not to do so; that Mac had never once asked his advice on anything and had not even responded in any way to the very intelligent series of memoranda Henry has been writing about Berlin; that, when the President had expressed a desire to see him, Mac had never made clear to him what he wanted to see him about, and that Henry was in consequence both so ill-prepared and so tense that he could not do himself justice; and that the whole experience had been humiliating for him. I counselled him to be patient and let me check into the President's views of his usefulness. Henry has been excellent on the whole negotiation problem; and it seems to me a great error not to put him into the center of the political/diplomatic planning.

My completion of the White Paper on Wednesday finally liberated me. On Thursday morning, I had breakfast with Don Cook, just in from Paris, and Rowland Evans. Don confirmed my feeling about the disinclination of the Europeans to fight over Berlin and the growing desire for some form of political solution. Of course, Kennedy's military measures are an indispensable prelude to negotiation [on Berlin]. Without the military build-up, Khrushchev might suppose that he could push us out of West Berlin. The rearmament program should much increase the incentives for a negotiated solution.

August 1

On the plane back from Otis [Air Force Base], JFK asked me to come forward to his stateroom. He had read [my] draft White Paper on the test suspension and expressed general approval. The President's immense reluctance to resume testing became increasingly apparent in the course of the talk. He also said that he thought six on-site inspections would be adequate—that the risk of being caught was so great that, given six tries, even the Soviet Union would be extremely stupid to try and get away with anything.

The President then mentioned Scotty Reston's column in Sunday's *Times*. This column was a general indictment of the Secretary of State for his failure to mobilize the full resources of the government in the political planning for Berlin. It reflected in part (alas) a talk I had with him on Thursday. The President said that Rusk had called him up, deeply hurt, and had reported that Reston had told him that all this came from the White House. JFK looked at me shrewdly and asked whether I had recently talked with Reston. I said that I had, and about this subject. JFK said mildly that he wished hereafter I would make my complaints directly to the State Department rather than through the *New York Times*. Actually I do not think that the column did much harm—it ought to spur Rusk into getting the right people into the Berlin situation. What the hell Scotty was doing telling Rusk that he got the story from the White House I shall never know.

The President complained of the press concentration on the allegedly prospective appointment of Frank Morrissey as federal district judge in Massachusetts and the simultaneous neglect of the excellent judicial appointments under way in the rest of the country. Mac said that this was one more sign that Morrissey's appointment would cause a lot of unnecessary trouble. The President said, "Look: my father has come to me and said that he has never asked me for anything, that he wants to ask me only this one thing—to make Frank Morrissey a federal judge. What can I do?" Mac answered forthrightly that his father really knows that he shouldn't ask this, that JFK knows that he should reject the request, and that his father will know that he was right to reject the request. The President looked gloomy and said that Morrissey couldn't have worked for him for eleven years without picking up something in the way of a sense of public service and that in any case he would be greatly superior to his predecessor.

August 12

On Tuesday morning, August 8, the National Security Council met to hear a report from the Panofsky Panel on the nuclear testing situation. The report said, in effect, (a) that it was technically feasible for the Soviet Union to have been testing clandestinely, (b) that there was no evidence that it had done so (or had not done so), and (c) that there was no urgent technical need for immediate resumption of testing by the U.S. The Joint Chiefs of Staff had filed a paper questioning both the premises and the conclusions of the Panofsky report. The Joint Chiefs of Staff paper, however, was assertive, ambiguous, semi-literate and generally unimpressive.

The meeting began with a presentation by [nuclear physicist Wolfgang] Panofsky. General Lemnitzer, that sweet but dopey man, was then invited by the President to set forth the Joint Chiefs of Staff position. He summarized the Joint Chiefs of Staff paper. Then he said, "I would like to emphasize that we are not advocating atmospheric testing. Our memorandum is at fault if it suggests otherwise. And we have no objection to a reasonable delay in the resumption of testing. But we do see urgency in testing for small-yield weapons development."

The President: "Does your doctrine assume that it is possible to use tactical nuclear weapons without using strategic nuclear weapons?"

Lemnitzer: "Our doctrine is that it will be possible to use tactical weapons without escalating into strategic weapons. I know that many people disagree with this."

The discussion then moved to the question of the neutron bomb.

The President: "Is it accurate to say that testing would speed the development of the neutron bomb?"

Foster (the scientist who is the most ardent proponent of the neutron bomb): "Yes."

The President: "What advantage do we get from the neutron bomb?"

Wiesner: "Economy is the main advantage. We could have large numbers of relatively inexpensive bombs."

General [Maxwell] Taylor: "This weapon offers us the first real possibility of offsetting the Soviet superiority in gross manpower. Our present tactical weapons have no discrimination in their effects. The new weapon would be more precise. It would not destroy the territory in which it is used. It would open up great opportunities for us."

Wiesner: "Actually no one knows anything about the field effects of the neutron bomb. We don't even know how quickly it kills. Its effect might be to wound people fatally but still leave them active enough for 24 hours to strike back—and, since they knew they were dying, to strike back with everything they have. It might transform the population into a kamikaze squad."

The President: "If we test, we will presumably test underground alone. The USSR will resume testing if we do, and they will test in the atmosphere. If you were satisfied that the Soviet Union was *not* testing, would you favor our resumption?"

Panofsky: "No."

Foster: "Yes."

Bradbury: "No. There is no point in our resuming testing if we only test underground. The Soviet Union will test in the atmosphere and will overtake us."

Taylor: "We have four disadvantages in our present military posture. (1) We must accept the first strike. (2) They have or will have an anti-missile missile. (3) They have manpower superiority. (4) They have submarine superiority. All these things can be overcome only if we develop much greater flexibility. The one means of developing that flexibility is through our gaining a great advantage in light nuclear warheads. We cannot achieve this without testing."

[John J.] McCloy: "It would certainly be unwise to resume testing till after the meeting of the UN General Assembly. The decision can be postponed till the first of the year with reasonable confidence that we are not impairing the security of the country."

The President: "We have a major problem. The Soviet Union will support the Indian resolution, which in essence provides for a moratorium without inspection. But we have them at a disadvantage over the test ban treaty. We can't jeopardize this by giving indications that we intend to resume testing."

It is evident from the above that JFK has no wild passion to resume testing. The general pressure for resumption seems to have subsided, but it will no doubt resume after the UN General Assembly meeting.

Later George Kennan dropped by. He was concerned with the military implications of the Berlin crisis. He spoke with great earnestness: "I am expendable, I have no further official career, and I am going to do everything I can to prevent a war. You and I are historians—or rather you are a real historian and I am a pseudo-historian. We both know how tenuous a relation there is between a man's intentions and the consequences of his acts. There is no more presumption more terrifying than those who would blow up the world on the basis of their personal judgement of a transient situation. I have children, and I do not propose to let the future of mankind be settled or ended by a group of men operating on the basis of limited perspectives and short-run calculations. I figure that the only thing I have left in life is to do everything I can to stop the war."

August 27

On Wednesday, I went in with Averell [Harriman] to see the President. Averell first reported on the Laos negotiations. Both he and the President were obviously opposed to intervention in Laos. We then turned to the subject of a possible Kennedy counterstatement to [a] recent Communist manifesto. Harriman had cabled Kennedy about this from Geneva, citing an editorial in the *New York Times* of August 14 "For a Manifesto of Freedom." JFK was very much interested in this. He spoke rather wistfully (as I have heard him speak before) of Castro's capacity to enlist Cubans in public efforts. "Each weekend 10,000 teachers go into the countryside to conduct a drive against illiteracy. An immense communal effort like this is attractive to people who wish to serve their country. And there seems to be no way of doing it in a country like Peru." He went on to discuss the sources of Communist appeal. "There seem to be two main things," he said. "One is the power of the police apparatus. The other is the Communist identification with economic and social well-being at the expense of political freedom, which is after all meaningless in so many of these countries." It was decided that I should try my hand at drafting a free world manifesto.

The President said: "I have discovered finally that the best way to deal with State is to send over memos. They can forget phone conversations, but a memorandum is something which, by their system, has to be answered. So let's put as many things as possible in memoranda from now on."

August 30

I spent most of Monday, the 28th, at boring meetings on virtuous subjects. As one grows older, one knows more and more definitely what people one likes and what subjects one is good at. It is perfectly clear that I am good at political subjects—anything involving the conflicts of political factions and forces. When it comes to economic subjects, I am much less good. When it comes to developing programs for something like the United Nations, I am really not much good at all. My present assignment therefore is not precisely congenial.

September 4

The central excitement of the last few days (so far as I have been concerned) has been the Soviet decision to resume nuclear testing. Word first came through late Wednesday afternoon, the 30th, when Foreign Broadcast Information Service intercepted a routine newspaper alert from Warsaw. There was a flurry of activity, and that night the President put out a statement (prepared in first draft by Adrian Fisher of the U.S. Disarmament Association).

On Thursday morning, the President called a meeting to consider next steps. Present were the Vice President, [Dean] Rusk, [Robert] McNamara, [Glenn] Seaborg, [Allen] Dulles, [Lyman] Lemnitzer, [Maxwell] Taylor, [Charles] Bohlen, [Ed] Murrow, Fisher, [McGeorge] Bundy, [Herbert] Scoville (CIA) and myself. Dulles began by reporting on indications of actual testing.

If the Soviet Union continues its policy of secrecy, he said, we ought to take full advantage of our opportunity to speak out as the conscience of the world.

Dean Rusk then proposed a statement for the President announcing the U.S. decision to resume testing. The President had to leave the room at this point to take a phone call from Adlai Stevenson (in which Stevenson argued that a special meeting of the Security Council should be convoked to consider the Soviet decision). While he was away, Mac Bundy set forth what he thought to be the President's position—that, the longer any announcement of our decision to resume testing could be put off, the greater the international political advantages for the United States. When the President returned, he elaborated on this line: "Why should we put ourselves into this business right away? [Indian prime minister Jawaharlal] Nehru said last year that whoever resumed testing would win the opprobrium of mankind. There may be a storm of exasperation in the United States if we don't announce resumption, but we can stand that for two or three days."

He then asked Johnson what he thought of the mood on the Hill. Johnson said he had spent an hour that morning hearing Gore, Symington and others give speeches demanding immediate resumption. "There will be a lot of talk of this sort," Johnson said. "But I personally think it would be a good thing if you let Khrushchev take the heat for a few days. Also you ought not to give the impression of reacting every time he does something. I think that you should say these things to the congressional leaders, while at the same time saying that preparations for the resumption of testing are under way."

The President meanwhile was fooling around with the Rusk statement, changing it from an announcement of a decision to resume to an announcement that preparations making resumption possible had been ordered.

The meeting was taking place under some pressure; it began shortly after 10, and at 10:45 the congressional leaders were due to arrive. As the deadline approached, it looked more and more as if the meeting were going to approve the diluted version of the Rusk statement. Even this diluted version seemed to me all wrong from the viewpoint of political warfare. Its effect would be to take the Russians off the hook, to share with them the limelight of world obloquy and to cancel out the windfall the Soviet decision had given us. I whispered this to Ted Sorensen, who said he completely agreed and suggested that I say it to Murrow, who had sat silent thus far. When I spoke to Murrow, he said that he intended to say something. "If we issue that statement," he said, "we destroy the advantages of the greatest propaganda gift we have had for a long time. At present, the Soviet decision is causing the Communists great trouble everywhere in the world. It is cutting the legs off the Ban-the-Bomb movements. We have a great asset here which we will waste if we move too quickly." Rusk then spoke up and said that he agreed with Murrow's estimate of the international political effect of the proposed statement.

The real case for Rusk's original statement, so far as I can make out, is (a) the domestic political demand for immediate U.S. resumption will be irresistible, and (b) that against the Berlin backdrop it is essential for the President to appear as tough and resolute as the Russians. There may be some point in (b). But, so far as (a) is concerned, domestic reaction thus far had been exceedingly restrained. It is all too typical of Rusk that, instead of speaking for the interests of U.S. foreign policy, he capitulated and put forward a statement which might have been drafted in the Defense Department or the Joint Committee. Fortunately Murrow and Kennedy were present to represent the interests of U.S. foreign policy.

On Friday morning (September 1), McCloy (who had been on holiday when the Soviets made their announcement), [Arthur] Dean (who had just returned from Geneva), Mac and I met with the President. Dean told a little about the atmosphere in Geneva; but we spent most of the time discussing the statement he would issue after his meeting with the President. He had his own text, but it was characteristically legalistic and long-winded, and the President and Mac finally decided in favor of a statement written by me.

I should have said that earlier in the morning Ed Murrow, Ted Sorensen, Spurgeon Kenney and I met with Jerry Wiesner (also Scoville of the CIA) to consider what should be said when the first nuclear test took place. I wrote a statement which the U.S. Information Agency adopted with some emendations and which the President appeared to like at the 11 o'clock meeting.

At three, I was sitting in my office when Mac called to say that we had what seemed clear indication that the Soviet test had taken place. "We haven't wakened the President about it," he said. "We are trying to figure out what to say. You had better come over." When I arrived in Mac's office, McCloy, Dean, Murrow, Scoville and Wiesner were already there. It soon became evident that there was sharp disagreement over what should be said. McCloy and Dean favored a statement announcing our decision to resume testing. The rest of us favored a statement along the lines of the one we had drafted that morning calling on the world to condemn the Russians for their action. After some discussion, it was decided to bring two statements to the President.

We then trooped over to the Mansion. The President came out of his bedroom in a bathrobe. He listened a little impatiently to the statement of the issues; then asked for the statements. McCloy argued that the necessary thing now was for the American President to show that he was capable of hard and tough leadership—that we could not continue to stand by and let the Communists kick us in the teeth. Murrow and I made the opposite case. The President was not in a mood to listen to the arguments through. He knew what each side was going to say, completed our sentences, slashed each statement to bits, said he was not inclined to announce our resumption at this point but did not know how much longer he could refrain from doing so, and briskly ushered us out. I felt it was all over a little quickly.

When I went back to the White House, it occurred to me that nothing had finally been settled about the question of taking the matter to the UN. So I went again to see the President to find out his wishes on this matter. He was back in the Oval Room, but fully dressed now, and much more relaxed than he had been an hour earlier. He motioned me to sit down, and came over and talked in an easy and leisured way. "McCloy was certainly reverting to Republicanism," he said, "—and to think that only a few days ago he was all over Khrushchev!" He then spoke with great and profane acrimony about the neutrals now meeting at Belgrade, comparing the meagerness of their reaction to the Soviet action with what they would have done if the U.S. had announced the resumption of testing. We then discussed the Security Council question. He thought aloud for a minute, then sat silent in his chair, obviously going through a process of visible concentration on the problem. I have never seen him thinking through an issue in this way before. After a moment or two or silence, he said, "I don't see how we can do it. It would look hypocritical for us to take the question to the Security Council when we have already decided to resume testing. The two things seem to me incompatible." In a few moments he left cheerily for Hyannis Port.

When I reported this conversation to Harlan Cleveland, he argued strongly that there was no such incompatibility. The next morning Rusk called a meeting on this subject—Cleveland, Bohlen, Dean, Mc-Cloy and myself. Dean, McCloy and Bohlen argued strongly against bringing the matter before the UN on the ground that we would gain nothing and might end up in a position which restricted our own freedom of action. When Cleveland mentioned the effect on world opinion, McCloy snorted and said, "World opinion? I don't believe in world opinion. The only thing that matters is power. What we have to do now is to show that we are a powerful nation and not spent our time trailing after the phantom of world opinion." He later said, "I now believe that the Russians have been cheating us all along. I believe that they have been testing secretly, that they have reached the point where their weapons development requires atmospheric testing, and that we must answer them in their own terms." Chip [Bohlen] disputed him on the point of Soviet cheating. I must say that I do not find McCloy especially impressive. Rusk expressed no clear opinion and finally proposed a meeting with the President on the question on Tuesday.

For the first time, I feel really gloomy about the state of the world. The Soviet decision to resume testing, on the top of other recent events, convinces me that Khrushchev has decided on a very risky power play over Berlin. I fear that he had decided to make the USSR the embodiment of terror and power in the world in the expectation that all lovers of peace, terrified of war and recognizing the futility of trying to alter Soviet policy, will concentrate their energies on making the West give way over Berlin. This is brinksmanship with a vengeance, and it may get us very close indeed to war.

September 5

This morning, on the plane down from Otis, the President called me into the forward stateroom. He first said, "I didn't realize that you had become a film critic." The reference was to *Show* magazine in which my long frustrated critical ambitions have finally found an outlet. I blushed and mumbled something. He then said that he had seen *L'Avventura*—that, one by one, all the others had stolen out until only he and Jackie were left—that it all seemed so slow that he had asked the projectionist to skip the intervening sequences and run the final reel—and that it had still left him mystified. I asked him whether it embarrassed him at all for me to do this. He said not at all; then he asked, "Do they pay you well?" I said, "Fairly well." He said, "How much? Five?" I said, "Yes."

One thing we did *not* discuss was the question of our resuming nuclear tests. Mac told me later that the President has been harder and harder to restrain on this matter. Apparently, there was an animated discussion on this question yesterday afternoon. The President finally said that he would not announce our resumption right away, but felt it absolutely necessary to do so if there were a new Soviet test. When the third Soviet test was reported today, the President's patience was exhausted. The statement was released (without much consultation among his advisers) at five this afternoon.

I assume that he did not raise this question with me because he had heard my view and was not interested in listening to more liberal guff on this matter. As a matter of fact, my own view has hardened somewhat as my sense of gloom over the situation has deepened. At this point, I really could not have argued with total conviction against the announcement. The gains from restraint have proved so marginal, and the danger of appearing inert and even alarmed is so considerable, that we might as well go ahead.

September 10

Since JFK has been kidding me a good deal about my new role as film reviewer, I began to wonder whether it might not be an embarrassment to him; so I sent him a note saying that, if so, I would of course be glad to stop forthwith. The following memorandum came back from

Mrs. Lincoln: "The President says it is fine for you to continue to write for *Show* as long as you treat Peter Lawford with respect."

September 22

On Tuesday night, the 19th, I had dinner with Jimmy Wechsler, Joe Rauh and Hubert Humphrey. Jimmy had come from a forty-five minute interview with the President. He was, as usual, wholly disarmed and delighted by Kennedy—and particularly by the new note of impatience with Eisenhower, the Republicans and the business community (the same thing I encountered when I went to the White House for dinner the next night). Hubert was in marvelous form, overflowing with wit, charm, energy, eloquence and sheer animal vitality. I asked him what he thought ought to be done next. He replied, "The first thing I would do is fire Dean Rusk." He feels that Rusk has been dangerously inadequate both in formulating foreign policy and in presenting it to the people. Hubert is really unique: George McGovern, who lives next door to him, told me today that he heard shouts of exultation outside his window this morning, looked down, saw Hubert striding around his lawn and saying "What a wonderful day," looked further, saw absolutely no audience of any sort—what a pure and charming expressing of Humphreyan exuberance!

September 20

[On Wednesday the 20th we had] dinner at the White House with Joe and Susan Mary Alsop. The President was in excellent form—very lively, pungent and vigorous. I was delighted to see that he was particularly concerned with the role of the business community. He began by saying that he was struck by the paradox that, while labor leaders individually were often mediocre and selfish, labor as a body took generally enlightened positions on the great issues; while businessmen were often enlightened as individuals but invariably took hopeless positions on public issues. He said several times that he now understood FDR's attitude toward the business community and that he only wished there were no Cold War so he could debate the future of America with the businessmen.

After dinner, at about 10:30, we adjourned to the projection room for a movie—*Blood and Roses*, directed by Roger Vadim. It was terrible; and the President left after 40 minutes, saying over his shoulder that he would be content to read my review in *Show*. He also recommended that I see *The Girl Without a Suitcase* and *A Cold Wind in August* (or September?) and review them as contrasting treatments of the same theme. He had not liked *Breakfast at Tiffany's* and expressed a general view that Hollywood had no guts any longer and could not do a sharp or interesting film.

We talked a bit about Berlin. I think that I forgot to note a major theme in his remarks to Charles Wintour, the editor of *London Evening Standard*—that the American people had no conception what a nuclear war was like; and that, if they did, they would not be half so bold in their attitudes toward foreign policy. He recurred to that tonight; but also said (what is doubtless true) that mankind's recuperative powers after a nuclear war would probably be greater than anyone supposed.

JFK was also rather concerned about the Metropolitan Club. The Board of Governors has just sent a letter of reprimand to George Lodge for his offense in bringing his successor, George Weaver, a Negro, there for luncheon. Bobby, Lodge, Charlie Bartlett and others have consequently resigned. JFK said that he did not see how anyone could remain in the club under those conditions.

On Friday Norman Thomas came by, deeply perturbed over the administration's Berlin policy. He reported a general impression in liberal circles that JFK's attitude was rigid and menacing, that he had no interest in negotiation, that military considerations were predominant in the administration's thinking. I did my best to reassure him on these points.

October 8

The big news of the week was the announcement on Wednesday September 2 of the appointment of John McCone as new head of the

CIA. The story was broken in the morning's *Times*, and I promptly fired off a memorandum to the President at Newport predicting that this appointment would cause infinite trouble.

The possibly consoling thought is that the President has a habit of designating "liberals" to do "conservative" things, and vice versa. Thus, when he wants to keep Red China out of the UN, he gets Adlai Stevenson to do it; when he wants to move toward an acceptance of the existence of East Germany, Lucius Clay is the man. The only problem is that McCone is not charged with a single mission but with a continuing and undefined responsibility. I am sure JFK knows what he is doing, and possibly my concern here will turn out to be as unwarranted as my concern last December over the appointment of Doug Dillon, but I doubt it.

October 22

On Wednesday, the 11th, Harlan Cleveland and I went to New York and the UN. We arrived in the middle of two active issues—the Secretary Generalship; and nuclear testing. I met U Thant of Burma a couple of times on Wednesday afternoon. He disarmed me instantly by saying that he had just finished reading *The Politics of Freedom* (the English edition of *The Vital Center*). He seemed calm and intelligent, with an incisive grasp of issues and an easy competence about negotiation. Both Harlan and I were impressed by him. Adlai was, as usual, fussing and complaining, but enjoying it all (I believe, at bottom). He has been much concerned over a possible quick resumption of atmospheric testing.

It is essential to visit the UN from time to time in order to reacquaint oneself with what is a separate world—and a world so vivid and hectic and compelling, so filled with excitement and crisis, and those who dwell in it all the time begin to believe that nothing else exists. And yet . . . I cannot resist the feeling that the UN world is really an immense and picturesque form of make-believe, and that its problems and crises are remote from the serious issues of the day. I am sure that this feeling is wrong, certainly it is wrong in the long run; but it enables me to understand the inevitable gap between Washington and New York. Considering the fact that JFK is surrounded every day by State Department people, who believe essentially in bilateral diplomacy, and by generals and admirals, who don't believe in diplomacy at all, I think he does exceedingly well to keep the UN as considerably in the forefront of his attention as he does.

On Thursday night we went to dinner at Kay Halle's with Mark and Raymond Bonham-Carter and their wives. Randolph Churchill arrived from Los Angeles in mid-evening and regaled us all with an account of a dinner given by Otto Preminger at Mike Romanoff's the night before, in which Randolph so successfully insulted so many guests that eight people left the table. Evidently this explosion had gotten much pent-up temper out of his system; I have never seen him so moderate, amiable and charming. He told a splendid story about his father and his remark about British politics: "I know both the Conservative and Liberal parties well—and I hate them both." Apparently on Saturday night, however, the strain became too great, and he became his testy and explosive self. Kay later told me that, when Ethel Fowler mentioned Averell Harriman to him, he turned on her and said, "Averell Harriman is the man who cuckolded me when I was away in the Army—cuckolded me in the Prime Minister's very house." Seeking to lighten the conversation, Kay said, "But Randolph, how many men did you cuckold when you were away in the Army?" To which Randolph replied, "Perhaps—but never in the house of a Prime Minister."

October 17

[On the 17th] Marian and I dined alone with the President and Jackie. JFK was, as usual, exceedingly relaxed, pungent and charming. The talk, as usual, encompassed a tremendous range of subjects, with swift transitions from one to another. Let me try to recapture a few recurrent themes.

Germany. He was very critical of all West Germans except [Konrad] Adenauer. Adenauer, he said, was a great man, greater than de Gaulle because his objectives transcended his nation, while de Gaulle dedicated himself to the aggrandizement of his nation. All other Germans, he said, seemed to him terrible. "They say that we are betraying them after all their services to us. They act as if they had been our allies."

Eisenhower. He was derisive about Eisenhower, spurred on by the Felix Belair piece in the *Sunday Times* and by the Eisenhower press conference today. He said that Eisenhower had been "too stupid to know what was going on." We talked about the similarities and contrasts of the Truman and Eisenhower administrations. The President remarked that he had written David Lawrence the other day to commend him for having noticed the number of former Truman appointees now serving in the Kennedy administration. "Truman's appointments were excellent except in the National Committee, the regulatory agencies and the Department of Justice." He then commented on Eisenhower's determination to send Matt Connelly to prison for some trifling sum and his toleration of Sherman Adams and Tom Stephens.

Metropolitan Club. JFK returned with zest to the Metropolitan Club. He [said] that he could understand newspapermen who stayed in the club, but he could not understand senators—he named especially Stuart Symington and Claiborne Pell—who made speeches on the floor about civil rights and then retired to the Metropolitan Club for a drink and dinner.

1962

❖

January 14

At 10 Wednesday night [January 10] I went to the White House to join Ted [Sorensen] and Mac [Bundy] for a final review of the [State of the Union] speech with the President. I felt that the domestic section, to which I had tried to give a philosophical coherence, had been reduced again to a laundry list, and I strongly urged that a paragraph be added to tie the program together and relate it to the New Frontier. The President agreed. We then went over the foreign section and the peroration. This process came to an end a little after 11. The Bradlees had been dining with the Kennedys, and Jackie now asked us in to hear the Jimmy Dean recording of "PT 109" (Goddard Lieberson had sent me an early pressing, which I had passed along) and have a glass of champagne. Jackie and Tony Bradlee both essayed the twist with great and lady-like charm. Jackie does an absolutely enchanting combined twist-and-charleston. As she finished, she said, "I will bet that Mary McCarthy can't do this."

We then dispersed. I went off to write the domestic paragraph.

The next morning the President called to ask about the paragraph. I brought it to his bedroom about 9:30. He was eating his breakfast in bed. He had only his pajama pants on. Newspapers were strewn over the bed; also a new book by Gerald Sykes. He read the paragraph, nodded approval, then read and signed the letter. We chatted as he dressed himself (strapping a corset around his waist; his back is still giving him trouble). He has been a little irritated by the liberal attacks, and especially by John Oakes's editorials in the *Times*. He keeps saying—as he said to Sam Beer at noon—"What more do the liberals want me to do that is politically possible for me to do? So far as I can see, the only thing they want that I'm not doing is a bigger deficit. And I'm not against that in principle. I don't see how we can keep the economy growing unless we run a deficit at least two out of every three years. But we have the balance of payments to look at, not to speak of the Congress."

The speech went off with considerable success. Mac told me later that, in the last moments, Ted had said to the President, "I really don't see much need for that new paragraph." After Ted left the room, the President said to Mac, "What do you think?" Mac said, "I think you should say it." The President said, "I think so too," and did. He added, "Ted certainly doesn't go for additions to his speeches!" In the afternoon he called to thank me for helping on the speech. He said that he had been most surprised by the volume of applause for his defense of the UN. The next morning, he called to ask me whether I had read the "Quotation of the Day" in *The Times*. I had not, and it turned out to be from the new paragraph. "Ted will die when he sees that," said the President.

I returned from a meeting [on Thursday, January 11] to an appointment with Harold Wilson. I had not met him before, and most of my friends in the Labour Party regard him as an opportunist—a socialist Nixon. I expected a small, natty, young man and found a small, portly, graying middle-aged man. He is immensely clever, immensely self-satisfied, and skates on the edge of pomposity. He conveys no sense of principle whatever but a considerable sense of competence and intelligence. On Friday night I gave an informal dinner for him—Harriman, Fulbright, [Wayne] Morse, Galbraith, [Carl] Kaysen, [Harlan] Cleveland, Goodwin, Augie Heckscher. It was an interesting evening. We tried to smoke out Wilson on the subject of socialism and of the Common Market but with little success. He struts but is amusing.

I have decided this week to resign from Harvard. A return-or-resign letter came from [Harvard President Nathan M.] Pusey, accompanied by a phone call from [history professor] Bobby Wolff saying that, if I resigned, the Department would undoubtedly welcome me back any time in the next two or three years, though if I did not return this year, I would probably lose the intellectual history course to Fleming. I asked Mac what I should do, and whether the President might be relieved if I went back. He told me later that he had asked the President about the cases of Jerry Wiesner (who can stay away from MIT indefinitely but must inform Stratton whether or not he will be back in the fall) and myself. According to Mac, JFK said that he would be sorry to see Wiesner go but he imagined that he could find another scientist to take his place, but that I was irreplaceable. I expect that the presidential reaction has been improved by Mac's generosity, but it is probable that he would like me to stay; and, since I do not feel that I have come near exhausting the value of the experience for myself, or the fun, I feel that I should do it a little longer.

January 21

On the 16th I went to Cambridge for a talk with Pusey. I called JFK Monday evening before my departure. He said, "I think you would be more useful down here than teaching those sons of privilege up there."

When I met with Pusey, he was, as usual, courteous. He did not argue much with my decision, especially when I invoked my father and Bundy to support it. At one point he burst forth against scholars and government, suggesting that he regarded it as a corrupting relationship.

We dined at the White House on Thursday evening, the 18th. The dinner was in honor of [Igor] Stravinsky, who turned out to be an amiable man, very tiny, with a manner of twinkling gravity. The President toasted him at the end of the dinner, and Stravinsky, obviously moved, responded with immense charm.

When we joined the ladies, I went over to talk to Stravinsky. He said, "Lean over—I want to say something in your ear." When I did, he said, with a smile of great content on his face, "I am drunk."

Marshall [Field, a guest] kept complaining that all the good columnists were liberals. JFK objected to the term—"Liberalism and conservatism," he said, "are categories of the thirties, and they don't apply anymore. Our problems today are mostly technical and require above all sophisticated thinking. The trouble with conservatives today is that most of their thinking is so naive. As for the liberals, their thinking is sophisticated; but their function ought to be to provide new ideas, and they don't come up with any."

This discussion, as I say, depressed me a little. The President has been quite impatient recently with liberal criticism, when he ought to be grateful to it for offsetting pressure from the right and thereby expanding his menu of alternatives.

Saturday was a frantic day. I dictated a great many letters, finished up material for Bob Kennedy's Japan trip and finally made Andrews Field in the later afternoon in time for the plane to Montevideo [for the Organization of American States Conference in Punta del Este on Cuba]. I called Bobby from the airfield about his Berlin speeches. He said, "The President is mad at you. I have just been talking to him, and he said, 'Let's check that with Arthur.' I said that you had gone off to South America. He blew up at that and said that he knew nothing about it, and that everyone was leaving him." I could not make out how seriously to take Bobby's rendition of this and in a way was a little relieved, since I had somewhat the impression the other night that the President might be getting impatient about his liberal advisers. I told Bob that I would, of course, get off the plane if he thought the President really wanted me to stay in Washington. He told me to go ahead.

February 22

We arrived in Berlin on a cold, snowy day. Willy Brandt, General [Lucius] Clay and Al Lightner (head of the U.S. Mission in West Berlin) met us at the airport. As we got off the plane, the band played "When the Crimson in triumph flashing, Mid the strains of victory." After a brief airport ceremony and gallant but incompetent tries at German by Bobby and Ethel, we set forth on a motorcade to the Rathaus. The streets were lined with cheering people, who had waited for hours in the bitter cold. It was all deeply moving until one remembered that a good many of them were cheering just as hard twenty years ago for Hitler.

A vast crowd had gathered in front of the Rathaus—perhaps 100,000 people. Bobby made a fine impromptu speech. When balloons with red flags floated over from the Communist zone, he observed, "They will let their balloons come over—but not their people." After he had signed the Golden Book and departed to inspect RIAS [the Radio in American Sector radio station], Lightner and I stayed behind for a talk with Brandt.

I had met Brandt before but had never had the opportunity for a long talk with him. He seemed calm, intelligent and detached and inspired confidence. I asked him about the Wall—whether in retrospect he feels that steps should have been taken to prevent its erection or to tear it down. He replied, "If I were to say that now, it would be inconsistent with the things I said at the time. On August 13, 1961, no one proposed that we try and stop the erection of the Wall. We all supposed that such action would run the risk of war." He went on to say that counteraction might have been justified if one believed that the East Germans had put up the wall on their own, but most indications were that they had prior Soviet approval and support. He added that he was critical of the allies because of their slowness to note and condemn the East German action—but even if they had spoken out immediately, he said, it would not have brought down the Wall.

He expressed great interest in steps under way to assure the future of West Berlin. Apparently the flight from West Berlin has come to a halt; at least the outflow is now balanced by the inflow. But Brandt wanted to know what could be done to encourage private investment, develop educational centers and the like.

In the evening Brandt gave us a dinner. This occasion was made most notable by Bobby's remark that this was the birthday of two distinguished Americans—George Washington and Edward Kennedy— and by his teasing insistence that Teddy (who had joined us in Berlin) and his sidekick Claude Hooten sing a song in honor of the day. They finally obliged with "Bill Bailey, Won't You Please Come Home"—a performance which thoroughly mystified the Germans at the dinner.

We then went on to the Free University where Bobby gave his speech. It went over, I thought, exceedingly well. The most uproarious applause came when he said, "We have not forgotten those in East Germany"; but the non-Berlin sections, showing that free society was the best means to individual liberation and social progress, also seemed to go over well. They were largely ignored in the press reports, however. These concentrated on the ritual of reassurance—i.e., the reaffirmation in the first couple of pages of the commitments to West Berlin, which every American visitor faithfully renews as soon as he lands at Tempelhof.

After breakfast [the next day], we embarked on a tour of West Berlin. A good deal of the trip was along the Wall. No matter how much one reads or how many photographs one sees nothing prepares one for this ugly and sordid reality. The Wall is an obscenity. Not only is its conception barbaric but its execution—the crude, gray concrete blocks, the bricked-in windows of apartment houses along the sector line, the vicious tank traps, the tall picket fences erected to prevent East Berliners from waving to sons or fathers in West Berlin—is repellent and hateful. It was a sobering and maddening experience.

March 31

[When I got to Paris,] George Kennan asked me to come over for a private talk. I found him in a fairly irritated state of mind. He said that he greatly admired Kennedy; that his every talk confirmed him in his high opinion of the President, his admiration for his approach to foreign policy and his sympathy with his objectives. Because he wanted to do everything he could to help the President, he had gone to Belgrade, and he would not leave the administration in any way which would hurt the President. But, so far as Belgrade was concerned, he thought his mission was doomed to frustration. He had no sympathy at all, he said, for Rusk or for [ambassador to Russia Foy D.] Kohler or for their approach to foreign affairs. He characterized Rusk as a "parliamentary diplomat" and said that he had no instinct at all for the problems involved in bilateral relations. As for Kohler, he was rigid, cold and sterile—a Cold Warrior of the [John Foster] Dulles school. Both these men had at one time been subordinate to him, and he found it impossible, given Rusk's approach to foreign policy and Kohler's views about foreign policy, to work with them now.

His messages to the Department, he said, were ignored. At the President's request, he had worked hard on a statement to explain our policy of aid to Yugoslavia. Basic to this statement, he said, was a clear definition of the ideological differences between the two governments and the limitations these differences imposed on the effectiveness of our aid. Such a clear definition was necessary, he said, not only in justice to the Congress but also to remind the Yugoslavs that they could not continue denouncing the United States with impunity. But someone reworked the statement for Rusk, and Rusk's exposition of the case before the Senate Foreign Relations Committee, Kennan said, misconceived the whole base of our Yugoslav policy. This and other incidents had convinced him that no one in State respected his views. Accordingly he felt the time was approaching when he should follow the advice of Isaiah Berlin, resign his embassy and get to work on a history of the Russian Revolution. He did not want to do this precipitately; but he wanted the

White House to know how things looked to him so no one would be surprised when he finally decided to leave.

I guess I spent the weekend of March 3 recuperating from my travels. We dined with the Kennedys and Peter Lawford at the White House on March 5, and then with the Kennedys and the Bartletts on Jackie's last night, March 7. Each time we went down around 10 o'clock to the projection room for a movie—*Sergeants Three* on Monday and *Last Year in Marienbad* on Wednesday. *Sergeants Three* was one of the worst films I have ever seen, and *Marienbad* one of the most enthralling. The President walked out of both with great expedition; but Jackie stayed to the end of *Marienbad* and seemed to watch it with fascination.

It is criminal not to have made extensive notes about these two evenings; all I have is some semi-legible scrawls. On Monday he talked a good deal about the decision [to resume testing in April]. He had called up both Truman and Eisenhower, he said, to communicate his decision. Truman was sympathetic and seemed to understand how difficult the decision had been. Eisenhower was cold and grumpy and said, "Well, I thought you should have done this a long time ago."

On the 7th, the issue of raising children came up. The President, probably in order to provoke Marian and Martha Bartlett, said that he did not see why children should not be brought up in community nurseries. This led to a discussion of the role of the family. I asked why the Kennedys had turned out so well and the Churchills and Roosevelt so badly. JFK said, "Well, no one can say that it was due to my mother. It was due to my father. He wasn't around as much as some fathers; but, when he was around, he made his children feel that they were the most important things in the world to him. He seemed terribly interested in everything we were doing. He held up standards for us, and he was very tough when we failed to meet his standards. This toughness was important. If it hadn't been for that, Teddy might be just a playboy today. But my father cracked down on him at a crucial time in his life, and this brought out in Teddy the discipline and seriousness which have made him a possible political figure."

Another episode of this week proceeded from my old friend Richard M. Nixon and his noxious new book *Six Crises*. Doubleday sent me a copy, and I glanced at the account of the 1960 campaign. I was immediately struck by Nixon's assertion that [Allen] Dulles had told Kennedy about the Cuban operation during the campaign. When we dined at the White House on the 7th, I brought the book along and read the hot passage to the President. He said, "Of course that is not true. I never heard of the Cuban operation until Dulles and Bissell told me about it at Palm Beach after the election." He asked me to get Mac on the phone, which I did, and he asked Mac to confirm the President's recollection with Dulles, which Mac did and which Dulles did. I read some of the other Nixon passages, including his account of the first debate (which, according to him, he lost because he concentrated on substance while Kennedy concentrated on image). The President seemed mildly amused and absolutely unsurprised by all this. His opinion of Nixon is obviously so low and his contempt so ingrained that he cannot bring himself to become angry over anything that Nixon does. He was particularly amused by Nixon's contention that the working press favored Kennedy because Salinger had unlimited entertainment funds at his disposal.

I personally find the book almost beyond belief in its remarkable (and unconscious) revelation. Everything I wrote in *Kennedy or Nixon* about Nixon's self-absorption, his obsessive concern with the impression he is making on others, his lack of taste and lack of style—all these things are given overwhelming documentation in *Six Crises*. I do not see how his political career can survive this book.

The President expressed great irritation over the *New York Times* and "your friend" John Oakes. I really do think this is a weakness. As I have said to him a number of times, "How much better it is to be criticized in the *Times* from the left rather than from the right!" I have argued that this increases his flexibility and gives him something to offset the Harry Byrds. He agrees in an abstract way, but the *Times* continues to annoy him nonetheless. The fact is, I guess, that it is much easier to take criticism from one's enemies than from one's friends. I can see this in myself. I bear the asperities of *Human Events* with total equanimity, but I get very mad when attacked in the *New Republic*.

When the President returned from California, I asked him about Eisenhower. He said, "I have never found him pleasanter. He was relaxed and seemed really glad to see me. Usually he is such a cold bastard. This time he was really genial." JFK added, "You know what he said to me? We were talking about Laos. Eisenhower said, 'A State Department man told me—*and it was odd coming from him*—that Laos is a nation of homosexuals.'" The President repeated the phrase I have italicized with a kind of wonder.

On Friday, March 23, Scotty Reston asked me to have lunch with him and Jean Monnet. I saw Monnet again on Sunday for an hour or so. A talk with Monnet enforces a fascinating change of perspective. Washington life inculcates a tremendous concern with the immediate and especially with the personal. Monnet could not care less about personalities. He has a lucid and profound sense of deep-running historical tendencies—tendencies which, he is confident, no personality can arrest and no politician deflect. He could not care less about the attitude of Tory or Labour politicians in England toward the Common Market whatever its politicians may think. Similarly de Gaulle can confuse but not confound the inexorable movement toward economic integration in Europe. Monnet has seen inexorable tendencies effect so many revolutions in his own lifetime that his confidence in the future may be easily understood. I must confess that his perspective had the effect of underlining the transience and triviality of so many things that concern me.

April 5

We have observed in the last few days the more recent stages in the decline of Richard Nixon. *Six Crises* is an incredible book. I cannot bear to read it, partly because of the vulgarity of the diction, partly because of the nakedness of the self-exposure, partly because of the frustration over not being able to review it. I cannot recall any political autobiography in American history which has represented quite such an orgy in unconscious self-revelation. The very title is symptomatic: imagine writing a book called *Six Crises* which is not about Laos and Berlin and the Congo and the arms race but about six episodes in one's own personal history! Nixon portrays himself as an intensely self-absorbed, intensely insecure and wholly incapable of serious responsibility. The sketch of Nixon in *Kennedy or Nixon* has now received full and conclusive documentation. And Nixon has compounded all this by a series of errors in California [where he was running for governor]. He seems a badly rattled man, and he is behaving in March with the ill-concealed panic which campaigners ordinarily reserve for late October. I was talking with Lyndon Johnson the other day about it. His theory is that, as long as Nixon was on the national scene, he was surrounded by men (Johnson named Len Hall) who vetoed his worst impulses. Now he is by himself in California, surrounded by men who defer to him because he was once nearly elected President, and the consequence is that there is no longer anyone to save Nixon from himself.

On Sunday, April 1, Marian and I and Ken Galbraith were invited out to Glen Ora. We left Washington shortly after four and arrived around five-thirty after an agreeable drive through the pleasant Virginia countryside. It was like visiting anyone in the country. We turned off the main road and then off the side road through a gate with a single guard. Then, in a few moments, we were at the house. It is a relatively modest early-19th-century house, surrounded by stables and slave quarters. It had rained most of the day, but had suddenly cleared, and Caroline was sloshing around in the puddles by the swimming pool. The President and Jackie were still napping or reading, so Ken and I took a walk around the estate. We returned at dusk for tea. Jackie soon joined us. At 6:30 NBC put on an hour's film about [Jackie's] Indian trip. The President joined us as the film began. He said to Jackie, "Well, while you and Ken watch yourselves on television, Arthur can read his books and I will listen to some of my old speeches."

The television program amounted to no more than superior home movies, improved by color and by the Jackie-Ken commentary. I gather that the trip was a considerable success. Jackie much preferred India to Pakistan. Pakistan, she said, was a man's country: the women were still mostly in purdah; the men were interested, not in women, but in hunting and soldiering and in talking to each other. India, on the other hand, had many intelligent and able women, and its men (or at least Nehru) were agreeable and responsive.

After the TV show, we completed our drinks and went in for dinner. Just as we sat down, Caroline appeared, her eyes filled with tears and a book clutched under her arm. Jackie said, "Oh, I promised Caroline that I would finish her story" and disappeared for a few moments to complete her assignment.

We talked about the appointment of Byron White [to the Supreme Court]. The President said that this was one of the hardest decisions he had had to make—that he hesitated for a week over it—and that he finally chose White because White, besides his other qualifications, had worked so hard for his nomination and election. He acknowledged that Paul Freund had been for him too and said that this was what had made the decision so hard. He also said that he had once asked Max Freedman to ask [Justice Felix] Frankfurter whether he would be willing to resign if he and the President could agree on his successor. I asked what Frankfurter had replied. The President said, "I guess he decided that he was indispensable to the Court."

The President spoke with contempt about Nixon and said that his book showed him to be a "sick" man.

Ken and the President talked about Laos. The President made clear that he had no intention of ever committing American troops to Laos in force.

It was, as usual, an extremely pleasant evening, the conversation discursive and wide-ranging and the atmosphere entirely beguiling. We left about eleven and returned to Washington around midnight.

April 8

[On Friday the 6th, Hubert Humphrey and I] lunched at the White House. The dowager Duchess of Devonshire was the guest of honor. I sat next to Lorraine Cooper, who was interesting on Nixon. She said that Eisenhower disliked him. I asked why. She said, "Well, how could Eisenhower stand this tense, insecure, self-absorbed man, always look-ing for marks of favor. Nixon bored Eisenhower and probably made him feel guilty too. Eisenhower liked rich, self-assured, relaxed peo-ple like George Humphrey." I remarked on the obvious hostility to Eisenhower in the Nixon book. She said, "Of course. Nixon knew that Eisenhower did not like him, and disliked him for that. Besides, the re-lationship between the President and the Vice President is always un-easy. The Nixons felt all the time that they were being ignored and left out." Then, lowering her voice, she said, "Don't think that the Johnsons don't have the same feeling today."

May 3

[On the] evening [of April 17] we dined at the White House. It was a curious evening. The other guests were B. K. Nehru and his wife, Oleg Cassini accompanied by a nice Philadelphia girl named Robin Butler and a couple from *Paris-Match*. The last four represented international café society, and I cannot imagine what prompted Jackie to have them with the Nehrus. I suspect that we were invited as a desperate bridge. The evening was not so hopeless as one might have supposed, but it was not a great success either.

[The President] spoke a little about religion during dinner, argu-ing that all the Ten Commandments except one were derived from na-ture, and almost implying that all religion was so derived. After dinner, he made one of his quiet disappearances. The rest of us tried to dance the twist in a desultory way and finally dispersed. I do not think that the Cassini crowd brings out the best in Jackie; and I rather imagine that she might be much more like Lee if she had not married JFK. But I love her.

[On the 2nd] I met with Adlai Stevenson and the President at 10:30. I should mention here the curious effect that Kennedy seems to have on Stevenson. In New York on Monday night and Tuesday morning, Adlai Stevenson was at his best—relaxed, funny, quick, pungent, informal. He was very funny, for example, on the subject of Francis Plimpton, whom George Ball had asked to handle the UN bond issue before the House committee; "Francis is my oldest friend," Adlai said, "but he has all the political sex appeal of a dead mouse." In Washington on Wednesday, however, he was solemn, prissy, verbose and insistent. That tight little lip-smile, which used to be so unbearable on television, came in to play. The President was equable and courteous. He said to me later, "Adlai seemed in good form today." I weakly agreed; but the fact is that Adlai was not in good form at all. I wish that they had become friends before they became rivals. I do not think that JFK has ever seen Adlai at his best.

May 14

I forgot to record a remark of the President's last Friday. He was commenting on the Eisenhower press conference the day before. "The thing I liked best," he said, "was the picture of Eisenhower attacking medical care for the old under Social Security as 'socialized medicine'— and then getting into his government limousine and heading out to Walter Reed."

June 17

The President has been more and more concerned in recent weeks with domestic policy. The reasons are evident: first, steel; and then the Wall Street trouble. He has become increasingly disturbed, baffled and irritated by the problems of living with business and getting businessmen to face the serious problems of the economy.

On June 4, I dropped into his office in the afternoon. He was talking over the question of coexistence with business with Sorensen and

O'Donnell. When I came in, he said, "I understand better every day why Roosevelt, who started out as such a mild fellow, ended up so ferociously anti-business." He went on to say, "There are about ten thousand people in the country involved in this—bankers, industrialists, lawyers, publishers, politicians—a small group but doing everything they can to say that we are going into a depression because business has no confidence in the administration. They are starting to call me the Democratic Hoover. Well, we're not going to take that."

One consequence of the emergence of domestic issues is to project me increasingly into the political picture. The business community has never admired me wildly in any case, and the exhumation of a piece I wrote for the *Partisan Review* in 1947 as a contribution to a symposium on "The Future of Socialism" has supplied ample ammunition for attacks in trade papers and in newspaper editorials. A columnist named Henry J. Taylor has been working particularly hard on me, and so has old Walter Winchell. I have a feeling that JFK is a little edgy about all this and may even be beginning to wonder whether I am not more of a political liability than a working asset. On June 15 I had to speak at a foreign policy conference called by the Americans for Democratic Action in Los Angeles. Ted Sorensen called me urgently that morning to say that the President was much concerned over what I might say and did not wish me to touch on government-business relations. I explained that I was sticking to foreign policy.

June 25

I am in Wellfleet for the moment, at a pleasurable distance from the events of the last week—my worst week in Washington, and no doubt the harbinger of more to come. My downfall began innocently enough at Robert Kennedy's on Saturday night, the 16th. It was their annual dance. We dined al fresco around the swimming pool; I sat between Mrs. Joseph P. Kennedy and an old friend of Ethel's named Sarah Davis. Lester Lanin's band played during dinner. In due course Sarah Davis and I rose to dance. Ethel meanwhile had set a table for three on a plank thrown rather precariously across the swimming pool; this table was intended for John Glenn, Byron White and herself. Only Glenn and Ethel were sitting there when Sarah Davis and I danced by, and Sarah, in an excess of midparty exuberance, rushed out on the plank and began jumping up and down on it. After a moment, I followed, rocked myself a little on the plank, and suddenly Ethel's chair, with Ethel on it, slipped quietly into the pool. We stood there aghast, Glenn and I, while Sarah Davis ran appalled to the other side. I recall thinking that it was hardly chivalrous for Ethel to be in the pool by herself, but I helped her out from the side; and, while I was still contemplating this, was suddenly (I believed) nudged into the pool myself, carrying Ethel back with me. The question of whether I was nudged, and if so by whom, remains obscure. Most eyewitnesses have no notion how I got in, though one person told me that Lee Udall, convinced that I had pushed Ethel in, pushed me in for retaliation. Later in the evening Harry Belafonte, having been told by Ethel that Sarah Davis had been responsible for her having been pushed in, pushed Sarah Davis in. This concluded the evening's immersions. I found that Bobby's clothes fitted me perfectly and stayed till five.

On Wednesday Betty Beale published a somewhat garbled account of this in the *Star*. On Thursday, the *Herald Tribune*, in its frantic anti-administration mood, ran a front-page story with big headlines and photographs of Ethel, Glenn, Bobby and myself.

[A few days later] Gretchen [Schlesinger's longtime secretary] gave me a copy of that afternoon's *Washington News* with a column by Henry J. Taylor giving a false account of the telephone conversation we had had some weeks ago and then charging that I was violating government policy by accepting payment for articles published by the *Saturday Evening Post* and the *New York Times Magazine*. Taylor wrote, for example, that I began the conversation by calling him an idiot. That is an absolute lie. The conversation had been preceded by a telegram from him asking whether I would repudiate views I expressed in an article in the *Partisan Review* in 1947, by a reply from me and by a Taylor column misrepresenting those views. When he called, I made the mistake of accepting his call but thought that, by talking reasonably with him, I might be able to do some good. His first words were, "I want to ask you about your article in the *Saturday Evening Post*." I told him to go ahead, assuming that he had some questions about the substance. He said, "How much were you paid for it?" I replied that this had been handled by my publisher, that the article was part of a forthcoming book, and that I had stayed away from all financial detail. I then said, "If you are going to write about the *Post* article, I hope you will do me the courtesy of reading it first and reporting accurately what was written. Your column on the *Partisan Review* article wholly falsified my views." He said, "What do you mean?" I then read him portions of his column with appropriate comment. By this time, the conversation began to deteriorate. When I pointed out that he had cited obviously ironic passages about patriotism and religion as proof that I was anti-patriotic and anti-religious, he said with heavy sarcasm, "I guess I was too dumb to appreciate your irony." I said, "I guess that maybe you were." Later on, when he made some particularly outrageous accusation, I may well have said, "If you believe that, you are an idiot." In the end, I hung up on him.

Exhausted by all this, I then went to Bob Nathan's office, where a fund-raising party for George McGovern was in progress, had two stiff drinks and gave an eloquent speech on behalf of George. I then returned to my office and sent the President a memorandum mostly dealing with certain policy questions but concluding with a heartfelt apology for the trouble I was causing him and a statement that I would be glad to resign at any time. Bill Walton was with JFK when he received the memorandum that evening. Bill later told me that the President was both amused and touched by it and that he felt I was taking the whole thing too seriously. I did not, however, know this at the time.

At the end of the afternoon I steeled myself to go and see the President on a minor matter (the text of the Yale speech to be put out by the Yale University Press). We talked briefly about this. Then he asked me about my troubles. I said that it had been a bad couple of days. He said in a kindly way, "Don't worry about it. Everyone knows that Henry Taylor is a jerk. No one pays any attention to him. All they are doing is shooting at me through you. Their whole line is to pin everything on the professors—you, Heller, Rostow. When the market fell, *Time* put Heller on its cover—not Doug Dillon. Don't worry about it. This is the sort of thing you have to expect."

July 1

I should report on Norman Mailer's diatribe against Jackie in the current *Esquire*—a mad piece, not without flashes, but basically and transparently animated by Mailer's sense of grievance over the fact that he won the election by his *Esquire* piece of November 1960 and that, since then, Jackie had not answered one of his letters, had declined to give him an interview and had not invited him to the White House. Jackie's reaction, according to Bill Walton, is that she rather agreed with Mailer's account of the image she presented on television.

July 13

I have been resting agreeably here in Wellfleet for the last two weeks and thinking intermittently about our problems in Washington. As I look back over the last year and a half, the main—and persisting—error of the Kennedy administration has been the appeasement of business. This appeasement has been political and psychological rather than intellectual: that is, the President does not believe in the business ideology of the business community but does believe that, because of the weight of pro-business sentiment in the Congress and because of the need of active business collaboration in economic growth and in foreign policy, it is necessary to propitiate business and yield to its particular prejudices. From the start, the President has shown an unfortunate disposition to consult those whom he regards as enlightened and responsible business leaders (Lovett, David Rockefeller) and make a special effort to meet their wishes. I would guess that he does not have much respect for their ideas but has considerable for their experience and feels that this experience gives them certain clues to the operation of the economy which the intellectuals, for all their superior theories, do not possess. At times, he resents this process of appeasement and vents his resentment in private cracks about businessmen. But, when the chips are down, given the state of opinion in the Congress and in the country, he seems to feel no alternative but to pursue the appeasement line.

The Kennedy Administration has also capitulated too much to the existing momentum of government as embodied and urged by the executive bureaucracy. Wherever we have gone wrong—from Cuba to fiscal policy—it has been because we have not had sufficient confidence in the New Frontier approach to impose it on the government. Every important mistake has been the consequence of excessive deference to the government service. In area after area, we have behaved exactly as the Eisenhower administration would have behaved—in spite of everything we said during the campaign and of every hope and intention we brought to Washington. The essential reason for this is the power of the permanent government and its ability to sabotage and dominate the political government.

Another reflection uncomfortably forced upon me is the power of the hostile press to neutralize people in government through external attack. They did it with Chester Bowles; they are now trying it on Heller, Rostow and me. I think that I am fairly unmoved by attack *per se;* but I am obviously concerned over the extent to which my vulnerability to such attack creates further problems for the President and the administration. I know that all this has somewhat cramped my style— that I will speak and write less in the coming months—that I will make telephone calls instead of sending memoranda—that I will try to narrow the target I present to the enemy—and that, as a consequence, whatever limited effectiveness I may have had will be diminished. Thus far, JFK has been fine on these matters—and he must be, as a matter of elementary presidential self-protection. The moment that the opposition knows it can determine the composition of his personal staff, then they will know that they have him truly on the run.

August 5

In the course of a talk with the President on Thursday, he brought up my father's article in last Sunday's *Times* describing how the historians rate the Presidents. He said that he had liked the article very much and had read it with great interest. He was pleased that Truman's qualities were so generally recognized and was delighted with Eisenhower's rating (22). He said, "At first I thought that it was too bad that Ike was in Europe and would miss the article, but then I decided that some conscientious friend in the United States would probably send him a copy." What surprised him most, he said, was the high rating given Wilson— why, for example, was he put ahead of Jackson? After all, he said, Wilson was barely reelected in 1916, he mishandled the League fight, and, though a great speaker and writer, failed in a number of basic objectives.

August 6

I must confess that the report yesterday of Marilyn Monroe's death quite shocked and saddened (but did not surprise) me. I will never forget meeting her at the Arthur Krim party following the JFK birthday rally at Madison Square Garden in May. I cannot recall whether I wrote anything down at the time, but the image of this exquisite, beguiling and desperate girl will always stay with me. I do not think I have seen anyone so beautiful; I was enchanted by her manner and her wit, at once so masked, so ingenuous and so penetrating. But one felt a terrible unreality about her—as if talking to someone under water. Bobby and I engaged in mock competition for her; she was most agreeable to him and pleasant to me, but one never felt her to be wholly engaged. Indeed, she seemed most solicitous of her ex-father-in-law, Arthur Miller's father, a baffled and taciturn man whom she introduced to the group and on whom she constantly cast a maternal eye. The only moment I felt I touched her was when I mentioned that I was a friend of Joe Rauh. This produced a warm and spontaneous burst of affection—but then she receded into her own glittering mist.

Late yesterday afternoon I went out to the Rauhs' for a swim. Both Joe and Olie were saddened by the news. Olie talked about Marilyn as a guest, her fear of facing people, and the complicated stratagems she went through when she finally, for example, had to confront a press conference. After keeping the group waiting for two hours and a half, she examined herself in the mirror, saw the outline of her panties through her summer dress, removed them, put on white gloves, saying to Olie, "You don't know these people; if they saw my hands, they would write that my nails were not polished enough," and walked in agony downstairs. Later the CBS man said to Olie, "I have never seen anyone so nervous at an interview in my life."

August 19

On Wednesday, the 15th, I went to Cambridge and spoke to Henry Kissinger's International Seminar. I talked about the presidency and concluded with a description of the developing new restraints on the presidential power. Most people, I said, think that the President has grown more powerful because the national government has grown more powerful; but this is not necessarily the case. In certain respects, the President today is less free to act on his own that the President fifty or a hundred years ago. There were two reasons in particular for this: as the national government grew in size and function, so too grew (a) its dependence on appropriations and (b) its commitment to the federal bureaucracy.

The more the acts of government require appropriations, the more the Congress acquires a veto over national policies. Thus, in the realm of hemisphere affairs, Monroe could unilaterally promulgate the Monroe Doctrine and FDR could unilaterally promulgate the Good Neighbor policy—and Congress could do very little about it. But the Alliance for Progress is dependent on congressional support every step along the way—because the Alliance for Progress requires appropriations. I argued that this was true for foreign policy down the line.

As for the bureaucracy, I said, this had become the great deadweight on executive innovation. As the functions of the national government multiplied, a bureaucracy developed dominated by vested interests of its own—vested interests in ideas, in procedures, in institutions. The American government really has today four, not three, coordinate branches—the legislative, the judiciary, the executive and the presidency; and an active President would encounter as much resistance within the executive branch as he would from Congress or the Supreme Court. The increase in the size of the bureaucracy created a split between the "political government" and the "permanent government"; and many members of the bureaucracy exuded the feeling that Presidents come and Presidents go, but they go on forever. The problem of moving forward was in great part the problem of making the permanent government responsive to the policies of the political government. FDR had solved it brilliantly by carrying on his war against the depression outside the permanent government—through a set of emergency agencies, staffed from top to bottom by men who believed in his policies. If he had tried to combat the depression through the Departments of the Treasury and Agriculture and Commerce and Labor, we would probably still be in it. That option, however, is no longer open to Kennedy. The result is that the bureaucracy has an infinite capacity to dilute, delay, obstruct, resist and sabotage presidential purposes.

1961 was the free-wheeling year of the Kennedy administration, when we all felt free to act and intervene when we thought we had an idea or when we thought we saw something wrong. But the ice is beginning to form over government again; the press, the Congress and (tacitly) the bureaucracy have begun to pick the New Frontiersmen off as if from ambush; and the old continuities, the Eisenhower-Dulles continuities, are beginning to reassert themselves.

August 23

When I saw the President today, I told him, among other things, that my disposition was to turn down the various invitations I had received to speak in the campaign. He agreed, saying that he thought it would be a mistake for me to get into the limelight again; "after all, you and Ethel are just now beginning to emerge from the shadows."

September 1

Yesterday afternoon I went out to the Bethesda Naval Hospital to see my old friend John Bartlow Martin, who came back from the Dominican Republic ten days ago because of a revival of stomach ulcers.

We reminisced about our first meeting—just ten years ago in Springfield, Illinois, at the Elks Club. We all met there, a bunch of amateurs engaged in trying to elect Adlai Stevenson President of the United States. Where are we now? There are two cabinet members (Bill Wirtz and Ed Day); three ambassadors (Ken Galbraith, Bill Blair and John Bartlow Martin); one judge of the court of appeals (Carl McGowan); one director of the budget (David Elliott Bell); one undersecretary of state (George Ball); one chairman of the Federal Communications Commission (Newt Minow); one special assistant to the UN Ambassador (Clayton Fritchey); one special assistant to the President (me). I suppose that had some soothsayer told us one night at the Elks Club that we would all be occupying these positions, we would not have been wildly surprised; but if the soothsayer had gone on to say that the agency for this would be John F. Kennedy, we would have been incredulous. All this suggests the unpredictability of politics, and of life.

September 4

[I have been pondering] the question of what is required to be *effective* in government. For example, when studying the New Deal, I used often to marvel over the fact that a bright and original man like Adolf Berle was far less effective in government than a slow-witted man like Henry Morgenthau. I do not mean to compare myself to Berle, because I have been far less effective than he was in the 30s. But effectiveness seems somehow to derive from a sense of administrative weight. Over

Cuba in March 1961 I was right in an ineffective way—ineffective at the time, and ineffective in persuading anyone of any particular cogency in my judgment; while people like Rusk, McNamara, Dulles, Bissell, Bundy were wrong in an effective way—in a way which did not much impair future confidence in their judgment (Lemnitzer and [Charles P.] Cabell, on the other hand, were wrong in an ineffective way). I have the feeling that the President somewhat discounts my views, primarily because he regards me as a claimant agency for standardized liberalism, partly also because he considers me to be, after all, an intellectual and insufficiently practical and realistic.

September 22

[On Monday, the 17th,] I lunched at the British Embassy. I drove back with Bobby Kennedy, and we discussed the impending trouble at the University of Mississippi [over the admission of a black student, James Meredith]. I made some suggestions about the historical status of the "interposition" doctrine. Later that day Ed Guthman called and said that Bobby wondered whether I could supply some of this background for a statement on the Mississippi crisis. I went over to Justice about six thirty and found the legal group in Bobby's garish office. Everyone was in shirtsleeves except Nick Katzenbach, who sat saturninely in the background and said softly that he saw no reason to issue a statement at that time. Guthman had drafted a statement, to which I added a quotation from the Mississippi Legislature in 1832 denouncing the interposition doctrine. Bobby pondered this and then engaged in quiet conversation with his people about the best mode of protecting the Negro student when he tried to register. The mixture of shirtsleeved casualness, soft voices and evident determination was impressive. In the end, Bobby agreed with Nick about the statement, and it was deferred. Instead, he issued quiet orders and his troops dispersed. He told me, by the way, that he regarded Governor Barnett of Mississippi as genuinely loony—that he had been hit on the head by an airplane propeller last summer and had never been the same since.

[After a trip to New York,] I got back to Washington in time to go to the *Mr. President* opening. The show was really terrible. I saw Josh Logan at the party following. Unable to say anything else, I said, "What a good party!" He said, "Yes—but don't say anything about the show." The party was not only good but great—the best since last spring at the White House. Ken O'Donnell came up to Cissy Ormsby-Gore and said in heartfelt tones, "This is the best party I have ever been to in my life." The girls were pretty, the drinks were plentiful, the music good, and everyone had such a sense of liberation after the show that they were preternaturally vivacious for that hour of the evening on that day of the week. The President stayed till two, and I stayed till four. I had a good talk with Jackie. At one point she feared that the President, then deep in conversation with some unidentified person, might become bored and want to go home. "Bring a pretty girl," she said, "and divert him." I suggested Evangeline Bruce. Jackie made a face and said, "No. Everyone knows that she is a bloody bore. That's what Isaiah Berlin called her." I do *not* consider Evangeline any kind of bore; but I suppose this shows how fashions change.

Ted Sorensen went to the hospital on Wednesday for an ulcer (which appeared to evaporate by Sunday), so I received the assignment to write the Wheeling speech for Thursday. As usual, I was overwhelmed by the utter casualness of the speech-writing process. On Wednesday morning I asked the President what he wanted to say. He issued a few general injunctions about West Virginia, the argument for a Democratic Congress, etc. I spoke to the state chairman, Ken Hechler and one or two others and got some more ideas. I wrote the speech in the afternoon, revised it early the next morning and took it to the President before luncheon. He read it quickly, suggested omitting a couple of things, wanted a passage added with statistics showing the extent of Republican opposition to welfare legislation, and handed it back. I asked whether it was OK to release it. He said, "Sure." So the advance text was handed out in the afternoon; and he actually followed it moderately well in the evening, until the rains came and he cut the speech short.

Ted's absence brought me back into the Mississippi affair. On Friday Bobby asked me to come over to prepare a presidential statement explaining the necessity for federal intervention. Ed Guthman spirited me into the Department through a side entrance and installed me in a room behind the Attorney General's office. Bobby came in and said that he understood better now how Hitler had taken over in Germany. "Everyone in Mississippi is accepting what that fellow is doing," he said. "There are no protests anywhere—from the bar or from professional men or from professors. I wouldn't have believed it." I asked him how his talks with Barnett had been. He said, "Some of them have been hard to believe. Today Barnett said to me, 'Why can't you persuade Meredith to go to another college? I could get some money together and we could give him a fellowship to any university he wanted outside the state. Wouldn't that be the best way to solve the problem?' " Bobby couldn't believe it.

I wrote the statement next morning and then went over to the Cosmos Club to lunch with the American Historical Association's Advisory Committee on the Relations between Historians and Government. I had barely been there for 15 minutes when O'Donnell's office summoned me back to the White House. I entered the President's office to find Bobby, Kenny and Burke Marshall. Matters were approaching a climax, and the President was about to call Barnett. As the phone rang, the President, with the air of a master of ceremonies, announced, "And now—Governor Ross Barnett." Bobby said, mocking a prize-fight manager, "Go get him Johnny boy." The President, rehearsing to himself, said, "Governor, this is the President of the United States—not Bobby, not Teddy, not Princess Radziwill." Then the call came through, and he got down to business. The following notes, taken at the time, report obviously only his half of the dialogue.

JFK: "I am concerned about this matter as I know you must be." . . .

"Here's my problem, Governor. I don't know Mr. Meredith, and I didn't put him in there. But under the Constitution I have to carry out the law. I want your help in doing it." . . .

"I've talked with him [Bobby]. We've gone over our situation. . . ."

"Yes, he talked to Mr. Watkins [Barnett's personal attorney]. . . ."

"Wait just a minute. The Attorney General is in the outer office. . . . He says he talked to Mr. Watkins. The problem is whether we can get help to get this fellow in this week. The Attorney General did not feel that he and Mr. Watkins reached any final agreement on this. . . ."

[Barnett proposed that Watkins come to Washington.]

"I'll talk to Mr. Watkins when they meet. . . ."

"The difficulty is this—we have two or three problems. First, the Court's order to you gives you till Tuesday to permit the entry of Mr. Meredith. What is your position on that? [Bobby runs in from the outer office and whispers in the President's ear.] The problem is I have my responsibility as you have yours. The Attorney General can talk to Mr. Watkins tomorrow. I want to work this out in an amicable way. I don't want a lot of people down there to be hurt or killed. . . ."

[Long silence while Barnett speaks.]

"The Attorney General will see Mr. Watkins. After that I will be back in touch with you. . . ."

After he hung up, the President said, "You know what that fellow said? He said, 'I want to thank you for your help on the poultry problem.'" He and Bobby discussed the problems of talking to Barnett. Bobby said, "One day Barnett said to me that the reason he could not admit Meredith was that a state law forbade registering anyone convicted of a crime. [Meredith had been convicted in a ten minute trial of registering from a county of which he was not a resident.] I said, 'Governor, you really don't mean that. Isn't the real reason you won't admit Mr. Meredith because he is a Negro.'" The President said, "You've been fighting a sofa pillow all week." As they analyzed the Barnett conversation, it became evident that he had said nothing substantial. I asked Bobby what [attorney and Barnett friend Tom] Watkins had said in previous talks. He replied, "Nothing very much—something about not having his troops fire on our troops." Watkins also said that Barnett would yield if he could be confronted with a dozen soldiers pointing unloaded guns at him.

The more they talked, the less point there seemed in Watkins's coming to Washington unless he was prepared to negotiate a change in Barnett's position. Bobby accordingly put in a call to Watkins.

He began by saying that he had two questions: "Will the Governor defy or follow the order of the Court? If he means to defy that order, will we have a pitched battle down there when we arrest the Governor? . . ."

"Is there any possibility of finding out what we need down there? Must we send an army, a division or what? This depends on what the Governor will do. We are at least entitled to know that. . . ."

"If the Governor is going to stand up and bar the way, that's one situation. If he is going to tell everyone to go home, that's an entirely different situation. . . ."

"But he can't do that. You can't tell others to behave if you yourself are obstructing the order of the court. . . ."

[Aside to the President: "His understanding is that the Governor will physically bar Meredith. He says that the situation is very explosive—the law enforcement officials can't control it." JFK: "Will they try?" Bobby asks the question and whispers to JFK, "He doesn't know."]

"I have three questions. 1) Will the Governor cooperate in enforcing the court order? 2) If not, will he attempt personally to obstruct it, or will those under his direction attempt to obstruct it? 3) Even if he doesn't help with the court order, will he take the responsibility for maintaining law and order? I need the answer to these questions."

Time elapsed in order to give Watkins a chance to call Barnett. Then the President called Barnett. Watkins, however, had not called or reached him. Bobby then recapitulated his conversation with Watkins.

"Watkins said that Meredith's entrance would create problems which could not be overcome. I said that, unless he had concrete proposals which might form a basis for agreement, he was wasting his time in coming to Washington. These proposals would have to include strong and vocal action on your part."

[Barnett evidently asked what.]

"At minimum, an order that people could not congregate in Oxford in groups larger than three or five; that students who commit disorders are liable for expulsion; that all people carrying guns or clubs in Oxford be arrested. Such steps would indicate interest in maintaining law and order. 'Cool heads' [evidently referring to a phrase used by Barnett] are not enough; there must be orders so that people will not congregate. . . ."

"Sneaking Meredith off to Jackson for registration doesn't meet the problem. It doesn't really make much sense, does it? . . ."

"Are you going up to Oxford Monday? Is that your plan? . . ."

"The President has some questions to which he wants answers in order to make his own determination."

JFK: "I know your feeling about the law of Mississippi and the court order. What we are concerned about is whether you will maintain law and order. I want positive assurances from you that you will maintain law and order—prevent the gathering of a mob and action taken by a mob. Can you stop that? What about the Attorney General's proposals to stop a mob? . . ."

"As I understand it, you will do everything you can to maintain order. Next, Governor, *can* you maintain order? . . ."

"The only thing is that I have my responsibilities. This is not my order. But I have to carry it out. I want to do it in a way which will cause least damage to the people of Mississippi. That's my interest. . . ."

"At what time would it be fair? . . ."

"Would you undertake to register him in two weeks? Unless we have your support and assurance. . . ."

"Do you want to talk to Mr. Watkins?"

That ended the conversation. The President reported that Barnett had said, "Just tell 'em to cool off and you can sneak him in. I'll bring everyone up to Oxford—and then you can register him in Jackson."

Bobby: "What a rogue!"

October 15

Tonight Hickory Hill* convened at Bob McNamara's to hear a discussion of Soviet cybernetics by John Ford of the CIA, Dr. Robert Livingston of the National Institutes of Health and Dana Durand.

---

* Hickory Hill, which was the name of Robert Kennedy's estate, was also the name given to the intellectual seminars that were arranged by Schlesinger at RFK's request.

I had a few moments of private conversation in which McNamara, as usual, displayed his great intelligence and candor. He said that he had told John Gunther (whom I had asked McNamara to see) that no sane western leader could for one moment envisage the initiation of nuclear war. "This is the only realistic conclusion," McNamara said. "But the Pentagon is full of papers talking about the preservation of a 'viable society' after nuclear conflict. That 'viable society' phrase drives me mad. I keep trying to comb it out, but it keeps coming back.... Everyone knows that we won't go to nuclear war over Berlin. That is why we have to develop a conventional capability. Now in Europe they say that emphasis on a conventional capability weakens the credibility of the nuclear deterrent. This seems to me wholly unreal. A credible deterrent cannot be based on an incredible act."

October 28

On October 19, Adlai Stevenson called up, said that he was in Washington and asked when we could get together. We agreed to go down to the State Department together the next morning; he was staying at Paul Magnuson's across O Street. On Saturday morning, he beckoned me into the Magnuson house. "I don't want to talk in front of the chauffeur," he said; and then, "Do you know what the secret discussions this week have been about?" I had heard of no secret discussions; the President was out of town campaigning; and, surprised, I ventured a poor guess: "Berlin?" He said, "No; Cuba." He then explained to me that aerial reconnaissance had revealed the presence of offensive missile bases in Cuba. The President had learned this Tuesday morning, he said, and had told him after luncheon that day. I gathered that there had been a steady argument all week between those who wanted a diplomatic solution and those who wanted a military solution. He indicated that there had been pressure for a direct air strike to knock out the bases but felt that this had been put aside in favor of a quarantine on further shipments of offensive arms into Cuba. He said that he would have to make a speech early in the week in the Security Council justifying the quarantine and asked me whether I would begin work on it.

I subsequently heard from other sources a more detailed account of the secret debate. When the President first heard the news, he ordered an intensified surveillance. Then a small inner group began to meet to consider what course should be followed. At first, there was considerable sentiment for a strike; but, as people began to reflect on the implications, the preference shifted to the idea of a quarantine. On Friday, the 19th, however, there was a sudden revival of the strike. Dean Acheson was sitting in preparatory to going to Paris to brief the North Atlantic Council. Some one asked him what he thought, and he argued vigorously for knocking the bases out by an air strike as soon as possible. Douglas Dillon, John McCone and then Mac Bundy supported this argument, Bundy saying that it was now or never, that the bases had to be attacked before they became operational, and that the attack should be launched on Sunday morning. At this point Bobby Kennedy spoke up and, according to my information (not Adlai Stevenson, who wasn't there), held forth much as follows: "For 175 years this has not been the kind of country which launches Pearl Harbor attacks on Sunday morning. The first American President to do anything like this would not be forgiven by history, by his own people, or by the world." The discussion continued, and finally it was decided to appoint two teams to prepare the case for each alternative—a strike team, captained by Bundy; and a blockade team, captained by Alexis Johnson. Rusk, I am told, took no part in this discussion; Maxwell Taylor implied that he went along with the Bundy view; McNamara that he was against a strike. By the time the group met again late that afternoon, the blockade was in ascendancy, perhaps because of work by Rusk behind the scenes.

The secret was superbly kept. Late Saturday—as the President abruptly returned from the campaign and as Rusk cancelled a speech—a sense of excitement and anticipation began to flood Washington. That night at Jim Rowe's dance there was great speculation as to what was up. By Sunday morning speculation was beginning to settle on Cuba;

and by Sunday afternoon Scotty Reston was able to call me up with what substantially was the whole story. *The Times* did not print it, however, because Orville Dryfoos had told the President on Saturday evening that he would print nothing without first consulting with the President about its implications for our general position. I suppose that they must have talked later on Sunday because *The Times* withheld the story on Monday morning (while surrounding the Washington speculation with a host of Cuba stories, so that the intelligent reader would know where the trouble was centering).

My connection with all this was—and remained—peripheral. During Sunday I continued work on a draft for the UN. On Sunday evening I went over to State and considered the speech with Harlan Cleveland, Joe Sisco and Tom Wilson. The President called me around ten to find out how things were going. I told him that a draft would be ready in the morning.

I saw the President about 10 o'clock on Monday morning, the 22nd. He noted how strange it was that no one in the intelligence community had anticipated the possibility of a Soviet attempt to transform Cuba into a nuclear base; all the intelligence people had wholly excluded this on the ground that the USSR would not be so stupid as to offer us this pretext for intervention. (I must note that I had been as wrong as the intelligence community on this point.) I asked JFK why he thought the USSR had done this. He replied that, first, it would help bring Russia and China closer together (I did not quite grasp his point here, unless it was that the display of this capacity for drastic, anti-U.S. action would wipe out some of the elements of discord between the USSR and China); second, that it would radically redefine the setting in which the Berlin situation would be reopened after the election; and third, it would deal the U.S. a tremendous political blow. I said that the Russians must have thought that we would not respond. The President said, "They had us either way. If we did nothing, we would be dead. If we reacted, they hoped to have us in an embarrassed and exposed position, whether with regard to Berlin or Turkey or the UN."

The establishment of nuclear bases in Cuba would have made the Soviet medium-range missiles effective against American targets and thereby about doubled Soviet nuclear striking power against the United States. The speed and stealth of the Soviet plan made it imperative that we react in time to prevent the completion of the job. That is why we had to impose the quarantine quickly and could not wait for a fortnight while the matter was debated in the Security Council, vetoed by the USSR and then debated and voted on in the General Assembly.

On Monday the President told me to go to New York and work with Stevenson on the UN side of things. At 11 o'clock, I returned to the office to meet with Rusk, Bobby and others. They read my draft for the Security Council. It was generally applauded. The President called for a few omissions—including a passage threatening an American strike if the Cuban build-up persisted. I went down to New York after luncheon, intending to stay for the night if necessary.

The next three days were a kind of continued pandemonium. I had never before been exposed to the UN process in a very sustained way; and I came away with a heightened respect for Stevenson and the UN crowd. It is like a permanent political convention: there are so many people to be considered and cajoled; so many issues all going at once; and such an inherent unpredictability about the parliamentary sequence that the result is a sense of continuous and unrelenting crisis. Stevenson, for example, had to spend so much of his time in meeting with UN delegates from other nations that he had little time left to consider his own speeches and strategy. Nonetheless he was unperturbed and effective.

The actual speech process was dismally reminiscent of the 1952 and 1956 campaigns. Adlai Stevenson worked hard on the draft, but at the last moment, so that both the main speech, delivered on Tuesday, and the rebuttal, delivered on Thursday, were still in the works when he had to go over to the Security Council to begin speaking.

On Wednesday night Averell Harriman called me from Washington. He said that it seemed clear to him that Khrushchev wanted us to help him get off the hook and that he was sending desperate signals to us to cooperate with him in moving toward a peaceful solution. His letter to Bertrand Russell, his instructions to Soviet ships to avoid confrontation and his well-publicized visit the night before in Moscow with Jerome Hines, the American singer—all these seemed to Averell evidence that he was seeking a way out. Harriman said that Khrushchev had sent out similar signals directly after the U–2 affair in 1960, and that Eisenhower had made the mistake of ignoring him; we must not, he said, make a similar mistake. "If we do nothing but get tougher and tougher, we will force him into counter measures. The first incident will engage Soviet prestige and infinitely reduce the chance of a peaceful solution." Averell said that the key to all this lay in two Khrushchev remarks—his statement that the Soviet Union must now be dealt with as an equal; and his observation to Robert Frost that the democracies were too liberal to fight. "We must give him an out. If we do this shrewdly, we can downgrade the tough group in the Soviet Union which persuaded him to do this. But if we deny him an out, then we will escalate this business into a nuclear war."

I asked Averell whether he had told this to anybody. He said, "I haven't talked to Rusk. He has never asked my advice about anything outside of the Far East." Accordingly I reported his view in a memorandum which I sent that night to the President, who apparently read it because he called Harriman the next day and asked him questions about it.

On Thursday Adlai Stevenson had his confrontation with [Valerian] Zorin in the Security Council. Zorin, who seemed to be laboring without instructions, was not effective, and Stevenson even won a favorable notice from the *Daily News*. On Friday morning Adlai Stevenson went to Washington. He returned relatively optimistic. Nonetheless at the end of the week the rumors of an impending invasion reached a new height of intensity.

In the course of Friday, the Cubans at the UN began to hint to unaligned delegates that a settlement might be possible, that the missiles bases might be dismantled and removed, if the U.S. would guarantee the territorial integrity of Cuba. Then on Friday night came Khrushchev's impassioned and deeply personal letter to Kennedy concluding with substantially this proposition. On the other hand, work on the bases continued, and this strengthened the case of those who still argued for direct military intervention. Invasion remained a live possibility through Saturday. Khrushchev's public letter Saturday morning, suggesting a swap of Cuba and Turkey, complicated matters. Our response to this seemed to Harriman, Mike Forrestal and me unnecessarily negative; but we did not know that at the same time we were readying a more affirmative response to the letter of Friday night. This response and Khrushchev's answer on Sunday morning ended the crisis.

So it was a near thing. I am sure that for the next few days the national relief over the resolution will overwhelm everything else. But I wonder how long it will be before the opposition starts shooting at the non-invasion guarantee as one more example of the "no-win" policy. In a sense, it might have been more acceptable politically in the US if we had traded away our Turkish bases (which McNamara wants to get rid of anyway) instead of committing ourselves to tacit recognition of the Castro regime in Cuba.

October 29

I stopped by to see the President after the staff meeting this morning. He seemed relaxed and chipper but far from complacent. He said that it was too bad that all this had happened in the midst of a campaign because the Republicans would now feel compelled to attack the settlement. "Too many people will think now that all we have to do in dealing with the Russians is to kick them in the balls. . . . I think there is a law of equity in these disputes. When one party is clearly wrong, it will eventually give way. They had no business in putting those missiles in and in lying to me about it. They were in the wrong and knew it. So, when we stood firm, they had to back down. But this doesn't mean at all that they would back down when they felt they were in the right and had vital interests involved."

He discussed Eisenhower with his usual rueful detachment. "I can't make him out. Here Truman and I cancelled all our speeches last week, and Eisenhower had a perfectly good excuse to do so. Instead, he gave two speeches attacking me in the most bitter way—and all the time he claims he doesn't like politics! Do you know what has really driven him into this campaign? It is your father and his poll. For years, Eisenhower has gone along, basking in the glow of the applause which he has always had. Then he saw that poll and realized how he stood before the cold eye of history—way below Truman; even below Hoover. That is what is eating him now. He hates me because I am his successor; but his real quarrel is with what he now fears may be the judgment of history. That is why he is going around the country trying to defend his administration and to blacken us—to show what his administration saved the country from."

November 1

Stevenson complained—and with entire justice—of the fact that he had filed a report Wednesday night to the State Department on U Thant's conversations with Castro; and that by Thursday afternoon the substance of the report was in the newspapers, causing much embarrassment to Stevenson and to U Thant. I reported this late in the afternoon to the President. JFK, much irritated, called Bob Manning, learned that the Stevenson message had been distributed in 100 copies and that the newspapers had it within two hours of its distribution. He swore briefly and directed Manning to send a note to each recipient of the report, to be signed by Rusk, pointing out the trouble the leak had caused to the nation at a delicate moment of negotiation. The President is on a crusade against leaking. All members of the White House staff are now required to report to Pierre each day the names of newsmen with whom they have talked and the subjects discussed. (I wonder how long this system will last.)

While we were talking, there was suddenly a clatter outside and an avalanche of children poured into the room, followed by Jackie and by

Tony Bradlee. The President seized Caroline and John Jr. with delight and induced John to dance, clapping his hands to provide the accompaniment. (The night before was Halloween. On one occasion when the bell rang, Chrissie went to the door and discovered a collection of small masked creatures, one of whom was particularly eager to have her basket filled with goodies. After a few moments a masked mother in the background called on the children to go to their next house. The voice seemed familiar; then Chrissie suddenly recognized it. It was, of course, Jackie, and the eager little girl was Caroline. I told Jackie what a thrill it had been for Chrissie. Jackie said that they had stopped next at Dean Acheson's and then had gone on to Joe Alsop's.)

November 14

I saw excerpts from Nixon's Farewell Address on television on Wednesday. It was an astonishing performance, and it must be said that Nixon went out in character. The pale face, the furtive smile, the spurious air of reasonableness, the exposed vanity, and the profound incomprehension—all were there; and, just when one began to feel a little sorry for him, he would say something so terrible as to abolish all compassion. Oddly enough, he spent his time denouncing the press and praising television which destroyed him. I am really quite pleased in retrospect at the characterizations of the two men in *Kennedy or Nixon*. I believe that this tract stands up very well.

Mrs. Roosevelt died on November 7. I felt a strong sense of personal loss (as did several hundred million others), not because I had been especially close to Mrs. Roosevelt, but because one regarded her presence as a permanent guidepost and blessing in American life. She was, of course, much more than an image of liberal idealism. She always seemed to me most impressive when she talked about politics, especially New York politics. This brought into play her penetrating vision and her pungent common sense. She was, in many ways, a tough and salty old lady. No one could deflate a person or idea more artlessly and devastatingly than Mrs. Roosevelt. I will never forget the 1956 convention when Harry

Truman came to Chicago determined to destroy Adlai Stevenson. He did his best in a press conference; then Mrs. Roosevelt came to town and proceeded, in the kindest possible way, to destroy Mr. Truman. There was a delight in watching those two old pros conduct their duel—and I never felt that the outcome diminished President Truman's affection for Mrs. Roosevelt. I was never close to Mrs. Roosevelt—those really close to her were those she could do something for, and I did not fit into that pattern. But I greatly admired her, enjoyed her company, valued her counsel—and wish that I had dared invade her time and energy more systematically on behalf of *The Age of Roosevelt*.

[On Monday, the 10th,] we landed at a military field and helicoptered to the Vanderbilt estate [for Mrs. Roosevelt's funeral]. It was a somber day; at noon there were still streaks of sunshine. We lunched with the Alsops, Tom Corcoran and Ben Cohen and had considerable New Deal reminiscence. Tom said, "This is the last assembly. There will be no other occasion on which all these people will gather together." I thought of this as we sat in the Hyde Park church—Henry Wallace was there, and Jim Farley; Henry Morgenthau and Frances Perkins; and the three Presidents. I have never seen Mr. Truman look so anguished. I had not seen Eisenhower since Armistice Day, 1944, when I watched him (I think) walk up the Champs Elysees to the Arc de Triomphe. I found myself a little surprised by his bearing and presence; he is a more impressive looking man than I had imagined.

By the time we reached the grave-site, a gentle rain had begun to fall. A local rector delivered a few remarks of exceptional banality. The mourners lined the four sides of the rectangle; it was deeply moving. We then adjourned with Jack and June Bingham to the John Roosevelts' for a final drink. All the Roosevelt children were there—Anna, handsome and haggard; Franklin, that wreck of a man of talent and potentiality; Jimmy, that charming cypher; Elliott, old and stout, a meaningless, aging man; my classmate John, a hopeless slob. As I saw them, I could not help thinking of the Kennedys at the White House the night before—so young and confident, so full of energy and charm and purpose. One felt an historic contrast, one dynasty giving way to another, like the Plantagenets to the Yorks.

One footnote to the Hyde Park visit: as we drove from the church to the grave, I reflected that, if anyone had said in 1940 that the next three Presidents of the United States would be Harry Truman, Dwight Eisenhower and John F. Kennedy, it would have provoked total incredulity. The second and third names would have been unknown, and the first would probably have seemed almost the least likely member of the Senate to succeed. Having pondered this, I swore not to hazard any predictions about the man who will be inaugurated in January 1969.

December 25

The President called me on Sunday morning, the 16th, and, among other things, discussed the Khrushchev speech. He expressed, as he has before, his wonder that Khrushchev makes much the same set of charges against the West that the West makes against him; he credits Nikita S. Khrushchev with sincerity in this, and the mirror effect reinforces his own detachment and his refusal to regard the world contest as a holy war. He read two sentences aloud with admiration and said, "Khrushchev certainly has some good writers!" The sentences were: "Those militarists who boast that they have submarines with Polaris rockets on board, and other surprises, as they put it, against the Soviet Union, would do well to remember that we are not living in mud huts either" and "At the climax of events around Cuba, when there began to be a smell of burning in the air. . . ." (I said that we could do as well for him if he would only give some two-hour speeches.)

We have decided to make one more try to force [Congolese politician Moise] Tshombe to permit the integration of Katanga [province] with the Congo. I have kept away from this, partly because most of my friends—like Stevenson, Ed Gullion and Mennon Williams—take the opposite side; but I might as well note here that I regard the policy of deepening U.S. involvement in the Congo as a mistake.

The battle for identity is part of the ordeal of nationhood, and it can only be fought out by the nation itself. I agree with the English comment: "Every people have a right to their own Wars of the Roses." I cannot help thinking that for the UN to try to act as midwife is depriving the Congo of part of the shared agony necessary to lay a solid basis for nationality.

Beyond this, I am very doubtful that we should be doing very much in Africa at all. My guess is that no outside force will make much of a dent of this great, chaotic continent, so much of which is only in this generation beginning to emerge out of tribalism, fetishism and cannibalism. Communism and democracy are equally irrelevant. The Communists have got nowhere in Africa, and I doubt if they would do much better if we withdrew totally. We are not going to get anywhere either. I suppose that we must do what we can to help those Africans who wish to keep things moving in a democratic direction. But I can't help thinking that, if we could add the talent and resources presently invested in Africa to our effort in Latin America, we might stand a chance of succeeding with the Alliance for Progress. And both the ideas of communism and democracy are relevant to Latin America.

1963

January 6

The New Year opened quietly, with the President still in Florida. On Friday, January 4, I went to the National Archives for the opening of an exhibition celebrating the centennial of the Emancipation Proclamation. Bobby gave the speech—it was derived from a speech I had written for the President for use on January 1 by television from Palm Beach, but which the President had decided not to use on the grounds that a segregated city was hardly the best place from which to make an emancipation speech. It was a good speech; and, at the end, Joe Rauh passed me a note saying "Poor Lyndon." I asked Joe what he meant. He said, "Lyndon must know he is through. Bobby is going to be the next President."

January 10

We dined tonight at the White House. The other guests were Joe and Susan Mary Alsop and Lee Radziwill. I thought Joe looked a little disappointed when we entered the room, but he accepted the situation philosophically. The President and Jackie were both in great form. The talk ranged widely. JFK discussed his conversation the night before with [André] Malraux. He said that he had tried to say to Malraux that all the talk about European nuclear deterrents, multilateral forces, etc., was unimportant and irrelevant, since it was all based on the expectation of a Soviet attack on Europe, "than which nothing is less likely." In this connection, he derided the notion that nuclear weapons are essential for prestige in the international community. "What matters," he said, "is the strength of the currency. It is this, and not its nuclear weapons, which makes France a factor. Britain has nuclear weapons, but the pound is weak, so every one pushes it around. Why are people so nice to Spain these days? Not because Spain has nuclear weapons, but because of all those lovely gold reserves." Instead of worrying about improbable formulas to meet unlikely contingencies, people should begin thinking about the Far East and the consequences of a Chinese nuclear capability. This was the real issue—and people in Europe were too preoccupied with a series of unreal issues. I asked how Malraux had responded. The President said that he had not displayed any very clear reaction and that he seemed to be retreating in order to think it over.

The President was amusing on the subject of the candor of wives. He said, "Whenever a wife says something, everyone in this town assumes that she is saying what her husband really thinks. Last night I suddenly heard Jackie telling Malraux that she thought Adenauer was 'un peu gaga.' I am sure that this has already been reported to Paris as my opinion."

March 21

On Thursday evening, March 7, I dined at Averell's with Ambassador [Anatoly] Dobrynin. Walt Rostow, Charlie Thayer and Mike Forrestal were also present. Averell was in great form, directing the conversation in high spirits and with an iron hand. He obviously had designed the evening to make certain points with Dobrynin. His first point—that the U.S. and the USSR had a common interest in restraining Communist China—did not elicit much reaction. He did better with his second point which had to do with nuclear testing. Averell emphasized the President's problem in gaining ratification of a test ban unless he could make a strong case that the national interests were fully protected. Both leaders had internal problems, Averell said, but on the whole it seemed probable that it would be easier for Khrushchev to go up to six on-site inspections than for Kennedy to go down to three. The point seemed to register with Dobrynin.

April 14

[On April 8] I met with Walter Reuther and Hubert Humphrey [at the White House]—and thought about the differences in style between the New Deal and the New Frontier. Reuther, Humphrey and Bowles are all essentially New Dealers, though Hubert has adapted better than the others to the Kennedy epoch. One difference certainly lies in the penchant for talk. Judging from contemporary testimony, the New Dealers were always great talkers and philosophizers; and Walter, Chester and Hubert remain faithful to this tradition. Moreover, the New Deal had its distinctive rhetoric. Walter and Hubert could talk about "the people," about their ultimate wisdom, and about the importance of doing things for them in a way quite alien to the New Frontier. The heart was worn much more on the sleeve then. The New Frontier has a deep mistrust of what it regards as the pat liberal sentimentalities and clichés of the thirties. I sympathize with both sides and can see all too clearly why each is baffled by the other—all the more baffled because of a substantial agreement on policy (though the New Dealers are still more audacious, less impressed by business wisdom and more willing to damn the torpedoes and go ahead). The difference in rhetoric does probably signify a deeper difference in commitment—a change, in a way, from evangelists who want to do something because it is just and right, to technocrats who want to do something because it is rational and necessary. The New Frontier lacks the evangelical impulse—in part no doubt because there is no audience for it.

I wish I could figure out the terms in which the idealism and imagination of the New Deal could be infused into the anti-sentimental, anti-rhetorical, understated mood of the New Frontier.

On Monday afternoon, I attended the swearing-in of Averell Harriman as Deputy Undersecretary of State. George Ball gave a graceful speech, recalling the early days of the New Deal, when he and Averell had first met, and saying how exciting these days had been, when the New Dealers believed that anything was possible and that everything done in the past was wrong. Averell picked up this theme in his own remarks, saying that he had lived through four times of immense excitement and creativity—the early New Deal, the war years, the Marshall Plan and now today. After the ceremony, Averell asked me to come into his new office. He said, "Of course, I had to say all those nice things about the spirit in the State Department today, but it isn't so. This place is dead, dead, dead. What I want to do is to give it a little of the crusading spirit of those earlier times. I want to bring it to life." If anyone can, he will.

He then said, "What is wrong with the President when it comes to dealing with the Congress? These people spend all their time obstructing and sabotaging his program, and yet he treats them with constant consideration and respect. I suppose that it is because he still views them as one senator viewing his colleagues and equals. . . . I am used to Presidents who understood their power over Congress and who would not stand this nonsense. Roosevelt wouldn't. Truman wouldn't." I said that it had taken Truman nearly three years to get over his senatorial habits, and that JFK had only been in office two years. Averell allowed that that might be so, made clear his basic admiration for JFK and said that he was going to change the State Department's line of undiscriminating deference.

On Wednesday night I attended Marie Harriman's birthday party— a most agreeable occasion. Among those present were FDR Jr., Randolph Churchill and Bobby Kennedy—an unusual representation of the great dynasties of the 20th century. The dominating figure of the three, it must be said, was Bobby, who kidded the others mercilessly. He had, of course, the moral advantage of being on the way up while both of them had a consciousness of spoiled and wasted lives.

I left for Warm Springs on Thursday evening. [It] was an enjoyable interlude. The Little White House surprised me by its utter simplicity—a combination living- and dining-room, three small bedrooms, a simple frame house with a refrigerator on the back porch. The experience increased my feeling that the time is approaching for me to cut loose and return to historical labors. (But disengagement is going to be extremely difficult: this life is far too much fun.)

May 8

On Saturday, May 4, a group of Americans for Democratic Action local leaders came in to see the President. This was the result of an intervention by Ken O'Donnell, who thought that the President had seen enough businessmen recently and that it would be a good idea for him to see some liberals. The session, which lasted 45 minutes, was animated and useful. The President dominated the proceedings; he was charming, witty, forceful and disarming, and one could see even the most critical melting in spite of themselves.

He was hardest pressed on the question of civil rights, especially in view of the photograph on the front page of the *Times* that morning, showing a Birmingham police dog lunging at a Negro. The President said that the picture made him "sick" but that there was nothing he could constitutionally do about the situation. I must confess that I have found his reaction to Birmingham disappointing. Even if he has no power to act, he has unlimited power to express the moral sense of the people; and, in not doing so, he is acting much as Eisenhower used to act when we denounced him so. He questioned the timing of the Birmingham demonstration, wondered why it could not have been deferred until the new city administration came to office (in a few days), but then added, "I am not asking for patience. I can well understand why the Negroes of Birmingham are tired of being asked to be patient."

On Monday, May 6, I dined with Alfred Knopf. He was talking about [Joseph] Conrad, who apparently used to give himself airs, but added: "I don't mind a man pretending to be first-rate when he actually is, like Conrad. What I find hard to take is a second-rate man pretending to be first-rate . . . Thomas Mann."

May 21

A few days ago, on a Saturday morning, Mike Feldman and I were together with the President. This provided us an opportunity to raise a matter which we have been discussing among ourselves for some time: i.e., the condition of the White House tennis court. We said that the court was not in good condition, that its surface was cracked, and that the White House deserved a better court. The President listened skeptically. He said that he saw no particular need to resurface the court since Jackie couldn't play until the fall but, after listening to our complaints for a while, finally said that he would take a look himself. Later in the morning I was back in the office, seeing him about something else. Suddenly he said, "I went down to take a look at the court, and it looks fine to me." Unfortunately Mac Bundy, who was present, said, "Yes, the court's in great shape. All it needs is a new center tape." So, with that, the Feldman-Schlesinger project for court reform appears to have lapsed, at least until the fall.

On May 10, I went to Venezuela to open a seminar sponsored by the American Embassy.

On Saturday morning, the 11th, John Plank and I visited a Peace Corps project. Deep in a Caracas *barrio*, along alleys turned into mud by several days of pouring rain, we found a playground at one end of which a young Negro from Denver, Colorado, was in charge of a group of about 25 slum boys, all hammering and sawing away. We learned that a soap-box derby was impending, and Jerry, the Peace Corps man, had got some lumber and specifications and set the boys to work. I had a long talk with him. He has apparently struck up an alliance with the local Catholic priest, and they are working together, both to keep the boys in school and to improve the school. Later he drove us out of the quarter in his jeep. The walls were chalked with amiable slogans like "Death to Betancourt" and "Death to Kennedy," but Jerry received friendly waves and greetings all along the way. When I mentioned this later to Allan Stewart, he said, "The Peace Corps has been wonderful. It has worked miracles in changing the Venezuelan image of North Americans. Before the Peace Corps, the poor Venezuelan supposed all Americans to be rich, selfish, callous, reactionary. Now they are seeing an entirely different kind of American, and it is transforming their whole theory of the United States."

June 2

This has been an exciting fortnight. The civil rights movement has suddenly turned, following Birmingham, into a Negro revolution. It has been a long time since I have felt things to be so vividly in motion in our country. Old institutions and ideas, which have held firm for so long, seem to be giving way all at once. Of course, this is optimistic; and there will be much ugliness and sadness before we are out of the woods. Yet I feel that this is a turning-point—and nothing is more heroic than the role of the Negroes themselves, and nothing more ominous than their inevitable feelings of frustration, resentment and even hate.

It is hard to know how widespread such feelings are. But they have recently come to the surface with intensity in the Negro intellectual community. I had a foretaste of this a year ago, after the Nobel Prize dinner, when James Baldwin attacked Joe Rauh in this house over civil rights. Baldwin's basic belief, I think, is that all whites hate all Negroes and that, in consequence, all Negroes hate all whites. Feeling this, he finds white liberals the hardest of all to take because they are too hypocritical, in his view, to own up to their true feelings. That may be why he turned on Joe so savagely a year ago, and why his meeting with the Attorney General last week was such a flop.

They met first for breakfast. Baldwin's plane was late; Bobby had a meeting to which he had to go; so their talk was cut short. Bobby thereupon suggested that they meet the next day in New York, where he had to go for other reasons. Baldwin agreed, proposing that he bring along some friends. On Friday about a dozen Negroes, mostly writers and performers, appeared at the Kennedy apartment. I reconstruct the meeting from an account provided to me by Bobby, supplemented by Jimmy Wechsler's discussion with a number of the participants. It was doomed from the start when Jerome Smith, a Negro Freedom Rider who had been beaten up in the South, began by saying, "I feel like vomiting being here in this room with you." Smith evidently meant to say that he felt like vomiting to have to go to the Attorney General to plead for the rights he should have as an American, but it came through to Bobby as an expression of personal contempt and hatred. This startled him, and he was startled even more by the evident agreement of the rest of the group with Smith's sentiments.

From this point, the meeting continued steadily downhill. Bobby says that he tried to discuss problems rationally and practically; that he was in search of ideas and wanted to see whether the group had anything to propose. "They didn't know anything," he later said to me in despair. "They don't know what the laws are—they don't know what the facts are—they don't know what we've been doing or what we're trying to do. You can't talk to them the way you can talk to Martin Luther King or Roy Wilkins. They didn't want to talk that way. It was all emotion, hysteria—they stood up and orated—they cursed—some of them wept and left the room." He was particularly shocked when one said, and others seemed to agree, that the Negroes would not fight for the United States, and he was even more shocked when some of them spoke of sending arms to the South to continue the fight. The tone grew worse and worse. Ted Poston of the *New York Post,* who arrived late, entered the room to hear the lovely Lena Horne say, "Mr. Attorney General, you can take all those pious statements and stuff them up your ass." There was considerable talk about Birmingham. Baldwin said that the only reason Bobby had ordered federal troops into Alabama was because a white man had been stabbed. When Bobby said that he had consulted with Dr. King over the use of the federal troops, the group derided him. The group seemed possessed, he said; they reacted as a unit; it was impossible to make contact with any of them.

All this was a great shock to Bobby, who sees himself (correctly) as the Attorney General who has labored hardest for Negro rights in our history. He was both hurt and angered by the attitude he encountered—especially by what seemed to him a purposeful desire *not* to communicate. After nearly three hours, the meeting broke up. Then two incidents further increased Bobby's shock. Dr. King's lawyer, who was present, drew Bobby aside and said, "I just want to say that Dr. King deeply appreciates the way you handled the Birmingham affair." Bobby said, "You watched these people attack me over Birmingham for forty minutes, and you didn't say a word. There is no point in your saying this to me now. You should have said it then." Then Harry Belafonte, an old friend of Bobby's and a regular at the Kennedy parties, came up and said, "Of course you have done more for civil rights than anyone else." Bobby said, "Why do you say this to me? Why didn't you say this to the others?" Belafonte said, "I couldn't say this to the others. It would affect my relationship with them. If I were to defend you, they would conclude that I had gone over to the other side." Finally, when Baldwin took the story to the press and to television, Bobby had a feeling of ultimate betrayal.

When he told me this on Monday, he was still bitter over the experience—so much so that I was worried myself for fear that his final reaction would be a sense of the futility rather than of the urgency of trying to bridge the gap. He may have felt himself that I might have had this idea, because he called later in the evening on another matter and seemed thoroughly calm. Certainly—though I have not been close to it—the government's reaction since has expressed a complete recognition that the pace has to be stepped up. This means a much stronger civil rights bill this session than anyone had previously contemplated. As for Baldwin, Bobby told Dick Goodwin later in the week that Baldwin had destroyed the only channel of communication through which he might have influence. (Bobby is, of course, wrong here; Baldwin's words and pen will have even more influence than his capacity to call up the Attorney General.)

June 16·

On Friday, June 7, Mac Bundy, Walt Rostow, Carl Kaysen, Ted Sorensen and I met to consider the draft of a speech on peace written by Ted Sorensen for delivery by the President on June 10. The President had been seeking an opportunity to give such a speech for some time; and a few days earlier Mac had asked the staff to send any ideas along to Ted. His draft was affirmative and hopeful in its general spirit; and it contained the announcement of a moratorium on nuclear testing. So far as I can tell, neither Rusk nor McNamara had seen the draft nor, perhaps, even knew of the proposed announcement. We all thought the speech fine and suggested only minor changes. Defense and State were informed in the course of the afternoon. Then Ted flew to Honolulu, where the President was addressing the Mayors' Conference, the next day.

I suppose that, from the viewpoint of orderly administration, this was a bad way to prepare a major statement on foreign policy. But the State Department could never in a thousand years have produced this speech. The President is fortunately ready from time to time to assert control over the policy of his administration, however deeply it may offend the bureaucracy.

In this connection, I have increasingly the impression that Rusk is on the skids, though the final execution may be delayed until after the election. He has become much more sensitive about his position than before, more bristling, and more intent on asserting his prerogatives on small matters, while continuing not to assert them on major ones.

The big issue in Washington continues to be civil rights. My guess is that May-June 1963 will go down in history as the great turning-point in the fight for Negro equality. There has been nothing like it in the way of spontaneous mass democracy in this country since the surge of labor organization in the summer of 1937. Characteristically, one began with "sit-downs," and the other with "sit-ins." In each case, ordinary people took things into their own hands, asserted their rights, and outstripped not only the government but their own organizations. FDR responded by pronouncing a curse on both houses; JFK, in a more clearcut case, responded by giving (on June 11) what I would regard as the best speech in his administration on civil rights.

June 22

On Tuesday I lunched with Averell Harriman and Ray Cline. We talked a good deal about Averell's impending mission to Moscow. Averell said, "Each of the nations has an urgent political interest. We want to get the Russian troops out of Cuba. The British want a test ban agreement. The Russians want a guarantee against the nuclear armament of Germany—and I agree with them on this point." He was, as usual, exceedingly trenchant on everything. He has no belief in the multilateral nuclear force and still would be prepared to go quite far to meet the Soviet wishes on Germany in order to get them to give in some other area, such as the test ban. None of us had any optimism about the chances of an agreement on the test ban, and it is not clear why this meeting is taking place or what purpose it will serve. Averell, nonetheless, the old war horse, is delighted to go to Moscow and rather relishes the opportunity to put Khrushchev on the spot.

It is indispensable for the liberals to bring pressure on a [Democratic] President to do things and to complain about his slowness to act: this is indispensable in order to enlarge his range of alternatives. But, as they do this, liberals must understand that theirs is a contributory role, and that he may well be more correct than they are about the moment when the balloon goes up. [In a recent speech,] I cited the exchange of letters between FDR and my father in 1935 and FDR's invocation of what he called "a strange and weird sense known as 'public psychology.'" The fact that one man is President and another isn't creates a presumption that he knows more about "public psychology" and has a better sense when it is possible to act. I tried to say that, if men like Roosevelt and Kennedy could achieve objectives by declaring them, they would of course do so all the time. What held them back was a sense of feasibility and an instinct about the price to be paid in other areas. Thus the

President's civil rights message in February, though less impressive in substance, was as urgent in tone as his civil rights message this week, but no one paid any attention to it; James Baldwin, for example, had not even been aware of its existence. If the President had given his June 11 speech six months ago, it would have died before an indifferent nation. No one is so well placed as the President to feel the balance of pressure; and, while those on the left must bring all possible pressure to offset pressure from the right, they should not be so certain that the President is wrong in the timing of his ultimate decisions.

The Attorney General called me early Saturday morning and asked me to come to the meeting with Martin Luther King, Roy Wilkins, James Farmer and the other civil rights leaders.

The meeting, which took place in the Cabinet Room, was about the best I have attended in government. The President, who was in much better form, it seemed to me, than in the larger meetings, gave a crisp, precise, articulate account of the [civil rights] situation.

Bobby said a few words, and then the meeting was open for discussion. Whitney Young of the Urban League began by saying that the President's statement against action in the streets and mob pressure on Washington was being interpreted as meaning that he was against all forms of demonstration. The President replied that what was important were the kinds of actions which would contibute to the enactment of the legislation. "We want success in Congress, not just a big show at the Capitol. Some of these people are looking for an excuse to be against us; and I don't want to give any of them a chance to say, 'Yes, I'm for the bill, but I am damned if I will vote for it at the point of gun.' It seemed to me a great mistake to announce a march on Washington before the bill was even in committee. The only effect is to create an atmosphere of intimidation—and this may give some members of Congress an out."

A. Philip Randolph then spoke about the President's effort to shift the matter from the streets to the courts. "The problem of the streets is very difficult," Randolph said. "The Negroes are already in the streets. It is very likely impossible to get them off. If they are bound to be in the streets in any case, is it not better that they be led by organizations dedicated to civil rights and disciplined by struggle rather than to leave them to other leaders who care neither about civil rights or about non-violence. If the civil rights leaders were to call the Negroes off the streets, it is problematic whether they would come."

The President agreed that the demonstration in the streets had brought results—that it had forced Congress to entertain legislation which had no chance a few weeks ago, and that it has made the executive branch act faster. "This is true. But now we are in a new phase, the legislative phase, and results are essential. The wrong kind of demonstration at the wrong time will give those fellows a chance to say that they have to prove their courage by voting against us. To get the necessary votes we have, first, to oppose demonstrations which lead to violence and, second, to give Congress a fair chance to work its will."

Martin Luther King then said, "It is not a matter of either/or, but of both/and. Take the question of the march on Washington. This could serve as a means through which people with legitimate discontents could channel their grievances under disciplined, non-violent leadership. It could also serve as a means of dramatizing the issue and mobilizing support in parts of the country which don't know the problem at first hand. I think it will serve a purpose. It may seem ill-timed. Frankly, I have never engaged in any direct action movement which did not seem ill-timed. Some people thought Birmingham ill-timed." [The President interjected, "including the Attorney General."] King added that he thought the public accommodations section was the most critical section of the bill from the Negro viewpoint.

Someone brought up the question of police brutality. The President said, "Yes, but I know what southern mayors and police chiefs will say. They will say that all they are doing is trying to maintain law and order. In any case, I don't think you should all be totally harsh on Bull Connor. After all, he has done more for civil rights than almost anybody else."

JFK went on to say: "This is a very serious fight. The Vice President and I know what it will mean if we fail. I have just seen the new Gallup poll: national approval of the administration has fallen from 60 to 47 per cent. We're in this up to the neck. What would be the worst trouble of all would be to lose the fight in the Congress. We'll have enough troubles if we win; but, if we win, we can deal with those. A good many programs I care about may go down the drain as a result of this—so we are putting a lot on the line. What is important is that we preserve confidence in the good faith of each other. I have my problems with the Congress; you have yours with your own groups. We will undoubtedly disagree from time to time on tactics. But the important thing is to keep in touch."

Then he concluded by saying: "What seems to me terribly important is to get, and keep, as many Negro children as possible in schools this fall. It is too late to get equality for their parents, but we still can get it for the children—*if* they can go to school and take advantage of what educational opportunity is open to them. I urge you to get every Negro family to do this at whatever sacrifice."

July 5

I continue to have the impression that Rusk [Dean Rusk, then Secretary of State] is nearing the end of his rope, though I may be excessively influenced by Carl Kaysen's mounting contempt for him. According to Carl, his vanity became an increasingly disturbing factor in the European trip. Thus his feeling of being left out of things led him to accept with unbecoming eagerness the proposal that he meet with the Spanish Foreign Minister in Rome. And he seems to have blocked the idea that Harriman should have gone to Birch Grove [MacMillan's house in Sussex] in order to consult with [Tory cabinet member] Lord Hailsham (whom Averell has never met) and discuss the Moscow mission with the President and the Prime Minister. Averell was all set to go; but at the last moment he received word from the Secretary that his presence was not necessary.

July 21

Averell prepared for the Moscow trip in his usual astute and jugular manner. He had no overwhelming expectations; on the other hand, he wanted to give the thing the best possible try. But there has been a remarkable change in the climate of the negotiations. Three weeks ago, no one anticipated very much. The general feeling was that the test ban talks had been forced on Khrushchev by Macmillan's passion, derived from domestic politics, for an agreement. In the last fortnight, everything has changed.

On civil rights, the most interesting development has been the intimation of northern political discontent over the President's recent initiatives. John Bartlow Martin stayed with us after a few days in Chicago. He revisited his old home in Oak Park and found this suburb, predominantly Jewish and hence predominantly Democratic, liberal and pro–civil rights, in considerable anxiety over the President's civil rights speech. People there seemed alarmed over the pace of the integration movement. Then Jim Lanigan dropped by the other day (on his way to India). Jim could not have been more gloomy. He said that civil rights might very well lose the election for Kennedy in 1964; that there was widespread and intense panic in the suburbs; that even good Democrats were appalled by the nightmare of an inundation of their neighborhoods and their schools by Negroes; and that speedy counteraction was necessary. The President has never had illusions about the political benefits of a civil rights fight, but has felt that he had no alternative if he wanted to hold the country together.

August 11

While in Salzburg, I heard (from Charles Wintour in London) the news about Phil Graham's suicide. I was shattered by it. Though I have not seem much of Phil in recent months, he was in some ways my closest friend in Washington. He was also in some ways the most brilliant member of my generation. He was a man of extraordinary charm, vitality and insight, gay and witty in company, generous and wise in counsel, filled, it would seem, with the life force. Suicide always remained a possibility; but I had subconsciously supposed that his innate vitality would win out over the demons within. Before I left Washington, I had a long talk with Kay, in which suicide was mentioned; but she said that the doctors felt this to be less of a danger this time than in previous periods of depression. There is no one like Phil, and I shall miss him sorely.

August 20

I saw the President briefly on the 15th. He expressed a little concern about the March on Washington, scheduled for the 28th, on the grounds that it might not be large enough. The leaders have committed themselves to producing 100,000 people. The President fears that, if they fall materially short of this, it will persuade some members of Congress that the demand for action on civil rights is greatly exaggerated.

I also saw him today. We talked mostly about the forthcoming session of the General Assembly and whether he should attend or not. In the course of the talk, he said, almost shyly, "I don't think that Adlai has written to Jackie [about the death of her infant son Patrick], and she is upset about it. Everyone else who ought to write has written—she got a very nice letter from you—except Adlai. I can't believe that he didn't write; but, if he hasn't, I wish you would tell him to send her a letter. Don't mention that this came from me; but I have spent most of my life in the midst of people getting hurt because someone doesn't write a letter or attend a funeral, and I want to avoid this sort of thing as much as possible. I don't want Jackie to feel badly about it, so get Adlai to write."

October 2

On Monday, when Philip Kaiser and I were walking over to the West Wing for luncheon, we ran into the Kennedy family. Caroline, at her mother's bidding, shook our hands and curtsied. Young John, delighted at this, rushed up, put out his hand and, as he shook ours, curtsied too. Jackie said: "I think there is something ominous about John curtsying." John said indignantly, "Mummy, I wasn't curtsying, I was bowing."

October 13

I saw the President for a while about 7 o'clock [on Friday, October 11]. I asked how Jackie was. He said that she was having a good time in Greece and added that Franklin [Roosevelt Jr.] had, through no fault of his own, got in the spotlight. The President said, "He did not want to take a trip on the Onassis yacht, but I didn't want Jackie to be out there alone, so I asked him to go along." I suppose that Franklin thought that Onassis on top of [Rafael] Trujillo might be a little too much for New York voters.

When I came in, the President was looking at some books on his desk. "No, these are not right," he was saying to Evelyn Lincoln. "I wanted Peter Quennell's *Lord Byron in Venice*." As I was leaving, he called after me, almost a little wistfully, "What are you doing tonight?" I told him that we were going to a dance at the Walter Ridders'. The President gossiped for a moment or two. I hate to repeat the cliché about the loneliness of the job, but it *is* a lonely job.

Tonight we dined at the Stewart Alsops'. The Herters were there— a somewhat sanctimonious and poisonous couple, who preserve an indestructible Republicanism under an eastern cosmopolitan cloak.

Frank Wisner and Mac Herter went into a long bit about how terrible it was for Jackie Kennedy to go off on the Onassis yacht. Wisner said that "everyone" in Europe knew that Lee Radziwill was having an affair with Onassis, and that Jackie was along as cover. The gossip of the idle rich is exceedingly boring.

October 27

However, to continue the previous item, there is no question that the Greek trip has caused a certain amount of doubt and resentment. Even my mother feels there is something wrong about *la dolce vita* in the isles of Greece while the President slaves away in Washington. I try to point out Jackie's distress, her exhaustion, her need for a rest; but the trouble is that her idea of a rest (with which I wholly sympathize) strikes too many Americans as unduly gay and energetic. But this will soon blow over.

On Thursday I attended the President's luncheon for Tito. I went with considerable curiosity. Tito is one of the heroic figures of our epoch, for better or worse, and I wanted to see what he was like. I expected a rather massive, powerful man. I met instead a small, plump, old man, with rimless (or steel-rimmed) glasses, a benign expression and a high-pitched voice. He looked rather like the owner of a successful department store in, say, Akron, Ohio. The luncheon passed agreeably, though Averell thought (and I agree) that the President was a little defensive and stressed unnecessarily the existence of ideological differences. Of course the differences exist; but emphasis on them did nothing to appease the opponents of the Tito visit, while it introduced a faint note of reserve so far as Tito was concerned.

Against my inclination, I have been doing more and more in the way of speech-writing in recent weeks. I wrote the speech the President gave before the National Academy of Sciences on October 23 (on the basis of material supplied by Jerry Wiesner); and on Wednesday the President called me in, handed me a draft Ted Sorensen had written for Amherst on Saturday, said that it seemed to him thin and stale, and asked me to try my hand at it. Accordingly I wrote a speech on the place of arts in a democracy. The President read it and said that it was fine except for a number of sentences which sounded too much like Adlai Stevenson. On Friday night, he called me and invited me to go along with him to Amherst. He worked over the speech on the plane north, toned down the fancier passages and added an opening section of his own on the obligations of young men of privilege. The result, I think, was most successful. Certainly no previous President has ever talked this way about the arts.

We chatted about the Eisenhower reminiscences on the way up. The President commented on their self-righteousness. "Apparently he never did anything wrong," he said. "When we come to writing the memoirs of this administration, we'll do it differently."

November 23

I heard the terrible news as I was sipping cocktails with Kay Graham, Ken Galbraith and the editors of *Newsweek*. Kay and I had flown in from Washington; we were to discuss the future of the back of *Newsweek*'s book. A man entered in his shirtsleeves and said, a little tentatively, "I think you should know that the President has been shot in the head in Texas." It took a few seconds for this to register. Then we rushed for the radio. The President's condition was unclear for a time. I said that we should go back to Washington immediately; so Kay, Ken and I went out to the airport. We reached the White House about 4:30. Sargent Shriver, composed and pale, had already taken charge of the funeral preparations. The plane was due in from Texas at six. I went out to Andrews Field. A small crowd was waiting in the dusk—Averell looking haggard and old, Mac very intent, Bob McNamara stunned and silent. As I was standing on the side of the crowd, a man brushed by. It was Lyndon Johnson. I shook his hand and told him that of course we wanted to do everything we could to help him. Then I returned to the White House. Ken and I dined in the mess. Afterward I went back to O Street. Chrissie said, "Daddy, it was so hateful. I feel as if I do not want to live in the United States anymore."

Then I returned to the White House and helped Shriver and Goodwin and others work on the funeral lists. About midnight, I went up to the Mansion where Bill Walton was supervising things in the East Room. Jackie has sent a message that she wanted the President laid out as Lincoln had been. David Mearns, whom I called, had gone to the Library of Congress and found a newspaper article and drawing showing Lincoln lying in state in the East Room. It is now twenty minutes to two. The casket will arrive at the White House around 3:30.

It has been a day of shame and horror. Everyone is stunned. Fortunately the practical details of the funeral engage everyone's attention and sidetrack us from the terrible reality. I still cannot believe that this splendid man, this man of such intelligence and gaiety and strength, is dead. The wages of hate are fearful.

No one knows yet who the killer is—whether a crazed Birchite or a crazed Castroite. I only know that the killer has done an incalculable disservice to this country and to all mankind. It will be a long time before this nation is as nobly led as it has been in these last three years.

5:15 A.M.

When I went upstairs again, at about 2 A.M., workmen under Bill Walton's direction were draping pillars and windows with black crepe. After a time, a military guard arrived and took up its places. The casket was expected first at 2:30 and then at progressively later times. We sat or walked around, exchanging forlorn scraps of conversation, trying to fight off the appalling reality. Walton and I walked through the rooms in which we had had such happy times, filled with memory and melancholy.

Eventually the car arrived from the Bethesda Naval Hospital. The casket was carried into the East Room and deposited on a stand. It was wrapped in a flag. Jackie followed, accompanied by Bobby. Jean Smith, Ethel, Kenny, Larry, Bob McNamara, and Dave Powers also came from the hospital. Already at the Mansion were Walton, Shriver, Ralph Dungan, Dick Goodwin, Pierre, Chuck Roche, Andy Hatcher, Louis Martin and Frank Morrissey. A boy appeared to light the tapers around the bier. The third taper took a painfully long time to light; and, in lighting the fourth, he extinguished his torch. He struck a match, rekindled his torch and then discovered that the taper was feebly flickering. A priest said a few words. Then Bobby whispered to Jackie. She approached the bier, knelt in front of it and buried her head in the flag. Then she walked away. The rest of us followed.

Jackie went upstairs with Bobby, Ethel and Jean. Bobby came down in a few minutes and disappeared into the East Room with Bob McNamara. After a time, he came out and asked Nancy Tuckerman and me to go in, look at the bier and give our opinion whether the casket should be open or shut. And so I went in, with the candles fitfully burning, three priests on their knees praying in the background, and took a last look at my beloved President, my beloved friend. For a moment, I was shattered. But it was not a good job; probably it could not have been with half his head blasted away. It was too waxen, too made up. It did not really look like him. Nancy and I told this to Bobby and voted to keep the casket closed. When Bill Walton agreed, Bobby gave instructions that it should be closed. He told me that Jackie preferred to have it closed, and I reassured him about the precedent by remembering that Roosevelt's casket had been closed.

After this we quietly dispersed into the mild night. I drove Bob McNamara home. He said that the country had suffered a loss which it would take ten years to repair, that there is no one on the horizon to compare with the President as a national leader.

Later. I talked briefly with Bobby, Steve and Sarge. All seemed composed, withdrawn and resolute. Around noon I took Marian and the children past the bier. Afterward, we lunched at an upstairs room at the Occidental—Bill Walton and his son Matt, Ken and Kitty, the Sam Beers, Paul Samuelson, Dick Goodwin, Walter Heller. I left for a 3 o'clock meeting with the Bundy staff, in which Mac explained how the show must go on.

After the meeting he told me that my letter of resignation (which I had sent to the President the first thing in the morning) had arrived when Johnson was having his meeting with Eisenhower. Johnson read the letter, thrust it at Mac and said, "Please take this letter back and have him withdraw it. And send out instructions that I do not want any letters of resignation." Eisenhower quite correctly demurred, saying that Johnson must preserve his freedom of action, and that he did not have to accept resignations right away. So the present line is that the staff should resign, but that, "for the time being," Johnson plans to accept no resignations.

Mac said that he intended to stay on as long as Johnson wanted him. He said that he was worried about Bobby, that Bobby was reluctant to face the new reality, that he had virtually to drag Bobby into the cabinet meeting, and that, if Bobby continued in this mood, he had probably better resign. Mac said this a little more sympathetically than I have reported it, but not a hell of a lot more so.

A telephone call from Ken reported that he had seen Johnson, and that Johnson had asked him to work with Sorensen on the message. Ken seemed in high spirits. Like Mac, he is a realist. He would infinitely have preferred Kennedy, but he is ready to face facts and make the best of them. Like Kenny and Bobby, I am a sentimentalist. My heart is not in it.

November 25

The agony continues, and one can still only intermittently believe it. I keep supposing that tomorrow morning, I will come down to the White House, Evelyn will be in her office and Kenny in his, and in a few minutes the President will be along, with some jokes about the morning papers. The thought that we will never see him again is intolerable and unacceptable and unendurable. But we never will, and nothing will ever be the same again.

Newt Minow told me this afternoon that Pat Moynihan had been asked on television whether we would ever laugh again. He replied: "Yes, we will laugh again. But we will never be young again." Later he said, "We Irish always expect our hearts to be broken, so we are not surprised. But we thought we had a little more time."

Yesterday afternoon, I did a piece on the President at Stewart Alsop's request for the *Saturday Evening Post*. Late in the afternoon and again in the early evening I went up to the Mansion. The family was there, quiet and composed. Dave Powers was marching Caroline, John and Sidney Lawford up and down the central hall, making them count out and execute right turns. Ethel and Lem Billings were in the Lincoln bedroom watching the murder of Oswald on television. Ken O'Donnell and Larry O'Brien were drinking quietly in the Oval Room. Jackie was in her parlor behind shut doors.

As I was leaving, Teddy, Eunice and Mrs. Kennedy arrived from Hyannis Port. I asked Mrs. Kennedy about the Ambassador. She said,

"We have told him, but we don't think that he understands it." Apparently the news produced no visible reaction. Someone told me later that it had been decided to tell him on Saturday morning rather than on Friday evening—I suppose so that he would face a day rather than a night.

I came back around 8 o'clock. Jackie came out, looking very pale but most composed. She said, "Susan Mary Alsop called me to say how wonderful I have been. How did she expect me to behave?" She made the remark with a certain contempt. Then she talked about Evelyn Lincoln and Dave Powers. "At least, I have my children. They have nothing, nothing at all." She had in mind using them in the Kennedy Library, which of course would be fine. We chatted for a few moments. Then Bobby appeared to take her to the Rotunda. The rest of the family went downstairs for dinner, except for Sarge Shriver. He and I ate sandwiches and drank bourbon upstairs for another half hour. He reminisced about the past with sad cheerfulness.

Today was the funeral. The service at St. Matthews was incomprehensible to me; but the ceremony at Arlington, against a background of wildly twittering birds, was solemn and heartrending. De Gaulle was there, and Eisenhower, and Truman, looking shattered. Evelyn Lincoln said to me, "The thing he hated most of all was fanatics." The day was sunny, crisp and cold. I have never felt so depressed.

The inevitable changes are taking place. I gather that the new team will move in on Monday. Johnson has behaved, in the main, with great consideration. He has made a general request that everyone stay and has followed this up with personal calls to most of the staff (notable exception: me). He has assured Heller and Galbraith that he is a Roosevelt Democrat, not an Eisenhower Democrat; that he always felt Kennedy to be unduly conservative on fiscal questions; and that he plans to continue and enlarge Kennedy's social and economic programs. My guess is that he will be pretty good on issues, and that in some respects he will be more liberal than JFK. An obvious reason for this is that he must convince the industrial states that he is more liberal than they think he is if he is going to be reelected. Ken Galbraith is more worried about his views on foreign policy than on domestic policy and fears that he may accept too easily the Achesonian line. But on the only issue that I know about so far—the reaffirmation of the joint moonshot—Johnson has made it clear that he does not want to retreat one inch from the position taken by Kennedy. There has been only one disturbing story thus far—that, on the plane back, Johnson asked O'Donnell to bring Jackie from her rear compartment for the swearing-in. Since Jackie had been resting there, Kenny hesitated for a minute. According to this story, Johnson said coldly to him, "When I tell you to do something, I want it done—and *fast*."

I must add an unpleasant note about Adlai Stevenson. He arrived Friday night at the White House and came to Dungan's office. We were all sitting around in various stages and forms of distress. Stevenson came in, smiling and chipper, as if nothing at all had happened. Marian and Clayton say that he was the same at Averell's later in the evening. Clayton and I later discussed this at length. We agree, I think, that we have practically never heard Stevenson make a generous remark about Kennedy. I fear that the resentment of 1960 went too deep. He may well now feel that he will have a freer hand, and perhaps more influence, under Johnson than under Kennedy. In any case, it is a most disappointing reaction, and one that it will take me long to forgive.

November 26

I encountered the new President today when Dick Goodwin and I went up to the East Room to attend a meeting of Latin American diplomats called to enable Johnson to reaffirm our national commitment to the Alliance for Progress. He said that he wanted to speak to me in the next day or so. He then read fairly well a few remarks prepared by Dick. Jackie came down and attended the ceremony. She is heroic.

Afterward the President called and asked me to come over. I took the long familiar, sad walk to the West Wing. In the past the door to Evelyn Lincoln's office was always open and welcoming; I have never seen that door closed. It is closed now; and behind it, where Evelyn reigned in unhurried amiability, three girls were efficiently typing away. After a moment, the President came out and took me into his office. It is stripped bare at the moment, the desk is new, but a rocking chair remains. We sat down on the sofas before the fireplace. He said, "I just want to say that I need you far more than John Kennedy ever needed you. He had the knowledge, the skills, the understanding himself. I need you to provide those things for me. . . . You have a knowledge of the program, the measures, the purposes, of the history of the country and of progressive policies, you know writers and all sorts of people. I need all that, and you must stay. . . . I have your letter of resignation and that is fine as a gesture but I reject it as a fact. If you act upon it, I will have you arrested." At one point, I intervened to say that I thought every President to have his own men around him. He replied, "I consider you one of my men. I hope you will consider yourself that way too. I just want you to know that I have complete and unlimited faith and confidence in you. I want you to stay. I know it will be a sacrifice for you, and I know that you have many other things you can do. But I am asking you, for my sake and for the sake of the country, to stay with me for at least a year. By that time I hope I will have earned from you the same confidence and faith which I know you had in John F. Kennedy." He said all this with simplicity, dignity and apparent conviction.

I must confess that LBJ's presentation of the case could not have been improved. Yet all I could think, as I sat in the office, was JFK rising, as he so often did, opening the French doors, beckoning one out to the colonnade outside, and then clapping his hands, at which signal all the dogs and/or children on the lawn would come running toward him.

I am a little perplexed as to what to do. I am sure that I must leave, but I can see the problem of disengagement is going to be considerable.

November 28

When I got back from the movies Tuesday night, I found a note from Stephen: "President Johnson called at 10:55 P.M.—you are to call the White House immediately." It was now nearly 1 A.M.; and, when

I called, I was put through to a man named Cliff Carter, who told me that the Johnsons wanted me to sit in Mrs. Johnson's box during the President's address to the joint session the next day. Lady Bird herself confirmed the invitation the next morning. Reasons?—personal kindness? liberal reassurance? a quick way to knock down stories which spread around town yesterday (and were used by David Brinkley) saying that I had had a disagreement with Johnson about the speech and had resigned or been fired?

I had not intended to go to the Capitol at all, remembering too vividly the bright hopes when we had all rushed down to JFK's first State of the Union message two and a half years ago. But I am glad that I went. Johnson had an excellent speech, delivered it with dignity and force and achieved a genuine success. I have never heard him deliver a speech so well. The reference to the civil rights bill and the appeal against hate won the loudest applause. I watched Bobby during the speech. He was pale, somber and inscrutable, applauding faithfully, but his face set and his lips compressed. He has been under desperate strain these past few days, and this must have been a particularly unbearable moment.

December 5

The first few days of the Johnson administration move along. The new President continues to display much energy and astuteness. He has been particularly careful to touch base with the Negro and labor leaders and has, in general, maintained a strong liberal line, except in connection with government economy, implying that he is slashing the budget considerably beyond the Kennedy point; but this is explained to the Keynesians—and accepted by them (and it is probably true, and it may well also be true that JFK would have had to go through the same motions) as a tactic designed to hasten the passage of the tax bill. On the whole, it is hard to fault the new President thus far on issues. On taste, there is the expected infusion of corn.

On Wednesday I went to New York and had a long talk with Adlai Stevenson. He began by saying, "You know, things are ten times better for me now than they were before." He described his talk with Johnson after the funeral: "We were in the President's office, and Johnson said, 'I know, and you know, that you should be sitting behind this desk rather than me. You could have been the nominee for Vice President if you had come out for Kennedy in Los Angeles. But you kept your word to me that you wouldn't back any of the candidates, and as a result I am here instead of you. But I haven't forgotten.'" Johnson went on to say, "There has been no consultation around here. You know, they put in the tax bill without ever talking to me about the timing or what should be in the bill. I know they haven't consulted you either. So far as I am concerned, that is all changed. I want you to call me whenever there is anything on your mind. I want you to play a big role in the formation of policy." Adlai said to me, "I have known Lyndon for thirty years. I used to play golf with Dick Kleberg when Lyndon was his administrative assistant. We talk the same language—much more than I did with Kennedy. I think that, if I said the word, Rusk and Bundy would go; but I told Johnson and [Abe] Fortas that they both should be kept." Much more of the same—never a generous word about Kennedy. In the course of the evening, Jackie called me and, knowing I was at Adlai's, said, "Tell Adlai that, in looking through a box in which Jack kept his studs and cuff-links, I found a silver shoe, which Jack must have kept since '56. I thought Adlai might like to have it, and I sent it to him." When I told this to Stevenson, he put on a sickly smile and said, "How sweet."

This morning, December 5, I joined Bobby, Teddy and Evelyn Lincoln in a melancholy flight to Boston on the *Caroline* to incorporate the Kennedy Memorial Library. On the way back, we had a fairly frank conversation. Bob asked me whether I thought he should go for Vice President. My first reaction was negative, though, when he asked me why, I found it hard to give clear reasons. I think, first, that it seems to me a little too artificial and calculated; second, that Bobby should develop his own independent political base; and third, that LBJ might well prefer Shriver on the ground that Shriver would bring along Bobby's friends without bringing along his enemies. Bobby added that he did not like the idea of taking a job which was really based on the premise of waiting around for someone to die. In the course of this, I made clear that I hoped he would be President some day and wanted to do what I could to bring this about, but that I just doubted whether the vice presidency would be the best way.

He asked what I thought he should do. I said that, after staying as Attorney General for an appropriate period, he should go into private life. He might do something in the humanitarian field in which he was already interested—civil rights; or international exchanges; or juvenile delinquency. This would help erase the national impression that he was a demonic prosecutor. Or he might buy the *New York Post*. Then in 1966 he should run for Governor of Massachusetts; or, if he decided to go to New York, Governor of New York.

I showed him letters I had received from Isaiah Berlin and Reinhold Niebuhr. As he read them, his immense control faltered for the first time in my vision, and he wiped away his tears.

He remarked that there had been a revolt of the FBI since his brother's death. He said that the FBI had always in recent years been used to having direct contact with Presidents—better contact than the Attorneys General—and that his appointment had changed all this. For the first time in 30 years, the FBI had had to accept the control of the Attorney General and knew it could not bypass him and go directly to the President. Bobby set up a system of FBI liaison with the White House through his office. As soon as the President died and Bobby went to Florida, everything changed. Nick Katzenbach could not get reports from the FBI. The White House liaison went, in effect, out of business. Bobby said grimly that this is something with which he would gladly occupy himself in the next 11 months.

In the course of the talk, he said that the President intended in due course to make McNamara Secretary of State. (I said that I thought that McNamara would make a better Secretary of Defense. It has always seemed to me that McNamara's one weakness was his deficient sense of politics; he is far too rational a man to sympathize with the political world. But perhaps I underestimate the power of sheer intelligence to grasp the realities of life, however untidy and irrational.)

It was a melancholy journey. Bobby obviously has no confidence in and no taste for Johnson and obviously wants to be President himself (an ambition I thoroughly applaud and will support).

I had a luncheon with Bill Moyers and then met with him later in the day. He seems bright, efficient and attractive. He told me that his main thing was administration and neither policy nor politics; but I imagine that he is as good on the second two as he is on the first. He seems liberal, quick, receptive, candid and effective. I like him very much.

We also talked about Latin American affairs, including the proposal that an Undersecretaryship be established for the western hemisphere. Bill asked me what I thought of Tom Mann in this connection. I replied that Mann was an able man, but that he would be a "disaster"—that he was a free enterprise ideologist, that he did not really believe in the Alliance for Progress and that his appointment would mean a reversion to the days of John Foster Dulles. I also said that it might be possible to head Mann off by urging the appointment of Robert Kennedy. This briefly fascinated Moyers, who said he was sure that Johnson would give Bobby anything he wanted.

In the evening I brought the matter up with Bobby. I said that I thought the appointment would be great for the Alliance and for Latin America but might not be the best thing for his own political future. He agreed with me on Tom Mann (as, according to Bill Moyers, Sarge Shriver does also) but said that he could not possibly take another assignment for 11 months—he must stay at Justice until the civil rights bill is passed, which would be in March or April, and thereafter he would be busy in the campaign, until November. He suggested that the word be passed to Johnson that, because of President Kennedy's intense personal concern with Latin America, no appointment should be made to the Latin American post without due consultation with his Latin American executors—himself, Shriver, Goodwin and myself.

I asked him, perhaps tactlessly, about Oswald. He said that there could be no serious doubt that he was guilty, but there was still argument whether he did it by himself or as part of a larger plot, whether organized by Castro or by gangsters. He said that the FBI thought he had done it by himself, but that McCone thought there were two people involved in the shooting.

December 13

Late in the afternoon Dick Goodwin and I went to see Bobby. The purpose of the call was to report progress on the organization of the Kennedy Library, but we inevitably discussed a good many other matters.

I first told him about a State Department meeting that afternoon on the question of travel restrictions. For some time, State has had under consideration a proposal which originated, I believe, with Abba Schwartz and had Averell's strong backing to remove travel restrictions in the case of all countries (including Communist China and Albania) save Cuba. However, Bobby, as he contemplated the Cuba question, saw that Justice might be faced next summer with the obligation to indict several hundred college boys who were determined to visit Cuba. As Bobby said to us, "And what's wrong with that? If I were 22 years old, that is certainly the place I would want to visit. I don't see how we can prosecute every student who wants to see Cuba." So he sent a memorandum over to State recommending that travel restrictions be lifted everywhere, including Cuba, and that any qualified American should be able to travel anywhere (with provision, of course, for holding back people who might be going to Cuba to become agents or saboteurs).

As we were leaving, Bobby talked for a few minutes about larger political issues. He said, "The important thing for us to do now is to stick together. Our power will last for just eleven months. It will disappear the day of the election. What we have to do is to use that power in these months to the best permanent advantage." I interjected that it seemed increasingly that the vice presidency would be the key to the situation. He indicated agreement and said, "In due course we will have to decide who we are going for. In the meantime, we must work together. There are a hundred men scattered through the government who are devoted to the purposes for which we came to Washington. We must all stay in close touch and not let them pick us off one by one. . . . The thing is we worked hard to get where we are, and we can't let it all go to waste. My brother barely had a chance to get started—and there is so much now to be done—for the Negroes and the unemployed and school kids and everyone else who is not getting a decent break in our society. This is what counts. The new fellow doesn't get this. He knows all about politics and nothing about human beings."

It was an impressive performance. I am more and more persuaded that he should go for the vice presidency—and more and more persuaded that I am for him whatever he wants.

December 15

Mike Forrestal came by for a drink in order, as he said, to relieve his sense of depression. He had had a certain amount to do with the new President on questions of Southeast Asia, especially Vietnam. He said that LBJ had kept silent during all the formal discussions of Vietnam, explaining once privately that he had made it a rule not to speak until he knew what the President had decided and then to do everything he could to help carry out the decision. However, once in a confidential talk with Mike the Vice President violated his rule, declared his belief in the unconditional support of [Ngo Dinh] Diem and said that "you fellows in the White House" were making a great mistake in trying to disengage from Diem. On Friday, LBJ said to Mike, "Don't you think that the situation in Vietnam is more hopeless today than it has ever been before"—a remark indicating that he still holds to his earlier views.

We dined at Bill Wirtz's with Adlai Stevenson, the Carl McGowans and the Ed Days. Most of the evening was spent on an agreeable, nostalgic chat. But we had a certain amount of contemporary comment, and I took the occasion to give Stevenson my views, perhaps too forcibly, on Tom Mann, Frank Coffin and other recent events. Adlai listened silently, only to say that he knew no reason to salute the Mann appointment. After he left, Bill warned me against speaking so freely in his presence. I think Bill feels that Adlai is going to try for the vice presidency, and he also quite clearly feels that this would be a tremendous error. Bill also said, "I think there are very few people in this town for whom the hurting continues—Bobby, Ted, Ralph Dungan, you—and myself."

December 16

Tonight I went to Jackie Kennedy's to see a preview showing of Teddy White's *The Making of a President*. Present were the Whites, the Harrimans, the O'Donnells, Don Wilson, Pam Turnure, the Franklin Roosevelts, Nancy Tuckerman, the Dave Powers, the Ted Reardons, the Ted Kennedys, Bobby, the Ormsby-Gores, Ted Sorensen, perhaps two or three others. The film was a very skillful and evocative portrait of the 1960 campaign. I found it almost unbearable to watch that graceful, witty, incandescent personality in the presence of his widow, his brother and two sisters (Eunice and Jean were also there).

Later I talked to Jackie, who was marvelously self-possessed and bright, yet with a certain latent liquidity of eye and expression which was most appealing and demoralizing. She talked about evenings at the White House. She said that the President could not stand seeing anyone at dinner who would bring up the problems of the day, that he wanted to have his mind taken off these things. Also it was essential to have people who would be available at the last moment. She told of asking the Ormsby-Gores at the last moment and learning later that they had cancelled a ball at which they were guests of honor in order to accept a White House command performance.

December 23

And so the year—and the era—draws to a close. Yesterday we went out to the candlelight ceremony at the Lincoln Memorial. It all began on a fiercely cold day 35 months ago, and it came to an end on a fiercely cold day yesterday. Today it is snowing—almost as deep a snow as the inaugural blizzard. The White House is lovely, ghostly and alien. My own depression does not abate.

I have had several talks with RFK. He thinks our bargaining power is greater than I suppose. He rests this primarily on the Kennedy relationship to the big city machines—Daley, Green, Buckley, Peter Crotty, etc. My own belief is that he overestimates the power of these machines. Daley, yes; but Buckley and Crotty are weaker than I think Bobby supposes, and Bill Green died a couple of days ago. Bobby feels that LBJ will have to consult the Kennedys about the vice presidency, and that the Kennedys will be able to exert some influence about the choice of Secretary of State in the next cabinet. I said that it is awfully hard to impose a deal on a President. Bobby said, "It is not so hard. I will be perfectly willing to ask President Johnson what his plans are for the State Department before we decide the role we are going to play in the campaign." I said, "We will all have to play a role in the campaign, or we will be finished forever in the party." He said, "Yes, but there is a considerable difference between a nominal role and a real role. We can go through the motions or we can go all out. It may make a difference, for example, whether Jackie appears with Johnson at the last big rally, or whether she goes to Europe in the autumn for her health."

It is clear that what Bobby would like most of all is to be Secretary of State, presumably with Sarge as Vice President. This would, of course, be wonderful, and I shall do anything I can to help bring it about. In the meantime, LBJ will do everything he can to develop alternative avenues to the Kennedy constituency—i.e., to the northern machines, ethnic groups, labor and liberal groups—avenues not controlled by or patrolled by the Kennedys. This is the significance of the Stevenson and Humphrey maneuvers. It can be argued that, if LBJ has Stevenson or Humphrey on the ticket, he will not need the Kennedys in order to carry the big electoral vote states. This might involve a risk with the Catholics, especially Stevenson and especially if Nixon is the Republican candidate (which I gather is what Johnson expects); but the alternative would be to entrench the Kennedys in the executive branch and give them the great powers of being the heirs-apparent. In the end, it will all depend on the polls and on LBJ's own sense of how badly he needs the Kennedys. If it looks as if he could win without them, he will try and do so. If it looks close, he will probably swallow hard and bind them to him.

December 30

And so this wretched year draws to a close. I find it hard from my isolated position to gather what is going on; but there are signs that my frustration is not so unique as I generally imagine.

Part of this is natural enough; and I tell myself ten times a day not to succumb to the temptation to draw invidious comparisons between the old President and the new. LBJ is quite right not to be stampeded into decisions. This is happily a time of lull; and he can afford to feel his way, get to know the men he is dealing with and take time in assessing the consequences of decision. He is not Kennedy, and he is bound to do things in his own manner. And there are many things he does not know and must learn (though some of these are startling: Mike Feldman told me that LBJ called up Bromley Smith on Friday and said, "Can you tell me in one clear sentence what the Kennedy Round is?"). I gather that the new President is a quick study in the sense that he can be briefed effectively before a meeting, but that, unlike JFK, he does not retain what he has been told beyond the meeting and must be told it again a few days later. His basic trouble, I imagine, is that he has never in his political career had to concentrate on substance. He has always assumed substantive alternatives and supposed that the correct alternative is the widest degree of political assent. Policy for Johnson has always been determined by the balance of political pressures. Now he must begin to examine the merits of policy *per se*, and he is not intellectually or psychologically prepared to do this.

My own position remains baffling—or perhaps not. I have not had a single communication from the President or his staff for the last month—not a request to do anything, or an invitation to a meeting, or an instruction, or a suggestion, not even the photographs or swimming or cocktail invitations which have gone to other members of the Kennedy staff. This simplifies things a good deal; for, when I reaffirm my desire to resign, it will be hard for LBJ to insist again that I am indispensable to him. At the same time, the *Times* has called me a couple of times to check the story that I am about to be replaced by Eric Goldman. When I inquired whether they had heard this story from "Johnson sources," I was told that they had. It seems clear that they are prepared to have me fade away, which is OK by me.

1964

January 18

Life continues to run down. I spend most of my time doing things about and for the Kennedy Library. My relationship to the new administration could hardly be more meager. I have had no private talks with President Johnson since early December; and the only piece of ongoing business in which my participation was invited was the preparation of the State of the Union message.

I would say that the essence of the Johnson administration so far is motion without movement—but again I must guard against my commitment to his predecessor and my dislike of the current style and corn; because in most public respects he has done well, and held the line on the big issues. I am sure he will be a good President, but I am also sure that it's not my sort of thing.

January 31

On January 27 I submitted my resignation. It was accepted with alacrity. LBJ received it at 8 P.M. Monday evening, and his letter of acceptance was in my hands by noon the next day. The letter, which I believe to have been drafted by Bill Moyers, could not have been more cordial. It is all rather odd. I guess Johnson decided from the start that I was among those whom he could not hope to win over; certainly he made no effort to involve me in the processes of the new administration.

It now seems to me that it may be possible to create a situation where LBJ will find it very difficult to turn down RFK for the vice presidency. If Bobby continues to lead in the polls, if the Reuthers and labor in general demand him, if the big city machines indicate a preference for him, if the Negroes and the liberals support him, LBJ may not be able to reject him very easily. Obviously LBJ threw Shriver's name into the picture in an effort to confuse and derail the RFK movement. But I think that this effort has failed. At the moment, I am reasonably optimistic about Bobby's chances.

March 11

LBJ differs from JFK in a number of ways—most notably, perhaps, in his absence of intellectual curiosity. Again, he has the senatorial habit of knowing only what it is necessary to know for the moment and then forgetting it as soon as the moment has passed. Thus a senator knows everything about railroad legislation one week and about urban renewal the next and about foreign aid the next—by which time he can no longer remember anything about railroad legislation. LBJ lacks the supreme FDR-JFK gift of keeping a great many things in his mind at the same time, remembering them all, and demanding always to know new things. This is particularly unfortunate in foreign affairs, where he knows little and yet seems disinclined to add to his knowledge as, for example, by talking to foreign visitors.

One senses a certain insecurity in his relations with people, except senators. He alternates between effusive cordiality and absent and preoccupied indifference. He apparently dislikes to do business on a face-to-face basis and requires single-page memoranda which he takes back to the Mansion, broods over and decides (or postpones) without discussion with the person who has brought up the problem. There is no easy access to his office; even [Jack] Valenti, Moyers and [Walter] Jenkins have to request permission before they enter; the old informality of the Kennedy days has gone.

March 25

There is nothing more dangerous, so far as I can see, than being accepted by Johnson as one of his own. I think he has been meticulously polite to those in the White House whom he regards as Kennedy men. But, when he starts regarding them as Johnson men, their day is over. He begins to treat them like Johnson men, which means like servants. This is what happened to Pierre Salinger. Of all the Kennedy people, he seemed to make the transition most easily—which meant that LBJ began shouting at him, ordering him around and humiliating him just as if he were Jenkins or Valenti. Teddy White told me a terrible story in which Johnson made Salinger eat a plate of bean soup at a White House luncheon out of pure delight in the exercise of authority. As soon as people become Johnson men, he seems to stop listening to them and to use them only as instruments of his own desires.

Evelyn Lincoln told me at luncheon that all LBJ's phone talks are taken down on tape. They are immediately transcribed by the girls in her old office and then given to the President the first thing in the morning, so he can see what he said. What a treasure trove for the historian! and what a threat to the rational and uninhibited conduct of government!

At luncheon with Evelyn Lincoln, she gave a rather amusing and acid account of LBJ as Vice President. He used to call her up when he heard of a meeting to which he had not been invited and ask whether this was not an oversight. She would check with the President, who sometimes would say yes and sometimes no. She confirmed my impression that he was in the White House much less often after the first year. She thinks that he talked too much in meetings for the President, and that he began to get on JFK's nerves. She said that he always seemed very nervous and ill at ease while waiting in her office.

She added that she would never to able to forgive him for his behavior after the President's murder. She resents first the fact that LBJ and his entourage moved into Air Force One instead of letting JBK [Jackie] and the President's friends take the body back to Washington by themselves. She says that there was much hurrying around, talking, typing, laughing on the plane by the Johnson people. Then, on Saturday morning, she went to her office at 8. LBJ arrived about 8:30, called her in and said, "I have a meeting at 9:30 and would like you to clear your things out of that office by then so my own girls can come in." Evelyn, grief-stricken and appalled, ran into Bobby and told him what had happened. Bobby saw LBJ and got the period of grace extended till noon. But Evelyn had cleared out by 11:30.

March 27

I might add a few remarks by JBK which do not appear on the oral history tape. She does not like Ted Sorensen, and the reason is that in 1956 he gave people around Washington the impression that he, and not JFK, had written *Profiles in Courage*. JBK says that for a couple of years she could not bear to speak to Ted, but that luckily JFK had preserved the long, yellow, legal-sized sheets on which he had written the first draft; so, when Drew Pearson wrote that he had not written the book, Cass Canfield was able to obtain a public retraction. She also said that the first question Bob McNamara asked JFK at their first meeting was whether he had written *Profiles in Courage*.

JBK also said that JFK, wanting to do something for Ted and not supposing that the book would do exceptionally well, made over all the royalties to him. I found this hard to believe and checked it with Bobby who said, yes, it was true—that Ted had received all the royalties up to the new edition (the royalties from which go to the Library). This must have amounted to nearly $200,000. Bobby also was exceedingly cool about Ted. I said that he had served the President well in the White House. Bobby said, "Yes. Ted loved only two people in his life. In the White House he finally decided that he loved one more than the other." I said stupidly, "Who was the other?" Bobby said, "Himself."

A few days before he left for Cambridge, Ted had called me and asked about his own original drafts of Kennedy speeches—for example, the inaugural address. Should he destroy them? Might they not damage JFK's historical reputation? I said that he should destroy nothing—that his historical reputation rested on many other things besides speeches, and that in any case a President deserved credit for the writers he chose and the texts he approved. Later, in one of my interviews with JBK, she described JFK writing the inaugural address at Palm Beach, coming into her room in the morning (she was still recovering from Caroline's birth), smoking a cigar and reading her passages, again on the yellow legal-sized sheets. I asked her to go into this in detail so that the story of the way the inaugural was composed could be clearly on the record.

June 16

I went to New York on Tuesday night for a dinner in honor of Jackie to thank contributors to the Library. Afterward we went to the Smiths'. I had a long talk with JBK. She started to tell me about the trip back from Dallas and the effort made to get her to change her dress when Jim Fosburgh came up and we had a change of subject. A few nights ago (June 5) at the French Embassy, Godfrey McHugh gave me a long account of that ghastly afternoon. Godfrey told me that they did not know that the Johnsons were on Air Force One. He and Kenny kept asking the pilot to take off, and were told that the plane had to wait for Mrs. Johnson's luggage—a mysterious excuse, since none of them knew that the Johnsons were already occupying the presidential apartments in the back of the plane. Godfrey also said that LBJ was in a panic at the hospital, convinced that there was a conspiracy and that he would be the next to go. Godfrey also gave me a horrendous account of his visit to the LBJ Ranch before the [Ludwig] Erhard visit in December—Johnson's crudeness, discourtesy, drunkenness, etc.

July 23

Last Wednesday, July 15, Bobby and I flew to the Cape together. The Dillons were anchored off Hyannis Port on Henry Ford's yacht, and we were going up for a party that night.

Bobby seemed philosophical about the vice presidency. His thoughts are still turning to the idea of spending a year at Oxford reading and writing.

We talked a good deal about his relationship to LBJ. Obviously Johnson's actions in the first 24 hours after JFK's death left wounds which will take a long time to heal. Bobby commented that Sarge Shriver had taken it on himself to harmonize the situation then and had only made it worse. Bobby said, "I told Sarge that if I wanted him to intervene I was capable of asking him to do so." His references to Sarge were fairly cool, and he seemed scornful of the notion that Sarge might be a serious possibility for the vice presidency.

After a silence Bobby said, "You know the worst thing that Johnson has said? . . . Once he told Pierre Salinger, 'When I was young in Texas, I used to know a cross-eyed boy. His eyes were crossed, and so was his character. Sometimes I think that, when you remember the assassination of Trujillo and the assassination of Diem, what happened to Kennedy may be divine retribution.' "

On that same day Ken Galbraith was summoned to Washington by LBJ. He spent three hours with him that evening and another hour the next morning. LBJ (as he had done with Jimmy Wechsler the Saturday before) went through a long list (18, I think) of vice presidential possibilities and then narrowed the list down to six: Humphrey, Kennedy, McNamara, Stevenson, McCarthy, Shriver. He spoke of McNamara with great admiration, Humphrey with warmth. On RFK, he simply gave pros and cons. Then he went on to complain of the coldness of the

Kennedy people toward him—"They never come in to see me. Schlesinger sent me a nice letter about the civil rights bill but hasn't come in to discuss with me his objections to our Latin American policy." Ken pointed out that he would not have been there had Valenti not called him and said that people who knew how pressed any President was were not inclined to break into his day unless they had something of vital importance to communicate.

I have the impression that LBJ is playing a vast game with everybody on the vice presidency and doing so with great relish. He evidently talks to everyone about the problem and leaves behind a trail of cryptic hints and possibilities which only tease and torment both aspirants and observers.

July 29

Bobby phoned me today (in Wellfleet) to say that "Lyndon Johnson," as he calls him, had asked him to come to the White House earlier today. [LBJ] explained that he had given a great deal of thought to the problem of the vice presidency, that he had not decided who he wanted, but that he had decided whom he did not want, and that one of those was RFK. I asked Bobby whether anything further could be done. He said no.

August 2

We went over to Bobby's yesterday afternoon. After tennis (during which I sprained, or wrenched, my ankle), we got on the *Marlin* and set out for Martha's Vineyard and Tony Lewis. It was my first trip on the *Marlin* without JFK, and I felt sad. The Harrimans, the Hacketts and Mike Forrestal were also there.

Bobby described his Wednesday meeting with LBJ. He said that LBJ seemed nervous; that he outlined what he regarded as the vice presidential requirements and then said, rather flatly, "In my judgment, you don't have them." He then became more effusive and said that he would help Bobby to get anything he wanted—any place in the cabinet, any embassy, London, Paris, Moscow—anything he wanted, concluding that he was sure that Bobby would be President some day and that he hoped he could help bring it about. Bobby said that he wasn't interested in anything at the moment.

Mac Bundy called him up the next day and suggested that he put out a statement saying that he was withdrawing from the vice presidential contest on his own initiative; such a statement, Mac said, would be good for the President, for the party and for Bobby. Bobby replied that he could not say this; in the first place, it wasn't true; and, in the second place, it would be hard to explain to his supporters why he had withdrawn from the contest without consulting them. LBJ's device of excluding all those who regularly attend cabinet meetings was then the makeshift substitute for the statement they wanted from Bobby.

Bobby does, of course, want to be Secretary of State. He, Mike Forrestal and I talked a bit about probabilities and strategy but did not get very far. We can perhaps do something to get the foreign policy establishment—Lippmann, etc.—to do more to give him a mantle of respectability in the field. But I think LBJ wants most of all a man who would have strength on the Hill, like Cordell Hull. Bobby's own thoughts are inclining much more toward the New York Senate seat. As he told me later, he has a great desire to be independent of Johnson and the administration and to have his own base. I asked him about Massachusetts. He said wryly, "Well, that's really Teddy's state now, and I wouldn't want to interfere."

August 22
Atlantic City

Here I am in Atlantic City for my fifth Democratic convention— and for the first time since 1948 without any particular interest or role, except for the American Broadcasting Company. The ins and outs of politics are fascinating. Jim Rowe, for example, back in the center of things, and the old Kennedy people on the sidelines.

The great speculation is about the vice presidency. The party is strongly for Hubert, now that Bobby is out; but there are intimations that LBJ does not much want him—primarily, I think, because he does not want a competitive Vice President. If he decides on Hubert, my guess is that he would postpone things to the last possible moment on the theory that the torment would be good for Hubert's soul. LBJ rivals FDR in his delight in mystification and in his semi-sadistic teasing.

August 29

A strange convention, wholly, but not altogether happily, dominated by Lyndon Johnson. It is, I think, the first convention in the history of the Democratic party which did not have a single roll call vote. The result is a party which is united and confident, but the mood of the convention was none the less tinged with a certain mild frustration.

When Hubert came in on Saturday, I asked him how things looked. He replied soberly, "I think they look pretty good." But still there was apparently nothing definite. He maintained a marvelous public facade in the next three days, always ebullient and happy; yet those who saw him off guard, as Jimmy Wechsler did late Monday night, thought that he was under intense strain.

My guess is that LBJ had made up his mind some days or weeks ago, but enjoyed the game of mystification and thought that it would be good for Hubert's soul to keep him in torment. I understand that Muriel Humphrey was miserable during this time. (Someone repeated to me a remark which LBJ had made about the vice presidency in general: "Whoever it is, I want his pecker to be in my pocket.")

It all came out happily. I found myself in the middle of the Minnesota delegation when LBJ made his announcement. I asked Orville Freeman when he thought Hubert had had the word. He said that, so far as he knew, Hubert had known nothing definite until he went to the White House that day. I then wondered what he and LBJ had talked about in their hour together. Freeman said, "Whatever they talked about, I bet that Hubert had to sign it in blood."

The one great spontaneous moment at the convention came on Thursday night when Robert Kennedy introduced the JFK film. His appearance set off a sustained and deeply-felt ovation. They stopped the organ after a moment or so, but the demonstration continued neverthe-less and, indeed, gathered steam whenever Bobby, who stood there, a wistful half-smile on his face, tried to bring it to an end. Then they showed the JFK film, which cast a spell on the convention; but it was followed by other memorial tributes—Stevenson on Mrs. Roosevelt, the best speech in the convention; [James] Farley on Rayburn; [New York mayor Robert] Wagner on [Herbert] Lehman; and the Kennedy effect was dissipated by the time LBJ arrived.

The convention wholly ratified LBJ's control of the party, in case anyone had any doubt, and it supplied further evidence of his political wizardry, if such evidence were required. It was his convention—every controversial issue deflected and disposed of; no roll calls; plus the hectic melodrama of the vice presidency. And his presence dominated the convention. It would have been hard to tell from the external trap-pings that Kennedy had been President of the United States during three of the last four years; in the symbolism of the convention, he was a remote icon, along with Truman and Roosevelt. And the LBJ party emerged: western rather than eastern; middle-aged rather than youth-ful; conciliatory rather than aggressive; bland rather than intellectual; centrist rather than liberal. These adjectives refer perhaps to form rather than substance. On issues and programs, I have no doubt that LBJ will continue to carry forward the Kennedy policies. He under-stands that to be a great President you must do great things—and he is determined to do them. The test will come when he runs out of ideas. Up to this point he has been living intellectually off the Kennedy years.

1965

January 20

Today is the first day of the Johnson era, at least in its technical sense, and I suppose that I ought to put something on the record. But anything I say at this point is subject to discount. I have been in a state of depression ever since the inaugural preparations began. The memory of the happiness and hope of four years ago is too much—this and the ruthlessness of history and power which makes so many in Washington today act as if JFK never existed.

I have avoided all the formal inaugural occasions (indeed, I was not invited to any), but I did go to a dance that Mary Lasker and Abe Fortas gave after the Inaugural Concert last night. Johnson was there, lowering and somber, doggedly plowing his way across the dance floor, a smile of self-satisfaction playing about his lips. The contrast with the Vice President–elect is so striking. Humphrey is the only thing I have seen this week which has lifted my spirits. He is the happiest man in the world—the incarnation and exaltation of happiness—and when *he* danced, it was so filled with gaiety and charm and life that everyone else stopped, formed a circle around him and applauded.

I continue to believe that Johnson will achieve a great deal as President; but the irony is that he has been so dependent thus far on the man whose memory he is trying to erase. It is not only that he has been living intellectually off the Kennedy program but that his own formulations have been so largely made by Kennedy people. Dick Goodwin invented the Great Society (Johnson had started out himself by talking feebly about something called the Better Deal), and Goodwin has been responsible for almost every significant Johnson speech (except the New Orleans speech on civil rights, which seems to have been a largely inspired improvisation by LBJ himself) since Sorensen left.

Still I think that Johnson will probably go down as a considerable President. He *wants* to be a great President, and he knows that a great President must do great things. Where Presidents like FDR and JFK had some idea themselves what those great things should be, LBJ has no idea of his own but consensus; yet he is eager for suggestion and has immense capacity to make a new idea sound innocuous and to mobilize congressional and business support behind programs which they would otherwise suspect.

Ken Galbraith gave a luncheon yesterday at the Jockey Club. Bobby and Teddy were among those present. Teddy's recovery from an airplane crash is remarkable, and I am sure that in retrospect his interlude will turn out to have been one of the luckiest things that ever happened to him. I remember how dismayed I was when JFK told me that they were going to run Teddy for the Senate; and I must say now that I have no doubt that he will be an effective and hard-working senator. He is conscientious, he has a strong practical intelligence, and he has a superb political temperament. But a gap remains between Teddy and his two older brothers. Teddy said to me yesterday, "I've been trying to read that list of books which Jack said were his favorites. Could he really have enjoyed those books? I tried to read Bemis on John Quincy Adams and Allan Nevins on the coming of the Civil War, and I just couldn't get through them." Of course, JFK really adored books like these (and Bobby too reads and enjoys them).

After lunch, Bobby came over to my office, and we talked for a while. His mood is excellent. He said that he thanked heaven every day that the vice presidency had fallen through; it would have been a miserable and hopeless relationship, and nothing but trouble could have come from it.

Everyone remarks on the change of atmosphere in Washington. The old exhilaration is gone. LBJ as a personality lacks excitement. The presence of the President causes little stir. Last night many people did not even know that Johnson was at the dance and, when told, did not seem to care. The State of the Union message is very radical in its implications; if JFK had come out with the same program, half the country would have been enraptured and a quarter deeply hostile. LBJ's ability to transmute boldness into banality may be, in the short run, a source of strength. His sponsorship of a program does not arouse antagonism, and his old-shoe approach creates the impression that he is proposing only the most moderate and sensible policies.

I have just heard the inaugural address. The first half is much as it was when Dick Goodwin showed it to me yesterday. The last part is new and good. On the whole, a fine address. Credit goes first to Dick and then to Adlai Stevenson, who submitted (according to Dick) the only usable draft and who conceived the device of the perspective on the earth created by the rocket traveling to Mars.

May 25

I stayed around the White House Saturday morning and lunched with Bundy and Goodwin. [Romulo] Betancourt was in town, and I urged strongly that the President see him; if not the President, then Mac or Bill or Dick. Mac called Johnson and suggested this but Johnson was cold to the idea. As Mac talked, I could see one of the problems of the new White House. Johnson's staff has to figure out how to put things to him without irritating or boring him; this very much impedes the speed and candor of communication. In general, I felt a little sad about Mac. He was, as ever, bright and charming but not his old confident, active self.

July 16

Another chapter of my life sadly ended. Dick Goodwin called me from the White House a minute or two after one o'clock on Wednesday, July 14, to say that Adlai Stevenson had died in London. Marietta was with him. They were walking in the sunlight along Grosvenor Street toward Hyde Park when he felt faint, clutched an iron railing nearby and then pitched over, obviously felled by a massive heart attack or stroke. We drove out with Ed and Mary Louise Day to Andrews Field the next afternoon when Air Force One came in from London with the casket. One's mind spun back to November 23, 1963. Ten years ago both Eisenhower and Johnson had heart attacks; who would have dared predict then that they would both be alive and hearty and Kennedy and Stevenson dead a decade later?

I saw him last about six weeks ago. He appeared deeply disappointed and a little hurt over the limited role he was playing in the formation of policy. He had thought—Johnson had led him to think—that he would have a much larger role than he had under Kennedy; that the Stevenson-Johnson generation, prematurely pushed out by the Kennedy generation, would have their long postponed chance to run things. In the first weeks, as I believe I have recorded elsewhere, Johnson wooed Stevenson in an all-out manner. But Adlai's expectations were all disappointed. Indeed, he played less of a role under Johnson than under Kennedy, not because of any lapse in his personal relations with LBJ, but because LBJ rarely thought about the UN or the Third World and thus rarely thought about Adlai. He hoped for a time that he might be the vice presidential nominee. Ed Day told me that Stevenson had asked him to call a list of big businessmen and get them to call Johnson recommending

Stevenson. And to the end he probably still hoped to become Secretary of State. But I think he knew that these things would never happen. One can never know to what extent these disagreements and disappointments contributed to his death.

Stevenson was a great creative figure in American politics. I have written about this in *A Thousand Days*, and I am glad that I do not feel now, in the horror over his death, the need of changing anything. He turned the Democratic party around in the fifties and made JFK possible. In 1952 and 1956 he stated most of the leading themes of the New Frontier and the Great Society. Both to the United States and the world he was the voice of a reasonable, civilized, elevated America in a time of self-righteousness and conservatism. He was also a most warm, forgiving and generous friend. He was not a perfect man, and I am glad that Carl McGowan suggested this in his remarks at the National Cathedral. He had many moments of petulance, querulousness, indecision. As talk with [Clayton] Fritchey and McGowan in these last few days reminded me, he rarely said nice things about those close to him—Bill Blair, for example, who served him so faithfully and so well for years. I said to Clayton, "I do not think I have ever heard him say a generous thing about John Kennedy." Clayton said that he had not either. Stevenson never forgave Kennedy for denying him the two things he wanted most—the Presidency and the Secretaryship of State—and even after Kennedy's death he could never bring himself to say a magnanimous word about him; in private, that is, for no one was more felicitous and perceptive about JFK in public.

Yet Adlai won one's love and admiration wholeheartedly, gathered to himself a brilliant collection of men, brought a new generation into politics and moved millions of people in the United States and around the world who never saw him in person or shook his hand. He had somehow the quality of inciting and fortifying one's better self. He had an unsurpassed gift of public utterance. And he was one of the most enchanting human beings that any of us will ever know.

1966

January 21

I have been meaning for some time to put down the substance of the evening of January 6 when I assembled Carl Kaysen, Dick Goodwin and Ken Galbraith for a dinner at 3132 O Street with Bob McNamara.

The subject was, of course, Vietnam. Bob combined frankness about issues with discretion about personalities in his usual fashion. But it became evident that he was strongly in favor of the pause in the bombing of North Vietnam and had advocated it ever since he had felt the military equilibrium had been restored in the autumn. One gathered that the Joint Chiefs of Staff and Rusk had opposed the idea, but that the President was eventually won over.

McNamara said, as he had before, that he did not regard a military solution as possible. The military advantages of the bombing, he seemed to feel, were marginal and were outweighed by the political disadvantages. The infiltration rate had increased steadily (fourfold?) since the bombing had started. He seemed skeptical about the value of enlarging our ground forces. At the 8:1 ratio, we could put in 80,000 men, the North Vietnamese could put in 10,000, and we would all be even again. He seemed deeply oppressed and concerned at the prospect of indefinite escalation. Our impression was that he feared the resumption of bombing might well put us on the slippery slide. When I asked whether the North Vietnamese had increased their commitment in response to or independently of American action, he said flatly the first.

He defined his objective in South Vietnam as "withdrawal with honor." The establishment of a neutralist government in Saigon would meet that standard. When we asked whether there was a South Vietnamese Souvanna Phouma [the prime minister of Laos, who governed on a platform of national reconciliation], he said he thought there was: [Phan Huy] Quat. One gathered that he might even be prepared to consider Viet Cong participation in such a government—presumably on the Laos model (implying that the Viet Cong, like the Pathet Lao, would turn against a genuinely neutralist regime).

In times past, I have always thought that Bob lacked a political ear— that he had little instinct for the political and diplomatic dimensions of the problem. We were all deeply impressed by his apparent evolution. He obviously now has a clear and free grasp of the intangible factors in the Vietnam situation and is determined to prevent the conflict from billowing up into nuclear war with China. Evidently the Secretary of Defense and the Secretary of State have exchanged roles—with McNamara asserting the political and diplomatic interests of the government and Rusk defending the views of the Joint Chiefs of Staff.

March 11

I have been meaning for some time to put down some notes about Vietnam. Things have got much worse since January. Probably the critical mistake, the point of no return, was, as George Ball insists, the decision to send in combat units in March 1965. The pause and the peace offensive, however, held out the hope, if not of a change of policy, at least of a halt in the momentum of enlargement. I do not doubt that LBJ seriously hoped for success in Vietnam. I am sure that the last thing he wants is a large war in Asia; among other things, he cannot have forgotten what the Korean War did to the fortunes of the Democratic party a dozen years ago. Then, toward the end of January, he decided to end the pause and resume bombing. The essential reasons for this, so far as I could find out, were psychological and political rather than military.

The resumption encouraged insurrectionary sentiments in the Senate. For a long time, the pro-negotiation senators had refrained from public criticism of the administration on the ground that this would freeze LBJ in hawk-like policies. After resumption, they began to despair of the value of private letters and meetings and decided— Fulbright especially—to bring their opposition into the open.

Bobby Kennedy has become increasingly disturbed but reluctant to seem to lead a revolt against LBJ. He has been thinking about the processes of negotiation and reached the conclusion that the sticking-point was the role of the Viet Cong. When this point did not emerge in the hearings, he decided to make it himself. There followed ten days of confused controversy. His first statement was not as precise as his later ones (especially on *Face the Nation*, February 27); but what he said consistently was that, if we meant business on negotiation, we had to persuade Hanoi and the Viet Cong that we were asking them to come to the conference table for some other reason than to demand their surrender; this meant that we had to assure the Viet Cong a seat as an independent body, that, if the negotiations resulted in an interim government with Viet Cong participation, we would accept that, and if free elections resulted in a coalition regime, we would accept that too. Bobby's point was that, if we were not going to exterminate the Viet Cong, we had to indicate that, if they laid down their arms and took part in a supervised free election, they would have a say in the future political life of Vietnam.

On Sunday morning before *Face the Nation* Fred Dutton and I went out to Hickory Hill to run through possible questions. By this time, Rusk had said that Viet Cong participation in the talks was not an "insurmountable problem," Bill Moyers had said we would not exclude

Viet Cong participation in an interim government, and everyone (except the Vice President) had said that we would abide by the results of a free election, even presumably if it brought the Viet Cong to power.

An hour after Bobby, Hubert went on the air on *Issues and Answers*. We all watched it before lunch at Hickory Hill (except Bobby, who was both so irritated and upset by Hubert's performance that, after a few minutes, he went silently away). It was a new and different Hubert—hard-faced, except for some unctuous smiles, and uncharacteristically coarse in his language. His trouble, I fear, is that he cannot say something publicly without deeply believing it privately; and when, as now, he has no choice in his public utterances, he whips up a fervency of private belief. I fear also that Max Kampelman or someone has persuaded him that this is the issue on which he can knock out RFK. His sense of splitting with the liberal community, a probable feeling of guilt over the positions he is taking—all this has made him self-righteous and irascible.

The effect of Bobby's intervention, I think, was to make the administration think concretely about the meaning of negotiation—and, having thought about it, they did not like it. Or, to put it more exactly, having thought about it in the context of the military optimism now sweeping Washington, they feel it would be a great mistake. One has the impression that very little would embarrass the administration now more than a peace overture from Hanoi. The military have the bit between their teeth and are confident that they can "win" the war—i.e., that they can force a retreat of the regular Hanoi forces back over the 17th parallel and a dissolution of the Viet Cong. If they are right, LBJ may still pull himself out of this. But if they are wrong—and the Joint Chiefs of Staff are almost always wrong in their military predictions—then we are committed to a steady enlargement of the war; for, if one thing does not break the resistance, the pressure will increase to do something more—to bomb large population centers, harbors, the industrial complex, to strike along the Chinese border, until we force China into the war.

March 13

Last night the Gridiron [Club dinner]: Russell Long, a great success; John Lindsay, a flop (including surprising and stupid indulgence in blue material). The show contained a vicious attack on Fulbright and ended with a hymn of reverence to Rusk; after which Rusk was introduced and received a standing ovation. Along with Herblock and perhaps 10 percent of the audience, I stayed seated. Afterward, at the Cowles party, President Lyndon B. Johnson came over and grasped my hand. After a moment of chat, he said, "Well, Arthur, I noticed that you had a little trouble with your chair when there was that ovation with Dean." Then he turned to Chalmers Roberts of the *Post*, who was standing nearby, and said, "Don't print anything about that. It is very important to maintain the unity of the Democratic party—from Rusk to Schlesinger." He seemed entirely cordial—but how characteristic that he should have peered out over the audience during the ovation and beadily noted who were remaining seated.

July 28

The big issue, of course, has been Vietnam. I would say that this period has marked, if not a change in Lyndon Johnson, at least a change in my own perception of him. I had thought until rather recently that the tendency toward a widening of the war represented a triumph of his advisers over his instincts—that the last thing he wanted was American involvement in a ground war in Asia, or, even less, a war with China, and that his dearest hope was a negotiated solution making possible American withdrawal. If this was once his mood, I fear it is so no longer. He would seem to have turned a corner toward the systematic enlargement of the war. Why? I cannot resist the feeling that domestic politics—his precipitous decline in the public opinion polls—constitute a major factor. He once told Dick Goodwin that there was far more chauvinism in the United States than easterners understood, and it now looks as if a course of playing the war to the hilt has recommended itself to him as the best way of reversing the polls and bringing about Democratic gains in November. There may be other, deeper pressures working on him. Dick has hinted that he may have a streak of personal cowardice (as demonstrated in his panic after the murder in Dallas), which may force him into public virility in order to prove something about himself (in the sense that a war hero, like JFK, felt no need to prove himself by invading Cuba after the Bay of Pigs or the missile crisis). In any case, whatever the motive, LBJ now seems to have committed himself to pressing the war *a l'outrance*. He seems to have accepted the Rusk thesis that this is Munich all over again, that the issue is democratic resistance to Chinese aggression, and that, if we don't hold the line in Vietnam, we are condemned to "wars of national liberation" all through the underdeveloped world. And he now seems to have become a hard-liner. At the time of the Johns Hopkins speech in April 1965, LBJ seemed to be clearly on the side of negotiation. He instructed Dick to make negotiation a central theme of the speech; and the White House upheld negotiation against Rusk's complaint that it would upset the government in Saigon (McNamara told Dick that the speech was fine and that he should not change a word of it). As late as December 1965, LBJ acquiesced in McNamara's plea for a suspension of the bombing of North Vietnam. But that mood appears to have faded away.

I suppose that the illusion of a military victory lies behind LBJ's decision to widen the war—this, plus the feeling that widening the war will enable him to pursue the domestic strategy of rallying the country around the flag. The notion that victory is possible—which McNamara has always denied in the private talks I have had with him over the past two years—comes, I imagine, from the sheer momentum generated by the size and power of the American military presence in Vietnam. The idea of military victory, at whatever cost in obliteration of the country, has begun to overwhelm the political purposes which brought us into the area in the first instance. The problem now is how to restrain the pursuit of military victory before it leads us into war with China.

Dick [Goodwin]'s argument is that the only thing likely to reach Johnson is vigorous political opposition; and we have discussed the possible formation of a committee against the widening of the war as a means of rallying the resistance.

We discussed this with RFK at dinner in New York on July 20. Bobby suffers from a sense of bafflement. He listened carefully while we outlined our thoughts, but he had, or at least offered, a skepticism about a mass [antiwar] movement. Such a movement, he said, would have to tie itself to an issue or to a man. The issue of widening the war, he said, was too complicated and ambiguous. LBJ could always justify each specific step of intensification on the ground that it was necessary to save the lives of American troops and that it would shorten the war. As for tying it to a man—here he paused, for the polls have clearly demonstrated that he is the appointed and expected leader of the opposition (polls in California, Iowa and other states have shown that Democratic voters prefer him as President to LBJ, and that the electorate as a whole would go for him against any Republican). Dick then made the point that, the more the anti–widening of the war movement seemed a RFK movement, the less likely it would be that LBJ would respond to it. In other words, RFK's appearance as head or beneficiary of the movement would only confirm LBJ in his present course. Bobby again listened carefully but withheld comment.

I discussed much of this obliquely with Averell at dinner at George Stevens's on July 22. Everyone has his weaknesses, and Averell's is the desire to be near power—compounded in the present case by the passion to be the negotiator in the case of Vietnam discussions, a hope held out to him more than a year ago by the President. I think that he sees the Vietnam negotiation as the climax of his public career and, to keep himself eligible for this, he is prepared to make all sorts of compromises (though, of course, Rusk would die rather than let Averell do it). This means that, like Hubert, he defends the administration line on public occasions. But, unlike Hubert, he does not altogether believe his own defense.

The conversation was resumed over the weekend of July 24, which I spent at Ken Galbraith's in Newfane, Vermont, with George McGovern and Seymour Harris. But now I had begun to think for the first time of the possibility of RFK's going for the nomination in 1968. Of course, this is a long time away—and two years would give LBJ plenty of opportunity for all the escalation he seeks and needs. But, assuming he follows the present course without getting into a nuclear war with China, there might be just the possibility of reversing all historical precedent and rejecting the nomination of an incumbent President.

George said that he would be all for it; adding that he thought that LBJ had a "great yellow streak" and might conceivably be bluffed out of trying for renomination, citing his health and the 22nd Amendment as reasons for not running again. This is all remote and unlikely, but a month ago none of us would have thought it worth a moment's consideration.

"Fear always runs the State Department," Averell said. "They always follow what they are most afraid of. When Bobby was Attorney General, they were most afraid of him. Now they are afraid of Congress, the Joint Chiefs of Staff and the White House." He expressed the deepest anxiety about the people around the President who were urging the intensification of the war. As he left the Stevenses', I told him that I was spending the weekend with Galbraith, McGovern and Harris [in Vermont]. He said, "What are you up to?" I said, "We are planning a coup d'état." As he and Marie disappeared into the darkness, he waved his hand and said, "Count me in."

I find McNamara especially puzzling, as does RFK. When he talks to us, he dismisses the military value of bombing the north, asserts the importance of limiting the war, denies the possibility of a military victory and looks wistfully to the neutralization of South Vietnam and the withdrawal of American troops. Nothing seems to alarm him more than the prospect of provoking a war with China. Yet publicly he is the spokesman for the widening of the war; and it is hard to believe that he urges his private views on the President with the force that he does with his old friends of Kennedy years.

Walt Rostow has suddenly emerged from a long eclipse and is now established as the Pangloss of the White House, telling the President with great authoritativeness all the things the President wants to hear.

Everything, according to Walt, is getting better and better; and I can see him when the bombs begin to fall on Washington, assuring LBJ that the deep-running historic tendencies are on our side, that we are turning the corner in Zambia and Tasmania, and that all is for the best in the best of all possible worlds. I last saw him at dinner at Jane McBaine's in Washington on June 14. He exuded self-satisfaction with his resurrection and set forth a tedious and misconceived analogy between LBJ and Lincoln, casting the opposition to the war in the role of the Copperheads and saying that, if LBJ only kept up the military momentum, he would be in the clear in another few months.

As for RFK, he has been extremely impressive in these months. He has exposed himself to a series of unpredictable situations—South Africa, Mississippi and Alabama, Vietnam, foreign aid, the Negro revolution—and has not, so far as I can see, set a foot wrong. And he does this primarily, so far as I can see, on his own instincts. His apparatus, like JFK's, depends, not (as the press assumes) on supernaturally efficient organization—his ideas of organization are exceedingly casual—but on surrounding himself by bright people and then making his own judgments out of a sense of what is right—i.e., faithful to his own character—for him. The Machiavellian myth of RFK—the notion that he is a rigorous and premeditated calculator of chances and opportunities—dies hard. But, in fact, he is a fatalist, who has determined to be the best senator he can and do what he thinks is right, supposing that if by 1971 this commends itself to the party and the nation he will try for the presidency, and, if not, then he could not honestly aspire to it.

August 1

I am not sure that my notes have adequately recorded one interesting development of recent weeks: that is, serious discussion for the first time of RFK's running for the Presidency in 1968. I have not yet broached the topic with him, though I have no doubt that he has it well in mind. But LBJ's evident commitment to the widening of the war makes the thought of RFK's candidacy both possible and necessary.

I would imagine the speculation was provoked by the (to me) quite surprising results of various state polls this summer, especially in California and (of all states) Iowa, showing RFK running well ahead of LBJ both in voter preference among Democrats and as matched against various Republican possibilities.

So we have begun to take this seriously. Dick Goodwin, Ken Galbraith and, what is more important, George McGovern all feel that we must now begin to look quietly to the prospects. George, in spite of his old friendship and deep affection for Hubert, says that he thinks the only hope for the country is the nomination of RFK in '68. But can this be done? All the historical probabilities, of course, are against it.

But yet, but yet. In 1948 the opposition to Truman's renomination included most of the northern city bosses. Had Eisenhower agreed to be a candidate, he would probably have beaten Truman in the convention. RFK retains his links to city and state organizations and would probably get their support. He seems to be the only truly popular political figure in the country today. By 1968 more than half the country will be under 25. More than that, a politician who decides to stick by LBJ and oppose RFK is not opposing a single-shot effort. He is opposing not only a man who will be around a long time but a political dynasty. No careful politician will back the aging Johnson against the youthful Kennedys lightly. If the RFK movement continues, there seem other possibilities than an open and damaging fight in the convention.

August 14

Just back from another Hyannis Port weekend. There is nothing pleasanter than these weekends, though I always return with every muscle sore from the incessant exercise. But there is nothing coercive about it: guests can disappear for hours pursuing their own lives, and nobody notices. RFK is really more interested in foreign affairs than anything else, and he was electrified by the news that North Korea has issued a declaration of independence against both Russia and China. No state is more in debt to China than North Korea or geographically more at its mercy; and this action reinforces RFK's conviction that communism will take increasingly nationalistic forms, especially in the underdeveloped world, and also that, if we had only left North Vietnam alone, it would be defying China too.

At one point in the weekend I came into the living room as he was sitting in a chair, holding his dispatch case in his lap and reading a book. I asked him what he was reading. It was Edith Hamilton's *The Greek Way*. He then showed me the passage he was reading: it was about the quality of life in Periclean Athens, and he mumbled diffidently something to the effect that Edith Hamilton's description could apply to Washington under JFK ("under President Kennedy," as he nearly always puts it, even in the most intimate circumstances). Then, almost shyly, he pulled out of the briefcase a copy of a paperback entitled *Three Greek Plays*—a well-thumbed volume, with pages loose and falling out—and asked me to read two passages from *The Trojan Women,* one describing the horrors of war, the other the importance of friendship and loyalty. They are both powerful passages and clearly had great meaning for him. He apparently carries these two volumes with him always.

October 30

I dined tonight at the Dillons'—RFK was supposed to join us, but did not arrive from campaigning (last stop: Connecticut) until about 10:30. Dick Goodwin came in a few moments before. Bobby seemed not at all tired; in fact, we left the Dillons' around midnight and went to [the New York saloon] P.J. Clarke's where we talked until 2:30.

Bobby talked about a great variety of subjects. He said that, so far as there were issues between himself and Johnson, he guessed that the voters would be 80 percent for Johnson and 20 percent for him; nonetheless he was wildly popular and Johnson was not. He attributes this in great part to the fact that people just don't believe Johnson anymore. He is rueful about his own vogue, which he regards as transient, at least at the present pitch of excitement.

He talked a bit about campaigning with Johnson. He said that, after a day together in New York, he said to Johnson back at the hotel, "Did you enjoy the day?" Johnson looked at him earnestly and said, "Of all the things in life, this is what I most enjoy doing." Bobby said to us incredulously: "Imagine saying that, of all the things in life, this is what you like most."

At Clarke's we talked about the [William] Manchester book [*The Death of a President*], and this led on to the question of the autopsy photographs and then of the Warren Report. RFK wondered how long he could continue to avoid comment on the report. It is evident that he believes that it was a poor job and will not endorse it, but that he is unwilling to criticize it and thereby reopen the whole tragic business.

November 16

A large party at Hickory Hill on November 14th to celebrate Averell's 75th birthday. It was great fun, though I felt that I misfired on my toast. The best speech was given by Hubert Humphrey—he was witty, charming, relaxed and *brief*. One felt that he was quite at peace with himself and very cheerful and comfortable in the Kennedy environment. Actually he and RFK quite like each other, though that will not, of course, prevent either from cutting the other up tomorrow.

1967

❖

January 4

Some random notes as we begin another hopeless year. On November 18 I lunched at the Century with Walter Lippmann, who has decided, after thirty years, to move back to New York. He really cannot abide the Washington of LBJ, and Helen, who was evidently the prime factor in the decision, can abide it even less.

I happened to be in Washington on December 14 when Bill Moyers's resignation was announced. I called him at the White House and told him that I had very mixed feelings over his departure: it was fine for him but sad for the country. We talked for a while and he finally said, "You know, Arthur, I would not be leaving if I thought I could do any good by staying." This is the most desperate commentary I have heard on the state of Johnson's government.

April 18

Last night Jimmy Wechsler and I went to Washington for a dinner with Hubert Humphrey.

The Vice President arrived around 8 and stayed until 12:30. The talk through dinner was mostly preliminary sparring: politics in Minneapolis; the farm crisis; Hubert Humphrey's troubles in securing the appointment of Karl Rolvaag as Ambassador to Iceland (a rather funny story). Finally I made a small speech, saying that everyone understood that the Vice President of the United States had no choice but to support the policies of the President; that we did not wish to invade his private thoughts; that only one question really mattered—Vietnam—and that perhaps he would like to listen to our doubts and, if he felt so moved, to answer our questions.

In the course of animated and occasionally heated discussion (this last mostly with me; it was my fault and I have no question that I behaved with greater discourtesy than did the Vice President), Hubert generally defended the administration position, but revealed along the way his own preference for the course of slowing down the war. He insisted that LBJ wanted negotiation now; that the Tet truce had met [Alexey] Kosygin's specifications about halting the bombing, and yet nothing had happened; and that the key paragraph in LBJ's letter to Ho [Chi Minh] was not the demand for an end to infiltration but the call for counter-proposals. All this seemed a trifle disingenuous to me; when pressed, Hubert Humphrey would say, "Well, you ask your friend Harold Wilson about that." He said that he had been striving to make two points within the government: the need for a physical barrier across the northern part of South Vietnam—this idea, he said with pleasure, [Nguyen Cao] Ky is now backing; and movement toward undeclared and reciprocal military de-escalation.

He did not seem on top of the military detail of the war. Thus he expressed surprise at the remark that there were only 50,000 North Vietnamese regulars in South Vietnam, though this has been the Pentagon figure for some time. When asked what the vital U.S. interest was in

Vietnam, he lapsed into Ruskese and talked about "militant, aggressive Chinese communism"—a phrase he used repeatedly. He quoted a number of Asian leaders to defend the thesis that they all felt threatened by an expanding China and protected by the American intervention.

At one point he reproached the liberals for having "ended the dialogue" with the administration and therefore thrown the President into the arms of Rusk and Rostow. Someone asked how we could resume the dialogue. He said, "Go and talk with your friends Averell Harriman and Bob McNamara." He went on to say, "I know that McNamara and Mac Bundy always used to regard me as some sort of clown, but McNamara could play a very important role in this."

None of us had mentioned the weekend photographs showing Hubert embracing Governor Lester Maddox of Georgia; but he brought it up himself before he left and launched into a long, labored, unconvincing and pathetic apologia. Maddox had said to him, "You know, Mr. Vice President, as governor of Georgia, I am governor of all the people—whites, Negroes, capitalists, socialists. A lot of my old friends don't understand this, and now they think I am betraying them." Hubert Humphrey said that he replied, "I know exactly what you mean." This psychological bond having been established, Hubert Humphrey tried, he said, to wean Maddox away from George Wallace and keep him a Democrat. As for taking Maddox's arm, this, he said, was to help him walk down the steps; he seemed old and infirm.

I think I was depressed most of all by the lack of the sense of the concrete human dimension of problems which characterized the old Hubert. Not once in his long discourse on Vietnam did he express any dismay over the human wreckage wrought by the American policy; nor did his discourse on Maddox show any understanding why so many people were disappointed and shocked by the picture. This trailing off of humanity is accompanied by an obvious delight in hobnobbing with statesmen—many mentions of the Pope, de Gaulle, [Sarrepalli] Radhakrishnan, etc., etc., etc.

After he left I said that I now saw no choice but to vote Republican in 1968—that this would be the only way to bring the war to an end.

April 27

We are reaching some sort of crisis on Vietnam. LBJ has evidently decided on a quick and brutal escalation of the war. It was clear in February that he did not wish negotiation until the existing military balance could be turned considerably in our favor; and his clear intention now is to bomb North Vietnam until Hanoi is prepared to sue for peace on terms which will meet Rusk's idea of a satisfactory settlement. More than that, the administration is apparently determined to advance the proposition that dissent is unpatriotic, and has brought General Westmoreland back for this purpose.

The irony is that all of us for years have been defending the presidential prerogative and regarding the Congress as a drag on policy. It is evident now that this delight in a strong presidency was based on the fact that, up to now, all strong Presidents in American history have pursued policies of which one has approved. We are now confronted by the anomaly of a strong President using these arguments to pursue a course which, so far as I can see, can lead only to disaster. It is not hard to assert a congressional role; but, given the structure of the American system, it is very hard to see how the Congress can restrain the presidential drive toward the enlargement of the war. Voting against military appropriations is both humanly and politically self-defeating. The only hope is to organize a broad political movement; and even this cannot take effect until, at the very earliest, the 1968 primaries, which may be too late.

May 13

On Sunday, the 7th, I went to Cambridge. In the afternoon I met with a group of Students for a Democratic Society leaders (a meeting arranged by Chrissie). A photograph of Che Guevara hung in the hall of a studiously bare and dreary apartment on Dana Street. The group ranged from disaffected young gentlemen to embittered figures from public high schools. One had a sense of deep frustration, decent concrete feeling and murky abstractions. When I asked them about their long-run vision of American society, they were exceedingly generalized and obscure; but they defended this plausibly by saying that, at the moment, they could not affect this much, so why think about it? Their interest, they said, was in things they could do something about—local organization of labor and the poor, Harvard matters, etc. This is really quite sensible and much to be preferred to the ideological megalomania of the leftists of the thirties. However, when they later got to their analysis of contemporary American society, they sounded exactly like a crowd of Trotskyites of thirty years ago and filled me with a certain irritated nostalgia. The big corporations run everything; thus someone said triumphantly to me, apropos of the CIA coup against [Guatemalan president Jacobo] Arbenz Guzmán under the Eisenhower administration, "What did Bedell Smith do after he left the State Department? He became a member of the board of directors of United Fruit." I tried to say that business motives dominated only in areas of limited government interest but that, in my experience, in vital areas political and strategic considerations were more important. They regarded this with polite skepticism.

That morning the *Times* had printed two stories in adjoining columns—one describing a recommendation from the National Rifle Association that its members form posses to put down violence in the cities; the other reporting that the New Left is developing an interest in "urban guerrilla movements." I asked how the guerrilla effort was coming in Cambridge (joke). They disclaimed any local efforts but acknowledged a growing sense within the New Left of the inevitability of violence—defensive, of course. "If the National Rifle Association is going to organize posses, why shouldn't we protect ourselves against them?" I can't make out how serious this is and retain the suspicion that 20 years from now most of the people in the room will be quiet insurance brokers or real estate men. But maybe not: there is plainly a massive spiritual defection of some sort from American society. I think we underrate the monarchical susceptibilities in any nation. The President sets the tone to an extraordinary degree. I can't imagine quite this conversation in the Kennedy years; however skeptical this kind of boy was about JFK, the leftists of the early sixties acknowleged a relationship; Kennedy was within their orbit of discourse. LBJ might as well be a creature from outer space.

I might interrupt at this point to note a curious encounter at a *Newsweek* party on April 25. I took Grace Kennan McClatchy, who happened to be in town. At one point we ran into Nelson Rockefeller. I introduced Grace as George Kennan's daughter. Nelson fixed her with an earnest look and said, "Is your father really sure about what he is doing?" Grace indicated puzzlement, and Nelson said, "Is he really sure that this woman who says she is Svetlana Stalin *is* Svetlana Stalin." Then he ascertained that George had met her only once in the thirties when she was a young girl, and he said triumphantly, "Well, how can he be sure she is the same woman?" He then outlined a James Bond theory that the alleged Svetlana Stalin may be a double agent endowed with a persuasive cover sent to the United States for some sinister purpose (presumably to pick up information at the Johnson estate on Long Island). He was completely serious, and the whole incident was preposterous and disconcerting. It reminded me that Rockefeller, for all his good qualities, is slightly obsessed on the subject of communism. One remembers his passion about building nuclear shelters and his opposition to the test ban treaty. I imagine that he may be more of a hawk on Vietnam than LBJ. It is too bad, because he would be the most powerful candidate the Republicans could nominate (though he would have an easier time winning the election than the nomination).

On May 3, I set out on a brief lecture tour to upstate New York. When I called Gretchen from the Syracuse airport late that afternoon, she said that Bob McNamara had been calling me. I called him back, and he came out of a meeting to say that he wanted to talk to me; when was I next coming to Washington? I said I would be there on Saturday, May 6, which turned out to be a day when he was tied up with the Heineman Committee. He asked me to be sure and let him know when I would next be down. I said, "Of course, I will, and I would be glad to hear what is going on." Bob said, "There's no point in your listening to me. I've been wrong from the start on Vietnam. The record shows that.

I want to hear your ideas." McNamara remains one of the most disarming men in the United States.

September 26

I went to Washington this weekend for the Americans for Democratic Action National Board meeting. The organization is on the verge of a split between the labor people who are irrevocably pro-Johnson, and most of the liberals who are deeply opposed to the widening of the war in Vietnam and are increasingly anti-Johnson. Neither side wished a showdown, however, so we voted down a "dump-Johnson" resolution to please one side and then vigorously attacked the war to please the other.

I had dinner at Hickory Hill on both Saturday and Sunday nights. Allard Lowenstein came out on Saturday night (along with Jim Loeb and Jack Newfield) and set forth in glowing and confident language his conviction that Johnson could be beaten in a string of primaries. I can't make Lowenstein out. Jimmy Wechsler is very high on him; Joe Rauh had been but now regards him as tricky and unreliable. All I know is that he is awfully sure about a number of things that no one can be sure about. I think that RFK is attracted, though, by his thesis that LBJ is more unpopular than the war, and that he would be more vulnerable to a campaign based on alternative candidacies than to one based on de-escalation.

October 18

George McGovern called yesterday and said, among other things, that he thought Eugene McCarthy had about decided to go—i.e., that he would enter the New Hampshire, Wisconsin, California and Massachusetts primaries against Johnson. The ironies of politics: Gene came to Los Angeles seven years ago hoping to be Johnson's vice presidential candidate. He has been a disappointing senator, especially in his laziness and in his acquiescence to the legislative views of the Minneapolis–

St. Paul banners. But he is a most intelligent and attractive man; he has evidently come to feel deeply about Vietnam; and I cannot see that his entry into the primaries will do anything but good. It might, indeed, open the way for a serious draft-RFK movement—a result which would vastly irritate Gene, who has never much liked the Kennedys (especially in view of the fact that Gene has been urging Bobby to run for some time).

November 7

I spent [Saturday] night at Hickory Hill and talked to RFK both that night and the next morning about 1968. I had sent him a letter setting forth my own recent change of views. His general feeling is that it would be a great mistake for him to challenge Johnson at this point—that it would be considered evidence of his ruthlessness, his ambition and of a personal vendetta. On the other hand, he fully recognizes that the situation has changed a good deal and may change a lot more. He thinks that McCarthy's entry into the primaries will help open things up, though he is perplexed as to how he should handle this himself. He acknowledges the danger that McCarthy might be successful enough to prevent the emergence of another anti-LBJ candidate, but feels he has no alternative but to wait. His hope is that, as McCarthy beats LBJ in primaries, state political leaders, faced with the prospect of local disaster if LBJ heads the ticket, will come to him and ask him to run in the interests of the party. In the meantime, he is refurbishing his national contacts.

November 29

After lecturing in Montclair, New Jersey, I returned to New York and met RFK around 11 at the King Cole Bar. Pierre Salinger, the vanden Heuvels and Tom Johnson were also there. Two dominating subjects, of course: McNamara and McCarthy.

On McNamara, RFK said that Bob had *not* had any intimation that Johnson had sent his name up for the [World] Bank. He had had a general conversation with Johnson about it last spring following George Woods's initial conversation with him; but that was all. Then suddenly he heard, not from the President but from a leak in London, that he was on his way out. I expressed incredulity at Bob's apparent acquiescence in this. Wouldn't any self-respecting man, I asked Bobby, have his resignation on the President's desk half an hour after he heard the London bulletin? Isn't that what you would do? I am not asking that Bob go in a public clamor; but why does he not resign quietly and go back to private life? Why does he fall in with LBJ's plan to silence him and cover everything up? Bobby listened silently and a little gloomily. He said that he thought that that was what would finally happen—that Bob would not take the World Bank job and would instead quietly resign from government. Obviously this is what Bobby had been urging him to do. When we broke up around one, we got copies of the morning *Times*. The headline: MCNAMARA TAKES WORLD BANK POST. Bobby was evidently surprised and sad about this.

As for McCarthy, Bobby said that he had come in to see him the other day and stayed for seven minutes. During this time, McCarthy said nothing about his own plans, with relation either to organization or to issues, and showed no interest in RFK's thoughts about these questions. "He is a very strange fellow," Bobby said. "After all, I don't want to blow my own trumpet, but I have a little experience running primaries. But he didn't ask a single question." Teddy apparently had had a similar experience. Also Gene told Bobby one thing and Teddy another on certain things—whether he would enter New Hampshire, Massachusetts and the like—but Bobby thought this was indecision and not at all duplicity. "He should go up to New Hampshire and hold a press conference. He should say that he does not expect to win and that he is entering the primary in order to give Democrats a chance to discuss the issues. Kennedy polled 44,000 votes in New Hampshire in 1960, so he expects that Johnson would get at least 40,000 this time. For his part, he does not expect to get more than 5,000 or 7,000. But he stands for the Kennedy tradition in the party, and he wants to carry that tradition forward in our national life." Then, Bobby said, he should walk the streets in every New

Hampshire town, without entourage or fanfare. He should not talk about Vietnam very much, since he has all the peace votes already. He should run against the organization, against the Democratic establishment, against the big shots. Bobby doubts whether Johnson can get more than 20,000 votes and thinks that McCarthy would have a good chance of actually winning.

Bobby says that the only primaries which really matter are New Hampshire and Wisconsin: McCarthy should concentrate all his effort there. He thinks that California comes too late to make any difference. As for himself, he says that he will have to fish or cut bait within a couple of weeks after the New Hampshire primary. If McCarthy should win in New Hampshire and Wisconsin, I think Bobby might well decide to enter the California primary himself.

December 7

I lunched today with Henry Kissinger at the Century. Walter Lippmann joined us. The central implicit subject of conversation was, of course, Rockefeller. I should perhaps say, if I have not done so already, that I have run into Happy Rockefeller a couple of times at dinner (at the Wrightsmans' and at Brooke Astor's) earlier this autumn.

Nelson was not present on either of these occasions (speaking engagements), and I was later told by Babe Paley (and by Joan Braden) that he had another girl—his present secretary. Henry Kissinger said that, if this might have been true once, it was not presently the case. Nelson, he said, always requires the emotional support of women who work closely with him. He got this from Happy; and, when Happy moved on from secretary to wife, she removed herself from the picture and made some sort of local succession inevitable. Joan Braden said much the same thing: that Nelson depends profoundly on feminine enthusiasm, and that Happy should have known what she was getting into.

Henry is bringing in a group of experts every week to brief Rockefeller on the big issues. We asked about Nelson's views on Vietnam.

Henry was reassuring, saying that Nelson's views were identical with his own. He made absolutely clear his own opposition to further escalation and his own skepticism about the administration's attitude toward negotiation. He had seen Johnson a few times this winter in connection with a Hanoi peace feeler with which he became accidentally but deeply involved; and he has come away with a conviction that LBJ's resistance to negotiation verges on a sort of madness. Henry feels that practically anyone would be better than Johnson.

Dick Goodwin feels the same way. We had a drink (several drinks) at P.J. Clarke's Sunday night on the evening of his return from England and Morocco. As he has many times before, Dick suggested, without especially documenting, his sense that the President was governed by motives so personal and irrational that his continuation in office would be disastrous. He told of one evening in the White House when Johnson, in a state of exasperation, said of the *New York Times* and the *Washington Post* that they were run by Communists—and he apparently meant this, not polemically or metaphorically, but quite literally. It is depressing to think that three of the great world leaders of 1967—Mao, de Gaulle and Johnson—are slightly crazy (and most of the rest are mediocrities).

This evening, moving to another phase of life, I had dinner with Marlene Dietrich, Angie Dickinson and Burt Bacharach. My friendship with Marlene began some years ago when I attacked Herman Wouk's *The Caine Mutiny Court-Martial* as a demoralizing play (because of its insistence that reverence for authority, even if the embodiment of authority should be, like Captain Queeg, cowardly and mad, is more essential to the preservation of society than the mutiny of rootless intellectuals like Keefer). One day in Cambridge I received a phone call from someone who identified herself as Marlene Dietrich. I naturally assumed this to be a joke; but it turned out really to be Marlene, and she congratulated me on my piece in the *New York Post*, saying that in her view *The Caine Mutiny Court-Martial* was, in effect, a Nazi play. Soon we met one night at dinner at Nat Benchley's. We have seen each other intermittently since.

December 10

RFK finally summoned a council of war today on 1968. It took place at a Sunday luncheon at Bill vanden Heuvel's. Present, in addition to Bobby and Bill, were Ted Kennedy, Ted Sorensen, Dick Goodwin, Fred Dutton, Pierre Salinger and myself.

The serious discussion began with my putting the case for his running in 1968. I said that, if the Democrats lost this time, it might change things the way the 1932 election did and lead to a long period of Republican supremacy; that, if McCarthy did moderately well in the primaries, he might expose Johnson without establishing himself; that state leaders would understand that their own tickets would go down if LBJ were at the head of the ticket; and that Bobby should then emerge as a candidate, rescue the party and end the war in Vietnam. The dissension in the Democratic party, I said, would tempt the Republicans to nominate Nixon, who would be the easiest candidate to beat.

Dick Goodwin then argued a slightly different case for running now—entering the primaries, assuming a McCarthy withdrawal, and carrying the fight through to the convention.

RFK then said that the talk up to this point had revolved around himself and the party. He did think another factor should be weighed— i.e., the country. From his own self-interest, the renomination and re-election of Johnson might be the most desirable thing; but he was not sure whether the country or the world could survive five more years of Johnson. Whether or not he was sure of winning, was there not a case for trying in 1968?

Ted Kennedy and, later, Ted Sorensen put the case for waiting. Ted Kennedy's view was that LBJ is sure of reelection and that Bobby is sure of nomination in 1972. Dick suggested that LBJ, if reelected, would use all his wiles and powers to prevent RFK's nomination. (Bobby interjected, "He would die and make Hubert President rather than let me get it.") Ted felt that he would try this, but his capacity to do damage would be limited. To do anything now, Ted said, would be to jeopardize, if not destroy, Bobby's future.

Ted Sorensen thought it would be futile to go into the primaries and impossible to buck up the McCarthy effort without implicating the Kennedys in his failure. RFK added that, if Gene had any success, he wouldn't get out, no matter what he might be saying at this point. The most important thing, Ted said, was to make RFK President, and the sooner the better; but 1972 seemed to him the propitious year.

Pierre, who said afterward that he agreed philosophically with me and politically with Ted Sorensen, questioned the inevitability of LBJ's reelection. He said that no one should underestimate the total alienation from the President, especially among the young.

Ted said that maybe we should consider how Johnson might be induced not to run again. Three things might lead him to such a decision: being beaten in the primaries; or sinking even lower in the polls; or being urged by party leaders not to run again. The general feeling was that he would do better in the polls as the election approached, and that McCarthy would not do well in the primaries. Ted also suggested that options be kept open and quiet preparations made for every contingency: space in Chicago, contacts around the country, etc.

Bobby said that he was by no means sure he would be any stronger in 1972 than he is now. He would have been around five years longer, taken more positions, estranged more interests, gained more enemies. Perhaps he would never be stronger than he is today. Suppose he entered the six primaries and won them: would he then get the nomination? Ted Sorensen said no; LBJ would still get it. RFK rather disagreed. A series of primary victories, he said, would have an impact on other delegations and change the picture. There was then some discussion about filing dates, etc.

It seemed evident that Bobby is sorely tempted. He would in a way like to get into the fight, and he also is deeply fearful of what another Johnson term might do to the world. But he said that practically he did not suppose he would have much chance of getting the nomination, though he thought, if he did, he could beat Nixon. He added that people in whom he had confidence were strongly opposed to his doing anything, nor, so far as he could see, were many people in the party for it. So he supposed he would do nothing, and nothing would happen. He said this regretfully and fatalistically. But he said no final decisions had to be made for a few more weeks, and in the meantime everyone should keep on brooding about the problem.

The meeting, as is evident, was troubled and inconclusive. Bobby was torn, rueful, enormously attracted by the idea of moving, but at the same time impressed by the lack of belief on the part of serious politicians that he should.

1968

January 10

RFK was at Jackie's on Monday; and last night (Tuesday), after dining with Roger Stevens at La Grenouille, I joined Bobby, George and
Liz Stevens, Sidney Poitier and John Glenn at Orsini's. Bobby said that
the California politicians—Jesse Unruh and others—wanted him to enter the California primary and assured him he could win; but he was
skeptical of their motives—they wanted this, he thought, to help themselves, not to help him.

January 19

While on the slopes of Sun Valley a few weeks ago, RFK evidently
decided it might be a good idea to have a talk with Walter Lippmann.
As a result, they had a meeting on Wednesday (January 17), and Bobby
asked me to come along with him. As we drove to the Lippmann apartment, I warned him (a) that Walter had known every top American

political leader since Theodore Roosevelt and, having survived so many generations of politicians, was no longer impressed by any particular generation; and (b) that Helen, having abandoned the Catholic Church, could not help thinking there must be something wrong with those who stayed. I also said that Walter was by nature diffident and often gave the impression of coolness, but this should not be taken personally.

When we arrived, Walter met us at the door and greeted Bobby with surprising warmth. Helen joined us, and we had a drink and about an hour's talk. Bobby did most of the talking. I have never heard him more eloquent. After a preliminary chat about Arizona (from which the Lippmanns have just returned) and Vietnam, RFK began talking about the McCarthy candidacy. He said that he feared it would be ineffectual; that McCarthy might do tolerably in New Hampshire if he went about it the right way, but that he probably wouldn't; and that, if McCarthy flopped, Johnson would undoubtedly interpret this as a mandate to do anything he wanted about the war. He then said rather abruptly that he had to decide what to do himself. He set forth with evident feeling his concern about the country, the war, the young, the Negroes, his sense that we are drifting toward disaster and his conviction that there were so many things which might be done to improve the situation. Did this mean that he should run himself? Four more years of Johnson would be a "catastrophe" for the country; but so would be four years of Nixon.

Moreover—and this point worries him deeply—he does not see how he can overcome the advantage enjoyed by Johnson through his command of the war. Obviously nothing would restrain Johnson from manipulating the war in whatever way would help him politically—he would escalate, de-escalate, pause, bomb, stall, negotiate as the domestic political situation indicated. "For example," Bobby said, "suppose, in the middle of the California primary, when I am attacking him on the war, he should suddenly stop the bombing and go off to Geneva to hold talks with the North Vietnamese. What do I do then? Either I call his action phoney, in which case I am lining up with Ho Chi Minh, or else I have to say that all Americans should support the President in his search for peace. In either case, I am likely to lose in California."

And yet he felt that he had some responsibility and some remaining influence, and that he ought to do something. The Lippmanns listened intently and, for the most part, silently. Walter did not deliver a strong argument for Bobby's running, perhaps because he was impressed by Bobby's presentation of the complexities of the situation, perhaps because he does not regard it as his job to offer advice to politicians. When Bobby finally asked him what he thought, Lippmann said, "Well, if you believe that Johnson's reelection would be a catastrophe for the country—and I entirely agree with you on this—then, if this comes about, the question you must live with is whether you did everything you could do to avert this catastrophe." Bobby said that he agreed with that, he agreed that he must do something, but he was not sure that his declaring for the nomination might not make things worse, or ensure the election of a Republican.

I am now at St. Paul's School, where I am spending three days as a Conroy Fellow. I called George McGovern this morning to discuss Bobby's problem. George said that a month ago he had thought Bobby should go, and Bobby had asked him to take soundings. He had talked to Gaylord Nelson, Frank Church, Quentin Burdick, Governor [Harold] Hughes of Iowa and others, and the results had been, George said, most surprising and disappointing. He found universal reluctance even to consider the possibility, and certainly no one was prepared to do anything about it. There was general agreement that RFK would run better, but no one felt this strongly enough to consider either asking LBJ not to run or asking Bobby to run. "The trouble," George said, "is that everyone seems only interested in taking care of himself. This is the atmosphere Johnson has created. Everyone I talked to took the view: what would this do for me? No one was ready to stick his neck out."

January 25

The ordeal continues. I have never seen RFK so torn about anything— I do not mean visibly torn, since he preserves his wryness and equanimity through it all, but never so obviously divided. The decision in a sense seemed to have been settled by events a few weeks back. When we met before Christmas and the sense of the advice was against doing anything, that seemed to have settled it. Few would have been surprised if there were no further speculation. He has revived it himself; and I think essentially out of conscience. I think that he cannot bear the thought of consigning the country to four more years of LBJ without having done something to avert this.

I now really think he should [run]. I think that the tendency, with the polls and so on, is to view politics as a mechnical process. In fact, it is a chemical process. I think that his entry into the situation as a candidate would begin to transform the situation and create new possibilities not presently foreseeable.

Tonight Marian and I had dinner with Bobby and Ethel at La Caravelle. Bobby said that his brother Ted was the strongest opponent of his moving. Ethel, it developed, was, or seemed, very much in favor of his going ahead. We traversed fairly familiar ground, with Bobby still vividly concerned that his entrance into the contest would be attributed to his ruthless ambition, his feuding with LBJ and so on. He really thinks that he is a fairly unpopular figure through the country and he is impressed by the widespread lack of enthusiasm for his candidacy among his political friends in the party. He had seen Pat Lucey of Wisconsin in the afternoon, and Pat had advised him against running. Yet he can't give the idea up.

January 30

Close or not, [the decision] has been made, and he is not going to do it.

If I were to reconstruct his reasons, I would guess that three things in particular led him to the negative decision:

(1) the absence of any demand for his candidacy on the part of people who control delegates at the convention, apart from California. His best political friends through the country were opposed. Those who said they would come out for him, like George McGovern and

Governor Hughes of Iowa, concede that his candidacy would make their own contests more difficult; this might saddle him with the responsibility for their defeat.

(2) the difficulty of figuring out how to campaign against a President who is in command of the war and is prepared to manipulate his control in any way which will promote his political ambitions—to escalate or de-escalate, to bomb or stop bombing, to create incidents or to negotiate; and who would in addition give out the impression that he had been about to achieve a negotiated settlement, but, when the ambitious brother of a former President had challenged him, this encouraged Hanoi so much that they decided to continue the war, and that RFK in consequence would be responsible for the death of all American GIs after the announcement of his candidacy.

(3) his own odd conviction about himself that he is a rather unpopular figure, that people regard him as totally ruthless and ambitious, as animated by a personal feud with LBJ and so on.

Anyway that's where we are.

February 10

In our conversations since the last entry [RFK] seemed rueful but fairly philosophical. Others, however, have described him as sad and frustrated. My own suspicion is that the decision is not really final (how Stevensonian can we all get!).

February 19

On Friday, February 16, I lunched with Nelson Rockefeller and Henry Kissinger. The lunch resulted, I think, from a couple of talks at dinner with Happy Rockefeller last autumn and from the interest of Henry Kissinger. It took place at 13 West 54th Street in a high-ceilinged, second-floor apartment in a rather battered old brownstone. This had been an old Rockefeller residence, it developed. The furnishing was pleasantly masculine. A photograph of FDR was prominently displayed—"for my old friend, Nelson Rockefeller." The pictures in the dining room were superb.

When we sat down to lunch (good), I asked [Rockefeller] whether I could make him a short speech about the implications of the present political situation. I then made my point about the disenfranchisement of the young and argued the urgency of someone doing something to restore meaning to the presidential process. Otherwise the country risks a massive defection of the young to SDS [Students for a Democratic Society] or LSD. I said that he and RFK were the main hopes; RFK had decided for powerful reasons not to go; and therefore a good deal rested on his shoulders. He said that he thought Bobby had a greater appeal to the disaffected than he did. I agreed; but said that, in Bobby's absence, he would get tremendous support from the young. I then said that RFK had no interest in defeating Johnson in order to bring in Nixon. Nelson said, "I couldn't agree more."

Nelson did not state any positions on Vietnam; but the conversation skirted the subject a great deal of the time, and the tacit assumption of the talk was that he agreed with Henry and me on the futility of the present policy and the illusions of the Johnson administration.

At one point Nelson said to me, "You know, I have my roots in the New Deal. It was my experience those early days in Washington which has enabled me as governor to do imaginative things in social legislation, fiscal policy and so on."

On to Washington for a big, gay, pretty party at Hickory Hill in anticipation of Ethel's great charity telethon. The party was filled with television entertainers and professional football players, with a smattering of politicans and film stars—everyone from Bill Fulbright to Carol Channing, and from Alice Longworth to Roosevelt Grier.

I had a long talk with Bob McNamara, who looked gray and desperately tired. He said he could not wait for March 1 (the date on which he will be sprung). I congratulated him on his *Meet the Press* broadcast on February 4—on the tact with which he had made his own points about the fallibility of government officials without violating his loyalty to the administration. He said that he had been called at five minutes to eleven on the Friday night preceding, when he was visiting Margie in the hospital, and told that they wanted him to do it and planned to announce it in the 11 o'clock news. He said that from then until the broadcast on Sunday he had been acutely nervous, not wanting to say anything about our situation in Vietnam that he did not believe but fearful that he would either have to do this or appear to let the administration down.

I forgot to say that during an interval at lunch with Rockefeller, while he was taking a phone call out of the room, Henry Kissinger told me about a scene which he witnessed in the Cabinet Room: Johnson harrying McNamara, saying to him insistently: "How can I hit them [the North Vietnamese] in the nuts? Tell me how I can hit them in the nuts." Rusk, Henry said, was honorable but hopelessly rigid. Rostow, on the other hand, systematically put things to the President in a way which involved the President's ego in his own side of the argument— e.g., he would begin an argument against exploring negotiation possibilities with Hanoi by saying, "Mr. President, Hanoi does you the honor of regarding you as a serious man, and they would think that, if you did such-and-such, you were not being serious."

March 13

Here we go again!—if a little late. I went to Cambridge on Sunday (the 10th) for a meeting the next day of the Government Department Visiting Committee. While I was at the Galbraiths' Sunday evening, Ethel Kennedy called. She had just spoken to RFK, who was in California, and was now transmitting the long awaited message: he would definitely run if Eugene McCarthy could be persuaded to withdraw.

This decision came, of course, on the brink of the New Hampshire primary. It seemed obvious that McCarthy could not make any counter-decision until the count, and that, if he did well, it would be asking a good deal for him then to make way for somebody else.

McCarthy got 42 percent of the popular vote and, because of the way delegates are elected, at least 20 out of 24 delegates.

I went to dinner [Tuesday] at Ham Armstrong's—the Anthony Edens, Jack McCloys, Bill and Judith Moyers, Nin Ryan. I had a fascinating talk with Bill. He thinks that LBJ is now well sealed off from reality; the White House atmosphere, he said, is "impenetrable." He also feels that LBJ explains away all criticism as based on personal or political antagonism; Bill used the word "paranoid." He said that he had himself such a personal debt to Johnson that it had taken him a long time to reach these conclusions, and even longer to say them; but he felt that four more years of Johnson would be ruinous for the country.

[Later] at the 21 [Club] I found Bobby, looking a little subdued, with Bill vanden Heuvel and Tom Johnson. Sandy Vanocur and his wife were there for a time; but, after they left, we began a serious conversation. RFK felt that McCarthy's success had boxed him in. Obviously he could not now expect Gene to withdraw. "I don't blame him at all," he said. "Of course he feels that he gave me my chance to make the try, that I didn't and that he has earned the right to go ahead. I can't blame him. He has done a great job in opening the situation up." I suggested the possibility of his endorsing Gene on the theory that Gene could not possibly get the nomination, but he could, with Bobby's support, show the vulnerability of Johnson. Then, when McCarthy reached his limit, he would be obliged to come out for RFK; and, with the professionals (such as they are) now convinced that Johnson was loser, the nomination would inexorably go to Bobby. He listened but was not deeply impressed; he again cited the difficulty of saying, or seeming to say, that he really wanted Gene for President. We left, all perplexed and rather dejected, shortly after midnight.

The next morning Ken called with a better plan: that is, that Kennedy should run in some states, McCarthy in others, and that the weaker should support the stronger against Johnson in the convention. I spoke to Bobby, who was back in Washington, and he said there was to be a meeting at Steve Smith's apartment in the afternoon.

Present, when I arrived, were Steve, Ted Kennedy, Ted Sorensen, Burke Marshall, Bill vanden Heuvel, Tom Johnston, John Burnes, Jack English, Jerry Bruno, Pierre Salinger, Dave Burke, Milt Gwirtzman, perhaps one or two others. Ted Kennedy, who looked flushed and a bit unhappy, set forth the various options open—from total inaction to total participation. Ted Sorensen once again made the argument against moving in 1968. He proposed that RFK continue speaking on the issues but remain neutral as between McCarthy and Johnson.

I had to leave about 6:30 to speak to a Wall Street group at 21 (for $1,000). When I got back to Steve's, Bobby and Ethel had arrived; also Ken O'Donnell and Fred Dutton. The evening by this time had become thoroughly disorganized. Everyone was watching Bobby's (very effective) interview with Walter Cronkite. I had a long quiet talk with Ken and Fred, both of whom were dissatisfied with the way things were going. Ken was very emphatic. "What Bobby has to decide is who is first. Personally I think Uncle Sam is first and RFK second. Sometimes I think they tend to reverse the order. If he decides that Uncle Sam is first, he ought to do what is right for Uncle Sam and not worry about what is right for RFK. Hell, maybe it would be better to wait for 1972, when a hundred thousand Americans will be killed in Vietnam; but I don't think so. The right thing to do is for him to run and not worry about the consequences to himself." Dutton and Ken felt that the organizational talk and planning during the evening had been hopelessly amateurish, that we were weeks and months behind, that no one was focusing on the priorities.

Bobby asked me to ride downtown with Ethel. He said, "Are you happy about this?" I said I was. He looked searchingly at me and said, "But you have some reservations, don't you?" I said, no, I had no reservations. (Actually I have a reservation, but it does not have to do with his decision; it has only to do with the effect that decision will have on my plan to get started on volume iv of FDR.) I then said that he must make a decision soon. He said that he planned to do this in the next thirty-six hours.

He [saw] McCarthy [the next day]. The talk, he said, was friendly but did not go very far. He had congratulated McCarthy on his success and told him that he was reassessing his own situation. McCarthy had accepted that, said he had a perfect right to go ahead but that he did not intend to get out himself. He then repeated the bit about serving only one term as President—this apparently is a matter of constitutional principle for him—and saying that, "while I'm not making an offer," RFK might be the logical successor.

March 17

I had a quick luncheon with Bill vanden Heuvel [on Friday, March 15] and spent most of the afternoon at a Projects Committee meeting at the 20th Century Fund. Then Bill and I caught the 7 o'clock shuttle to Washington to spend the evening with Bobby in what we expected to be the last serious conference before the decision.

When Bill and I arrived at Hickory Hill we found—inevitably—a party in progress. Fred Dutton was there, visibly discontented at the lack of serious attention to the decision, and in due course Ted [Sorensen] arrived, also dismayed by the frivolity. Finally around 10:30 we settled down with Bobby for a serious talk, along with Adam Walinsky, Allard Loewenstein, a bright fellow named [Jeff] Greenfield from Bobby's office and George Stevens Jr.

Bill and I had been greatly impressed, and depressed, by the bitterness among liberals who had developed an emotional attachment to McCarthy. The newspaper reports that Bobby might now enter the contest himself had already begun to revive the theory of RFK as a ruthless opportunist; and we strongly emphasized the necessity of conciliating the McCarthy people. Ted, though he had opposed Bobby's going at all, had written the statement in this sense, and Bobby had accepted this as the essential strategy toward McCarthy. We discussed various expressions of the harmony approach—Bobby campaigning for McCarthy in Wisconsin, a joint delegation in California, etc., and finally went to bed around 1:30.

About four hours later I was awakened by someone in my bedroom hoarsely whispering, "Ted. Ted." It was Teddy Kennedy looking for Ted Sorensen. I asked him how it had gone with McCarthy. He said, "Very unsatisfactory; very unsatisfactory. His people had seemed to be for it, but he wouldn't go along. I think his wife was against it." (When he woke Bill vanden Heuvel, he said more succinctly, "Abigail said no.") This was depressing, but I was so exhausted that I went back to sleep. An hour or so later I was awakened again—this time by Bobby, wandering in rather gloomily in pajamas with short pants. He asked me whether I had heard about Teddy's mission. I said I had. He then said, "What do you think I should do?" I said that if McCarthy would not collaborate, and if a Kennedy-McCarthy contest split the anti-LBJ vote in any state and elected a Johnson delegation, it would take some people a long time to forgive him. He said morosely, "Well, I have to say something in three hours." I said, "Why not come out for McCarthy? Every McCarthy delegate will be a potential Kennedy delegate. He can't possibly win, so you will be the certain inheritor of his support. In the meantime, go on speaking as much as you can." He looked at me stonily and said, "I can't do that. It would be too humiliating. Kennedys don't act that way." He stayed a moment longer and then left the room.

I went downstairs where I found Teddy Kennedy, Ted Sorensen and Bill sitting around the breakfast table. Sorensen said, "Have you talked to him?" I said I had and told them what I had said. Someone said, "Where is he now?" Sorensen said, "He is upstairs looking for someone else to wake up in the hope of finding someone who agrees with him." We mournfully discussed the situation. By this point, Bill and I had proposed that he come out for McCarthy, and I think that both Teds thought that would be preferable to declaring for himself. Then Bobby himself came into the room; he may have heard the last part of our talk. He said, "Look, fellows, I can't do that. I can't come out for McCarthy. Let's not talk about that anymore. I'm going ahead, and there is no point in talking about anything else." With this he left.

Soon Bobby reappeared, now half dressed, and we reviewed the statement as redrafted by Ted in light of Teddy's meeting with Mc-Carthy. Bobby was in better humor. At one point, inserting something in the statement, he said, "It doesn't make sense without that—not that anything we are doing today makes sense anyway." Later he said, "Let's put something in about healing the wounds of the country" and added, "by splitting the Democratic party into three pieces." Finally he went upstairs to finish dressing. Then a barber appeared, and Teddy said to him, "Cut it as close as you can. Don't pay any attention to anything he says; cut off as much as you can." I went into the living room to read the morning *Times*. David Kennedy, a grave and sweet child, like all the Kennedy children, came to me and said, "Is Daddy going to run for President?" I said that he was.

Shortly after 9:30 we drove into Washington. The announcement took place in the Caucus Room in the Old Senate Office Building—where JFK had announced at the same age, eight years earlier. The room was crowded, and Dutton, vanden Heuvel and I decided to watch it all on television in Teddy's office on the floor above. It went off exceedingly well, and our spirits began to lift. Afterward Bobby went off to the St. Patrick's parade in New York, and we began to consider the campaign problems.

So this has been his own decision—and I now think he was probably right, which confirms my general theory that the principal knows better than his advisers, which is why they are only advisers and he is the principal.

This morning (Sunday) I spoke at a McCarthy fund-raising breakfast. I had agreed to do this a fortnight ago; but, especially in view of the policy of conciliation, it seemed best to keep the engagement. I explained that, now that he had announced, I was for RFK, but that I was for McCarthy in Ohio and Wisconsin and was glad to speak on his behalf. We raised about $8,000. In consequence, I was considerably irritated later in the day when Dick Wade read me from Chicago an item in the *Sun-Times* in which McCarthy made a sarcastic attack on me for abandoning his campaign. I was never in his campaign; indeed, I have spoken to him only once in the last six months; and he could have had no doubt that, if Bobby were to become a candidate, I would of course be with him. But Gene is given to self-pity and bitterness—traits which will probably stand us in good stead in the longer run.

March 19

RFK called about 9 and chatted for half an hour; or rather Ethel put in the call since he was at Hickory Hill, and then he came on the line; much like Jackie and JFK in 1960.

He seemed relaxed and cheerful and kept saying, "Are you glad I'm doing this?" I said that I am glad and that I now felt I had been wrong in telling him not to run on Saturday morning. He said, "Well, you were right earlier, and I was wrong then."

April 3

It is all moving faster than one could have supposed. On Sunday night, March 31, I went to my first meeting of the National Society of Film Critics, to which I have just been elected. In the midst of all this, some critic's wife telephoned to say that Johnson had announced he would not run again. For a moment the group regarded this as a misunderstanding or a put-on; but then I called Jimmy Wechsler, who confirmed it. RFK was supposed to arrive in New York that evening at 9:45, so, when the film critics adjourned, I made my way over to the apartment. I arrived to find total bemusement. Present were Dutton, Sorensen, vanden Heuvel, Walinsky and a group of younger men. Ted had already written a telegram to go to LBJ requesting a meeting and was at work on a statement. Bobby was on the telephone calling, and receiving calls from, political figures around the country. The mood was one of astonishment, a certain perplexity and a general, non-exuberant, incredulous feeling that RFK would be our next President.

Bobby himself looked terribly tired; he has been whirling around the country, has had little time for reflection and was plainly uncertain of what to make of the new situation. In the meantime, the telephone kept ringing.

On Tuesday night, April 2, I dined at Diana Vreeland's with Jackie and Paul Mathias (*Paris-Match*). We watched the Wisconsin results on Diana's prehistoric television, while Jackie reminisced about the difficulties of campaigning there in 1960; she found the people of West

Virginia much warmer. At one point in the evening she took me aside and said, "Do you know what I think will happen to Bobby if he is elected President?" I said no. She said, "The same thing that happened to Jack. . . . There is so much hatred in this country, and more people hate Bobby than hate Jack. That's why I don't want him to be President. . . . I've told Bobby this, but he is fatalistic, like me."

Ethel called about 7 this evening and then put Bobby on the phone. Bobby said that his meeting with the President had been friendly enough, that LBJ had said that he planned for the time being to stay out of the presidential contest and that he (RFK) had said that he would appreciate it if LBJ were to let him know if he changed his mind. I told him that he should begin to pace his campaign and not exhaust himself in the first few weeks. He bridled a little and said, "I know I look tired, but I'm all right. I know the limits of my strength very well. There is no need to worry about that." He agreed on the need for some sober, careful speeches and wants particularly to give one on how to avoid future Vietnams.

Why did LBJ get out? My guess is political cowardice: his polls showed him that he would be humiliatingly beaten in Wisconsin, and he decided to get out while it could still appear to be his own decision rather than one forced on him. Vance Hartke told me in Leningrad last summer that Johnson would not run again because he had a yellow streak and could not face the thought of being beaten. And, as Bill Moyers said on the night of the New Hampshire primary, Johnson cannot stand confrontations with equals. He is a bully who likes to flex his muscles and beat up his inferiors but avoids trouble with his peers.

April 4

David Karr called today. He had spent an hour yesterday with LBJ and says that it was "terrifying." Johnson was, first of all, filled with self-pity. He seemed very hurt over the Kennedy attitude toward him and kept talking about his "partnership" with JFK. "Then my partner died, and I took over the partnership. I kept on the eleven cowhands [the cabinet]. Some of the tenderfeet [Arthur Schlesinger, Jr.?] left me. But I kept on. If he is up there in heaven looking down, I know that he knows what I have done."

He was bitter about RFK. He said, for example, "On civil rights I was stronger than he was," instancing some issue about the guarantee of home mortgage loans, which, he said, Bobby would not put into the civil rights bill; this referred to his time on the Committee on Equal Employment Opportunities. He also talked about Bobby in connection with the Bay of Pigs (with which Bobby had no connection) and said that the credibility gap began then in the Kennedy administration and not in the Johnson administration. And he kept talking about an alleged affair RFK had with Candy Bergen in Paris.

April 5

Martin Luther King murdered: what in hell is happening to this country? And I am not cheered by the reactions. A taxi driver last night, a postman bringing me a certified letter this morning—both took a line that the Negroes were the great threat, and the whites had to prepare to deal with them. JFK's death produced a wave of shame and guilt, but King's death, as Alexandra [Emmet, now Schlesinger] said this morning, seems only to have increased hostility.

April 24

There is a general feeling that the campaign is not quite working; but, as Gilbert Harrison said yesterday, "I just can't put my finger on what is wrong." The basic trouble is that McCarthy, by the single act of prior entry, captured Bobby's constituency and, with it, a lot of the dynamism of the campaign.

May 5

I am baffled by the intensity of feeling some people have against RFK. It all seems to have been inspired by the way he entered the contest; or at least his mode of entry revived the earlier image of him, which his senatorial performance had so successfully obscured, as an unprincipled and ruthless opportunist. I cannot make out whether the bitterness is greater than the bitterness against JFK in 1960. I think probably it is, though it is easy to forget how savage many liberals and intellectuals were in their attitudes toward JFK then.

On May 3, I went to the Theater of Ideas to engage in a debate with Norman Mailer and Herbert Marcuse. I have known Marcuse for a quarter of a century—since the old days in OSS—and have always rather liked him, without ever really trusting him. He is charming and civilized, but one feels something sinister in him, some form of hostility transmuted into a soft reasonableness. He has lately become the guru of the New Left. His followers take his doctrine of intolerance and, since they are themselves charmless and uncivilized, apply it in a primitive and even brutal way. And, of course, this is in line with his doctrine, so Marcuse does not disown their actions; he told Shirley Broughton, of the Theater of Ideas, after the performance that he was pleased by the "spirit" of the audience. The "spirit" of the audience, or at least of the most ardent minority, was to howl down all speakers who said anything they didn't like, which most of the time meant me. It was a spirited evening, and I rather enjoyed it, but it filled me with despair about the New Left. At the end of the evening, a bearded little man, stoned on something—pot probably, came out of the audience and sat down beside me in an ominous way. He then started talking to me and, when the meeting adjourned, followed me out, saying softly, "You know what you are? You're a murderer, a murderer, and a traitor, and a mother fucker. It's against the wall for you. Do you know what is going to happen?—you're going to be executed." Before he began this tirade, he told me that his name was Jerry Bananas; and I was later told that he was an SDS leader.

How does all this compare with the left of my youth? The Stalinists of the thirties were equally rigid, dishonest and fanatical. But they did not have the cult of violence, nor the associated contempt for the mind. Many of the Stalinists were exceedingly well read; some even, outside politics, had cultivated tastes. The New Left seems to have read nothing and relies entirely on the proposition that feeling and acting are all that matter: the deed will eventually produce the doctrine; the act of revolution will lead to the program. The Stalinists believed that the end justified the means; the New Left believes that the means will create the end.

May 25

I [went] to Washington for the Americans for Democratic Action convention. I had thought there might be a chance to broaden the ADA endorsement to include RFK, but Joe Rauh and Jim Loeb told me when I arrived that this was impossible and that the best we could get was a friendly paragraph about Bobby in the statement reaffirming McCarthy's endorsement. McCarthy spoke at the banquet Saturday night. I was sitting next to Jimmy Wechsler at the head table. When Gene came in about the middle of the evening, he walked along the table shaking hands till he reached me, when his lips tightened, his eyes grew cold and he hurried by—adolescent behavior, it seemed to me. His speech went over well with this highly enthusiastic audience. But it seemed to me redolent with self-pity—it was all about how brave he was, how lonely he was, how he had changed the course of history, etc. I am prepared to concede him courage and nobility in the abstract, but he is rather sad in person.

May 27

Maybe fatigue encourages paranoia; but I am obliged to state that I have never felt so much in my life the settled target of hostility as I do here in New York City. I guess I have never been much liked by the New York literary people—the Lowells, Kazins, Epsteins, etc.— though they always accepted one's hospitality in Cambridge and Washington (something never repaid here); and now the McCarthy hysteria has turned this into real hatred. McCarthy himself, after declining to shake my hand at the Americans for Democratic Action dinner, is now attacking me in Oregon on the ground that I defected from his campaign! Of course, I was never a part of his campaign. Now I am hissed at practically every public appearance in this city. I have just been out to get the morning *Times*, and inevitably someone harangued and denounced me on Third Avenue—again a McCarthyite. I think these people are crazy. But I do feel curiously isolated here.

Before I totally succumb to self-pity, I must remind myself of other times in life when I have been bitterly attacked for brief periods—when I wrote the piece on the American Communist Party for *Life* in 1946; when I supported JFK and wrote *Kennedy or Nixon* in 1960; when I wrote the Cuba White Paper in 1961; when *A Thousand Days* began to come out in *Life* in 1965. All these things passed away because I was right on the issue. I am right on the issue today—RFK at least—and no doubt in time things will improve here too.

June 9

It is beyond belief, but it has happened—it has happened again.

On Tuesday, June 4, I went to Chicago for a conference on Vietnam sponsored by the Adlai Stevenson Institute. Saul Bellow and I had met at the airport on Monday afternoon and flown out to Chicago together; and he had suggested that I come over to his apartment Tuesday evening to hear the returns from the California primary. I took Frances FitzGerald over there that evening around ten o'clock. We listened until it became evident that RFK was winning. Then Dick Wade, who was there, dropped Frankie at the Center for Continuing Education and took me back to the Hotel Windermere. Feeling tired I listened to the results and then went to bed. I could hardly have got to sleep when the phone rang. It was Dick saying, "Kennedy's been shot. Steve Smith too, I guess." Filled with foreboding, I turned on the television and watched the rest of the night.

When I caught the 8 A.M. plane back to New York, I was still reasonably hopeful. A brain specialist from Georgetown University had explained over ABC that the bullet had apparently entered a part of the brain that didn't much matter; and he was now being operated on. When I arrived in New York, there was no real news. Around noon Dick Goodwin called me from the hospital; he sounded a little grim. So too did Frank Mankiewicz in his periodic appearances, delivering his briefings with weary precision, his face more haggard and ravaged on each appearance. On the way from Chicago I had written some new material for the commencement address; I now revised the address somewhat and took it to the office. I could hardly eat. Bourbon was again the great means of getting through the day, as on November 23, 1963. The address seemed to go off well. Chrissie had called me earlier in the day to suggest that I come to Cambridge, so I flew up that evening. The children—Kathy was in town too—were all profoundly depressed. Finally we went off to bed. At 7:30 in the morning Bill vanden Heuvel called to say that Bobby had died three hours before.

It is all too much. That evening I went with so many others to Butler Aviation to await the plane bearing the body from Los Angeles. It was all too familiar. The night was warm rather than cold; but the same sadness penetrated everything. In a way my friendship with Bobby had become closer than my friendship with Jack. How can one compare the two? JFK was eight and a half years older; Bobby would have been 43 in November, which was JFK's age in May 1960. One thinks of [Governor] Paul Dever's epigram: JFK, the first Irish Brahmin; RFK, the Irish Puritan. JFK, one sensed, was always a skeptic and an ironist; he had understood the complexity of things from birth. RFK began as a true believer; he acquired his sense of the complexity of things from hard experience. He remained a true believer to the end but at a far deeper level; he had long since shucked away the external criteria and the received simplifications and got down as far as one can in politics to the human meaning of things. JFK attacked conditions because they seemed irrational, RFK because they seemed hateful. JFK was a man of cerebration; Bobby was very bright and reflective, but he was a man of commitment. If JFK saw people living in squalor, it seemed to him totally unreasonable and awful, but he saw it all, as FDR would have done, from the outside. RFK had an astonishing capacity to identify himself with the casualties and victims of our society. When he went among them, these were *his* children, *his* scraps of food, *his* hovels. JFK was urbane, imperturbable, always in control, invulnerable, it seemed, to everything, except the murderer's bullet. RFK was far more vulnerable. One wanted to protect him; one never felt that Jack needed protection. In Bobby's case the contrast between the myth and the man could not have been greater. He was supposed to be hard, ruthless, unfeeling, unyielding, a grudge-bearer, a hater. In fact, he was an exceptionally gentle and considerate man, the most bluntly honest man I have ever encountered in politics, a profoundly idealistic man and an extremely funny man. JFK had much better manners. RFK was often diffident and had no small talk. He would do much better at Resurrection City than at the Metropolitan Club. There was for me such a poignancy about RFK—all the greater now that they killed him even before he had a chance to place his great gifts at the service of the nation in the presidency; Jack at least had two and a half years.

I think of all the good and gay times I have had with Bobby since coming to New York—the evenings, for example, when he would come up for one reason or another, and Angie [Novello, RFK's secretary] would phone and say, "The Senator wonders whether you can meet him at such-and-such a place a little after ten," and then one would go, and find a group, small or large, and have an hour or two of Kennedy conversation, with its easy shift from the light to the serious, and Bobby's endless curiosity and tremendous honesty. I think of all the pleasant times at Hyannis Port, Bobby deploying his children, kidding them, playing with them, and all the hundreds of times at Hickory Hill, on the tennis court or in the swimming pool or around the dining room table, with Ethel sweetly pronouncing grace, or dancing in the drawing room. I loved Bobby, I cannot bear the thought that he too is gone.

I loved my country too, and I cannot bear to think what this latest horror shows about the direction in which the nation is moving. I know Humphrey, McCarthy, Rockefeller and [John] Lindsay, and I know enough about Nixon, Reagan and Wallace: none of these men is in a class with RFK so far as intelligence, judgment and understanding are concerned. But beyond this is the sense one has of the progressive decomposition of the system. We have now murdered the three men who more than any other incarnated the idealism of America in our time. Something about our social ethos has conferred a kind of legitimacy on hate and violence. One shudders at future possibilities. There is the fact too that, for the poor and the non-white, RFK represented their only stake in the political process. Walter Reuther said glumly to me as we were waiting to get on the funeral train at Pennsylvania Station, "I'm afraid they will all opt out now. They will be like the college kids before New Hampshire—completely skeptical about any possibility of change within the system."

So I stood in the soft summer night waiting for the plane. At last it came; and soon the family appeared, all superb, as always, in composure in the face of calamity. Ethel looked rather beautiful in black. Jackie's face was pale and masklike. They whipped in to New York for a special mass at St. Patrick's. Ethel saw me, walked over, kissed me and suggested that I come back to the apartment. I walked over; and, when I arrived, I found her wholly composed and terrifyingly solicitous of her guests (mostly members of her family). Her first words to me were, "You were in Chicago for a meeting, weren't you? Wasn't it on Vietnam? How did it go?" And Mrs. Kennedy was there, also infinitely composed. At one point Jean and Eunice, who had arisen to go, went over to say good-bye to their mother. Mrs. Kennedy said, "I'm so glad all you children are home again." One felt impressed by the power of faith. What sustains Ethel Kennedy, what sustains Rose Kennedy, is the absolute conviction that Bobby is now happier than he has ever been, that he has been reunited with Jack, that soon all will be together again. Jackie told me that, after Dallas, Ethel said to her, "At least you have the comfort of knowing that he has found eternal happiness."

The next morning I went to a family mass at the Church of the Holy Family on 47th Street. Afterward there was lunch at the Dillons'. Jackie was there, and I told her that the first thing I thought of, when I heard the news, was her remark to me this winter (when she said she hoped he would never become President because, if he did, the same thing would happen to him which happened to Jack). She knew the remark I had in mind and said, "I told him the same thing, several times."

While all this went on, politics continued. My personal feeling is one of such outrage and despair that I do not want to get involved in politics again. Every political leader I have cared about is now dead; and I do not want to get attached to another, and then see something terrible happen to him.

On Saturday morning, the service. Ted delivered his eulogy superbly and made a very strong impression. Then we all went by bus to Penn Station, and by train to Washington. This was a most affecting journey. The tracks were lined with people, increasing numbers of whom, as the train fell more and more behind schedule, had been waiting in the hot sun for hours. Some were crying; some held up signs or American flags; all looked intently and sadly at the train. Stash Radziwill said, "To think that a few days ago they were calling this man the most ruthless man in America." At one point I said to Ken O'Donnell, "What marvelous crowds!" He replied gloomily, "Yes, but what are they good for?" Even boats clustered in rivers by the railroad bridges. One fireboat was named the *John F. Kennedy*, and its crew of three saluted proudly as the train went by.

We arrived in Washington after nightfall. Buses took us out to Arlington, and we all stood in the quiet dark while the last words were said over the casket. The moon was nearly full; it had rained, and the air was less heavy than it had been during the train ride. Mourners held candles, twinkling in the dark. One felt enveloped by the sadness and redeemed only by the fantastic courage of the Kennedys.

What kind of a President would he have made? I think very likely a greater one than JFK. He was more radical than JFK; he understood better the problems of the excluded groups; and he would have been coming along in a time more propitious for radical action. He would have re-created the excitement and exhilaration of the early sixties, and he would have restored the idealism of America.

As I rode up the Central Valley [of California] with him on May 30, who could have known that nine days later I would be riding with him on another train, from St. Patrick's Cathedral to Arlington Cemetery?

July 15

I spent the weekend of July 4–8 at the Cape—a sad time. Then on Monday I went on to Hyannis Port, where I have gone so many times in the last nine years and had such happy times. Now John Kennedy is gone, and Robert Kennedy is gone, and the effort to keep things going as they always were breaks one's heart.

We arrived shortly before noon. Ethel was playing tennis; I joined for a time. Then we went into the bay for the usual picnic. Ethel wanted to go on the sailboat.

Before dinner, Marian and I went over and had a drink with Jackie. (The old detachment remains between Ethel and Jackie; Ethel referred to her humorously but without affection as "her royal highness"). Jackie commented on styles of grief. She said that her own instinct after Dallas was to go off by herself and lick her wounds, but perhaps the Kennedy way—Ethel's way—was better; that the collective approach to total loss enabled everybody to keep busy and to reinforce and help everybody else. When the possibility of Teddy's return to politics was mentioned, she rejected it immediately; clearly she thinks he will be killed too if he takes a prominent role.

I stayed the night and saw Ethel again on Tuesday morning before Bill [Barry] drove me to the airport. She then asked me whether I would do Bobby's biography. Up to this point, I had rather dismissed this as a possibility and hoped that it would be worked out in some other way. But, when she spoke about it, I suddenly perceived that of course I should do it, and I think I will, though I cannot do it until I do another volume of *The Age of Roosevelt*. It is owed to Bobby, whom I loved so much, and it is owed to the country, which ought to learn so much from his life and death.

July 17

As for Humphrey, David Ginsburg, who is heading People for Humphrey, has called me a couple of times about consulting with him on HHH's acceptance address. In this connection, and in connection with a letter reproaching me for having come out for Rockefeller (which of course I did not), I wrote him a rather unguarded letter explaining why I could not come out for Hubert. He called me and asked whether I would mind his showing the letter to Hubert. Not recalling the letter in detail, I asked him whether there was anything in it which might be offensive to Hubert. He said he thought not, and that the letter could be useful in reinforcing points that he and others had been trying to make to Hubert. Mistakenly, I told him to go ahead.

Then yesterday I received a blast from Hubert—two and a half pages, single spaced—extremely egotistical, ungenerous, intemperate and, on occasion, even ugly in tone. I ascribed this to Hubert's extreme edginess over the fact that liberal opposition might jeopardize his nomination.

Stephen and I lunched with Henry Kissinger at the Century today. Henry told the following story of his first meeting with Johnson (in connection with the Hanoi negotiations). Henry said that we should not bomb Hanoi while he was passing messages back and forth to the North Vietnamese. Other people opposed this in front of the President, arguing that it would endanger American security. Henry finally said, "I cannot believe that the security of the United States will be endangered if for a little while we do not bomb within ten miles of the capital of a fifth-rate agricultural power." Johnson glowered at him and said, "OK, we will do it the professor's way. But (glaring at Kissinger) if it doesn't work, I will personally cut your balls off."

August 9

On Thursday I flew back to New York. On arrival, I received a message from George McGovern's office saying that he had decided to announce for the presidency on Saturday. Late in the evening I talked to George in South Dakota. He was detached and philosophical about it all, but said that [Jesse] Unruh, Frank Mankiewicz and [Pierre] Salinger had encouraged him to think that he could get perhaps 100 votes in California, that he had other prospects in Iowa, New York and (after the first ballot) in Massachusetts, that his people in South Dakota were urging him to go ahead, and that he thought why not?

August 24
[Chicago]

Here I am, contrary to intention and expectation, back at a Democratic convention. After Bobby's murder, I abandoned any thought of coming this year (missing the convention for the first time since 1948) and reinstated the trip to Japan which I had cancelled when he became a candidate. But when George McGovern entered the contest I said I would be glad to come out for the weekend (before Chrissie and I go to Hong Kong on Tuesday) and do what I can to help.

[Dick Wade and I] went up to see George. He was as placid, modest and agreeable as usual. We laughed for a moment over the fact that three American historians—McGovern, Wade and Schlesinger—should find themselves in this situation. George said that he thought he had 130 votes, not counting California (where he expects about 50) and New York. I asked him whether he had anticipated Abe Ribicoff's decision to come out for him. He said that Abe had called on his own initiative and asked whether he could be helpful. Mayor [Jerome] Cavanaugh of Detroit is supposed to come out for him tomorrow; and there is hope that [William] Fulbright, [Stuart] Symington, [Gaylord] Nelson, [Quentin] Burdick, Bartlett and one or two others ([Vance] Hartke, [Joseph] Clark) may also do so. I am impressed by George's easy competence—by his capacity to understand and meet all the conventional political demands. He has really done terribly well and would obviously be a better President than Humphrey or McCarthy.

By Monday morning the draft-Kennedy movement—or at least the draft-Kennedy story—had become very hot. It is evident that both Daley and Unruh see in Ted's candidacy the best solution for their own problems and are therefore pressing him to run. However, they are pressing him for *their* reasons, not for *his* reasons. Some California delegates had come to see me Sunday afternoon. They said that Ted could get the nomination only if he came in as an active candidate against Humphrey—which I am sure is the last thing he would do.

I have been going back and forth on [Ted's] question—originally opposed because I fear he will be shot; then half-persuaded on the ground that, even if young and in some respects unprepared, Teddy would still be a better President than Humphrey, McCarthy and Nixon and might, in addition, be the only Democrat with a chance of beating Nixon; then half-persuaded the other way by the thought that it would all be politically messy and that, in the end, he might not beat Nixon after all; now impressed by Moyers's point, which I used to argue to RFK in another context, that this would help convince the kids that the American political process isn't a fake.

[After] dinner [near the convention hall] I excused myself and went out to call Ted Kennedy, whom I had been trying to get all afternoon whenever I was alone. At last the line was not busy. I described the situation as I saw it. He said, "I have a gut feeling that this is not the year, that it is too early for me. I would rather try and do it as an individual in my own right, to carve out something of my own, establish myself to some degree in control of events. I don't want to do anything to besmirch our family name or seem to take advantage of people's sympathy. That's one side of it. On the other side, it is true that we have a hell of an investment in 1968. Bob's efforts to change policies and directions and the rest—I want to follow that up in every way I can. Moreover, I am realistic enough to know that it is a real question how many opportunities like this anyone can expect in a lifetime, 1972 is a long time away. I come from a family practical enough to know what these realities are."

He said he expected that Hubert would get it on the first ballot. "What I am going to do is to play it absolutely straight. We've called off [former Ohio governor Michael] DiSalle [who had announced that he planned to nominate Kennedy for President], and I don't plan to do a thing. If the convention wants me, they will be doing this on their own—which is the only way it can be done. You remember my father's old saying?—'Things don't just happen; they are *made* to happen.' All I can say is that we are not making this one happen."

September 25

Back to this wretched campaign. My desire for disengagement is so great that I have not been able to bring myself to put anything down. Let me sum up the apparent situation of the moment: Nixon, running a slick, evasive, Deweyesque campaign, way ahead; Humphrey, floundering all over the place and persuading no one; Wallace, coming up from behind as an American [Pierre] Poujade benefiting from sheer frustration. Nixon is still entirely capable of beating himself. But so is Humphrey. This is really the battle of the minnows. I cannot ever support Nixon, whom I regard as the greatest shit in 20th century American politics (the "20th century" bit is pure scholarly caution; I cannot at the moment think of anyone in the 19th century quite meeting Nixon's combination of sanctimoniousness and squalor). I expect that I will end by voting quietly for Humphrey. I cannot give him active support, however, unless he separates himself from LBJ on Vietnam (and comes out for ending the bombing of the north) and separates himself from Dick Daley on law and order.

I discover among the New York intellectuals a curious softness toward Nixon, stimulated largely by a rather mean passion to "punish" Humphrey. David Halberstam and I got into a momentarily angry argument about this the other night at John Gunther's, Halberstam insisting that he could never forgive Humphrey for Chicago and that Nixon really wasn't so bad after all; hadn't Bobby Kennedy changed through the years. I understand that Barbara Epstein of the *New York Review of Books* is strongly for Nixon. Last night at Peter Duchin's table at El Morocco, I got this nonsense at considerable length from Bob Silvers: Nixon is really not so bad, and he will get us out of the war in Vietnam sooner than anyone else! As Alexandra said, anyone predicting a year ago that Silvers, Halberstam and Barbara Epstein would be shilling for Nixon would have been considered loony. As I say, the ignorance/arrogance of New York intellectuals when it comes to politics is beyond belief.

October 14

David Ginsburg called me this morning and said that Hubert Humphrey had asked him last night whether I would be inclined to do anything for him in the election. David said, "I decided that the best thing would be to ask you directly. Will you do anything for Hubert?" I said, following the line enjoined on me by Rauh and Galbraith, "I will if he asks me directly." Dave said, "I will see that he does so."

Ninety minutes later Hubert called. He talked a good deal about the tide of reaction in the country and the need to rally the liberals. I asked him whether he planned to go further on Vietnam, saying that this would make it easier for liberals to support him. He said that he intended to do so but that Ben Reed in the State Department (for whom he said he had high regard, as do I), had suggested that he stick about where he is for the next few days. He remarked that Mac Bundy's Saturday speech unveiling himself as a dove had "legitimatized" the anti-bombing position. He said he had called up Mac last night—"no one suggested it; I just wanted to talk about things with him." He seemed to be about to ask me to do a speech, but I said that I really hadn't written speeches since 1963. He made a general allusion to our correspondence, saying he felt that "after certain matters" he hardly had the right to ask me to do anything.

I said that I would come out for him. He hoped that I would talk to some of my "academic friends." He sounded rather tired, rather friendly, but rather hesitant and hardly free-flowing. He must have dialed the call himself; at least he was on the phone asking for me when I picked it up.

October 18

On Wednesday night, the 16th, I went to a dinner at Marietta's. Very entertaining—Steve and Jean Smith, Ed Logue, and the Jim Perkinses, one or two others. The talk was largely political, and Steve was in excellent form. At one point he whispered to me, "We're going to have some surprises for you in the next couple of days." I assumed he meant political and said I hoped they would be pleasant. He said enigmatically, "Well, you'll just have to see." Then, as they were leaving, Jean drew me aside and [told me that Jackie and Aristotle Onassis were getting married on Saturday in Greece]. I thought she was kidding, but it became apparent she wasn't. My reaction was one of real horror. I hardly know Onassis; but one day last summer, when Leonard Lyons took Chrissie and me along with him on one of his evenings, we dropped by El Morocco and Lennie introduced Onassis. Onassis was sitting at what I gather to be his usual corner table surrounded by a collection of sycophants. He asked me to join him for a drink, saying "I have heard so much about you from Jackie and would like so much to talk with you." We talked for a while. He explained to me how splendid the Greek dictatorship was, etc., and finally I could bear it no longer and excused myself.

I called Jean the next day and asked her to say something to cheer me up. I told her the whole thing seemed terrible, that I felt it was an insult to JFK and a betrayal of everything he stood for. She and Pat were about to leave for Greece and the wedding. This is typical of these girls. I am sure they hate the whole affair as much as I do; but they feel that the only thing which would make it worse would be the impression of a family battle about it, so they are going along.

November 19

The election has come and gone. In the end, I came out for Hubert; and, in the end, he came out for himself, or rather as himself. He could have been elected so easily; if, for example, he had embraced the minority plank on Vietnam in Chicago, if he had come out strongly for ending the bombing in September instead of giving the half-assed Salt Lake City speech, if he had freed himself from Johnson by October 10 instead of by about October 25. There is a tendency now to blame his defeat on the liberals; but he did not make it easy for the liberals to come to his support. The real cause of the defeat, of course, was the war, and the architects of the defeat were the men who convinced LBJ he should pursue the policy of military escalation.

It is unfair to exploit the comedy of names; but it is odd that Nixon's three closest friends all have the kind of names Evelyn Waugh would give to American characters in his novels—Elmer Bobst, Jack Drown and Bebe Rebozo.

December 11

The Nixon administration is beginning to take shape. The best appointment from my viewpoint is Henry Kissinger. I talked for a few moments with Henry last week in Princeton. I asked him whether Nixon was turning out to be the kind of man Henry expected him to be. Henry replied enigmatically that he had been reassured on certain things that had previously worried him but was encountering other and unexpected qualities which might create problems. When I said how glad I was that he had been appointed, Henry said ruefully, "All I can say is I hope you will feel equally glad about it a year from now."

1969

❖

January 14

LBJ gave his last State of the Union message tonight—a curiously un-moving occasion. I am obviously not a great LBJ fan, but I was perfectly prepared to suffer a few sentimental twinges over his departure, as one could appropriately feel over any farewell performance. I felt nothing at all except disappointment over the flatness of the speech, irritation over the fake-benign smile he employed for the occasion and a horrible fear that five years from now he will be one of the beloved men of America.

I took part with Bill Moyers, Jack Valenti, Eric Goldman and Ted Sorensen (in Kansas City) in a National Education Television commen-tary. Afterward Bill and I went over to the Algonquin for a drink. We talked a bit about the problem of writing about Johnson. Bill said, as he has said to me before (and Dick Goodwin has said even more often), that one great trouble was that no one would believe it. He said he could not see how one could write about Johnson the private monster and Johnson the public statesman and construct a credible narrative.

"He is a sick man," Bill said. At one point he and Dick became so concerned that they decided to read up on mental illness—Dick read up on paranoia and Bill on the manic-depressive cycle.

January 22

LBJ's reaction to the National Education Television panel, as relayed by George Christians to Bill Moyers: Valenti was fine, Sorensen fair, Goldman an ass and Moyers and Schlesinger "traitors."

The Age of Nixon began two days ago. The inaugural address is not one of the higher art forms, and Nixon's was, in the main, a collection of unimpeachable banalities. There was, however, one notable line: "The American dream does not come to those who fall asleep." Apart from this, the speech was interesting not for what it said but for what it did not say. He said nothing, for example, about law and order, nothing about the implacable Communist conspiracy, nothing about the Republican idols of the past (damn little about the alienated groups either). The relevant comparison is with his acceptance speech; they could hardly have been more different.

January 28

Small dinner at Peter Duchin's last night for Averell. This is the first time I have seen him since his return. He was in excellent form, as usual. He talked a good deal about the Vietnam discussions and the people involved. On Rusk, he said, "That man has done more damage to America than anyone in our time." I said, "What about [John Foster] Dulles?" Averell thought for a moment and said, "No, Rusk has done more damage than Dulles." He added, "If the truth were told about Dean Rusk, no one would believe it." He described Rusk as "crafty" and "Machiavellian" and said that Rusk moved quickly to destroy his (Averell's) influence two months after JFK's death. Someone asked him how he accounted for Maxwell Taylor's role. "That's easy," Averell said. "He's a fool." He had high praise for McNamara—"all wrong about the war until about Christmas 1965; then good thereafter"—and especially for Clifford in the last few months. He was very hard on [Ellsworth] Bunker who, he says, regards the preservation in power of [Nguyen Van] Thieu and Ky as the central object of American policy.

He was also interesting on the subject of Presidents and instructions. "Roosevelt," he said, "would tell you what his goal was but left it to you to figure out the best way of achieving it. That gave you more flexibility and initiative and also enabled him to disown you if anything went wrong. Now Presidents and State Departments give the most detailed and minute instructions. This enables them to keep operating control, but it makes it impossible for them to disown their representatives if anything goes wrong."

Averell also said that at one point LBJ derived infinite consolation from a letter sent him by Allan Nevins, comparing him to Lincoln and equating their tribulations and objectives. LBJ, Averell said, used to carry the letter around in his pocket and show it to everybody.

January 30

A party at Steve Smith's Wednesday night (January 29) for Lauren Bacall. Ted and Joan Kennedy came in about midnight. I asked Ted about Nixon's visit to the Senate the day before. After the general visit Nixon lunched with half a dozen senators in the minority leader's chambers. Ted said that the President was "terribly ill at ease." "I suppose he has some sort of odd feeling about me," Ted continued. "Every time we are together in the same room I feel he has a particular awareness of me, and this means we keep getting thrown together and then have nothing to say. When he came into [Everett] Dirksen's room, he shook everybody's hand, and then we ended up standing together. He was very nervous. He said, 'Well, this is a strange room, isn't it?' so I looked around the room—it looked perfectly normal to me. Then in a minute he said, 'This is really an odd room.' Then he told me he was glad I had said what I had said about Biafra—'I don't agree with all your points, understand, but they were very interesting points.' A little while later, when we had all sat down for lunch, I heard [Richard] Russell say to him, 'I certainly hope you don't plan to go overboard on this Biafra matter.' Nixon said, 'Oh, no, Senator; I quite agree with you on that.'"

The Smith apartment is filled with photographs of the three brothers. Seeing these photographs in the midst of the hilarity of the party filled one with the saddest thoughts. There suddenly flashed into my mind a remark Ethel made to me in Washington a few days ago. I said that I had heard that the christening of the new baby (which I had not been able to attend) had been such a happy time. She said, "Yes, it's so marvelous to get the old gang together on a joyful occasion. We have spent too much of our time meeting around those black boxes."

One way Ted Kennedy differs from Jack and Bobby: he is the only one who seems to be affected by drink. JFK, of course, drank sparingly in the years I knew him well; RFK perhaps drank a little more but never showed it. Ted becomes a little high in an entirely merry way, lurches a little, his face grows a little flushed, and he wants to sing.

June 17

The Nixon administration has been aimless, boring and ineffectual. On major issues—Vietnam, the ABM—it has supinely resumed the policy of the Johnson administration. Nixon himself has generally preserved an external blandness, though the mask began to slip a few days ago when he gave an Old Nixon speech at the Air Force Academy, suggesting that those who dissented from the administration and attacked the military were lacking in patriotism and were isolationists. But even worse than this speech has been his inaction on every front. It all reminds one of the Chinese proverb JFK used to like: "There is much noise on the stairs, but no one comes into the room."

I have some random notes here. One is about the language of the young. Hippie talk, of course, is not so stereotyped that it becomes a means of avoiding the pain of thought. But a number of the locutions are brilliant and fill gaps; I don't know whether they designate new phenomena, but they certainly provide a crisper way of putting a number of situations. For example:

— "hang-up," meaning an obsession or inhibition
— "cop-out," meaning an escape from a problem or responsibility
— "turn-on," meaning to excite
— "turn-off," meaning to bore or antagonize
— "come on too strong," meaning to bring more pressure than the situation justifies or can bear
— "put down," meaning to deprecate or humiliate
— "put on," meaning to kid.

I have also been struck by the number of people roughly of my own generation who began to my left and who are now to my right. One has read often enough of those who start as radicals or liberals and end as conservatives, but it is still odd to see it happen among one's own acquaintances. Twenty years ago, for example, I used to argue with Teddy White about Henry Wallace and whether the U.S. was responsible for the Cold War; now I argue with him because he is (or has been until recently) a hawk on Vietnam and because he is a very definite hawk so far as the students are concerned. When I first met Howard K. Smith at Oxford in 1939, he was a Communist; now he writes homilies about the failure of liberalism and begins to sound indistinguishable from Bill White. Al Capp and I were great friends in the fifties when he spoke at the Americans for Democratic Action dinners and was hilarious on the subject of McCarthy (Joe); now he hates the poor, the young and the blacks and repeatedly attacks Galbraith and me as enemies of the republic. Oscar Handlin was once a good New Deal liberal; now he is Pusey's strongest defender at Harvard, a pillar of respectability and a Capp hero. Joe Alsop, of course, has been driven mad by Vietnam. He was once a very close friend; now, when we attend the same party, he glares across the room at me and tells people that Galbraith, Goodwin and I have ruined the Kennedy family and the American liberal movement. (Stephen Spender, who stayed a weekend with Joe this spring, says that Joe has a fantasy in which I will be under attack as a Communist or something and he will come to my defense, arguing that Schlesinger may have been mistaken but he was never disloyal.)

Of course one should not neglect those who grow more radical with age: Averell Harriman, Walter Lippmann, Tom Finletter, Francis Biddle. I have seen Averell a number of times in this period. He regards the ABM as a disaster and is privately most critical of the Nixon policy on Vietnam. He thinks that, so long as we regard the Saigon government as sacred, and that so long as we continue the policy of "maximum military pressure" in the field, we cannot hope for a negotiated settlement in Vietnam.

John L. Lewis died a few days ago. Jimmy Wechsler told me how, a few months after he had written a not altogether complimentary book about Lewis, they ran into each other in the men's room at the Carlton. As they stood next to each other, Lewis said, "Ah, Mr. Wechsler. The latrine is the great leveler." This prompted Jimmy to tell me another story he says he has told me before but which I do not remember. He lunched at the White House early in the Johnson administration and, after several hours, felt an irresistible desire to relieve himself. He asked George Reedy in a whisper where the bathroom was. The President, overhearing, said, "I've been hoping someone would say that. I've been wanting to take a leak myself. Come with me." He led Jimmy to the bathroom and, when Jimmy hung back, waiting for the President to go first, Johnson seized him by the arm, propelled him into the bathroom and insisted that they deliver themselves simultaneously. Jimmy felt that his organs were subjected to undue scrutiny until the President, evidently satisfied with the superiority of his own, began to piss into the bowl. Soon, on his insistence, the two streams mingled. What a man! I hope that someday someone will write the true story of the Johnson White House.

July 25

The last few days were, of course, shadowed by the distressing news about Ted Kennedy. We heard about it first on the yacht on Sunday afternoon and learned more details when we reached Paris. On Wednesday night in New York I called Jimmy Wechsler, Joe Rauh, Ken Galbraith and others and found general gloom. On Thursday I sat after lunch with Scotty Reston and Tom Wicker at the Century. They were both sympathetic; Scotty had been at the Vineyard that weekend and had personally driven over the bridge the next day; it was, he said, perilous even in broad daylight.

On Thursday night, July 24, I had dinner with Bill vanden Heuvel and Marcia Carter. Ted has asked Bill on Saturday to go to Pennsylvania and sit with the girl's [Mary Jo Kopechne's] family. Bill says that they were remarkable in their fortitude and in their compassion for Ted and for the Kennedys. On Tuesday, Ted, Joan and Ethel went to the funeral. Bill accompanied them. Ted, he said, was grim and sunk; he was "like a man in a catatonic trance." He told Bill, "I thought I was dead" and still could not imagine how he got out of the car and floated to the surface. Bill remarked that the affair could become a field day for the psychoanalysts; Ted had never wanted to run for the presidency in 1972. He was afraid that Ted might decide to resign his Senate seat and abandon politics. We all agreed that the private wounds would be deeper and more enduring than the public memories. That night I wrote Ted a letter urging against precipitate or drastic decisions.

His situation could not have been more difficult. His first statement was very poor. It left many of the most vital questions unanswered and encouraged suspicions—especially that he might have been drunk and postponed reporting the accident until the alcohol could be absorbed in his system. Moreover, the management of the affair was also very poor. At first, it looked as if he thought that, as a Kennedy, he should get special and favored treatment. Then the influx of advisers into Hyannis Port—McNamara, Sorensen, Goodwin, Marshall, etc.—made it look as if he felt himself in a terrific jam and could not afford to tell the truth. Even his friends were badly shaken. Rowlie Evans called this morning (July 25) and said that one could not escape feeling that there must be some "want of character sinew," that the whole performance seemed one of "running away from responsibility."

This morning he pleaded guilty, and this evening he made his television statement. Stephen and I heard it at the apartment. On balance, we thought it very good, though it still left unanswered questions: Why was he driving down the road to the bridge? Why did he go back to the island the next morning? Why did Gargan and Markham not inform the police? Nonetheless, the basic candor of his description of his own reactions that terrible night was impressive, and my guess is that the furor will now die down. I called Ethel this evening. She seemed cheerful. When I said that I had been afraid he might resign his seat, she said, "You will never know how close it was."

August 4

I have just returned from a weekend with the Galbraiths at Newfane [Vermont]—George McGovern, Gloria Steinem, Alexandra and Peter [Allen, Alexandra's son]. George was in excellent form and is preparing to run for the presidency. His state of mind, I guess, is why not? are Muskie, McCarthy, Humphrey, [Fred] Harris better qualified? And, indeed, why not? George is a first-class man, intelligent, brave and funny, a good debater and compelling speaker. He takes strong positions but does so in the most moderate and reasonable way.

We had some discussion about the future of liberalism, Ken arguing that liberals had become ineffectual and had lost contact with the young because they had grown accustomed to thinking "within" the system; to recover its energy and impact, liberals would have to begin thinking "against" the system and come out for "structural change." He agreed that his own earlier work, especially the doctrine of countervailing power, had strengthened the tendency to regard the system itself as OK, requiring only minor adjustment to dispose of remaining problems; but he feels now that a number of things—poverty, misallocation of resources, waste, pollution, inflation—are "inherent" in the system.

I am not sure how much this has to do with substance and how much with strategy. We were, indeed, too complacent about the economic aspects of the system; I remember in *The Vital Center* expressing uncritical optimism about the capacity of Keynesian methods to solve our economic problems. Also I am sure that the Cold War and the obvious cruelties of communism made us all tend to defend our system as a system. And it is undeniable that the system as such tolerates a continuing set of injustices and evils. Yet what does "structural change" mean? What changes, for example, would Ken recommend in the structure of ownership? We agreed that more land must be publicly owned if we are to preserve any rationality in urban and rural living; but Ken does not contend for more public ownership of industry. I think that in the end— and he seemed inclined to agree—that he is calling less for changes in structure than for changes in value and direction. Since values are part of the system, this does indeed imply the proposition that the system must be rejected.

August 27

The traffic [on the way to Hyannis Port] was terrible, but I finally arrived, was welcomed by the Smiths, took a swim, had a drink. There was great sadness at Hyannis Port. I thought how many times I had been there over the last decade—the excitement and hope and energy of 1959 and 1960; the serenity and power of 1961 and 1962 and 1963; the dark summer of 1964; then the revival of hope and energy with Bobby in 1965 and 1966 and 1967; then the second, incredible dark summer last year. Now it is sad again and in perhaps an even more painful way; for what happened to John and Robert Kennedy was beyond their control, while Edward Kennedy's wounds are self-inflicted.

We talked of very little else. The Kennedys are realists and waste no time in regret and recrimination. Moreover, they love Ted, they feel immensely protective toward him, and they know how he is accusing and punishing himself.

When I first saw Ted, we were playing tennis. He came in from sailing and sat down to watch us. He looked terrible and, for a moment, his glance was averted, as if he was not sure whether I would wish to greet him. We talked a number of times, but the extended talk about the affair was on Sunday morning. He says frankly that he behaved badly, that what he did, or failed to do, was inexcusable and indefensible.

He talked calmly and sorrowfully, but seemed to exude a sense of defeat. Only when he talked about the Senate—as we did on Saturday night—did his spirits revive. He cares about the Senate, is concerned about the bills coming up, loves his work as whip, admired [Majority Leader Mike] Mansfield and comes to life when he thinks about it all. It would be a disaster for him, I think, if he were goaded into resigning from the Senate. The Senate gives his life its framework. We also talked about presidential politics. He said that, if he had gone out for the nomination in 1972, it would have been by no means a foregone conclusion; Ed Muskie might very well, he said, have beaten him in New Hampshire. He thinks McGovern has a chance: "George ought to make his home in New Hampshire and Wisconsin for the next three years and let Muskie wander around the rest of the country giving speeches."

December 8

As for the Nixon administration, it has finally shown its hand. The President's November 3 speech on Vietnam expressed the final Nixonization of the war. His policy is to defend the Saigon regime until it is capable of defending itself—a policy doomed to futility and failure. The speech was full of Cold War rhetoric. Even more ominous was the statement that "we really have only two choices open to us"—his own plan and precipitate withdrawal. This statement plainly misrepresents the situation and misleads the country. Most ominous of all was the statement, "Let us understand—North Vietnam cannot defeat or humiliate the United States. Only Americans can do that." This, followed by the [Spiro] Agnew campaign against the press and television, indicates a clear purpose to rally the Great Silent Majority against the anti-war movement. Between them, Nixon and Agnew have stimulated and unleashed a startling amount of virulence on the right; this has further incited the virulence on the far left; and we are clearly in for a rough passage in the months ahead. Henry Kissinger has asked me to lunch with him on December 10. It will be interesting to hear what he has to say. I know what I mean to say to him!

On December 5–6, I went to Cambridge for an Oral History session with Averell Harriman at the Kennedy Center. Averell was in fine fettle and, needless to say, outlasted us all (John Kenney, Ted Tannenwald, Lincoln Gordon, Dick Neustadt, Don Price, Charles Maier, me). His recollections were detailed, exact and fascinating. At one point he said: "Many things I then [1945–50] thought Stalin did for offensive reasons I now believe he did for defensive reasons." Averell would include the Korean War in this category. He has no doubt in retrospect that the war was initiated in Moscow rather than in Pyongyang, but he believes that its main point was to tidy up local defense insecurities derived in part from the denial of Hokkaido to the Soviet Union as an occupation zone rather than to make a general test of Western will. He thinks that Dean Acheson's celebrated speech gave Moscow the green light, and that Molotov's visit to North Korea in the spring of 1950 produced the North Korean decision to go ahead. Averell added that he did not begin to understand this aspect of Soviet policy until he visited Tito in August 1951. Tito, who was requesting American arms, explained his defense strategy. Averell asked him whether he planned to go back into the hills. Tito said no; he would fight on the plains. Averell asked: do you think you can stop the Red Army on the plains? Tito said that it wouldn't be the Red Army; "Stalin will never deploy Soviet troops outside the borders of the Soviet Union"; and the Yugoslav Army could deal with satellite forces. Harriman also said that he felt the recent Soviet action against Czechoslovakia was also defensive in purpose.

Ted Tannenwald told a good Truman story [about how he] helped write the President's statement on the firing of [Douglas] MacArthur and kept trying to insert the sentence: "This action is taken on the unanimous recommendation of all my top civilian and military advisers." This sentence was not in the draft and, on the final go-around with the President, Ted summoned up his courage and said that he thought it should be added. With a twinkle in his eye, Truman said, "No, son. I am doing this on my own responsibility, and I don't want to share this with anyone. All that will leak out in twenty-four hours anyway, but let me have credit for this myself."

The timing of the discharge of MacArthur was stepped up when it was discovered that the *Chicago Tribune* had heard something and was keeping a wire open to Tokyo. As Charlie Murphy explained it to the White House group, "We're going to fire him tonight. The President said he is not going to give that SOB a chance to speak first."

December 14

I flew in the morning [of December 10] to Washington to lunch (at his invitation) with Henry Kissinger. I first dropped by the Senate Office Building and saw George McGovern. George says that the administration seems to have driven the Senate to cover for the time being. Many of the doves, he said, have been alarmed by the forces unleashed by Agnew; while Fulbright and Mansfield seem to have been beguiled by personal protestations of the President claiming his determination to get out of Vietnam. George said he still couldn't discover what the policy was but suspected it might be one of keeping the Saigon regime alive through the 1972 elections, so that Nixon could not be charged with having lost Vietnam to the Communists.

It was by now a day streaming with rain. It was with very mixed feelings that I went to the Southwest Gate of the White House and, after clearance, made my way to the West Wing. I had not been in the White House for nearly five years and could not repress a surge of memories. However, nostalgia quickly vanished when I entered the familiar door. Inside it is all wall-to-wall carpeting in the style of a Hilton hotel. On the walls hang what appear to be tinted photographs of the Nixon girls. (This, I hardly need stress, is in the working offices of the White House.) Henry was still in a National Security Council meeting, and I had a few moments to wait. When the meeting broke up, Dick Helms greeted me warmly and Mel Laird with astonishing cordiality. Then Henry took me into his office (unchanged from the Rostow-Bundy days) and there we lunched.

I asked him first how he was enjoying it all. He looked and sounded very cheerful, but said that his intention all along had been only to stay two years. I asked why; whether it was because he would otherwise have to resign from Harvard? He said, "The last thing in the world I want to do is to go back to Harvard given the present state of affairs. But the two-year limitation could provide a good excuse for me to get out of here." Then he added thoughtfully, "Of course, I might consider resigning earlier if that is what my friends think I should do."

He insisted throughout that the administration was determined to take out American troops and unwind the war. I said that I was sure this is what he wanted, but that I feared that the rhetoric and politics of Nixon's November 3 speech would foreclose the possibility of reaching this objective—the rhetoric by placing such emphatic stress on our stakes in Vietnam and the necessity for stopping Communist aggression; the politics by polarizing the country and unleashing the radical right in a crusade against the peace movement.

Henry also told about LBJ's visit to San Clemente. When he, Nixon and Henry were talking together, LBJ presented a long list of complaints about the treatment of his presidential papers. He wanted a team of ten from the Archives to go to Austin and work full time screening and declassifying his papers. Emphasizing the importance of opening up his papers as soon as possible, he turned to Henry, fetched him, Henry says, a karate punch on the arm and said, "You of all people should understand the importance of this, Dr. Schlesinger." Henry says that Nixon nearly fell out of his chair.

The talk was entirely friendly and agreeable. I like Henry very much, and respect him, though I cannot rid myself of the fear that he says one sort of thing to me and another sort of thing to, say, Bill Buckley.

On Thursday night (December 11) Alexandra and I went out to Pelham for dinner with the Max Jakobsons. He is the Finnish ambassador to the UN, a competent historian and a most agreeable man; he and his wife were very hospitable to us in Helsinki this summer. I sat next to [Soviet] Ambassador [Yakov] Malik, whom I found most genial. I asked him whether he had read Dean Acheson's new book. He said he had not. I said, "You are mentioned in it." He laughed. He did, however, tell a fascinating story about Winston Churchill when he visited him at Chequers when Churchill was Prime Minister and Malik was Soviet Ambassador to Britain. Churchill brought up the Fulton speech* and asked Malik whether he knew why he had given it. When Malik said he would like to know, Churchill said, according to Malik, "I believed that closer relations between the United States and the Soviet Union could only do harm to my own country." Malik then observed that he was perplexed by the fact that, though Churchill had first declared the Cold War, the Americans seemed to be conducting it more zealously than the British. Churchill said, "You must remember that the Americans are new on the world stage, and they always take generalities too literally."

Malik on the whole indulged less in those complacent, insinuating, anti-American generalities that make most Soviet representatives so irritating. He did, however, try one. He said, "And what about the future of your own country? A delegate from another country to the UN said to me the other day that he thought the future of the United States was fascism. What do you think of that?" I said, "Well, we haven't yet reached the point of sending our best writers to labor camps." He did not pursue the subject further.

December 31

For the first time in my memory, I look forward to New Year's Eve, ordinarily the most odious of all occasions, with positive pleasure. In the past, it has always been associated with the onward rush of time, absence of accomplishment, noisy parties, too much to drink, too much to smoke, boredom, hangovers. This year it means farewell to the sixties, the worst and saddest decade of one's life, that "slum of a decade," as John Updike has called it, the decade of the murder of hope.

---

* This was the March 5, 1946, speech at Westminster College in Fulton, Missouri, where Churchill first used the term "iron curtain."

1970

February 7

I lunched with Edmund Wilson today—as usual, at the Princeton Club. When we met, I asked him how he was. He immediately replied, "I've grown old." Then he said, "Trotsky used to say that people were always surprised when they found themselves growing old. They expected it in others but not in themselves. I find it hard to believe."

He had had no breakfast but had two Bloody Marys before luncheon, along with my two martinis. At the end of lunch he took two tarts from the *patisserie* tray. He was in excellent form and told about the book on which he was working—a fragment of autobiography beginning, as he says, in 1802 and going through the 1920s. He has discovered that Heber Kimball was a collateral ancestor. "Kimball had forty-five wives," he mused. "I have only had four." We talked about Ed O'Connor—"I still miss him," he said—about Penelope Gilliatt, whom he adores, about Isaiah [Berlin]—"never disappointing by himself, but tends to disappoint in company"—about [W. H.] Auden, with whom he is dining tonight—"he will give me a lecture about the British middle class as the source of all virtue"—and a dozen other things.

After lunch we walked down 43rd Street. He is very frail and walked very slowly—because of gout and because of angina. He had forgotten his nitroglycerine tablets, and he paused every few steps to regain his breath. When we parted on the corner, I said, with perhaps more emphasis than I intended, "Do take care of yourself." He smiled and said, "That's what I spend all my time doing" and walked slowly away.

A great man. I would not be surprised if this is the last time I shall ever see him.

February 11

At times one begins to wonder whether there is not some sort of madness loose in the country. On Sunday night Alexandra and I went to a preview of Antonioni's new film *Zabriskie Point*. It is a hymn to violence and revolution, done in the most heavy-handed and simple-minded way. In the course of the film I became vaguely aware of mutters in the row behind, and in a while I began to feel that the mutters were directed against me. Toward the end of the movie, a large house is blown up as a sort of metaphor of revolution. The explosion is repeated a number of times, and finally I whispered to Alexandra, "This is the film that ought to have been called *Blow Up*." This produced an angry reaction from the row behind. The next scene showed books and other artifacts hurled into the air by the explosion. From the row behind: "There goes bourgeois history." In another moment the film was over and the house lights went on. A young jerk in the row behind suddenly launched a tirade. "What are you doing watching this film?" he began. "It's about you and your kind and what we are going to do to you. It's a disgrace that you should have come to see it—or that you can walk the streets at all—and we're going to fix that, and very soon. We're going to rub you out." These agreeable sentiments, uttered in rather shrill tones, had an arresting effect for several aisles around. I started to answer when a man in a leather jacket who had been sitting next to me suddenly intervened. He turned to the revolutionary and said, "You shut up." When the revolutionary kept on talking, the man in the leather jacket said, "Have you ever heard of the Abe Lincoln Brigade?" The revolutionary allowed that he had. The man in the leather jacket said, "Well, I fought in the Abe Lincoln Brigade. I know what revolution is like. This man [gesturing at me] is OK. You just shut up." The revolutionary said, "If you fought in the Abe Lincoln Brigade, you were fighting the fascists. How can this man be your friend? He is one of the biggest fascists in America. He is responsible for people being killed all over the world, and he should be rubbed out." The man in the leather jacket told him to shut up again, and, as he subsided, we all moved out. This is not untypical of a sort of shrill, incoherent anger one occasionally encounters, especially among the young. It is also not untypical that it occasionally brings together members of the old left who previously might have been deeply divided over the merit of things like communism.

May 6

I find myself more depressed these days than I have been for years (except in particular moments, like Dallas and Los Angeles)—more depressed about the short-run movements of events and the long-run future of our country. Last week Nixon invaded Cambodia. With the evident failure of his Vietnamization policy, he accepted a plan the Joint Chiefs have been hawking around Washington for years and which even Johnson, to his credit, refused. Then he traveled to the Pentagon and denounced protesting students as "bums." When the President of the United States thus creates a national mood, I suppose one cannot be too much surprised if the National Guard of Ohio fails to exercise discrimination. At any rate, in the course of breaking up an anti-Cambodia rally in Kent, Ohio, the National Guard killed four students and gravely wounded others. I know Kent; I have often lectured at Kent State. It is the essence of an Ohio small town; the students are all from other small towns or off the farm; nothing could be more square, unradical and midwest-American.

The reaction has been one of gloom and fury—a fury derived from a sense of impotence, from the inability to get hold of the presidential process. Even more than the Johnsonian escalations, the Nixon Cambodian adventure reveals the anomaly in our process—the difficulty of getting control over a President determined to embark on foreign adventures. This anomaly did not matter as long as the foreign adventures seemed essential to the national security; but, when they do not seem essential to the national security, we have to confront a dangerous—I trust not fatal—weakness in our Constitution. The problem is compounded in this case by the political situation. Everyone's views are shaped by his experience. The experience of my generation, who had the luck of FDR, Truman and JFK, convinced us that the democratic process has been an effective way of changing things. But from the viewpoint of the young today, who were born way after FDR and Truman and can barely remember JFK, the democratic process has been a sham and a phoney.

In 1964 they backed Johnson against Goldwater—only to have Johnson after the election adopt the policy of military escalation he had denounced Goldwater for advocating. Then they watched the political tide begin to rise against the war. They flocked behind Eugene McCarthy and RFK in 1968. They saw Johnson forced to curtail the bombing of North Vietnam, to start negotiations in Paris and to withdraw from the presidential contest. Then they saw RFK murdered, McCarthy and McGovern defeated in Chicago, the police rioting against the protesters. Still, the administration which had escalated the war was beaten, and a new administration, pledged to end the war, was in office. Now, fifteen months later, the new administration has not only continued the Johnson policy but has actually widened the war—and it has done so against the opposition of probably half the Senate, nearly all the Senate Foreign Relations Committee, most of the great newspapers and most of the young. It is little wonder that the young are highly skeptical about the efficacy of the democratic process. What do we tell them now? To wait until 1973, by which time God knows how many Americans and Vietnamese, now alive, will be dead? And in the meantime what can be done?

On Tuesday night we went to Muriel Murphy's for dinner. Present were the Robert Penn Warrens, the Ralph Ellisons, the Holly Whytes and Willie Morris. Ralph, who did most of the talking, was emotional and incomprehensible. He seems to be the last hawk and very defensive/aggressive about his Vietnam record. At one point he said, "We never go out anymore. We never see people. It seems to be impossible to exchange ideas anymore." I thought he probably had the race question in mind. But his wife then interjected, "Ever since Vietnam," and Ellison agreed. A good deal of the time I could not, with the best will in the world, make out what in the world he was trying to say. I have always liked and admired him in the past, so I was quite saddened by seeing him in this mood. He gave the impression of a spoiled and somewhat conceited man incapable of expressing his ideas. Perhaps this is all bound up with his failure to come up with a new novel for so many years.

May 22

Yesterday I went to Washington to give a seminar and lecture at the Executive Institute. I lunched with Henry Kissinger at the Metropolitan Club. He had a Key Biscayne tan and looked well. He began by saying that he had read my letter and had thought a good deal about it. "I have been thinking a lot about resignation," he said. "In fact, I thought about it long before Cambodia. For a time I intended to resign after we completed the President's foreign policy report. There were problems in the situation well before this recent development." He did not explain why he had not resigned then but went on to say there were three reasons why he could not resign now. The first is that he is engaged in something he cannot talk about but which only he can pursue and carry through; if it works, he said, it would more than justify his staying. He did not say what this was; but I assume it to be secret negotiations of some sort with Hanoi. His second reason is that he feels it would be "dishonorable" for him to get out so soon after the Cambodian controversy; "I can't do anything at least for a month or two."

His third reason was less convincing and more Germanic. He said that he thinks the great need for the United States is to preserve institutions of authority. Johnson destroyed the authority of the presidency; if it is destroyed under Nixon too, it would mean by 1973 that the country had been without an effective President for 10 years; and, since the presidency is the supreme national institution, this would have a disintegrating effect throughout our national life. I said that there seemed to me no virtue in respecting authority *per se*. The relationship between authority and the people had to be a two-way relationship; and authority had to do something to earn respect. He rather glumly agreed.

I then went on to say what I thought about Nixon—his evident isolation within the government; the inability of cabinet members to get to him (Henry said promptly that this was not true of his area, State and Defense); his evident decision to intensify divisions within the country in the expectation that the silent majority would overwhelm the articulate minorities; the implied contempt in the fact that he thought students were mainly interested in sports and always asked them about their football teams (Henry said, "He is very shy"); and so on. Henry was gloomy and somewhat defensive during this recital. Finally he repeated, "He is a shy man, and he needs compassion." But he did not attempt much in the way of rebuttal. He said that he felt a majority of the people were behind Nixon and that he would probably be reelected; "he has enough support to win but not enough to govern."

August 10

Last night the Harrimans, George McGovern and Elizabeth Stevens came for dinner. Everyone was in lively form, and it was a most diverting evening. There was some talk about Hubert Humphrey and general expectation that he had not counted himself out in 1972. Averell asked George what he thought had happened to Humphrey.

George said that it was partly because Hubert had been Johnson's "slave" for four years and had lost his manhood. It was also partly because Hubert was determined not to repeat in 1968 the errors that he felt had lost him the nomination in 1960. He felt it was more important to have solid ties to Johnson, [George] Meany, Daley, etc., than to the liberals who in the past had promised so much and delivered so little. George recalled seeing Hubert after a breakfast with Meany and Reuther in the spring of 1960. He had never seen Humphrey so upset; he was crying out of anger and frustration. "For twelve years," he told George, "I've been taking the positions those fellows wanted me to take. This did me great damage in Minnesota. And now they say I am too liberal, too controversial, for them. To hell with those bastards." He was not going to be too liberal in 1968.

August 11

I lunched today with Henry Kissinger in his new headquarters on the ground floor of the West Wing—very light and much less claustrophobic than the old room in the basement. I felt that, with the cease-fire in the Middle East, the withdrawal of U.S. ground forces from Cambodia and the general subsidence of the Cambodian uproar, Henry enjoyed a certain tactical advantage as compared to our last meeting. On the State Department in general, however, he was scathing—even more so than when we last met. He said that, if he could reorganize the Department, he would begin by removing all the Foreign Service ambassadors and ministers; "some injustice might be done but still it would improve things greatly." The Department, he says, is essentially a cable-answering organization today; it must get away from this and begin to think about problems.

We went over the familiar ground on Vietnam without too much conviction on either side; the ground was too familiar. He said vigorously that there would be no re-escalation of the war. There were those who thought that the military situation had notably improved, "and in part they are right. Everything we can learn from foreigners who go to North Vietnam is that the war weariness there is intense. The military situation has really changed in our favor." He conceded that some concluded from this that we should try for military victory, and could probably get it in two years. I asked him what military victory meant; and he said that no one had been able to define what military victory might mean. Then he said emphatically that military victory was *not* the White House objective, and, should it become so, "I would resign rather than go along with it."

He asked, as usual, what I thought he should do. There was no point in my saying that he should resign, and I did not do so. He said he had little interest in returning to Harvard and would prefer to settle in New York; might even be interested in coming to the City University. Then he said, "I do not expect to be here during the second term." His deadline seems to be receding every time I see him.

August 25

On August 13 Pat Moynihan came to dinner with Kay Graham and Liz Stevens. I have always been fond of Pat and considered him an exceptionally lively and irreverent figure. This was a new Pat Moynihan. No one had any intention of harassing him about Nixon, but he was nonetheless on the defensive from the start—on the defensive, subdued and unamusing. His basic views then emerged when the conversation turned to Harvard. He regards Pusey as a "great president." His candidate for the succession is James Q. Wilson. I said that everyone I knew in the Harvard faculty thought that Wilson was a disaster. Pat said, with a sneer, "You've been talking to Ken Galbraith." It was apparent from his comments that he feels an intellectual kinship of a particular sort with Wilson and Irving Kristol. He could have added Henry Kissinger to this, but did not. They all have a distinctive view which, I suppose, is the intellectual case for Nixon. The case, as I gather it, is the vital necessity of defending the institutions which make up the fabric of American society on the grounds that, if those institutions go, we move into a stage of chaos. Of these institutions whose legitimacy must be sustained, the presidency (as Henry has said to me) is the most central; and therefore, whether or not one especially agrees with Nixon, one must defend and protect him because, if people lose faith in the presidency, then they lose faith in everything. The key thing appears to be the proposition that one has a duty to sustain the institutions, regardless of what the President may do, lest opposition to the President challenge the legitimacy of authority and subvert the structure of American life.

October 13

We spent last weekend in Washington, staying with Averell. When we arrived, Chip and Avis Bohlen, fresh and tanned from Martha's Vineyard, were there for a drink. After they left, Averell said, "Chip is one of my oldest friends, but he is far too fixed in his views of the Soviet Union. He thinks that nothing has fundamentally changed. The trouble is that he takes Marx and Lenin far too literally." The next night, Chip and I were talking at Joe Alsop's 60th birthday party (at Kay Graham's). Chip said, "I admire Averell greatly, of course, but his trouble is that he tries to be a Russian expert without knowing any of the basic documents. I doubt whether he has ever read anything by Marx or Lenin."

The party for Joe was highly ecumenical so far as Vietnam is concerned—everyone from Ben Cohen, who tried (in vain) to alert me to the Vietnam catastrophe as early as 1961, to Walt Rostow, who still thinks it was a great idea. (When I discussed the party with Kay a few weeks ago and expressed a certain surprise that I had been asked, she said, "We regard you and Averell as the furthest out we could go.") Joe was tight, flushed, extremely genial and generally moved and affectionate. Stewart and John Alsop gave very funny speeches.

At one point in the evening I fell into conversation with John McCone, who was in an unusually loquacious mood. He said that, as soon as he heard the news on November 22, 1963, he had gone over to Hickory Hill—a few minutes, of course, from the CIA. He found Bobby and Ethel alone in the upstairs bedroom. After a short time word arrived that the President had died. Ethel's first words were: "Can you imagine the country in the hands of Lyndon Johnson." Later RFK and McCone walked back and forth, back and forth, between the tennis court and the swimming pool, Bobby (as I understood McCone) continuing to repeat Ethel's phrase.

December 11

I lunched today at [the] 21 [Club] with George McGovern, Mike Feldman and Henry Kimmelman. George plans to announce on January 18. On all these matters, one must yield to the candidate's instinct, and George feels he must go ahead. The usual indicators are not very encouraging. In spite of his clear and courageous record and a tolerable amount of public attention, he does not rise much above 2 percent in the public opinion polls. But he has a lot of devoted support and feels that, in the end, and if Ted Kennedy stays out, the liberal Democrats will have to unite behind him.

1971

January 2

Another year; another house; a new life. I left 166 East 61st Street on December 1 and spent most of the month getting settled at 118 East 82nd Street with my beloved Alexandra.

January 15

Last night I spoke at the annual dinner of the Century. I sat next to Mac Bundy and we discussed, among other things, the Khrushchev memoirs. I remarked on the curious resemblance between Khrushchev's account of the life around Stalin—the domineering and obsessive dictator, the total boredom of the social occasions revolving around him, the horror when invited to attend and the even greater horror when not invited—and Albert Speer's account of the life around Hitler. Mac said, "When I read Khrushchev, I was reminded of something else in addition—my last days in the White House with LBJ."

January 20

Ten years ago today JFK was inaugurated. By chance I sat next to Ted Sorensen at a dinner at the Council on Foreign Relations tonight, and we discussed the melancholy decade. Revisionism has, of course, set in; this week's *New Republic* has a mean-spirited and rather bitter attack on Kennedy. It is true that the inaugural address reads much less well today than it sounded then; but people tend to read back the current Soviet-American mood into 1961 and suppose that JFK was some kind of gratuitous and hectic cold warrior. After all, the inaugural address was in part a response to Khrushchev's truculent Moscow speech a fortnight before; 1961 was the year of the Berlin crisis; 1962 the year of the missile crisis. The Cold War was hardly a figment of someone's imagination; it was a hard and visible reality; and one main reason why the world's mood has changed and we seem in some respects to have moved beyond the Cold War is precisely because of the initiatives JFK took after the missile crisis, culminating in the American University speech and the test ban treaty.

Ted remembered a wise statement that Clark Clifford made to him about ten years ago: "Every President has to remember that any laundry clerk in Kansas City would make a better President that he is—by hindsight." Apt enough for the revisionists.

February 2

We gave a small breakfast for George McGovern [Monday] morning. He was, as usual, candid and straightforward. He thinks that his first weeks as an official candidate have been good and is glad that he decided to announce; among other things, it has given his statements better coverage and more attention. (I agree with this; though I disagreed with his decision to announce so early, I was clearly wrong—which gives me more faith in George's political intuitions.) He is aware that fifteen months is a long time and hopes to pace his campaign, both by periods of silence and by special tours on specific problems. He is also concerned, rather fatalistically, about his failure to come over more strongly on television; he said that he can see himself freezing when he enters a studio. He said he would be willing to have a voice coach or anything else, but that thus far expert counsel had not helped much.

Last night the Bundys gave a dinner for the Alsops (Joe) and Moorheads. Jackie Onassis was there and told me about the White House visit. She found Mrs. Nixon more relaxed and toughly humorous than she expected and thought the girls nice. The President arrived toward the end and seemed quite nervous and uptight but was doing his best. At one point, everyone was trying to recall his earliest memory. Nixon said his earliest memory was when he had fallen out of a carriage as a three-year-old boy. He fell, he said, and gashed his head; but he didn't remember that; all he remembered was the carriage going along while he lay on the ground; "ever since I have had a phobia about being left behind." A revealing memory, I think; also Jackie thinks his use of the word "phobia" suggests psychiatric consultation at some point in his life. If so, it evidently didn't help very much, since she thought his extreme insecurity to be the most noticeable thing about him. But the occasion as a whole, she said, had been remarkably agreeable.

May 31

Averell called this morning in a state of amiable outrage over a piece I had sent him—an interview with Dean Acheson by Kenneth Harris which appeared in the *Listener* of 8 April. The interview was really Dean at his worst—filled with condescension and portraying himself as the single sane man in a world of fools, intervening from time to time to save statesmen from their folly. Averell objected to Dean's accounts of Truman and of Kennedy, but most of all to the account of FDR. Acheson said that FDR's belief he could deal directly with Stalin "was a complete mistake; it was just wholly wrong; there was no basis for it at all and this led us astray for quite a long time."

Averell exploded at this. "FDR was basically right in thinking he could make progress by personal relations with Stalin. My only difference with him was that he was more optimistic about how much progress he could make. Stalin was very much impressed by Roosevelt; you could almost say that he was in awe of Roosevelt. He saw in Roosevelt the power of the U.S.A., but he also saw in him the New Deal; he knew that something had been happening in America which did not fit the categories and which he had to take account of. . . . Stalin was not constrained by Leninism. He saw himself, not as the disciple of Marx and Lenin, but as a fellow prophet and was prepared to change things around to meet his own needs. So he rewrote Russian history and was prepared to rewrite Soviet ideology. . . . I don't know what would have happened if FDR had lived. I only know that things would not have been the same. He never had a chance to play out his policy. The Russians were utterly convinced that the change came as a result of the shift from Roosevelt to Truman. This was not quite the case. Roosevelt would have been tough too. Still things would have been different if he had lived. . . . Of course Roosevelt had his defects. He thought aloud to people, sometimes to the wrong people, and said things he did not really mean. Sometimes he kept talking because he didn't want to give the other fellow a chance to talk. He knew what the other fellow was going to say and didn't want to hear it or face it. Sometimes he was overly naive. He was at his worst when he was trying to be facetious, like the time Stalin angered Churchill by suggesting that 50,000 Nazi war criminals be summarily killed and FDR tried to smooth things over by suggesting 49,000. When he called Stalin 'Uncle Joe,' Stalin seemed taken aback; maybe there was some problem in translation, and he thought that FDR might be making fun of him. . . . [Acheson] Dean says that the great turning-point was Stalin's speech of February 1946. What he really means is that it was the great turning-point for himself. Up to that time he had refused to believe what others of us had been saying—that Stalin was going to cause trouble."

June 10

Again, death. On 30 May I delivered the commencement address at Muhlenberg College. This reminded me of the day 21 years before when I gave the commencement address there. Reinhold Niebuhr gave the baccalaureate, and we both received honorary degrees and had a fine time. The next day, back in New York, I dictated a letter to him recalling the incident. The following morning, I picked up the newspaper and read that he had died. This was not unexpected. Reinhold has had a series of strokes in the last 15 years and has evidently been especially weak this winter. I saw him every couple of months when he was still living in New York; but he went to Stockbridge permanently perhaps three years ago, and I have not seen him since, though we have talked over the phone and exchanged letters.

He was a great man, and he had more intellectual influence on me than anyone I have known. His Christian interpretation of democracy as resting on the mixed nature of man—"Man's capacity for justice makes democracy possible; man's inclination toward injustice makes democracy necessary"—provides far the most convincing basis for the democratic faith. His emphasis on the role, overt and covert, of pride and self-interest in history, was very important for me. His realism armed one against both the ideologists on the right and the utopians on the left. Even more important, he embodied the Christian virtues he talked about—the wisdom, the trenchancy, the very genuine modesty and humility. He was a robust man, warm and open, with strong appreciations and reactions. I will always remember him pacing the floor as he talked (before his illness, he could not bear to remain seated for long) or gesturing at the pulpit as he delivered a sermon. He had been a man of unlimited energy and activity; and his last years were a torment for him. I imagine he must often have wished himself dead. For the first time in his life he experienced physical limitation; he could not work or write as he once had; in the last months he could not even converse for very long.

It is odd to me how little read Niebuhr seems these days. We are inundated by new forms of the old utopianism he exposed so effectively. The New Left is based either on antinomianism or on the perfectibility of man. But we are bound to go back to Niebuhr, because we cannot escape the dark heart of man and because we cannot permit an awareness of this darkness to inhibit action and abolish hope.

June 19

The topic this week has been the publication of the so-called Pentagon Papers—the secret Pentagon account of the Vietnam involvement,
compiled in 1967–68 at Bob McNamara's order—in the *New York Times*
and later in the *Washington Post* and elsewhere. There are the usual cries
about violation of national security, and so on; and the government is
engaged in trying to prevent further publication.

Most of the principals have said nothing, except for Maxwell Taylor,
who made a most dispiriting television appearance in which he said
he did not agree to the people's right to know as a general proposition; they needed to know, he said, only enough to be good citizens—
a sentiment which would have seemed more appropriate on the lips
of a Communist or Nazi general. Someone who had gone to Ken Galbraith's commencement day party on the 17th reported Jim Gavin as
saying: "Didn't it do your heart good to watch Max Taylor squirming!"

July 13

Two events of more than routine importance in recent weeks.
First, and most important, Alexandra and I were married last Friday,
9 July. Since this is not a very personal journal, I will not make personal comment, except that we have had an exceptionally happy life
already here at 118 East 82nd Street, and that I have no doubt this
happiness will grow for the rest of our lives. I am astonished by my good
fortune.

The other is the release of the Pentagon Papers. These papers don't
really contain many revelations—i.e., previously unknown facts. Most
of the "disclosures" have long since been printed, either in the newspapers of the time (as Richard Harwood of the *Washington Post* and Peter
Arnett of AP have demonstrated in interesting pieces) or in subsequent
memoirs and histories.

What the publication does is to accentuate the basic mystery: that is, why anyone ever supposed that Vietnam so involved the American national interest or so threatened the security of the United States as to justify the frightful slaughter and destruction we have brought to this remote and alien country. And what it also displays, at interminable length, is the frightening combination of certitude, misjudgment and ignorance that went into the making of decisions. There is far too much deception here, especially in connection with the Tonkin Gulf resolution. But there is also a terrifying amount of self-deception. It is not a record of wickedness or criminality; it is rather a record of glibness, illusion and intellectual mediocrity.

I said some of these things yesterday in Washington when Bill Fulbright, Walt Rostow, John Tower, Max Frankel, Crosby Noyes and I taped a discussion for CBS on "The Pentagon Papers: What They Mean." The hawks on the program were critical of the publication on the grounds that it undermined confidence in government, but this, of course, is precisely why the publication seems to me so happy an event. It is a very healthy thing for a democracy to be made to realize that government is not infallible and very often consists of exceedingly limited, presumptuous, mistaken and even stupid men. The great lesson, I concluded by saying, is: Don't trust your leaders—until they earn and justify that trust by telling the people the truth.

July 29

I lunched today with Bill Fulbright in the dining room at the New Senate Office Building. Capitol Hill dining rooms are always splendid places for strange encounters. As we came in, Scoop Jackson waved genially at me, and I chatted with him for a moment. Then, as we sat down, I looked at the next table and saw a man with an astonishing resemblance to Dean Rusk. I mentioned this to Bill, who wheeled around and said, "My God, it *is* Dean Rusk." A little later Dean got up and came over, saying with a smile, "What kind of a conspiracy is this?" He then shook hands warmly with Fulbright and perhaps a little coolly with me (for which I hardly blame him). I must hand it to him that he handled the encounter with the curious grace and dignity he often showed on private occasions.

Bill was, as usual, amusing about the Senate. We talked a good deal about the belated congressional struggle to recover purpose and influence in the government; and he conceded that members of Congress had often been willing collaborators in their own impotence. "About 20 percent of the Senate," he said, "really don't want responsibility in foreign affairs. Take John Sparkman, for example. He occasionally might differ with some detail of policy, but he always ends up by saying, 'He's the only President we have, and I think we have to back him.' I can't remember a conversation with Sparkman on foreign policy in which he didn't end up by saying that."

I said he looked well. He said he was tired and had been feeling depressed but felt a good deal better since the publication of the Pentagon Papers. I wonder what would have happened had JFK followed through on his original intention and made Fulbright Secretary of State instead of Rusk.

August 4

We are staying at Hickory Hill—the perfect place, of course, to meditate on a book on Robert Kennedy. In the heap of books by Ethel's bed I found *The Cassell Book of English Poetry*—actually an exceedingly inferior anthology; the kind that prints nine poems by Rossetti, one by Yeats, one by Eliot and none by Auden. In paging through it last night, I noticed that the corner of one page was turned down. It marked Emily Dickinson's "Parting":

My life closed twice before its close;
   It yet remains to see
If Immortality unveil
   A third event to me,

So huge, so hopeless to conceive
   As these that twice befell.
Parting is all we know of heaven,
   And all we need of hell.

Luncheon today with Henry Kissinger at the Metropolitan Club. He arrived a little late, explaining that he had been held up because the President had called a small press conference in his office. "I hate these things," he said. "I'm always afraid that the President will say something he shouldn't say. When he knows something, he is like a little boy and can't wait to tell somebody. And he really can't remember whether he has read something in a newspaper or in an intelligence report." I assured him that Presidents were always the weakest security link in any administration.

We talked most of the time about Peking. I remarked that here at least the President had kept security remarkably well. Henry said, "The reason nothing got out about this is that we didn't tell anybody." It soon became apparent that he included the State Department high in the list of those not told. "We've never told the State Department anything that wasn't leaked," he said.

As for the trip itself, he talked about it with enthusiasm and charm. He was obviously enchanted by the Chinese. "I could not possibly understand anyone young and militant wishing to dedicate themselves to the cause of the Soviet Union," he said. "European communism is dreary and sterile. But I could fully understand it if someone decided to dedicate himself to Communist China." He added that, of course, his view was limited. Outside of two hours in the Forbidden City and two hours at the archaeological museum, he had spent all his time with Chou En-lai and four of his aides. But he was very much impressed by their grace and subtlety. "The Russians seem at bottom peasants, elemental and rigid. You can never have a ranging conversation with them." Chou, on the other hand, was much freer and more curious. "The Chinese are less doctrinaire than the Russians and more idealistic." He was particularly taken by their "elegance" of manners. "Even their communications," he said, "have a style which you never find in Soviet diplomatic documents."

Henry is quite optimistic about the outcome of the talks (and I entirely agree with him). He thinks that the Chinese have already lost their revolutionary purity by issuing the invitation; if they should make trouble later and try to humiliate Nixon, they will not recover that purity; it will seem only a pragmatic decision. Moreover, their interest in breaking out of isolation is too great.

Walking back to the White House, he said that he did not plan to stay beyond the first term (I will believe this when I see it). "I feel that if we have a new Chinese policy and get out of Vietnam, I will have done everything I could do to justify the confidence of my old friends in the scholarly community." He asked how I thought the Democratic presidential contest looked. When I gave him my view, he said that he liked McGovern very much but was entirely mystified by the popularity of Muskie, whom he had found unimpressive.

September 15

Last night we dined at the Peter Duchins'. We arrived a little later, and Averell, Pamela Hayward and Madeleine Sherwood were already there, as well as Cheray and Peter.

We went into dinner. I sat next to Pam. Suddenly I heard her whisper to me, "It's the most incredibly romantic story. Imagine, after twenty-five years!" Then I began belatedly to realize that something was up. Pam and Averell, I knew, had an affair in London during the war. Then they met at the party Kay Graham gave for Alexandra and me in Washington in early August; and I had heard that they were seeing each other on the subsequent weekends. But I had not imagined the speed with which things have progressed. Soon Averell, with a cheerful and contented smile, told us that they were going to be married. After dinner they sat together on the couch holding hands.

It is an incredibly romantic story, and Pam took me aside much later in the evening to tell me more about it. She was 20, the daughter-in-law of the Prime Minister. He was 49, the President's special representative in London. They were thrown together by Max Beaverbrook. In retrospect, Pam feels that Beaverbrook engineered the whole thing in order to get something on Averell and thereby influence American policy. She loved him madly. Harry Hopkins was disturbed, fearing stories to the effect that the President's envoy was breaking up the Prime Minister's son's marriage. After six months, Averell felt he had to break things off; but then there was another Beaverbrook weekend, and he could not bring himself to do it. They lived together for the rest of the war, until Averell went to Moscow. He turned down jobs in Washington to stay with her. (Recently she said to him, "How fortunate it was that you stayed; where else could you have got your experience in world affairs." Averell said, "Yes, but, if I had gone back to Washington, I might have been Secretary of State instead of [Edward] Stettinius.") She never thought they would marry; he seemed too old, and the affair was an episode of war, when all the rules were suspended. Except two or three times at very large parties, they had not seen each other for a quarter of a century.

I asked Pam whether the Prime Minister ever knew. She said, "He only mentioned it once." For a moment, her blood froze. She thought that old Winston was the one person she could not lie to about it. Then he said something about the triviality of gossip in the midst of the mighty concerns of war.

October 26

I lunched today at the Century with Pat Moynihan. He is a member of the U.S. delegation to the General Assembly and was full of last night's vote admitting Peking into and expelling Taiwan from the UN. He said that the atmosphere on the floor was exceedingly disquieting— a kind of exultation about the American defeat. Apparently the ambassador from Tanzania was particularly arrogant and nasty in his effort to rub the American nose in humiliation. He also expressed some bitterness about the Cypriot ambassador who had promised George Bush support and had then abstained. George, by the way, was really quite good on CBS this morning.

Pat was considerably more open about Nixon than he was when we last talked a year or so ago. "The most important thing about the President," he said, "is that he is dominated by his hatreds. The last thing he wants to do is to give satisfaction to people he hates—people like you, for example." I asked him whether this wasn't also true about Johnson. He said it was different; LBJ never really began to hate people until he became obsessed with Vietnam; hatred, he suggested, was more organic in Nixon's personality. Nixon, he added, is "an intellectual," and cares considerably about intellectual opinion; but has come to feel that nothing he will ever do can win intellectual support and therefore hates intellectuals more than ever. He went on to say that he found personal relations with Nixon easy; there was no problem, he said, about saying anything to him, even things he might not like to hear.

November 11

I lunched today with Bill Moyers. We were musing about LBJ and the Indochina War. Bill remembered a session with LBJ when the President recalled a meeting at Sam Rayburn's office with Truman early in 1945. "The Russians are testing me," Truman said. "They think I'm just a little haberdasher, and they're testing me." Bill thinks this sense of being tested played a considerable part in Johnson's reactions to Vietnam. What happened, Bill said, "was an atrocious marriage of ego and nationhood, so that Johnson saw himself as America involved in some sort of challenge to manhood."

December 7

We spent the weekend after Thanksgiving with Steve and Jean Smith at Hyannis Port and saw a lot of Ted Kennedy. He was in a jolly mood, and we played a good deal of tennis but talked very little politics. The Sunday *Times* on 28 November had a rather favorable piece about him implying that he was preparing the way for a presidential run. Jean asked him what he thought of the piece, and he said, "Very straight." I think he is still rather fatalistic about it all, probably prepared to accept the nomination if he is asked but also prepared to see many advantages if he is not asked.

1972

April 15

Incredible as it may seem, it really looks as if George [McGovern] will get the Democratic nomination. As Muskie continues to collapse, it is turning into a contest between McGovern and Humphrey; and it is inconceivable to me that Humphrey can beat McGovern in California and New York, the two largest states and the two last primaries. And I find it hard to conceive that the convention will deny the nomination to the man who carries these two primaries.

This is essentially a tribute to George himself. He was right to declare so early, and he has shown an accurate intuition on issues. It is more than ever evident now that the polls, in the early stages, register name recognition more than anything else—hence naturally favored Hubert, who has been in politics for the last 150 years, and Ed, who had a distinguished national campaign in 1968, and Ted, who bears (and has earned the right to bear) a famous name. But wherever George has had time to campaign in a state, he has moved swiftly ahead.

I spoke last week for McGovern in Ohio and was impressed by what seems to me a quiet underground strength in a state where labor is supposed to rally votes for Humphrey and Jack Gilligan votes for Muskie. George (to whom I talked to this morning) says that they plan a media blitz in Ohio as an experiment.

George attributes his recent gains to his success in addressing himself in simple and believable terms to the distresses of the low-income whites. "My advantage over Wallace," he said, "is that Wallace whips up excitement and says, 'We have to send a message to those bastards in Washington,' but then he never tells them what the message is. I can tell them things that hold out a chance of relieving their distress." He said that he had had an astonishingly warm reception yesterday in the factories of Lowell and Lawrence, especially from women workers. I asked what they said to him, and he said, "They say things like 'I like the way you answer questions—you don't duck the hard ones' or 'It's time we got someone who tells the truth.' "

We discussed the Stewart Alsop–[Rowland] Evans & [Bob] Novak line that his nomination would do to the Democratic party what the nomination of Goldwater did to the Republicans in 1964. "I don't think I am perceived as a left-winger," George said (and I think he is quite right—as the number of Republican cross-over votes he received in Wisconsin demonstrates). He added, "I do think the old politics of the center is dead. The old center is not an attractive political ground. People who say they stand for the center are taken as standing for the Establishment, for the status quo. The thing that strikes me is that there is a nationwide revolt against the center in that sense. What our politics needs is a new center." He added, "I hope the regulars will understand that actually I would be a more reconciling candidate than Hubert. What we have to do is to construct a new coalition, and that is what I am trying to do."

May 7

George continues to do splendidly in primary and non-primary states alike. But the campaign against him is beginning. It takes several, somewhat contradictory forms. Some condemn him as a sectarian candidate, a left-wing extremist, a Democratic Barry Goldwater, committed to positions on pot, abortion and amnesty which, once the electorate realizes what they are, it will repudiate. Others condemn him as a tough and ambitious pragmatist who, in his drive to become President, has been all over the map on issues. The second theory is nearer the truth. As George made clear in our last conversation, he fully understands the political necessity of reassuring regular Democrats and persuading them that they can live with him—though he will not do this at the expense of his position on the defense budget, tax reform and Indochina.

Later. I went to a party given by Goddard and Brigitte Lieberson at the St. Regis for a hero of my youth, Groucho Marx. He is a small man with a weary, astute face, a beret and a line of compulsive, almost automatic, verbal response. He looks exactly like Groucho Marx. Goddard Lieberson said, "I want you to meet an old friend of mine, the distinguished historian Arthur Schlesinger, Jr." Groucho looked at me amiably and said, "Oh yes, I've read his lies for years." Betty Comden, who was sitting next to him, asked me where Alexandra was. I said that she was feeling exhausted and had stayed home. Betty explained to Groucho that Alexandra was pregnant. Groucho said, "By whom?" Both these remarks sound in print less funny and more offensive than in fact they were.

May 11

These have been rather discouraging days. On Monday evening our President delivered what are, in effect, ultimatums to Hanoi and Moscow and announced his intention to mine the North Vietnamese harbors and seal off the country from foreign supply. The speech was appalling in tone, and the actions proposed seem wholly gratuitous.

Yesterday I went to Washington to testify before the Senate Foreign Relations Committee on the origins of American involvement in Vietnam. By this time a theory had arisen that Nixon's bellicose tone was simply a mask for a cave-in; that, if one read his "conditions" for stopping the mining and the bombing, they would not only leave the North Vietnamese in control of the territory they have gained in the new offensive but might even imply the dumping of the Thieu regime. Thus Frank Church has said that he thinks the administration has dramatically softened its negotiating position. I asked Bill Fulbright before the hearing whether he thought there might be anything in this theory. He was skeptical about it.

Though the subject of the inquiry was of course historical, the senators—also the witnesses—were so filled with present apprehensions that the talk kept turning to the Nixon speech. The senators were in a state of intense frustration and kept asking what we thought they could do to prevent the President from further escalation. One's suggestions were lame—a fund cut-off bill; demanding a meeting with the President; going to the country. One can understand their sense of impotence and their rage. Nixon has gone further, I guess, than any President in ignoring even the forms of congressional consultation. I fear that those uncritical theories of the strong presidency that historians and political scientists, myself among them, were propagating with such enthusiasm in the fifties have come home to roost.

May 29

On the 26th I spent the day campaigning for McGovern, beginning in Ithaca and ending in Suffolk County. I left the house at 6:30 in the morning and returned at 11:15 in the evening. I could not help reflecting on the contrast between this excursion and my sallies on George's behalf last November and December. Then one spoke to gallant but rather forlorn groups who were standing by principle but had no great faith in George's ability to get anywhere. Indeed, I had no such faith myself. He was my friend and stood for the right things; I felt that, the more impact his candidacy might have, the greater likelihood the party would end up with a candidate and platform pointed in the right direction. Now one feels everywhere a strong and happy surge in his favor. If he wins California, as Ken Galbraith assures me he will, he cannot be stopped for the nomination.

June 27

At 11:04 tonight I became, after an interval of 24 years, a father again. I took Alexandra to the hospital about 5:30; two hours later she was given something to accelerate her labor, and I was told that I might as well go back to 118 and await developments. A few minutes before 11, Dr. Truppin called and said I had better come back to the hospital. Around 11:30 he picked me up in the lobby and took me to the second floor, where the offspring was revealed—a cunning little boy, weighing 7 pounds, 11 ounces. I had rather hoped for a girl on the grounds that a 60-year-old father would not be very good playing touch football with his young son. We had chosen a name for a girl—Elizabeth Emmet, after my mother and Alexandra's family. But I am already reconciled to this unexpected development; and we can figure out a name tomorrow.

Odd how this is by far the most exciting human experience. I had thought that, with age, my capacity for undue nervousness had disappeared. I cannot recall being nervous for years—whether meeting Presidents or Prime Ministers, or addressing large crowds or testifying before congressional committees. I was not even particularly nervous when Alexandra and I were married a year ago. But, rather to my surprise (since this whole event has had for me an air of unreality), my stomach tightened early in the day, and I found myself in an increasingly tense state. I had to go to a television show after luncheon (the first in the History Machine series—on the first successful flight in 1909 of the first plane purchased by the army—and with Colonel Ernest Dupuy, a delightful man of 85, Walter Lord and Najeeb Halaby—rather good show); then rushed to the doctor's office. By seven I was filled with a curious feeling—not quite apprehension but anxiety, I guess—and felt quite sick. When I came back to the house, I had several bourbons in quick succession, followed by a steak, and felt much better.

June 30

McGovern called about nine this morning. He said, "I know you don't like writing speeches anymore, but I still think you know my thinking better than anyone else, so I would be infinitely grateful if you could do an acceptance speech." I said that, in the circumstances, I would, and asked him what he had in mind to say. He then outlined his ideas with some eloquence. He is taken by a remark that Clayton Fritchey made to him some days ago—that this period is comparable to the Jacksonian period in the emergence of new forces in politics; and he wants to make the point that we are on the threshold of a new political era. The convention itself stands as an expression of these new forces and of the new era of citizen participation. The mainstream of American politics has moved beyond the traditional power brokers on substance as well as on process. And, while he does not want to sound isolationist, he wants to attack Nixon for his indifference to domestic affairs and for his evident feeling that Peking and Moscow are more important than Keokuk and Kalamazoo. "After thirty years of obsession with foreign policy, probably the greatest contribution we can make to the world and to ourselves is to put our own house in order."

July 8

Here I am—Room 1208 at the Doral, Miami Beach—my seventh Democratic convention. I look out my window and see a parking lot, a swimming pool, the narrow and dirty beach and the Fontainebleau. It is a hazy Sunday morning.

As usual, walking through a crowded convention lobby is like some weird form of class reunion. I encountered Pat Donovan, who told me that McGovern had liked the acceptance draft I had (with some reluctance) done for him much better than the others. Warren Beatty later told me much the same thing; "George said that he could give your draft as it stands, without changing a single word, and it would be the best acceptance speech ever given." This sounds extravagant. And, of course, he will (and must) change quite a lot of words.

July 9

The remarks about my draft were unwarrantedly optimistic. Ted Van Dyk later told Stephen that McGovern found it too literary—too much like a Kennedy speech. (Kennedy used to say that my drafts were too Stevensonian.) Hardly a line survived in the final speech. In the end, McGovern himself wrote most of it, and it turned out very well indeed.

July 13

When [I] got back to the Doral, I found a message saying to call Senator McGovern, URGENT. This was about 3:20. I did my best to call for some moments but could not get through the McGovern headquarters switchboard. After a time I went up to the 16th floor and was told that the candidate would be tied up until the press conference. This was the press conference announcing the choice—OK, I think—of Tom Eagleton as the vice presidential nominee. A couple of hours later, Blair Clark dropped by, and, when I told him this story, said I should go up and see McGovern now. I demurred; having been through these things before in closer association with candidates, I know the problem of intrusive friends who waste people's time and harass the candidate for their own need, not his. This is why I have made no attempt to approach McGovern all week. But this time I weakened, and Blair steered me through the security up to the 17th floor. We were ushered in rather quickly to see McGovern. He was in a small sitting room with a splendid view of the shining inland waters of Miami Beach.

McGovern was as composed, natural, unaffected and wryly humorous as ever. I don't know why one always expects that winning the nomination will produce an immense change in a man you know well; but one always does (or at least I always do), and then one is astonished to see that they are about the same today as they were yesterday. (It is different, though, when they are elected President.) He talked first about

Ted Kennedy. To my surprise, he said that Ted had not finally taken himself out of the picture until 2:30 that afternoon; he had been up and down on the question, George said, for the last 48 hours.

George said he had been trying to reach me about Kevin White, the mayor of Boston, whose name had inexplicably boiled up in the last moments of vice presidential consideration. I might say that I have never seen any candidate engaged in a struggle for the presidential nomination give serious thought to his vice presidential choice until he is safe home himself—and then everyone is always tired, somewhat emotional and under the gun of a twenty-four-hour deadline. McGovern proved no exception. A group of mayors, George said, urged [White's] selection; and some of the staff (especially Dick Dougherty, Dick told me later) pressed the idea. I told George that, in my view, Kevin White simply did not carry the guns for this job.

Around 2 A.M., Ted Kennedy arrived, and I went out to see him in one of the stationary trailers established for dignitaries behind the convention hall. He was in a moderately jovial mood, and we chatted lightly for a time, with the convention on television in the background. Then the telecast cut from the convention to a picture of McGovern getting out of a car and, surrounded by Secret Service men and photographers, walking to another trailer, perhaps fifty feet from the one we were sitting in. I glanced at Ted while we were all watching. His face was suddenly reflective, almost somber. One could not help but wonder what thoughts were in his mind. A few moments later, he strode out on the platform, and the convention hall exploded in cheers and applause. His introduction of McGovern was smashing— all the more so for those standing to the south of the platform, like George Stevens and me; for we could see Ted in profile and, beyond him, huge photographs of Bobby and Jack hanging on the north side of the hall.

George Stevens and I had wondered whether George would be able to top Ted; but, at the very least, he held his own. The acceptance speech sounded a good deal better than it had read (when Marty Nolan of the *Boston Globe* had shown me a copy earlier in the evening). George delivered it with a certain flat force and earnestness that became a kind of eloquence, and the audience gave him round after round of applause.

It was an unusual convention—unusual not only in the composition of the delegates, the unprecedently large numbers of women and blacks, the total absence of sexism and racism, the seriousness with which the delegates took their responsibilities but, above all, in the spirit of amiability that pervaded the proceedings. If any one had said that the convention would throw out Dick Daley and put down every one of George Wallace's platform proposals without breaking up into ugliness and rancor, no one would have believed it. But most of the time the atmosphere could only be described as benign.

August 6

We are now through the Eagleton phase of the 1972 campaign. I was originally for him for the vice presidential nomination. He seemed agreeable and intelligent when I met him at Rowlie Evans's 50th birthday party; his record was good; and his ties with the Democratic regulars, with labor and with the Catholic church all commended him. After seeing him on television for a few days, he became more identifiable. He appeared the most radical member of the country club.

Then came the bombshell. As I told McGovern (in a message phoned through Pat Donovan to the Black Hills on 26 July and subsequently in a letter of 29 July), the fact of his psychiatric history mattered a good deal less than his failure to communicate this fact to McGovern. His subsequent TV appearances were rather appalling: voluble, compulsive, filled with self-regard and generally oblivious to the issues of the campaign. He seemed a man on the manic phase of a manic-depressive cycle. He could not stop talking about himself—and he incessantly referred to himself in the third person: "Eagleton" believes this or that.

I thought he went out with a certain amount of class; but his persistent self-serving TV postures thereafter quickly cancelled the sympathy one felt for him.

It is Sunday as I write; Sarge Shriver will be the nominee; and I have just spoken to McGovern. He said that it had been a rough week, but that he felt it had come out all right. He noted rather bitterly that some people who had told him with the greatest urgency that he had to drop Eagleton were now saying how hard-hearted and ruthless he had been in doing so. As for Shriver, he felt that he would be, on the whole, better than Muskie. He said that Ted Kennedy had not been wildly enthusiastic but had understood the necessity for Shriver and would, of course, campaign. Ted also told George that his mother was pleased and had said, "Now I will have to get new dresses for the campaign"— which George interprets as meaning that she plans to take an active part herself, which cheers him.

I had been a little negative during the week about Sarge, but I must confess that I feel very good about it now. He is attractive, articulate and endlessly energetic. He has always attracted first-rate people, who swear by him (Moyers, Goodwin, Mankiewicz, [William] Haddad, etc.). He has support on the Hill, among the blacks and with the young. I have always found him amiably impenetrable as a person, somewhat ingenuous and Boy Scoutish; and I know that the Kennedys (except for JFK) have always doubted his depth and his loyalty. But he has been quite right to wish to live his own life, and no doubt he has had to take a lot from that strong-minded, spirited and overwhelming family. His own buoyancy and resourcefulness will stand the campaign in good stead. The reception thus far has been excellent; the campaign after this fortnight of dithering has had a lift; and I think the Eagleton episode will now fairly rapidly fade into history.

August 27

We have been here at Aspen for a week. The pretext has been one of the executive seminars put on by the Aspen Institute; I am invited as what is somewhat unhappily called a "resource person." The sessions themselves can hardly be considered stimulating, but there are a good many lively people around, and we have had a good time. Chrissie and Andy joined us on the 25th.

One unexpected development has been a reconciliation with Eugene McCarthy. We ran into each other the first day—I don't think that either knew the other was within a thousand miles—and, caught off guard, without time to meditate a policy, we reverted to our cordiality of an earlier time. This week we have been playing tennis every morning: McCarthy and Jack Valenti vs. Gus Tyler (of the ILGWU) and me (after the first day Tyler and I won every set, to the mounting irritation of our opponents). Throughout Gene has been disarmingly agreeable and charming, except, of course, when he talks about George McGovern or other of his former senatorial colleagues.

September 14

The campaign is moving along, but heaven alone knows in what direction. The Harris poll in the *Post* this afternoon gives Nixon a fantastic 34-point lead, with an 11-point increase in the past month. This sounds impossible to overcome. Yet a crazy optimism surrounds the McGovern effort.

September 23

And still we seem to drift along. Every few days a particular crowd or speech strikes a spark, and the word goes out that the turning-point has come. But the next day the campaign appears to slip back to the sloughs. Yet the crowds are large and, reportedly, enthusiastic; but so they were for [William Jennings] Bryan, and so for Al Smith.

I cannot rid myself of the expectation that a surge will come and that the contest will be much closer than anyone supposes. I also must confess (as I said during the week to Dick Wade and to Joe Rauh) to a certain disappointment with George as a candidate. He seems never to have recovered his stride after the Eagleton mess—perhaps because so many long months of campaigning have really depleted and exhausted him. He does not seem to have the energy now to pull his organization together, put the issues in focus and convey a sense of purpose and mastery. He had to move to conciliate the regular Democrats after the convention; but, instead of doing this as from strength, in the style of FDR in 1932, he seems to have done as from weakness. He seems too intent on pleasing the audience of the moment.

October 4

We went tonight to the Liberal Party dinner—an all-star cast, [John] Lindsay (better than usual), Ted Kennedy (not so good as usual) and McGovern (good, but not so good as he had been Monday night at the Waldorf). As the dinner broke up, George suggested that we meet him back at the Biltmore, where he was staying.

We got there before he did. Soon he arrived with Valerie Kushner, a POW wife who has been campaigning with him. She left after a time. Shirley MacLaine had meanwhile dropped in, and Frank Mankiewicz was in and out during the conversation.

George seemed tired and a little discouraged, despite his success of the evening. Ruminating about the campaign, he said that the Eagleton affair had been "a devastating blow. . . . If it hadn't been for that, I think we would be even with Nixon today." I asked him whether he had known Eagleton well. "No," he said, "hardly at all. And I never liked him." He then explained how it had all happened. On Wednesday night after the nomination he still hoped to get Ted Kennedy. He talked to Ted till about 2 A.M. Ted said he would think about it some more and call back in the morning. In the morning he gave a press conference announcing his unavailability.

George then went to Ribicoff. "Ted and Ribicoff were the two men I would really like to have had." When Abe said no, he decided to talk to Humphrey and then to Muskie. "But I asked them in a rather perfunctory way, and was rather relieved when each said no. Perhaps if I had really gone after them, I could have got one or the other. It's funny, because this is what I did later." In the meantime, the clock was ticking away; the absolute deadline was 3 P.M. in order to give time for the circulation of petitions.

Various names were considered. George tried [Walter "Fritz"] Mondale, but he excused himself on the same grounds that George himself had used in 1968: he was running for reelection. Leonard Woodcock had been twice divorced and the rest of labor was against him. Pat Lucey and Larry O'Brien were both "dying for it"; but George did not think either was right. He considered Frank Church, but Frank was an ex-Catholic, he had been operated on for cancer, "and there were a couple of other problems." Various people kept recommending Eagleton, but McGovern did not like the idea and did not take it seriously.

Then Gary Hart and others came up with the proposal of Kevin White. George called Ted Kennedy, who "exploded" at this suggestion. George then said that, if Ted thought Kevin was a disaster, perhaps he should reconsider his own position, for otherwise George might have to go to White. Ted said he would think about it some more and call back in an hour. It was now about 1:30. Ted called back after two o'clock to give his final no. "In retrospect," George said, "I think that Ted and Ken Galbraith did a disservice by taking on so strongly about Kevin White. We would have been better off today with White. I figure that the most desirable quality in a vice presidential candidate is not to attract too much attention." By this time everyone was getting a little desperate. George went around the room: all his advisers were now for Eagleton. Mondale had already recommended Eagleton. Kennedy had said that he was an attractive and fresh face who would help the ticket. Fred Dutton was strongly for him. But George still did not like the idea. "I thought there was something wrong. I didn't know what. I couldn't put my finger on it." So he balked, declined to call Eagleton and instead called Gaylord Nelson, with whom he argued for a long time. But Nelson said that he had promised his wife when he ran for the Senate that, if she would not divorce him, he would never run for another office. By this time it was almost 3 o'clock. Eagleton seemed the only name left. (I asked George whether Shriver had been discussed. He said that he had inquired about Shriver but had been told that he was in Moscow and no one knew how to get hold of him.) George said he still hated the idea, but, with the deadline drawing closer every minute, could see no alternative. When he called Eagleton, Eagleton said yes, he would accept immediately, before George changed his mind.

"I still think I'm going to win," George said as we said goodnight. He said it a little sadly, I thought. Of course he is incredibly tired. He also conveys a certain remote bitterness over the fortuity of events.

October 29

I cannot recall ever having been so depressed about a presidential election—not (I think) in 1948 or 1952, certainly not in 1968. Every (quasi) statistical indication is for a Nixon landslide; the *Daily News* poll this morning has him leading 65–35 in New York. My own instinct is that it will be very close, but my instinct has been wrong. Still I simply cannot believe the polls. I cannot believe that the electorate will be this indifferent to the crookedness of the Nixon crowd.

Nixon continues to get away with murder. Now it is the progress toward a Vietnam settlement. Does no one think it is odd that the only times of dramatic progress toward such a settlement have been just before presidential elections—in '68 and now in '72. My old friend Henry Kissinger held a press conference the other day explaining his diplomatic triumphs. He was, as usual, subtle, disarming and disingenuous. What is most obvious is the spectacular and unprecedented concessions we have made. But the press, following Henry, has written about it all as if we had made no concessions at all.

What is saddest of all is that if Nixonger (as Isaiah Berlin would say) had been willing to make these concessions in 1969, we could have had the settlement then; and 20,000 Americans and God knows how many Vietnamese, now dead, would be alive.

November 5

Two days to election—and the question now horribly appears to be not whether Nixon or McGovern will win but whether Nixon will carry fifty states.

Evidently McGovern misread the national mood, though I still think he was right to discern a widespread desire for change. But a sensed need for change can produce anxiety as well as hope; it can move the country in two different directions, sometimes at once, and apparently it has. McGovern's personal failure has been his inability to bring the campaign into focus and more particularly to reassure voters about his strength and competence in making change orderly; he thus failed to do what JFK succeeded in doing in 1960. He was, in addition, the victim of terrible luck, above all, Eagleton's fatal lie, followed by Eagleton's even more fatal determination to make a fight to stay on the ticket. Then George has been up against the richest political party in the history of democracies— the Republicans will have spent nearly $50 million on the presidential contest alone. The press has been overwhelmingly against him (over 700 endorsements for Nixon; less than 50 for McGovern) and has applied an unblushing double standard throughout the campaign—Nixon's mind-changing is an evidence of growth, McGovern's of wishy-washiness; McGovern is held personally accountable for all the troubles of his campaign organization, Nixon for none of the crimes of his.

Behind everything else has been the concealed but all-pervading issue of the election—race. When this issue has come to the surface, it is under an alias—welfare, crime, busing, schools, quotas. People are ashamed to acknowledge racist feelings to pollsters. But I would imagine that the one thing which, more than any other, has pulled traditional Democrats to Nixon (the so-called "ethnics"—terrible word—every human being is equally ethnic) is the belief that he can be relied upon to keep the blacks down.

No doubt Nixon will interpret victory as public approval for his methods and objectives. Oddly, he is still not popular or trusted, though there is some strange illusion about his competence and "professionalism."

Actually he has been strikingly incompetent in his conduct of domestic affairs; his anti-inflation policy, for example, was hopelessly wrong and concluded in a 180 degree reversal. Even internationally, despite the nonsense put out (and too widely accepted) about his calm mastery of foreign affairs, he has not been, except for the China trip, very successful. His Vietnam policy remains a scandal. Most offensive of all is the peculiar combination of sanctimoniousness and duplicity with which he faces the people. Nothing is more ironic than this self-styled "strict constructionist" doing more than any of his predecessors to usurp authority in both foreign and domestic matters; or than this vigilant champion of law and order, this keeper of the national morals, presiding over a quite exceptionally crooked administration.

November 8

Well, the worst has happened—not quite the worst; the Democrats did well in House and Senate—but Nixon and his collection of crooks will be running the country for another four years. I feel so badly for George—to have suffered what he can only regard, in view of the Democratic success in Congress, as a sharp personal repudiation and to have enabled a third-rater like Nixon to win by perhaps the largest margin this century. George's concession address was generous and effective; Nixon seemed to me smug and false, but I guess my fellow countrymen disagree by a vast majority. Yet can even Republicans like him or believe him?

George called about 7:30 this evening. He sounded tired but entirely composed and easy; there were traces of bitterness only when he spoke about Nixon. He said, "Nixon is really a diabolical son-of-a-bitch. He knows all the ways to divide the country—and to profit from division. Remember how he made a bee-line from Miami Beach to Michigan after the Republican convention, all to dramatize his point about busing. He has been using code words to hit the racial nerve all through the campaign—'welfare,' 'crime,' 'quotas,' and so on. . . . I wonder what would have happened if Wallace had been able to run on his own. I think we would have won."

He feels about Nixon as the Kennedys used to—a man with no class. "He was such a slob in his victory speech," McGovern said, "that after a while I just had to leave the room. . . . He sent me the most graceless telegram possible for a human being to compose—empty, flat—he must have written it himself; it sounded so much like him." George dismissed the Vietnam negotiation as a deception (he is probably right, but we shall see) and characterized the Nixon administration as "so dishonest and so crooked, corrupt from top to bottom."

November 26

Just back from a couple of nights with Jean and Steve Smith at Pawling. [Saturday] night at dinner we chatted with Ted Kennedy about the future of the party. Ted, by the way, is a much changed person from the Ted Kennedy of a decade ago. He still likes physical movement and is entirely capable of noise and boisterousness; but he is fundamentally much more serious, and his table talk, for example, constantly comes back to issues—the Common Market, trade, Ireland, his health program and so on. He spoke warmly about McGovern and felt that he had aroused a genuine intensity of support in the country, but, of course, in far too small a group. He agreed with the view that race was the hidden issue of the campaign and felt rather pessimistic about the possibility of stopping the drift of low-income whites, who feel threatened by racial change, into the Republican party. If Ted is right, this will make the years ahead very difficult for the Democrats, especially if Republican candidates continue sufficiently unscrupulous to follow the Nixon example and manipulate the race issue for party advantage. Ted was especially scornful of Nixon as the first President since Hoover who did not move the racial justice issue forward, if even a little, during his administration; who, indeed, by moving it back, threatened to undo a good deal of the progress that has been so painfully made.

December 29

The year comes to an end in great gloom. Nixon's resumption of the obliteration of North Vietnam is the most shameful and tragic thing in American history.

1973

I have just finished reading the manuscript of Wallace Stegner's life of Bernard De Voto. It has brought back a flood of memories of another time in my life and of a man whom I owed and from whom I learned a great deal. Still, well as I knew Benny and fond as I was of him, I was really not conscious at the time of the sheer desperation of his life, or of the extent of his intellectual exhaustion and physical decline in the years immediately before his death—years when I saw him and talked to him constantly. I suppose it was partly his own desire not to seem weak before one of his surrogate sons, partly my own activities and preoccupations; in any case, though he was always a man of a certain repressed rage, and though he thundered and grumbled as usual in these years, I never realized how much he was evidently at the end of his tether. Stegner's manuscript brought back so much—Cambridge in the early fifties, late Sunday afternoon at 8 Berkeley Street with Benny mixing the martinis, and Benny himself, with his mixture of public pugnacity and private sweetness, even sentimentality, with his absolute, if somewhat driven, fearlessness, with his passion about this country and its history. I first got some sense of the writer's craft and vocation from the composition course I took from him when I was a sophomore at Harvard, 1935–36. I first got a sense of the West when I went with him along the Santa Fe Trail in the summer of 1940. I always benefited from his limitless generosity to his friends. Stegner's book is very good—filled with affection and understanding, and quietly honest about his temper and his inner torment. The account of Benny's relationship with Robert Frost is excellent, and so, I think, is his judgment of Benny as a failed novelist and a successful historian.

Benny was 58 when he died, and somehow at the end of his string. He had (rightly) given up on fiction; he had abandoned literary criticism, where he had been invigorating on specific works but unnecessarily sweeping and truculent in general indictment; and, after completing his superb trilogy on the West, he had, Stegner says, used up his consuming historical theme. Also he was in a chronic condition of financial uncertainty. But he concealed most of this on those Sunday afternoons when The Hour struck and the ceremony of drink and friendship began. It was another world, and I had forgotten how much I miss him.

I sat next to Mac Bundy at a dinner for Bob Schaetzel at the Council on Foreign Relations on Thursday, 4 January. He had lunched with Henry Kissinger at the White House on 26 December and reported the irony of Henry, with his still marked German accent, sitting in his office and complaining of "the Germans" at the White House. Mac's account was of Henry beleaguered but still hopeful of a Vietnam settlement. I said that I thought Henry should go, both for himself and for the country; that the argument has always been that he might be able to stop Nixon from doing disastrous things, but obviously this argument had now collapsed; that, if we were going to have a primitive foreign policy, it would be better for the country if it were accompanied by a primitive rather than a sophisticated explanation; that Henry was impotent and disgraced and should get the hell out and let General [Alexander] Haig or someone like that take over. Mac said he disagreed, but I am not clear why he thought so.

January 21

Yesterday was inauguration day: the United States of America sentenced (self-sentenced) to four more years of Richard Nixon. I got back to the house in time to see and hear the great event. What is it about Nixon that is so hard to take? I think that it is, among other things, the air of ineffable unction he conveys. But I imagine that the problem is worse than that.

The Constitution is premised on the assumption that Presidents of the United States will be basically reasonable men, ultimately sensitive to their constitutional responsibilities. There is really no procedure for dealing with nuts. On the whole, the assumption has worked. But we seem now to have had two Presidents in succession with very bizarre psyches. LBJ, crazy as he could be, did have a final sense of reality. He often hated reality; but he did read the newspapers, look at television, talk to members of Congress and the press, and a sense of what things were like somehow filtered through his wishes and rages. Nixon seems to have walled himself off from reality much more effectively. He obviously cannot abide scrutiny and challenge. As a result, his reality principle seems to grow steadily weaker, and he drifts off more and more into a world of fantasy. Four more years.

January 26

Lyndon Johnson died the other day—an event that left me curiously unmoved, though I always found LBJ personally impressive and, in his relations to me, entirely courteous, and though I fully acknowledge the authenticity of his social concern. For all this, he was not likable; and he had, in addition, compulsive, even lunatic, strains that were enormously disturbing when he was in power. One does not feel at all about Johnson as one did about Truman. Still, the press reaction has been surprisingly warm. One of Nixon's salient accomplishments has been to create a nostalgia for LBJ.

February 5

We arrived back in New York in time for Norman Mailer's 50th birthday party at the Four Seasons. In an act of monumental impertinence, he decided to charge his guests $50 per couple. We declined to go, but then Jean Campbell sent us some tickets. The restaurant was crowded with a wild variety of people—from the Javitses and the editors of *Time* and *Newsweek* through Jessica Mitford and Lord and Lady Melchett to a flock of hippies or ex-hippies. The high point was supposed to be a speech in which Norman was billed as making a world-shaking announcement. But the birthday boy, evidently trusting to charisma and afflatus, gave a most disconnected series of remarks, beginning with a dirty joke that turned off some of the audience and concluding with a proposal for a "people's FBI" and a "people's CIA" to investigate the government's FBI and CIA. Among other things, this proposal was some years late. The FBI and CIA are far from sacrosanct institutions now, and it requires no particular audacity to attack them. The speech was a disaster, and we left as speedily as possible. Norman is a most gifted writer who should stick to writing. He is a victim of a society that consumes writers not as writers but as public personalities; it must be added that he is a self-chosen victim, and only half the blame attaches to the society.

April 28

Teddy, who was confronting an interview with Scotty Reston Thursday afternoon on the Kennedy legacy after ten years, wanted to have a talk about all this, so we had an early breakfast Thursday morning before I left to catch the plane for Palm Beach. Our conversation was almost entirely about the past rather than the future. There were some digressions into the present, however, when we saw the headlines in the *Washington Post* underneath large pictures of John Mitchell, bluff and unctuous, and those two all-American boys John Dean and Jeb Stuart Magruder. According to the story, Magruder had now implicated Mitchell and Dean in the Watergate affair. This gave us intense pleasure. There is something splendidly comic in the disclosure that this most righteous and moralistic of all administrations, after five years of going on about its supreme devotion to law and order, was really a collection of third-rate crooks, all beginning now to rat on each other. It is the ultimate impertinence on Nixon's part, after months of denial and cover-up, now to cast himself as the zealous investigator who, as he said on television Tuesday, was intent only on finding out the truth. Ted cannot believe that he did not know about and approve the campaign of espionage and sabotage, nor can I.

Bill and Betty Fulbright were on the plane to Palm Beach, and I spent the second half of the trip talking with Bill. He began by talking about the Middle East. He is fed to the teeth with the immensely successful Israeli lobbying operation in the Senate. He is quite right: it makes the Clan-na-Gael, which used to irritate Henry Adams so much, seem like a Boy Scout troop. Scoop Jackson, he said, could rely on about 80 votes in the Senate for any Israeli issue. The other day Fulbright had a couple of Arab diplomats for lunch. He asked a number of senators; most made excuses; one said he would come by after luncheon but didn't; and only three or four accepted.

May 3

Averell called to say how pleased he was that we had decided not to sell the Hobe Sound [Florida] house and to offer (again) to help us get into the Club (which we are not inclined to do at this point). We laughed a good deal about Watergate. Averell reported a conversation earlier today with the former Chief Justice. Averell said, "The news gets worse each day." [Earl] Warren replied, "No, I think the news gets better each day."

Warren seems to me everlastingly right. This is the healthiest thing that has happened to the presidency for years. It will take a long time before another President and another White House will conceive themselves in the Nixon style as above the law. And it is also healthy for three other American institutions without which the mess would never have been exposed: the independent judiciary (Judge [John] Sirica); the free press (Kay Graham); and the Senate (Sam Ervin). In short, it is all a great tribute to the separation of powers.

August 13

At last, *The Imperial Presidency* is finished! I began it in March, expecting that it could be done in a few weeks. The original idea was to concentrate on the presidency and the war-making power. But the book grew as I got further into it and as I thought harder about the inner pattern of the Nixon presidency. Then Watergate came along to provide the climax and, I trust, denouement. The hearings did not make it easy. For a time I tried to type and watch at the same time, but the only result was that I did both things poorly. But now, thank heavens, it is all done, and I am done too.

October 21

Two intensely dramatic days. On Friday night word came through that Nixon had made a deal with Sam Ervin and Howard Baker regarding the tapes. According to Nixon's statement, he would prepare a summary of the tapes, John Stennis would verify the summary against the tapes, and this would satisfy the "spirit" of the order of the Court of Appeals. Nixon concluded his statement with peremptory instructions to Archie Cox to cease and desist in his attempts to get tapes and other evidence from the White House. I went to bed more depressed than I have been for a long time. It looked as if Nixon had thought he had recovered enough to force Cox's resignation, and I had long supposed that the long-run hope of exposing this crowd lay with Cox and not with the Ervin committee.

I flew to Minneapolis Saturday morning for a speech on the presidency. As I was holding a press conference, I was told that Archie was about to hold one of his own; so we adjourned mine, turned on the television and listened to his. He could not have been better. Though he looked dead tired, he spoke with total control; his tone was moderate, almost relaxed; his line strong and right. It was clear that he believed Nixon in contempt of court and would ask the court next week to declare him so. I learned that Nixon had tried to get Elliot Richardson and then William Ruckelshaus to fire Archie; both had refused and were fired themselves; then Robert Bork, the Solicitor General and a professor at the Yale Law School, was made acting Attorney General, from which eminence he fired the professor from the Harvard Law School.

This morning Ted Kennedy called. He wants to call a meeting of the Senate Judiciary Committee in the next day or two to begin to focus public attention on the essential issues and to start pressure on the House to prepare the case for impeachment.

Ted sees no alternative to impeachment—an apparent change of position. He is a bit skeptical about the will of some of his colleagues. "Every time we have a caucus," he said, "all the talk is about how Congress must reassert its prerogatives—budget ceiling, impoundment or whatever. Now that they have a real chance to reassert their prerogatives, we'll see what they do." I said that Carl Albert, who stands next in the line of succession, would be a good deal better than Gerald Ford. Ted said, "I would certainly buy that." Then he said with a laugh, "Three months from now, we'll all be in the East Room of the White House watching Carl Albert announce his Vice President." It occurred to me later that, consciously or not, Ted must be thinking that President Albert's choice might well fall on him.

November 18

We returned from Europe Monday afternoon; and Tuesday morning Jean Smith called to cancel a tennis engagement with Alexandra, saying that she had to leave right away for Washington, that Teddy's 12-year-old son was dangerously sick. It turned out to be cancer. Yesterday was also Kathleen Kennedy's marriage to a tutor in History and Literature from

Harvard. We went down for it. Ted appeared at the church looking very haggard and concerned. The Kennedys, with their usual indomitable spirit, had added "When Irish Eyes Are Smiling" to the service. As the congregation sang this oddly melancholy song, one's mind went back through the sad years and wondered at the future.

Bob Coles was at the wedding reception. He has been acting as general psychiatrist for all the Kennedy children, and was called in to help break the news to young Teddy. He said that the little boy was deeply upset and lay in bed for a long time in silence, throwing a towel over his face so he would not have to look at anyone. Then Nixon called, spoke to Ted, then asked to speak to the boy. The phone was passed over, and young Teddy talked to the President for a few moments; his side of the conversation was monosyllabic—"Yes, sir," "No, sir." After he finished, everyone asked, "What did the President say to you?" Teddy fell silent again and would not say anything. Then, Bob said, his father in the most jovial and at the same time delicate way, went into a long, kidding speculation. "I bet he told you where those missing tapes were," and so on—until young Teddy, for the first time since he had been told about himself, began to laugh.

December 16

Ted Kennedy was at the Smiths' for dinner Friday night. He thinks that the House will vote for impeachment but doubts whether there will ever be two-thirds of the Senate for conviction. He believes that the effort should be made anyway. As we were leaving, he took me aside and said he wanted to talk at length some time about 1976—whether the views for which he had stood, especially on racial questions, would have any prospect of success. I think he is right in continuing to see race as the basic domestic election issue. Joan was there; she had drunk too much, alas, and was forlorn.

1974

January 2

It is fashionable to say that 1973 was a bad year, but I found it personally and politically most enjoyable. It is the first year since 1945 that the bad guys really began to get what was coming to them. And for an historian it has been fascinating to observe the process of rediscovering the ability of the Founding Fathers to foresee the problems of our polity. I only hope that the nation will resort to the constitutional remedy before too long. If Nixon does not deserve impeachment, one wonders what limits there will be on the capacity of future Presidents to abuse their power and betray the trust confided to them.

March 6

On Monday night we had dinner with the Smiths and Sam Spiegel. In the chat of the evening the name of Greta Garbo came up, and Sam told the following story. Garbo, he said, was a great admirer of JFK.

George Schlee had been saying that he was sure the President would like her to come to dinner at the White House, but she had been shy and reluctant. But he finally overcame her doubts. They went a few weeks before Kennedy left for Dallas. It was a small party. After dinner JFK took her for a tour of the White House. They paused for an hour or two, by themselves, in the Lincoln bedroom and had a long, searching conversation. When the time came to leave, JFK took an ivory figurine off one of the shelves and said to her, "I want you to have this." As Garbo later told the story to Sam, she wept. She is wholly non-political, Sam said, and not only was moved by JFK, and what happened to him so soon afterward, but by a sense of the exclusions of her own life, of the forces that played upon the world to which she had been till then oblivious. She felt "touched by history" and decided that she would never in her life go to Washington again.

On Tuesday Alexandra lunched with Jean Smith and Lem Billings. Lem had actually been at the dinner, and he told the following story. Lem had got to know Garbo slightly through Mary Lasker. "I was always trying to think of things to tell Jack that would interest him," Lem said; so he used to report to him on Garbo when he met her and in time urged him to invite her to the White House. JFK did so in November 1963. It was a small party. When Lem arrived, Jackie was in charge; the President had been delayed. Lem rushed over to Garbo and said how nice it was to see her again. She looked stonily at him and said, "You must be mistaken. I do not recall that we have ever met before." Lem tried to refresh her recollection, but to no avail. Considerably cast down, he went off to talk to someone else. Eventually JFK came, and they all went to dinner. Garbo, who had been perceptibly nervous, drank one glass after another of vodka and was now rather merry. Seated between the President and Lem, she turned her back on JFK and talked steadily to Lem. This finally attracted the attention of Jackie, who thought that Lem was monopolizing the guest of honor and began to make what Lem regarded as mean cracks to him. The dinner drew to an end, and the President took the whole party for a tour of the White House. As Garbo admired some scrimshaw, JFK opened the case, selected an uncarved piece and gave it to her. Then the party broke up, with Lem pursuing Jackie into her bedroom to complain of her treatment of him at the table. "The evening was a disaster," Lem said. "Then the next day I discovered that it had all begun as a joke. Jack had called Garbo and said, 'My friend Lem boasts how well he knows you, so, when he comes in, pretend you never met him before.' The only trouble was that Jack was held up and wasn't there when Garbo and I were introduced. If he had been there, the joke would have come out at once. As it was, I was hurt and sulked all evening; Garbo was confused; and Jackie was no help *at all*. . . . As for the scrimshaw, Jack said to me the next day that he liked Garbo but he really didn't want to give her a piece of his *good* scrimshaw."

May 1

Last Friday, 26 April, Pat Lawford gave a large Kennedy party ("exorcise your fantasy") in her splendid new apartment on Sutton Place overlooking the East River. As we were leaving, Ted Kennedy took me aside and told me a little about his trip to Russia; he had returned the day before.

Ted saw [Leonid] Brezhnev for four hours (how do the Soviet leaders arrange to have so much time for foreign visitors?) and found him cordial and surprisingly frank. Ted was surprised in particular by his bitterness about Kissinger. Kissinger, Brezhnev claimed, had deceived him into thinking that Moscow would have a role in the Middle Eastern negotiations and then had excluded Moscow from the negotiations. He implied that, until Moscow was given a role, his government would have no choice but to continue sending arms to Syria. When Ted asked Brezhnev what he considered the three most important world problems from the Soviet viewpoint (a typical Kennedy question), Brezhnev listed them in this order: the nuclear arms race; overall relations between the USSR and the USA; and the Middle East. Oddly China did not make the top three.

On the question of the Soviet Jews, Brezhnev vigorously rejected the reports that those seeking exit visas had been harassed and mistreated. Ted, who saw a number of Soviet Jews during his trip, had no doubt at all about the harassment, but thinks that Brezhnev may honestly not know what the bureaucracy is doing.

On Monday Ted talked about his Russian trip at the Council on Foreign Relations. It was the largest audience I have ever seen there. Most came, I imagine, filled with doubt and suspicion. I think on the whole he reassured them, though he seemed to me far from his best. He was nervous and rather inarticulate and imprecise in speech—much less fluent and cogent than in private conversation. I could not help thinking that Jack or Bobby would have begun with a series of jokes about the Council as the "invisible government" of the United States, while Ted instead spoke respectfully of the Council and said how privileged he felt to be there. He was excessively statesmanlike for my taste, and he came over as an earnest young man with establishment views. But this worked well for the establishment part of the audience (95 percent). Only once did he reveal much passion or edge of phrase. Someone asked a question that suggested that he and [Scoop] Jackson agreed on a certain approach to arms reduction. With a certain vehemence Ted explained how their two positions differed and, without mentioning Jackson by name, went on to inveigh against "those who marched to the beat of distant drums from another age."

May 10

We continue to make progress. I have never really doubted, since Watergate began to unravel, that Nixon would be removed or would resign before January 1977. This confidence was based essentially on a sense that Nixon was the greatest shit—probably the only shit—ever elected President of the United States, and that no disclosure about his greed and knavery would ever be the last. So, when he went on TV on 29 April and said, with apparent perfect confidence, that the release the next day of his expurgated version of some of the tapes would show "once and for all" that everything he had done with regard to Watergate was "just as I have described them to you from the very beginning," I did not believe it for a moment.

One's sense that he is now hopelessly immured in a dream world leads me to believe that he will not resign, at least without a deal. I am also more sure than ever that the Senate will convict and remove him. This is the most solemn vote most of those senators will ever cast, and then, if ever, they will vote their consciences. Moreover, none among them has any personal affection for or loyalty to Nixon, and those Republicans up for reelection know they will do far better if Gerald Ford is President.

I may well change this view, but Henry Kissinger, despite his work in the Middle East, seems to me one of the most disgusting figures in this whole business. Yesterday Dick Rovere, Martin Mayer and I were chatting at the long table in the Century about Kissinger and especially about his mania for secrecy and about the panic he evidently fell into when Dan Ellsberg handed over the Pentagon Papers. After a moment I said, rather loudly, "In my view Kissinger and Ellsberg deserve each other." A short while later, as I left the table, I was hailed by someone sitting directly behind me. I need hardly say that it was Ellsberg. He gave no indication that he had heard my remark, though he could hardly have missed it, given the authoritative tone in which it was uttered. We talked a few minutes. He seemed more egomaniacal than ever and affected to think that further and harsher prosecutions lay in store for him.

The movement toward impeachment moves slowly ahead. I encountered in my two Washington trips a certain pessimism as to whether anything will happen. Peter Lisagor thinks that Congress is such a cowardly body that Nixon will survive. Rowland Evans also thinks that Nixon will pull through. I continue not to think so.

July 19

Stephen and I lunched today at the Century. Cliff Case, who was at the long table, joined us, and we chatted about impeachment. It is evident that he is prepared to vote for conviction, though, of course, he carefully refrained from saying so. He said that he had asked Hugh Scott the other day why in the world Nixon had arranged to have all his conversations taped. Scott replied, "Greed. He thought he could make a lot of money out of the tapes and transcripts after they had been sanitized."

August 19

This is a belated recognition of the fact that it is all over, the matter that has preoccupied us for so many months—belated in part because I have been so damn busy, but more fundamentally perhaps because the denouement was, in the end, so flat, such an anti-climax. I have believed for a long time that, when Nixon went, he would go rather quickly and that the margin in the Senate would be overwhelming against him. The reason for this belief was essentially my confidence that the corruption was so widespread and organic in the Nixon presidency that there would never be an end to revelations of lawlessness—and that there would be an end to national patience. My only regret is that I did not stake more money on my conviction at a time when I could have gotten splendid odds—as in my 100–1 bet with Bill Fine, then the President of Bonwit Teller.

What happened after the Supreme Court decision and more especially after Nixon's own admission that he had been in on the cover-up from the start was a massive and spontaneous withdrawal of support. The Republicans became as eager for him to go as the Democrats. The movement was so strong and unmistakable that it finally broke through the cocoon of unreality in which the White House had enveloped itself. By Thursday 8 August it was clear that we were in the last act. That afternoon we motored to Westport to spend the night with Jimmy and Nancy Wechsler. We heard Nixon's obtuse and unrepentant speech that evening and, by a lucky chance, his weird remarks to the White House staff the next morning. We paused for a moment during tennis to hear Ford's swearing-in and quasi-inaugural—straightforward and disarming.

Everyone has said that this would be a great national trauma, however it came out. I had always quoted Adam Smith—"there is a lot of ruin in a nation"—but even I have been surprised at how painless it has all been—the least traumatic trauma in history. Nixon's departure brought a huge sigh of national relief; thus far Ford has shown how far a little candor and decency will go in restoring confidence in the presidency.

September 9

The Ford truce came to an abrupt end yesterday morning when he announced his unconditional pardon of Nixon. A mysterious move, unless Ziegler and Haig convinced him that Nixon, unless he received a pardon, would kill himself. At one stroke, Ford has terminated his honeymoon, revived Watergate as an issue, tied himself irrevocably to what Jimmy Wechsler well called in today's *Post* "the ultimate cover-up" and put every Republican candidate in this autumn's election on the spot. This is quite apart from the double standard of justice displayed, the anomaly created in prosecuting those who executed Nixon's wishes while Nixon himself basks in the sun at San Clemente, and the reinforcement given to popular cynicism about politics and politicians. In addition, by stopping the process of justice now, Ford makes it impossible to place the full story of Nixon's implication on the record and therefore facilitates Nixon's resort to a stab-in-the-back theory about his resignation. In time he may well begin to mistake San Clemente for Elba and plan an irredentist campaign.

September 22

We returned late last night from four days in the West—Wednesday and Thursday in Long Beach, where I gave a lecture that paid for the trip, with Chrissie; Friday and Saturday in Santa Fe with Andy.

In the questions after the Long Beach lecture someone asked me whether I thought, as a matter of principle, Ford should retain Nixon's cabinet or move on to a cabinet of his own. I replied that, as a matter of principle, I thought Ford should appoint his own men; then I added, "including the Secretary of State." I thought as I threw this in that it would create headlines in excess of the point; I thought also, what the hell. Someone soon asked me why I thought Kissinger should go, and I made the obvious points: he was good with our enemies but not with our friends; he was good at political and military problems, not at economic, monetary and commercial problems; he preferred authoritarian governments, because they could reliably deliver their countries, to governments based on consent. In response to another question I said that I thought Bill Scranton might make a good Secretary of State. As I feared, this series of unpremeditated questions and answers produced in the next morning's *Los Angeles Times* the headline SCHLESINGER URGES THE FIRING OF KISSINGER. The story made its way across the country and appeared in Friday's *New York Times*. I am sorry that all this has the aspect of a crusade on my part, since it could not have been more accidental. But I also feel, what the hell. I do think that Henry has outlived his usefulness as a decider of policy, however useful he will always be as a negotiator, and, though I did not intend to get into this, why not.

This morning Ken Galbraith called and said he was coming to New York this afternoon. So we asked him to dinner along with Jean Smith; Steve had gone to Hyannis Port to meet with Ted Kennedy in advance of Ted's press conference tomorrow morning, in which he will withdraw from the 1976 contest for the Democratic nomination. I expressed my surprise that he should have made this decision so early. Ken thought it right. I guess I agree, though, if we have a large economic collapse, I still can't see anyone else at the moment with big qualities of leadership. I asked Ken where he thought we should go now. He said, without conviction, "I suppose Fritz Mondale," but did not press the proposition.

October 13

In the evening Osborn Elliott, the editor of *Newsweek*, had his 50th birthday. We had dinner at the Peter Petersons'—pleasant enough, except for the food, which was curry; and then on to the Elliott apartment, also at 10 Gracie Square. Both apartments have magnificent views of the East River. The most rewarding part of the evening was a reconciliation with my old friend Ben Bradlee. I can't remember whether I noted this in the journal; but a year or so ago Tom Guinzburg of Viking and later Bob Manning of the *Atlantic Monthly* mentioned to me that Ben was circulating his notes of his conversations with JFK in 1962–63 and that they thought them mischievous and damaging. Unfortunately after hearing all this I ran into Kay Graham one night and asked her about the Bradlee manuscript—and this before Ben had told her about it. She brought it up to Ben, who was irritated. This summer when we were in East Hampton over 4 July I ran into Barbara Howar who said that Ben was upset and angry. In the meantime his brother Freddy told Alexandra that Ben thought I was mad at him because he was divorcing Tony, of whom I was vary fond, to marry Sally Quinn. I had it in mind to write Ben but never got around to it. Then Alexandra ran into him at the Elliotts' and said that I thought he was mad at me. He said that he thought I was mad at him. So Alexandra brought him over, and we had a good talk.

God knows what his book will be like. I have no doubt that it will be an invaluable contribution to the future biographies of JFK. But I fear it will be greatly resented by the Kennedys, because I am sure it displays JFK in relaxed, gossipy and somewhat irresponsible moods in the evenings. The Kennedys as a couple did not on the whole like many other people as couples. They liked the wife or the husband, or one liked a couple and the other didn't; but about the only couples they enjoyed as couples were the Bradlees and, to a lesser degree, Charlie and Martha Bartlett. Ben said to me, "I really don't think that Jack liked me very much. He always thought I was a spiv, in the British sense—a little glib and scheming perhaps. But I think he was rather in love with Tony. He fucked Mary but he was in love with Tony. But I do think I entertained him. He adored gossip, and I could tell him what was going on around town. You must understand that—that was one reason he liked you. . . . I could never figure out in my own mind whether I was a friend or a newspaperman. So for a while I kept no notes on our conversations. Then after a time I began to keep notes. . . . I know my own limitations. I think I know a lot about the uses of power. But I have never been interested in power for myself. I never tried to sell people to him, get ambassadors appointed and so on, or sell policies either. That's for Joe

Alsop. I just had the opportunity to see him when he was very relaxed, and all I have written about is that. It's part of a picture. But I think you will find it fascinating." No doubt I will, but I have the feeling that his book will cause transient trouble. Still I really am fond of Ben, and I am glad that we had this conversation.

December 19

Last night ABC put on a three-hour television show about the Cuban missile crisis called *The Missiles of October*, and the Sorensens had the brilliant idea of having a missile crisis reunion. They assembled Jackie, the Bundys, the Kaysens, the Don Wilsons and ourselves (Alexandra, alas, could not come because she was at the hospital with Robert, who had sprayed his mouth with oven cleaning fluid).

The film, which involved impersonation and reenactment, could have been much worse. The Kennedy brothers were played with exaggerated Massachusetts accents; and some of the casting—Dillon, for example, and Senator Russell—was ludicrous. But, except for the suggestion of a military ultimatum to the Soviet Union toward the end, the script was a simplification rather than a falsification of history. The audience watched many moments with considerable hilarity—the appearance of Pierre, played by an actor who looked rather like the original, provoked particular applause—but also, from time to time, especially when RFK was arguing against drastic action, with real emotion.

I had not had a talk with Jackie for some time. She was easy, charming and beautiful. The whole evening was in a curious way most agreeable. Despite disagreements and tensions at the time, the White House in that remote period was bound together not only by devotion to JFK but by a real commonality of values.

1975

January 1

Another year, and before it is over I will have had my 58th birthday. In two years more I will be 60. In five years I will be 63—FDR's age when he died. I continue to feel (and, I believe, look) younger than all this. I don't know about my health, since I have not had a comprehensive medical examination for half a dozen years. But if there is anything wrong it has not yet affected my daily sense of well-being.

We spent New Year's Eve happily at home. There was a light snow, melting on contact. We had caviar and champagne; I grilled a steak in the garden; then we watched musical films on TV—*Top Hat*, *Dames* and *Where's Charlie*. I felt less gloomy than usual on New Year's Eve, even though I did not do nearly as much in 1974 as I had hoped to do. In particular, I had hoped to begin writing the RFK book in November. The pressure is slightly off with Ted Kennedy's withdrawal; I had originally wanted to bring the book out well in advance of the 1976 campaign. But, with Marian receiving the first $60,000 I earn, the financial pressure is acute. However, I have a certain feeling of confidence about the book now, which I did not have before, though technical problems remain—especially that of providing adequate coverage without repeating stories everyone has heard before.

January 3

Ted Kennedy came to dinner last night for a general consultation. The guest list (his own selection) consisted of Steve Smith, Bill Moyers, Ted Sorensen, Bill vanden Heuvel plus Paul Kirk and Cary Parker of his own staff.

Ted was just in from Sun Valley, looking very ruddy and healthy. The great object of (largely unspoken) concern among the group was to find out how resolute Ted is in his determination not to be a candidate in 1976. It seemed clear that everyone, except for Ted [Sorensen] (who seems to oppose Ted's running in 1976 as he opposed Bobby's running in 1968), hoped that he would not shut the door in the end. My own strong impression is that, if no other liberal candidate emerged and if there were an authentic draft at the convention, he would accept; moreover, that this possibility figures seriously in his calculations as to how he should spend his time in the next months. At least he did *not* say at any point, "I am out of the picture so far as 1976 is concerned. My decision is final, and let's not talk about it any more."

Moreover, he continues to think that [Scoop] Jackson is a "dangerous" man and is obviously hostile to his candidacy. And he seems to think that, in the absence of strong competition, Jackson will be very hard to stop. He said that he had had a long private talk with George McGovern recently, and is satisfied that George will not be a candidate for the 1976 nomination. He did not say much about other liberal possibilities—which again contributed to the general picture of himself as the only alternative to Jackson. He seemed to have little use for [Lloyd] Bentsen.

Like all such evenings—it reminded me of so many in the past, with Adlai, with JFK, with Bobby—the talk was discursive and inconclusive. But this, I have come to recognize, is part of the process by which politicians crystallize their own views. Ted was impressive in the discussion and showed mastery of facts and issues. He was also full of charm and good humor. He affected some concern about Massachusetts, where he comes up for reelection, on the ground that the busing fight will cut deep into his Irish support. He said he would do much better running against Elliot Richardson, who could not use busing against him, than against a conservative Republican.

Our advice, in general, was that he should proceed on the merits of issues, say what he really believes and accept this respite of liberation from political calculations—and that this in the end would turn out to be the best politics.

January 9

Alexandra and I went to Washington yesterday for the Walter Lippmann memorial service at the Cathedral. We went down in the late morning and lunched with George McGovern. George seemed cheery and is pondering whether to seek the chairmanship of the Foreign Relations Committee's subcommittee on the Middle East. Fulbright had personally held this chairmanship himself, in order, as he told George, to prevent its falling into the hands of someone who would be too responsive to the Israeli lobby, and he has encouraged George to take it on. "If there is anything that will really make it clear I am not a candidate in 1976," George said rather wryly, "it would be doing this; but maybe I could help strengthen the hands of those in Israel and in Egypt who feel the need for some sort of accommodation."

George did seem fully in earnest (as Ted Kennedy had said the other night) about not being a candidate. We asked whether his view of Jackson had improved. "Certainly not," he said, "and on top of everything else he is such a crashing bore." As I recall, he had been rather kindly toward Bentsen last spring, but now he dismissed him as "smooth to the point of oiliness." Hubert, he said, had gone out of his way to be friendly and cooperative in the last session. When I advanced the theory that Hubert, if his health is really OK, might well become a candidate again, and might do well in the primaries, George said he didn't think it impossible. My vision is of Jackson offering himself as the man who can save the party from Wallace, and Humphrey offering himself as the man who can save the party from Jackson.

The [Lippmann] service was rather good—nice speeches all around. When I was chatting with Gil Harrison before the service, he confided that he had just resigned as editor of the *New Republic*. "It seems appropriate," he said ruefully, "to resign on the day of the memorial service for Walter Lippmann"—who had, of course, helped found it. I said that I thought Gil had been assured editorial control for three years in the sales agreement. The assurance had not been strong enough, however, to block [Marty] Peretz, and Gil said somewhat enigmatically that money had talked. He well remembered that I had warned him against Peretz, who has always seemed to me an unprincipled egomaniac. When I first heard that he was after the *New Republic*, I wrote Gil saying that, if he ever got hold of it, he would destroy it. "I couldn't have been more surprised," Gil said yesterday. "He seemed perfectly decent and reasonable during the negotiations. It has been a disquieting experience for me. It has really made me lose faith in my judgment of people."

In the evening Kay Graham (with whom we were staying) gave one of her large, sprawling and genial parties. Nelson Rockefeller and the Kissingers led the guest list. Nelson was even more affable than usual. He thanked me for the admonitory material I had been sending him about the vice presidency. I said that I hoped he would make a go of it, though I had my doubts, but that we all ought to agree on regarding this as the last experiment; that, if he and Ford could not make something of the vice presidency, then let us abandon the whole thing. He did not endorse the conclusion but seized upon the phrase "the last experiment" and heartily endorsed that.

After dinner Kay found me in one room and said that Henry wanted to have a talk. We sat together for half an hour or so on the sofa. He was warm and friendly in manner, said (most unconvincingly) that I had had a great influence on him at Harvard and hoped that we would have time in the near future to discuss our differences on foreign policy. He mentioned his problems during the Watergate period—this in partial explanation of his Salzburg press conference—and I seized the opportunity to ask him whether he had been surprised by the eventual Watergate revelations. "You won't believe it," he said, "—I find it hard to believe in retrospect—but I was totally surprised. It never occurred to me that they were all lying when they said that the White House knew nothing about it." He said that he had gone to [H.R.] Haldeman, who told him that he knew no more about it than Henry did and suggested that he talk to [John] Ehrlichman. Ehrlichman and Nixon had been similarly reassuring. It was [Leonard] Garment who warned him, without detail, not to get involved. Henry said that he had talked regularly with [George] Shultz and [Arthur] Burns about the situation (two people less likely to know what was going on I cannot imagine). The Nixon revealed in the tapes, he said, was totally astonishing to him. He had never heard Nixon use such language or talk with such cheap cynicism. "He was a very strange person," Henry said. "I realized that. When I conferred with him, he would be rambling, prissy and inordinately repetitious. But he never talked to me the way he talked on the tapes."

My own guess is that Henry is far too intelligent a man to have been as naive as he now pretends to have been; but that it (understandably) suited his purposes to accept the reassurances and not pursue the matter further.

January 27

I flew to Washington this morning and back this afternoon—the weather crisp, sunny, rather exhilarating. I first spent a couple of hours with David Hackett, a sweet and thoughtful man, talking about Robert Kennedy. Then I lunched with Henry Kissinger. As I said to Dave when I left his office, lunching with Henry seemed to me a waste of time since I did not know how seriously to take anything he said to me and he did not pay any attention to anything I said to him. Actually it was more interesting, and agreeable, than that.

He is established in the new State Department building now, of course, though he told me that he tried to spend his mornings in his White House office. I waited for a moment or two on the terrace with its wide sweep of Washington from the Lincoln Memorial past the Washington Monument to the Capitol. The sun gleamed on the landmarks. For an instant Washington seemed tranquil and serene.

I love the State Department portrait gallery—all the old faces of the Secretaries, with (as they like to say in the Department) the best Secretaries getting the worst portraits and the worst Secretaries the best portraits. I mentioned this to Henry when he arrived, which led to a discussion of the redecoration of the eighth floor. He said that before he left he hoped to redecorate his own office, which looks, he said, like the office of the chairman of a board of a large corporation, but that he would not try to do it for himself, only for his successor. Attempting a lame joke, I said, "Yes, I understand. After all, you spend so little time in the office." He looked perplexed for a moment; but, when I labelled it as a joke, brightened and laughed mildly. In his humor, as in his analysis, he likes to command the field.

The food and wine were not bad; the cigars were mediocre and confirm the case for the restoration of relations with Cuba. Henry, who looked plump, was genial and rather definite in his conversation. He began by discussing the problems that arose when Congress tried to run foreign policy day-by-day. The abuse of executive power, he said, seemed to have led to an over-reaction in favor of congressional power, with liberals taking unaccustomed positions. I mentioned [Lord James] Bryce's point that the legislative branch should determine the ends of foreign policy and the executive prescribe the means, and I said that in the end it was all a matter of confidence, and Congress had lost its habit of trusting the executive. The problem was that of reestablishing confidence. He had mentioned military aid to Turkey, the Jackson amendment and the discrimination in the trade bill against Venezuela and Ecuador as members of OPEC as examples of harmful congressional interference with the conduct of foreign affairs. I said that I was afraid the Vietnam debate (over a pending appropriation of $300 million) would cause great trouble, and damage the hope of rekindling the confidence that would permit a wider measure of executive discretion. I asked him what he saw as the future in Vietnam. He said, and repeated, with considerable emphasis that in no condition would there be a renewal of American military intervention; "I can give you my word on that."

The most interesting part of our talk had to do with Nixon. Henry had seen him at San Clemente last week. He looked pretty well, Henry thought, adding that the atmosphere out there was that Nixon would regain political popularity and influence in a few years. He paused and said, "It's impossible to tell now how Nixon will look ten years from now," implying that he might look pretty good. This started him into a lengthy and fascinating stream-of-consciousness on Nixon. "He was both more evil and better than people supposed," he said. "He was at his best when he was under pressure and cornered. That brought all his faculties into play. . . . It was a great myth that he was a hard worker. He was one of the laziest men I have ever seen. I don't think he ever read the Vietnam armistice agreement, for example, or the SALT agreement or the preliminary papers on China. He worked in spurts of energy, as at the time of Cambodia or Laos or the mining of the North Vietnamese harbors. Then he would collapse into a condition of lassitude that would go on for weeks. His work habits were very much like Hitler's as described by Speer." Henry added, by the way, that he had agreed with the invasion of Cambodia and the mining of Haiphong, only he felt less clear and certain about it than Nixon had. "He was unquestionably a weird President, but he was not a weak President. . . . But everything was weird in that slightly homosexual, embattled atmosphere of the White House." I would love to have pursued the implications of "slightly homosexual" but did not wish to interrupt the flow or appear too intrusive.

"One trouble with him," Henry continued, "was that you could not believe a word he said. It wasn't that he was a deliberate liar. It was more a Walter Mitty thing. He often lied without point or purpose. He lied to people whom he must have known knew that he was lying to them. Once he told Haig and me, as if from a participant, something that both of us knew Haig had briefed him about only a few hours before." At San Clemente, Henry said, Nixon had remarked about Watergate: "Haldeman, Ehrlichman and Mitchell did me in." Obviously all the evidence, including his own voice on tape as well as the total devotion of these men to him, refuted this proposition; yet, Henry said, Nixon uttered it with total conviction. Henry also said that, according to one of the tapes (not relevant to the trial and therefore not yet released), Nixon ordered [Charles] Colson and Haldeman to start putting around damaging and discreditable stories about him.

He was obsessed with the Kennedys, Henry said, and wanted to destroy their reputations—from JFK to Ted. Hence his preoccupation with trying to prove that JFK had ordered the assassination of Diem. First, Henry was asked to have someone search the State Department files for the evidence. He declined to do so, he told me, because he felt that if one President started using the files for political ammunition against a predecessor, it would be destructive of government. "My refusal is on the record," Henry said. "I wrote memoranda." Then the White House tried an end run by instructing David Young to get the documents without Henry's knowledge. When the documents showed only knowledge of the coup but not complicity in the assassination, Nixon was dissatisfied; the next thing [E. Howard] Hunt started forging the documents.

"I didn't realize how much pressure Nixon was putting on me," Henry said, "until I started meeting with Ford. You can't imagine the difference." At the end we got back to his relations with Congress. He professed vast admiration for Fulbright, saying that he met with him every week, showed him the relevant cables and told him what was in his mind. [John] Sparkman, he said, doesn't understand what it is all about. He thinks that the congressional reforms in the mode of selecting committee chairmen will weaken the congressional structure and make it harder for the executive to locate the levers of collaboration with the Hill.

After hearing some lugubrious ruminations about the impossibility of running a government if the authority of political institutions is

systematically undermined, I took my leave, it now being 2:40 P.M.
I must say that, with all the reservations I have about Henry and his
policy, he is a highly intelligent and charming man.

February 12

We had dinner last night at Quo Vadis with Franklin and Felicia
Roosevelt—very agreeable. I was very fond of Sue, Franklin's previous
wife, a lovely, fragile girl. Felicia is less feminine and rather brisk,
downright and funny. Franklin remains Franklin, filled with charm
and energy; more mellow now than he was when ambition was still
dominant in his life. Much talk about the Kennedys. I have always been
fascinated by the interplay between these two great American political
dynasties. Franklin told of receiving a call from Joe in the late winter or
early spring of 1960 asking him to come to a meeting at Palm Beach.
The Ambassador said to him on arrival, "You know, Franklin, if it
hadn't been for that ginny [Carmine De Sapio], you would have been
elected governor in 1954, and now we would all be working for you."

The Palm Beach meeting discussed whether JFK should go into
West Virginia. FDR Jr. argued strongly that he should—that victory in
West Virginia would persuade the politicians that Catholicism was not
an issue. Someone asked whether he would be willing to spend six
weeks there himself. He said that he would, and of course did (and, next
to JFK himself, was probably most responsible for the result). "I made
only one mistake," he said. "That was bringing up Hubert's record during the war. Bobby had been bringing pressure on me to mention it. He
kept calling—five or six calls a day. Finally I did. Then there was a lot
of criticism, and Kennedy repudiated the statement and cut the ground
out from under me. That was the beginning of the break between
Bobby and me."

He was very fond of Jack, though one feels that he felt he had been
used by him. (Franklin would have done the same had the roles been
reversed.) At the beginning of January 1961 JFK called him and said,
"Jackie's very upset about the new life. She's in a panic. Could you come

down and reassure her—tell her it won't be so bad." So Franklin did so. And in 1963 JFK asked Franklin, who was on official business in Somaliland and Israel, to join Jackie and Lee on the famous Onassis cruise, when Jackie was trying to dissuade Lee from marrying Onassis. After Dallas, Jackie asked Franklin and Sue to come to Hyannis Port over the Thanksgiving weekend. They took him to see the Ambassador, now paralyzed by his stroke. Franklin sat down beside the bed and took his hand. The old man began to cry, and cried for some moments. Franklin tried to say words of sympathy and realism. Finally Joe Kennedy struggled to say something and got out a few words. Ann Gargan interpreted them as: "I am so glad that Jack had you as a friend." This was probably as much a dynastic as a personal comment. Perhaps in it there was contained a sadness about the end of his own relations with Franklin's father.

April 5

We are back in Hobe Sound, relaxing and recuperating by the shining sea while the miserable war in Vietnam drags to a miserable end. But let me retrace our steps. I forget when I issued my last bulletin; but I should record the party we gave for Dick Wade and his fiancée, a pleasant young woman named Cynthia Whittaker. It was an uproarious evening. Dick, Jimmy Wechsler, Dick Dougherty and Bill vanden Heuvel are all quick and funny men; but Steve Smith, with all his notable talent for mimicry, satire and extravagant comic improvisation, was undisputed star. I have never seen him in better form. He stayed for a while after the others left (Jean was visiting her mother in Palm Beach), and the talk turned to Jackie and her future after Onassis. There has been great speculation in the press about the number of millions she would receive. Steve electrified us by saying that he did not think she was going to get anything. When she married Onassis, the trust fund set up in JFK's will was automatically cancelled. Reminding her of this, Steve told her before the marriage that she ought to arrange a premarital settlement. She was angry at this suggestion and said that she had no doubt that Ari would provide for her. Subsequently, Steve told us, Onassis had a law passed in Greece exempting him from the Greek law assuring a widow one-eighth of the estate. Nancy Tuckerman said to Steve the other day, "You were so right in what you told Jackie in 1968." I asked Steve why Onassis would have cut Jackie out. He said, "I suppose he may have wanted to stick it to the Kennedys, saying 'OK, I've had her; now it's up to you to take care of her.' " I suppose too he may have wanted to prove to the world that he had not bought Jackie. Pam Harriman, who had heard rumors to the same effect in Washington, said to Alexandra yesterday, "Jackie should have known better. Greeks never leave their money except to Greeks."

[After we arrived in] Hobe Sound, we went to dinner at the Harrimans'; they came to us last night and left for Washington this morning. There was, as always, a lot of fascinating reminiscence. I asked Pam about Joe Kennedy. She said that she always liked him, that he was a man of great charm, endlessly kind to his children's friends and that, if his reports to Washington about Britain were defeatist, that is what he honestly believed and that though, thank God, he was mistaken, he could not be expected to tell the President anything but the truth as he saw it. I asked what she supposed Churchill thought of him. She said she couldn't recall Churchill ever mentioning him. Averell interrupted gruffly, "Winston despised him."

May 15

I lunched today with Jan Wenner, the publisher of *Rolling Stone*. I have seen him from time to time in recent months, initially through Dick Goodwin, who at one time was scheduled to be editor of a political review to be financed by Wenner. Dick decided he could not work with Wenner, and Wenner decided he could not work with Dick; but they apparently remain wary friends. I find Wenner entertaining and sympathetic and enjoy lunching with him, though I am not clear why I should always be taking him to lunch, since his income must be considerably greater than mine.

In any case, he observed today, "The generation gap is dead." He, I suppose, should know, since his magazine is the favored reading of the rock music/political activist residue of the late sixties. I asked him why he thought so. He said that the older generation has concluded that their children were right on Vietnam and that marijuana is not a mortal threat; while the younger generation has concluded that aimless agitation is not the answer to everything. Also recession has had a sobering influence: "it greatly contracts one's scope for frivolity."

September 5

This afternoon news came of an assassination attempt on Gerald Ford. I found this deeply troubling. In a nation as large and incoherent as ours, one can count on a sufficiency of homicidal lunatics. Yet it would be a betrayal of our democracy if we reached a point where Presidents never dared venture among our people except in bulletproof cars and vests. Among other things, this will make it much harder to press Teddy to run. If so innocuous a man as Ford is a target, Ted Kennedy will inevitably attract many more and fiercer assassins.

1976

January 4

It has been a good year. Personally I could not be happier and thank heaven every day for the blessing of Alexandra and the children. I have made substantial progress on the RFK book—about 500 pages written; though this only goes up to 1960 and raises the question whether the book should not come out in two volumes. Of course I am behind on everything, but then I always am, though I keep promising myself that next year will be different. I am putting on weight again, alas. A certain austerity is the hallmark of my New Year resolutions.

We are entering another presidential year; how fast the years race by! For the first time in my life I do not have a candidate. I am not sure whether this is a commentary on me or on the candidates. I still doubt whether the primaries will yield a strong Democratic front runner. This means that the odds in case of a deadlock will be on Humphrey, though I still think that the younger delegates will rally around someone else. At the moment [Hugh] Carey has troubles of his own. It continues to look as if Ted Kennedy is really out of the picture. But I would not totally exclude the possibility of a change. I still would predict Reagan–[Elliot] Richardson for the Republicans. It will be politically an interesting but rather depressing year. A poor way to celebrate the Bicentennial, but then 1876 was not all that hot a year either.

February 16

Dick and Doris Goodwin came to luncheon yesterday with Stephen. (The Goodwins were in town to take young Richard to the Star Trek convention. Peter and Robert are equally devoted Trekkies, and the Goodwins left their tickets—$20 each for a weekend's admission—when they returned to Lincoln so that our two could go today.) Much conversation about presidential prospects. Dick thinks that [Jimmy] Carter will win in New Hampshire, do well in Massachusetts and Florida and begin to gather serious momentum. In the end the liberals, he thinks, will have to rally around Humphrey in order to stop Carter. He seems moderately reconciled to that prospect. (Oddly enough so is Norman Mailer, who came to dinner the other night with the Isaiah Berlins.) I am less reconciled to the prospect of Hubert. I think he is fine—perhaps the best—on domestic policy, but I fear undue deference to the national security establishment in foreign affairs and I fear even more the kind of entourage he would bring to the White House.

There was much speculation about Carter. Stephen thinks he is a devious right-winger who, once in power, would show his true colors. Stephen also thinks he is authoritarian in his instincts. Dick rather agrees with this, saying that he could not otherwise understand how Carter could have spent 11 years in the Navy. I tend to regard Carter as an intelligent, ambitious opportunist, who will move to any position that he thinks would help him in his upward course. For that reason, I am not unhappy that people like Bill vanden Heuvel, Ted Sorensen, Dick Gardner, Frank Mankiewicz are gathering around him. Nor do I think we should denounce him too drastically in the primaries lest we have to support him in the election. Nor am I altogether in the end sure what sort of man he is. But I must confess he continues to turn me off—his steely eyes, fixed grin, righteousness and ambiguity on issues.

February 27

Last night we went to Elizabeth Hardwick's for dinner—a small party, Mary McCarthy, Susan Sontag, Bob Silvers, and an uncommonly pleasant evening. Mary and I became quite close in the fifties and early sixties; then cooled somewhat, it may be; but are good friends again now. I have had ups and downs through the years with Liz Hardwick too, though recently we have been restored to the mood of the fifties when she and Robert Lowell briefly lived in Boston. Susan I knew moderately when I first came to New York and liked a lot but have seen little of in recent years. I received a letter a few weeks ago from Alfred Kazin saying she had cancer, was undergoing chemotherapy and had no money; would I ask Jacqueline Onassis whether she could contribute to a fund. I wrote Jackie without high expectation, and she promptly sent a check for $300. Susan looked very well and seemed cheerful and unperturbed, though, as we left, she spoke about it calmly. Bob Silvers said later that the treatment works in about 40 percent of cases, fails in about 60 percent.

Much talk about Gore Vidal, who is suing Truman Capote for a million dollars. Truman had an interview with *Penthouse* magazine in which he said that Robert Kennedy and I threw Gore bodily out of the White House after he got drunk and insulted Janet Auchincloss; and that this is why Gore turned so bitterly against the Kennedys. Gore claims that this does irreparable damage to his reputation as a writer and wants his million. Truman unfortunately has the detail of the story wrong but his basic point is indisputable. On checking my White House diary, I find that I put down Gore's version of the very brief episode with RFK. I did not put down what I remember as the sequel. Later Gore, who was staggering drunk, got into an altercation with Lem Billings, who may have been drunk too. Someone—perhaps the President, but more probably Jackie or Bobby—asked me whether I could get Gore out of there before he caused any more trouble. I enlisted George Plimpton. Together we persuaded Gore to get into a car, took him back to the Hotel Jefferson, watched him lurch into the lobby, and we returned to the party. My own feeling is that basically Gore and Truman deserve each other, but that, since Truman is in bad shape and Gore is riding high, it is awful of Gore to press the suit. Mary agreed. Liz, who is fonder of Gore, also regretted the suit. I asked her why he did such things. She said, "Vanity."

March 11

Reading John Bartlow Martin's biography of Adlai reminds me of the really quite active role I had in national politics in the 1950s. I was close to candidates, consulted, asked to serve as intermediary, overflowing with advice and so on. I have been totally out of things since RFK died, and never more so than this year. I am frank to say that I miss it. Politics is the best of all spectator sports.

May 10

I was in Denver on the morning of the Humphrey press conference. Bill vanden Heuvel called me on the assumption that Humphrey was going in and said that I had a great chance to make a contribution to history. He had in mind the moment in 1960 when Ken Galbraith, Joe Rauh, Arthur Goldberg, Henry Commager and I put out a statement for JFK at a time when the belated Stevenson movement was gathering force. I said that Carter did not need us; that he could beat Humphrey and would get the nomination. Bill said, "Carter doesn't need the liberals. But the liberals need Carter. It is imperative that, when he gets the nomination, he feel that he got it with the support of the liberals, not over their dead bodies." I said that I did not have it in my heart to come out for Carter at this point and that in any event I was sure that his reaction would be not one of appreciation or gratitude but rather more one of contempt—"Those sons of bitches are trying to scramble onto my bandwagon."

May 14

Bill Moyers called today, and we chatted about Carter, whom he interviewed at length in a recent TV show. He asked me what I made of Carter. I told him, concluding that he might turn out to be a damned good President or he might become a Democratic Nixon, and that at this point no one could know. He said he agreed. He found Carter cold, tough, terrifyingly self-confident. "He's not a real Baptist," Bill said. "I know the Baptists. He's Calvinist. I recognize the type. I've been struggling against Calvinism within myself for years. He's the sort who would burn people at the stake." I asked whether he liked Carter, whether Carter relaxed at all off camera. "I don't like him," Bill said. "And I don't dislike him. I respect him, and I'm afraid of him. He never seems to relax—always businesslike, always the consummate politician."

May 25

We dined tonight at the Smiths' with Mrs. Kennedy. This has been another interesting week in this unpredictable campaign. It has turned into a rather gripping contest in spite of the fact that the contenders are not in the same league with the heroes of one's youth. Carter, after his brilliant beginning, seems to have hit a plateau. His campaign has simply not evolved: he is giving the same speech in May that he was giving in January, and it is beginning to wear thin. The recent results in Maryland, Nebraska and Michigan were less a surge toward [Jerry] Brown, [Frank] Church or [Morris] Udall than an expression of unease with Carter. The voters don't want to give him the nomination until they know more about him.

In the midst of all this, Ted Kennedy has suddenly come to the forefront again. Last week James Wieghart of the *Daily News*, a good reporter, said that Kennedy was reconsidering his candidacy. Wieghart had indeed seen Teddy, but I imagine that he hardened a Kennedy meditation into a decision. Probably at the minimum Ted wants to smoke out Carter and find out where he stands on social policy. Beyond that he probably oscillates between staying out, his general view, and going in, a later possibility forced upon him in a sense by the Carter recession.

I suggested that, if Carter faltered, it was not easy to see where it would go. I said that I doubted Humphrey would be the automatic beneficiary; the Carter people would regard him as the contriver of their frustration, the young would be against him on principle. The serious choice, I thought, would swing to Ted. Mrs. Kennedy looked very unhappy. She said, "Would it not be too dangerous?"; then, musingly, "It only took someone with a gun on the sixth floor. . . ."; then, her voice trailing off, "I have already lost two. . . ."; then stopped. Jean was somber and silent. Steve said he thought it would be very difficult, if Carter and Humphrey were out, for Ted to turn down a draft. Jean looked unhappy. My impression has long been that the Kennedy family is deeply and genuinely opposed to Ted's running; that Steve thinks that Ted would be best for the country and that his candidacy may become inevitable, and is fatalistic about the risks. I believe that Ted shifts according to time of day from one of these positions to the other.

Mrs. Kennedy is a remarkable combination of sentiment and realism, of humor and indomitability. She and Jean were teasing each other in a way hard to reproduce without suggesting callousness. Mrs. Kennedy, complaining about tourists in Hyannis Port, said, "I have discovered it is much more effective to say not 'Please keep off the grass and stop trespassing,' but, 'Oh, our family has already suffered so much.' " This is an Irish style of distancing oneself from events.

May 28

We went last night to dinner at Zbigniew Brzezinski's in remote Englewood (New Jersey). The other guests were the Harrimans, the

Punch Sulzbergers, the Augie Heckschers and a local couple. I have known Zbig for, I suppose, nearly 20 years. For most of this time he seemed to me an unduly opinionated, dogmatic, cocky and rigid fellow; but in recent years, as we have encountered each other here and there, he has seemed (or become) much more open, humorous and flexible. On a number of occasions we have surprised, or dismayed, each other by the extent of our agreement. He is now Carter's leading foreign policy adviser. Bob Shrum told us the other night that Carter's general reaction on any international question was to clear it with Zbig. He is the putative Kissinger of a putative Carter administration.

I never liked him more than last night—because of the impressive honesty and candor with which he discusses Carter. My old friend Dick Gardner is another Carter adviser on foreign affairs; but Dick in politics is like a young man with his first girl. Dick is an intelligent, lucid and well-organized man on issues (and the author of an excellent historical work called *Sterling Dollar Diplomacy*); but he is also exceedingly ambitious and somewhat insecure, and he sees Carter through a romantic haze. Brzezinski is detached, realistic and rather sardonic. Both Zbig and Dick got to know Carter in the Trilateral Commission. Alexandra asked Zbig what he thought. Zbig said that Carter had not struck him at all until, at one point, he asked Zbig to appear at a press conference with him. The poise and cleverness with which he answered questions made Zbig take him seriously for the first time.

Zbig says that he has known several Presidents and none of them had the systematic, controlled, cool intellect of Carter as exhibited in the exercise of interrogating experts. Kennedy, he said, asked penetrating questions, but was incomplete, intuitive and "romantic." Johnson, Nixon and Ford were not in the same league. Carter is methodical and exhaustive. Then he said that one striking difference between Kennedy and Carter was that Kennedy was surrounded by his "peers"—by people of roughly equivalent age, experience and self-confidence with whom discussion took place on a certain plane of equality. Carter, on the other hand, was surrounded by people 10–15 years younger who deferred to him and were definitely his subordinates. It was possible to disagree with Carter, he said; Carter was always imperturbably courteous; but one could tell from a certain tightening of the expression that he didn't like it too much. He is, Zbig said, "super-calculating," cold, determined. (His wife interjected at that point, "He sounds like Nixon.") Zbig also said that he was ruthlessly precise in his use of language while at the same time contriving to give a politically different impression. For example, his statement to Abe Beame, which produced Beame's endorsement, said, not that he favored the federalization of welfare, but that he would "consider" the federalization of welfare. During the New York primary he was quoted as supporting Israeli settlement on the West Bank, but what he in fact said was that, if he were an Israeli, he would support settlement on the West Bank. On the other hand, Zbig is greatly taken by his high intelligence and his unlimited self-confidence and obviously thinks, quite apart, I believe, from his own ambitions, that Carter might make a formidable President.

June 24

Alice Mason, who has been raising money for Carter, called a couple of days ago and asked me whether I wanted to meet Carter in a small group this week. I said sure; and she brought me in to one of a series of meetings Carter had yesterday with $1,000 contributors. I sat with Dick Dougherty; another ringer, Elizabeth Taylor was there, looking darkly handsome but perhaps a little fat. Howard Samuels, who introduced Carter, noted my presence, and Carter made some reference in his remarks. He spoke softly and pleasantly; then answered questions at too great length. He is not crisp, but he may have been tired; this was the last of several such meetings. He showed more humor than I expected. When Elizabeth Taylor asked a question, he said that he first wanted to say how honored he was to have a question from her and that he had done his best to keep his mind on the question while she asked it.

After about 45 minutes, the meeting adjourned. Bartle Bull came up to Dougherty and me and said that Carter wanted to talk to us in the side room. (All this was at the Waldorf.) We went into the side room, where he soon joined us. He has a ruddy face, much better in repose than when crinkled into the manic and artificial grin he affects much of the time. He was pleasant, thanked us for coming and was wholly soft-sell; no requests for support. For some reason we fell to talking about the campaign coverage. He greatly admires [R.W.] Apple of the *Times* (who has been writing pro-Carter stories from the start) and is critical of [Jules] Witcover and [David] Broder of the *Washington Post*.

In general, Carter gives an impression of very considerable intelligence, confidence and competence. He does not move one to rush to the barricades. I decided not to ask any questions—the group was too large, and I did not wish to strike a discordant note—but I am encouraged by this meeting to contemplate sending him a letter expressing my reservations about his attacks on the horrible, bloated, unmanageable, etc., bureaucracy. In working on the RFK book, I have come across the presumptuous letters I used to send to Stevenson, Kennedy, Humphrey 15–20 years ago; so, now that I am beginning to be really an elder, I might as well exploit my seniority.

June 29

Lillian Hellman. For many years, though I liked her early plays, I regarded her with mistrust as an unreconstructed Stalinist. Some time in the late 1960s, Ed O'Connor, who had come to know her, brought us together. She later told me that she had regarded me with equal mistrust as an unreconstructed red-baiter. We hit it off well, and in recent years I have acquired a considerable fondness for her. She is a woman of quality and charm, sharp, elegant, amusing and great fun. We have always avoided politics, partly, I suppose, in order to avoid argument but more essentially, I think, because she does not understand politics and is really not greatly interested. Her Stalinoid leanings derive especially, I imagine, from her long association with Dashiell Hammett and an un-thinking contempt for the party members who repented and turned state's evidence.

She has now written a highly successful book called *Scoundrel Time*. The book is slight and impressionistic but well written and effective. She has a marvelous portrait of Joe Rauh, who emerges as, next to herself, the book's hero. She also has a biting attack on Jimmy Wechsler, whom she describes as a "friendly" witness before the House Un-American Activities Committee. (In fact, he was a responsive but hostile witness before the McCarthy Committee in the Senate.) Lillian [does not] under-stand that, just because there were bad reasons to be anti-Stalinist, [does not mean that] there were no good reasons to be anti-Stalinist.

Jimmy was naturally upset by her references to him and briefly threatened a libel suit. Joe offered to put out a public statement in de-fense of Jimmy. This would have been effective because of Joe's role in Lillian's book. But Jimmy, properly and nobly, declined to take up Joe's offer. Murray Kempton wrote a good review for the *New York Review of Books*. Nathan Glazer has a crude anti-Hellman piece in *Commen-tary*. Dick Rovere, Joe Lash and other veterans of the period are dis-turbed by the book. But in general it has won great acclaim. My own view is that these things balance themselves out in the end.

July 12

Here we are at another convention—and I continue to feel more dis-engaged than ever before in my political lifetime. We went out to the Smiths' at Pawling on Saturday and had a relaxed time playing tennis, swimming and watching an old movie called *I Wake Up Screaming*. Jean had just come from a camping trip with Teddy in western Massachu-setts. Carter has made no overtures to Teddy—odd, it would seem, from Carter's own viewpoint, since Ted is the best campaigner in the party and Carter's victory in the autumn is not precisely guaranteed. Ted is strong especially where Carter is weak—in the Northeast and the West. I gather from Steve that, if Carter had asked Ted to nominate him, Ted would have felt compelled to do so. Jean is quite sharp about Carter and is plainly reflecting a protective concern about her brother.

I saw the Humphreys at a *Time* party earlier in the day. I like Hubert, though obviously (judging by his acid references to me in his memoirs) I offended him deeply somewhere along the way. But politics is a rather jovial profession, and he was friendly enough in his greetings. So indeed was Muriel.

July 13

We went to the Steve Smiths' for dinner with Ted Kennedy. Also present were Candice Bergen, John Seigenthaler [Sr.], David Burke, Art and Ann Buchwald, Pat Lawford, Michael Kennedy and a girl. Afterward I had a long talk with Ted. He is highly uncertain what to do about Carter—not that Carter has asked him to do anything. "I don't want to appear a bad sport," he said. "My brothers and I have always played by the rules. I can't change on that. But a lot of people have put a lot of work and belief in things. I can't go to them and say they must trust Carter or that he believes in the things they believe in. I don't know what he believes in myself." He was speaking, as he often does, in a rush of words and somewhat cryptically. He has the Kennedy habit of articulating enough of a sentence to open up a point and then, assuming the point is made, jumping to the next sentence. So I am not altogether clear whether he was talking about Carter in general or in particular relation to national health insurance.

There was a certain sadness about Ted. One felt he could not escape the apprehension that history may have passed him by. The highest expectations have been instilled in Ted, and now it looks as if Jimmy Carter, whom no one ever heard of, will be President for the next eight years. Yet one must never forget the unpredictability of life. And Carter will always have the felt presence of Ted Kennedy on his left. Ted is quite clearly prepared to go into the opposition if he feels that Carter is moving too far to the right. In short, Ted will serve as the ideological conscience of the Carter administration—and no doubt make Carter a better President than he would be without pressure from the left.

It is perplexing that Carter, with all his talk about party unity, has made such negligible effort to bring in Kennedy, Udall, McGovern and Humphrey. I know that he has done nothing about the first three—they have all told me this in the last couple of days—and I believe that Hubert is equally in the cold. I suppose the reason, at least in connection with Ted, is that Carter wants to prove that he can do it on his own and does not need the Kennedys. I also imagine that he will become more conciliatory after the convention. But it must express too the sense of contempt for people that seems to lie near the heart of Carter's personality.

July 19

And so the convention passed. On Wednesday, the 14th, we heard Ted Kennedy speak, effectively, at the health caucus; then went on to a party given by Hugh Carey at the World Trade Center, watching Manhattan glow in the sunset; then back to a steak in our own garden while watching Carter win the nomination. On Thursday we heard the acceptance addresses with the Smiths. I thought Carter good for about five minutes in the middle, but generally it seemed to me a poor speech, banal in language and rambling and repetitive in argument. No phrases; no structure. I must report, however, that most people found it an effective speech—even Norman Mailer, whom we encountered at a party afterward given by Irving Lazar at 21.

The convention seemed anti-climactic. Maybe I am getting old. Carter should win the election and probably will be a good President. He is a curious combination—an original as a person, but quite conventional, it would seem, in his views; a prudent and methodical manager, I would think, not an innovator. I am glad that Mondale is on the ticket; it provides what JFK used to call "visual reassurance" to the liberals. In the longer run, Fritz has my sympathy.

July 27

We are back from a weekend at the Galbraiths in Newfane. The idea was to assemble a group of notables to comment on issues raised in Ken's BBC series on "The Age of Uncertainty"—i.e., the impact of industrialism on society. The notables included Ted Heath, Jack Jones, Shirley Williams and Rolf Dahrendorf from England, Kukrit Pramoj [prime minister of Thailand], Georgi Arbatov [Soviet expert on the United States] from the U.S.S.R., Henry Kissinger, Kay Graham and Tom Winship from the U.S.A. It was easy and pleasant for us and, I hope, useful for the BBC.

I was much impressed by Jack Jones—a marvelous and winning combination of gentleness, toughness and wisdom. Heath was surprisingly genial and charming; also intelligent and articulate. He was much concerned about the rise of nationalism in the British Isles, especially about Scotland. Scottish nationalism, he said, fueled by "greed and revenge," had become a serious movement; and he did not exclude the possibility of an independent Scotland before too long. Every once in a while, though, one encountered rather hard strains in Heath. On the Vietnam war, he said, "You Americans could have won the war if it had not been for the newspapers. I warned Johnson about this. The newspapers destroyed your will to win. It was great folly." He was also somewhat malicious about Roy Jenkins. "I have known Roy for a long time. We were at Balliol together. He is not without courage but he isn't a fighter. He will love the life in Brussels. There will be enough duchesses and fine Burgundy to keep him happy."

Henry was affable and relaxed. He said he had been speaking around the country a great deal (he had just come from talks on the West Coast, ending up at the Bohemian Grove) and doubted whether Reagan's anti-détente position commanded much support. He was quite funny about Tony Crosland. "Every foreign minister has to put up with platitudes," he said. "Eighty percent of diplomatic discourse is platitudes. But Crosland suffers visibly. He winces each time he hears a cliché. But he plays games with himself and manages to get through.

When Peter Rasbottom was late for a reception with the Queen, Tony awarded himself one point. When Tony wore a black tie at a white tie dinner for the Queen, he awarded himself two points. He keeps going by figuring out ways by which he can frustrate protocol."

Arbatov was his usual rigid but outwardly genial self. Henry was tough on the subject of Angola, to which he kept recurring, but otherwise very strong and clear on détente (though he said at one point, "I want the record to show that I did not introduce the word 'détente' until it was brought into the discussion by our Soviet friend"—he is evidently still irritated by Ford's ban on the word). He argued that political and nuclear détente could not be separated and that détente in Europe could not be separated from détente in Africa; "there can be no selective détente." I said that, given the nature of life, I could not imagine anything but piecemeal and selective détente

Once again Henry talked about the Chinese. Mao, he said, embodied more *will* than anyone he had ever met, except de Gaulle. He radiated extraordinary personal strength and extraordinary intelligence. He exuded domination without throwing his weight around. His style was to lead people to conclusions through sharp questions softly asked, not to lay down the law. On their last visit, Mao could hardly speak; but the interpreter, partly through lip reading, managed to make sense out of his babble. Henry is most puzzled by the succession problem: Mao always turned against his No. 2 men, which is why Chou was so wise to keep himself as No. 3 man, but there are indications (Henry said) that toward the end Mao was turning against Chou too.

He was aggressive/defensive on the subject of the Italian Communists. If they succeed in getting into the Italian government, he said, this would lead quickly to the disintegration of NATO, leaving NATO as an American-German alliance. I said that maybe Western European Communists would stand by NATO as the means of protecting Eurocommunism from the fate of Communist deviations in Hungary and Czechoslovakia. Henry evidently though I was being facetious and did not respond. I was only half facetious.

August 20

The Republicans have now given us Ford and [Bob] Dole—two four-letter words. Everyone feels that Ford gave the speech of his life last night in accepting the nomination. I heard it on television, but it sounded like the same old stuff and did not raise my head from my book.

Carter remains a mystery. Frank Mankiewicz, whom Carter was courting at one point, told George that everyone north of Atlanta was now "out." Even the Peter Bournes in Washington are regarded as having been taken over by the Georgetown crowd. Frank's calls are returned only after several days, if at all. Campaign planning is very tightly held.

Fritz Mondale called me last week. I had sent him a letter of commiseration and enclosed a copy of my *Political Science Quarterly* essay on the vice presidency. He said that, after reading the piece, he had told his wife that maybe they ought to reconsider the whole thing (goak, as Artemus Ward would say). He seemed rather cheerful, said he thought things were going well in his relations with Carter, agreed that Carter was hitting too hard too early (in New Hampshire) and said that Carter agreed on that too. He wondered whether I would take a look at his basic speech, which I said that of course I would be glad to do.

September 18

I lunched today with Paul (Red) Fay—an interesting return to older days. Red said: "I always felt much more at ease with Jack than with Bobby. I always knew where I stood with Jack. I was never sure where I stood with Bobby." Odd: I think I always had somewhat the opposite feeling. Odd too because the Fays and the RFKs took their holidays together regularly during the 1950s.

We talked about the relations between the brothers. Red thought that JFK was much easier and more relaxed with Ted than with Bobby. RFK was too intense, too much involved with issues, too demanding for a President at the end of a long day. JFK would say of his father, and by extension of himself: "Ted can do no wrong in the old man's eyes. . . . When Teddy comes into a room, you know you are in for a good time." Fay: "He related to Teddy more than he did to Bobby." But he greatly admired Bobby on the serious questions: "I'd put Bobby's judgment against all those other guys."

He had the same question I had about Ben Bradlee's book—that is, the profanity that Ben constantly attributed to JFK. As Red Fay said, "It all sounds much more like Ben than like Jack. He was putting his own way of speaking into Jack's mouth." This is very clearly my memory. Once or twice when JFK got very mad, he would be reasonably foul-mouthed in the Second World War Navy style, but this was rare. It is particularly inconceivable that he would have spoken this way in the presence of Jackie and of that gentle girl Tony Bradlee. Franklin Roosevelt and I had a similar conversation a year or so ago, and he expressed similar incredulity about Ben's rendition of Jack's table talk. Both Red and Franklin knew Jack longer and better than I, and their testimony on this point is impressive.

October 7

The second debate last night—Carter much better than before, assured, articulate and crisp. His performance ought to arrest his downward slide at a point well above what he needs to win. Ford was stalwart but made one awful boner when he denied that Eastern Europe was under Soviet domination. Carter was slow to exploit that break but finally did so; he seems to lack the instinct for the jugular.

We heard it at Karen Lerner's with the George McGoverns, Jacqueline Onassis, Pierre Salinger, the Dick Doughertys, the Robert Bernsteins (Random House), the Richard Walds (NBC) and the Cuban minister to the UN and his wife. George was reluctantly impressed by Carter this time. He said, by the way, that he had not exchanged a word with Carter since the convention. One would have thought that, as a matter of courtesy, Carter would have invited McGovern to Plains and asked him to do some campaigning. He seems a mean little man. But he was not bad last night.

Later. Jackie called; we chatted about last night. She said, "I felt so sorry for George McGovern. What a nice man he is—especially compared to that stiff, prissy little man on the screen! How different things might be if he had won!" She went on to indicate great reservations about Carter. Without thinking, I said, "Well, if Carter should lose, we can console ourselves; this will probably mean Ted in 1980." There was an intake of breath at the other end. I knew at once what she was thinking. She said, "You are ahead of me on this. Maybe, maybe it would be better for Carter to win. . . ."

October 19

I saw Ted Kennedy this evening at Pat Lawford's. We exchanged our incredulities about the campaign. He cannot make out Carter (any more than the rest of us can). He spent some time with him recently in Massachusetts. "You know," he said, "with most people you meet—American politicians or foreign statesmen—you can make a connection. There is something they want to talk about, something they care about, something on their mind. I have never seen anyone like him. Once you get beyond the merely perfunctory and try to talk about something substantive, a glazed window seems to come down, and there it is. I suppose he has a feeling about the Kennedys. Jim King [a Boston figure, who has been travelling with Carter and running the organization on the road] says he is filled with disdain and contempt about the Kennedys. But I didn't want to take this all personally, so I specifically asked McGovern, Humphrey and Muskie, and they all had the same treatment. He has not been in touch with them, has not asked them to do anything serious in the campaign—not that any of them are passionate to work for him, but of course they would help if asked. I told him that I would be glad to go anywhere with him—East Los Angeles or Harlem or wherever he would like—but that I didn't want to be a surrogate and go by myself." I suppose Carter saw this as a somewhat double-edged offer and has no great desire to go anywhere and be overshadowed by Ted. "All they have asked me to do," Ted continued, "is to go somewhere with Rosalynn."

October 27

A week to go (from yesterday); and, as Henry Kissinger said last week at the Council on Foreign Relations, this long national nightmare will at last be over. Two worse candidates I have never seen. If the campaign were to go on still another week, I think that Carter would do himself in. But my guess is that he will win by a comfortable margin in the electoral college; by a smaller margin in the popular vote.

I vacillate every day and probably will not make up my mind finally until I have the moment of truth with the voting machine. Today I do not feel I can possibly vote for Carter. I note in the morning *Times*, very much played down, a report of a letter from Carter to the *Atlanta Constitution* in which he indignantly denies the statement that he read Genesis symbolically rather than literally: "I have never made any such statement, and I have no reason to disbelieve Genesis, Chapter II, verses 21, 22, or other Biblical miracles." I do not like to be influenced by a candidate's religion; but a fundamentalist in the White House seems a little too much.

The egregious William F. Buckley Jr. printed a flat lie about me in his column in yesterday's *Post*. He said that I "wrote [Carter] volunteering to serve as a speechwriter" and "got back from Carter a form letter advising him to apply to the nearest Carter-for-President office." Total fantasy, of course, and, as developed (I am described as "the most overbearing liberal ideologue in the United States"), filled with Buckley's usual malice. It is odd: whenever I encounter Buckley, he is excessively genial, as if he wanted to be friends; but, whenever I begin vaguely to soften under his personal courtship, something like this reminds me how odious he is. A simple phone call could have checked the point (it sounds like a garbled version of a story that Scotty Reston had about Ken, and that story, Ken tells me, is wrong too, though Ken did apparently write Carter offering to help). The last thing in the world that Buckley wants is to have facts violate his prejudices.

November 1

Election eve. We went across the street to watch the last respective national half hours for Carter and Ford. It was hard to decide which was more repulsive. I have resolved reluctantly to vote for Carter, on the grounds that the unknown is preferable to this particular known. I do so with great misgiving. Carter may turn out to be a sensational President. He may also turn out to be another weirdo, as incapable as Johnson and Nixon of listening to dissent or accepting the legitimacy of opposition.

I will be 67, God help me, at the end of Carter's second term, if this should be our destiny. I feel that his election will mean the exclusion of the tendency in the Democratic party with which I have worked for nearly thirty years—stemming from FDR and Truman and going through Stevenson, JFK, RFK, McGovern. That style of politics— open, curious, ironic, civilized, questioning—is, or appears to be, quite alien to the closed, sanctimonious, rancorous, punitive politics of Carter. Nor do I really think that Carter will do much more for the country than circumstance and the activist tradition of his party will compel him to do. As I may have noted before, his mind seems managerial, not in- novative, and his passion will be government reorganization, not social invention. So I am filled with foreboding. He reminds me too much of Nixon. Yet one can't vote for Ford.

November 3

The deed has been done. In the end I could not bring myself to vote for a man who believes that Adam and Eve once existed and that Eve was literally made out of Adam's rib (as he explained in a letter to the *Atlanta Constitution*) and believes he has seen flying saucers. So I left the presidential space blank. I would have voted for McCarthy if his name had been on the ballot (as the only one of the three who had no chance of winning). What a dismal election! Sinclair Lewis should have covered it: Babbitt v Elmer Gantry.

I turned the television off about 1 o'clock, confident, as I had been all evening, that Carter would win. Around 4 A.M. the phone rang: it was Dick Gardner, soon followed on the wires by Zbig Brzezinski and then by Cyrus Vance, with sounds of revelry in the background. Evidently NBC had just given Carter the election. "We knew you would want to share our enthusiasm," Dick said with mild but understandable sarcasm. I congratulated them all warmly. In the morning I turned on the television to see Carter promising the people of Plains, Georgia, that he would give them a government as fine, wise, upright, beautiful, etc., as they are. He really seems to me a total phoney. I don't know whether it is worse to think he believes this junk or doesn't believe it. Eight years of righteous homilies masking a punitive nature may be hard to take. I see him as the smiler with a knife.

December 26

Our friend Sylvia Marlowe, whose husband Leonid Berman (one of whose Venetian paintings Alexandra gave me for my birthday a year ago) sadly died a few weeks back, came for Christmas dinner. It was she who called us to tell of Lionel Trilling's death; and, when she asked us to come today to have a drink with Diana [Trilling], we asked at once, of course, how Diana was.

Sylvia, who is a realist of the most humane sort, said in effect that Diana had become very difficult—that she was so obsessed with Lillian Hellman, and with protecting Lionel's reputation against the most invisible of aspersions, that it was hard to deal with her anymore. I saw what she meant when I dropped over to Sylvia's this afternoon. (We had no baby-sitter, so Alexandra stayed behind.) Roger and Dorothea Strauss were there, also Joel Carmichael; and for the 45 minutes I was there the conversation, commanded by Diana, was almost totally about Lillian. I have always liked Diana, as I have come in recent years to like Lillian; and, on the political points of disagreement, I stand with Diana

in opposition to (and in contempt for) Stalinists. S[...]
Monomania is boring. Diana, perceiving my want [...]
particular subject, said, "This talk makes Arth[...]
Lillian too much." The premise was right, the c[...]
simply felt after a time that it was all too much [...]
Diana is an intelligent and brave woman. She is r[...]
is wrong to let herself be possessed by the matt[...]
exorcism.

One story is perhaps worth recording. The tal[...]
supposed sexual irresistibility. Some incredulity [...]
Strausses told the following tale. Lillian had them [...]
along with Philip Roth and Richard Poirier. At the [...]
Strausses and Roth took their leave. Poirier stayed [...]
tor Dorothea Strauss discovered that she had forgot[...]
took the elevator back from the ground floor and [...]
door. After a delay they heard Lillian's voice askin[...]
identified themselves and explained their mission.[...]
Inside were Poirier still wearing jacket and trouser[...]
Lillian, in miniskirt nightgown with ruffles and [...]
aplomb, Lillian handed the Strausses the gloves, an[...]

1977

❖

January 1

The years rush by. In nine and a half months I will be sixty. I don't *feel* sixty, or anything like it (or at least anything like what I always imagined sixty to be). I had hoped to finish the RFK book in 1976; I retain great forebodings about Carter in the White House. Still I find myself on New Year's Day singularly and inexplicably cheerful. It is really not beyond explanation. With Alexandra and Robert and Peter as constant company, it is hard not to feel buoyant about life.

The Duchins invited us last night to Tavern on the Green, where Peter is playing. We danced a bit; I chatted pleasantly with Lee Radziwill, who was sitting next to me; at midnight I embraced Alexandra, and then we watched George Plimpton's fireworks bursting over Central Park. It was a dry, clear, freezing night. We were in bed by 12:45, thereafter watching Fred Astaire and Bing Crosby in *Blue Skies*. A harmless way to pass a noxious night. And now for 1977. My resolutions are to give up drinking and cigars, for at least three days.

April 7

We got down [to Hobe Sound] last Friday, nearly a week ago. On Saturday we went to Palm Beach and lunched at Mrs. Kennedy's. Jean and Pat were there. I had never been to the Palm Beach house before. Like all Kennedy houses, it was designed for comfort and family rather than for elegance. Rose Kennedy is indomitable and went in swimming with a large bonnet tied under her chin.

Isaiah [Berlin] was in New York on his way to Japan. I called him and expressed particular pleasure over his listing Hannah Arendt in the *Times Literary Supplement* as one of the most overrated writers of the century. He said that he had promptly received a postcard from Mary McCarthy, which said, "In case your conscience should trouble you, the rating was mutual. Mary West." He replied: "Thank you for giving me this information. I had no idea! Perhaps we are both right." Years ago, I brought Hannah and Isaiah together. He was convalescing from flu in Lowell House. The meeting was a disaster from the start. She was too solemn, portentous, Teutonic, Hegelian for him. She mistook his wit for frivolousness and thought him inadequately serious. She did write one good, though wrongheaded book, *The Origins of Totalitarianism*. Subsequently she confused intellectual history with philology. Or so it seemed to me.

May 30

We have endured the late Nixon's resurrection at the hands of David Frost. He was almost more odious than one remembered, a grotesque parody of himself—so much so that one began to feel it was not Nixon at all, but one of those nightclub mimics impersonating Nixon and maliciously accentuating all the awful mannerisms, smiles, turns of speech. One felt more keenly than even before that he is nuts.

June 1

[My brother] Tom called me this morning around 11 to say that Mother had died. She had been in a semi-coma for several days. I had asked Tom yesterday whether I should go down to Williamsburg; but he said she did not speak any more and did not appear to recognize anyone; that she was barely conscious, if conscious at all. She was not in pain. I know that she has been wishing to die for some time, and I am glad that she was able to do so peacefully, and in her own room and bed. Still, no matter how much one expected it and how much a deliverance it was for her, it is a shock. I have felt strangely disturbed ever since Tom's call.

She was quite a marvelous woman in her spirit, her range of interest, her high standards, her absence of righteousness and rigidity and her passion. Her acuteness of concern used to get on my nerves from time to time, a fact I naturally regret bitterly now, but I think she knew how much I loved her and how indebted I feel to her. I know I owe some of my better qualities to her—my strength of feeling, my readiness to trust intuition, my capacity for affection; not to mention my reading speed. My father was more reserved, almost austere perhaps; more a man of consecutive reason, though with much repressed emotion; more consistent, disciplined, purposeful. I believe they were very happy together. I also guess that I combine qualities from them both.

In particular, Mother did a great deal—my father too—to cultivate my taste for literature. She was a patient and enthusiastic reader when I was small, and I adored being read to. In later years she loved reading to her grandchildren.

She would have been 91 in a month—a full life; a happy one too; even these last years were infinitely brightened for her by Robert and Alexandra. I don't suppose any grandmother ever loved any little boy as Mother loved Robert. He was always great with her, responsive and appreciative. Oddly when I called her nurse the other day to find out how she was, Robert suddenly burst into the room. I don't know how he knew that I was talking to Williamsburg; nor has it recently been easy to get him on the phone with his grandmother; but he suddenly cried, "I want to speak to Grandma! I want to speak to Grandma!"

August 11

I am sitting on the balcony of Ken Galbraith's apartment in Gstaad [Switzerland], a green valley stretching out before me, snowy peaks in the distance, a bright sun over all. The book was finally done about 3:50 P.M. on Tuesday, 26 July. The last weeks were rather like the last weeks, a dozen years earlier, of *A Thousand Days*. Alexandra, Robert and Peter went to London on 21 June. This had all been arranged on the assumption that I would finish by the end of June. Alas, I still had far to go. But, working night and day in a silent house, I managed to do 13 chapters in five weeks. I could not have sustained the pace much longer. But finishing a book is rather like finishing a political campaign. One has just enough energy to get to the end. Thereafter, collapse.

I would have finished earlier if I had not become embroiled in a disagreeable controversy with Bill Moyers. Early in June he put on for CBS a television "documentary" entitled *The CIA's Secret Army*. This show, which was masterminded by George Crile, seemed to me an extraordinarily shabby and tendentious polemic in which Bill gave his imprimatur to the proposition that the CIA was an innocent agency bludgeoned into excesses toward Cuba by the insensate demands of the Kennedys. I wrote a piece for the *Wall Street Journal* setting forth carefully the flaws and lacunae in the presentation. I recalled Gilbert Seldes's piece on Ed Murrow's McCarthy show and expressed the hope that this would be a single lapse in Moyers's otherwise honorable record. Bill took this very personally and responded, not by dealing with the issues I had raised, but by impeaching my integrity as an historian. He also proposed a personal meeting in which he could show me the errors of my way. I responded by listing the questions about the show that he had declined to answer. As for a personal meeting, I said fine; but why confine the pleasure to ourselves? Let us instead have a television debate which CBS could use as an epilogue if it put the show on the air again. Needless to say, Moyers did not take up the challenge.

I was sorry about the escalation, because I have always liked Moyers. His attack on RFK seemed to me singularly unfortunate because RFK had a high regard for him and would very probably have made Moyers Secretary of State if he had won in 1968—a recollection that Ethel Kennedy confirmed when we had dinner with the Smiths on 27 July. However, maybe I was wrong about Moyers. A surprising number of people expressed great dubiety about him since the controversy began. Dick Goodwin says that he is deeply neurotic. Teddy White says that Moyers is one of the few people in politics who has lied to him—"not once but several times." Bill White, who was a great LBJ pal in these years, says he never trusted Moyers—"too sanctimonious for his own good." Jack Valenti has been warning me against Moyers for years. Still I have a regret about the episode.

September 7

[Our] European interlude was highly agreeable, though it was said to be the worst summer for forty years. This was certainly the case on the Riviera, where the mistral blew and then the rains rained and [Sam Spiegel's Yacht] the *Malahne* never sailed beyond Monte Carlo (at least during our stay).

Grace Kelly, her daughter Caroline and Caroline's somewhat dubious fiancé came aboard [the yacht] in Monte Carlo. I remember seeing Grace at the White House in, I think, 1962. I said to JFK, "What an astonishingly pretty girl." "Yes," he said. "Very pretty, and very boring." She is less astonishingly pretty 15 years later, though still very good-looking, but I found her not in the slightest boring. She talked most amusingly about her family. My father had always been a great fan of George Kelly, who stopped writing his plays about the time I started going to the theater, though he lived for another thirty years. I asked why he had abandoned the theater. She said, "FDR." I sought clarification. "He hated FDR," she said. "Thought he was wrecking the economy and the theater along with it. My father was a great admirer of FDR. He and Uncle George had a long and very funny correspondence about the New Deal." Caroline is rather beautiful, intelligent I would think, strong and, on this occasion, somewhat sulky. M. Junot, the fiancé, looked like an aging beach boy. The prognosis, I would say, is poor.

Back in the United States I now for the first time scent the possibility of denying Carter renomination. His popularity remains low in the polls, compared to that of Truman, Eisenhower, Kennedy or Johnson at the same point, and people regard him indifferently. He excites neither love nor hate. His economic conservatism grows more evident every day. His instincts are better in foreign affairs, but the world is intractable. The trouble is that Jerry Brown, who is presumably straining to challenge him, would be no better so far as one could tell; perhaps not even greatly different. Of course I would prefer Ted, but he has become a familiar face. Yet I think that in the right circumstances he could become an exciting figure again. He would plainly make by far the best President of the lot.

September 23

I lunched yesterday with Marietta [Tree]. We talked about John Bartlow Martin's second volume, which she had not seen. I told her that she came out as Adlai's top girl and that the sons were quoted as saying they always expected their father to marry her. She was not displeased. But she added, "I am so glad the book was not published when Ronnie was alive." She told an amusing story about AES and his women after the 1960 convention. Alicia Patterson and Marietta were invited by Adlai to come and stay at a ranch owned by Susie Zurcher's family but ended up in a motel nearby. Exasperated by it all, Marietta decided to accept an invitation from John Huston to watch him shoot *The Misfits* near Reno. When she went to Reno, John gave her a small part (saying good-bye to Clark Gable in the opening reel). Adlai meanwhile kept calling and insisting that she join him at the Heller place near Lake Tahoe. She agreed to meet him at the Reno airport and, without saying so, gave Huston the impression that she was flying back to New York. She could not dissuade Huston from taking her to the airport. When he found Stevenson waiting there, both men were furious and hardly spoke to each other. Marietta then went off to Stevenson. The next day Huston called and told her she had to come back to Reno for retakes on her performance in the film. (She went.)

October 15

Sixty years old, God help me! I find this hard to credit. I do not feel sixty—ninety sometimes, about thirty-five most of the time, but never sixty. My illusion of youth is due altogether to the miracle that incorporated Alexandra and Robert and Peter into my life. With three such spirited young presences around the house, it is impossible to feel old. I weighed myself this morning: 176 pounds. This I regard as about 5 pounds above fighting weight; but it is still 5 pounds less than my inordinate weight when I returned from the French eating tour in August. I continue to shrink and am now under 5'10". I have finished the RFK manuscript and am now engaged in trying to cut some 75,000 words in order to bring it down to marketable length.

October 24

Jackie had a dinner last night for Hugh Fraser and Sonia Melchett. Others present were Bill Walton, Karen Lerner (replacing Alexandra, who was at Peter's bedside, Peter having broken his ankle in a remarkably complicated way) and Pat and Liz Moynihan. Pat, I thought, was more than usually intolerable. He swells like a bullfrog and punctuates his speech with a repertoire of sweeping gestures and smug expressions. Like the late Dean Acheson, he tells stories all of which illustrate his triumph over someone else. He was superficially cordial but obviously detests me (manners and feelings I reciprocate). He is filled with egotism and rancor. He launched into a vicious attack on the Labor Party as a virtual branch of the Comintern. When I observed that Jim Callaghan had, I thought, done a valiant job in dishing the left wing, he exposed his real reasons for hating Callaghan—because Callaghan had instructed Ivor Richard to attack him at the UN.

November 7

I lunched today with a young fellow named John Taft who threatens to do a profile on me for the *New Republic.* I told him over the telephone that that was the last thing I wanted. However, when it came out that he was the grandson of Robert A. Taft, I remembered that 30 years ago his grandfather had given me considerable time when I was doing a piece on him for *Collier's;* so I decided I owed some time to the Taft family. To my surprise, I had liked Bob Taft back in 1947. He was candid, direct and had a sort of pawky charm I had not expected. He also could be dogmatic and even, I guess, mean; but I saw little of that side and found him quite agreeable. Later, when I got to know Charlie Taft, the liberal brother, I found, again to my surprise, that I rather preferred Bob to Charlie, though I was in much greater agreement on issues with Charlie; a step in education comparable to my reluctant recognition that I would rather spend an evening with Alice Longworth than with Eleanor Roosevelt. Politics, I came to conclude, is not everything.

November 12

Carter. I have been watching the decline with a certain dismal relish. As I surmised, he is conservative, unimaginative, filled with solicitude for business, and tight and defensive in his personal relations. I did not expect, however, that he would be as weak and vacillating as he appears to be; or so poor a manager—not that this last is a necessary presidential virtue, but it is one he was supposed to have.

His administration is badly in the doldrums for the moment. He has seized gratefully on the excuse offered him, with their usual irrelevance, by the Washington reporters—that he has been trying to do too much too quickly and has thereby "overloaded the circuits." His defect, he has implied in recent press conferences, is that he is too much the activist President. In fact, he has tried to do rather less than Wilson, FDR, Truman, Kennedy or Johnson tried to do in their first years. His trouble is that his recommendations have come as disparate and unrelated shots rather than as parts of a coherent program. This is what people mean, I think, when they speak of his "lack of vision." The other trouble is that he does not understand politics as an educational process. He seems to think that if he has reached a conclusion, the mystic communion he thinks he enjoys with the people should lead to immediate popular support and congressional enactment. Only under pressure does he try to explain why something is important or necessary.

It is an idiotic point, but he is the first Democratic President since Cleveland who has not had a label for his program. We have had the New Freedom, the New Deal, the Fair Deal, the New Frontier, the Great Society. Carter has proposed nothing. It is, I think, more than a public relations point. It reflects the evident facts that (a) he is not an innovator and (b) he has no vision to project, no underlying pattern or unifying purpose behind his random proposals. I do not suggest, of course, that if Pat Cadell or Jerry Rafshoon could come up with a label, this would solve Carter's problems.

He is low in the polls now, but will come up a bit once he gets some sort of energy bill. But one gets no impression of popularity as one travels around the country. People neither love nor hate him. On the whole, they regard him with indifference. He is rarely mentioned. He is a remote, abstract figure; not a factor in people's lives or hopes. It is, in a way, like Eisenhower; except that Eisenhower was a national hero with a great fund of public affection on which to draw. Carter has none.

The great question is whether or not he is a learner. If he is, this dreary beginning will not be held against him. After all, he has done nothing nearly so disastrous as we did in our first months with the Bay of Pigs. If he is a non-learner (my bet), then there will be more of the same, and we can run someone against him in the primaries in 1980.

(Ted? can he be asked to affront the 20-year curse? every President elected every 20 years beginning in 1840 has died in office.)

December 13

Lunched today at the Century with Henry Kissinger. The conversation turned inevitably after a time to Nixon. I had asked Henry about his book. He said, "You know, I had the greatest difficulty in bringing myself to think about Nixon. It wasn't until the Frost interviews—seeing him dancing around questions, hearing him give his own incredible recollections—that it all came flooding back. . . . One thing you have to remember about Nixon is that he only worked about three hours a day. Every once in a while, as over Cambodia, he would work for twelve hours a day for a week. Then he would disappear, and you couldn't get in touch with him. The rest of the time he worked very little." I asked what he did to pass the day. "He wouldn't see any visitors. When he did, he would ask for a memorandum anticipating what the visitor would say and how he should reply. Then he would commit them to memory. But this took time, so he saw few visitors. And he hated seeing members of his cabinet. He liked to call in members of his staff and ruminate—about the liberals, the Hiss case, the people who were out to get him. It was impossible if you had other things to do. I would sit there, almost hoping that war would break out so I would be released and be able to get back to work. Whenever there was an interruption, I would scoot out as quickly as I could."

Henry said rather regretfully that [Frank] Gannon and Diane Sawyer, who are writing Nixon's book, are doing a careful job. "From a Machiavellian viewpoint, it would be much better for me if they printed all his fantasies. But they are checking everything, so I am afraid it will be a pretty good book. . . . Nixon doesn't lie. He invents his own truths."

Henry was mutedly critical about the administration. He considers Vance "very decent and a professional" but without ideas. As for Carter and Brzezinski, he finds them "petty," determined to score short-run political points at the expense of foreign policy. He resents particularly their desire to prove that their SALT deal is better than the Kissinger-Ford SALT deal. On balance, he continues to think that his own deal was marginally better. Brzezinski is "gimmick-minded." Carter reminds him of Nixon in his passion to protect himself from argument and from diverse human contact. "There is something very weird about him."

He said that Donald Rumsfeld was the rottenest person he had known in government—that it was Rumsfeld who, in pursuit of his own ambitions, had set Kissinger and Schlesinger (J.) against each other, and had persuaded Ford to make George Bush head of the CIA so he would be extinguished as the vice presidential candidate in 1976 (and thereby, Henry added, probably lost Ford the election).

1978

January 1

Another year has rushed by. At least I have finished the RFK book—though since October I have been at work cutting it down by some 75,000 words, much improving it in the process. Once one has changed gears from creation to destruction, it is a rather absorbing exercise. I should finish in another month or less.

January 12

A call this afternoon from Jim Fallows at the White House. He is working on the State of the Union message and said he had persuaded Carter to include more historical material. "I felt we had too much engineering talk last year and that we ought to have more historical talk this year." We chatted about the historic crises and the manner in which past Presidents had personified and clarified great ideas in the life of the nation. I then asked what there would be in the way of content; it would ask for trouble to begin by implying grand historical comparisons and then offer little in the way of grand programs. "That is the problem," he said. "The content will be on the thin side. It will be mostly the economic program." I said, "I hope you are to show how the Carter economic program differs from what Ford would have done if reelected." He said, "Between us, that is the question I have been asking at every stage. The real answer is that the difference is only incremental. All we are doing is fiddling at the margins." He seemed throughout candid and sympathetic.

Last night I sat next to Margaret Truman Daniel at Barbara Kerr's. Margaret was enraged by her aunt Mary who, it appears, went into the Truman Library, managed, with Rose Conway's connivance, to sneak out the great series of "Dear Mother and Aunt Mary" letters that HST sent every week from the White House and burned them. There were no copies. Margaret fortunately used some of them in her book, but the rest are now permanently lost to scholarship. "Daddy wrote those letters for the historians," Margaret said. "I told Aunt Mary that she had burned history." I asked why she had done it. "She is very old," Margaret said. "She said she felt the letters were too personal." Margaret said that she had stopped speaking to her aunt and to Rose Conway. It really is an appalling story.

January 14

Hubert Humphrey died this morning. He was a nice man, but I doubt that history will make much of him. He was extremely intelligent and quick, filled with charm and gusto, concerned and generous by instinct, but vulnerable, insecure and, at critical moments, fatally weak. He was, as Harding's father said about Harding, like the girl who couldn't say no. He was corrupted by the desire to please.

I have known him for over thirty years. We met first in the early days of ADA. He was the liberal mayor of Minneapolis, bright, voluble and impassioned. We all thought he was great then. He turned the Philadelphia convention around in 1948 by his eloquence in support of the minority plank on civil rights. I had had to leave the convention because of an attack of mumps; but I still remember lying in my bed on Irving Street hearing Hubert saying over the radio, "We must come out of the shadow of states' rights and move into the sunlight of human rights" and hearing the hall go wild. Actually he did not, at the end, want to give the speech and had to be shamed into it, and physically transported to the convention hall, by Joe Rauh, who had written the speech. That, alas, was typical. He always faded in the crunch. His spirit enlivened the Senate; but I do not feel that the history of the last thirty years would have been much different had he never gone there. Unlike Douglas, Kefauver, Fulbright and others of his Senate generation, he has left no legislative monuments. He did not excel at investigation. He always had a third-rate staff.

Of course Vietnam sticks most in my mind. I suppose he had no alternative except to believe or to resign. But I will never forget the sad evening at Joe Rauh's house in 1967, nor the chilling correspondence Hubert and I had at a later point. We made up in recent years, at least on the surface. I have never felt that he really forgave me for what?— going with Kennedy in 1960 (which in fact I did not do till after West Virginia)? or criticizing him later? He got back at me a little in his book. I have never been able to go along with those who describe Hubert as the politician who never bore a grudge.

Still he stood, most of the time, for the noble causes, communicated joy in living and in politics, endured much and died gallantly. He will be greatly missed.

January 22

On Thursday night we went to Brooke Astor's for a small dinner for the Nelson Rockefellers. Nelson looked trim and went into a long business of how liberated and tranquil he felt. Happy alleged cheerfulness, but she is sad, I think, and looks as if she is drinking too much. She said darkly at one point that, knowing what she did of what was going on in the Ford White House toward the end, she couldn't possibly vote for Ford's reelection. As Nelson came by and said it was time to go home, she said, "Oh, Nelson, I hope I haven't done anything to disgrace you tonight." She is the remnants of a woman of spirit and charm crushed by his hyperactivity and infidelity.

February 15

Dinner last night at Jan Cushing's. Norman Mailer was also there and talked a bit about Gore Vidal. "He was very kind when I was in a lot of trouble," Norman said. ". . . in the period after that business with Adele, Gore is really a most avuncular fellow. Then we broke. If I ever see him again, I will smash him. . . . Still he and I are in some way bound together forever, like a bad marriage." Norman is beginning to sound pretty avuncular too.

May 7

New York Jew, the third volume of Alfred Kazin's reminiscences, has just been published. When I greeted him the other day in the Century, he responded so dourly that I sensed guilt as well as hostility and concluded that he had paid back scores in the book. Subsequently I looked at it in a bookshop. He goes over once again the whole business of the luncheon I arranged for him to have with JFK. He claims that he showed me his piece on "Kennedy and the Intellectuals" *before* the luncheon, that I said that Kennedy would not mind, that the luncheon took place and that Kennedy was furious. I no longer recall the episode in detail; but I don't see why Alfred wanted to see JFK if he had already written his piece; my memory is that the lunch took place, and the piece was written afterward. But, since I can't recall, I don't insist. Perhaps I thought Kazin would change the piece after he met JFK. In any event, JFK was *not* furious; it was not a major issue in his life, even though it appears to have been in Alfred's. Alfred also draws a ludicrous picture of high life in Wellfleet. When I think of the bare, two-room piece of wartime emergency housing in which Marian and I lived, with an equally bare shack for the children nearby, I wonder at Alfred's reportorial conscience. Actually he reports poorly but evokes rather well, only too often inaccurately.

I am vaguely juxtaposed against Dick Hofstadter—the power-loving stablemate of statesmen as against the pure, dispassionate, incorruptible scholar. There is something in this, except for Alfred's pretense of intimacy with Hofstadter, which, like his pretense of intimacy with Edmund Wilson, is grotesquely overdone. Kazin and Hofstadter were indeed close in the early 1940s, but, according to Beatrice Hofstadter White, much less close thereafter. When Dick was dying, she told me the other day, Alfred used to keep calling on him at the hospital; and was so boring and exhausting that Dick finally asked her to keep him away.

Alfred *is* exhausting. I first got to know him well twenty-five years ago in Cambridge. I liked him a lot for a while. He was bright, enthusiastic, sensitive, filled with the excitements of discovery. After a time I began to feel an insistence on response from him that was at first distracting and then annoying. He *demanded* that you see things as he saw them. Still his intellectual qualities far outweighed his social defects. To this day I am not sure what scores he thinks he is repaying—probably the fact that I had him invited for luncheon to the White House. His life, one feels, has almost been stultified by obscure wounds and invisible slights. *On Native Grounds* is still, I suppose, his most enduring work—and an astonishing achievement for one so young.

May 31

Once one becomes 60, age is preoccupying; but I have been much cheered about the prospects of growing still older as a result of spending Monday evening with Averell Harriman (86) and Tuesday evening with Rose Kennedy (87).

Averell and Pam had us to dinner in their suite at the United Nations Plaza Hotel with a dramatic view of midtown New York from one window and an equally dramatic view of the East River from another. They are here for a few weeks while Averell is on the U.S. delegation to the special UN session on disarmament.

Averell was in a rage over the recent and rather suddening harden-
ing of the American line toward the Soviet Union. He thinks Brzezinski
is a "fool" and a menace with "absolutely no understanding" of the Russians. His whole idea, Averell said, is that we can scare them into changing their policy. This will only strengthen the hawks in the Soviet
Union. The fact is that we both have a vital interest in getting a SALT
agreement. Here he interrupted his flow and said to Pam, "Tell them
what [young] Winston told you," adding to us, "As you know Winston
is a real hardliner." Pam said that Winston is in Japan and had recently
called from Hiroshima. He was badly shaken, Pam said, and told her
that everyone in the world should go there, that people were still dying
from the first A-bomb and that the world must understand that nuclear
weapons can never be used again. "That is the point," said Averell.
"The Hiroshima bomb is trivial compared to the bombs we have now.
We can't let anything stand in the way of a good SALT agreement. And
we had better act while Brzezhnev is still around."

He said that [Andrei] Gromyko had never been more genial than he
was at the beginning of the special session and he supposes that the Russians must be totally confused by the Carter hard line. "They have always understood détente to mean specific and limited agreements, not a
general standstill," he said. "They have always made it clear that they
would of course continue to back liberation movements around the
world." I asked him why Carter listened to Brzezinski. "He thinks it
will strengthen him in the polls," Averell said. "He thinks the hard line
will help him politically." Vance, Averell says, has the right views on Soviet policy but is too courteous and passive to be effective against
Brzezinski. "He should have built up Marshall Shulman as Brzezinski's
offset," Averell said. "Instead he won't take Marshall to the meetings,
and thereby allows the debate to be defined as Brzezinski v. himself."

I completely share Averell's concern. In the last few days Zbig has
done his best to start a Chinese-American alliance against the Soviet
Union and to carry us back to the old Cold War. I am sure that Carter
thinks this will help him politically. It may in the very short run, but its
longer effect will be to renew the impression of the Democrats as the

war party. In the long run peace remains a good deal more popular in this country than war. Brzezinski aspires to be the Henry Kissinger of this administration. I fear he will end up the Walt Rostow.

We dined the next night with Rose Kennedy at the Smiths'. She has shrunk with age, but still very bright-eyed, animated and responsive. During dinner she conducted a grammatical quiz in her old style, testing the young (Jean and Alexandra) on such questions as "who" v. "whom" and "between you and I." When we went upstairs after dinner, she sat down at the piano and played "Sweet Adeline" and a couple of other tunes with considerable dash. She is much taken with General Vernon Walters—Dick Walters, whom I first knew as Averell's translator in Paris 30 years ago and who tells lies about me in his memoirs (for which he has apologized and which will be deleted in subsequent printings)—and was amusing on that subject. She went on strong till almost 11 o'clock. Amazing vitality.

June 10

On Wednesday, before leaving for New Orleans, I lunched with Ted Kennedy. He was in good form. To my relief he did not defend Carter, though he said that a good part of Carter's troubles was caused by the "collapse of the Congress." The trouble with Congress, he said, is that "it is owned lock, stock and barrel by private interests." I wondered whether this was more true now than fifteen years ago when he had first come to the Senate. He said that it was—the private interests are better organized now, and the mood of the country is more in their favor.

He was just back from the arms reduction talks in Geneva. He was somewhat concerned about the Brzezinski drift in foreign policy but even more about the essential waywardness and unpredictability of Carter's personal attitudes. This, he said, was really what worried the Russians. I said that it worried a lot of Americans too. "You talk to Carter," I said. "Where does he really stand on things? He gives the impression of a man without a center. Is there a center?" Ted said, "That's the question."

For the first time I had the feeling that he is beginning to think seriously about 1980. This feeling was strengthened when I had dinner with Jean and Steve last night. It was, on this subject, one of those cryptic Kennedy conversations. Steve said, "I suppose he would have to announce by January 1980." I said that I did not know how the new rules adopted by the Democratic National Committee would affect this. He said, "In any case, he couldn't do it later than January."

June 15

Very entertaining dinner last night: the Harrimans, the Wechslers, the Chancellors, Kitty Hart. As he was leaving, [Harriman] noticed the blown-up *Life* cover (1938) of FDR that Alexandra recently had framed and now hangs in the front hall. He paused for a moment and said, "You know why he was such a great President? . . . Because he did not yield to feelings of personal loyalty. He picked men, gave them jobs to do, gave them plenty of discretion. If they did the job well, fine; if not, he cut them off without a second thought. He did not allow personal loyalty to get in the way of the public business." He paused again. "Also, you know, he was something of a sadist. He liked to set people against each other. He liked to keep people off balance." I reminded him of Emerson's statement on Napoleon: whatever else could be said for or against him, everyone had to admit that Napoleon "understood his business." Averell said, "President Roosevelt sure understood his."

August 5
Midsummer in Europe

We drove on yesterday from Portofino to Florence in time for dinner with Marietta, Pam Hartwell and Joe Alsop. I have never really appreciated Florence, I guess, nor even much liked it. It does not have for me the active charm of Venice or of Rome. I am just back from the Uffizi, that stupefying collection of masterpieces, far too many to absorb in a single visit, badly hung and lit. The galleries were crowded with

Japanese. I had forgotten the Bronzini portraits—very sharp and elegant. But it was hot, and I emerged exhausted after an hour and a half.

Joe says he is never going to travel again—too much trouble, too little reward. I have not reached that point and hope I never will. But I do feel that the age of 60 confers certain liberties. As I went into the Duomo, it occurred to me that I have been visiting churches in Europe for 45 years, and that they have really done very little for me—my fault, not theirs, of course; but there it is. Why should I waste my declining years going into churches? I have been reading *Mt. Saint Michel and Chartres* to see what excited Adams so much about churches. I broadly understand his intellectual interest in these noble edifices as expressions of their age; but I am not equipped to get the direct aesthetic shock. So I will simplify life by abandoning the inspection of churches, as in earlier years I have abandoned ballet, metaphysics, linguistics and other subjects that, however estimable, are, alas, not for me.

September 21

We returned on Sunday from San Francisco. Directly after Labor Day I began the promotional tour for the book—first in New York, then on to Chicago, Denver, Los Angeles, San Francisco, where Alexandra joined me.

I stayed in Chicago at the Ambassador East, where I had stayed so often in the past. It has fallen on sad days. Its atmosphere is now one of faded elegance, and the lobby is filled with tieless men wearing double-knit trousers. I still remember it during the 1952 convention when Joe Alsop maintained a table in the Pump Room and the hotel was the center of stylish activity.

With the exception of Studs Terkel, who was sympathetic and imaginative, most of the interviewers seemed to be disconcertingly hostile, to RFK or to me or to both of us. The usually affable Irv Kupcinet even planned to put Roy Cohn on the show with me (along with Bob Novak). I said that I would not appear on the show with Cohn, so he was scrubbed. This general mood of hostility continued until we reached

San Francisco. Everyone was pleasant there—whether because San Franciscans are more civilized or because Alexandra accompanied me to the interviews and the presence of a beautiful wife enjoined a greater degree of courtesy.

In Chicago the wiretapping of Martin Luther King was the big issue. The question is entirely legitimate, but the explanation as to how it all came about was viewed cynically and the fact that King and his associates never held the tapes against the Kennedys dismissed. In Denver and especially in Los Angeles Marilyn Monroe became an obsessive concern—a question I do not regard as legitimate. All along the way there were the cheap and obvious cracks about canonization, hagiography, *Love Story,* etc.

As I traveled, I interpreted this reaction rather personally. It seemed to me to indicate such a strong undercurrent of hatred of the Kennedys that I began to think Ted should not be encouraged to run in 1980. Part of it, it seemed to me, is that the great RFK themes—the plight of the underclass, and our capacity and obligation to help them help themselves—are forgotten today. No one seems interested in the fact that an American politician ten years ago cared deeply about the poor and the powerless. Perhaps in order to deal with guilt about their own indifference, the interviewers impeach RFK's motives. He must have been opportunistic, a demagogue, a man out only for a political base and power. I encountered a consistent refusal to believe that his concern was genuine. Then the whole litany would come up—McCarthy, Hoffa, "ruthless" and so on. I felt as if I were back campaigning for him again. When one tries to explain the exact nature of his entanglement with McCarthy, then one is triumphantly told: See, you are finding excuses for him. It was idle to point out that these were not excuses, simply facts.

Later I reflected that this may have been not so much personal resentment of RFK or of the Kennedys (or of me) as the prevalent style in the communications world. In the aftermath of Woodward and Bernstein, the hot thing to do is to expose scandals and ferret out secrets in the lives of public men. This may explain the indifference to RFK's public career, the fascination with the stuff behind the scenes and the general cynicism about motives. Even if this is so, however, it does not greatly reduce the strength of the argument against Ted's running. Even if the anti-Kennedy feeling is not so great per se as it appeared to me in gloomier moments during the trip, the compulsion to tear people down will rekindle such feeling in the case of a man who, with all the qualities that make him the most commanding of presidential possibilities, has a sufficiency of vulnerabilities in his private life. I believe in the exposure of public vice but the obsession with personal lives has degenerated to the point of prurience.

All this gives me moments of depression about the reception of the book. But readers apparently like it. I also reflect that the same criticism—excessive partiality—was made of *The Age of Jackson, The Age of Roosevelt* and *A Thousand Days*. I also reflect that the nadir of a man's reputation often comes about ten years after his death (as I pointed out over twenty years ago in the foreword to *The Crisis of the Old Order*—a book sympathetic to FDR hurled into a quite anti-FDR climate). And I recall Churchill explaining how it was possible for him to go to sleep every night when he was being so vehemently criticized— "I simply say 'God damn them all,' and then I sleep like a baby."

December 28

I suppose I should add a political note. I detect a certain fatalism now pervading the Democratic party about Carter. His success at Camp David arrested his decline, and people stopped speculating that he would not run in 1980. While Democrats don't much like him, they don't dislike him enough, for the moment anyway, to start organizing against him. Still, no one was organizing against Lyndon Johnson in 1966. And inflation remains the problem to which Carter has no answer save the old Republican remedy of recession and unemployment. Ted Kennedy made a great stir by converting a panel appearance at the midterm party conference in Denver into a ringing attack on the cuts in the social budget. I asked Steve whether this was a calculated move in a larger campaign. He said not; that a few days before, when he was in

Washington, John Culver came over to Ted's one night, and the two fed each other's indignation over Carter's plan to increase the military budget and cut back social spending, thereby placing the burden of a fiscal attack against inflation on those least able to bear it. They finally decided to express themselves at Memphis, which both of them did. I still think it most unlikely that Ted will challenge Carter, though he might conceivably be drafted to save the Party from Brown or Moynihan.

1979

January 17

John Chancellor and I lunched yesterday with George Ball, just in from Florida, looking tan and fit but very white-haired. He was extremely entertaining about his recent Washington experience. Brzezinski had asked him to come down to conduct a special study of our policy toward Iran, evidently expecting that George would endorse the Brzezinski recommendation of all-out support for the Shah. George instead told them that the Shah was finished and that American policy should be directed toward replacing him by a moderate government and finding him a face-saving exit. ("Zbig made two miscalculations," George said, "—about the Shah and about me.") When he concluded his work and reported to Carter, Carter said, "But I can't tell a fellow head of state what to do."

George said that [Ardeshir] Zahedi, the Persian ambassador to Washington who went back to Teheran in an effort to save the Shah, was in effect dictating American policy during this period. Zahedi told

Brzezinski that the Shah had no confidence in Bill Sullivan, our ambassador in Teheran, and that all communications should go through Zahedi. "Zbig was on the phone to Zahedi twice a day," George said, "getting his instructions." The State Department had virtually no role. "The trouble with Cy is that he is a trial lawyer, and a trial lawyer can conduct only one case at a time. He was involved in the Israel-Egypt negotiations and couldn't focus on Iran." I asked what he made of the policy process under Carter. "You wouldn't believe it," he said. "I have never seen anything like it. A mess. Vance can prevail whenever he wants to intervene, but Brzezinski has the advantage of being there all the time. Carter is intelligent but ignorant, only he doesn't know how ignorant he is. A poor show." Jack Chancellor, who had interviewed Carter on Saturday, told how Carter kept talking about Iran's "2,500 years of self-government."

At one point Brzezinski was all set to go to Teheran and take charge himself. Ball told Carter this would be a great mistake, would identify the White House irrevocably with the Shah and would reduce the value of any concessions the Shah might thereafter make. Carter cancelled Zbig's trip. Zbig was furious.

George inevitably blamed the whole trouble on Kissinger. Under Kennedy and Johnson, he said, the Shah was held at arm's length. Then in May 1972 Nixon and Kissinger visited Teheran. George said he had to get the record of the meeting from the Nixon Papers—rather shocking this, because anything essential to the continuity of the public business ought to be retained in the government files. This, George said, was the time when the all-out embrace began. Nixon asked the Shah to be our "protector" in the Gulf. The Shah said he would, on one condition: the most sophisticated military equipment for his army. When the party returned to Washington, Kissinger sent out a directive saying that the government of Iran should get all cooperation from the relevant departments and that it was to be the judge of its own military requirements. Carter continued the policy of unconditional support and now is blaming the CIA for the mess. "It wasn't a failure of intelligence," George said. "It was a failure of policy." At one point in his Washington tour, he had a long talk with Admiral [Stansfield] Turner. "The CIA could save the Shah," Turner told Ball. George asked how. "All we need to do is to send some good people to Iran." What would they do? "First of all," Turner said, "we need a good PR man, someone who would get the Shah good coverage in the media. It's really an image problem out there." Chancellor and I protested that George must be kidding. He assured us he wasn't.

I asked whether it was possible that Brzezinski still wanted a military coup and was waiting for Khomeini to return to Iran before springing the trap. Once Khomeini was back, then the army might take over, arrest and execute the revolutionary leaders, decapitate the movement and establish a military dictatorship under the Shah. George said that something like this seemed to him wholly possible, but would not work because the lower ranks of the army were underpaid, badly treated and disaffected and could not be relied upon to shoot down their fellow countrymen in order to give power to their officers, whom they loathed. George does not take too tragic a view of the immediate consequences of the Shah's collapse.

We asked whether any Democratic senators had been in touch with him—Frank Church, for example. He said only one senator had called him—Ted Kennedy, who is not on the Foreign Relations Committee. (I am writing Church today urging him to ask George to meet privately with the Democratic members of the Committee.) I said that, in view of Carter's incompetence, should we not try to get a better candidate in 1980? George's view is that Carter is sure for renomination and that a primary fight would only make things worse.

In the evening we dined at Henry Kissinger's—an engagement I did not dare confess to George at lunch. This was at their new and curiously unlovely apartment at River House. Henry is now turning his powerful intelligence to sharp and contemptuous criticism of the Carter administration, though rather of a heads-I-win-tails-they-lose kind. One feels that, whatever the administration did, Henry could show why it was wrong. He detests Brzezinski, likes Vance but thinks him ineffective and thinks Carter is highly intelligent but intolerably self-centered—more so than Johnson, "even" more so than Nixon. (This remark was interesting in view of Carter's reaction to Ball's recommendations, not in terms of the national interests of the country but "*I* can't tell a fellow head of state what to do.") Henry was less all-out for the Shah than I expected and dismissed the Brzezinski military-coup scenario on the ground that military rule would not bring stability. He is far more pessimistic than George, however, about the immediate future of the Gulf, the repercussions for Saudi Arabia, etc. He thinks that the Shah's collapse will accelerate an Israel-Egypt settlement but diminish its importance. He was jovial and winning, but many of his remarks were tinged with bitterness.

February 12

Here it is February in my 62nd year, and I seem to have done nothing substantial since finishing the RFK book nine months ago. God knows where the time has gone. I have been working as long and hard as ever; but I have frittered the hours away in a variety of stupid and transient tasks. I have not even done what I have promised myself to do for years—straighten out the books in the house and get rid of as many of them as I can.

The days have gone inconsequentially by. On 26 January we went to Boston where I spoke to the Massachusetts Historical Society. I stayed over the next day to go to a luncheon of the Saturday Club, a venerable Boston institution of which I was a member many years ago. The Boston visit was all right, but I left blessing my fate that I decided not to return after the Kennedy years. I don't know what is so deeply depressing about it all. Henry Adams had it right when he recalled his days as a member of the Harvard history department: "Several score of the best-educated, most agreeable and personally the most sociable people in America united in Cambridge to make a social desert that would have starved a polar bear." I had forgotten the peculiar social gracelessness of Cambridge. In the 1950s, we often entertained for visiting dignitaries. The Harvard people, instead of talking to the visitor, would ignore him, cluster among themselves and engage in local gossip. There were exceptions, of course, like Galbraith, Bundy, Seymour Harris; but they were distinctly exceptions. Now that I was the visitor, I was subjected to the same treatment myself.

February 28

Much travel in the last few days. On 21 February I flew to Dallas. I have abstained from Dallas ever since November 1963, less out of principle than out of pain, but it seemed pointless to run a permanent boycott, so I had agreed to go. After the lecture a nice couple, returning me to the hotel, took a detour to Dealey Plaza. It was night, there was soft rain, the streetlights glinting off the wet street. I was astonished by the intimacy of the scene. The Book Depository, the narrow street, the grassy knoll, the underpass—all packed into each other. I had imagined something grander; more Texan. For a moment the horror all came back, and I recalled the deep depression that overtook me for some weeks 15 years ago. We went on and saw the JFK monument—a slab enclosed by a tall, unadorned wall; at first, awfully stark in its impact; but then one wonders what could be done. At least this memorial was understated. What a long time ago it all seems, like an event that had taken place sometime before the Second World War.

The sense of Carter's incompetence deepens every day. Actually he has been rather prudent and sensible—i.e., restrained—in major foreign policy issues, though there is considerable, primitive pressure these days for *macho* diplomacy. But he has no real instinct for foreign affairs, as shown by his misunderstanding of the Persian situation, and even less instinct for popular education and persuasion. The result is a pervading impression of vacillation and weakness. Lou Harris went to see him the other day; and, Jimmy Wechsler tells me, came away with the feeling that Carter may very well not run in 1980. He has aged greatly in two years, has developed a facial tic, and must be aware, since he is an intelligent man, that he is miscast in his present job.

March 4

I got back from Richmond in a heavy fog about noon today, 40 minutes late, and then lunched with Arthur Burns at the Lazard Frères suite in the Waldorf Towers. He was in a reminiscent mood and told stories about George Humphrey, whom he regarded as a great phoney, Eisenhower, whom he respected, Kennedy, for whom, he said, "I came to acquire great respect and affection; he always did his homework." I asked what his estimate was of Nixon's intellectual qualities. "Oh, he would have been a first-rate professor of political science or law in any of our best universities," Burns said. "He had a powerful, well-organized mind. It was a pleasure to watch him take hold of a problem and break it down. Of course he was much more interested in foreign than in domestic affairs." I asked him whether he had been surprised by the Watergate revelations. He paused for a moment (he is a great pauser), then said slowly, "No, I was not. I had a foretaste of it." He described an incident in 1971 when he had come out for an incomes policy and Nixon, one evening on the *Sequoia,* had told Charles Colson, "The time has come to cut Arthur down to size." There followed a series of White House leaks designed to discredit Burns. After Colson found God, he came to Burns, told him the story and sought his forgiveness. Arthur said: "I wouldn't have minded it so much if Nixon had said that to Colson in a passing mood of irritation. But he said it a very cool, collected, considered way." I asked whether he ever saw Nixon anymore. He said, "Well, I'm not sure you would approve, but I call him every New Year's Day to wish him well. It takes hours before I can bring myself to do it, but he is such a lonely man living such a sad life; so I grit my teeth and do it."

We discussed this morning's Gallup poll, which shows John Connally roaring up to 15 percent for the Republican nomination. I begin to feel that Connally may have a real chance. The country is hungry for strong leadership, and no one better projects a sense of confidence and masterfulness than Connally. "That is why Nixon liked him so much," said Burns. "He was what Nixon longed to be. Nixon once said to me,

'There are only three men in the country who understand power—I do, and John Connally, and *perhaps* Nelson Rockefeller.' " Burns could not be more unhappy about Connally. "He has the prejudices of the business world but none of the convictions," Burns said. "He is a dishonest man. And he would be a disaster abroad. None of our allies has forgotten him. . . . I don't want to get involved in politics, but, if Connally should get the Republican nomination, I feel I would have to declare myself publicly on him. He is a real menace."

In our 20th Century Fund days I used to regard Arthur Burns as pompous and boring. Once again, I was wrong. He now seems to me a rather sweet, shrewd and entirely decent man.

April 13

I embarked for lectures in New Jersey and Georgia the week of March 27 and in Texas the next. The subject of the Texas lectures was (on request) "The Kennedy Years." Rather to my surprise the audiences, most of whom were 4–5 years old when JFK was killed and 9–10 years old when RFK was killed, seemed interested and sympathetic. I encountered none of that disillusion that set me back when I toured on behalf of the RFK book last September. Perhaps it is a generational difference. People who are 35 now were 19 when JFK was killed. I have the impression that many of that age who invested emotion in him then feel disillusioned now, whether because they have been persuaded by revisionist historians that he was a fanatical Cold Warrior or by the sensational press that he was an inveterate womanizer. The college generation is spared this particular problem.

May 3

I now begin to feel that Ted Kennedy may be planning to run after all. I base this feeling on various emanations in the atmosphere. Much as we see and love the Smiths, I would not dream of asking a straight-out question about Ted's intentions. Steve, I have always felt, has hoped that

Ted would run in 1980. My guess is that in his view the assassination danger is always there, whether or not Ted runs, and that you cannot turn your back on opportunity too many times. When the EMK line was to support Carter, Steve was unexpectedly pro-Carter; but there has been none of that in recent months.

Jean a few months ago was desperately opposed to the idea of Ted's running. There is little of that now. When we were in Williamsburg last week, James MacGregor Burns reported that Doris Kearns (who has been in Palm Beach interviewing Rose Kennedy) had told him that Mrs. Kennedy is no longer opposed to Ted's running in 1980. I mentioned this to Steve last night, who said, "Grandma is an old trouper. She will support whatever Ted decides." I told Jean that, when I traveled around the country, I was constantly asked if Ted would run in 1980. I asked her whether she wanted to hear how I answered. She said she would. I told her: "I say that I do not expect Ted to initiate a candidacy against Carter, that his family is opposed to his running and that, after what happened in 1963 and 1968, it is asking a lot of the Kennedys to expose a third son. However, if Carter were to pull out, or if Brown appeared likely to beat him for the nomination, and if party leaders came to Ted and said he had to run to save the party and the country, I could not predict what might happen."

Alexandra and I still think that Ted will be shot if he runs.

May 23

Pressure is building on Teddy. Steve called this morning. He thinks it is getting increasingly difficult for Ted to maintain his present line—i.e., saying he expects Carter to be renominated and expects to support him, while at the same time not quite taking himself out of the picture. Steve thinks the five congressmen ([Richard] Nolan, [Richard] Ottinger, [John] Conyers and a couple of others) are going to press their campaign and that this will make it hard for Ted to continue dodging the issue. Also, as liberal frustration builds up, some will begin to feel that Ted's indecision is preventing the emergence of another liberal alternative to Carter. (Mo Udall has told Ken that he would be prepared to go again if Ted took himself out.) "If it were just the political side of things," Steve said, "there'd be no problem. The road looks pretty clear there. It's the personal side. Apart from the first point [by which I think Steve means the risk of assassination; when he talks politics, he becomes awfully cryptic], there is Joan, who is a loose cannon; no one can tell what she might say in another interview. Then there are the kids. I don't know what they are ready for it. . . . I don't know what the hell to tell Ted."

My guess is that Carter's hopes are riding on SALT. If he can get Senate ratification (which ought to be possible), he can demonstrate "leadership," assert a claim to liberal support, overshadow Ted (who will be for SALT himself of course) and win a new lease on life.

May 26

Henry Kissinger at Bill Paley's the other night and Joe Alsop at lunch today were both filled with indignation over our treatment of the Shah of Iran—ingratitude to a loyal and devoted friend; why should any other political leader go out on a limb for us in the future; general indecency, etc. All very surprising on the lips of such devotees of *Realpolitik*. Everything the Shah of Iran has ever done has been in his own interest, not ours. He has never taken a risk or made a sacrifice to help the United States except when he was helping himself more at the same time. He misused the aid we lavished on him and won the hatred of his people on his own. I don't see that we owe him anything. As for the example set for others, the proper conclusion surely is that the United States gives no unconditional support to anybody; which ought to be an incentive to leaders propping themselves up with American assistance to use that assistance more wisely than the Shah did.

June 5

We spent the weekend, as we have spent so many (and so happily), with the Smiths in Pawling. More cryptic talk about 1980. I think that what really worries Steve most is Joan. He feels that she is not in control of herself, that she does not want to be hostile but cannot always contain unconscious hostilities and that someone may get to her in an unguarded moment and lead her to say things that might cause great trouble. He appears to feel that this is the gnawing and perhaps inhibiting uncertainty in Ted's situation.

June 18

After a quarter of a century I am back again at Hyde Park and the FDR Library. It has been a long detour. But I have been consoled by the example and memory of my putative collateral ancestor George Bancroft, with whom through the years I have had such a keen sense of sympathy, almost perhaps of identification—with his politics, his passions, his urbanity and taste for high living (Newport and Washington), his admirable friendships (from Emerson and Van Buren to Henry Adams), his weakness for public jobs, his instinct for narrative history informed by a larger democratic vision and above all, his commitment, despite all distractions, to his central work. His first volume of his great history came out in 1834; the tenth and last volume in 1874—and then, with his awareness of the modulations of style, he revised the whole business, pruning his work of rhetorical excess (to which he, like me, was all too susceptible). It is no longer possible to have Bancroft's splendid faith in the radiance of democracy—did he have it himself toward the end?—and in this regard I feel closer to Adams. But Adams felt close to Bancroft, who was one of the few to whom Adams showed the manuscript of his great work. I wish I knew more about their relations; despite 38 years' difference in age, they obviously had an affinity; perhaps the kind of affinity and affection I feel toward Harriman (36 years' difference).

At any event, here I am again, back to FDR. So much has been declassified since I was here last that I have to cover a lot of the same ground. I cannot hope to see everything; I have never learned how to use research assistants (and doubt whether they are of great use in my kind of history, since you can never program an assistant to know what may suggest a scene or an insight to oneself); and I must begin to write shorter books. So this is a process of updating and reimmersion, out of which I will in due course begin to write volume iv. A mysterious figure, FDR, rendered more mysterious by his own insistence on appearing casual and impromptu; or was he in fact casual and impromptu, and at the same time bright and lucky? Certainly he was at once aggressive, in the sense of being curious and of raising and forcing issues within his administration, and at the same time circumspect, in the sense of recognizing, especially in foreign affairs, his dependence on the processes of consent. In consequence he was devious; also deviousness came easily to him; it had always been his way of avoiding trouble in his personal life—Sarah v. Eleanor, Eleanor v. Lucy, Eleanor v. Louis Howe, etc., etc. A fascinating figure—not probably a great man but certainly a great President.

June 20

Does a time come when archival research seems a disproportionate investment of remaining time? I wonder how much time Bancroft spent in archives after the age of 60. It is not that research in original documents palls. I have no trouble working from 8 in the morning to 4:45 (when the search room closes) in the evening; indeed the time passes all too quickly. Twenty-five years ago, however, I did not grudge the time spent in relation to each day's return. Now I do. I also recognize that I cannot do the rest of *The Age of Roosevelt* on the minute scale of the second and third volumes; and certainly not on the scale of *A Thousand Days* or the RFK book. I once had a gift for impressionistic, as against voluminously detailed, history. *The Age of Jackson* was essentially that; so was *The Crisis of the Old Order* which a reviewer (Stephen Oates, who wrote a good short life of Lincoln) describes in the June *Reviews in American History* as possibly "the most perfectly sculptured work of historical art produced in this country, a book distinguished for its novelistic use of time, its symphonic organization, its vivid scenes and graphic vignettes, its telling quotations and dramatic narrative sweep." Can I return to that mode? Why did I abandon it? One reason is a desire to guard myself against academic criticism by providing all the evidence. But I will have to discipline myself against the hopelessly long book—if for no other reason than that otherwise I will never carry FDR through to 12 April 1945.

How much more time should I spend in archives? I will do what I can in the next month here at the FDR Library; perhaps do some work at the Library of Congress this winter and at the British Public Records Office in the spring. Then I must figure out a fresh structure in which to contain the material, eschew fanatical detail and strive for pattern and distillation. This will require a massive shift of gears. But no one person can look at all the evidence in 20th century history, and God knows I already have a fantastic mass of notes. OK: back to sculpture, symphonies and novelism.

July 11

Back to Hyannis Port last weekend—we flew (with Robert) from Poughkeepsie to Boston and thence to Hyannis, where Jackie, driving her own car, met us at the airport. Our plane was a little late, and she was having a cup of coffee in the cafe when we arrived—I was about to write, "Just like anyone else," but thought that may sound wide-eyed, she is a form of American royalty. I continued to be impressed throughout the weekend by her easiness, directness, simplicity, lack of front or pretention—impressed and finally perplexed, because it is hard to understand why so "real" a girl would have cared about marrying Onassis and living that kind of life. I can only conclude that there are dimensions to Jackie I never see. The dimensions I do see I greatly admire and adore.

Caroline was there—totally unspoiled, so far as we could see, and awfully nice. When we all flew back on Monday, she cried, not for any specific reason, but evidently because of the general principle of leaving Hyannis Port. She and Jackie get along well, and Jackie has obviously done a fine job bringing her up. It was a jolly house party—one of the best. Jackie even provided a couple of instant playmates for Robert, and he had a splendid time.

Ted was up, and we saw him a couple of times. My feeling is confirmed that, so long as he is not out, he is in; but that he will not initiate a contest against Carter nor even declare a candidacy; instead, he will submit himself to events and let events take their course. His predominant attitude toward Carter remains one of bemusement. He simply can't understand why Carter lets so many opportunities slip and handles so many things so badly; but he certainly does not detest him as RFK did Johnson. In general, Ted seemed cheerful and unconcerned.

July 13

We dined last night at FDR Jr.'s. His new wife is young, rather British, rather clipped, obviously a strong personality. She reminded me curiously of [his previous wife] Felicia, another strong personality. Franklin has given up drinking—"forever," he says—doesn't miss it, has lost 35 pounds and: "You can't imagine how it improves your sex life." He added that Averell had given up drinking at about the same age, and look what it did for him. Probably this is not a bad idea. I think that hereafter I will not drink unless I really, strongly want a drink.

Franklin said about Carter: "I was an early Carter man. He asked me to campaign for him in Pennsylvania, and I did. Afterward he said that he owed his success there to me. Then came the election. In the next couple of days I tried to call him. The calls were never returned. Later I wanted very much to be ambassador to Canada. Carter and his people showed no interest at all."

Franklin looked fine under his new regimen and was as charming as ever.

September 7

The Carter decline continues, and the Kennedy speculation grows. Since my return, I have had a number of calls and letters from people around the country asking for a signal of some sort from Ted. My impression is that he has decided to encourage the draft-Kennedy movements, but I will hope to have a clearer idea as to what is going on after the coming weekend in Pawling.

Ben Bradlee called up today to chat about Kennedy. He said inter alia, "Our relations with the Carter White House are worse than they ever were with the Nixon White House." I expressed surprise at this. He said, "The Nixon White House ignored us. These fellows keep hammering away at us. The Nixon people were awful, but they never took it out on Carroll Kilpatrick [who was covering the White House then]. These jerks hammer away at our reporters." Carter sent him a handwritten letter the other day complaining about the *Post*'s coverage of the passage of the trade bill. "You would have handled it differently in 1962," Carter said. The implication was that Bradlee would have given Kennedy much more credit because of his personal friendship. Of course Ben was not at the *Post* in 1962 and, as he added feelingly, "No one can say I am close to the Kennedys today."

September 10

Here we go again, or so it seems. It looks now as if Ted is going to run. Steve thinks it is about 85 percent certain. When I said that of course he must be the campaign manager, Steve said no; perhaps young Joe Kennedy could do it. As for myself, I said, rather glumly, that my misgivings were well known; but, if he were going ahead, I would of course do everything I can to help.

Ted lunched with Carter on Friday. This was at Carter's initiative, and he had been rather insistent about it, suggesting a number of earlier dates, and then proposing that they plan to have both luncheon and dinner together so that they would have plenty of time to talk. On Thursday night, after the vanden Heuvel reception, Jean, Steve and Ted had dinner together. Steve said semi-jocularly, "If [Carter] asks you why you are reassessing your situation, you should say to him that maybe he ought to be reassessing his situation." Ted said, "No, no, I can't say that." At the luncheon, he talked about mental health and retardation with Mrs. Carter; then she left, and the President got down to business. He wanted Ted to issue a Sherman statement. When Ted said he couldn't do that, Carter seemed surprised. Ted did *not*, as the *Atlanta Constitution* claimed yesterday, ask Carter to withdraw. Steve surmises that Carter wanted to force the issue one way or another: to get Ted either out or in and thereby end his present favored situation, when he has the advantages of being a candidate without incurring the disadvantages. Once a candidate, Ted will become a target. The press will be after him—not only Chappaquiddick but what he would do about inflation, about Russians in Cuba, about energy, etc. Reporters, determined to show they are not playing favorites, will be especially hard on him. Voters will begin to wonder whether he may not be too liberal. He will inevitably decline in the polls.

Yesterday I lunched with Felix Rohatyn. He is one of the few original people around. His mind is direct, unfettered, practical and ingenious, and he has the gift for recognizing fresh connections and possibilities.

Felix and four other Wall Streeters had dined in Washington last night with Hamilton Jordan, Charlie Schultze and some lesser White House people. The purpose of the dinner was evidently to reassure the business leaders that they could trust Carter to hold the line of fiscal conservatism against Kennedy. At one point, one of the White House subordinates said, "Besides, he's not going to survive the primaries." Felix said, "Would you mind repeating that?" The fellow did. Felix said, "I am appalled. When the President's mother said that, I thought it was just an old lady speaking. But if you fellows say it, it is beginning to look like a considered and orchestrated White House line." Felix told me that the clear implication was: don't go with Kennedy because he will be killed, and we will remember who was loyal and who wasn't.

September 21

I lunched today with Jackie at the Quo Vadis. She had not known about the possibility of an invitation to Nixon [for the JFK Library dedication] and was appalled. "It would destroy the whole occasion," she said. "I am going to tell Teddy I won't come if Nixon does. . . . But suppose they say all right? I really don't want to miss it." She reminisced about Nixon. "He phoned me before his book came out. He had been calling me all over New York and reached me just after I had left my office, and they caught me and I took the call. He began by saying something about the letters that John and Caroline and I had written after we had visited the White House. He said, 'You remember that letter of condolence I sent you? Manchester published it in his book, but no one asked my permission.' I didn't know what he was talking about. He went on in his meeching, slimy way. Finally I understood that he wanted my permission to publish our letters in his book. I weakly said yes—but said it as haughtily as possible so that he would know how I really felt. If he hadn't caught me off guard, I would have handled it differently. I don't ever want to do any favors for that scurvy little thing. . . . It would be absolutely impossible to have him at the dedication of Jack's library."

She said she was rather thrilled at Teddy's entry. She did not seem as much oppressed by the assassination possibility as she was a decade ago when Bobby decided to run. She adores Ted, especially his readiness to assume all sorts of family responsibility, but does not think his judgment is as good as Jack's or Bobby's. "Neither of them would have considered having Nixon for an instant," she said. In fact, I think that both would have considered it, but not for much more than an instant.

Why besides being so astonishingly beautiful and intelligent is Jackie so fascinating? Because of the impression she gives of total, exclusive and absorbed concentration on oneself, as if she felt she were talking to the most fascinating person in the room. One knows it is simply her way, but it is irresistible all the same.

September 28

I was rushing back [from a Washington trip] to go to the Board of Management meeting at the Century. The chief subject on the agenda

was the admission of women, and the meeting was full. The issue arose
when Jack Greenberg nominated Joan Ganz Cooney (of *Sesame Street*).
Dick Dana as secretary replied that the Century, by by-laws if not by the
constitution, was a "men's social club" and the nomination was therefore rejected. This reply dissatisfied the committee on admissions, several members of which feared that the issue was being buried. A
discussion followed. I was struck by a significant change of mood. A
few years ago, if anyone had proposed this, a number of members
would have condemned the idea roundly. This time, though some
people were plainly unhappy, no one openly attacked the idea. It reminded me of the first civil rights debate, I think it was in 1960, when
southerners stopped giving speeches about white supremacy. Louis
Auchincloss spoke spiritedly in favor of admitting women; the day of
the "monosex club," he said, was over. Opponents advocated delay and
insisted—quite rightly, I think—that this is a matter the entire membership must decide. I have a sense now that it is only a question of time.
(And, though I am strongly in favor of the change—because life has
changed—I do feel a certain admixture of regret at the alterations it will
inevitably bring to the character of the club.)

We went to a dinner dance last night for the New York Public
Library at the St. Regis roof. Very pleasant—I sat between
Lauren Bacall and Phyllis Newman and had the additional pleasure of
dancing with my glorious wife, who looked exceptionally beautiful in
what had once been a ball dress of her grandmother.

Afterward we went over to Lally Weymouth's where I encountered
Joe Califano. He said, "I have decided what the essential power of
the presidency really is." When I played the straight man and inquired,
he said, "The power to pick people." He then went into a fascinating
disquisition about Carter—his staff, so inadequate that it did not even
recognize its own inadequacy; and Carter himself, so insecure that disagreement made him upset and angry. Joe gave new detail on the familiar picture of a man who really dislikes face-to-face discussions. "I

didn't know Kennedy very well," he said, "but I gather that he quite liked debate in his presence. Johnson loathed disagreement but understood perfectly that it had an essential role in government and steeled himself to listen to people who disagreed with him. I used to send Johnson occasional lists of people whom I thought he should see about one or another problem. He mostly saw them. I did the same with Carter. He never asked one of them in."

I ran into George Kennan today at the Century. He said, "I am 75 years old and constantly resist the notion of the necessary inferiority of the present to the past. But really I have never in my life seen such dillettantism, amateurism and sheer bungling as that shown by American diplomacy in the last few months." The climax of ineptness, in his view, came with the hopeless mishandling of the so-called problem of the Soviet troops in Cuba. "The way the Carter administration handled that violates every elementary diplomatic rule. We got our facts wrong; we overreacted wildly; we pushed the Russians against a closed door; we preferred domestic politics to foreign policy; and now we have painted ourselves into the corner and don't know how to get out. And we have dangerously jeopardized SALT in the process." George thinks that Brzezinski is hopelessly out of his depth. Then he said, "If Ted Kennedy becomes President, I hope he will make George Ball Secretary of State. The Israelis will be unhappy but they will accept it. George is the best qualified man for the job."

October 3

I am in Chicago in the cause of the paperback edition of *Robert Kennedy and His Times*. Alexandra has called to say that we appear to be having a new neighbor over the back fence. I asked who it was. She said, "Guess. It is not someone you like very much. In fact, it is someone you have no use for." I thought for a moment and said, reaching as far down as I could, "Roy Cohn?" She said, "No, even worse. Someone you think ought to be in prison." I said, "I can't believe it. Richard M. Nixon."

October 5

The *New York Times* had called Alexandra on Wednesday to tip her off and get her reaction. Today the *Times* printed the story. Alexandra, having finished her morning exercises, was in the kitchen in her leotard having a cup of coffee with Joe Alsop, our house guest. Suddenly she said, "Look, Joe, someone is photographing us through the window." Our kitchen looks out on 64th Street, and an eager ABC television crew was on the stairs, its camera pointed at the window. I was summoned to deal with the situation. Asked for my view as I stood in shirtsleeves on the front steps I said, "There goes the neighborhood."

ABC returned in the afternoon with the hope of filming Nixon's house through our garden. A CBS crew arrived at the same time with the same idea. The best view in fact is from our bedroom window on the second floor, from which we gaze squarely into the Nixon garden and house. We turned down these requests, but I submitted to another front-steps interview, this time with CBS. Robert, now back from school, held my hand as we faced the camera. I repeated my usual stuff about having been on Nixon's Enemies List and "there goes the neighborhood." Robert meanwhile climbed up the balustrade, perched just behind my shoulder, put his arm around my neck and rolled his eyes. The interviewer said, "Robert, what do you think of Nixon's coming into the neighborhood?" Robert said, "I think it is just fine." The interviewer, surprised, said, "Why do you think that, Robert?" Robert said, "So I can trick and treat him on Halloween." I added feebly, "Tricks and Treats for Tricky." Later that evening Robert was thrilled to observe his television debut, with the legend below: "Robert Schlesinger—seven years old."

October 12

We went to California October 7–9, and I was asked a couple of times about our new neighbor. I said that this marked my declension in life. "When I lived in Cambridge, Massachusetts, I had John Kenneth

Galbraith over the back fence. Now I have ended up with Richard M. Nixon." When an interviewer asked whether I did not consider Nixon a tragic figure, I added, probably unfortunately, "I don't think there is anything very tragic about him. He is a very lucky man living out his days in luxury when he ought to be in the federal penitentiary." What I had in mind, of course, was William Cullen Bryant's obituary note on Nicholas Biddle, the president of the Second Bank of the United States: Biddle's end, wrote Bryant, "came at his country seat, where he had passed the last of his days in elegant retirement, which, if justice had taken place, would have been spent in the penitentiary."

Speculation continued about the arrival day. The prevailing theory, based on I know not what, is that the Nixons will move in on November 1. In the meantime, the house still seems to have inhabitants or at least is lit at night. There are few signs of preoccupancy activity. But some people prowling on a roof next door aroused the suspicions of Alexandra, who was certain that our wires were tapped when we lived on 82nd Street when Nixon was President and I was on the enemies list.

Phyllis Ferguson Seidel called Alexandra to remind her that Nixon had bought the house in which her grandfather Learned Hand lived for half a century. Our 64th Street handyman, John Blanco, says, "Do you want to know why Nixon wanted that house so much? He wanted to live next to David Rockefeller." And a local philosopher at the Herb Shop across the street opined to my wife, "Well, the Bible says Love thy neighbor. Maybe those who hate each other too much get put together in the end."

October 16

Sixty-two passed lightly yesterday. We held a joint birthday celebration with Ken (seventy-one)—a stellar evening, I thought. We gave a dinner for about thirty-six, the cast led by the Galbraiths, the Harrimans, Jackie, Lauren Bacall, Marietta, Evangeline, Charles Addams, Paddy Chayefsky, Kay Graham and Lally [Weymouth] (not speaking to each other), Denis Healey, the Smiths, Bill Paley, Sam Spiegel, the

Fritcheys, Stephen and Andy and their girls, Alexander Cockburn, our Venezuelan friends the Revengas, Bill Walton, Leonard Bernstein, etc. There were supporting dinners given by the Finletters and by Jan Cushing, and still others who came in after dinner, from the Norman Mailers and the George Plimptons to the Harrison Salisburys and the Jimmy Wechslers. Lennie wrote a canon called "Historeconomy" for Ken and me to sing and then rehearsed us in it till we had it down. He has never had such intractable material. Romulo Betancourt called from Caracas to wish us happy birthday. All in all a smash, save perhaps for the disapproving presence of Kitty Galbraith, dowdily dressed as if to show what she thought of handsome and stylish women and wearing a pained and unhappy expression on her face every time I noticed her. Ken, though, is imperturbable and goes cheerfully along his own road.

Considering all the emotions I generally have on birthdays, this one aroused no particular emotion at all, except that I do not feel sixty-two, and do not expect to feel sixty-two so long as I have Alexandra, Robert and Peter to keep me young.

October 20

We are back from the dedication of the JFK Library at Columbia Point—a most agreeable occasion, filled with good friends from the old days. The completion of the building must have been a particular satisfaction for Steve Smith, without whose constant intercession nothing would ever have happened, and of course for I. M. Pei, who has conceived another dazzling, soaring triumph.

Last night there was a splendid dinner at the Library, and this morning the dedication. President Carter was quite good, and so was Ted Kennedy, but I was most taken by young Joe Kennedy who seized the occasion to give a fiery radical speech that would have pleased his father. John Kennedy Jr. read the Stephen Spender poem which I quoted in the last pages of *A Thousand Days*.

We lunched at the Ritz with Bob and Margaret McNamara. Bob, I was pleased to discover, is for price and wage controls and made an eloquent case that I urged him to repeat to Ted Kennedy. He was equally eloquent on the subject of SALT and its opponents—Paul Nitze and Eugene Rostow ("they seem to have lost their senses") and James Schlesinger ("an arrogant boor").

I said to Bob, "This will probably be the last time that all these people will get together." He said, "I hope there will be one more time." We agreed, though, that it is going to be a rocky and uncertain road to EMK's inaugural.

Jackie came by during lunch. I said that she had seemed to recoil visibly when Carter kissed her. She said she thought it was too much. He did not dare kiss Eunice, Jean and Pat, and in fact he had hardly met Jackie before. This tendency to kiss women on first meeting does not sit well in the East. "He acts as if the presidency carries with it the *droit du seigneur,*" Jackie said. Nor did the passages in his speech about kneeling down after hearing the news of Dallas and crying as he had not cried since the death of his father go over too well in reticent New England. Again too much.

November 1

Yesterday was Halloween. Alexandra took Robert and two friends on a neighborhood tour. They rang the Nixon bell. No one answered. The house was dark. Yet by eight o'clock, when the trick-and-treaters had gone home to bed, the Nixon house, as viewed from our bedroom window, was ablaze with light on the first and third floors—almost as if the inhabitants had laid doggo when children were about and now thought it safe to proceed with their business. Can it be that the Nixons are actually coming, as the word mysteriously has it, today?

November 16

I went down to Washington last night for Averell's 88th birthday. I stayed at the Harrimans', and, when we got back to the house, Averell and Pam expressed dismay about the first weeks of the Kennedy campaign—a dismay I share. I think there are several reasons why it is stumbling along:

1. Circumstances compelled them to start before they were ready. As Steve said in September, this was the biggest improvisation of them all. Bobby's campaign was improvised organizationally but not intellectually. The groundwork on issues had been well laid. Teddy has been floundering all over the place in the last two months on issues. Yet clear themes are what he needs more than anything else to justify challenging an incumbent from his own party.

2. Ted himself lacks the grasp of things his brothers had. His staff is far more conservative than their staffs were. All this prevents him from developing substantive themes distinguishing himself from Carter. Instead he slaps away at Carter before small crowds of enthusiasts, responding to the people in the hall and forgetting about the much larger crowd who will see the result on television. He is too strident too early. Most voters aren't yet that interested in the 1980 election.

3. Steve Smith is the great hope for remedy. But thus far he has been totally involved in finance, organization, endorsements. And traditionally he has stayed away from issues. That was OK in the JFK and RFK campaigns, when both the principal and his staff were good on issues. It is causing trouble now.

4. The Kennedy challenge is making Carter act like a President, as George McGovern remarked to Steve Smith. He has become unwontedly forceful. His people may not know how to run a government but they know how to run a campaign. Jordan and [Jody] Powell seem happier than they have appeared for months, as if they were at last back in their element. Carter is exploiting the advantages of incumbency more systematically and grossly than any of his predecessors.

Still it is all very early, and things will doubtless improve. Yet it is a shaky start.

December 1

Still no action across the [Nixon] fence. In the meantime, Mexico has rejected the Shah of Iran; no other country (except Egypt) seems to want him; and New York Hospital is determined to get rid of him. Alexandra's fantasy is that David Rockefeller will invite him to recuperate on 65th Street—Nixon in one house, the Shah in the next.

December 2

Carter has flown the Shah to Texas and placed him under direct U.S. military protection. A bizarre political decision, but a local relief.

December 5

Gretchen said this morning, after seeing Henry Kissinger on the Merv Griffin show last night, "I just can't believe that that is the humble little fellow who used to sit in our anteroom and wait to see you at the White House." It is interesting to speculate about the overpowering ego so long repressed under Henry's apparently unassuming demeanor. He does appear, by the way, to be something of a casualty of the Iranian affair—deservedly so, in view of his history of intercessions for the Shah. He has been going around denouncing the administration for not being tough enough—odd from the fellow who wouldn't let [Alexander] Solzhenitsyn visit the White House lest it upset the Russians. When I was in Denver last week, the *Rocky Mountain News* (28 November) had a full-page headline on the editorial page: "A Message To Kissinger: Shut Up." A widespread national reaction. Henry is a splendid example of Prichard's Law: Absence of power corrupts, and total absence of power corrupts totally.

December 6

Ted Kennedy is in trouble. He has committed the heresy of criticizing the Shah and has brought the foreign policy establishment down on his head. Of course his presidential rivals in both parties are having a fine time contrasting his "irresponsibility" with their "statesmanship." But he is quite right on the central issue, though his formulation was awkward and hyperbolic. The central issue, as I see it, is the importance of separating the question of the hostages from the question of the Shah. Carter is fusing these issues, especially by incredibly placing the Shah under the protection of the Air Force. Kennedy is trying to show that those who detest the Shah feel quite as strongly about the hostages as those who embrace the Shah, and that we therefore stand, not on our belief in the Shah, but on our belief in the inviolability of diplomatic personnel. The foreign policy establishment, its code violated, has landed on poor Teddy with the same relish that it landed on Jack in 1957 when he came out for the independence of Algeria and on Bobby in 1967 when he opposed the escalation of the Vietnam War. Why can no one understand that the establishment is more likely to be wrong than to be right? Yet everywhere one goes one hears how terrible Ted's intervention is. I have written a piece for the *Wall Street Journal* in an endeavor to clarify the issues, but Gretchen and Mary think it is going to get me in trouble. I have been in trouble before.

December 15

I went to Washington yesterday and stayed for luncheon with Steve. I have had several talks with old Kennedy hands in the last week: Fred Dutton, Ted Sorensen, Dick Goodwin. We are all filled with really *intense* concern over the absence of theme and direction in the campaign, over Ted's stridency and hyperbole and over the want of steady and experienced counsel. I don't think any of us except Dick or possibly Ted want to go into the campaign, though I am sure the senatorial staff resent old-timers and suspect our intentions.

Steve was cheerful on the surface but worried and depressed underneath. They are running low on money; and he does not see much chance in Iowa so long as the hostages are detained; no one is going to repudiate the President before the world at such a time. I think he realizes that the campaign needs focus.

1980

January 1

A new year, a new decade (technically, I suppose, the new decade will begin a year from today, the first decade having begun with the year 1; still . . .). We had an uncommonly painless New Year's Eve. Hugh and Vanessa Thomas are staying with us, and we began by hearing Pavarotti sing at Avery Fisher Hall. He was in superb voice, sang with that enchanting hint of vast powers in reserve and concluded with "Auld Lang Syne" in Italian. We moved on to a party at I. M. Pei's Sutton Place house; then, for the rites of passage, to John Chancellor's; finishing by inspecting the scene at Woody Allen's mighty party. This last was held in Rebekah Harkness's school of the dance, which meant four floors filled with notables affably circulating—Elizabeth Hardwick, Tammy Grimes, Arthur Miller, George Plimpton, Kevin McCarthy, Tony Randall and so on.

Having drunk nothing but ginger ale after the Peis', I feel not bad on this glittering, fortyish morning. I did damn little in 1979 except write an inordinate number of fugitive pieces, but I am not too unhappy; after all, Alexandra and Robert redeem daily existence; I do not feel sixty-two; and I hope to get some work done in 1980. The world fills one with pessimism at the moment (the hostages are still in captivity, the Russians have moved into Afghanistan, Carter is still President), but genes or whatever infuse a certain *joie de vivre*.

January 11

George Kennan spoke last night at the Century. He told me privately before dinner that he had been "shattered" by the mood at the White House breakfast in Washington on Tuesday, when Carter briefed foreign policy leaders about his assessments and intentions following the Soviet invasion of Afghanistan. "Everyone is rushing to define political and diplomatic problems in military terms and to insist on military responses. . . . I have been involved in Soviet-American relations for fifty-two years, longer than anyone else on either side. I have had my share of frustration and agony. I know what the Soviet leaders are like. But I have never been so depressed by the state of the relationship as I am today."

January 13

Averell, with whom I talked this afternoon, is also considerably depressed by the breakdown in Soviet-American relations, though he is not so tragic about it as George Kennan. "We've had crises before," he said, "and we'll have them again. Ten months after the Cuban missile crisis we had the test ban treaty. The important thing is to keep SALT II alive." He feels that we have made it very difficult for Brezhnev to hold out against his own hard-liners—especially by the March 1977 effort to revise the SALT terms, an effort which, he says, not only lost a year but gained a lot of suspicion and mistrust. He says that we had known for some weeks that the Soviet Union was planning to move into Afghanistan and that we failed to tell them how seriously we would take it; hence their irritation now. He felt as Kennan did about the Tuesday briefing at the White House. "All the hawks spoke their stuff," he said, "and the doves kept silent." I forbore to ask why he and George had not spoken up.

January 17

The children keep the [Nixon] house under steady surveillance. There have been signs of activity: lights dimly on, workmen plodding through, Christmas wreaths hung (adorned incongruously with doves of peace); still no curtains. But the second coming impends. Today Alexandra was meeting in the living room with a group working on the Kennedy campaign. Suddenly one of them said, "You won't believe what I see through the window." They all looked. There was the unforgettable profile briefly framed in the window across the fence. He was there for an instant, oblivious, then he turned away. A daughter was with him. Apparently he was inspecting the property.

January 22

[The Iowa caucus] was even worse than I expected—Carter by more than 2–1. I feel very sorry for Ted today; but also rather mad at him, for having kicked away the opportunity to deliver the nation from four more years of Carter and incompetence.

Jean called from Washington. I said that I thought he [Ted] must stay in through New Hampshire. Actually it had not occurred to me that getting out was a serious consideration yet; nor am I sure that this was more than an abstract canvass of alternatives. On the other hand, funds will dry up from now on; staying in will burn remaining bridges with Carter; defeat in New England will injure future presidential prospects, perhaps fatally. "He who fights and runs away lives to fight another day." I told Jean that, if he continues, as I trust he will, he must seize the peace issue and say that a war party has arisen in Washington,

Carter has allied himself to it, and that the exploitation and exaggeration of an international crisis for domestic political purposes may endanger the peace of the world, and that Ted will have to say this.

I then wondered aloud whether Ted really wanted to be President; whether he may not be going through the motions in order to get the problem out of the way while unconsciously not wishing to succeed.

Later—talked to Jean again. They are going ahead.

January 27

On Thursday morning the 24th shortly after 8, Ted Kennedy called. He wanted to discuss Carter's address to Congress the night before, in which he announced his "Carter Doctrine" committing the U.S. to military intervention in the Persian Gulf area. "The great trouble," he said, "is that foreign policy is swallowing everything else up. All our polls show that. When we began, inflation was high and foreign policy was low. Now everyone has forgotten about inflation, and all people seem to care about is Iran and Afghanistan." I told him my skepticism about the Carter Doctrine and suggested that he announce a major foreign policy speech for next week, in which he could take a hard look at the new policy.

[On Friday, January 25,] I arrived at Ted's house around 8 [to help draft a speech]. [On Saturday,] Ted seemed to me in very good form. During the morning discussion on the drafts, he was most impressive, noting gaps and inconsistencies in argument and insisting on pursuing the hard questions that lay behind verbal formulas. He was cogent and coherent. In general, he seemed rather buoyant. Those who think that he does not really want to be President would argue, I suppose, that the almost certain prospect of defeat has cheered him up. On the other hand, Steve told me that he had spent two days after Iowa arguing to Ted that he should get out at once, and that Ted was determined to carry on. Still the atmosphere was permeated by the sense that it was probably a lost cause but that, when Ted went down, he must go down with style.

Some time was spent Saturday in discussing what to say about Chappaquiddick. I was against saying anything at all, on the ground that most people had already made up their minds one way or another. I was told that, on the contrary, the polls showed a steady and accelerating loss of support on the issue and that something had to be done to arrest further loss. The people running the campaign in New England all say that he has to talk again about Chappaquiddick. Ted looked somber through all this discussion. Everyone under-estimated the impact of Chappaquiddick; and the themes of Kennedy's dubious character, panic under stress, resort to cover-up, have recently been given new life by articles in *Reader's Digest*, the *Washington Star* and the *New York Post*. I had used the phrase "panic reaction" to describe the Carter Doctrine. Bob Shrum said to me, "He won't say that. He won't use that word. We will have to find some other way to say it." It was finally agreed to omit Chappaquiddick in the speech he gives Monday morning at Georgetown but to include a passage in the version of the same speech that he is taping on Sunday for release on New England television stations Monday night.

February 1

The speech has been a great success. Even Bill Safire yesterday morning said that it "revived the art of the political speech, which has been dormant for nearly a decade." The campaign has had a genuine lift, I think, and necessary issues have been raised. But the time is so short—25 days to New Hampshire—and Carter continues to manipulate the patriotism issue with some dexterity. Three months from now the hollowness of the Carter Doctrine will be evident; whether it will be three weeks from now is another matter. I have had nice calls from Ted and from Steve about the speech. I asked Ted how he felt. He said he felt much better after the speech. I said, "Free at last?" He said, "Yes, that's exactly right."

Yesterday I went to hear Alonzo McDonald, the managerial genius of Carter's White House, hold forth at the Lehrman Institute. He is a tall, bland, smooth Georgian speaking fluent managerialese. It was an astonishing performance. The people present—a dozen or so executives— asked him no relevant questions: e.g., why does Carter require a staff five times as large as the staff FDR needed during the depression and four times as large as the staff FDR needed during the war? McDonald, innocent of any knowledge of history, talked about current problems of the presidency as if they were some dire novelty. When he got to substance, he was deeply conservative. One cannot imagine him in any other Democratic White House this century. One can easily imagine him in any Republican White House (except for TR's).*

March 4

On February 14, Nixon came at last to 65th Street. I returned late on March 2. The next morning, Sunday, Peter called, "Look out the window." I did and saw the unmistakable figure on the terrace picking up some logs. He returned to the house; then inexplicably came out in a few minutes, still carrying the logs. He deposited them, picked up some other logs (perhaps shorter?) and disappeared.

Logs seem to be the dominating theme of the presence so far. Peter reports an earlier appearance, in which he filled his arms with logs and, as he approached the door, dropped them. Mr. Pashkoff, who installed some energy-saving storm windows during our absence, later told me that he too saw Nixon in search of logs. This time the door closed behind him. When he approached it, he discovered that he was locked out. He began banging on the door and, after a few minutes, someone opened up, and he was rescued. One recalls the White House accounts of his passion for log fires, often accompanied by intensified air conditioning in order to make the room cold enough to justify a fire. Actually the weakness for open fireplaces must count as one of his more disarming characteristics.

March 20

A sad few days: the Kennedy campaign [has come] to an end. Last Thursday we dined at the Smiths with Bob Shrum; and on Saturday,

---

* Kennedy lost to Carter in the New Hampshire primary on February 26, 1980.

Steve, Steve Jr. and young Steve's girl came to dinner. We love the Smiths, including young Steve, an exceptionally sensible, bright and attractive boy; and one's heart goes out to them in this time of acute disappointment. As Kennedys, of course, they are well accustomed to disappointment and sorrow; so the tone remains gay and sardonic/ hopeful. On Sunday I saw Ted at the press conference welcoming Erberto Padilla to the United States; he looked terribly tired but is sustained by some inner drive. Late Tuesday night we watched the returns from Illinois: Ted savagely beaten.

The next morning I left for Michigan to give a lecture at Albion College. When I called Alexandra from La Guardia, she said that Steve was trying to reach me. I called him, and we chatted a bit. The Illinois result, Steve said, had been "a blow in the stomach" for Ted; he had expected to do better. Steve ran over the figures, comparing the situation as of now with his own calculations as of late February. He figures that Ted would have to carry the remaining primaries by 58–60% to have any chance. The New York figures for the primary next Tuesday are discouraging. Should he get out now? I argued strongly for his staying on through New York.

The Carter bubble is bound to burst; between his manifest incompetence, his panic-mongering abroad and a near 20% inflation rate at home, a revulsion is bound to come. But people disenchanted with Carter are not going to Kennedy. Beyond Chappaquiddick, Joan, women, etc., I think there is a deep resentment of the Kennedys in the land—the kind of resentment I encountered when I went around promoting the RFK book. I guess we like dynasties up to a point, but then begin to hate what are taken as dynastic pretensions and expectations. Ted Kennedy is the victim of the same backlash that destroyed TR Jr. in the 1920s and FDR Jr. in the 1950s.

Where do we go from here? Joe [Rauh] and I both feel that Reagan, contained by a Democratic Congress, would be no worse than Carter compromising and confusing a Democratic Congress. In California Reagan's bark turned out to be considerably worse than his bite.

Jean called to say that Averell is going to come out for Carter. I love Averell, but that love is terribly strained by this. I know his penchant for staying in with Democratic Presidents, and with potential winners; but at eighty-eight he need not go out of his way to keep on good terms with power. And he could at least have waited until after the New York primary.

March 26

The pessimism of last week turns out to have been premature. I have not for a long time enjoyed myself so much as I did last night. I could not hear the bemused television reporters announce Kennedy's upset victories in the New York and Connecticut often enough. It was all richly satisfying.

I talked to Steve Smith this morning. He was in high spirits, describing conversations he had just had with Hugh Carey (who said, "Tell Ted it really was a personal victory—he won it despite you and without me") and Pat Moynihan. Ted is changing plans to go into Wisconsin, where I would think he might have a chance. John Anderson is not wearing too well as a candidate; he has a weakness for righteous lecturing; and New York might swing many who inclined to Anderson when I was in Wisconsin a fortnight ago to go for Kennedy now.

April 7

Lunch today with Jack Valenti. The thought had flickered through my mind that Jack might be an emissary from Bob Strauss, commissioned to tell me that the Kennedy people must get behind Carter in due course lest they elect Reagan—and the luncheon was in fact interrupted by a telephone call from Strauss for Jack. But Jack's own frame of mind could not have been more different. His contempt for Carter equals mine; and his informed distrust of Jordan and Powell, whom he regards as intolerably "arrogant," exceeds mine. We mutually confessed that we were feeling our way toward the possibility of learning to live with Reagan. What a confession!—who could have imagined that we would come to this. Yet Reagan's governorship demonstrated that his bark is a good deal bigger than his bite; he is obviously not a man who, like Nixon or Carter, has enemies lists; and we might come out better with Reagan surrounded and contained by a Democratic Congress than with Carter compromising and stultifying the liberal opposition. The old Johnson crowd is evidently quite as disaffected as the old Kennedy crowd.

April 10

Very few [Nixon] sightings. I don't think I have seen our neighbor at all, though when I throw open the curtains in the morning, around 7 o'clock, a fire is usually blazing in his fireplace. Lest he get too much moral credit for rising so early it should be noted that the Nixons seem to dine around 6 o'clock, an hour or so before we start pre-prandial drinking, and the house is generally dark by 9. Not New York hours.

Alexandra reports that the old fellow trots out himself on bright days for an interlude in the sun. I asked her what he looked like as a sun-bather. She said, "Like a man wearing a Nixon mask."

One day Robert and a friend played in the garden, climbed on the jungle gym and Robert eventually climbed to the top of the wall be-tween our lot and Nixon's. Nixon came out on the terrace briefly, Alexandra said, and waved at Robert—a forlorn, hopeful wave, she thought. I asked Robert that evening what Nixon had done. "He waved at me to get off the wall," Robert said.

April 16
West Branch, Iowa

Here I am, in the Presidential Motel, West Branch, Iowa, ten miles from Iowa City, where I lived sixty years ago. I mean to drive in tomor-row afternoon and see if I can find 427 South Johnson Street, where I lived from 1918 to 1924. But Iowa City has changed from the quiet lit-tle town of 5000 or so people that I dimly remember. I lectured yesterday at Creighton University in Omaha and came on here to do some work at the Hoover Library.

April 17

After the Library closed today, I drove into the metropolis—Iowa City—in search of my childhood. When I live there, it had a population of perhaps 5000; now it is around 50,000. I remember only two places: the old State Capitol, and the house at 427 S Johnson Street where the Schlesingers lived. I found the Capitol without much difficulty. As I walked over to see it, I remembered how I used to walk past it so many years ago holding tight to my father's hand; and this brought back a surge of vivid memories about my father, whom I loved so much and to whom I owe so much—a kindly, reserved, disciplined man whose apparent austerity concealed, I believe, much intensity of feeling. It was harder to find S Johnson Street, but somehow I hit upon it, and found the hill down which I careened one day when I was sitting with Margaret Olsen, the little girl across the street, in the front seat of the Olsen automobile and accidentally released the brake. The car banged into something, the windshield broke and Margaret's forehead was cut—superficially but with profuse and scary bleeding. The house, alas, has gone. In its place there is a small, quasi-modern apartment house. All this, God help me, nearly sixty years ago.

May 5

I have not seen anything of Nixon in recent weeks. He has been away; so have I. Alexandra has witnessed some of his fitful sorties—even collided with him the other day as she was running to a taxi—but the neighborhood has been without drama—until, that is, a few days ago, when the Secret Service installed a set of cameras, including one on the wall between the Schlesinger and Nixon houses. I am presumably half-owner of the wall, though I have not had a chance to check my deed; and no one consulted with me about placing a camera on it—especially a camera that appears to be trained at us.

The last few days have been a chaos as we gathered our forces to leave for two months in England (where I will go to the Public Record Office and see how the British Embassy in Washington reported the evolution of American foreign policy in the late 1930s). I had a thousand things to do, a dozen deadlines to meet, but I did manage to draft a letter to the chief of the Secret Service asking about the cameras and wondering why their installation (or at least the installation of the one on the Schlesinger-Nixon wall) had not been cleared with me.

When I returned from delivering a despatch case full of things to do to Gretchen, I discovered that the crisis had escalated. This was yesterday, May 4. Peter and Adam had been sitting on the wall, as they have been doing for years; and a Secret Service man had told them to get off. I told Peter that he had as much right to sit on the wall as Nixon had. Soon he and Sophie West were out there again. The Secret Service agent reappeared. "Last time I asked you," he said (as they described it to me immediately afterward), "but this time I am telling you: get off that wall." I was summoned, clambered up on the jungle gym, stuck my head over the wall and found the Secret Service man, complete in jacket and vest, in the Nixon backyard. I took the offensive, asserting my half-ownership in the wall (I hope I am right about that), asking why these infernal instruments had been put on the wall without consultation with me, adding that my children had played on the wall for years without causing any harm to anybody and wondering by what authority anyone was ordering them off the wall now. The Secret Service fellow was rather more courteous to me than he had been to them (though later he professed ignorance about me, asked my name and did not appear deeply moved when he heard it). He said that the appearance of the children on the wall had caused one of the cameras to malfunction. I repeated my earlier points and asked what the camera was doing on my wall anyway. The agent said he was not familiar with the policy, only following orders. He also said that, if he were in my position, he would be mad too. I said that I had already written to the head of the Secret Service. He asked whether the children would stay off the wall until the matter was resolved. I said yes, adding that this was an act of courtesy and did not reflect any doubts about my rights.

It is really rather infuriating to find old Tricky causing this sort of entirely unnecessary problem in the neighborhood. And the whole thing is so idiotic. The enormously tall apartment house covering the west side of Lexington Avenue between 64th and 65th Streets commands Nixon's garden as well as mine. If a sniper wished to rid the world of Tricky, he could rather easily do it from the apartment house. But the apartment house is impossible to cover. So they train their equipment at the neighbors. God knows what they are doing—photographing us; listening to us? perhaps beaming cancer-inducing rays of the kind the Russians beamed on the American Embassy in Moscow? And all for a man who, if justice had been done, would be in the pen himself instead of becoming this object of technological solicitude at the taxpayers' expense.

August 6

I dined this evening with Steve. Alexandra, who is not feeling well, did not come, but Chrissie, who arrived in town today, joined us. Steve talked a good deal about the campaign. "I have never seen a worse managed campaign," he said, "—mismanaged by me, and mismanaged by others." He went into considerable and entertaining detail, but it had been a long day, and I had much to drink, and can't recall much now. At one point, he said, "And now the candidate and I aren't speaking," but whether that is to be taken literally or means only that the candidate isn't seeking his advice I don't know. Steve agreed that Ted has in the end come out quite well, and attributes this to Ted's own character and conviction triumphing over the incompetence of his managers.

August 11

Another Democratic convention, and this one perhaps the most dispiriting of all. Alexandra, still not feeling well, took Robert out to

East Hampton to stay with Jean Smith on Thursday, and I flew out to join them on Friday evening. Late that evening Ted Kennedy called to discuss the speech he is giving Tuesday night. He wanted me to see the Parker-Shrum draft, and arrangements were made to bring it out to East Hampton on Saturday. The speech was, I thought, a poor, tired job, a random laundry list interspersed with demagogic polemic against Reagan and rhetorical claptrap. A later version even concluded with the following incredible doggerel (as if from "The Star-Spangled Banner"):

> Then conquer we must when our cause it is just
> And this be our motto: "In God is our trust."
> And the star-spangled banner in triumph shall wave
> Over the land of the free and the home of the brave.

The rest of the speech did not particularly rise above the conclusion.

I read it with a sinking heart. Where the occasion calls for a dignified, elevated, thoughtful vindication by EMK of his effort, the draft abandons his major issues, concentrates on attacking Reagan and the Republicans and in so doing raises the question: if Reagan is such a national menace, why did Kennedy not withdraw after Detroit instead of carrying the fight into the heart of the Democratic convention? In essence, it is not a vindication speech but a concession speech, almost a capitulation speech; and damn poorly written too.

Soon I received a disturbed phone call from Dick Wade, to whom Ted had also sent a copy. I set to work to produce an alternative draft, flew back to New York early Sunday morning, ran it through the type-writer, consulted with Wade, who amended and endorsed the result, and then sent it over to Kennedy's office at the Waldorf Astoria. My fear was that Parker and Shrum would intercept it, incorporate a few sentences in their next revision, tell Kennedy that they had seen my suggestions and taken them into account and withhold the text from him. This, judging by the draft I received this morning, must have been what happened. When I had a few words with Ted this morning at a fund-raising breakfast organized by Abba Schwartz at 21, he gave no indication of having seen the alternative draft and said he wanted my reaction to the new draft of the morning. When I received the new draft, any improvements were marginal; so I wrote out my reservations and took them over to Steve's office.

There I found Steve with young Joe Kennedy. Neither had seen the Parker-Shrum draft. Joe read it with incredulity and said, "If Ted gives that speech, I am not even going to the hall. If that is really what he thinks, what the fuck have I been doing over the last nine months?" Steve was more reserved, questioned the paragraph on controls (even Doug Frazier, he said, is no longer for controls) but, I think, sympathized with the comments about tone and style. He said he would try and make sure that Ted read the alternative draft before a final decision was made. But Ted is spending the day going from one caucus to another, and Parker-Shrum already have their draft set up on teleprompter. He also said that he would try to get me in to see the candidate.

I then went off to lunch with Alexandra at the Quo Vadis. George McGovern called when we were there, and then joined us. He read me his speech. After a sentence in which he mentioned having supported Democratic presidential candidates, he paused for a moment after the name Carter (which concluded the list) and said: "Well that isn't entirely correct. I did publicly endorse Carter. But I voted for Gerald Ford." So of course did Alexandra, and I think she and George were right. Had Ford been reelected in 1976, we would have had the Panama Canal Treaties without trauma, SALT II would have passed, domestic policy would have been the same as with Carter and the Democratic party would have been liberated to be itself again. The election of Carter was a disaster to both the party and the country.

August 12

All over now, and I am not surprised but depressed all the same. We went to the convention last night in time to hear George's speech. Then came the roll call. It became evident almost at once that the closed convention crowd was piling up a commanding lead. After the vote, filled with gloom, we drifted from Madison Square Garden up to 21. There we joined George and Liz Stevens for dinner. Hugh Carey came in. He was quite funny and emphatic about Carter, whom he detests. Pam Harriman came up (we were dining on the second floor) and said, "Have you heard? Teddy has withdrawn." The source turned out to be Art Buchwald, who soon joined us. Then Averell came. Pam said, "What are we going to do now?" thereby infuriating the Stevenses, since, after initial interest in Teddy, she saw where things were going and scurried back to Carter. Averell is talking stoutly pro-Carter, but Pam told me at Isabel Leeds's on Sunday night, "You know, he hates Carter worse than you do." It is sad, though, to see this fine and dear old man's inability to do things that would keep him out of the center of things.

August 13

Contrary to my expectations, the speech was an enormous triumph. I never heard Ted deliver a speech better, and my guess is that the text sounds better than it will read. My representations may have somewhat moderated the capitulationist aspects, but it remains essentially the Parker-Shrum version, and they deserve the credit.

We had scheduled our mid-convention party for 6–8. Ted was supposed to speak at 6:45, then at 7:30 and finally began well after 8. A good many people left the party for the Garden; others stayed to hear it in the living room.

Everyone was naturally in a mood of high exhilaration. It was at first mostly family; later a number of politicians dropped by. Around midnight Ted summoned Bill Dougherty of South Dakota, Frank Bellotti of Massachusetts, a couple of others and me and asked what we thought he should do on Thursday night. I said "Go to the podium; and afterward support Carter in the campaign with the same zeal that Reagan supported Ford in 1976." Most of the others said the same. Ted appeared to argue against this, though I suspect he may have been doing this in order to test the arguments. "Isn't the mood different this time?" he said. "Look at John Anderson. He is popular because he is perceived as an anti-politician. You fellows want me to do this because this is what politicians always do. Maybe that is an argument against doing it. Maybe the people are looking for something different now." Underlying his words was an evident and ill-concealed contempt for Carter. I think it will be personally difficult for Ted to go to the podium Thursday night. My bet is that he will do it. We left with the Smiths about one o'clock. The day had been hot and sultry, but the night was soft.

This morning confirmed last night's exhilaration. We received one call after another, beginning with Averell who said how magnificent he thought Ted had been. A little late.

So another adventure comes to an end. Short of winning, it could not have ended better.

August 15

We stayed at home and watched the obsequies on television. Fritz Mondale gave a speech in the Humphrey manner, but, though he has the words, he doesn't have the tune. Then Carter came on and gave the most random, self-serving and generally horrible acceptance address I remember. He cannot stop talking about himself; he is, as William Lee Miller has said, "the autobiographical president," the center of every concern and every discourse. The speech appeared to fall flat.

Then came the aftermath. Dick Goodwin had called around eight to say that he thought it would be a ghastly error if Ted went to the platform. I said I didn't think so; in fact that I had recommended that he do it but that he do it coolly. Dick, not persuaded, asked for Ted's phone number so he could carry the argument to him directly. None the less Ted appeared in due course, arriving at the Garden accompanied only by John Douglas. He moved politely to the platform, shook Carter's hand, towered over him for a moment, waved to the crowd and moved on—a brief courtesy call, as Jack Chancellor described it on television.

Absolutely perfect. Carter stood with an inane smile on his face and hatred in his eyes; Mrs. Carter's lips were pursed, and her expression was
grim. The hitherto listless crowd was now roaring. It was highly enjoyable. We called Jean and Steve in East Hampton. Steve, still laughing,
said that the platform scene could hardly have been funnier if it had
been staged by *Saturday Night Live*.

August 16

Convention vignettes: in the midst of the hurly burly of the week I
glanced one morning out of our bedroom window. Below, sprawled on
a deck chair, wearing jacket and tie, was Richard Nixon. Seated
near him, wearing an afternoon dress and high-heeled shoes, was one of
his daughters. A grandchild was playing. The two Nixons looked as if
they were dressed for a garden party: even in his own house, his own
garden.

August 19

Alexandra and Robert went out to East Hampton today, while I
stayed behind to try to bring a modicum of order into my study, closet
and office. As I was struggling away, Steve Smith called around eight
o'clock and proposed dinner. We went off to the Quo Vadis (where we
encountered Irving Lazar, Bob and Helen Meyner, Oliver Smith, Gar-
son Kanin and Ruth Gordon, etc.) and had a jolly evening.

Steve talked a great deal about the campaign, in a mood of mingled
frustration, defensiveness, anger and humor. He says that he does not
understand Ted Kennedy, that he does not think he will ever be President, that he had no sense of the way his staff used and abused him, but
that his own instincts none the less brought him to a kind of triumph in
the end. The whole experience was obviously a searing one for Steve—
a fact he succeeded in disguising while it was all going on. "I stayed at
the house far too long," he said, meaning Ted's house in McLean; in the

late spring he finally left and went off to live in Abba Schwartz's house in Georgetown. Steve has always been involved in the fundraising side of campaigns, which may have prejudiced his remarks; but he thinks the great difference is that, as a result of the new campaign finance laws, the family money was for the first time not available to a Kennedy. The family money, he said, made all the difference for JFK in 1952 and 1960 and for RFK in 1964 and 1968. He feels that he was miscast and misused in the campaign and that he should never have got into it. He thinks that Ted lacks the sense of political reality that his brothers had, but also agrees that it has ended much better than anyone could have expected because of Ted's ultimate reliance on his own intuition and conviction.

We talked a bit about Anderson. Steve finds him thin, preachy, somewhat repellent. This is probably so. He plainly does not think I should back him, on the ground that he will end up a very bad third. I said that I found it impossible to vote for either Carter or Reagan. He said, in a stage whisper, "I plan to vote for Reagan."

September 19
[Dinner party at Marietta Tree's]

Last night we went to Marietta's for a dinner given in honor of Dick Gardner. Max Frankel, the editor of the *Times*'s editorial page, was there too. The *Times* has a terrible effect on people who work for it. They cannot bear any criticism of anything the *Times* ever does; they act as if it were lèse-majesté. To question the *Times* is as if one were questioning their religion. Frankel had recently run an editorial denouncing Bill Sullivan for writing his version of the events in Iran. I sent a letter to the *Times* saying that, as an historian, I welcomed such disclosure and, as a citizen, I was entitled to it. Frankel disagreed. He said he had attacked Sullivan because his article was a "cheap shot" at the President. Stimulated by a couple of pre-dinner bourbons, I exploded. Why, I asked, did the *Times* feel compelled to rush to the defense of the most powerful man in the land against the testimony of an ex-ambassador now consigned to a trivial job as head of Columbia's Arden House? What had happened to the "people's right to know" about which the *Times* became so pious on other occasions? Max became furious—a fury that took the form of glum and angry silence. He simply could not bear the thought that anyone might doubt the *Times*'s infallibility. Abe Rosenthal is the same. Harrison Salisbury and Tom Wicker are not.

September 24

John Anderson spoke today at the Council on Foreign Relations—a serious, intelligent, unimaginative, rather boring speech. It went over fairly well, I think, and was well attuned to the particular crowd. Teddy White told me afterward that it was the best speech he had heard Anderson give in the campaign.

I cannot recall so idiotic an election. Both Carter and Reagan are so addicted to the dissociation of words from things that nothing either says can be taken seriously for a moment. Each is going around the country promising anything that might win votes, and neither has any intention of discharging such promises if elected. Campaigns have never been sacred covenants with the electorate. Still, as late as Eisenhower and Kennedy, candidates intended to preserve some connections, however tortuous, between what they said and what they meant to do. The process of total dissociation began, I think, with LBJ. Now, with Carter and Reagan, candidates are entirely cynical and manipulative.

I have decided in the general doldrums—"Sir," said Dr. Johnson, "there is no settling the point of precedency between a louse and a flea"—to support John Anderson. I do not see that his effort is accomplishing the signal function of the historic third parties—introducing bold ideas into political discourse—but he compares favorably as a man to the two clowns the major parties have imposed on us, and an outpouring of national disgust in the form of a vote for Anderson offers the best means of rebuking the major parties. Or so I have written for the *Wall Street Journal*.

October 18

I went down to Washington for a luncheon given by Ed Muskie to discuss the FDR centenary in 1982. I had no sooner sat down on the 11 A.M. shuttle than I saw my old friend Bill Casey lumbering down the aisle. I first met Bill in London in 1944 when he was chief of the Secret Intelligence branch of OSS under David Bruce. We have kept up with each other through the years, and he is now Reagan's campaign manager. So I hailed him, and, after introducing his companions—Ed Meese, Reagan's confidante, and Richard Wirthlin, his pollster—Bill sat down with me for the trip.

He seemed reasonably cheerful and believes that Reagan will win. He will carry everything west of the Mississippi, Bill thinks, and is presently ahead of Carter in half the southern states, and he does not see how Carter can expect to carry everything else. But he agreed that the Reagan progress had slowed up. I said that war and peace were in my view the vital issue, that Carter was succeeding to some extent in painting Reagan as a warmonger and that Reagan had played into his hands by making SALT an issue. Bill said, "Our polls show that Carter has lost 3 points on decency while Reagan has lost 12 points on capacity to keep the peace—a pretty good trade-off from Carter's viewpoint." When I asked why Reagan hadn't fudged SALT instead of saying he would withdraw it, Casey rather shrugged and said, "Sometimes it is hard to get him to fudge things."

He told me in some detail the story of his acquaintance with Reagan. He hardly knew him before this campaign, but was asked at an early point to take a look at things and finally was despatched to New Hampshire a couple of weeks before the primaries. He sensed that something was wrong; soon came to believe that John Sears had decided Reagan would lose and was preparing a "soft landing" for himself. Reagan had come to feel the same thing and impressed Casey by the expedition with which he decided to fire, and then fired Sears. I asked Bill where Sears had made his reputation. "He is like Henry Kissinger," Bill said, "he cultivates the press. When Henry was Secretary of State, he spent half his time calling reporters either to praise stories he liked or to denounce stories he didn't like."

I said that, if Reagan were elected, the one thing he could do that would instantaneously dispel international dismay and concern would be—when Bill interrupted and said, "I know what you're going to say. Henry.... Well, we've been bringing him into the picture." I said I supposed that the right wouldn't much like it. Bill agreed but added that the right had been disappointed in a number of things Reagan had done and would probably be more disappointed in the future. I like Bill, and it was an interesting trip.

October 23

Down the home stretch at last, to everyone's undisguised relief. What a wearying and demeaning campaign this has been! There has been no serious discussion of anything and, even if there had been, it would have been useless, since there is no reason to believe anything that either Carter or Reagan might say. Carter will say with ringing sincerity, "I pledge never to use unemployment as a weapon against inflation" at the very time when he is doing precisely that. Reagan, who has been used to reading lines all his life, will play whatever script is required. But emotions boil up nevertheless, and one now notes the phenomenon of people who could not stand Carter a few months ago now arguing that the future of the republic depends on his reelection.

Thus at the Carter-Kennedy dinner in Washington last weekend Lennie Bernstein apparently, after explaining how the election of Reagan would release the forces of American fascism, then paused and shouted: "And this is a message I want to send through you to my liberal friends in New York, especially Phyllis Newman and Arthur Schlesinger." We ran into Lennie last night. He was quivering, intense, emotional; not the usual affectionate Lennie at all. He said that I did not know what I was doing. I said, "Do you really want four more years of Zbig Brzezinski?" Lennie said almost furiously, "I can guarantee that won't happen." At this point my old friend Irene Pappas who was with Lennie intervened, and the conversation lapsed. On the other hand, I encountered Dwight MacDonald at the same affair, and, somewhat to our mutual surprise, found we had substantially the same views—a relaxed view of Reagan and a determination to vote for Anderson.

Earlier in the day, I ran into Happy Rockefeller at a party at Doug Fairbanks's. She expressed great relief at seeing the Anderson button I was wearing and said she felt that Anderson was nearer to Nelson's view of life than either of the other two.

Later. I talked to Jackie today. She is going to vote for Anderson. She cannot bear the thought, she said, of pulling the lever for Carter. "But Teddy tells me just to write in *his* name."

November 5

The long national nightmare is finally over. The Reagan landslide, which I anticipated in some of my moods, has indeed come to pass. I couldn't care less what has happened to Carter. But I feel badly about the fine people he dragged down with him—George McGovern, John Culver, Birch Bayh, Gaylord Nelson, Frank Church, John Brademas. As Joe Rauh said this morning, "If I hated Jimmy Carter yesterday, I hate him twice as much today when I see what he has done to the Democratic party."

George said, "I voted for Carter this time. Last time I voted for Ford. I told no one, not even Eleanor. Then at Thanksgiving we went around the table, and I discovered that, without any consultation, all the McGoverns—Eleanor and our children—had voted for Ford. No one would have believed that the entire McGovern family voted Republican in 1976."

I lunched today with Jackie, fascinating as always. We talked about growing old. I mentioned that I had just had my 63rd birthday. She said, "You know, Ari was 63 when we were married." I was astonished at this; I recall him as seeming immeasurably old at the time. She said, "He was so filled with energy that he wore me out. Then, after his son was killed, he suddenly grew old." She spoke of him with a certain affection.

December 23

Christmas harassment!—always a sneaky holiday, it seems to have crept up more sneakily than ever this year; plus the fact that the term goes remorselessly on, so that I have a seminar this afternoon, than which nothing at the moment, for a Christmas shopper with much yet to do, can seem more incongruous. But I write this only to note the relaxing influence of the Century and, more especially, of a Century Martini. I went over to luncheon at 1:30, fairly despairing in mood, but, after drinks gently provided by Arthur, the Barbadian drink waiter, followed by an entertaining luncheon at the long table, I have returned filled with equability and cheer about the seminar, Christmas shopping and all else.

"Tis the season to be jolly."

1981

January 8

Irving Lazar dropped in after dinner last night. The guests (Max Jakobsen and his wife from Finland, Bill and Melinda vanden Heuvel, the Harrison Salisburys, Sidney Urquhart) interrogated him on Reagan. Irving said that Reagan pronounced his name Reegan until he married Nancy. She made him change the pronunciation to Ray-gan lest he be taken for shanty Irish.

Irving, just back from Washington, was delighted at having signed up Zbig Brzezinski for a book. Everyone expressed dismay at the prospect of a book by Zbig. Lazar said, "Can you think of anyone else in the Carter administration likely to write a book that anyone would want to read?" I can hardly imagine a sadder verdict on these four wasted years.

January 20

Inauguration day. Reagan will be my 13th President—which, since he is No. 40, means that I will have lived through the administrations of one-third of American Presidents (precisely, since the figure of 40 counts Cleveland twice).

I heard the speech at the office—skillfully projected, banal in language, reeking with sincerity. About as memorable as Carter's inaugural four years ago. This is not a notable art form, however—about in the same category as commencement addresses.

February 4

At Kitty Hart's last night, Henry Kissinger came in after dinner. He seemed cheerful and was on his on way to Acapulco to work on his second volume. He now plans three volumes, the third on the Ford years. Betty Comden asked him whether he had been offered anything in the administration. Henry said no very emphatically. Why Haig? George Shultz had told him, Henry said, that he kept reading in the papers that he was the top choice for State and that he was entirely interested until one day he received a call from Reagan, saying, in effect, I understand that you don't want to come to Washington and would rather stay in Bechtel. Henry speculated that one problem may well have been that Reagan did not want to recruit both State and Defense from Bechtel and that, in addition, Shultz and Weinberger do not get along all that well. When I referred to Haig as Henry's "protegé," Henry said, "We should all have such protegés."

Henry spoke dismissively of Richard Allen but evidently regards Jesse Helms as his major enemy, and thinks that antisemitism is at the root of it. "I get along well with Reagan," he said. "I spent an hour and a half with him only a few days ago. He is a nice man, a decent man. One odd thing, though. When he talks, all his illustrations are drawn from the movie business. He never says, 'We had a problem like that in Sacramento,' never brings up his eight years as governor. It is always, 'We had a problem like that in the Screen Actors Guild.'"

February 10

A film has been made about [the civil rights struggle in] Little Rock. I invited Norris Church Mailer, Norman's beautiful new wife (and, over a longer period, companion), [to see it.] Norman first spotted her when she was a schoolteacher in Russellville, Arkansas, and the girl friend of Bill Clinton, who later became Arkansas' governor. Norris was six years old at the time of Little Rock, but she is highly intelligent and retains a great interest in her native state. After the film we went to the River Café for luncheon, at which Norman joined us.

I have known Norman for nearly thirty years. We first met perhaps at a debate in Columbia where Mary McCarthy and I debated Norman and Norman Podhoretz on, as I recall, the Thirties. I believe that Podhoretz has an account of the debate in his recent volume of memoirs. I used to see Norman from time to time on the Cape in the later 1950s, when he was at Provincetown and I at Wellfleet. He drank a good deal in those days and was generally contentious, though often likeable. We have seen him increasingly in recent years. Norris is serene and calming; Norman has grown genial with the passing of time, or perhaps has finally yielded to this natural sweetness and warmth; and we like them both very much.

February 12

Lunched today with Emmet Hughes. He is back with Time, Inc., working as an editor, not as a writer, for *Fortune* and seemed vaguely melancholy. He wanted to ask what I thought of the possibility of his going to Washington to do for Reagan what he did so well for Eisenhower; apparently a few people, including Bill Rogers, have proposed this to Bill Casey. I said I thought it would be a fine idea. Privately I would consider any such invitation most unlikely. As a Rockefeller man (and a liberal), Emmet would be a red flag to the rightwing zealots, and friends of Reagan, recalling *The Ordeal of Power,* would warn him of the book that Emmet would inevitably write. I said that instead I wished Emmet would write a biography of Nelson Rockefeller. He seems to me ideal; a book combining political observation with personal testimony—the sort of book John Bartlow Martin did about Adlai (and I about RFK). He said, "You know, it is very funny now that I think it, but that idea has never occurred to me." He did not seem uninterested in the possibility, though, and I hope he will think about it seriously. One of the areas of difficulty would be dealing with Nelson's private life, and we chatted about that for a bit. "Nelson was just compulsive about women," Emmet said. "He made Happy go through the misery of a divorce, and two years later was fooling around with a new girl in the office. In 1968 we were concerned all the time that the press might get on to this new involvement. . . . All his girls were the same type—the wholesome, hearty, simple, innocent American type. Except possibly the last one: Hugh [Morrow] tells me that she was a bad one."

We chatted also about Eisenhower. "I think I got him about right in *The Ordeal of Power,*" he said. "I think that that was a fair book. He was much more of a man than most liberals thought at the time. But Eisenhower revisionism has gone too far. Take Fred Greenstein of Princeton, for example. He is a nice fellow—but his thesis these days— Eisenhower the Activist President—is a lot of bullshit."

March 7

I guess I was wrong about the Reagan crowd. They turn out to be considerably more doctrinaire than I expected them to be. In domestic policy they seem really to believe that reducing the budget and cutting taxes will produce prosperity without inflation. The more likely effect, it seems to me, of cutting taxes for the rich and social programs for the poor is to rekindle social tensions. Still I think Reagan should have the chance to play his hand. If his policy succeeds, it will be a miracle, but a pleasant one; if it fails, then we will at least have got free-market therapy out of our system, and then can move on to something else. In the meantime, the Reagan policy will be hard on the poor people and on the northern cities; but, as Adam Smith used to say, there is a lot of ruin in a country. Nor do I think it too bad an idea for government agencies to have to make do on smaller budgets. So we will survive Reagan's domestic policy.

"Domestic policy," JFK used to say, "can only defeat us. Foreign policy can kill us." Here I am more worried. Reagan and Haig obviously see the entire planet, and all recent history, through the lens of the Cold War. They have decided that the civil war in El Salvador is the product of Soviet-Cuban intrigue, and that El Salvador is the place where the U.S. can show how decisive and tough it has recently become. So we seem to be heading for unilateral intervention in circumstances where we will have little (expressed) Latin American support, where our actions will encourage right-wing dictatorships throughout the hemisphere, and where our success, if achieved, will have no effect on the Russians, who already believe we are capable of licking El Salvador. I wrote a column to this general effect for the *Wall Street Journal* of February 23, but only two newspapers picked it up, nor has anyone even inserted it into the *Congressional Record*. There seems a general mood of acquiescence in the Reagan-Haig nonsense. I did get though a letter from George Kennan, who thought the column "superb—the best thing of its sort I have ever seen on that subject."

March 31

I was working away yesterday afternoon at home when Gretchen called and said that Reagan had been shot (at). We turned on the television—Stephen was there talking with Alexandra, who was indisposed and spending the day in bed—and we sat by the set for the rest of the afternoon. I could not care less about Reagan and am sure George Bush would make a better president, but the whole business rekindled old emotions and left me surprisingly upset. In the hours since, I have had a flood of newspaper, television and radio requests for op ed pieces or interviews. I have declined everything. What can one say? Whatever I have to say about assassinations, I said long ago, and I have nothing arresting to add now. The logical conclusion is a severe national policy on handguns, but I suppose Reagan will continue to take the National Rifle Association line. And yet Hinckley nearly killed him with what Nancy Reagan would describe as a "teeny-weeny" gun.

April 4

I am just back from a meeting of the Library of Congress Council of Scholars in Washington. I find that in discussions of the organization of scholarship, and equally of programs of education, I am struck dumb. I am a scholar and a teacher; nevertheless my mind does not run naturally in academic categories. Had the topic been foreign affairs or economic policy, I would have been filled with reactions and suggestions. As it was, I contributed nothing and experienced excruciating boredom.

This is part, I suppose, of a larger dilemma. What I like most of all, apart from love and family, is writing history. I am even willing to put up with teaching history in order to secure the facilities for writing. This inevitably lands me in academic life. Yet I have always felt uncomfortable, even alienated, in academic life. My academic friends are mostly those like Ken Galbraith and Dick Wade for whom academic life is also a means rather than an end. The historians with whom I feel instant sympathy are those like George Bancroft and Henry Adams who abandoned academic life for the world of affairs. I tried during the discussions at the Library to define my feelings about pure academics— what is it?—the sense they give of collective unreality? collective complacency? collective pomposity? collective futility? And their jokes are so bad! Yet individually they are mostly agreeable, admirable, rewarding people. Why does the academic environment, as distinct from the academic discipline, seem to bring out the worst in otherwise decent individuals?

April 8

Spring has come briefly to New York. Yesterday morning, as I was changing from work clothes into a suit for the office, I glanced out the window, and there was Nixon, formally dressed in a three-piece suit and necktie, rather stiffly throwing a large rubber ball to a grandchild. Later in the day Alexandra and Dial Press gave a cocktail party for Sally Belfrage and her new book. Sally, a charming girl, shared an apartment with Alexandra in New York in the early sixties. She is also the daughter of Cedric Belfrage, the old-time Stalinist. When the guest list for the party appeared, I was appalled to discover a large infusion of Stalinist and neo-Stalinist names—Alger Hiss, Victor Navasky, Victor Rabinowitz, etc. However, what the hell. Because of my seminar, I arrived late at the party. There indeed was Alger Hiss. I had not supposed he would come, because I have long since publicly declared my belief in his guilt; I do not think I would come in his position; but he was in my house, so I went over and greeted him. We talked mostly about his brother Donald, who is now nearly blind, and his niece (and goddaughter) Joey, who was a friend of Chrissie's.

How odd, I thought, to begin the day with Nixon and to end it with Hiss!

April 24

I went down to Washington yesterday to speak at a session of the American Society of Newspaper Editors. I arrived in time to hear George Bush speak at the luncheon. He was very cordial at cocktails before the luncheon, and we had an agreeable but meaningless talk. His speech was suitably vice presidential. After lunch someone asked him what he would have done differently if he were President rather than Vice President. He said wryly, "You certainly don't expect me to answer that, do you?"; then, suddenly aware that this might imply he would have done some things differently, he hastily added that, of course, he was heart and soul for the Reagan program. The vice presidency remains a humiliating job, though I guess Carter-Mondale and possibly Reagan-Bush have made more of it than has been the general experience in the past.

The first session after luncheon brought together Lester Thurow and George Gilder, two young men very full of themselves, in a debate.

Thurow seemed to me to win on points; he is bright, but bolder in analysis than in remedy and much given to quoting himself ("As I said . . ." or "As I have written . . ."). My own session was on the Democratic Party—Is There Life After Reagan? The others were John Glenn and Gary Hart, both of whom would like to be the presidential nominee in 1984, and Elinor Holmes Norton. Glenn was conservative, Hart opportunistic, Norton abstract and wordy. I represented the left wing. When I said that the 1980 election meant the rejection, not of liberalism, but of a failed presidency, Gary said, "It is too early to decide whether the Carter presidency was a failure or not." It was a fairly entertaining session.

May 18

We spent the weekend with the Harrimans at their place near Middleburg in Virginia. Averell, in his 90th year, still walks and swims, surrounds himself with guests and seems no deafer than usual. He is getting old, though, and it is all a little melancholy. Pam is now deeply involved in setting up her own political action committee and combatting the National Conservative Political Action Committee—a most worthy endeavor, but one that dominates her conversation well beyond the point of diminishing returns. When she can be persuaded to talk about England in the 1940s, she is charming and funny; but on America in the 1980s she is, I hesitate to say it but it is alas true, a bore.

I interviewed Averell for *American Heritage*. (Typically he asked me whether I was being paid. I said I was. He then said that he thought he ought to be paid too. I said that I would see whether *American Heritage* would not make a contribution to some cause in which he was interested—the moribund FDR Foundation, for example.)

In the interview he mentioned his father's break with Theodore Roosevelt. Later I asked him what he thought about TR. He said, "I disliked him very much. He wrecked the last years of my father's life. He was a vengeful man. I have always regarded him with contempt."

Pam told a story about Winston Churchill in his last years. She was sitting with him in a garden holding his hand. Churchill said, "I have lived a long life and have served my nation to the best of my ability, and now I wish they would let me depart." I can't make out whether Averell is approaching that point. But he still has zest for life and is rather optimistic about the future.

June 11

We lunched with Joe Alsop. The big current topic is the sneak Israeli attack on the nuclear installation in Iraq—an appalling action, in my view. If preventive war becomes the international rule, then why not India taking out the Pakistani nuclear installation next month? Russia knocking out the Chinese plants the month after? In this light the Japanese took entirely justifiable precautions at Pearl Harbor. But Bill Paley, with whom we dined Tuesday night, and Joe at lunch yesterday were delighted by the Israeli action. The *Wall Street Journal* applauded, and even Jimmy Wechsler, to my surprise, wrote a mild defense in the *Post*.

We went to Henry Kissinger's for dinner—an odd company, the Lane Kirklands, the Peter Duchins, Joe, a Dutch foreign affairs expert and, after dinner, George Shultz, who had been speaking at the Council on Foreign Relations. Henry was asked what he thought about the Israeli raid. He gave a typically convoluted answer. "Privately," he said, "I am pleased. I think even many Arabs are pleased. No one trusts Saddam Hussein. Still, there are problems. One can be pleased and still not condone," etc. He arrived late, having been to see Reagan. "This was at his initiative?" I asked. "Always," Henry said. "I make it a strict rule never to volunteer advice." "Does he take it all in?" "He listens," Henry said, "and tries to understand, in so far as he is capable of understanding foreign policy. But I don't have the impression that he ever ingests anything you tell him. I used to brief him for Nixon when he was governor. I find that years later he could tell me almost verbatim something I had told him back then. He remembers exactly, but I have the feeling that the item has lain unused in his mind all those years."

I had not met Shultz before. He is bluff, confident, terribly sure of himself, quite impervious to argument. Henry asked him, "Do you think the Reagan economic policy is going to work?" Shultz said, "Of course it will work. No question." Lane Kirkland and I tried to explain why we doubted his certitude. It was like talking to a blank wall. I was less impressed by Shultz than I expected to be.

The prettiest sight of the evening was Alexandra, Nancy Kissinger and Cheray Duchin standing together in a row—three exceptionally pretty girls in exceptionally pretty dresses.

June 12

Stephen and I lunched today with Carlos Fuentes. Carlos is recently back from Paris, where he attended [François] Mitterrand's inauguration as part of an invited group of writers, among them Bill Styron and Arthur Miller. Jimmy Baldwin was also invited but told the French government that he never traveled by himself. The French said that the other writers had asked whether they could bring their wives and had been told no. Baldwin said that he did not care about the others but that unless he could bring a companion he would not come. They sent him two tickets on the Concorde. On arrival in Paris Jimmy and his current lover (male, of course) took off at once for the Côte d'Azur, spent the weekend in the sun, returned to Paris and took the Concorde back to New York, never going near Mitterrand and the inauguration. As Carlos summarized Baldwin's probable explanation, "Well, all you wanted was a token black, so this is what you deserve."

October 8

The season has begun. On Monday night we went to Jan Cushing Olympitis's for dinner—Margaux Hemingway, Pat Lawford, etc., and the Mailers. I had a long talk with Norman about Jack Abbott, whose release from prison he helped to secure and who soon thereafter killed a man. Norman has been in consequence the object of much savage attack and was sad and stoical about it. "You have been through this sort of period," he said, "so you know what it is like." He found Abbott quiet and considerate, but tense and constrained, not inclined to open up. "He talked like an old con," Norman said, "who knows that he must never be pinned down to anything, because that will only get him into trouble." His response to questions about prison life were general and evasive. Norman attributed this partly to the fact that Abbott had not levelled with him about the circumstances that led to his release. Abbott, Norman now believes, made a deal with the prison guards, who told him that, if he cooperated with them by turning in other prisoners, they would get him released, and that, if he refused to cooperate, they would beat him to death. So he became a fink and, in Norman's gloomy view, will be killed by other prisoners when sent back.

Norris Mailer found Abbott easier to talk to. She said that Norman made him nervous, but when alone with her, he was inclined to open up, partly (she thinks) because she is a woman, partly because her Arkansas accent and upbringing made her a less unfamiliar type. She liked him, found him gentle and helpful, but said she was not altogether surprised by the denouement. Abbott was captured a few weeks ago and has sent messages saying he would like to see her. She said, "I can't see him. What can I say to him? I can't say that I hope he gets out, because that would not be true. He killed a harmless man, and he deserves to get his punishment. If I were to see him, I would have to tell him that I am on the other side, and I don't see much point in that." I am very fond of Norris—not only beautiful but sensitive and intelligent.

1982

January 10

Apart from the normal attrition of life, I have taken on two new jobs, neither of which I felt I could quite refuse. The first was to become president of the American Academy/Institute of Arts and Letters, a venerable establishment institution. I was told that the job would not take much time, and indeed we are lucky to have a most efficient director in Margaret Mills. But "for every benefit you receive a tax is levied" (Emerson); and the Academy/Institute cuts into time in all sorts of minor but persistent ways. Then I suggested to Hugh Carey a year ago that he establish an FDR Centennial Commission for the state of New York. He retaliated by making me chairman. The appointment was announced on 30 January a year ago—FDR's 99th birthday. I promptly submitted a list of possible members, possible projects, etc. Nothing happened. For several months I tried to get some action. I could not help reflecting that, if this had been the 100th anniversary of Greek independence, Carey in his present mood would have been considerably more forthcoming. In August I managed to see Carey. He appeared interested, even enthusiastic, and promised quick action. Finally in September he put out a proclamation establishing the commission. Gradually telegrams of invitation went out. In December we had our first meeting in Albany. FDR Jr. came; so too did two indomitable old ladies, Anna Rosenberg and Dorothy Rosenman. Carey, who retains the gift of rising to occasions, was good. But that was six weeks before the 100th birthday. Since then I have been struggling with the problem of organizing and stimulating centennial programs. Again more vagrant and persisting cuts into time.

Then, for an exceedingly generous sum, I have been hired as a consultant for an ABC FDR special, to be televised on 29 January. Pamela Hill, a bright, capable, attractive woman who is married to Tom Wicker, is the producer; and Roone Arledge, who remembers my suggesting the idea to him some time back, is the top ABC executive on the project. Also Andy is an associate producer, which increases my interest in the show. But this means I have to review scripts, watch rushes, answer questions and otherwise justify my fee.

The Academy/Institute + the FDR centennial + ABC + my course at CUNY + various pieces and reviews I agreed to do, either because I had something to say or because I thought I could make some quick money or (more generally both) + our hyperactive social life—all this has meant that the FDR book thus far is dying the death of a thousand cuts—and that 1981 was the most frustrating year for a long time—all the more frustrating since I figure that I will have, if lucky, a dozen more book-writing years left, and I hate wasting a single minute.

Pat Moynihan is up for reelection this year. He is a brilliant and entirely opportunistic man. He anticipated the neo-conservative swing and in 1967 gave a talk to the ADA in which he said, in effect, liberalism had gone too far, government could not solve all our problems and, in particular, the young and the blacks were becoming pains in the neck. I think that Pat had a bum rap after his 1964 study on the black family, but that he took it too personally and expended too much energy in subsequent years paying people back. By 1969 he was working for Nixon, portraying him as a new Disraeli and as a man whose respect for civility recalled Wilson and Adlai Stevenson. His great friends became people like Irving Kristol, a likable and intelligent ex-radical, and Norman Podhoretz of *Commentary,* an odious and despicable ex radical. Pat, with his alert antennae, foresaw the disgrace of Nixon and began distancing himself in the early 1970s. Then he had his splurge at the UN, where he practiced a nationalist demagoguery that isolated the United States at the UN but prepared him as a senatorial candidate—a Democrat once again—in New York. During this period my relations with Pat grew prickly and then cold. As a senator, Pat has been excellent on New York issues, hopeless on Cold War issues. But, with Reagan, he began to anticipate new reactions. In a Gridiron speech a year ago, he suddenly came out with an eloquent vindication of government. As his reelection campaign has come nearer, he has moved again to the left, and has begun to mend his liberal fences. Early in November he called me and suggested lunch. We lunch regularly on Saturdays at P.J. Moriarty's, and I asked him to join us. We arrived together and sat at the only vacant table in the main room. Then I noticed that Steve and Jean Smith and a couple of their children were at the next table. Pat and Steve are not great pals, and it seemed to me that Pat was somewhat dismayed by the proximity. Alexandra soon joined us. Pat seemed nervous; and, after downing one glass of sherry, asked for a large tumbler of sherry, which was duly provided. By now he was beginning to sweat visibly and kept mopping his face. When the food arrived, he suddenly said, "I am humiliated, but if I stay a moment longer, I am afraid I will become sick." He then got up and staggered to the door. Alexandra said I should follow him and put him in a taxi, which I did. Later in the afternoon he called to say that he had been suffering mysterious pains for some days, that the day before his doctor had diagnosed his trouble as shingles, and that he had been quenching the pain with codeine. Apparently codeine and liquor (even sherry) are a lethal combination. Subsequently he wrote a charming ("Dearest Alexandra") letter of apology.

February 6

In 1973 or thereabouts, when the Nixon tapes were on everyone's mind, a reporter asked me whether JFK would ever have done anything like that. I imprudently said no, the whole idea of Kennedy's doing it was "inconceivable." Steve Smith called me and said that, before I went farther out on a limb, I should know that there were some Kennedy tapes.

I more or less forgot about this until on my return from Wake Forest College on the morning of 4 February I saw a sensational headline in the *New York Post* about JFK's taping the Oval Office. The *Post* had picked up the story from the *Washington Post*. (The *Washington Post* had run my 1973 comment, dating it correctly; the *New York Post* had typically run it under a headline "Kennedy Aides Stunned" as if it were a response to the 1982 disclosure.) By the time I got to the office there had been about 20 calls, but I quickly decided on a "no comment" policy and spoke to no reporters during the story's 24 hours.

In fact, I have two feelings. As an historian, I think it is fine to enrich the historical record. As a government official, I don't think it makes much difference. As a person, I think it is a poor idea to record other people's conversation without their knowing it. If anyone had asked me at the time, I would (I think) have counselled against it. I rather agreed with Pierre Salinger on *Nightline,* who said that he understood JFK's motives in having the recordings but wished he hadn't done it. There will of course be much rejoicing among the Nixonians, though of course the outrage over the Nixon tapes was aroused much less by the fact of taping than by the contents of the tapes.

On that Thursday night we gave a party for Joe Alsop and his new FDR book. Douglas Dillon was one of the guests, and I asked him whether he minded being taped. He said, "Certainly not. I never said anything to the President that I wouldn't be happy to see on the historical record." Joe too thought that the indignation about the tapes was self-righteous and hypocritical and quoted Macaulay, "We know no spectacle so ridiculous as the British public in one of its periodical fits of morality."

On 21–26 February we were in Claremont, California, while I gave five lectures at Pomona College. On our only free evening we went into Beverly Hills, where Angie Dickinson had arranged a dinner party at Dinah Shore's. The other guests were Kirk and Ann Douglas, Paul and Mickey Ziffren, George and Joan Axelrod, Robert Wagner and Tommy Thompson, a writer who did a successful book a few years back about a murder in Dallas. Though I like most of the people, the evening was a little depressing. This was only partly because of the strong atmosphere of sympathy for Reagan, a mood that even infects the Ziffrens. This was partly a movie reaction: everyone was pleased by Reagan's tolerance of films like Warren Beatty's *Reds* and Costa-Gavras's *Missing*. Jack Lemmon had recently been in Washington doing publicity for *Missing*. Reagan invited him over to the White House. Lemmon went with some trepidation, expecting to be chastised for his participation in a film that had already been formally denounced by the State Department. Instead, Reagan was affable and charming and reproached him not at all. But what was really depressing was the way the evening degenerated until all these quite intelligent people were talking with some avidity about Elizabeth Taylor's sex life and such subjects. Angie must have sensed some boredom, because she said, as she drove us back to the Beverly Wilshire, "I'm a little sorry, but I guess you saw a typical Beverly Hills evening." Conversation would have been very different with the same people in New York.

Meantime, the Reagan administration continues to crumble. We will survive his failures in economic policy, but his foreign policy gets scarier all the time. God knows what they think they are up to in Central America, but it doesn't make much sense to me, and policy is conducted with a technical incompetence reminiscent of the forgotten days of Jimmy Carter.

April 3

Yesterday, at Kitty Hart's party to celebrate Irene Selznick's 75th birthday, I congratulated Henry Kissinger on the skill with which he had written about Nixon in his second volume, just out, of memoirs. I said, "You wrote about him with such insight that those who dislike Nixon recognize the man that has afflicted them for so long, and yet with such sympathy that Nixon must recognize himself." I forebore adding that this mastery of ambiguity helps explain Henry's success as a negotiator and also introduces a certain equivocalness in his personal relationships. Henry said, "Oh no, you are quite wrong. Nixon will hate what I have written about him. He won't recognize himself at all."

Then he added: "You know, I have much less sympathy for Nixon now than I had in 1974–75. I think what really finished it for me was the trip to [Anwar] Sadat's funeral—when I went along with Nixon, Ford and Carter. As soon as we got into the plane, Nixon was his old self again, trying to manipulate everybody and everything, dropping poisonous remarks, doing his best to set people against each other. Later, when we were in a car by ourselves, Ford said to me, 'Sometimes I wish I had never pardoned that son of a bitch.' "

May 22

We got caught in a bad traffic jam on the Long Island Expressway and barely got back to 64th Street in time for dinner. Our guests were Gianni and Marella Agnelli, Henry and Nancy Kissinger and Lally Weymouth. Someone asked Henry whom he would like to see the Republicans run for President. He said after a moment, "Howard Baker." He was scathing about George Bush—"a very weak man"—and even more so about Jack Kemp, whom he believes makes no sense at all. "I like Ted Kennedy very much, but not for President." Henry and Nancy both talked a lot about Nixon (we were dining in the garden, which led to speculation about what had taken place over our back fence). They both said that he hates women. "I never liked Nixon," Henry said, "but now I actively dislike him," and he told again the story of the trip to Sadat's funeral, including Gerald Ford's great line: "Sometimes I am sorry I ever pardoned the son of a bitch." Henry, by the way, alleges a very high regard for Ford, a man whose intelligence, he says, is much underrated. One is never sure whether for Henry intelligence in Presidents may not mean amenability to advice. It was an agreeable evening under candlelight in the garden. Gianni Agnelli, who has been through a series of Job-like afflictions over the past year and a half, culminating a couple of months ago in a heart attack, seemed a trifle subdued; Marella has never looked prettier.

June 30

On 27 June I took Robert to the Yankees game for his 10th birthday; then Alexandra and I got on the plane to fly to Albany for a dinner Hugh Carey was giving (in association with the FDR Commission) for Queen Beatrix of the Netherlands. I had met her briefly a couple of months ago when the Dutch gave an evening party for her on one of their ships and was favorably impressed. This time I sat next to her at dinner and was bewitched. She is bright, pretty, rather sexy, filled with life, charm and humor and endowed with a marvelous capacity for (seeming) candor, though one imagines that she knows perfectly well what she is saying and makes few errors. She is a delight to talk to. She was amusing, for example, on the subject of Gerald Ford, having just returned from Michigan where she visited the Ford Library in Grand Rapids. "I said to him how nice it was to see him again. He looked blank, and then said, 'I know we have met, but where was it.' I finally told him that it was at one of the Bilderberg conferences, where I played a very modest role, listening at the back of the room. He pretended to remember me, but I am sure he thought I was one of the secretaries." At the end of the evening, I told her that she had transformed my attitude toward queens. She laughed.

Yesterday we went to a cocktail party given by John and Mary Lindsay for Carroll O'Connor—"Archie Bunker" of *All in the Family*. He is an engaging man, well read and politically liberal though compelled to work hard to make it clear that he is really not an Archie Bunker. He had just returned from the Joyce centenary in Dublin. He had recently accompanied his wife on a visit to someone at the Institute for Advanced Study. He asked about the office next door. He was told that it was George Kennan's office. O'Connor then ventured into the office and found Kennan standing by the window, looking out gloomily at the rain. O'Connor said, "Are you worried about things?" Kennan replied, "I am worried about everything." They chatted for a few minutes. As O'Connor left, Kennan said, "Are you one of the new professors here?"

In public affairs, disintegration continues. The Reagan crowd is rapidly coming to seem as amateurish as the old Carter act. Haig finally resigned this week, to be replaced by George Shultz, who struck me as rather pompous and dogmatic when I met him this winter at Henry Kissinger's. He will no doubt be better than Haig in the Middle East, if for the wrong reasons, and he will probably rather take the European line on economic issues; but he knows nothing about arms reduction, which is the biggest issue of all.

July 5

We are just back from a long weekend at Campobello. Flawless weather the whole time—hardly a cloud in the sky. On Saturday, July 3, FDR Jr. took us on a tour first of the old family cottage and then of the island. Ed Muskie, the American chairman of the Campobello Commission, arrived in the course of the day. He was in genial form and, except for his addiction to bad puns, is an impressive man. We had some talk about Carter over the weekend. "One of his troubles," Ed said, "was that he was incapable of reaching out to people. When he came in, I told him that he ought to begin by making one close friend in the Senate. It didn't matter who it was; but he had to have somebody on the Hill he could talk frankly to and who could talk frankly to him— someone he could bounce ideas off, someone who could tell him what the atmosphere was on the Hill and what he could and should do to improve relations. He never made that close friend. Nixon had more friends in the Senate than Carter ever did. . . . You know that, during the whole time I was Secretary of State, he never once asked me for advice on political matters." Muskie of course was by far the most politically experienced member of Carter's cabinet.

August 5

On Sunday 1 August we returned from ten days in the USSR. What follows comes from notes made at the time.

On Thursday, 22 July, we flew to Moscow. The occasion was a conference of American and Soviet writers in Kiev. I went with foreboding. This was my fourth trip; the last was in 1969. On each previous trip my only real sensation of pleasure (apart from admiring pre-revolutionary monuments in Leningrad and Moscow) had come when I stepped on the plane that would take me back to the democratic world. I anticipated the usual routine of frustration and deception, and went simply because it would have seemed foolish to turn down a free trip at a time of such uncertainty in Soviet-American relations.

We stopped briefly at the Hotel Sovietskaya before taking the night train to Kiev, where the conference was to take place. No caviar: it had been abundant in 1969. By this time the delegation was beginning to form its internal patterns. The Salisburys of course were old friends (I met Charlotte first in Leningrad in 1967), and I have always liked Susan Sontag; so we went around mostly with them. Erica Jong is a naive, breathless, bouncy, amiable, self-involved girl; Susan took to collecting her remarks. ("Is Kiev to the north or south of Moscow?" . . . "I've never been on a trip like this before. I usually just go to appear on the Phil Donahue show.") Studs Terkel is said to have had a Stalinist past, but I have always liked him after the careful and very good interview I had with him in Chicago on the RFK book, and I liked him more on this trip. He is rumpled, informal, direct and funny. [Robert] Bly seemed a pleasant fellow. Vera Dunham, Russian by birth and a specialist in Soviet literature, is 70, lively and amusing. Gwendolyn Brooks, the black poet (and not a very good one), seemed lost and rather dopey. Irving Stone is a genial fool, very full of himself, very pleased with the Soviet Union because his books have been translated and so many people, he claims, came to see him on his trips to Russia to tell him how reading him has changed their lives.

The night train was OK. We arrived in Kiev at 11 A.M. on Friday, 23 July. It was a lovely, sunny day, not too hot, and Kiev, a city of wide boulevards, parks, trees, gushing fountains, now spruced up for its 150th anniversary, was rather more attractive than I remembered from my visit there in 1969. We were given a perfectly agreeable suite at the Hotel Kiev.

In the early afternoon we had a motor tour of the city. The first session of the conference took place at 5 P.M. in a nice old building that had been a girls' school before the Revolution. [Nicolai] Federenko, a smooth, cynical fellow who looks rather like Ted Heath, presided. The Americans sat on one side of the table, the home team on the other.

The alleged theme of the conference was "History and Modernity." The Soviet participants had been instructed to prepare papers; we had not; so they gave the appearance of much more careful preparation, even if the papers were generally abstract and hortatory. After a while we adjourned.

When we met again in the morning, the exchange of speeches continued, rather windy and self-congratulatory on the Soviet side, unduly deferential (it seemed to me) on the American. After the intermission, I told Salisbury that I would like to interject a note of realism into the proceedings.

The Soviet delegates invariably spoke about (1) the immense Soviet losses in the Second World War and (2) the urgent need to avoid nuclear war as threatened (they implied) by the American government. I began by saying that we all shared the concern about nuclear war, but the irony was the way that each country fed the fear of the other. I recalled Norman Cousins's account of a conversation with JFK in 1963, in which the President had said that he and Khrushchev were in the same position—each striving for peace, but each opposed by the hard-liners in his own country. The hard-liners in both countries, Kennedy told Cousins, reinforce each other. In the spirit of mutual candor, I said, the Soviet colleagues should know that actions of the Soviet government—the invasion of Afghanistan, the deployment of the SS-20s in Europe, the pressure on Poland—had supplied ammunition to those in the United States who were skeptical of détente; such actions had done more than anything else to revive the Cold War mood in America.

One difference, I said, troubles us. "In the United States, we are free to criticize our generals and our leaders, their plans, conceptions and budgets. Every member of the U.S. delegation has done this. The American press is filled with such criticisms, led by our most eminent newspapers—the *New York Times,* the *Washington Post.* We look in vain for comparable criticism by our Soviet colleagues of the Soviet government and the Soviet military establishment. Surely as writers we have the obligation to speak truth to power; and, if history tells us anything, it is that no group of moral men is infallible. A society in which the citizen cannot criticize the policy of the state is a society without the means of correcting its course.

"This point applies especially to the writing of history. The purpose of history is to tell the truth about the past as best we can—for the past is irrecoverable. To write history one must have access to documents. The Bolsheviks set the world an admirable example by opening up the imperial archives. Alas, they have not followed this example themselves. In Britain and the United States, nearly all government documents are open to 1950—and to Soviet scholars. But there is no reciprocity in the USSR for Western scholars. . . . Also to write history one must not be constrained to sacrifice the past to the present. One must not distort the past to meet the supposed needs of some ruling group. Myths have their function in society, but we must preserve the distinction between myth and history. We must respect the dignity of the past, as we must hope that our descendants will respect our own dignity. That Trotsky was subsequently considered an enemy of the state is no reason to deny the reality of his role in the Revolution. History is not a myth to be manipulated in the interests of one or another ruling class. History is a debt of honor we owe to the past.

"Lasting relationships cannot be built on deception and hypocrisy. They can be built only on candor. We cannot deny or disguise the difference between a society marked by mistrust of dogma and by faith in free inquiry; and one based on a faith in the infallibility of a single ideology and of a single political party; indeed, of a single leader. These differences do not outweigh the great fate we have in common. They do not justify tensions that threaten war. They must not prevent us from working together to subdue the generals in both our countries and to move toward the control and reduction of nuclear weapons. We are willing to press our government to this end—we hope you will do the same. But let us not pretend agreement on issues of individual and intellectual freedom on which no agreement exists. And, until there is a free flow of argument and ideas throughout the planet, there can be no real, full and lasting peace."

Federenko, who looked increasingly pained through this discourse, swallowed a couple of times and said that Mr. Schlesinger had raised interesting issues to which he was sure the Soviet delegates would wish to respond. The response came at once from a fellow named Y. N. Zasursky, dean of journalism at Moscow University. He was furious; said that the Soviet delegates did not need instruction from me as to how they should behave; that this was interference in Soviet affairs, unacceptable interference, outrageous interference; that Soviet writers liked their system and did not propose to change it to please me; and that in any case my argument was founded on a false doctrine of "symmetry." By this he meant that Americans were right to criticize their bad government but had no right to demand in the name of symmetry that Soviet citizens criticize a government they respect and trust. Western scholars, he said, had better access to Soviet documents than Soviet scholars have to Western documents, etc.

Harrison Salisbury has surrendered to a sense of futility derived from too long an experience with these people. His advice to Susan Sontag: "You can either be tough, and you won't get anything useful back. Or you can say something that they will hear, and maybe you will get something back."

The Russians care mainly that the conference is held, not that it should accomplish anything. Holding the meeting is the end in itself.

Anything said is potentially dangerous; so let us talk generalities, pieties and platitudes.

Ten days in a country can yield only cursory impressions. But I fear that those who think the Soviet Union is on the verge of economic and social collapse are kidding themselves.

The USSR is an increasingly bourgeois society. The consumer ethos is on the march. The government has given much ground on state control of the economy. Private farmers' markets are crowded. Even the black market is accepted as a means of keeping the economy going. One feels increasingly that the essence of communism is not state ownership of the means of production and distribution but state ownership of the means of information and communication. Private inroads on the economy are much more acceptable than private inroads on press and television.

There remains basic incomprehension on the question of free speech and press. Most Soviet citizens cannot see the need for it and can see infinite possibilities for mischief in it, from subversion to pornography. The USSR inculcates a respect for authority that should win the admiration of those neo-conservatives who regard the decay of authority as the master source of America's troubles. This respect for authority obviously long predates communism—and is part of the explanation for communism's success.

August 19

This morning I had breakfast with Henry Kissinger at the River Club. He looked tan, having just come from Southampton where the Rohatyns have lent the Kissingers their house (while they have gone to Salzburg). He was candid, amusing, intelligent, with hardly a good word to say about anyone. He said that he liked George Shultz through the years, but that "George has no knowledge of foreign policy, none at all; worse than that, he has no feel for it. In the dozen years I have known him we have never had a conversation about foreign policy. He just doesn't think in terms of foreign policy. Making him Secretary of

State would be like making me Secretary of the Treasury. Hard as I might work to master the subject, I would never be sure in my bones that what I was doing was right. This means that George will be at the mercy of the State Department bureaucracy." I asked whether Shultz listened to him. "Yes; he listens to me. But it is hard to have much continuing impact at a distance. I think I will concentrate on speaking to him about arms control. He is *very much* against SALT II, but only because people on whose judgment he relies tell him it is a bad thing. He couldn't name three provisions in the treaty that he objects to. I will try to bring him around on that." I said that I doubted that much progress was likely on arms control so long as the negotiations did not want an agreement that did not result in American superiority. Henry: "Well, you have to distinguish among them. [Edward] Rowney doesn't want any agreement that the Russians could conceivably accept. [Gene] Rostow, I think, is crazy—really a madman. But [Paul] Nitze—Nitze is another matter. Like many older men, I think he would like to accomplish something at the end of his life. Also all he cares about are the strategic forces: he would have no problem making concessions in other areas."

He was caustic about the administration in general, from the President down. "I have known a number of Presidents and of presidential candidates," he said. "With all the rest, when you talk to them, you can feel them translating what you are telling them into 'What can I do about this?' With Reagan, you feel him translating it into 'What can I say about this?' Words are the reality for him—probably natural enough for an actor. He is the only President with whom I would rather have someone else in the room when I see him. If you talk to him alone, you can be sure that nothing will ever happen." Henry also denied that Reagan is such a nice man. "Of course he is very genial and pleasant. But he is a mean man underneath. And, if you don't believe me, just ask Howard Baker."

September 24

Mario Cuomo, to the surprise of everyone except Dick Wade, won the Democratic primary for governor yesterday. I supported him, as I had for mayor some years ago, but was surprised (though I was quoted in the *Poughkeepsie Journal* of 30 August as predicting a Cuomo victory). I have long disliked Koch as an unbridled egomaniac and an incipient racist. (The dislike is reciprocated: when he held an FDR centenary event last spring, he specified that Wade and I were not to be invited.) I have long liked Cuomo, who is an intelligent, ruminative fellow of considerable charm. Having seen Cuomo's mayoralty campaign at first hand, I had decided, however, that he was self-destructive as a candidate, and I doubted this time that he would be able to put things together. I was wrong. Dick, who was the top issue man, says that the three most important people in the campaign were Mario himself, Matilda, his nice wife, and his son Andy.

October 23

Friday was the 20th anniversary of the resolution of the missile crisis. I have given half a dozen TV and radio interviews over the past few days. Judging by these, the revisionist thesis—that JFK brought the world to the brink of war for macho or for political reasons—has not caught on. The tendency of questions was rather the opposite: did Kennedy not concede too much? was it not in the end a Soviet victory?—the Jupiters out of Turkey, and Castro still flourishing in Cuba.

November 2

Last night at Norman Mailer's Ed Doctorow asked me rather tentatively how I felt about Ted Kennedy. I explained how I felt. Doctorow said: "I am glad to hear you say that. I am for him 100 per cent. But no one I know is. I can't understand it, but I never run into anyone who is for him for President."

November 3

We spent election night at the vanden Heuvels' with the Wades, Greens, Dick Gardner, Lennie Bernstein, Bartle Bull. An entertaining time, but I was disappointed by the results. I had predicted 30–40 seats for the Democrats; instead the gain was only 26. I cannot understand why the Cuomo–[Lewis] Lehrman contest was so close; I thought Cuomo would win in a walk. Reagan has had a rebuff, but not nearly so large a one as he deserves.

I began to think about writing memoirs, which I suppose I will do one day; not that I am a natural memoirist, but I am after all a writer. One thing I must remember to do—to write about the things that really make all the difference in life: not just the great decisive things like (1) love, and (2) children, and (3) politics; but the minor things that make idiosyncratically an abiding difference—popular songs, musical comedy, food, movies, How can one do justice to the exact proportions of happiness?

December 1

We dined at Bill Paley's last night; and, shortly after we got home, the *New York Times* rang to say that Ted Kennedy would announce today his decision not to run for President in 1984. I am not altogether surprised, after the resistance I have encountered everywhere (and reported here); but I felt a great surge of regret. What the country needs is a radical departure from the existing frameworks of both domestic and foreign policy—from the domestic policy of using unemployment to fight inflation, and from the foreign policy of an indefinitely escalating nuclear arms race. Ted has stood steadfastly for alternatives to Reaganism; and he seems to me the one candidate who would have challenged the framework of policy. I don't see Mondale doing it, or Hart, or Glenn, who would now seem the most likely candidate (but remember what happened to Ed Muskie). There is no point in another Carter—someone who would only fiddle with details within the framework. We need a new framework.

George McGovern called this morning from Pittsburgh. He talked a bit about what he should tell the papers. His instinct was to confine his remarks to an expression of regret. I strongly encouraged that. He then discussed his own situation rather realistically. He asked, "Do you think I should give consideration to trying again?" I said, "Well, I don't think you should move precipitately. It will take a few days to see what the impact of Ted's announcement is. Even then I don't think you should do anything unless there is a groundswell of demand." He laughed and said, "No groundswell is visible at the moment. I have the impression that a lot of people feel I have had my chance, that it was a disaster and that I shouldn't try again." I said that I feared this was the case, and that he didn't want to be another [Harold] Stassen. "Or another Gene McCarthy," he said. "Gene runs for office every couple of years now, and is looking more and more pathetic. . . . Still, I wonder sometimes whether the feeling I shouldn't try again isn't the feeling of our own generation. Maybe the young feel differently. I get a tremendous reception these days on the campuses." Obviously George would love to be encouraged to try, but I hope to hell he doesn't. I fear I am too fond of him to present the case against his trying as bluntly as it ought to be presented to him.

December 11

The Kennedy gap remains a problem. Ken says without great enthusiasm that he expected in the end to go for Mondale, but I find no great interest in Mondale elsewhere. I dined Wednesday evening (the 8th) at Ted Sorensen's with the vanden Heuvels, the Gardners and Chick Chaikin and his wife. Ted said he regarded Gary Hart as the most intelligent of the lot, and both he and Gillian appeared to be leaning in that direction. Ted and Dick had both just come from hearing Mondale at the Council on Foreign Relations (I had meant to go, but had forgotten about it); both had found Fritz platitudinous and hortatory. Dick was particularly disappointed, and Danielle acutely so. On the plane to Washington yesterday I ran into Jack Valenti, and he too seemed inclined toward Hart.

Most people allege great relief over Ted's withdrawal.

1983

January 7

We had a dinner for Roy and Jennifer Jenkins last night (Bill Paley, Marietta, Kitty Hart, Sam Spiegel, the Smiths, the Kissingers, the Dick Gardners, Tom Wicker, Pamela Hill). Henry, playing to a liberal house, expressed careful dismay about the Reagan course on arms control. Roy having said that the "zero option" was a defensible starting position but one that would have to be abandoned in the course of negotiation, Henry said that he had always thought the zero option a poor idea. When asked about his quoted comment that the KGB may well have been behind the attempted assassination of the Pope, he said that his point had been that, even if [Yuri] Andropov had ordered the assassination, this should not stop us from trying to get progress on arms control; the two were entirely separable questions. I said that it seemed to me that, far from wishing arms control, the Reagan people really saw a nuclear arms race as the way of doing the Russians in: either they would try to keep up, in which case they would wreck their economy, or they would give up, in which case we would have decisive military superiority. Henry remarked that some people in the administration thought this, but that the real trouble was the absence of any considered position at all. He was leaving for Washington the next morning in order to urge on George Shultz the necessity for a full study and review of arms control policy.

Nancy Kissinger, whom I like a lot, sat on my left at dinner. She said that Nixon, though highly intelligent, was an awful man, "weird," who dripped poison whenever he talked and found no greater satisfaction than in setting people against each other.

January 18

Reagan has fired Gene Rostow and rebuked Paul Nitze. It is a desperate state of affairs when inveterate hard-liners like Gene and Paul are regarded by the American government as excessively soft on the Russians. All this confirms my impression that Reagan does not really want an arms agreement. A document leaked this week from the depths of the Pentagon says, in effect, that we want an unlimited arms race on the theory that it will either wreck the Soviet economy or result in unquestioned American nuclear superiority. These people don't seem to realize that they are playing with the future of humanity.

Jan Olympitis called this morning from Florida. Claiborne Pell, who was sitting with her beside some fragrant swimming pool (it is 18 Fahrenheit in New York), came on and said, "Do you remember when Joe Clark, Hubert Humphrey and I came to see you one day in the White House? It was when Kennedy was planning to establish the Arms Control and Disarmament Agency by executive order. We thought it should be done by statute, and you agreed, and eventually Kennedy did it that way. Thank God he did. Otherwise we would be in a hopeless position."

January 24

Bob Wagner had another one of his breakfasts for Democratic aspirants this morning. The guest was Gary Hart, who spoke earnestly and intelligently but not very excitingly; or so at least it seemed to me. Dick Gardner and Angie Duke, on the other hand, were greatly impressed. I have noted that Ted Sorensen, Mac Bundy and Jack Valenti are all favorably inclined toward Hart, and Kingman Brewster, when I encountered him the other day, gave me a strong Hart pitch (not necessarily a recommendation so far as I am concerned). I began to wonder, as I kept from yawning during the presentation and the questions, whether I have not been around the track too often. One becomes so familiar with the clichés of politics, the phrases, the pieties and evasions; it is like the discovery that, after a certain age, one is never likely to fall hopelessly in love again. I don't suppose I will ever enjoy the careless rapture of my engagement with Stevenson or JFK or RFK. Of course I had a genuine enthusiasm for Ted Kennedy, but that was somehow different. In any event, Gary Hart, for all his concern and (I think) decency, left me rather cool. I was somewhat cheered to discover that Tom Wicker, who was also there, felt the same way.

February 2

We went last night to a party given by Pat Lawford in honor of Norman Mailer's 60th birthday. (His actual birthday is on the 31st of January—a birthday he shares with Zane Grey, John O'Hara, Eddie Cantor and, felicitously, Norris Church.) One could not help contrasting the scene with Norman's 50th birthday and the party ten years ago at the Four Seasons, when Norman gave a birthday harangue to the audience, beginning with a dirty joke that fell terribly flat and then (as he tells the story now) going downward from there as he called for the establishment of a counter-CIA CIA. This time he was soberly dressed in a pinstripe suit with vest, looking like a jolly banker. Ted Kennedy acted as master of ceremonies, calling on people for toasts. It was a typical, high-risk Kennedy affair with much heckling. Norman accepted the adoption into the Kennedy family with evident relish and underwent a lot of kidding from Ted about his enthusiasm for Jimmy Carter in 1976.

February 7

I had breakfast this morning with Gary Hart at the Plaza. I liked him more than I expected. He is pleasant, earnest, with a genuine interest in the substance of issues. He described his childhood. He comes of Irish stock; his father was hardworking but poor. "I don't suppose he ever made over $5,000 a year. But he and my mother had one consuming purpose: to put me through college." Gary had just returned from two days in New Hampshire. I am generally a defender of the status quo in political process, but the quest for the presidential nomination has really become ridiculous. A year before the primary, and Hart, [Alan] Cranston, Mondale, etc., are already on the New Hampshire track—as if New Hampshire were representative of anything but the calendar.

Hart showed some recognition of his problems as a speaker. "You get caught either way," he said. "If you are too general, the press says it is rhetoric. If you are too programmatic, the press says it is dull. I know that I haven't been able to strike the right balance." I told him, as I had told Cranston and [Dale] Bumpers, that I wasn't in the endorsement business (as if my endorsement mattered a damn anyway) but was ready to help any liberal candidate. When I mentioned I had talked with Bumpers, Hart said, "He's my best friend in the Senate. . . . Do you think he is going to run?" I said I thought there was a 70 per cent chance he would. Hart said, "If Mo Udall pulls out next week, I suppose Dale will almost certainly go in."

March 5

We wound up the New York FDR Centennial with a ceremony at Hyde Park yesterday commemorating the 50th anniversary of the first inauguration. Like everything else the Commission has done, it was an astonishing success. In collaboration with the Four Freedoms Foundation, which Bill vanden Heuvel has now taken over, we presented (as we had done in the Netherlands in October) five Four Freedoms medals—a general one to Averell, plus a Freedom of Speech medal for

Joe Rauh, Freedom of Worship for Coretta Scott King, Freedom from Want for Bob McNamara and Freedom from Fear for Jack Javits.

Mario Cuomo gave the major address and spoke well about FDR. He seemed relaxed, though one senses considerable tension within. Demonstrators are following him around the state these days protesting cuts in the state payroll. McNamara said to him, "You have no idea how relieved I was to know that the demonstration was against you, not against me." Cuomo: "Well, we would be happy to put on one against you. I don't want anyone to feel left out."

Then we adjourned to luncheon at the Rectory. Fritzy Goodman, my wonderful collaborator on the Centennial Commission and a splendid organizer, had been vague when I asked her about the luncheon program; and it turned out to be a celebration of me. I would have stopped it had I been consulted in advance; and I always feel hopelessly inadequate and graceless in response; but I suppose I am glad that it happened.

I am vastly relieved that the Centennial Commission is now concluded. It took far more time than I expected and delayed starting the next FDR book by a considerable period. But it was a useful thing to have done, gave pleasure to many people and, I think, helped revive the Roosevelt ethos for a new generation.

As we were driving to Hyde Park on Thursday, I heard over the car radio the disconcerting news that Arthur Koestler, who has been suffering from leukemia and Parkinson's disease, had killed himself. His wife [Cynthia Jefferies], much younger and healthier, had joined him in the suicide pact. The news was disconcerting but somehow not surprising. It is the kind of final gesture that would have appealed to him, an eminently rational but outrageous act; also the final note of selfishness, in persuading his wife to go with him, was characteristic. I knew Koestler well for half a dozen years, from the founding of the Congress for Cultural Freedom in Berlin in 1950 through his American years to the mid-1950s, when he abruptly turned his back on politics and on people he had known during his last political phase. I liked him a great deal, and liked Mamaine Paget, his beautiful and poignant [previous] wife, even more. He was a dangerous man, always poised, one felt, on the edge of some unforgivable slashing remark or some indecipherable explosion. But he was brilliant, funny in a sardonic way, loaded with charm when he was in the mood and darkly vibrant with a somewhat melodramatic sense of history. I will never forget one evening when Koestler and [Gaetano] Salvemini came to dinner in Cambridge, and a generation apart, talked about the experience of totalitarianism, both men of passion, eloquence, humor and intense historical irony. I can't remember when I saw Arthur last; it was in London a few years ago; we chatted a moment but nothing remained. Politics had become a closed chapter in his life, and he had long since moved on to science, his youthful vocation, and meta-science, the obsession of his last years. A strange, intense and remarkable man.

June 20

We lunched yesterday with Bill and Wendy Luers. I first met Bill Luers some years ago when he was our ambassador to Venezuela, and a highly successful one.

We talked a good deal about Central America. This is intellectually a tough problem. My own inclination is to stay out and let nature take its course. "Every country," David Harlech once said, "has a right to its own Wars of the Roses." I do not see the Soviet Union assuming the financial burden of keeping Nicaragua and El Salvador afloat nor the military risk of converting them into missile bases. If Marxist victories in these countries are a threat to the hemisphere, they are initially a threat to Mexico, Costa Rica, Panama, Venezuela, Colombia; so these countries should take the lead in the formulation of remedies.

Bill thinks that we cannot reject responsibility. He is against the CIA attempt to overthrow them. He feels that the Sandinistas are lost to democracy. Because it so difficult for the Latin American countries to go along with our policy, on balance, he thinks we must make an effort in El Salvador, provide economic and military assistance conditioned on reforms, but assure the regime of our continuing support.

I said that, as soon as we assured the regime of our continuing support, it would forget about reform, and in time we would become its prisoner, as we had become the prisoner of successive regimes in Saigon. Also, once our prestige became involved, then, given the fighting (or non-fighting) qualities of the regular army, our combat troops would in time become involved too. Already one hears talk of avoiding the alleged fallacy of our approach to Vietnam—incrementalism—and sending in overwhelming force at once. I said that I did not think the Marines could go into El Salvador and clean out the guerrillas in a few weeks or months. Bill agreed.

Bill also agreed that my dismal larger scenario was a possibility, but still thought we had no alternative but to try for "constructive engagement." Maybe I am getting tired and cynical, but I despair of our capacity to go into other countries and set things straight. On the other hand, our friends—our democratic friends, not the D'Aubuissons—surely deserve at least as much support as Cuba and the Soviet Union are giving *their* friends. All choices are terrible. Before parting, Bill and I agreed that the top priority had to be the development of a program that the neighboring Latin American countries would support.

July 23

Alexandra and I returned this morning from a sad journey to Charlottesville. Two weeks ago my brother was stricken by an aneurism, which ruptured, hemorrhaged and flooded the frontal lobes of his brain. For a time there was hope of recovery, but Tom then lapsed into a stuporous condition close to coma. After this went on for several days, we decided to go down.

We visited Tom three times yesterday in the intensive care ward of the University of Virginia hospital. Tom and I have not really been all that close; but this experience affected me more than I would have expected. There was my kid brother, lying unconscious on the bed, tubes running into his nostrils, other wires recording sensations in various parts of the body, one eye still caked with blood from his last hemorrhage. He responds on occasion to stimuli, especially in the morning. When I spoke to him—"This is Art, Tom"; Tom is the only person in the world who calls me Art—a convulsive tremor shot through his tanned and quite powerful body, and for a few seconds his lips trembled as if he were straining to speak. Catherine, his charming, highly intelligent and tremendously devoted wife, has noticed similar reactions to the sound of her voice and the pressure of her hand. It was heart-breaking, and I was considerably shaken.

What is more heartbreaking is the growing conviction on the part of Tom's doctors—T. R. Johns and Richard Winn, both of whom struck us as admirably candid, realistic and concerned—that he has almost certainly suffered irreversible brain damage resulting in permanent intellectual impairment and grave distortion of personality.

This is the kind of situation that one reads about in the papers and considers in the abstract. At a distance it is easy to say: if a person is going to be dangerously incapacitated, better let him die. Alexandra and I have signed declarations saying that we do not want in such circumstances to be kept artificially alive. Yet when faced with a concrete person—husband, father, brother—it is not so easy, especially in view of the responses that Catherine and I think we have seen. The fact that he has not recovered consciousness confirms the apprehensions of the doctors; patients with a prospect of full recovery do not stay for so long a time in coma.

I shudder as I write these lines and am overcome with sadness—in part the sadness of things not done and not said over the years.

Tom's tragedy comes on the heels of another great sadness: my faithful Gretchen Stewart, who has been my secretary (except for a brief interval) since I went to the White House twenty-two years ago, is down with cancer of the liver. She is dangerously sick and has gone back to Kansas to spend these last days in the midst of her family. I don't suppose I have ever noted in these pages how much I owe to Gretchen. Through the years she has eased and ordered my life, saved me from excess and error, acted as my conscience and my protector, stayed far too long hours and worked far too hard—and has done it all with such an exacting sense of responsibility, such incomparable tact and efficiency and with such inexhaustible sweetness of temper.

I have entered the orbit of mortality and will never leave it.

August 19

On Thursday the 16th I lunched with Henry Kissinger at the Four Seasons—his invitation. When Reagan appointed him chairman of the commission on Central American policy, I had written him a letter outlining some of his problems, as I saw them. Luncheon was his response. He was his usual charming/funny/devious/satisfied self, and we had a good time. On Reagan: "Most politicians translate everything into: what do I do about it? He translates everything into: what do I say about it?" Henry commented, as he had before, on Reagan's tendency to illustrate everything by Hollywood anecdotes. On Shultz: "He is tone-deaf when it comes to foreign policy. . . . I still can't figure out how foreign policy decisions are made in this administration. In the Carter administration, whether the decisions were good or bad, you could at least figure out the structure. And Brzezinski and Vance at least knew something about foreign policy. Have we ever had decisions made by people with less knowledge of foreign affairs? Reagan? Clark? Shultz? Weinberger?"

We talked mostly about the commission. Nancy, who had called here a few days before, had told me that she was strongly opposed to his taking the job and ascribed his acceptance to the "immigrant boy" complex—the idea that you can never refuse to do anything a President asks you to do. Henry claims he vacillated a good deal, turned against the proposal when Clark made it, moved toward it when Shultz seconded it but decided he wanted first to talk to Gerald Ford and asked Shultz not to have Reagan call him unless he decided to accept. He then put in a call to Ford, who was on the golf course at Palm Springs. He waited for Ford to call back; and, when the phone rang and the operator said "The President is calling," Henry assumed it was Ford. It turned out to be Reagan, who pressed him to take the job. Henry accepted. Then Ford called a few minutes later and thought Henry had made a mistake. Much distressed, according to his account, Henry went out to dinner and decided to turn the offer down. He immediately called Shultz and said he could not do it. Shultz said, "You are too late. The announcement is already on the wires."

He is of course well aware of the pitfalls. He says he has rigorously separated himself from current operations. (In other contexts he has argued that operations determine policy.) He does not think, however, that large-scale military intervention is likely, or that options will be seriously foreclosed by the time the report is made (early next year). Bill Rogers and Winston Lord will write the report. I asked whether he had had any voice in the selection of the commission. He said, "No. I had sort of a veto power. I did stop a couple of nominations." He did not say who they were but went on to say that he had not wanted [Robert] Strauss and has proposed Muskie (who would have been infinitely better) but had not got him. His aim is to rebuild a foreign policy consensus by getting a unified report. I said that I didn't think this likely unless the commission was prepared to repudiate the Reagan course of militarizing the remedy. He said that he hoped to get agreement on the diagnosis; this would leave room for disagreement on the tactics.

He decided to ask the living ex-Presidents to appear before the commission. "Nixon, as usual, immediately started making conditions. Above all, he insisted that he would meet the commission only in New York, not in Washington, and that they would have to come to his office. So we dropped that. Carter was agreeable until I emphasized that we were concerned, not with immediate policy, but with the longer run—3–5 years. For some reason Carter took this as a personal criticism and went off in a long tirade about how he always took the long view; in his administration they always were thinking ahead, not 3–5 years, but much longer. Later I told Ford that I was prepared to certify in writing that he is our only sane ex-President."

Henry affected to regard Jeane Kirkpatrick as the evil genius of our Central American policy. "I used to like her when I saw her around New York," he said; then shrugged expressively. Bill Styron had put him in touch with Carlos Fuentes, whom Henry said he liked very much and agreed "generally" with. I would like to have seen those two con men charming each other. Rose Styron tells me, however, that Carlos reported an enjoyable talk with Henry but little agreement, which I suspect is closer to the truth.

At one point Henry said, "What do you think of the Seymour Hersh book [*The Price of Power*]?" I said truthfully that I had not read it. This did not deter him from going on for a few moments about how inaccurate the book was, how unfair, how Hersh did not understand foreign policy, etc. Whatever else Hersh did he struck a nerve. There are even those who say that Henry took on the commision in order to distract attention from the book. Later in the week I saw Bob McNamara reading the book on South Beach. I asked him what he thought. "A prosecutor's brief," he said, "but interesting." He obviously did not feel that the book should be burned.

August 22

We dined last night at Jackie Onassis's in her new house near Gay Head. Maurice Tempelsman was there.

We had heard on the car radio earlier in the day the shocking news that Benigno Aquino, the leader of the anti-Marcos opposition, had been assassinated as he returned from exile to Manila. I knew that Tempelsman was a good friend of Bill Blair, and I knew that Bill detests the Marcoses; and, without thinking, I started to mention the affair, of which the company had not heard. Once I was irretrievably embarked on the recital, it suddenly occurred to me that this was the last household in the world to start talking about assassination. Jackie is very tough, though, and did not appear to notice. She is also highly intelligent and very witty and was in excellent form last night.

September 17

I testified before Henry Kissinger's National Bipartisan Commission on Central America. I took in general a neo-isolationist line and doubted whether the Alliance for Progress could work in the absence of political parties and leaders committed to democratic social improvement. The questions were interesting, but my mind was elsewhere and I don't think I handled them as well as I might have done. Afterward Henry said, "I hope you won't be surprised if our group comes out for something like a revival of the Alliance for Progress. That is one thing we all seem to be in agreement on, and it's the only way I will be able to move them away from the military remedies." I said that I hoped my negativism had not hurt this laudable strategy. He said no; it had helped; but did not explain why. He also said during the hearing that Jeane Kirkpatrick had been one of those recommending that I be called, and that Tom Mann and I had made much the same argument. I said that I was sure Tom Mann would be as much surprised by this as I am.

October 15

A crisp, brilliant fall day—the temperature about 66, and so am I. It is hard to believe. I sometimes feel 99, and sometimes 33, but never 66. When I see a person designated as 66 in the papers, my automatic reaction is "really old" till it occurs to me that I am on (now over) the verge myself. But in this summer of intimate death it is splendid to be alive. (As Maurice Chevalier used to say, "Consider the alternative.") I am in pretty good shape (I hope)—at least I feel OK most of the time. I bicycle 5 miles every morning on the stationary bicycle upstairs and walk home from my office (1^1/$_4$ miles) every afternoon. I smoke too many cigars, but am trying to cut down. I drink before luncheon and dinner but never after. Nor dare I underestimate the extent to which Alexandra, Robert and Peter keep me feeling young, or least keep me from feeling old.

October 30

On Tuesday, the 25th, Reagan invaded Grenada. An enormous triumph for the republic—a nation of 230 million launching a surprise attack on a small island of 110 thousand. Fortunately we won. This will certainly make the Russians think twice. Reagan obviously hopes to make us the terror of the world but he is more likely to end up making us the world's laughingstock.

I made these and similar remarks Wednesday night before a group of IBM executives and customers. Never have I given a talk that went down with such a dull thud. It is obvious that the Grenadan victory fills many Americans with enormous pleasure and pride. The polls report immense approval. I trust that the nation will return to its senses before too long. I am sure that the residual impact will be to increase apprehension over Reagan as a trigger-happy President.

November 13

On 9 November I left for Rochester, Michigan, where I spoke at Oakland University about JFK.

On the plane to Michigan I ran into Abby Hoffman. I did not recognize him at first: face furrowed, neatly trimmed beard, manner subdued—quite a change from the Abby Hoffman of 1968, but then he has been through a lot in the years since. We had a nice talk. His consuming interest now is conservation of the Great Lakes. I asked whether any of the Democratic candidates moved him at all. He said, with a flash of the old Abby, "Well, I guess Jesse Jackson more than anyone else."

The next day I went on to Texas, where I spoke at the University of Texas in Tyler. East Texas is the most reactionary part of the most reactionary state in the union; but here, as elsewhere in Texas, there is a staunch if beleaguered liberal underground. I let go on the subject of Grenada, pointing out that during the missile crisis RFK had turned the tide against a sneak military attack on Cuba by arguing that such a course was contrary to the best American traditions and ideals. How we have progressed since 1962! Pearl Harbor is a date that will live in infamy, I continued, and why? because it was a sneak attack, delivered without warning; but at least the Japanese were picking on someone their own size, not on a pathetic island of 110,000 people without army, navy or air force. When I finished, about a quarter of the audience gave a standing ovation, and the other three quarters seemed ready to form a lynch mob. The sad fact is that our glorious victory over the Grenadans seems extremely popular, and no one cares how it came about. Pearl Harbors are evidently OK when we are the perpetrators; wicked only when we are the victims.

November 26

Last Tuesday was the 20th anniversary of JFK's murder. I have been involved in a lot of interviews, television and radio shows, etc., in connection with the anniversary. It has all stirred a turmoil of emotions in me, partly remembrance of things past, partly exasperation over the incomprehension of the present. Nothing is more exasperating than the revisionist idea that JFK was a reckless, risk-taking, macho Cold Warrior. On the contrary, he was cautious, circumspect and conciliatory. There can be no doubt about this whatever. On the morning of the 22nd Ted Sorensen and I appeared together on the *Today* show in Washington, and in the evening David Harlech came for a drink in New York. Both Ted and David probably knew JFK better than I did, and both agree completely on the total falsity of the revisionist portrait. Nor can this portrait be reconciled with his constant refusal of escalation and search for negotiation. Yet the revisionists cannot be dissuaded; do not wish to be dissuaded. One feels almost an obscure and sour envy of Kennedy and of people like him—too handsome, too popular, too rich, too beautiful a wife; and historians have their own way of paying back.

We went to Washington for the mass. We spent the night at Joe Alsop's and went to dinner at Kay Graham's—old times. The mass was quite beautiful; Ted, as so often, rose superbly to the occasion in his own remarks. We had been invited to Ethel's for luncheon afterward, but I had to return to New York for my seminar. In a way I was sorry, because there were people whom I would like to have seen. In a way, not, because of the turmoil of emotions.

November 30

At 3:15 I went off to Kitty Hart's to meet the Harrimans. Bill Walton had given us a rather depressing account of Averell in advanced dilapidation, but this turned out to be an exaggeration. Soon after I arrived I heard him call "Arthur" from an inner room. This recalled at once a spring afternoon in 1948 when I was sitting in Joe Alsop's garden, and Averell was coming by. I can still remember his call in advance of his appearance. It was then he asked me to go to Paris with him and work on the Marshall Plan. He is increasingly blind, but not too blind not to notice and admire the red striped Hilditch & Key shirt I was wearing. He was good humored and perfectly lucid about everything he could hear. He went off with Pam to the house of Mike Sovern, the president of Columbia, for a meeting of the board of the Harriman Institute, during which Averell stayed awake rather more successfully than I did.

George Kennan and Clark Clifford were among those present, and the talk turned to the present state of Soviet-American relations. One could not help reflecting that, in the revisionist lexicon, Harriman, Kennan and Clifford were arch-villains in bringing on the Cold War. Clifford said, "The relationship between the United States and the Soviet Union is at the lowest and most dangerous point in history. I don't blame the Soviet people for regarding the United States as the enemy. How can they not when they hear our President's talk? Our leaders display a deep and implacable misunderstanding of the motives of the Soviet Union." Kennan said, "Treat them as outsiders, criminals, crooks and so on, and they will begin to act that way. Their primary feeling is insecurity. . . . This is the most dangerous minute I can remember in Soviet-American relations. . . . The deterioration since 1973 seems to me basically unnecessary. We all know how difficult they are to deal with, but the failure to work out practical if limited relations is mostly to be blamed on us." Clifford: "Every other President has tried at some point to get along with the Soviet Union. This President alone has chosen *not* to get along with the Soviet Union." Averell applauded these sentiments. All very depressing.

December 9

Political update; it looks more and more certain that Fritz Mondale will get the nomination, but people look to this result with, at best, weary inevitability. I have not encountered a Mondale enthusiast. I imagine it will end up a Mondale-Glenn ticket, since Glenn will do everything for Mondale in the South that a southern candidate could do, and will do more for him in the North; also Glenn on the ticket will nullify Republican attempts to use Glenn's current "weak-on-defense" attacks on Mondale.

I have known Fritz for many years. He is a fine man, decent, intelligent, conscientious, humorous, basically liberal. He is also a repressed and somewhat irascible Scandinavian and, I fear, too weak and too anxious to please. He comes from the Minnesota or rather Humphrey school of politicians who hate saying anything that would displease the person or audience they are addressing. I don't see Fritz regarding the counsel of the Joint Chiefs of Staff with the scorn it deserves. He lacks the proper irreverence for the establishment. I will have no problem in voting for him. But I doubt that he can beat Reagan.

December 15

Lally Weymouth gave a dinner last night for a West German named Karsten Voight, an SPD spokesman on Soviet-Western relations. He was fluent and intelligent but not especially impressive.

George K. was in particularly good form. Ruminating about American self-assertion and chauvinism, he said that he supposed it to be in part because "we are a nation populated by immigrants, who are under the constant need to prove that they are really loyal Americans." Europe, he said, had had a "deeper historical experience than the United States." America lacked a sense of sin; and "a sense of sin about oneself is the first prerequisite when judging others." He concluded by saying that he had been accustomed for years, when people were deploring Soviet behavior, to say, "You have to be patient with them," but it never had occurred to him that at some point he would be saying about his fellow countrymen, "You have to be patient with them."

December 22

Typically New York round yesterday night. We went to dinner at the flat of a woman named Judy Green. Mixed crowd: Cleveland Amory, Julie and Maggie Styne, plus a lot of people I have never seen before.

We left around 11 and made our way to the west side for a party at Mick Jagger's. The whole thing was rather mysterious—especially why were we asked. But Jerry Hall, who is seven months pregnant with the Jagger heir and may or may not be making an honest man of him in the next few weeks, is an amiable, very pretty, tallish Texan, who likes Alexandra, who no doubt makes her feel short. So A. was invited to her baby shower the other day, and we received the invitation to the party last night. We expected a packed house with a lot of drinking, cocaine, noise, etc. Instead, it was a party of only moderate size and, so far as we could see (we left shortly before 1 A.M.), entirely seemly. Most people were young, except for Norman Mailer, Andy Warhol, Jean Stein and Ahmet Ertegun (who could not get over the fact that we were there—actually we met Mick Jagger first at his house). The house was quite fine—not large, but a c. 1890 brownstone with elegant moldings and panelling, including marble in the stairwell. Mick Jagger appeared from some upstairs retreat and sat down and talked for half an hour or so, mostly about communism, war, the threat of Cap Weinberger and so on. He is alert, funny, intelligent (Alexandra told me later he had attended LSE [the London School of Economics]—can this be so?) and interested in public affairs; he speaks in a rather impenetrable cockney accent, with much expression and vivacity. Very graceful in body movements when he danced. As we were putting on our coats to go, he suddenly reappeared to say goodbye. Well mannered. I liked him. But I still could not understand why we were there.

December 26

Christmas passed equably yesterday—indeed, very cheerfully.

I have sometimes reflected (perhaps I have already confided the reflection to this journal) that, when Robert goes to college in 1990, it will be the first time since 1942 that I will have lived in a household without children in it. Nearly half a century—and I wonder whether I will be able to stand it. Children, heaven knows, can be pains in the ass. But they add immeasurably to the fun, the fulfillment and the wonder of life. As I look at my contemporaries who write book after book, I think occasionally (more than ever these years, when I have not written a book for five years and when I must recognize that I have only a finite number of book-writing years left) how many more books I might have written had there not been children always around. But I am absolutely clear in mind that, if I had the choice to make again, I would have made it the same way. Last night, as Robert was going to bed, we talked for a moment about what a nice Christmas it had been. He left, then returned and said simply, "I love you, Dad." The best words in the world.

December 28

We went to Newport on Monday (on Jan Cushing's private plane) for a pleasant dinner party with Alexandra's beautiful and entertaining cousin Minnie Cushing, Claiborne and Nuella Pell, my old friend John Slocum and his wife, Noreen Drexel and her husband, etc. I came back the next morning with Margaux Hemingway and her rather intelligent husband Bernard Fouchet. Margaux is a charming, open, agreeable girl, not especially bright but warm and good-hearted. I like her.

I mentioned Margaux to George Plimpton when we lunched today. This led him into Hemingway reminiscence. I recall two stories in particular. Once, after they had spent a morning deepsea fishing together,

George asked Hemingway about the bird imagery in his sex scenes. Hemingway growled, "What do you mean?" George thought it would help if he were more specific, so he mentioned the scene in *Across the River* when the colonel penetrates the contessa in a gondola, and, after climax, a white dove flies out of the boat. Hemingway's eyes narrowed, his face turned a furious red, and he said to George, "Do you think you could have done it better?" I asked George whether Hemingway was angry because he felt threatened by psychological interpretations of his imagery or because he resented criticism of his literary tricks. George said emphatically the second; "it was a poor device, and he knew it, and he hated having it pointed out." He hated it so much that in the midst of lunch he challenged George to a fight. No sooner had they put on gloves than Hemingway shot a blow to the head that staggered George and made him see stars. It might have become an ugly scene, George thinks, but he had the presence of mind to drop his fists and say, "That was amazing, Poppa, how did you do it?" Poppa loved playing the role of teacher, George says, and he quickly relaxed and took pleasure in showing George how he had contrived the punch.

The other story involved a meeting arranged by Ken Tynan between Hemingway and Tennessee Williams. This took place in Havana in 1959 shortly after Castro came to power. Williams, evidently in a nervous dither, arrived an hour late, dressed as if he were the commodore of a small local yacht club. Hemingway looked at him with great wariness and said nothing. Williams desperately tried to break the ice by saying, "I knew Pauline [Hemingway's first wife]. Whatever happened to her?" Hemingway replied, "She died, and now she is dead." Silence. Williams tried again. "This reminds me of my first meeting with Faulkner," he said. "It took place in Rome. We met at a bar. When I arrived, his head was bowed, as if in reverie. When he raised his head, I could see that there were tears in his eyes." Hemingway looked at Williams and said: "Good try." Things improved in due course, and finally Williams left for dinner. Hemingway said to Plimpton, "What in Christ's name was that costume he was wearing?"

December 31

More on the Nixon revival. Last night we dined at Mortimer's with Jerry Brown and Lally Weymouth. Jerry said that, if he were President, he would send Nixon to Moscow to negotiate an arms control agreement. I said I thought anything that rehabilitated Nixon was a bad idea. "Yes," Jerry said, "but suppose you got arms control in exchange? That would be worth the price of Nixon's rehabilitation." Perhaps he is right, and very likely Nixon is the one man who could negotiate an agreement that would be simultaneously acceptable to the Kremlin and the hard right.

I recalled the old story about Pat Brown listening to the election returns in 1968 and saying, "Why I thought I finished that fellow off in 1962"; to which someone responded, "Yes, but you forgot to drive a stake through his heart." Jerry Brown to my surprise said he had never heard the story before.

This was the longest time we had spent with Jerry Brown, and we both liked him. He is bright, eager, interested and unpretentious. The Zen Buddhist side of him, if still there, was not evident. He is spending his time these days running various research institutes and political action committees. He is for Cranston in 1984 and seems to have genuine regard for him.

1984

❖

February 11

I went to Washington last Wednesday to give the American Film Institute's annual Patricia Wise lecture. Kay Graham asked me to lunch at the *Post* with David Broder, Brigitte Weeks and a couple of other people. Broder, just back from New Hampshire, said that Mondale was still well ahead, that Jackson and Hart were gaining and that Cranston was faltering. "One man this campaign has changed my opinion of," Broder added, "and that is George McGovern. He has been excellent on the issues and excellent in his attitude toward the others and toward the party. A very classy performance."

After luncheon Kay asked me to stay for a while. She said she had decided to write her memoirs. She plans to do it herself. Unfortunately, she says, her memory is not very good, nor does she seem to have much in the way of personal letters, but she plans to interview people—Bob Lovett, Prich, Joe Rauh, etc.—in order to prime the pump. I think she really has two things in mind—to tell the story of her parents, and to assemble her ideas on management. She plans to write the book herself. I encouraged her to go ahead.

February 24

I have not written recently about politics because I have shared the general assumption that—as I assured people in Berlin and London—Fritz Mondale had it all wrapped up. Wrong again. Gary Hart's strong win in New Hampshire yesterday reminds one once again why politics is so much fun—the best of all spectator sports (and not a bad participant sport either). It is not clear how far Gary will be able to go; he is not well set up for the southern primaries. But he has destroyed the idea of Mondale's inevitability and opened up the contest. What happens now will be, among other things, a test of Mondale. I remember when Estes Kefauver beat Adlai Stevenson (backed by Hubert Humphrey and the state organization) in Minnesota in 1956. This was a great shock, but it galvanized Adlai who came back vigorously and demolished Estes in subsequent primaries. If Mondale can do this, he will have added the human touch (return from adversity) and ignited the drama that his campaign has lacked. His trouble is that no one I have encountered is really enthusiastic about him; his great strength has been the conviction of inevitability. Now he has a chance to generate enthusiasm.

I am glad that Hart won in New Hampshire. The Mondale crowd is second-rate and filled with complacency, and it needs to be shaken up. I think Fritz is better than the people immediately around him (at least the issues people), and his capacity to respond to this setback will be a measure of his capacity to be an effective President.

March 20

They are voting today in Illinois, and we will have a better sense of things tomorrow. In the meantime, I am inclined to vote for Gary Hart in the New York primary a fortnight today but disinclined to endorse him (not that my endorsement will make any difference to anything).

Why am I inclined to vote for him? Because I think he will be the strongest candidate against Reagan, because I think he will introduce new possibilities into our politics, because I think he is much better on foreign policy, especially on Central America, than Mondale, because I was impressed when we breakfasted a few months ago by what seemed an authentic interest in substance and remedy. The trouble with Fritz is the collection of old Washington hacks who have been planning to ride back to power on his coattails. The time has come for some new hacks.

Why am I disinclined to endorse him? Because he is a self-created figure, and in consequence surrounded by legends of his own fabrication. The *Wall Street Journal* the other day had rather a touching story about his beginnings in Ottawa, Nebraska. The progress from a severe Nazarene household in a small Nebraska town is almost a Dreiser story. But he invented himself along the way. If Nixon is the Clyde Griffiths of American politics, Gary Hart is the Gatsby. Now the legends are catching up with him. We know that he changed his name from Hartpence (but who can blame him? otherwise he would be known as Gary Hotpants; yet he should have admitted that he changed it himself and not said it was his father's idea); that he has changed his birthday, his handwriting, his church; that he has a phoney naval commission. None of these things is significant in itself. The cumulative effect is disturbing, if only because one wonders how many unexploded land mines remain ahead. On the other hand, one can be sure that Lane Kirkland's research staff is working day and night to explode them as quickly as possible.

There is also a "man of destiny" sense about Hart. FDR and JFK never saw themselves as men of destiny. They had no doubt they were better than the competition, but they retained a sense of irony about themselves. Hart laughs a lot and tells jokes, but I am not clear whether he has the distancing value of irony and I fear the Nazarenes may have instilled a messianic strain before he abandoned them.

March 26

Edna O'Brien has been delightfully in town, and on Saturday I took her to Tom Wicker's for dinner. Carlos and Sylvia Fuentes were guests of honor. Jerry Brown was there too and took a fancy to Edna. I was very tired for some reason, made no contribution to the evening and, when the others wanted to go off to Elaine's at midnight, I begged off and went home. Edna called the next morning to say that Jerry Brown, whom she liked, had taken her back to the Algonquin around two, stopped for a drink and, when they discovered the bar was closed, had taken her to some dance hall around the corner, where they stayed till six. "When I got back to the hotel," Edna said in her lovely, lilting Irish voice "they looked at me as if I were a fallen woman." She went to bed, and at seven the phone rang. It was Jerry saying that his plane was not leaving at eight, as he had supposed, but at eleven, and would she have breakfast with him. (She didn't.)

April 26

David Kennedy was found dead in Palm Beach yesterday. I still remember that March morning in Hickory Hill sixteen years ago when David asked me, "Is Daddy going to run for President?" He was then 12, a sweet boy. The murder devastated him more perhaps than it did the others, or he was at a more vulnerable age or had a more vulnerable psyche. Ethel was loving, unpredictable, demanding and hysterical and could control neither her children nor herself. David went on drugs and in time became a desperate young man, with haunted eyes, filled with anger against his family and himself. He made intermittent efforts to come back and, according to Michael Curtis of the *Atlantic Monthly* on television this morning, did well as an intern there and was much liked. But he had been so deep into heroin and for so long that he had ended in a land from which few travelers return.

I had taken Alexandra to a birthday luncheon at the bar of the Four Seasons. Suddenly a hand fell on my shoulder. I looked up, and it was Henry Kissinger. I had not seen him since I wrote a critique of his Central American report for the *Times*. He said, "I just wanted to say that your piece in the *Journal* last Friday was the most brilliant, the most perceptive, thing I have ever read on Reagan." I was a little surprised since the piece, while no doubt brilliant and perceptive, was hardly favorable. Then Henry added, "The only trouble is that the alternative is worse, so, grudgingly, I am going to have to support Reagan." I could not help thinking that this was a characteristic Kissinger counterpoint. We chatted amiably for a few moments. He finally said, "What has happened to the old Democratic tradition—social reform and a strong foreign policy—FDR and JFK—the tradition of the Democrats I used to meet at your house in the 1950s?" I said that it still existed and was just as determined to save Central America as he was but doubted that military intervention was the answer. He said, "Yes, but diplomacy cannot work without the military factor—but we will have to discuss this at another time."

April 28

I attended David Kennedy's funeral mass yesterday. It was held on the terrace at Hickory Hill—a lovely day, fragrant with spring, the deep green grass rolling away toward the swimming pool and tennis court. I thought of all the happy times I have had through the years at Hickory Hill, and the sad times too. The younger brothers read prayers; Kathleen spoke charmingly about David; so did Ted Kennedy, choking back tears. I looked at Ted and Sarge Shriver, once so young and slim, now both gray and portly; even Steve's hair is now white. Ethel was composed, pale, rather beautiful. It was a profoundly sad occasion.

The cover of the program was a letter that David, then 12 years old, had sent his mother after Bobby's death—the Donne quotation, "Death be not proud . . ." carefully written and decorated—heartbreaking.

May 14

I did the Ted Koppel show with Bill Buckley and the Undersecretary of State, a smooth managerial type named Kenneth Dam. I am compelled to confess that my old dislike of Buckley has given way to a certain liking, if not affection. I surmise that a reciprocal change has taken place on his side. I surmise also that Alistair Horne, and also perhaps Pat Buckley, whom I greatly like, are responsible for the mutual softening. We differed, of course, but amiably; we had enjoyable talk off camera; and when we went our separate ways in the night, Buckley said improbably, "Good night, my dear."

May 19

We sold the Hobe Sound house this week. Sad—at least Peter, Robert and I feel so; Alexandra, who enjoyed it less, is, I think, rather relieved. The reason we sold it is financial. I have not published a book for five years, and have none immediately in prospect. Alimony consumes my CUNY salary. We live from lecture to lecture and piece to piece. I do not even have a savings account. I have also had to put aside the FDR book for the time being, much to my sorrow, in order to do a political/historical book (*The Cycles of American History*) that will bring me a large advance ($350,000) and keep my name alive. I hope to do that this summer; it will be based largely on articles already written; and then get down to FDR in the winter.

But it is sad about Hobe Sound. I loved the house and the beach and the swimming; nothing was more restful and restorative. The only trouble was that we got down there so seldom ourselves. Rental barely paid the taxes and repairs. It was simply not practical to keep it. But sad all the same.

Last night we saw Shirley MacLaine's one-woman show at the Gershwin. She is a prodigy of energy, talent and charm. She is on stage for more than 90 minutes, singing, dancing, reminiscing, chatting— always vibrant, lithe, funny, inexhaustible. Afterward we (Alexandra,

Sam Spiegel and I) took her to dinner. She wanted to see a show in a nightspot at 11:30, so we ate at Garvin's (where Stephen and Judy had their wedding party) and then went over to the Bottom Line for a brilliantly choreographed though excessively loud rock performance. I had never really liked rock music before, but I liked this one a lot, apart from the decibel level. Shirley was adorable, less manic and crazy than in other years. She is highly intelligent, interestingly reflective and rather amused, if stubborn, about her mystical convictions. I like her very much. In fact, I find great pleasure in the company of intelligent actresses, of whom there seem to be quite a number around.

Pat Moynihan and I are going to be co-hosts of a fundraiser for George McGovern on 30 May. George and Nixon have made contact with each other, and George is pleased by this, a little too pleased in my view. The other day someone called from his office and said, "We want to pass an idea before you. What would you think if Nixon were to be invited to the party?" I said, "I think it is a terrible idea; and, if Nixon comes, I won't." She said, "Well that is what we want to know and why we called. It seemed a far-out idea, but we thought we would find out what people thought." Query in my mind: did George put her up to calling? I love George, but sometimes he goes off the rails.

July 2

I returned [from a trip to Europe] to find the political scene extremely gloomy. Pamela Harriman told me yesterday that Pat Cadell says his polls indicate a Reagan landslide, comparable to 1936. Mondale now has the nomination wrapped up; but he is engaged in a demeaning series of interviews, a la Jimmy Carter, with vice presidential possibilities and is embarrassed by Jesse Jackson and his pal [Louis] Farrakhan. He appears a man in a mire.

I had written him before we left saying that I thought the time had come for the party to rally around his candidacy and set to work to beat Reagan. On Friday Fred Martin, John Bartlow's son and a Mondale speechwriter, called me. He said that Fritz thanked me for the letter and would like to have my thoughts about the acceptance speech. I asked Fred what thoughts Fritz had—had he given any indications about the line he thought the speech should take? Fred answered, rather uncomfortably, "No. That's not the way he works. He doesn't tell us what he wants. We give him drafts and learn what he wants by his reaction."

I found this a little depressing. Mondale is seen by too many voters today as a man who is the sum of the special interests that support him. This is unfair, since no politician has ever served more special interests than Reagan. But Reagan gives the impression of a man of vision into which his special interests fit. The question is whether Mondale has a personal vision that will include and transcend the special interests that back him. The only hope is to let Mondale be Mondale. His acceptance speech must not appear to be more calculation and contrivance. It must spring from his head, heart and gut. He must say what he really thinks. It is his only chance of winning. But what if there is no thought there?

Later. Stephen has described to me Mario Cuomo's meeting over his keynote address. While he asked each of the several aides assembled for ideas, it soon became apparent that he had the whole speech figured out in his mind and knew precisely what he wanted to say and how he wanted to say it. What a contrast with the candidate!

Lillian Hellman died last weekend. I cannot honestly say that I wept many tears. I first met her with Ed O'Connor more than a quarter of a century ago. My anti-Stalinism made me an object of suspicion to her, as her Stalinism made her an object of suspicion to me; but we hit it off rather well at the start and became friends. She was capable of great wit and charm and was one of those fairly unforgettable characters. In later years I fell afoul of her over some political point and was expelled to the outer darkness for a season. Then the relationship renewed somewhat, but was rather polite and potentially prickly. Her suit against Mary McCarthy finished her so far as I was concerned, and I have avoided her the last couple of years (as on the Vineyard last summer—not that she evinced any desire to see me). She was of course a pathological liar of the

Harold Laski order, spinning her fantasies with total conviction; probably she believed them herself. She was cruel and vindictive, and hate kept her going. I rather admired her force of character, she was a powerful woman, but I will not miss her.

July 11

Alexandra, Marietta and I went out to the Harrimans' in Yorktown Heights tonight. This evening Averell was in even better shape. He cannot see very well, but prides himself on seeing what he can see—noting, for example, the color of my shirt (red checks with white collar—hard to miss). We had considerable despairing talk about the Democratic party; Pam is leaving tomorrow for the convention. But the most interesting part of the evening had to do with Roosevelt and Churchill.

I have just finished reading the first two of the three volumes of FDR-Churchill correspondence, edited by Warren Kimball of Rutgers. One question that arises from this grand and affectionate exchange is whether the two men really liked each other, or liked the theory of liking each other in the great historic context. I asked Averell and Pam: if they had not been President and Prime Minister, if there had been no Hitler and no world war, would they have been friends? Pam said very definitely no. "They had nothing in common," she said. "They were not each other's type. They were not amused by the same things. They did not like the same sort of people. Churchill liked men. Roosevelt liked women. They had a different attitude toward the past. Churchill revelled in tradition. Roosevelt was much more a pragmatist. But they had to get on with each other, and both worked at it." Averell said, "Each asked me at various times how best to get on with the other." We asked what he had told them. He said, "I told them to be natural, be yourselves."

The one exception to their having different kinds of friends is, of course, [Harry] Hopkins. (I am sure that Churchill regarded Arthur Murray, FDR's closest English friend, as a bore.) Why, I asked, was Hopkins such a pal, a man that both of these very different men could relax with? He was such an "endearing" man, Pam said; also, she surmised, as a professional social worker, he was skilled at winning confidence. Also I imagine that Hopkins's irreverent sardonic style was compatible both with FDR's rather simplistic humor and with Churchill's stylistical polished wit. Pam added that Churchill considered Louise Hopkins a bad influence, not so much on Harry as on FDR. Returning from a White House visit after Harry's marriage, Churchill talked of too many martinis before dinner stimulating FDR into rambling talk and discouraging his focus on specific problems. (An odd complaint from a notable drinker.) But, even if each loved the theory of the other more than he loved the other, they shared an exultation in responding to the heroic moment.

July 18

Midway in the Democratic convention. Alas, the convention is in San Francisco, and I am here. I rather miss not being there. I greatly enjoy conventions. On the other hand, there is little more frustrating than being at a convention without a candidate or a function; so I am probably better off watching it all on television.

The designation of Geraldine Ferraro as vice presidential candidate is fine, even though one cannot repress the thought that Gerald Ferraro with the same record would never have been in the picture. Margaret Thatcher got to the top in spite of being a woman; Geraldine Ferraro approaches the top because she is a woman. But her example will open the way for women who have really earned it. I do not mean to belittle Mrs. Ferraro, who, on small acquaintance, seems a bright and pleasant woman in the Joan Blondell style.

August 27

On Sunday we heard the news of Truman Capote's death. He was an old, though never close, friend, or acquaintance. I met him first in the late 1940s, perhaps with or through Newton Arvin. We had a mild acquaintance. I remember when his play *The Grass Harp* opened in Boston running into him after the first act. I thought the play terrible and could only manage, when I encountered him, a feeble "very interesting evening." He saw through me at once and darted a venomous look at me. However, I was never really on his enemies list—not rich or social enough. I used to see him at the Paleys' in the 1960s. New York still remembers the Black and White Ball he gave for Kay Graham's 50th birthday in 1967—a great party. Then bitterness generated by years of sycophancy began to overtake him, plus drink, drugs, unrequited homosexual love affairs, and he began to publish pieces containing thinly veiled portraits of people, like Bill Paley, in whose drawing rooms he had starred for so long. Doors now closed on him, though a few people, like C. Z. Guest, remained faithful. I had not seen him for some time when Jan Cushing, hearing that he was alone, brought him to Christmas dinner a few years ago. He was, as I recall, charming and rather pathetic. I don't think I have seen him since. At his best, he was a master of a certain feline malice, often devastating and sometimes very funny.

September 1

Yesterday afternoon the Styrons gave a cocktail party for Carlos and Sylvia Fuentes—a characteristic Vineyard gathering on the broad lawn in the twilight with the waters of Vineyard Haven harbor glimmering in the distance. Afterward Alexandra, Andy and I went out with Kay Graham and Dick Darman for dinner. Darman is married to Alexandra's cousin Kathleen Emmet. He is the bright young man in the White House, Jim Baker's assistant, an Elliot Richardson protege whose resignation is regularly demanded by the Republican right. We had met him last summer, but this was the first time we have had an extended talk.

We both liked him more than we expected. In quick takes last summer he had seemed slightly pompous and forbidding, but last night he was charming and funny. He has a saturnine wit, high intelligence and surprising candor. He prefaced his remarks about Reagan by saying, with emphasis, "I like him *very much*," but went on to describe him with admirable detachment. I asked, for example, about his reading habits. To Kay's horror, Darman said that, when the President picked up the *Washington Post,* the first thing he read was the comics. "Which ones?" "He reads them all." I inquired about his policy reading. Darman said, "He values information that accords with his prior personal prejudices. It doesn't matter where the information comes from—*Reader's Digest, Human Events* or a top-secret CIA report; if it fortifies his prior convictions, he grades it high. And he downgrades sources that supply information that goes against his prejudices. No matter what they have done in the past, they are off the A-list." Darman said that Reagan receives two copies of *Human Events* so that he can clip it. Darman expressed the highest regard for Reagan's political instincts; also for his sense of humor. "He cannot talk for three minutes without a humorous turn." I asked whether these were witticisms or anecdotes? He said, "Often anecdotes, but sometimes witticisms, though they may be only the punch lines of anecdotes so old that my generation has never heard them."

Much talk about Nancy Reagan, who is plainly a key figure. Kay finds her quite sympathetic when they lunch together. Dick Darman compared her to Jackie—insecurity derived from a mixed-up and somewhat fatherless childhood, combined with very definite tastes and views. "She is more ideological than her husband," Darman said, "but also more political in the sense that she wants more than anything else that the world think well of him, and therefore, when she senses strong movements of opinion, she can be a force for compromise." She adores him, but also can be tough with him. Reagan, Darman said, is afflicted by allergies and therefore loves air conditioning. Nancy Reagan cannot abide air conditioning and likes rooms at a very high temperature. So Reagan arrives wheezing at the Oval Office every morning, grateful to be at last in an air-conditioned, pollen-free environment.

Kay described a White House evening in which, after dinner, they all saw a film. During one vivid sex scene, Kay said, Nancy was convulsed with laughter while Reagan looked grimly ahead. Darman said that this latter was probably for Kay's benefit. "He tells dirty stories often."

Darman added that in Dallas during the convention Reagan turned on the porno channel on the hotel television and watched it for a while with amusement. This was the one story he put expressly off the record.

We talked about the election. My view is that the economy favors Reagan; that a foreign policy crisis would help Reagan in the short run, because of the rally-round-the-President effect; and that Mondale's hope must be that Reagan will say or do things to remind the voters that he is far and away the oldest President we have ever had. Darman expects the gap to narrow but does not seem unduly perturbed about the outcome. "Mondale is known in the White House as Wimp 2," he said, Carter being Wimp 1. In the White House view, Hart would have been a far more formidable opponent, because, Darman said, his profile of support is much like Reagan's—strength in the suburbs, with the professional classes and among the young.

I asked why Reagan chose to run again: "If he had stepped out after one term, he would occupy an interesting niche in history. But a second term will probably mean four years of misery and wreck his historical reputation." Darman: "You may well be right. I think the next four years may be difficult, though I would put the probability of 'misery' at 60–40 while you would probably put it at 90–10. I sometimes think that Reagan may provide eight years of continuous Republican rule, and then the Republicans may not be in the White House again for a long time to come. . . . But he chose to run a second time first because he is an optimist; he does not think things are going to go bad; he really doesn't. And, even if he did, he would have chosen to run, because he is not a quitter."

September 30

Marietta asked me for luncheon today with John Huston. (Alexandra and Robert are visiting Peter in Middlebury.) I had met Huston years ago at a (large) dinner at Marietta's, but we had not had much time for a talk. He greeted me with the quiet complicity of a man who knows that the other had been in love with the same woman at a later time. He is infinitely beguiling, highly intelligent, elaborately courteous. He had a short gray beard and surrenders periodically to coughing bouts of emphysema. I liked him very much.

I asked him about B. Traven, who, I had read somewhere, had appeared on the set when *Treasure of the Sierra Madre* was filmed. He said that a man calling himself Hal Croves (?) had indeed appeared, bearing a letter from Traven in which Traven said Croves was his representative and knew more about his work than he (Traven) did, etc. Huston did not much like Croves, whom he found bland and studiously furtive. Later some said that Croves was Traven. Huston doubts this. He received a number of letters from Traven, filled with emphatic opinions, emphatically expressed. Croves, John said was nothing like that. He thinks that Traven may have died at some point and that Croves later assumed his identity, or allowed others to assume it.

The talk drifted to Dashiell Hammett. Huston had known him well before *The Maltese Falcon*. Hammett, however, had nothing to do with Huston's *Falcon*. Huston sent him the script before production began; Hammett never replied, and did not comment on the film when it was released. Some years later in New York, Huston summoned up his nerve and asked Hammett what he thought of the film. Hammett said, "I liked it fine," and nothing more. He was full of curious knowledge, Huston said, about subjects like Rosicrucianism. He knew all about the existentialists before existentialism became an American fashion. Despite his membership in the CPUSA, he rarely talked politics. He liked his tour in the Aleutians during the war and did not mind his later tour in federal prison. He was "elegant" in his appearance, Huston said, more like William Powell than like Humphrey Bogart. "In fact, the three most elegant men I have ever known were all writers and all alcoholics—Hammett, Eugene O'Neill and William Faulkner."

I asked him about Reagan. Loyal Davis, John said, was a great friend of his father, so he had known the Davises forever and Nancy since she was a little girl. He said that Davis was not the reactionary ordinarily imagined, nor Nancy the political influence on Reagan sometimes represented. He likes Nancy. Reagan, he thinks, was converted to conservatism by General Electric. Huston found him "a hopeless bore. . . . I often wonder why he thinks he has any right to hold opinions on the questions with which he has to deal."

An enchanting man. He is in town making a film from a Richard Condon novel.

Last Tuesday (the 25th) I lunched with Brian Urquhart. He described a "working luncheon" that he and [Javier] Perez de Cuellar had with Reagan on the Sunday before. Reagan's ignorance of international affairs, Brian said, was deeply disturbing. Also Brian began to wonder whether there was something wrong with Reagan's neck, because he kept it stiff in a curious way as he leaned toward a bowl of flowers in front of his place. Brian mentioned this later to Perez de Cuellar. The Secretary General said, "Didn't you notice? He had an index card with his agenda in the bowl of flowers."

On Friday we dined at Perez de Cuellar's—a dinner for [Fernando] Belaunde [Terry] of Peru. Bob McNamara was there. For some reason we talked about the 1968 campaign. He said, "Mac Bundy and I persuaded Hubert that he must repudiate Johnson on Vietnam and strike out on his own. An appointment was arranged for Hubert to go to the White House and explain to Johnson why he was doing this. Lyndon must have surmised what was impending. He kept Hubert waiting for 45 minutes, thereby reducing him to a state of nerves. Hubert did not dare bring up Vietnam. The effort failed. If Hubert had been a stronger man, he would have been elected President."

October 8

The first debate took place last night—an evident victory for Mondale. Fritz looked well, radiated confidence and humor, was never shrill or whiney and seemed always in command. Reagan looked well too and tried to prove competence by a deluge of statistics; but he appeared on the defensive, nervous and toward the end quite tired. The Mondale campaign will get a desperately needed boost, and the second debate (which will take place when we are in Japan) may be quite crucial.

The Columbus Day parade took place today, and Alexandra and I walked over to Fifth Avenue to take a look. First we saw George Bush in a limousine, leaning out the window and waving preppily at the crowd. He looked a little gray and wan. A little later Mondale and Ferraro appeared, walking along with Cuomo, Moynihan (in his cloth hat) and the ineffable Koch. Fritz spotted me and came over with Mario to say hello. I congratulated him on his success last night. He leaned over and whispered, "Wasn't he incredible? I mean Reagan? . . . The easiest debate I have ever had."

We went [on Saturday, October 6] evening to a party at Mick Jagger's. I don't know why we are on their list; I guess that Jerry Hall is fond of Alexandra. It was rather fun. I had a nice long talk with Anjelica Huston, who has a lead in her father's new film. She had worked with him once before (in *A Walk with Love and Death*) and hated it; it was a time, she said, when she felt great tension with him. But that is over, and everything is going well this time. She is bright, and I liked her. Jack Nicholson was there too and even more enthusiastic about working with Huston, from whom, he says, he has learned a great deal in a short time—"and I thought I knew most everything I needed to know already." Nicholson struck me as genuinely brilliant; he talks awfully well and has a fresh slant on things. Perhaps he was on some kind of high; the words poured out in a flashing cascade. We knew very few people there; most were young and looked like models or rock stars. Andy Warhol was there and appeared stunned to see me. We brought Peter and left him there when we went home well after midnight.

November 1

On Sunday last we returned from Japan. *Asahi Shimbun* had offered me a comfortable fee plus two first-class round-trip tickets to speak at a symposium on "A Message to the 21st Century." The symposium, like all symposia, was boring.

On Friday the 26th we went to Hiroshima, accompanied by Hiroshi Fujita, the bright and charming husband (a newspaperman, working for the Kodyo Agency) of my CUNY student Fumiko Fujita. Hiroshima today is a thriving, ugly city of nearly a million, as against 370,000 in 1945. A newspaper friend of Hiroshi's, Akira Tashiro of the *Chugoko Shimbun,* met us at the museum devoted to the bomb, and the museum's director, who had been himself in Hiroshima when the bomb fell, took us around. The museum was shattering. It plunged Alexandra into a deep depression and left me with an appalled sense of the end of the world. Groups of school girls in middie blouses, grave and giggling, crowded the museum and looked at the horrific exhibits. Later I asked Hiroshi why there was not more dislike of the United States in view of Hiroshima and Nagasaki; a poll had just shown the U.S. to be far the most popular among foreign nations. He said, "It is partly our own guilt over Pearl Harbor. We know that, if there had been no Pearl Harbor, there would have been no Hiroshima. And it is partly that the immensity of the common fate transcends national frontiers."

I found a letter from George Bush on my return. He had given a speech on the vice presidency, and I had written for a copy, reminding him of my long interest in the vice presidency (an office I think should be abolished). He sent the text along, with a scrawled postscript: "Don't abolish my job. I need the work."

November 3

A few weeks ago I received an invitation from the Association of Former Intelligence Officers to attend an off-the-record talk by Bill Casey. It was held at the University Club, and the guests were instructed to look for "William G. S. Smith Reception." Bill was his usual smooth, affable self, concealing steel purpose under a shuffle of mumbles. He looked well, despite the recent trouble over the CIA "assassination manual" for the Contras in Nicaragua. He is a man unperturbed by trouble.

He began by saying that he had been around long enough to know that there was no such thing as an off-the-record talk to 200 people. Then he told the old Johnstown [Pennsylvania] flood story—the survivor of the Johnstown flood, who, when admitted to Heaven, insisted that a group be convened to listen to his story; after he embarked on the tale, St. Peter whispered to him, "I forgot to tell you, but Noah is in the audience." Casey said, "That is the way I feel when I look at this audience and see John Wilson and Arthur Schlesinger sitting in front of me. They were in the intelligence business long before I was." Not true of course. John Wilson was a Harvard economist who became one of Bill Donovan's assistants in OSS; an able fellow. After such pleasantries, Bill read a rather more routine defense-of-the-agency, Cold War speech and then dealt with questions in his bluff, humorous, dismissive way.

Bill and I became friends in Paris during the war when he was running SI/OSS. After the war, he hired me to do occasional Washington reports for the Research Institute of America, which he was then running with Leo Cherne. We have encountered each other through the years and, in spite of manifest political disagreements, have remained joshing friends. When his nomination as chairman of the SEC was before the Senate, he asked me to write a letter to Bill Proxmire on his behalf, which I did. When he became head of CIA, I hoped that, as an old SI man who used to complain vehemently about Special Operations during the war, he would restore the primacy of intelligence over covert action. But Bill loves action and loves power, and covert action has apparently become his baby. I think his influence on American foreign policy has been malevolent. Yet I continue to like him personally. Why? Should one dislike people who do evil? Probably.

December 21

Another year rushes to an end. Time whirls by faster than ever in these autumnal years. One Christmas is barely over when it is Thanksgiving again. And one of the great illusions is that age brings simplification in life. On the contrary, the older you get, the more obligations you assume, the more burdens you carry, the harder it is to find time for oneself and one's work. I don't mean familial obligations which I embrace with pleasure, but obligations to institutions, to causes, to strangers, to the social round. I keep trying to retrench but to little avail.

But I cannot complain. My health continues good. I arise at 6:45, do five miles on a stationary bicycle and five minutes of back exercises, drink a glass of grapefruit juice for breakfast, walk with Robert to the bus stop and then set to work. I work till about 11:30, then go to the office for mail, phone calls and appointments; then luncheon (ordinarily at the Century); then I always walk home—a mile and a quarter; twenty minutes. I weigh about 175 pounds, which is thirty pounds more than I weighed fifty years ago but ten pounds less than I weighed twenty years ago. I appear to have lost an inch or so of height with the contraction of age, and now am about 5'9".

I can work as long and hard as ever, though, if I write in the evening, it leaves the mind in motion and I find it difficult to get to sleep. Research never tires me. Writing depletes after a while, but a break for luncheon or dinner (always with a drink) is restorative. I take it that one can practice history as long as one can amble about. My father did; Sam Morison did. There is inspiration in the letter George Bancroft, aged 84, wrote to O. W. Holmes: "I was yet strong enough to rise in the night, light my own fire and candles, and labor with close application fully fourteen hours consecutively, that is, from five in the morning till eight in the evening, with but one short hour's interruption for breakfast; and otherwise no repast: not so much as a sip of water." I now keep Marian Adam's photograph of old George on my desk.

1985

February 4

Some notes on people.

MAC BUNDY: We had an exceptionally good time with the Bundys in Barbados. Mary of course is a sweetheart—intelligent, humorous, staunch, generous-hearted. Mac has been chastened by the vicissitudes of experience. His incisiveness has lost its patina of arrogance. He was always, with his high intelligence and spirits, excellent company. And even in the old days he had one very disarming social quality—a readiness to talk to the person in the room whom other people were ignoring. When we gave dinners in Cambridge in the 1950s, Mac could always be depended on to carry his social weight. Harvard society was extremely self-centered. People would dwell on local matters and make little attempt to bring strangers—even eminent foreign visitors—into the conversation. Mac always made the effort, whether the outsiders were someone's unknown aunt or Hugh Gaitskell.

I had brought with me to Barbados a paper on the Kennedy White House that had been submitted to the *Political Science Quarterly* and passed on to me as a reader. The thesis of the paper was that the Kennedy White House staff, far from being the "band of brothers" celebrated in legend, was riven by rivalry and feud. My reaction was along the lines of the old joke: "How's your wife?"; "Compared to what?" Obviously there was a lot of jostling for position in those years; but, compared to subsequent White House staffs, there was, I believe, a maximum of collegiality and a minimum of rancor. This is shown by the affection that has survived through the years. Mac, Ted, Pierre, Dick Goodwin, Ralph Dungan, Kenny when he was alive, Mike Feldman, Walt Rostow—all remain good friends.

I had one bad memory of Mac in those years. When JFK prepared to go to Europe in 1963, he asked me to think about the speeches he should give and to work with Mac on them. Mac was unresponsive, wanted to keep everything under his own control and eventually cut me out of the trip. Before he left, JFK said something to me indicating that he supposed I was going. I said I had not been asked to go. He appeared surprised but did nothing about it, not wishing, I imagine, to overrule Bundy. However, I felt that my grievance was cancelled out the next year when I was working on *A Thousand Days* and Mac gave me free access to the papers in his office. This enabled me to see and use the minutes of the Vienna meeting with Khrushchev, the Khrushchev-Kennedy correspondence and other highly classified documents and greatly strengthened the book. I was no longer in the government, and it was an immense help.

CASPAR WEINBERGER: I have known Cap now for more than half a century. We met first in the autumn of 1934 as freshmen at Harvard College. He is privately an amiable and civilized man, but as a public servant he is a menace. In the 51 years I have known him, he has never once, in my view, been right about anything (a view he holds as strongly about me). He is possessed of unbounded moral certitude that is impervious to argument and far outstrips both his knowledge of facts and his recognition of complexities. I well remember the 35th reunion in

1973 when Cap and I debated the Nixon administration. I brought up Watergate, and he behaved as if this were a cheap smear on a great and noble President. (Needless to say, most of our classmates applauded him.) I am sure that he really believes today that nuclear weapons are usable and nuclear wars winnable. If his efforts should drive us on to nuclear war, it will be inadequate consolation to think that the human race is being exterminated by a fellow member of the Harvard Class of 1938.

LAUREN BACALL: We have been friends since 1952 and the Stevenson campaign—a third of a century ago; and the friendship has grown steadily through the years. Last week Betty gave a party to mark the 25th wedding anniversary of Adolph Green and Phyllis Newman. This was a generally joyous occasion, except when Peter Stone arose to give a toast and raised his glass to "Adolph and Betty [Comden]." In a brilliant save, Mike Nichols arose and began his toast by saying, "On behalf of Elaine and myself." Betty told Alexandra later, "When Peter said that, I wanted to kill myself; but I wanted to kill Peter first." I am fond of Peter Stone; but Phyllis is still mad at him (or appeared to be when we lunched with her and Adolph yesterday). He has not apologized, sent flowers or made any other gesture. Bridges will have to be mended.

Betty is filled with affection, slashing judgment, raucous fun and boisterous humor. I love her.

May 3

This is the week of Bitburg—Reagan's visit to the Nazi cemetery. The whole thing is a mystery. Why this sudden concern about reconciliation? One had supposed that reconciliation had taken place in the age of Adenauer, with West German rearmament, German admission to NATO, Kennedy's "Ich bin ein Berliner," etc. What further reconciliation is suddenly required in 1985? Obviously [Helmut] Kohl wanted the Reagan visit as a means of helping his party in the impending election; but why did Reagan fall for so obviously self-serving a request? Where was the State Department? Where were Arthur Burns and our embassy in Bonn? Reagan never served overseas himself in the Second

World War (and was the only President of military age not to do so); and I guess he does not understand how the people who fought the war feel about the SS.

We discussed this at luncheon today at the Century. Drew Middleton blames the fiasco on bad staff work. He thinks that Robert McFarlane, the National Security Adviser, was not even consulted. He recently asked McFarlane what would happen to Mike Deaver, who served as advance man for the German trip. McFarlane said, "In a well regulated society, Deaver would be taken out and shot."

May 8

Monday the 6th, was Teddy White's 70th, and Beatrice gave a dinner for him. It was much less of an affair than his 50th; I still remember Harry and Claire Luce competing for the credit of having discovered Teddy. How the years rush by! I have known Teddy now for more than half a century, and we have ended living across the street from each other.

I lunched today with David Garrow, the young political scientist who wrote the book on Martin Luther King and the FBI. He has now got (through the invaluable Freedom of Information Act) the transcripts of the FBI wiretaps of the phone conversations King held with Stanley Levison and is planning a book on King's last years. He has two great problems, he says: how to treat King's "real wife," who is now a dean at Cornell, without permanently alienating Coretta; and how to deal with King's determination in his last months to fire Jesse Jackson without causing great troubles with the black community. He spent a weekend recently travelling about with Jackson and was rather impressed by his intelligence and by his relationship with his two teenage sons. But Jesse has Dr. King's weakness for dalliance. "Two things I always admired about Martin," Jesse told Garrow, "are that he never embarrassed his wife publicly and that he never got a divorce." Garrow says that many of the people close to Jackson are white. He also says that Jack Odell, the real Communist close to King in the early sixties, is now an intimate Jackson adviser. He tried to warn Jackson about possible repercussions, but Jackson, he felt, does not regard it as a serious problem. Garrow is a bright fellow with sensible views.

May 15

I have been giving a seminar this term for faculty members from community colleges awarded fellowships by the Mellon Foundation. The fellowships release them from their heavy teaching and administrative burdens and give them time to work on their own projects. The Mellon Fellows are also required to take a seminar at the Graduate School, given in various years by Irving Howe or Alfred Kazin or Herb Gutman or me. Since the Fellows are both well-informed and ardent, I find these seminars enjoyable; indeed, probably learn as much at them as the students.

The topic this year was Literature and American Society, and I persuaded Norman Mailer to make an appearance, which he did on the 14th. It is interesting to see how much Norman fits into the American literary tradition—and how little aware he is of the character of that tradition. He is what Tocqueville prophesied—"strong and rapid emotions, startling passages, truths or errors brilliant enough to rouse [the readers] up and then plunge them at once, as if by violence, into the midst of the subject. . . . Style will frequently be fantastic, incorrect, overburdened, and loose, almost always vehement and bold . . . immense and incoherent imagery, with exaggerated descriptions and strange creations. . . . Man himself taken aloof from his country and his age and standing in the presence of Nature and of God, with his passions, his doubts, his rare prosperities and inconceivable wretchedness, will become the chief, if not the sole, theme."

When I say that he is not aware of the tradition, I mean only that he has absorbed it without reflecting much on it. He did most of his reading in his teens, and the books evidently flooded his unconscious. I was struck in rereading *Why We Are in Vietnam* by the echoes of *Huck Finn*—both in the characters (two adolescent boys surrounded by adult phoneys) and in the style (the use of the most colloquial adolescent language to convey subtle insights and sensitive descriptions)—and I asked him about it. He said that he had read *Huck Finn* when he was 14 and never read it again until the *Times Book Review* asked him to do a piece last year on the centennial of its publication. But the early reading evidently got into his bones. His novels are very much in the tradition of "romance" in the Hawthorne-James-Faulkner-Richard Chase sense of the word.

Someone asked him about the formative experiences of his life. He was eloquent in explaining how the Second World War had molded his literary generation. We have had a spate of 40th anniversaries this year, and it has turned all our thoughts back to the war. For all those not killed or maimed in it, the war remains a decisive experience, the time when one lived with the most intensity.

My fondness for Norman and for his beautiful Norris continues to grow. Norman, once so prickly and exhibitionistic, has become in late middle age charming, funny, astonishingly considerate, even tender, but without any loss in seriousness and honesty. He has lived dangerously, and it has come out all right. He is getting a little fat, though.

June 2

I am just back from a few days in Cuba. About a fortnight ago I received a phone call from Robert White, who was our ambassador to El Salvador until he fell afoul of the Reagan administration. He retired from the Foreign Service and has been devoting himself to persuading the public of the dangers of the Reagan policy. I had encountered him a few times and have admired his general position. White asked me whether I might be interested in going to Havana with him and a small group. I thought why the hell not? and said I would go.

We flew through the night, arriving in Havana about 1:45 Monday morning, the 27th. I had last been in Havana in 1950 for the first meeting of Frances Grant's Inter-American Association for Democracy and Freedom. It was then that I first met Romulo Betancourt and Raul

Leoni of Venezuela, Eduardo Frei and Salvador Allende of Chile, German Arciniegas of Colombia, Pepe Figueres of Costa Rica, Juan Bosch of the Dominican Republic and received my first initiation into the Latin American democratic tradition. I was enchanted by Havana— and appalled by the way that lovely city was being debased into a giant casino and brothel for North American businessmen over for a big weekend from Miami. My fellow countrymen reeled through the streets, picking up 14-year-old Cuban girls and tossing coins to make men scramble in the gutter.

Things have changed. But Cuba still lacks the grimness and melancholy of the Communist countries of Eastern Europe. Perhaps communism is different in a hot climate.

On the afternoon of the 28th, Bob White and I, in order to avoid the semi-obligatory tour of day care centers, schools and hospitals, went to the Centro de Estudios sobre America for a not very profitable discussion with Cuban scholars and specialists. I discovered that my old friend Tad Szulc was in Havana where he is working on a biography of Castro; and in the late afternoon we (Bob White, Kathleen Kennedy Townsend, Caroline Croft) went out to his house for a drink and a swim. Tad is very interesting on Castro and especially on the problems of writing his biography. Cuba apparently lacks a strong historiographical tradition. There is little written Cuban history and little attempt even to collect a documentary record of the Revolution.

Tad drove us back to the Riviera on his way to a reception at the Palace for Perez de Cuellar, who was visiting Havana. When we arrived, we discovered that we had been invited to the reception too. The Palace, which was built by Batista, is a horrible block on the outside, but the reception room, filled with plants and small trees, is most attractive. As we advanced down the receiving line, Perez de Cuellar gave a double-take when he saw me approaching and an abrazo when we met. Fidel is a big man, six feet two I would judge. His black hair and beard now tinged with gray. He greeted us affably and later sent word for us to join him, Perez de Cuellar and the top people in a special dining room. The food was excellent, especially the roast suckling pig, and the drinks were plentiful. I had a nice talk with Senora Perez de Cuellar, when Carlos Rafael Rodriguez [the Cuban Vice President] came by and indicated that he would like to resume our conversation of earlier in the day.

We chatted for some time, mostly about the past. I asked him about the Bay of Pigs. He said that of course they knew about the training camps in Guatemala and that they expected an invasion. "We were not at all prepared to cope with an invasion. But we had a Russian military adviser. Fidel set him to work training some of our best people, and the people he trained trained others; so we did our best to prepare for the worst. Then came the attack on the airfields. This gave us the crucial warning. We still did not know where the invasion was coming, but we knew that it was on the way." I asked whether they had any doubt about the outcome. "Fidel was concerned that the Bay of Pigs attack might be a diversion and that American forces might attack at another point. This was our big worry. So far as the Bay of Pigs was concerned, we were confident we could deal with that."

Rodriguez asked me about Kennedy and what Kennedy thought about Castro. I said that Kennedy was greatly interested in Castro. I recalled how impressed Kennedy was by Castro's success in mobilizing the young people of Cuba and by the anti-illiteracy campaign. I recalled also Kennedy's looking at a photograph of Castro in a baseball uniform and saying, "It is hard to get angry at a fellow like that." On the other hand, I said, Kennedy was much concerned about Cuban intervention in other Latin American countries, especially Venezuela. I also said that Castro was not a major issue for Kennedy, who had much else on his mind—Khrushchev, the Berlin crisis of 1961, Southeast Asia, etc. Rodriguez said that Castro was initially very pro-Kennedy; then, after the Bay of Pigs, bitterly and angrily disappointed; then, toward the end, sympathetic again. We discussed the assassination attempts, and I explained why I believed that JFK had no knowledge of them. As we parted, Rodriguez surprisingly said that he had seen the RFK miniseries based on my book and liked it.

I then encountered an egregious figure named Armando Hart, the Minister of Culture, who lectured me in a hectic manner for what seemed an interminable time. Finally I broke away and joined a group around Castro. Fidel was in an exuberant mood, and there was much badinage back and forth. He is rather like Lyndon Johnson in his liking for physical contact—much touching of people—and he ended by kissing Kathleen good night.

We arose at 5:30 (White, Kathleen, Caroline [Croft]) to go to the Bay of Pigs. There was a long ride down a six-lane highway. We stopped at a town near the Bay and drove around, looking for the local Communist party headquarters in order to ascertain our luncheon arrangements. No one seemed to know where the headquarters were located, so we saw a good deal of the town. The houses were serviceable, sturdy and clean, and the general aspect was pleasant enough. One got no impression of poverty and squalor. After finding the CP, we drove on down a long narrow road to the Playa Giron. Here we visited a museum devoted to displays showing how Cuban patriots worsted the Yanqui imperialists and their Cuban mercenaries. Then we saw a film driving home the point. Bob White whispered to me, "I have had enough of humiliation."

When we got back to Havana, we were told the meeting had been postponed till 7. Fidel had spent the day with Perez de Cuellar at the Isle of Pines, where he had delivered a defiantly anti-American speech. We went to the Palace at the appointed time. A few minutes later Castro joined us. He was flanked by three men who had been serving as our hosts and escorts—Juan Antonio Blanco, who had accompanied us to the Bay of Pigs; Jorge Abrezo; and Alfredo Almeida. The first two are in the Foreign Ministry; the third is from the international bureau of the party. There were also a couple of stenographers and a photographer.

For the next four hours we received the full treatment—an endless, sometimes brilliant flow of facts, allegations, jokes, statistics, insights, parables, metaphors, sarcasm, punctuated by gestures and a splendid repertoire of facial expressions. I find in my notes: "Fidel Castro reminds me inexplicably of Joe Alsop." He came in with the tag end of

a long slim cigar in his mouth; then lit another but put it aside in an ash-
tray. From time to time, he would pick the cigar up, look fondly at it
and gesture with it; but he refrained from smoking most of the time.
Blanco told me later that they had been negotiating with Castro to stop
smoking and had at least persuaded him not to smoke the big black
cigars to which he was long addicted. Behind him was a painting of
guerrillas roasting a chicken in the Sierra Maestra, executed in the style
of Soviet socialist realism—an abominable job. Castro's own talk was
notably devoid of Marxist jargon. He was dressed in the usual olive gray
fatigues; no necktie.

After the usual formalities, he asked what we would like to talk
about. I made some suggestions, and then he proceeded to talk without interruption for the next hour and a half. I had mentioned his assessment of the relationship between Cuba and the United States.
"Prospects for improvement are non-existent," he said. (He spoke in
Spanish, rapidly and efficiently translated by a pretty, pregnant young
woman.) "We can't be blamed for that, Radio Marti, the use of Jose
Marti's name, the use of the date of May 20 [Cuba's traditional independence day]—all have deeply offended and insulted all Cubans. Moreover, it was done at a time when possibilities existed for improvement in
relations. The negotiations over the migratory persons agreement had
shown flexibility and respect. We had shown our desire to work for
solutions in Central America, in southern Africa, with regard to the
Latin American debt.

"Many mistakes have been made in history that could have been
avoided. You have been today at the Bay of Pigs. That is an example. It
was a Republican legacy, inherited from Nixon and Eisenhower. You
would have done better to cancel it. The same thing is true of your
adventure in Vietnam. The reaction to Reagan's embargo of Nicaragua
shows that Latin America today is not what it was in 1961 or during the
Dominican crisis of 1965. The war over the Malvinas Islands [the Falk-
lands] shows the potentiality of Latin American unity. If the United
States invades a Latin American country, the reaction will be ten times
what it was over the Malvinas. . . ."

He turned to the subject of the [hemispheric] debt, proposing that the U.S. cut back on arms spending in order to assume the Latin American debt and preserve the banking system. I broke in: "It is refreshing to see an old revolutionary like you so determined to save the American bankers." Castro: "Yes—you are right?—and why? It is essential to save the U.S. banking system in order to move toward the New International Economic Order. It is necessary to take measures that protect both the industrialized and the Third World nations.

"I am happy to be friendly with the conservatives. If a boat is sinking, it is not a question of progressive and conservative, socialist and capitalist, Catholic and Protestant, Moslem and Hindu—for we are all in the same boat. Better a calm and courageous conservative than a frightened progressive if you want to save the boat. . . . We are reaching the critical mass. A chain reaction will soon take place. But it will not be a controlled reaction. . . . Cancellation of the debt is the only solution."

I was rather taken by the Maximum Leader, though others in our group were frustrated by his monopoly of the interview. He is a man of high intelligence, boundless energy and ebullient showmanship. He is plainly too big a leader for a small country and would like to run the world, or at least the Third World, or at least Latin America. He is planning to ride back into the Latin American mainstream on the debt issue and would like to end, one imagines, as the beloved elder statesman of the southern hemisphere.

As we returned to the hotel toward midnight, after the Bay of Pigs and the four hours with Castro, I recalled that this was 29 May and that Jack Kennedy, if alive, would be 68 today.

June 23

Morty Hall, Dolly Schiff's son and an old friend, came for luncheon today. He was once married to Diana Lynn, a charming film star who died. Diana, he reminded me, was Reagan's co-star in *Breakfast for Bonzo*. This film was made in the days when stars still made personal appearances in theaters on behalf of their films, and the studio sent the

Bonzo stars on tour. Morty said that Diana's main recollections were (1) how boring Reagan was and (2) how humiliating it was that Bonzo got more applause than his human co-stars. While reminiscing on Ron and Hollywood, Morty also recalled Jane Wyman's remark about him— that he was the most unimaginative man she ever went to bed with.

October 2

Ahmet Ertegun is a record czar, a bon vivant, a cynic, a jolly rogue and an excellent raconteur. He wears glasses and a Van Dyke and looks like a psychiatrist, or perhaps the young Lenin. He told the following story at Bill Paley's a couple of nights ago. His father was the Turkish ambassador to Washington during the war, and young Ahmet was sent to Miss Shippen's dancing school. There he encountered Margaret Truman, the daughter of the senator from Missouri. Miss Shippen used to try to get the boys to dance with Margaret, but Ahmet much preferred another girl, who was a much sexier dancer, and avoided Margaret as much as possible. Cut to the 1950s, with Eisenhower as President and Truman out of the White House. One evening Ahmet took Didi Ladd to the Cote Basque for dinner. As they entered, Didi Ladd preceding, she said to Ahmet, "Oh, there's Truman. You go and talk to him while I get fixed up," and bustled off to the ladies' room. There indeed was Truman, sitting with Bess, Margaret and Clifton Daniel. Ahmet, a little confused, went up nevertheless to greet Truman, but, not knowing Truman, spoke to Margaret. Margaret said, "Ahmet, this is the first time you have spoken to me since Miss Shippen's dancing school, and you barely spoke to me then." As Ahmet desperately tried to make conversation, wondering where the hell Didi Ladd was, he suddenly saw her at the other end of the restaurant deep in conversation with Truman Capote.

October 6

We went down to Washington on Friday (the 4th) to attend the founding dinner of the Judson Welliver Society, an organization of presidential speechwriters summoned into existence by Bill Safire. The dinner took place at Safire's enviably large and rambling house in Kenwood. Sixty people showed up, and it was a lot of fun. Bill served as MC and asked one representative of each administration to introduce his colleagues and make some remarks. Despite partisan and ideological differences, the ghosts were bound together by the eccentricity of their trade and also by a sense of humor that seems to go along with the job.

Safire worked backward, beginning with the Reagan crowd. Robert Hartman, speaking for the Ford administration, told how he had composed Ford's first presidential speech. When he showed Ford the draft, Ford read it with approval and said, "There is only one line that has to go. That's the one 'The long national nightmare is over.' " Hartman protested, saying that this more than anything else is what the American people were waiting to hear. Ford said, "But it will hurt Dick's feelings." Hartman said, "But it has been a nightmare for Nixon and his family too. They are certainly glad it is over." Finally he persuaded Ford to keep the line. Of course it is the one memorable line that survives from his presidency.

James Keogh and Pat Buchanan spoke for Nixon. Buchanan turned out to be amiable and amusing and was quite funny describing Nixon in action. "I would go to him and say, 'The establishment is out to get you—the press and the liberals and the rest of that crowd.' He was extremely receptive to talk like that. He would say, 'We have to get back at them.' So I wrote a draft attacking them and brought it in to him. He read it and then looked up with a great smile on his face and said, 'This will tear the scab off those bastards.' "

Jack Valenti was good speaking for Johnson and, in Sorensen's absence, I spoke for Kennedy. I commented on the generational procession of ghosts, recalling how in the 1952 campaign Adlai Stevenson had one day told me with great excitement that Sam Rosenman and Bob Sherwood had agreed to do a couple of speeches. Later I was sent to New York to pick up the drafts. I met these legendary and venerable figures (actually they were in their mid-fifties, a good deal younger than I am now), discussed the campaign with them and took away the speeches. Returning to Chicago, I opened the envelope with trembling hand and then read the speeches with sinking heart. They seemed lustreless and useless. I wondered whether these men could really have written those great FDR speeches a decade earlier. Then a curious foreboding crept over me. In another decade, I wondered, would I do some drafts for a presidential candidate; and would some young smart-ass on his staff then look at them and say, "Could this fellow really have written those brilliant Adlai Stevenson speeches back in 1952?" And indeed, I said, this is what happened in 1960. I could feel the suspicion and resentment with which Ted Sorensen and Dick Goodwin regarded Ken Galbraith and me—so much so, that Kennedy had to meet with us surreptitiously, explaining that "otherwise it would upset Ted too much." I then added how much pleasure it gave me during Bobby's 1968 campaign in noting that Adam Walinsky and Peter Edelman looked on Sorensen and Goodwin with the same suspicion and resentment that Sorensen and Goodwin had looked on Galbraith and me eight years before.

Arthur Larsen spoke for Eisenhower, and Clark Clifford concluded by speaking for Truman. He began by saying, "Now that we are among ourselves, we can at last tell the truth about presidential speeches. You have been asked countless times, as I have been, how a President goes about making a speech. And I always reply, as I am sure you do, somewhat as follows. I go to see the President and remind him that he is to give a speech to the CIO in Detroit ten days hence. He says, 'Yes, I've been thinking about that, and this is what I want to say.' He then outlines his speech. I take extensive notes, writing down as many of his words and phrases as possible. Then I go away and write a draft, which the President then takes and rewrites. I have told that story a thousand times if I have told it once. But we all know what really happens. I go into the Oval Office and say, 'Sir, you are giving a speech to the CIO in Detroit ten days hence.' He looks up and growls, 'Who in hell scheduled that?' I say, 'Well, sir, it's been in the schedule for some time.' He says, 'I don't want to talk to those fellows. Where were they on that vote last week when I needed them?' We talk some more, and finally I go away. The next day I come back with a speech outline and hand it to the President. He reads it for a minute and says, 'Humph.' Then he reads a little longer and says 'Humph' again. Then he turns the page and says 'Humph' a couple of more times. Then he hands it back and says, 'OK, I guess this will have to do.' "

It was an agreeable evening, the camaraderie of the profession overcoming all other disagreements, at least for the moment. I particularly liked Peggy Noonan of the Reagan staff, an attractive young woman who told me how much she admired *A Thousand Days*. But it is too bad that speechwriting has now become a function in itself. The best speechwriters have been people who had other responsibilities and for whom speechwriting was secondary—Rosenman, Clifford, Sorensen. The divorce of the speechwriter from policy and operations seems to me a mistake. Apparently the sainted Judson Welliver, about whom Rick Hertzberg gave an amusing paper, confined himself to speechwriting; but not until the Eisenhower administration (Emmet Hughes and Kevin McCann) does speechwriting reemerge as a fulltime job. Under Kennedy and Johnson, the speechwriters were people mainly involved in policy. From Nixon on, the White House has had a team of people devoted only to speechwriting. And the anonymity that used to be the ghost's pride has vanished too.

October 22

A week ago today I became 68. What in the world has happened to all those years? My achievement is so much less than so many writers who were dead long before they were 68. I guess they concentrated their energies, while I have dissipated mine. I have got involved in too many things, wasted time and effort in fringe actions of one sort or another, and I have not been loyal to whatever I have in the way of a gift, which is presumably writing books.

I departed the [day after my birthday, October 16,] for Havana— another expression of the dissipation of energy. When we were down last May, Castro said he hoped we would come back in the autumn. I vaguely told Bob White I would come, though I hoped the trip would not come off. It is not that I mind Havana, and it is always interesting to see and hear Fidel; but I begin to recognize that I have a finite number of days left, and I don't want to waste them, and I have been to Cuba and have seen and heard Fidel. On the other hand, I did not want to let Bob White down; and, when I asked him whether it was really important to him that I come, he said it was, and so I did.

I flew down to Miami on Wednesday morning, the 16th, and caught the noon plane to Havana.

[A] visit [to an economic institute] was not interesting, and I experienced what has become an increasing problem in recent years—the tendency to fall asleep at meetings. Or even occasionally at dinners. Narcolepsy is usually a response to boredom.

[At our meeting,] Castro asked what we wanted to talk about. We mentioned several topics and he elected to begin with human rights, the hard one. Pat Derian set forth the case for more information and access. Castro listened attentively and took detailed notes in what seemed from across the table to be small, neat hand. Finally he replied. "I understand the humanitarian purpose of your statement," he said. "There is not only, as you say, confusion about the issue, but there is total misinformation about Cuba, not just about human rights but about Cuba in general. All revolutions are slandered. I believe that no revolution ever made such a systematic and tenacious effort in most difficult circumstances to preserve humanitarian values as the Cuban revolution. No revolution has had such a clean record. It is the only revolution in which no priest was executed. Compare it with the Bolshevik revolution, the Mexican Revolution, the Spanish Civil War." He went on for a while about the great humanity of the Cuban revolution, apparently forgetting the drumhead executions of 1959. There seemed no point in reminding him of them.

He kept on, his voice still soft, more hurt than angry, the weary voice of reason. "Many violent things happen in the modern world. But reactionaries and counter-revolutionaries are always more cruel than revolutionaries. It is true that most revolutions commit excesses. But our revolution is an exception. No torture, no missing people, no policy of cruelty.

"The reason I invited you for this meeting was to dispel the misrepresentations about our policy. We are a proud nation, jealous of our sovereignty. We have relations with many nations, right, center, left. It would never occur to me to ask another government about the prisoners in its country—in Italy, say, or Great Britain. Who knows how many cases we would find of people led to commit crimes by the social conditions in which they live—which makes them political prisoners. What if the Cuban government asked Italy about the Red Brigade prisoners—what prisons they are in, how they are treated, and so on. If we asked Italy that, Bettino Craxi would break relations with us. Why should the U.S. expect to supervise us? This causes great resentment—especially when things are demanded of us that are not demanded of Chile or El Salvador. Why should the Red Cross or some other international agency supervise us and no other nation? We have the right to be respected. My purpose in talking to you is to try and change our image. We have no objection to answering questions from people of good faith. It is useful for us to consider the points you have raised. Maybe we have been negligent. Maybe we can improve our ways. Prisoners who are not a danger to us should perhaps be freed."

All this, spoken with quiet passion, rather overwhelmed our human rights specialists. It was hard to see how to get a handle on this flow of intense language. After a moment I said that human rights embraced among other things a belief in the free exchange of information. If Castro felt such confidence in the triumph of his revolution, why would he not permit the sale in Havana of foreign newspapers—the *Excelsior* of Mexico City, the *New York Times*, the London *Times, Le Monde,* etc. Castro said he had no objection to this in principle, but they had limited foreign exchange and could not afford to spend it on things like newspapers, which were of interest to only a small minority. John Oakes then asked whether he would accept free subscriptions to leading papers for Cuban libraries, with the assurance that everyone would be free to read them. Castro finally allowed that this might be possible. Oakes is determined to follow up on this. We will see what happens.

At 11:30 we concluded. At no point in the five hours did I feel the slightest temptation to fall asleep—a tribute to the dramatic intensity of Castro's performance. Castro said he wanted us to come back again sometime after the Third Party Congress in March. He then noted that we had had nothing to eat and said he had laid on a buffet for us in the next room. The buffet was delectable, and we fell to with relish. Castro disappeared—to bed, I supposed. But forty minutes later he suddenly reappeared, vitality restored, and engaged in conversation. Craxi had resigned, and he told us what the Cuban cables had reported. It was then that he bragged of having gone 53 days without a cigar. He is an amazing character.

My feeling was reinforced that, despite Castro's agility and virtuosity, his revolution is in trouble. He cannot solve his economic problems. His main exports—sugar, coffee, tobacco, nickel—are all in trouble on the world market. His quarter-century attempt to diversify the Cuban economy has failed. The Russians are probably getting tired of subsidizing him. His only hope for economic viability is tourism, which may be one reason why he is refurbishing Havana. His other hope is to get into the U.S. market. So he wants to come to terms with the U.S. at least to the extent of ending the embargo. But, once he opens Cuba to American trade and tourists, I do not see how his revolution can survive. The embargo is his best guarantee of the integrity of the revolution. The irony is that Castro wants to end the embargo, though this may destroy him, while Reagan wants to maintain the embargo, though this will protect Castro and his revolution.

November 6

A dozen members of the Harvard class of 1938 are members of the Century, and Sinclair Armstrong and Wilson Binger decided to have a dinner, inviting Harvard '38 and Centurion Caspar Weinberger. So Cappy, as we all called him, falling into the habits of half a century ago, duly appeared, and we gathered Monday evening (the 4th) in an up-stairs room at the club.

Someone had to bring up what was on everyone's mind; and, since no one else seemed inclined to do it, I appointed myself to do the dirty work. Cap was as usual amiable and unruffled, explaining everything with the placid certitude and quiet lucidity of a madman. The Russians, he informed us, are "bent on world conquest," and everything follows from that. They are ahead of us in military power; they are further ad-vanced than we on Star Wars research; they are on the offensive every-where in the world. I said that other experts—Bob McNamara, Solly Zuckerman—questioned whether we had fallen behind in weapons and in research; Cappy waved that aside. I asked how they conceived the transition during the 25 years required to make Star Wars opera-tional: would not the Soviet Union build more ICBMs to overwhelm the space shield, more low-altitude delivery systems to go under it? would not Star Wars only intensify the nuclear arms race? Cappy re-plied that the Russians were doing all that anyway. I asked whether he was not choosing Star Wars over arms control. And so on, ships pass-ing in the night.

November 18

I took Evangeline and Marietta last night to hear Gore Vidal and Norman Mailer in one of Norman's series for the benefit of PEN. The last time the two met ended in a celebrated fight at Lally Weymouth's. This time both were on their good behavior, with respect to each other though, alas, in no other respect. Gore gave a (relatively) polished talk about the American empire, banal in content, cheap in tone and deliv-ered to the accompaniment of smiles of vast self-satisfaction. He began with a bad joke about Reagan that Bob Dole had told some weeks back about Jack Kemp and the *Times* reprinted. (Reagan is sad because his library burned down and he lost both of his books and he hadn't even finished coloring one of them.) Then, after half an hour of Gore's smirking, Norman came on and gave a series of awkward and incoherent remarks that made very little sense whatsoever. One had the impression that he must have spent all of three minutes in figuring out what he was going to say. Both men are better than their miserable performances.

One has a sinking sense of the consequences when talent is corrupted by personality. It was a low point on the American literary scene. We left at the intermission and had a jolly dinner at Mortimer's.

1986

❖

January 23

John Chancellor has just returned from a conference in San Diego bringing together former presidential "chiefs of staff." As moderator of one session, he asked the ex-chiefs how they prevented their Presidents from doing foolish things. Sorensen said, "Well, the long way was to say, 'Mr. President, we'll have to staff that out,' but the short way was to say, 'Mr. President, that sounds like something Dick Nixon would have done.'" Bob Haldeman, who was present, said, "We didn't have that option."

The whole concept of a presidential chief of staff is curious and recent. FDR, Truman, Kennedy, Johnson were in effect their own chiefs of staff. JFK had Ted as top man on domestic policy and Mac as top man in foreign policy, but the rest of the staff retained ample and easy access to them and to him. The notion of a chief of staff shielding the President began with Nixon. It has reached its culmination with Donald Regan, who, we read, decides himself what the President should read and whom he should see. Chancellor said that there was considerable criticism of Regan at the conference, on the part of Republicans like Donald Rumsfeld as well as of Democrats.

January 25

A movie we saw a few days ago lingers in mind. It was *Brazil,* a British film directed by Terry Gilliam, a graduate of the Monty Python team. Tom Stoppard contributed to the screenplay. Its portrait of the future is not all that original and draws much from *1984* and from *A Clockwork Orange.* But its vision of an electronic world in which nothing works, of cities drowned in filth and litter and divided between the stupid rich and the aimlessly violent poor, of an intrusive, incompetent and brutal state bureaucracy—all seemed peculiarly convincing. I find that I have no faith, none at all, in progress. I do not expect a better future. I shudder when I contemplate the world in which Robert will grow up. I pray that I am wrong, but nearly every amenity of life has declined in my lifetime. Only technology has improved, and even technology disappoints, breaks down and is impossible to get repaired. My heart sinks as I walk the streets of New York strewn as they are these days with paper and cans and bottles and garbage. However, I eat the best meals I can get, drink Jack Daniel's, smoke Havana cigars and prepare to enjoy life while it is still possible.

March 10

A great dynastic struggle is taking place in the Democratic primary for Tip O'Neill's seat in Massachusetts. Some time ago Jim Roosevelt, Jimmy's son, came to see me, said he was going to enter the contest and asked for my support. I told him that I doubted my support would do much for him but that he was free to use my name. Subsequently Joe Kennedy, Bobby's son, announced his candidacy. Franklin is much irritated by this, and he and Kate Whitney have been rallying the Roosevelt family behind Jim. Jim Roosevelt seems an earnest, straightforward, pleasant young man. Joe Kennedy is more aggressive and dramatic but perhaps less reliable. After Joe's announcement, I found myself in a dilemma and consulted Ken Galbraith, who lives in the district and for whom the dilemma would be presumably more acute. Ken said, "I don't see any great problems. I simply endorsed them both." That is what I have done, meanwhile sending Jim $50 and Kathleen Kennedy Townsend, who is running in Maryland, $100. I figure that Joe has plenty of money.

March 1

I find in my old age that more and more people ask my advice. I heartily dislike the responsibility of giving advice. When we were at the Kennedy house in Palm Beach I found the Riverside edition of Hawthorne and, reading *Our Old Home* for the first time, came on the following sentence in the chapter entitled "Consular Experiences," "I have always hated to give advice, especially when there is a prospect of its being taken." Right on.

March 12

An unusually pleasant New York evening yesterday, perhaps worth describing. My colloquium was on A. K. Weinberg's *Manifest Destiny,* still after half a century rather a marvelous book in the breadth of its research and reference and in its deadpan Veblenesque style. Then we took Kathy Sloane, who is staying with us, to a party celebrating the 10th anniversary of Mortimer's. Mortimer's has rather taken the place of P.J. Moriarty's in our lives. It is different from P.J.'s, though—less the neighborhood pub, more the resort of the chic and the jeunesse doree. Still, Glenn Birnbaum, the genial proprietor, has always been welcoming to us; the food is pretty good; the prices are astonishingly reasonable. So we tend to go there every weekend. It is a great place to take foreigners and show them the scene. The party was crowded—everyone from Abe Ribicoff to Klaus von Bulow.

We went on to dinner at the Rohatyn's—an extremely pleasant and cozy evening. The cast:

FELIX AND LIZ ROHATYN. I first met Felix some years ago through Jan Cushing, and we have become good friends. He is intelligent, cultivated, humorous and agreeable. I especially admire the broad scope and resourcefulness of his thinking on economic policy. Liz is a girl from Memphis, whom I first knew as Liz Vagliano when I first came to New York. She is pretty and lively, and I like her very much.

BROOKE ASTOR. I can't quite remember when and how we became friends, but I have grown very fond of her—not only for her enlightened philanthropies, but more particularly because of her breezy, informal charm, her unflagging energy (she has just completed a new novel) and other qualities I celebrate in a sketch I have done of her for *Architectural Digest* (above all, her permanent youth).

BILL PALEY. I have known Bill—through Marietta originally— for about thirty years. Like Brooke, Bill retains vitality, curiosity, humor and charm well into his eighties. He is always a delight to see.

HENRY AND NANCY KISSINGER. Henry I have known for thirty-five years and have watched evolve from an insecure and eager graduate student into the urbane global mover and shaker he is today. One of his disarming qualities is abiding loyalty to people who helped him when he was an unknown, so, despite our occasional and sometimes intense disagreements, he remains cordial. I like Nancy very much.

April 16

I am taking lessons every Monday at Robert's school in the arcane art of word processing—a weekly exercise in intellectual mortification, since I find it hard to master electronic techniques that eight-year-old children learn with ease. When I returned about 7:45, Alexandra informed me that Rambo had struck again [at the Libyan regime of Muammar Qaddafi]. What is most discouraging about the sneak attack on Libya is the near unanimous support it has received in politics (Lowell Weicker honorably excepted) and in the press (the *New York*

Times was especially unctuous and odious). Oddly enough I have not encountered many people who really like the action, and I imagine that the approval in the polls may conceal deeper apprehensions. Clifton Daniel at the bar of the Century yesterday was filled with foreboding and expressed relief to find a fellow worrier. We went to Sue Railey's last night, where Robin Duke, Evangeline Bruce, Bill vanden Heuvel and others were sharply critical. Only Morton Janklow defended the action. The French Ambassador to the UN was there and said that, when Dick Walters consulted with Mitterrand and [Jacques] Chirac, they were in total agreement and told Walters that France would back an all-out effort to overthrow the Qaddafi regime but saw no point in pinpricks. (As Emerson used to say, "If you strike a king, you must strike to kill.")

I confidently predicted last night that the bombing would solidify Libya behind Qaddafi and diminish the chances of internal upheaval. But this morning the news reported fighting of some sort in Tripoli—perhaps an anti-Qaddafi coup may be in the making. If this should happen, Reagan luck again.

April 19

The polls show overwhelming support for Reagan's bombing of Libya, but nearly everyone I have encountered is against it. This is no doubt a commentary on the restricted circles in which I move, but even when I went to Minneapolis on the 17th, I condemned the attack at a lecture and later before a live television audience and in each case got plenty of applause. My guess is that the initial approval is a result both of the prevailing frustration about terrorism and of the rally-round-the-flag effect whenever hostilities begin, and that it will fade away as soon as people start to realize that the bombing will stimulate rather than reduce terrorism.

Meanwhile Reagan seems loopier than ever. The *Times* quotes him today about the attack: "We weren't out to kill anybody." What in the world did he think would happen when he ordered the Air Force to drop bombs on a country? His remark confirms my sense that nothing is very real to him—that war in Libya is like war used to be in

Hollywood: a day simulating violence on the set; then home for a drink and a swim, while life goes on.

June 27

Robert's 14th birthday. He is now taller than I am, leaving me the shortest member of the household. He is also in a mild and generally amiable stage of teen-age rebellion against his parents—necessary, no doubt, to emancipate himself and define his personality but trying (at moments) for his father and mother.

July 3

My mother would have been one hundred years old today.

Mike Nichols asked us to a screening of *Heartburn* last night, along with Jackie, Caroline and Ed Schlossberg, her fiancé, the Smiths, and Maurice Tempelsman. Afterward he took us all to the Russian Tea Room for dinner. (The film was a brilliant exercise in weaving without straw—marvelously acted and directed, but very thin and repetitious as to story.) I sat next to Jackie at dinner, and taking up from the film she reminisced about her days as Inquiring Photographer for the old *Times-Herald* in Washington. "Jack used to help me think up questions," she said, "and one day he came up with this question. 'Suppose you came home and found your wife in bed with your best friend. Which one would you shoot first?' So I tried that question and was surprised that nearly all the men I asked said they would shoot their best friend first."

July 7

I had an Op Ed piece in the Sunday *Times* decrying the spread of me-tooism in the Democratic party. This produced a call this morning from Jesse Jackson, who praised the piece lavishly, said he wept after reading it and left the paper drenched with tears—"the soundest, sanest, boldest analysis I have seen in print . . . what I have been trying to say for years but could not say so well," etc. Naturally I was enchanted by his reaction, and we had an agreeable talk, culminating in an engagement to lunch next Monday.

When I later mentioned this call to Joe Rauh, he said, "Jesse is going to be a real problem for the Democratic party. He is quite capable of starting a third party. With Martin [Luther King], when we demonstrated to him that a third party would help the conservatives, that was enough to persuade him against it. But Jesse doesn't care about the result. He will be for a third party if he thinks it will enhance himself. . . . Still he says good things, and he is bringing blacks into the party. The trouble is that for every black vote he wins he loses a white vote. What you should say to him is that realistically he has to find ways to make points to black voters without scaring off white voters."

July 14

Bastille Day. I lunched with Jesse Jackson. He was nattily dressed, striped shirt, white collar, and brought along two of his sons—nice, polite, perhaps somewhat cowed boys. He is of course highly articulate but at the same time a little constrained. I called him Jesse and, after he called me "Professor Schlesinger," told him to call me Arthur. He continued to say "Professor." He said some more how much the *Times* Op Ed piece had moved him, spoke about the need for revitalizing the party, etc. I asked whether he saw his effort as within the framework of the party or as moving toward a third party. He said that he planned to work within the party. I posed Joe Rauh's question: how to make points to black voters without scaring off white voters? He said by concentration on economic issues; he added that just as Cuomo had his base in New York, he had his base in the black vote and could not neglect his constituency. I am still not clear why he wanted to meet, except that he said perhaps I could arrange an evening with people who could talk out some of the issues. I asked who might be good for such an evening, mentioning Dick Goodwin (who had travelled with him for a time in 1984). He was high on Dick; then, oddly, mentioned Edward Bennett Williams. I think I will try to do something in the fall.

When we had talked over the phone last week, Jackson had made a great and persuasive point about the drug epidemic. This was the "hound of hell" for this generation, he said, and the Democratic party ought to have a drug program. He is quite right. But when I asked him what the program should be, he was rather disappointing, resting everything on moral exhortation. His program really is to get athletes and rock stars to launch an anti-drug campaign.

[Caroline Kennedy's] wedding was at three in Centerville on Saturday. It was a happy day. I have never seen Caroline look more beautiful, and the groom went through the paces with commendable aplomb. I should have noted, in reporting the dinner with Mike Nichols after *Heartburn,* that Ed Schlossberg, who had given an impression of glum silence on earlier encounters, turned out to be intelligent and amusing. He obviously pleases Caroline. After the wedding, there was a reception at the Kennedy compound in Hyannis Port. The weather, which had been foggy in the morning and was still overcast in the early afternoon, suddenly became clear, with marvelous Cape afternoon light. The reception was like an alumni reunion, though with curious omissions. The only JFK cabinet member present was Abe Ribicoff, with Ros Gilpatric representing the subcabinet. I imagine that McNamara and Dillon must have been invited, but they were not there. The only senator or ex-senator (beside Ted) was John Culver. Where were Claiborne Pell and George McGovern? Still it was a most agreeable time. In due course, dinner was served in a tent with pennants flying in the wind. We ate with Ethel, young Joe and his wife, the Buchwalds and the Goodwins. In the evening there were toasts (Ted's voice breaking when he spoke of JFK), dancing, fireworks. These last were organized by George Plimpton, and some of the displays were dedicated by name to members of the wedding party or of the Kennedy family, except for one dedicated to Alexandra and me, evidently because it involved a rocket flaming into the sky (Alexandra) and becoming a bow tie (me). Unfortunately the clouds had returned, so, while the rocket was highly visible, the bow tie disappeared into the mists above. Probably symbolic.

We got back to New York in the evening. Pamela Harriman called to say that Averell was sinking. He remains lucid and won't let anyone help him, dismisses the nurses, tells her, "Leave me alone." She cried a bit as she told me that. I reminded her that Averell has always been an intensely proud man who hates to show weakness and demands to do things his own way. Alexandra says that he is like a great lion who wants to go off by himself and die.

July 26

Tuesday night, the 22nd, we spent with the Harrimans at Birch Grove (née Haywire). Diane Sawyer and Dick Holbrooke were there for dinner. Pamela is going through an ordeal with admirable temper and concern. She took me in to see Averell both that evening and the next morning. On both occasions he was lying asleep in his bed, mouth open, breathing heavily, sedated by morphine to relieve the pain. The family has properly decided against artificial life-prolongation measures. He cannot absorb solid food and receives only a saline solution. But he has been indestructible for 95 years, and his heart beats nobly along. He did not look pitiful as he lay in the bed; only profoundly tired. His doctor was there. He says that he may live for another ten days or so.

Pam called shortly after 8 this morning, weeping, to say that Averell had died in the night. This is the end of a long and wonderful chapter in my own life.

July 30

Averell's funeral took place yesterday. It was rather splendid. It took place at St. Thomas's on Fifth Avenue and 53rd Street, a block away from the site of the house in which he was born nearly 95 years ago. It was a regular Episcopal service, presided over by Paul Moore looking every inch (all 78 of them) a bishop. I was one of the ushers. Afterward a large delegation of family and a smaller one of friends accompanied the coffin to Arden for the burial. A buffet luncheon and drinks were served at Arden House. It was a nice, somber, sad day, redeemed by the sense that Averell had lived a full and marvelous life and that the death was not too lingering. Pam told me that the autopsy showed him to be "riddled with cancer." In 1972 he had an operation for cancer of the prostate. The cancer evidently went into remission for a long time but eventually metastasized and took the highly painful form of bone cancer. Averell was as ever stoic about pain, though the pain obviously became intense toward the end; hence the morphine.

Pam was a superb wife. She loved Averell, cherished him, surrounded him by people and events and gaiety and comfort, never showed impatience and more than kept her side of the bargain. My only regret is her abiding dislike of Marie [Harriman] and to a lesser degree of Peter Duchin and Mike Forrestal, who were the sons Averell never had and who adored Marie and her memory. When Peter began living with Brooke Hayward, who had been Pam's stepdaughter and who wrote scathingly about her in her own memoir *Haywire,* the breach became acute. After Peter married Brooke, things were patched up a bit. Peter was a pallbearer and went to Arden for the burial. Brooke was at the church but not at Arden. Mike is cruising off Canadian shores and could not be reached.

October 11

As I have no doubt complained before, it is a great illusion to suppose that advancing age brings any simplification of life. I seem to be busier than ever these days, and to less profit and purpose. We are broke, and my nice lawyer Jane Manopoli is coming to town in order to have a talk about my financial affairs. I have not yet had time even to begin filing my notes for volume iv of *The Age of Roosevelt.* I spend my days answering letters, reading colloquium papers, writing recommendations, talking to people about the past (having bothered plenty of busy people in my own time for historical purposes, I feel I must make myself equally available to historians and journalists today), seeing foreign visitors whom I do not want to see and generally wasting the most precious of commodities—time, which is inevitably running out for me.

Cycles is now in the bookstores. The first two reviews—by Jack Diggins in the *Boston Globe* and John Dizikes in the *San Francisco Chronicle*—are both generous and discerning, but I imagine that brickbats are lying in wait. The book will not be officially published until the 24th.

The press continues good on *Cycles*—a very nice review (and interview) by Peter Prescott in *Newsweek*. I ran into Pat Moynihan at the Century yesterday. He said, "Great book. I am a third of the way through, and it's a great book." I hope his enthusiasm survives the remaining two-thirds.

October 26

After an appearance on the *Today* show on Thursday the 23rd I flew to Chicago. The luncheon on the American flight was inedible; I would have been ashamed to feed it to [our dog] Polo. My Chicago book escort took me to a place called Riccardo's for luncheon, where in short order I saw Studs Terkel, Irv Kupcinet of the *Sun-Times,* a leading bookseller and a few local newspapermen. Afterward I went over to the *Tribune* for a meeting with the editorial board—an agreeable and liberal-minded group. It is hard for me to overcome my memories of Colonel McCormick's *Tribune* and to adjust to this new, civilized version. For many years I was never mentioned in the *Tribune* except as a sinister or ridiculous figure. Now I write for it on occasion, my books are favorably reviewed in it, and the editors listen politely to what I have to say.

November 10

For once, my political instinct was right. Election night was profoundly satisfying. The Democrats won eight seats—more than the most optimistic forecasts and a timely vindication of the cyclical hypothesis. We spent the night at the Smiths' in congenial company. A splendid time was had by all.

One consequence of Cuomo's smashing victory (67 percent of the vote) is to thrust him forward more vigorously than ever as a presidential possibility. Unfortunately the campaign brought out the worst in him; and, though this plainly did not affect the voters, it has aroused the press and alarmed the politicians. He played too many games on the question of debating [Andrew P.] O'Rourke, his Republican opponent, and then concluded the campaign by blowing up at the press. This he has continued to do since his victory, thereby acquiring the reputation of a sore winner. Stephen says that his performance has dismayed his staff as well as others. Some say that he characteristically has an emotional backlash at the end of campaigns. Others blame it on his back trouble, which apparently has been acute lately. Yet others wonder whether he does not have a self-destructive impulse and may not unconsciously be trying to remove himself from presidential consideration. Mario can be so good that it is discouraging when he puts on such a bad display. As I perhaps have written before, Mario, like Adlai Stevenson, has a great gift for throwing unnecessary obstacles in his own path.

A blow today—the review of *Cycles* in next Sunday's *Times Book Review*. It is written by Benjamin Barber, a third-rate political scientist at Rutgers without much reputation even in that third-rate field. He does not believe in representative institutions and favors direct democracy—town meetings, legislation by referendum and plebiscite, etc. As Bob Silvers says, he believes in Swiss, not in American, democracy. God knows why the *Times* uses him as a reviewer, which they do quite a lot; and God knows why they should assign a historical work to a political scientist anyway. The review is opinionated, snotty, obtuse and decidedly unhelpful. It is the first bad review so far, but inevitably in the most influential place. Bad luck.

November 18

I went to Boston on Wednesday the 12th to promote the book. A splendid review, by the way, in the new *New Republic* by Alan Brinkley. I am especially pleased that four of the best reviews have been by young historians—Brinkley, Jack Diggins, Robert Dawidoff, John Dizikes (not to mention the review by that eminent senior historian George Kennan).

November 23

Last night Chrissie celebrated her 40th birthday (which actually took place on Wednesday). She and Nancy gave a dance in their apartment, and it was a great success. It was also Robert's initiation into inebriation. He was helping to tend bar, and in the course of his duties sampled too much of the champagne. After a while he got sick. We then took him home, and he repeatedly threw up on the way, necessitating frequent stops by the taxi. I took him up the stairs and put him to bed. I could not get too irate about it, remembering my first debutante party when I was a sophomore at Harvard. Excruciatingly shy, a poor dancer, knowing none of the girls, I hung around the sidelines and drank champagne. On returning to Adams House, I got terribly sick and threw up over the bedroom floor on my rush to the bathroom. The odor lingered for weeks. It was a useful lesson. I have never liked champagne since.

November 28

This has been a most enjoyable week, at least from a narrow partisan viewpoint. The Reagan administration is beginning to collapse. After the 1984 election I wrote in the *Wall Street Journal,* "Every President in modern times who won an election with more than 60 percent of the popular vote has found himself in bad political trouble soon after—not only FDR in 1936, but Warren Harding (1920), Lyndon Johnson (1964) and Richard Nixon (1972). The euphoria induced by overwhelming support evidently loosens the presidential grasp on reality." Since Reagan did not quite make 60 percent, he might have been exempt from this particular effect, but evidently not. Like the others, he seems to feel that his mandate liberates him from normal accountability; and so he has plunged ahead on a secret course toward Iran, deceiving Congress, the American press and our allies along the way. How much did he know? When did he know it? These questions will dominate the next weeks. Don Regan, I imagine, will go; maybe Bill Casey too. Reagan's personal popularity will abide, but confidence in his leadership will plummet. It is rather like the climax of *The Wizard of Oz,* when Dorothy, having caught the Wizard manipulating his magical effects, says, "You are a bad man," to which the Wizard replies, "No, I am not a bad man. But I am a very bad wizard."

December 6

George Kennan said yesterday at luncheon at the Academy/Institute, "It is impressive how in recent times Congress has been far ahead of the executive branch in understanding foreign policy. I did not used to think that this could be the case, but I have had to change my mind." This is an understatement. George through most of his life has regarded foreign policy as a domain of the professionals to be protected by the executive from wayward and capricious congressional interference. Of course I too have traveled a considerable distance in acknowledging the indispensability of a congressional role in foreign policy; but George made the case against Congress more passionately and profoundly and in consequence has had to travel further. George's retraction is a rather moving recognition of the value in the democratic process.

December 7

Yesterday a Soviet political scientist came for a drink. Eventually we asked him to stay to dinner—an American family occasion; Bill and Pat Emmet are spending the weekend, and Chrissie and Nancy, Andy and Jenny were joining us for dinner.

His name is Fedor Burlatsky. He is a professor, vice president of the Association of Political Science and a political commentator for *Literaturnaya Gazeta.* What is more interesting is that he was in the 1960s a speechwriter for Khrushchev, Andropov and (briefly) for Brezhnev. Also he is the first Soviet citizen I have encountered who speaks with perfect freedom (apparently) about Soviet personalities, feuds and problems.

He remains a Khrushchev man and plans to write a biography of him. He is an outspoken anti-Stalinist and much in favor of Gorbachev's reform program. I asked him what it was like to work for Khrushchev. He said that Khrushchev was very polite and kind with his supporters and staff but crude and "vulgar" in his dealings with his colleagues on the Presidium; "he always wanted to put them in their place." Writing speeches for Khrushchev, he said, was a trial. On important speeches Khrushchev dictated his own first draft. These drafts, Burlatsky said, were a "mess"—rambling, confusing, disorganized, fragmentary. The writers had to extract a theme and impose a structure on the Chairman's stream of consciousness.

Burlatsky worked on the speech Khrushchev gave after the Cuban missile crisis. He had not been previously involved in the missile project but was called in after the debacle. I asked what Khrushchev thought he was doing. [Oleg] Troyanovsky, he said, had worked with Khrushchev on the messages to JFK during the crisis. Burlatsky said that he did not believe that deployment was originally Khrushchev's idea; he thinks the idea came from [Rodion] Malinovsky. Khrushchev embraced it, Burlatsky surmises, because he had the "naive hope" that, if he could sneak the missiles into Cuba, the United States would accept them as the Soviet Union had accepted the American missiles in Turkey—as a *fait accompli*. I asked whether he had come back from Vienna with an impression that Kennedy was weak and could be pushed around. Burlatsky said that the predominant impression that Khrushchev brought back from Vienna was not so much that Kennedy was weak but that he was "too young" and consequently inexperienced.

Burlatsky stayed on with Khrushchev. I asked whether the missile crisis was a prime cause of Khrushchev's downfall. Bourlatsky said that the real cause were the reforms that threatened the power of the state and party bureaucracy. Brezhnev represented the old guard whose privileges were in jeopardy. He did not want quite to carry the country back to Stalin, but he wanted to stop the reform movement. After Khrushchev's fall, Burlatsky remained in the speech-writing *apparat*. Brezhnev had to give a speech and was presented with two drafts—one from [Aleksandr] Shelepin, the other from the Bourlatsky team. The two drafts represented sharply differing positions, and Burlatsky tried to explain the differences to Brezhnev. He said that Brezhnev listened without comprehension, seemed wholly uninterested in issues and said, "That is not my field. I know about organization." Burlatsky decided that this was not for him. No doubt he was out of favor as a Khrushchev man.

I found this a rather astonishing conversation. Burlatsky talked about Soviet politics with the same lack of inhibition that an Englishman or American would talk about their national politics. Is this because he has a license from the KGB? Yet he made no effort to inculcate any particular line or insert pro-Soviet points. Or is this the new post-Gorbachev freedom? Or is he a man prepared to take risks? I called Marshall Shulman today to try and find out more about him, but could not reach him.

December 10

Last night I went to a dinner at Columbia in honor of Marshall Shulman. Marshall, Steve Cohen and Bob Legvold all say that Burlatsky is on the level.

Interesting change in manners: when people came up to congratulate Marshall, quite a number of the men hugged and kissed him. This is a custom unknown in my youth but now a rising tendency. I applaud it as an open expression of feeling but am too accustomed to more reserved ways to do it myself. Lenny Bernstein has kissed his male friends for years (I mean quite apart from any homosexual implications), and so has Sidney Lumet; but now the habit is spreading beyond musical and theatrical circles. It would have astonished the 1930s.

December 11

Last night I appeared on ABC's *Nightline* (Ted Koppel), leaving an entertaining dinner party given by Ahmed and Mica Ertegun for Irving Lazar. My combatant on the show was a fellow named Charles Krauthammer who writes particularly obnoxious neo-conservative trash for the *New Republic* and other rightwing journals. His special line is that a mature power must understand the vital need for an imperial policy and for unfettered executive secrecy in the conduct of foreign affairs. He argues this line with boundless self-righteousness and sublime ignorance of American history. He is also, alas, a paraplegic, having dived into a waterless swimming pool. The joy of dealing with Krauthammer perhaps tempted me into undue vehemence. I have been trying to establish a new and more benign television personality. His performance was surprisingly feeble, and I was unnecessarily testy. Still it gave me much satisfaction. Jules Feiffer called this morning and said, "If Krauthammer were not already in a wheelchair, he certainly would be now after the pounding you gave him last night."

The puzzle is that there are people who take Krauthammer seriously as a deep thinker.

December 18

The administration continues to twist slowly in the wind, giving boundless, though publicly unacknowledged, pleasure to nearly everyone I know. There is a good deal of hypocrisy among the opposition; much pious lamentation over the alleged sorrows of a weakened presidency. If a presidency is inclined to do dumb things, it is far better that it be weak rather than strong.

1987

❖

March 24

On Thursday I flew to Florida for a conference on the Cuban missile crisis organized by the Kennedy School at Harvard. The participants were partly veterans of the crisis and partly scholars (mostly political scientists, though, and no revisionists). I had argued in vain for Soviet and Cuban participation. The alumni reunion aspect was exceedingly pleasant, and I had delightful meals with George and Ruth Ball, Douglas and Susie Dillon and Bob McNamara.

Two points struck me with special force: JFK's absolute determination to avoid a military confrontation; and (a smaller point) the doubt that nuclear warheads ever arrived in Cuba.

Bob McNamara revealed himself as the biggest dove of all. At one point between the meetings he drew me aside and said: "The questions that really fascinate me are (1) did the installation of Soviet missiles in Cuba make any military difference to the security of the United States? and (2) if it made no difference—and I am sure that this is the case—could the acceptance of the missiles have been sold to Congress, our people and our allies? If this conclusion could have been sold—and I believe it might have been done—were we not running an unjustifiable risk of nuclear war by using confrontation to force the withdrawal of the missiles?"

My own view is that Bob views the balance-of-power questions too narrowly in military terms. The successful installation of the missiles might not have upset the military balance, but it would have seriously upset the political balance. It would have demonstrated the Soviet ability to act with impunity in the very heart of the American zone of vital interest; and the political implications would have been demoralizing for the West and destabilizing for the world. Certainly the Russians themselves believed that emplacement of the missiles would have altered the power balance. Nor, given the great American superiority in both conventional and nuclear weapons, do I think the risk of nuclear war was all that great.

McNamara in the meantime described with eloquence his riding hard on the military during the crisis. "Our quarantine was intended to be a political signal, a means of sending a message to Khrushchev, *not* a military operation. Trying to get that across to the military caused a lot of headaches. I slept for twelve days in the Pentagon not because I thought the military would challenge civilian authority but because I feared that they would not understand the real meaning of the quarantine."

A note on the political situation. 1988 should be a Democratic year. Hart is way ahead in the polls, but I think it is mostly the consequence of name recognition. I have yet to find anyone—even Ted Sorensen, who reverted to Hart after Cuomo's withdrawal—who is filled with genuine enthusiasm for him; and I believe his support is brittle. I think Hart is an intelligent fellow with a real interest in the substance of issues; but I continue to find a certain inauthenticity in him. He remains a self-created American type, like the Great Gatsby. Mike Dukakis is a cold customer too, but at least one feels that he knows who he is. I do not

feel that about Gary Hart, and I don't think the republic can afford
another weird President.

March 26

Andrei Voznesensky called last night (from Yoko Ono's apartment)
and asked whether he could stop by for a drink. He soon appeared,
wearing a white cap, and accepted some Stolichnaya. I said that we had
all been impressed by the astonishing developments in the Soviet Union.
Andrei said, "I would never have believed it if anyone had told me a year
ago . . . or six months ago . . . or three months ago." He is tremendously
pro-Gorbachev, but thinks that Gorbachev may be moving too fast for
his own good. I asked where Gorbachev found his main support. Andrei
said, "I can't think who is for Gorbachev in the Soviet Union, except the
intellectuals, and they don't count. The military are against him. The bureaucracy is against him. The KGB was for him at first, because he was
Andropov's protege, but I don't know how they stand now." I asked
whether there was any challenger. He said, "Well, maybe [Yegor] Ligachev. So people say. But it is hard to tell. It may be unfair to Ligachev."
Andrei's aim, he says, is to take advantage of the situation to rehabilitate
[Boris] Pasternak and [Marc] Chagall. He wants to establish Pasternak's
house in Peredelkino and Chagall's birthplace as museums.

He also told us about his meeting with Reagan during his last visit.
Reagan's first words to him were, "What an elegant jacket! Where did
you get it?" Andrei said it came from Valentino's in Rome. Reagan said,
"I have one just like it, only brighter." At the end of the interview, Voznesensky asked Reagan, "Which Russian writer influenced you most:
Dostoyevsky, Tolstoy, Chekhov?" As he asked the question, he glanced
at the faces of the people there with him—all somber, except for George
Bush, who smiled as if getting the joke. Reagan said, "In my youth I
read the international classics."

Andrei went off into the night, his white cap back on his head, to
dine with Norman Mailer at Elaine's.

March 31

I went this evening to a meeting of the advisory council of the Harriman Institute at Columbia. Arthur Hartman, who has been ambassador to the Soviet Union for the last five years, spoke after dinner. He says that Gorbachev is in his view a genuine Marxist-Leninist who truly believes, for example, that the United States is run by "ruling circles" made up of great industrialists and financiers. On the other hand, he also thinks that Gorbachev is a genuine reformer who realizes that the Soviet Union, if it is to survive as a great power, must modernize its economy. "Nothing has moved me more recently," he said, "than the phone call I received from Sakharov the day before I left Moscow. A year ago I could never have conceived for an instant that such a thing could happen."

He notes the great resistance to Gorbachev's reforms and doubts that Gorbachev will be able to carry them far enough really to liberate the Soviet economy. "In four or five years," he said, "Russia will be faced with a drastic choice: either much faster movement toward a market economy or a return to neo-Stalinism." Hartman thinks that the Russian people are so accustomed to authoritarian government that neo-Stalinism will win out. The mass of the people, he said, want an iron hand.

April 20

I lunched today at Aurora, an expensive new restaurant, with Harold Evans and Bill Rayner, who want me to do something for their new magazine *Traveler*. I could not help noting the generational differences in diet. I had a martini and grilled double lamb chops. They had Perrier and chef's salad. I suppose that their diet is better for them. But mine is more fun. I understand the disappearance of cigarettes these days; they are poison. But why has hard liquor, the staff of life, yielded to white wine and, heaven help us, Perrier?

May 23

The Gary Hart story appeared [Tuesday] morning in the *Herald Tribune,* and by the time we went to Washington on Thursday the 7th it was dominating all political conversation. I cannot say that I was altogether surprised. As I probably have written in these pages before, Gary always seemed to me a puzzling figure, the Gatsby of our politics, who in his upward rise from the bleak little Kansas town in which he was born has reinvented himself along the way to the point where he does not know who he is any more. I did not anticipate the denouement would take precisely this form, but I did believe that his inauthenticity would find damaging expression in one way or another and prevent his ever getting the nomination. One had heard stories of his escapades before—when we lunched with Antonia Pinter in London, she talked again about his enthusiasm for Diana Phipps—but I assumed from this fling that his taste was at least defensible. Donna Rice, the Louisiana lawyer [Bill] Broadhurst and the yacht the *Monkey Business,* are another matter. The names in the story are straight out of Evelyn Waugh—Gary's home address in Colorado is Troublesome Gulch. By Thursday the bad jokes had begun to spread—"Tailgate," as the name of the episode; "Where's the beef?" "It's in the Rice"; and "Gary should never have changed his name; he should have left it at Hotpants." It is a sad tale all the same, out of which only Lee Hart emerges with credit. I don't know whose behavior is worse: the *Miami Herald*'s or Gary Hart's. And I do think American politics reached a new low when a *Washington Post* reporter asked Hart whether he had ever committed adultery. Nor did the *Post* behave defensibly when, by threatening new disclosures, it forced Hart out of the race. The decision on Hart should have been made by the voters, not by the newspapers. All in all, a bad business.

It is worse because no one takes adultery very seriously *per se.* It wrecked Hart because it came as a culmination of a sequence of things that had raised doubts about his character and judgment. Nor can one suppress the suspicion that an impulse toward self-destruction was involved. As for the adultery standard, a valuable point emerged Friday when we were driving from Pam Harriman's house to Hickory Hill for the annual Robert Kennedy Book Award. The two winners— David Garrow for his biography of Martin Luther King and Elizabeth Becker for her book on Cambodia—were in the car with us. King, like Hart, was a man with a disorderly and compulsive sex life. But he was also a noble man who contributed formidably to the advance of justice in the United States. Pol Pot, on the other hand, was a model of marital fidelity and sexual scrupulousness. All he did was to murder 2 million or so of his fellow countrymen. So much for the adultery standard.

Where do the Democrats go now? This was a major topic at dinner at Pam's on Thursday night. As I see it at the moment, three candidates deserve attention—Mike Dukakis, Paul Simon and young Al Gore. The virtue of the primaries is that they will now provide the candidates a testing and the voters more evidence for judgment. The figure of Mario Cuomo haunts the background, and he is having a great time teasing the press. Perhaps in the end he might run. Stephen thinks that he need not make a decision till the autumn. There is also talk of Bill Bradley. Felix Rohatyn is for him, and so, I am told, is George Ball. I could not possibly support anyone who is for aid to the Contras and (I think) for Star Wars, and I don't see how George can either. Nor has Bradley identified himself with any liberal issue in domestic affairs. The cycle is changing, and we need a Democratic candidate who believes in the historic positions of the party.

I will let pass a gratuitous attack by a writer named Joan Didion in the *New York Review of Books*. Both Didion and her husband John Gregory Dunne have it in for me, and both have gone out of their way to drag me into their effusions on other matters. Heaven alone knows where this animus comes from. It is probably that they hate the Kennedys, and I become a derivative target. I have resisted Barbara Epstein's proposal that I send a reply. Life is too short for stupid controversy.

May 26

We went to Cambridge on Sunday the 24th for John Fairbank's 80th birthday—an agreeable occasion with a greatly deserved flow of tribute to America's greatest Sinologist. I first met John and Wilma in Peking in October 1933, and they have remained dear friends through all the vicissitudes of life. My classmate Ben Schwartz was one of the speakers. He put particular emphasis in his remarks on the way John revised the American approach to China by demanding respect for the "inner life" of other nations. This regard for the autonomy of other peoples is absolutely essential for the historian and for the diplomat and the statesman as well, and the failure to accord that respect is one of the most pernicious delusions of superpowership. I believe that I owe much of my understanding of this point to John's wry and gentle discourse through the years.

June 9

Last week I went to a couple of breakfasts for Al Gore (on the 3rd and the 5th—the first was a large breakfast of politicos and businessmen; the second, at Dick Gardner's, was more intimate). I like Gore. He is intelligent, articulate and agreeable, though a little hard to talk to at first, perhaps because of shyness. At the Wednesday breakfast he delivered rather extended remarks. "Ideas," he said, "are America's most powerful weapon," and he developed this theme effectively. At Dick Gardner's he was more informal. I asked him about his positions on civil rights and on aid to the Contras, and he answered forthrightly (and, from my viewpoint, very satisfactorily).

I guess what I like about him most is the sense one has that he is relatively at ease in the electronic, biogenetic age. This is of course because he is so young (39) and has the advantage over the other candidates of having grown up in the new era. Things other candidates will have to learn Gore has at his fingertips. (I feel all this especially keenly as I struggle to master the word processor.)

In his instinct for ideas and problems just beyond the horizon, he reminds me a bit of Jerry Brown—but a non-flakey, even perhaps plodding, Jerry Brown. If he lacks Jerry's dash, he also lacks his occasional weirdness. (Jerry, I understand, is now in retirement at a Zen monastery in Japan writing a book.)

August 12

Rex Brown, who is married to Sharon Bond, Helen Cannon Bond's daughter and my quondam niece, invited me to come to Denver and speak before the Education Commission for the States. The fee was not much, though every cent counts these days; but the real reason I went was to meet Governor Bill Clinton of Arkansas, the chairman of the Commission this year. I have heard about Clinton for several years from Norris Mailer, who used to go out with him, and I was curious to see what he is like.

I arrived Friday night, 10 July, in time for dinner. The Clintons were at the same table, and I had some initial talk with them. We talked again the next morning before my speech and lunched afterward (with the Browns and the Frank Newmans of Brown University). I was quite impressed by Clinton. He is articulate, personable, liberal (and not afraid to use the word) and humorous. I also liked his wife Hillary, whom he met at Yale Law School. She worked for Marian Edelman at the Children's Defense Fund, where she is now chairman of the board.

Clinton, who is a former Rhodes Scholar, was thoughtful and well-informed on issues and especially so on questions of international trade (where he is much closer to Dukakis than to Gephardt). He had called a press conference for the next Wednesday, and I left with the strong impression that he would announce his candidacy. In fact, he announced his decision not to be a candidate, but I gather that this was a last-minute change. When I asked him in Denver how he expected to differentiate himself from Al Gore, he said that he had more of a record on domestic economic issues, especially those of particular interest to the South. He did not see any great disagreement with Gore except over the Persian Gulf, where Gore, alone among the Democratic possibilities, has come out in support of the policy of reflagging Kuwaiti tankers. I find Clinton more relaxed and easy than Gore and more of an unabashed liberal, but they are both young, intelligent, clean-cut, southern, "new generation" types, and they would have appealed to the same constituency.

I asked Bill what he thought would happen if Jesse Jackson came out of the southern primary with most delegates. He said that this would probably mean there would be no first ballot nomination—unless one of the other candidates had won both Iowa and New Hampshire and had come in a strong second in the South. I remain skeptical about the possibility of a deadlock in the convention. Clinton suggested that the brokering might take place before the convention. If, for example, by May 1988 Jesse led in delegate count, the next three candidates might agree among themselves as to an alternative. He did not say this in any anti-Jackson sense but as a political fact of life. He seems to like Jesse personally, and one of his entourage told me later that he was closer than any of the other candidates to Jackson. Clinton also said that he was not at all sure that Jesse would run in the end. Mrs. Jackson, he said, had handled the adultery question masterfully, but there might always be problems about the book-keeping at PUSH.

Bill does not see any irresistible contender at the moment. While we were in the Far East, PBS had a show at Houston with the seven candidates. Clinton said that Dukakis was the only one he could really envisage as President; that Simon was unassuming and effective; that Jackson was subdued; that Gore had a strong moment when he destroyed Bill Buckley, the interlocutor, on an arms control point; that Biden was less rhetorical than usual; that Gephardt seemed too young but at the same time rather dominated the proceedings by focusing so much of the discussion on his own issues; and that [Bruce] Babbitt (whom Clinton likes personally) "eliminated himself" by coming across as a sort of mannequin.

July 30

I lunched today with Jim McCartney of the Knight-Ridder papers, a Nieman Fellow 25 years ago and now president of the Gridiron. In this capacity he sat next to Reagan at the Gridiron dinner this winter. I asked how it was. He said with considerable emphasis, "I think the man is nuts." He then described the conversation. Chernobyl was then a topic, and Reagan told McCartney that it had all been predicted in the Bible. He then cited the 8th chapter of Revelations with the account of the opening of the seventh seal, hail and fire mingled with blood, a great mountain burning with fire cast into the sea and a great star falling from heaven causing men to die from the bitter waters. The star, Reagan said, was called Wedgewood, and the Ukrainian word for Wedgewood is Chernobyl. McCartney looked up the passage on his return and discovered that the star was called Wormwood. Apparently Chernobyl may mean wormwood in Ukrainian, and McCartney later learned that the Biblical allusion had been widely repeated in the Soviet Union. But Reagan, he said, had not the flicker of a doubt that the Bible had it right from the start.

December 10

I have been unforgivably remiss in keeping up this journal. It has been a hopelessly busy autumn. There is no greater illusion than that age brings a simplification of life. On the contrary, it accumulates obligations. My great desire is to clear everything else out of the way and concentrate on volume iv of *The Age of Roosevelt*. In practice, I find I dissipate time and energy—in lectures, necessary because we are perennially broke; I do not even possess a savings account; in teaching, necessary because we are perennially broke and because I can't figure out any other way of getting a free office, secretary and space for several thousand books; in good causes, though here I have cut down, but still there is the Franklin and Eleanor Roosevelt Institute, the Schlesinger Library, the American Academy and Institute of Arts and Letters, the

20th Century Fund; in social life, diverting enough on occasion but too much, too much; in answering letters, a perceived duty ever since my father told me many years ago that, if a person took the trouble to write you a friendly letter, courtesy requires you to take the trouble to answer it (he told the same thing to Ken Galbraith, who complained to me the other day that he would have written many more books had he not been persuaded by my father's advice).

I dined with Pamela [Harriman] on the 14th [of September]; Bill Clinton was also there, and we renewed our friendship.

My notes: "Bill Clinton is expansive, easy, funny, intelligent. His anecdotes, which must be embellished in the southern style, are sometimes a little too pat and shapely but carry the ring of truth. He is shrewd and analytical about people as well as about issues. He is a liberal who takes care to protect his political flanks.

"Why did he not run? He thinks he could have won the nomination but says that his heart simply wasn't in it. His father had died before he was born; he is therefore acutely aware of a child's dependence on his parents. If he and Hillary set out on the presidential quest, it would mean a virtual abandonment of a seven-year-old daughter (a point illustrated by a slightly too pat anecdote concerning the daughter). In the end, he decided that fatherhood was more important than seeking the nomination. (I later heard from other sources—where I now forget—that Bill faced a version of the Gary Hart problem: not a serious and lasting extracurricular relationship, as Dale Bumpers is supposed to have, but a casual fling with a girl in the office, still not something likely to help with the inquisitive press.)

"He talked about Jesse Jackson with relish and a certain affection. Jesse, he observed, was an illegitimate child. His father lived next door where he had a son the same age as Jesse. Every day Jesse saw his father come home and play with his half brother. The desire to impress his father and win his love, Bill thinks, has been a vital motive in Jesse's life. (I could not but note Bill's sensitivity to the father question.)

"Bill had recently lunched in New York with Mario Cuomo and Gary Hart. Mario, he says, is not especially popular among the governors because he attends their conferences only briefly if at all and commands most of the publicity when he is there. The governors of New York and California, according to Clinton, hold themselves somewhat above the governors' conferences.

"Bill thinks that Mario is 'constantly thinking and reassessing'— that, while logically he does not see much chance for himself, he still does not entirely reject the thought that unforeseen things might happen and that he might end as the candidate."

15 October, my 70th birthday. Since I do not feel seventy (ninety occasionally, forty most of the time, but never seventy), it was a less traumatic experience than I would have believed a few years back. Bill vanden Heuvel, as chairman of the Franklin and Eleanor Roosevelt Institute (a merger of the old FDR Four Freedoms Foundation with the Eleanor Roosevelt Foundation), had planned a dinner at Hyde Park that night to honor the recipients of the Four Freedoms medals—Tip O'Neill, George Kennan, Herblock, Mary Lasker, Leon Sullivan. He said that he planned also something about the birthday, but I did not anticipate the proportions of the celebration.

It was really a glorious evening. The dinner took place in a tent by the FDR Library. After toasts to the medalists, it became a celebration of my old age. Stephen, Marietta, Ken Galbraith and Joe Rauh gave wonderful speeches—Stephen's by general account the best, and most moving it was, as were they all. Then Schuyler Chapin took over as master of ceremonies. Betty Comden and Adolph Green had written new lyrics to "There's No Business Like Show Business," now entitled "There's No Arthur Like Our Arthur," and Betty Bacall, Kitty Hart and Phyllis Newman joined with them in singing it. I was presented with an original copy of the *New York Times* of 15 October 1917 and with a beautifully bound book containing letters from American historians solicited by Bill vanden Heuvel and Bill Emerson. Our Dutch friends gave me a book of FDR essays written by Dutch historians in my honor. Friends came from all over—Jean Smith, Kay Graham, Pamela Harriman, Evangeline Bruce, John and Wilma Fairbank, Tobie and Franklin Roosevelt, Clayton Fritchey, Jim Burns, Frank Freidel, Brian and Sidney Urquhart, all my children except for Kathy, who was leaving for Europe that weekend and had to finish up some work in Boston. I was quite bowled over by it all and could only stammer a few inadequate words of response.

The medals were presented the next day at St. James Church in Hyde Park. I had a nice talk with Tip O'Neill, who seemed a picture of glowing health; in fact, a few weeks later he was rushed to the hospital for a cancer operation. Tip was full of stories illustrating the dopiness of our President—stories he tells with gusto and incredulity. I especially liked the one in which he briefed congressional leaders after the invasion of Grenada. After opening up the subject, he turned the meeting over to the Secretaries of State and Defense and promptly fell asleep. He then awoke to say that he recalled the crowds pouring into the streets when MacArthur returned to Manila and that he hoped this is what would happen when American troops returned to Grenada in the future. Tip later told this story to someone—Dick Bolling?—who had accompanied MacArthur on his return to Manila and said there had been no crowds at all.

1988

❖

February 25

On Monday, 22 February, I went to Washington for a second meeting of a 20th Century Fund task force on the vice presidency. I am resolute in believing that the office should be abolished; but, since this is not likely to happen, I am interested to see what, if anything, can be done to make more sense out of it. Michael Nelson, a political scientist from Vanderbilt, has written an excellent background paper, agreeing essentially that not much can be done about the office but arguing that events have given it a new and enhanced status and that there is no great point in drastic reform. The group is congenial, and the meetings are interesting. I still hope that, as we work our way through the problems, people will see the logic, if not the practicality, of abolition.

One member is Dick Moe, who was close to Mondale. He said at our meeting that Mondale and Carter had met only once before Carter raised the possibility of joining him on the ticket. Mondale was at first uninterested. Then Hubert Humphrey ("of all people," as Moe said) told Mondale that it was a great job and that he should take it. When Carter and Mondale talked in Plains, they agreed in principle that the Vice President should have an enlarged role but did not spell out what that might mean. After the election, they decided that the Vice President should be "chief adviser" on issues of his choice; that he should have no operational responsibilities; and that he should have total access to the President, to all information received by the President (Moe thinks that Carter lived up to this) and to all White House meetings. Carter also told the White House staff to regard instructions from Mondale as the equivalent of instructions from him, and efforts were made to integrate the two staffs through the presence of Moe at Carter's staff meetings. Carter's first suggestion had been that Mondale have no staff of his own and use the White House staff instead; but Fritz rejected this.

The relationship, according to Moe, worked pretty well on the advisory level. Rockefeller had urged Mondale to continue a custom he and Ford had instituted of a regular Monday luncheon—just the two of them; and this, Moe thinks, was the key to the relationship. The "most tense period" came when Carter retired to Camp David and formulated what has become known as the "malaise" speech (though the word does not appear in the text). Mondale went to Camp David and was "absolutely horrified" by what he found, especially by the influence of Pat Cadell. "Mondale really went to the mat with Carter on that," and the argument created "a major strain" in the relationship, finally healed when Ted Kennedy's candidacy "brought us all together . . . but it was never fully healed."

Jim Cannon, another member of the group, mentioned that Ford and Rockefeller never had a preliminary discussion of what either expected from the office before Ford sent Rockefeller's name to the Senate.

March 12

"We shall be obliged," Wilson wrote in 1908, "always to be picking our chief magistrates from among wise and prudent athletes,—a small class." Our weird process of presidential selection has done a reasonably good job in winnowing out the candidates, but I wonder whether it is not coming close to wearing out those who remain. I remember how exhausted Adlai was by the primary process in 1956—a minor effort compared to what candidates go through today. By the time the nominees get to the general election, they will have been through a punishing and relentless year; the election will drain them further; then four years in the White House? Fatigue is one item electoral analysis tends to leave out.

April 9

Life in New York: Thursday, the 7th, we went at 6 P.M. to Jean Stein's party for Andrei Voznesensky.

Yesterday afternoon Andrei called to say that he was going to be on the MacNeil-Lehrer show that night. I suggested that he come over to watch it and stay for dinner, which he did; Kathy Sloane also came to dinner. Andrei put on a good face during the TV interview and handled the question of his relationship to the regime pretty well. In private, he is quite pessimistic about prospects in the Soviet Union—more so than when we last met in New York. He is a great admirer of Gorbachev but fears he may be going too fast for the Soviet people.

"I would die for democracy," he said. "But I know my people. They do not want democracy. They have never known democracy. The czars? Lenin? Stalin? Khrushchev? Brezhnev? They fear democracy. They want to be told what to do. Gorbachev is asking too much of them."

"The fight is going on," he kept saying. He spoke about the "terrible" state of Soviet society, especially the corruption. "No one works," he said. "How will we ever get production if no one works?" The economic reforms will cause a short-run decline in living standards, and this will hurt Gorbachev. So will the Armenian riots and other nationalist manifestations. Ending the Afghan war will help, and he does have allies among the modernizers and realists in the various bureaucracies, including the KGB. "But it will be a long hard fight."

I asked him what the reaction to the serialization of *Dr. Zhivago* had been. He said, "It is a great anti-climax. No one can understand why it was ever suppressed."

We like Andrei. With his baby face, loud Italian suits, fluent, voluble English, sharp, ironic reactions, warm Russian affections, he is most engaging. I decline to judge his political stance, which has been halfway between the regime and the dissidents; pronouncing judgment on such matters from the safety of Manhattan is a precarious business.

April 10

Nixon was on television this morning—a *Meet the Press* interview with [John] Chancellor, [Tom] Brokaw and Chris Wallace. This interview should destroy the strange legend of Nixon the foreign policy virtuoso; but I suppose it won't. Here are three of his points:

1) Reagan is wrong to suggest that the Soviet Union has given up its ambitions for world domination. This is the inflexible Soviet purpose.

2) My greatest mistake was not to bomb Hanoi and mine the harbor in 1969 instead of waiting till 1972; then we could have won the war. If it had not been for Watergate, I would have bombed and mined some more, and I would have made North Vietnam respect the terms of the truce.

3) My greatest accomplishment was going to China. If I had not brought about Sino-American friendship, think what the world would be like today: the Soviet Union and China as staunch allies dominating the world. My China policy saved the free world from this terrible fate.

This last point is especially incredible from a man admired by some otherwise intelligent people as a foreign policy expert. Does he really not understand that China and Russia split for their own reasons and that the United States had nothing to do with it? Yet I have no doubt that his reputation as a great geopolitical maestro will abide.

April 21

We went to Washington yesterday to attend Pam Harriman's annual Democrats for the 80s dinner. (She will have to change the name soon.) Very pleasant, rather like a college reunion. I had a nice talk with old Senator Gore, who has been campaigning hard for Al Jr. I said I thought that young Al would be a significant figure in the party's future. His father said, fondly, "He is not always as liberal as I would like, but he is as liberal as can be elected these days in Tennessee."

Later I asked Dick Holbrooke, who has been working closely with Gore, whose fault the fiasco [of letting Ed Koch influence his campaign] was. "It was just one person's fault," Dick said. "It was the candidate. He tried to act as his own campaign manager. It was a disaster. No coherent strategy, no continuing themes, no adequate consultation even with his own people." Dick said that, though he was nominally a Gore foreign policy adviser, he did not even know that Gore was going to come out in support of [Yitzhak] Shamir.

Gore's New York campaign was badly misjudged. He went far too far in trying to win the Jewish vote by defending Israel 100 percent, this at a time when many Jewish voters are disturbed by the Shamir policy. Then he fell into the hands of Ed Koch, which, as Murray Kempton says, is the worst thing that has happened to a politician since Gary Hart met Donna Rice. Koch went through the campaign like a man obsessed. He seems at times off his rocker, and his harping on racial issues has done him lasting (I trust) damage. Al Gore's failure is the product, I would imagine, of immaturity, inexperience and fatigue.

Cuomo spoke effectively at the dinner. He was late in arriving and began his talk by explaining his tardiness: "I've been spending all day trying to convince Ed Koch that the primary is over."

May 22

There appears to have been an astonishing crystallization of opinion in favor of Dukakis in the last fortnight. We dined on the 17th last at the Dick Gardners' with the Sorensens, the vanden Heuvels and Lou Harris. Lou told us of his most recent poll, which, like the Gallup and other polls, showed Dukakis steadily widening a lead over George Bush. Since voters don't know a great deal about Dukakis and his views, this must be more an anti-Bush than a pro-Dukakis phenomenon.

Poor old GB is caught in the vice presidential trap: he is identified with the multiplying failures of the Reagan administration, yet cannot escape implication except at the cost of seeming disloyalty to the President. Moreover, the President himself, in the manner of all Presidents, is impelled to do in his vice presidential pretender to the succession, even mispronouncing Bush's name ("Bosh") when he issued a most tepid endorsement the other day. And scandals continue to spill out, some (Noriega and Panama) appearing to involve Bush himself.

In the meantime, Dukakis plugs along, conveying the impression that he is a secure, poised, integrated, intelligent man who knows who he is and wants to do good for the country. My guess is that he will grow on the voters as the campaign rolls on. I ran into Bill Safire at the New York Public Library dinner on the 19th. He said, "I guess you are right about your cycle theory, but the new phase is coming before its time." Bill is correct. The liberal tide should not begin running with full strength till the early 1990s. Probably this is why Dukakis, a genuine liberal, I believe, but a very cautious one, is well suited to the time of transition.

May 28

Politics has settled into a stage of quiescence, with both nominations more or less sewn up (well in advance of the conventions, as I predicted long ago; the day of the "brokered" convention is done). Dukakis is beating Jackson with regularity and will do so again in California a week from Tuesday. This irritates the Republicans greatly, both because the appearance of a contest keeps the Democrats in the news and because the particular contest puts Dukakis firmly in the center of the party when the Republicans would love to make him the candidate of the left. Jackson has done the Democratic party many services this year.

June 6

Robert Kennedy died twenty years ago today. I can still feel the anguish of that moment and that time. Grief does not abate. This anniversary has brought a surprising outpouring of interest and recollection. It is as if RFK's purposes, so exotic and unfashionable in the greedy eighties, are striking chords once more—another vindication of my father's theory of cyclical change. A mass will be held for RFK this evening at Arlington National Cemetery; but, alas, I am committed to various things at my Harvard 50th reunion and will not be able to go.

June 11

We are back from Harvard and the 50th reunion of the Class of 1938. It turned out not to be so bad; even Alexandra rather enjoyed it. The Schlesinger-Weinberger rematch took place, though with due exhortations from the reunion chairman to "avoid argumentative situations" (I quote the 50th Reunion Guide). Weinberger seems to have shrunk considerably in physical stature in recent years (in moral stature too, of course). Jane was in a wheelchair, attended by Caspar Weinberger Jr., a classmate of Chrissie's and a pleasant young man.

The confrontation, shared with Ed Barnes, the architect, took place on Wednesday the 8th. The title of the symposium was "Looking Back and Looking Forward." Cappy is incredible. He began by claiming that it was he who had suggested the title. "Looking Back and Looking Forward" is a title of such banality that it was not worth contesting the credit; but in fact I was the one who suggested it (and, moreover, can prove it: Dick Bennink, the reunion chairman, sent a circular letter to the three of us and the symposium's chairman on 26 February which begins: "I think

Arthur's suggested symposium title is great and reflects what we want to do—some nostalgia and history and some looking ahead.").

Why old Weinberger should make such a forlorn claim, God knows. He went on, after disclaiming polemics, to make an exceedingly polemical defense of our glorious military victory over Grenada, our Central American policy, etc., etc. We both avoided direct exchanges. Disagreements emerged in answer to questions. At one point Cappy spoke scornfully of the "euphoria" with which so many Americans contemplate Gorbachev, failing to note that one of the most euphoric of all is his recent boss, the President.

What was most interesting was the change from the 35th reunion in the reaction of my classmates. This time I received, instead of boos and hisses, the larger share of the applause. Many classmates that evening and the next morning thanked me for having said what I had said. Has enlightenment descended on the Class of '38? Or is it the change in the cycle?

July 15

Dick Wade called Tuesday afternoon, the 12th, to say that Bob Wagner had just told him that Lloyd Bentsen was to be the vice presidential nominee. I heard the news, I must confess, with dismay, though, as an aficionado of Franklin Roosevelt and John Kennedy, I am in no position to protest when a northeastern liberal goes to Texas for his running mate. I trust that Bentsen will have as much influence on a Dukakis administration as [John] Garner had on the New Deal.

Bentsen is actually not a bad fellow. He is intelligent, gentlemanly, agreeable (I had a nice talk with him at Pamela Harriman's dinner in the spring), public-spirited, but pretty conservative. Two episodes—his scurrilous campaign against Ralph Yarborough in 1970 and his charging lobbyists $10,000 for breakfast—are hard to reconcile with his generally patrician demeanor. Putting him on the ticket will make it harder to present Dukakis as some sort of wild-eyed liberal. However, unless he can deliver Texas, his choice will be considered a mistake. He means little to the rest of the South, and he will be a distinct drag in the North.

What is less defensible is the Dukakis treatment of Jesse Jackson. Perhaps the failure to notify him about Bentsen (he learned from a reporter when he got off the plane Tuesday morning in Washington) was an accident. But notifying Jesse should have been Michael's top priority as soon as he had talked to Bentsen. His people had Jesse's schedule and knew he was catching an 8 A.M. plane. If Dukakis really could not call until 8:15, then he should have asked Ted Kennedy or John Kerry to meet the plane in Washington, go on board before Jesse got off and break the news with full explanations and apologies.

I can't escape the impression that the low priority accorded Jesse was at some level quite deliberate. Dukakis is irritated by Jesse's determination to carry on to Atlanta instead of calling off his campaign at once.

Of course Jesse Jackson as the first serious black candidate has every right to have his day of glory at the convention, with nominating speeches, demonstrations and everything else. The party should rejoice and use the Jackson candidacy as a means of demonstrating what kind of party it is. But I am afraid that Dukakis, with his rather tight Greek/Yankee concepts of efficiency v. waste, and also with his own kind of inner arrogance (Bill Shannon has warned me about this), resents what he regarded as irrelevant Jacksonian pressure—irrelevant because Jackson doesn't have enough delegates. As Dukakis said rather callously on television yesterday, "In a political race some people win, other people lose"—as if this race were like every other race, and as if the Jackson candidacy were not a historic breakthrough.

July 22

It is all over now, and a triumph for Michael Dukakis. We heard the acceptance address last night (Thursday) with Bill and Melinda vanden Heuvel. Even Alexandra, heretofore a skeptic about Dukakis, was charmed and impressed. Jesse Jackson and Ted Kennedy had set standards for political oratory on Tuesday night that were hard to match, but Dukakis, after carefully lowering everyone's expectations, matched them.

I still don't know what to make of his handling of Jesse Jackson, though it seems to have come out all right in the end. I gather from a number of sources that the Dukakis people were really exasperated by and indignant over what they saw as excessive demands by the Jackson people, who, in the tidy Dukakis view, had lost and should have therefore shut up. According to some stories, Lloyd Bentsen played a useful mediatorial role. There may be some logic in Dukakis's selection of Bentsen as a political offset to Jesse.

The great disappointment at the convention was Bill Clinton's nominating speech. I have very high regard for Clinton, an intelligent, spirited and (I thought) sensitive man; and I find it hard to understand how he could have perpetrated so tedious and rambling a speech—and then persevered in it when the response from the crowd made it obvious it was not going over.

I also find it hard to understand how the Dukakis people permitted it to happen. In my day the presidential candidate took care to control the nominating and seconding speeches. In 1956 we (mostly I) wrote not only a speech for JFK to deliver nominating Adlai but a whole set of seconding speeches. We hoped thereby to orchestrate the occasion and make the various points about the candidate we thought most vital for the viewing audience. (Ted Sorensen did not think much of my draft for JFK and wrote a better one himself, but retained the themes.) In 1960 I wrote Orville Freeman's nominating speech for JFK (though the teleprompter broke down and Orville had to go ahead on his own, which he did with immense aplomb and hardly a break in stride). The Dukakis crowd should have given Bill a text—or at least vetted his text and cut it down to ten minutes. I hope that this speech will not go down in the folklore along with Paul Dever's 1952 keynote and Frank Clements's keynote in 1956.

Ann Richards's keynote was a rousing political speech filled with Johnny Carson–style one-liners (George Bush having been "born with a silver foot in his mouth"—a crack first applied to Newbold Morris when he was New York Parks Commissioner in the 1940s) and, more convincingly, Texas-style allusions (as, mysteriously, to telling "how the cow ate the cabbage"). It was not in a class, however, with the great keynote speeches of my time—Alben Barkley in 1948 and Mario Cuomo in 1984.

I did not feel that George McGovern, or Cuomo for that matter, received the recognition they should have had at the convention; even the acknowledgement of Ted Kennedy, who had helped Dukakis from the start, seemed grudging; and there was far too much of Jimmy Carter, smiling like a complacent basilisk. But on balance it was a triumph and left all Democrats with a feeling of optimism and hope.

August 17

Franklin Roosevelt died this morning—his 74th birthday (also Kathy's and Stephen's 46th). I am a little surprised at how deeply this news (relayed to me by Trude Lash early in the morning) affects me. Perhaps it is because Franklin's life must have been in some deep sense disappointing for him; and yet he bore every frustration with boundless grace and good humor. Of course he had his explosions through the years, and I have seen some of them. When he was younger, he could be wilful and self-centered. But in later years he has been marvelously at peace with himself, no doubt in great part because of the soothing and exhilarating effect of his marvelous Tobie. He was a man of wonderful charm, considerable talent, effective intelligence but in his crucial early years, without sufficient self-discipline. He discovered too early that his name, charm, facility and quickness could get him by. Some one once cruelly said, "What young Franklin needs is an attack of polio." But, as he grew older, his innate generosity of spirit emerged. He rejoiced in Jack Kennedy's success, instead of thinking that it should have been his own, and he was a warm and sweet friend.

I called Jackie a few days ago to alert her to Franklin's condition. She said, "Oh, I love Franklin. I always felt so badly that Jack couldn't give him what he wanted so much—the Secretaryship of the Navy. But Franklin understood Jack's problem, never complained, never reproached." I called her again this morning to say that Franklin had died. "I loved him so much," she said. "I only wish I could have hugged him and told him so."

In the meantime, the Republican convention goes on. George Bush's designation of Dan Quayle, a rich jerk from Indiana, as his vice presidential candidate makes little sense to me. Tom Kean of New Jersey gave a cheap, smirking keynote address—a great disappointment to me, for I had had a high opinion of Kean. Far and away the best speech on Tuesday was given by Gerald Ford—a direct, hardhitting, above-the-belt speech. I guess there is more to Ford than I have supposed.

August 22

George Bush's acceptance address. Bush for the first time looked presidential. His delivery slowed down; his voice was deeper; no whining, no jerky gesturing out of sync with words. The speech contained little substance and ended demagogically with the pledge of allegiance, but it would have done as much for Bush as Dukakis's acceptance did for Dukakis had it not been for GB's inexplicable choice of J. Danforth Quayle of Indiana as his vice presidential nominee. Quayle, a war wimp par excellence, is one of those members of Congress who are intrepid hawks now, all in favor of sending off young men to war, but who contrived when they were of fighting age to stay out of the wars of their time. Probably his offense is not heinous enough to force his withdrawal from the ticket, but he will be a drag on Bush to the end, and his designation reflects most adversely on Bush's judgment of people.

September 18

Franklin Roosevelt's memorial service took place on Thursday the 15th at the Church of Heavenly Rest. Tobie had been concerned that not enough people would come to fill the rather large church. She need not have worried. It was one of the most emotionally satisfying memorial services I can remember. All the speakers (including me) were good, and Trude Lash and Frank Roosevelt III were exceptional. Trude could hardly keep back her tears as she told of her affection and admiration for Franklin. Who in 1940 could have predicted that FDR Jr. and Joe Lash would one day become devoted friends? Yet they did, Mrs. R's son and her surrogate son, and Trude expressed her love for Franklin with quiet eloquence.

It occurred to me at the reception given afterward by Franklin's daughter Nancy Ireland that my own life has been curiously intertwined with the two great American dynasties of the century—the Roosevelts and the Kennedys. Many people have known one or the other of the two families better than I, but has anyone known both so well? And the families have been curiously intertwined too—not only the relationship between the two principals, but Elliott Roosevelt flying beside Joe Kennedy Jr. when Joe's plane exploded, Franklin helping Jack Kennedy to get the Democratic nomination in 1960 and later serving in his administration. Jackie, who was deeply fond of Franklin, was in tears at the service.

The campaign sputters along, drowned out this week by the roar of Hurricane Gilbert. Bush has gained a good deal since the Republican convention, despite his anointment of J. Danforth Quayle as his running mate. In particular, he has quite unscrupulously attacked Dukakis on such non-issues as the pledge of allegiance to the flag and Dukakis's membership in the American Civil Liberties Union. Bush's major theme so far is that Republicans are more patriotic than Democrats and that Dukakis is, heaven help us, a liberal. And this kind of assault seems to have worked, if one can believe the polls.

We went on the 8th to a New York dinner for Dukakis and Bentsen. The crowd was ready for red meat. They were looking for an all-out attack on the Republicans. Instead Mike gave them a lofty speech about the ideals of public service. My impression was that he had been taken aback by Bush's low blows, that he couldn't figure out how to respond and that he was rather depressed by the whole democratic process.

One reason he was slow in responding, I am sure, is that he is bone tired. I can remember how exhausted Adlai Stevenson was after the primaries in 1956, and the primary season was trivial then compared to what it is now. So far as I can recall, Dukakis has not had a real respite for a year or more. Bush had the sense to go fishing during the Democratic convention, but Dukakis went campaigning during the Republican convention. Wilson's prophecy about the approaching time when we would pick our presidents "from among wise and prudent athletes,—a small class" has come true.

Dukakis seemed weary and grim that night. He has perked up since, however, has gone on the attack and may be beginning to make up ground. I have a feeling that a recoil may be developing against Bush's cynical exploitation of the patriotism issue. I say cynical—George Bush surely knows better about the pledge of allegiance and the ACLU. I am risking my friendship with NBE [Nancy Bush Ellis], who is fiercely loyal to her brother, by writing about all this for the *Wall Street Journal*.

September 26

The first debate last night. I thought that Dukakis won by an emphatic margin. The others agreed too that he had won, but thought it closer. Dukakis was poised, unruffled, fluent, pointed. Bush rambled, often couldn't find his words or got them wrong and sometimes seemed quite incoherent. Commentators afterward said he was better than in his debate four years ago with Geraldine Ferraro, and he was certainly less unhinged than he appeared then.

Bush regurgitated his demagogic crap about liberalism, the pledge of allegiance, the ACLU, etc. For reasons of ancient loyalty, I have been leaning over backward in the last months to defend Bush as an honorable and intelligent man. But the smarmy cheapness of this line of attack is really too much. I have thought that George Bush knows better. I am beginning to wonder if he really does.

As for the campaign in general, Bush has built up a strong lead, in part, I fear, because of his slurs on Dukakis's patriotism. This kind of stuff probably pleases his rightwing zealots and may, ironically, permit him a certain latitude to move toward the center on substantive questions. I notice that on a number of specific issues—environmental protection, education, day care, the minimum wage, the plight of inner-city children, the rejection of abortion as a political litmus test—Bush seems to be shifting as if in rhythm with the incipient cyclical change.

But the cyclical change is probably coming too slowly to put Dukakis over the top. As I may have written here before (and as I have been saying since last spring), it is as if Kennedy had run against Nixon in 1958 rather than in 1960—and it was close enough in the popular vote in 1960. Dukakis is ahead of the cycle; Bush has the advantages of peace, prosperity, incumbency and money; and Bush should win—narrowly, I would think, in the popular vote; more decisively in the electoral college. Still Bush's capacity for gaffes and goofiness may save us yet.

October 18

I should add some other points to my hasty consideration of the reasons for the liquidation of Dukakis's early lead. It was not only Bush's harsh attacks but Dukakis's failure to answer them. He does not like negative campaigning, and he was encouraged in this dislike by people like me who wrote him in July that Bush's tone was hurting himself more than it was hurting Dukakis. I was wiser in my letter to him at the end of August in which I said he should defend his liberalism by identifying it with FDR, Truman and Kennedy.

By refusing to stand on the liberal record and instead saying he wouldn't argue about labels, Dukakis has tacitly validated the Bush strategy of converting liberalism into a dirty word. Walter Cronkite said to me the other day, "Dukakis should not be running away from liberalism. He should be embracing it."

Dukakis *is,* I believe, a liberal, and his evasion of the liberal issue not only plays into the hands of his foes but disappoints and discourages his friends. My guess is that he was the victim of bad advice and was too tired to try to think the question through on his own. All campaign staffs are possessive and jealous. The people on the Dukakis staff, having supposed that they had got their principal the nomination, believed that they knew everything and required no outside advice. In fact, they had little experience in national campaigns, and they knew very little.

November 5

In the course of the week Dukakis finally came out of the closet and identified himself as a liberal in the tradition of FDR, Truman and Kennedy (belatedly doing, I might immodestly add, what I urged him to do in my letter of 1 September and again in the *Wall Street Journal* of 21 October). Since then, his campaign has clearly picked up steam, though Stephen reminds me that George McGovern had his most enthusiastic crowds in the last week of the 1972 campaign. John Chancellor told me at luncheon on Thursday that, according to the latest polls, the gap was really narrowing. An engaging PBS documentary on "The Great Upset of 1948" has cheered a lot of people up and given new if romantic hope.

It is all, I fear, too late. My guess at this point is that we will have a 51% turnout, with the popular vote dividing 53–47%. I anticipate an electoral college landslide for Bush. 305–234 is the best I can figure for Dukakis, and 401–108 or worse seems more likely.*

November 22

Twenty-five years ago today! Hard to think that this quarter century has whirled by so quickly. It is now a longer span of time from JFK's death to 1988 than from the end of the First World War to the start of the Second. A third of the population today was born after he was killed; half is too young to recall him in the White House. Kids entering college this autumn were mostly born in 1970—seven years after Dallas. For them JFK is as much a figure from the historical past as TR (who died fifteen months after I was born) was for my generation.

---

* George Bush defeated Michael Dukakis 53%–46% and by 426–111 in the electoral college on November 8, 1988.

Yet there is tremendous interest and considerable emotion. Jean and Jackie are not happy over the tendency to build the assassination into the key anniversary. They think—rightly—that we should celebrate Jack's birth, not his death. We make a holiday of Lincoln's birthday, not of the day Booth killed him. But for so many Americans still alive JFK's death was a stunning, unforgettable moment, the one terrible memory shared with the rest of the country, and with the world. (For my generation the two other times that we all remember where we were when we heard the news are Pearl Harbor and FDR's death.) The impulse to relive those awful hours is uncontrollable. And JFK was the last President who addressed and elicited American idealism—and this strikes a chord of reminiscence and hope.

There has also been a considerable outpouring of snide and sneering comment by columnists, by TV people striving to seem objective and by revisionist historians. I particularly dislike the effort to paint JFK as a rigid and ardent Cold Warrior filled with a *macho* relish in crisis. In fact, he was a rational man who believed that things could ordinarily be worked out by negotiation and a cautious man who did not like getting involved in fights he was not pretty sure to win. One of his great strengths was precisely his ability to *refuse* escalation—as after the Bay of Pigs, during the Berlin crisis of 1961, during the Cuban missile crisis and throughout on Vietnam (at least so far as the commitment of American ground forces was concerned).

I also object to the snobbishness about JFK's legislative record. Like every Democratic President since 1938, he lacked a working progressive majority in the House of Representatives. Given this problem, he did as well as anyone could have done in getting some bills passed and in preparing the way for the passage of others. The 1964 election produced 37 new Democratic congressmen and gave LBJ a working progressive majority in the House. This made the burst of Great Society legislation possible. When the Democrats lost 49 seats in 1966, Johnson found himself in the same old fix and the Great Society legislative spree came to an end.

December 17

Christmas is suddenly upon us, as if leaping out of ambush. This has been a more frenetic autumn, it would seem, even than usual. I probably have noted before the illusion that age brings simplification of life. On the contrary: the older one gets, the more obligations accumulate, and time trickles away in a mess of imperative trivialities owed to a person or a cause or an occasion. I can't seem to fight myself free to finish the organization of my notes and to begin volume iv of the FDR series. I can't even find time to keep up this damned journal. I say "No" far more often than I used to do, but not often enough.

Consider this weekend. I have not paid medical bills for months; this means filling out Blue Cross forms, which takes time and defies comprehension. I haven't done anything to gather material to fend off the Internal Revenue Service and its critique of my 1986 tax returns; this has been hanging over me since the summer. I have to write something about the 1988 election for the textbook. I promised Jacques Lowe that I would write a foreword to the catalogue of his JFK photographic exhibition. I have to correct proofs for a *New York Review of Books* piece on advising Presidents. I have two score letters to answer—some of them complicated inquiries about events in which I have participated. Having bothered busy men in the past for their recollections of FDR and the New Deal, I feel conscience-bound to respond in like manner myself. I have to provide footnote citations for the published version of my Lincoln-FDR address at Gettysburg. I have to write something for a book honoring Vartan Gregorian on his greatly-to-be-regretted departure from the New York Public Library. I have to give Bob Merton a selection of immortal words of my own for his projected *Social Science Quotations*. And I have to start making Christmas lists.

It would help if I could stop teaching. I have never minded teaching particularly and have always striven to do a good job; but it has never meant much to me, as it has evidently done to others—I think of Henry Commager, who goes on teaching well into his eighties and would feel deprived if he could do it no longer. The only reason I still teach is that

I can't figure how else to maintain an office and a secretary or what to do with the 1,000 or so books in my office; there is no room for them at home. I am even ready to leave New York and the assault of interruptions if we could find a place in the country near enough to a reasonable university library.

1989

January 21

Yesterday was the inauguration. I find it hard to believe that George Bush is President; but then I was never able quite to believe that Ronald Reagan was President (or Carter or Ford, for that matter).

The address was low-keyed, agreeable, platitudinous, coming out strongly for generosity as against materialism and the heaping up of possessions (will the Reagans take this personally?). The *Times* gave me the "Quotation of the Day"—"I have just a slight sense that Bush may turn out to be more of a tribune of the people than he chose to suggest in the campaign. We may find noblesse oblige replacing greed as the White House style."

January 26

On Monday the 23rd we dined at Mike and Mary Wallace's. Mike, who has known the Reagans a long time, says that Nancy Reagan is considerably upset and irritated over the press adulation of Barbara Bush and the implied invidious contrasts with herself—breezy, natural, genuine Mrs. Bush, unashamed of being gray, fat and wrinkled, as against artificial, overstyled, glitzy, anorexic Mrs. Reagan.

February 22

The big event of the last few days, at least in literary circles, has been the call of the Ayatollah Khomeini for the murder of Salman Rushdie on the ground that Rushdie's book *The Satanic Verses* is blasphemous. The attack on poor Rushdie is very likely a function of political struggles within Iran, where the theocrats are very likely doing their damnedest to block the effort of the pragmatists to normalize relations with the West. *The Satanic Verses* lends itself brilliantly to that purpose, and the contract on Rushdie has already done grave damage to Iranian relations with the European Community.

The attack of course has roused great furor in the local community of writers. Last Thursday Waldenbooks, claiming the need to protect its bookshops and employees from Moslem fanatics, ordered the removal of *The Satanic Verses* from its shelves. This provoked me to fire off a letter Friday morning to [Harry] Hoffman of Waldenbooks, concluding with the hope that B. Dalton would not follow its disastrous example— which it proceeded to do later in the day.

In the meantime, a legend has arisen, propagated by Leon Wieseltier in the *Washington Post* and the odious Norman Podhoretz in the *New York Post,* that American writers have been afraid to stand up for principle in the Rushdie case. I don't know how this started. PEN and the Authors League both issued blasts, and any number of writers have declared themselves. Several, led by Ed Doctorow and Norman Mailer, are reading excerpts from the Rushdie book or making statements at a public meeting this noon (to which I can't go).

The Doctorows came for dinner last night along with Adolph and Phyllis Green and Jane Hitchcock to celebrate Jean's 61st (unmentioned) birthday. I like both Doctorows very much. Edgar is having a major success with his new novel *Billy Bathgate*. He retains vague traces from his youth of a Popular Front approach to politics; but his high intelligence, wit, skepticism and linguistic exuberance keep him in touch with reality. He has not read *The Satanic Verses* (nor have I, nor have most of those vocal on both sides of the controversy); but he is not impressed by the claim that the book transgresses the proprieties. "Every novel is a transgression," he said. "Every novelist, if he has anything original to say, must strain against the proprieties."

On Wednesday I flew to Portland where I lectured in the evening and debated Robert Bork the next evening at Pacific University. Bork turned out to be an affable, fat, bearded man, and we got along pleasantly. Indeed, he reminded me that we had met before in the lounge at the Yale Law School in 1962 or thereabouts, a meeting I now dimly recall. He seems *very* conservative. We had a couple of sessions with students, and at one of them we were asked what we saw as the greatest problems in the immediate future. I gave a banal answer—prevention of nuclear war, racial justice, renovation of the American economy. Bork said stoutly: "Soviet aggression. I don't think that Gorbachev has changed Soviet objectives in the slightest. He is just trying to make the Soviet Union more effective in attaining those objectives." Bork is a chainsmoker, his belly swarms over his belt, and one feels that he may not be long for this world. Nor do I think he is terribly bright. His "original intent" argument makes less sense the more he explains it. But he is likable, and we agreed at least on the indispensability of the dry martini.

April 15

Obligations are unrelenting. They are also the unrelenting enemies of achievement. I have finally done the new epilogue for *The Imperial Presidency;* but I had to do it in spurts. Sustained work on a single task seems the impossible dream. In the weeks since I last attended to this journal, I have also gone out of town seven times for lectures, held three seminars at the Graduate School, served as a host at two dinner parties, attended two memorial services (Jack McCloy and Beth Webster) and talked to scholars or journalists from Japan, Ceylon, West Germany, Italy, Great Britain.

Somewhere along the way, I think perhaps on 27 March, I had a talk with George Kennan at the Century about the Soviet elections. Soviet developments these days are really inconceivable. I never for a moment thought that I would be able to turn on television and watch a political rally in Moscow addressed by opponents of the regime. George has been enormously impressed by Gorbachev—impressed, and gratified too, since Gorbachev comes along as a kind of vindication of his own prediction forty years back that containment would bring about the mellowing and/or breakup of the Soviet system.

George is a happy man. He nearly died a couple of years ago, but his health seems fine now, and he basks in an atmosphere of belated but heartfelt recognition and approval. He testified recently before the Senate Foreign Relations Committee; and Claiborne Pell told me when we were in Providence that, after George finished, the whole room, including the members of the committee, broke into spontaneous applause. Claiborne also said that he had asked the committee clerk when the last time was that anything like this had happened. He was told that it had happened in 1966 in a hearing on the Vietnam War—and that the witness was George Kennan!

May 20

This has been an astonishing week. The defiance of the students in Beijing, following on Gorbachev's reform drive in the Soviet Union, shows communism as more vulnerable and malleable than most have imagined and democracy as more solidly grounded in fairly universal human impulses and needs.

The comeback of democracy has been one of the amazing things of this century. Looking back, one sees the First World War and the Great Depression as traumatic events that threw democracy badly on the defensive for the first half of the century. The First World War, by shaking the old structures of security, initiated the escape from freedom, and the Great Depression appeared as the fulfillment of the Marxian prophecy that capitalism would perish of its own internal contradictions. Fascism and communism arose as the twin totalitarian challenges to democracy. For a season they appeared to many, as to Anne Lindbergh, the wave of the future.

Fascism and communism, for all their differences, had more in common with each other than either had with democracy—as Hitler and Stalin recognized in 1939. Then, in his great miscalculation, Hitler turned against Stalin in 1941; and democracy in alliance with communism knocked out fascism in the Second World War. This left democracy and communism to confront each other, which they did in the Cold War. And now, after forty years, the Cold War, as George Kennan says, is obsolete—and democracy has won. (The *Wall Street Journal* put a good title on my column of the 17th: "Somebody Tell Bush We've Won the Cold War.")

Communism today is a burnt-out case. Its internal contradictions turned out to be far more destructive than the internal contradictions of capitalism. Lenin's talk about the "final stage" of capitalism looks ludicrous in an age when capitalism has prospered as never before—and when the Communist superpowers are trying to save themselves by adopting the incentives and disciplines of the free market. Moreover, the masses in Russia and in China, once presumed to have been indoctrinated beyond recall, are showing an unexpected appetite for regimes based on popular choice and an unexpected concern for human rights.

So democracy has won the political argument. The market has won the economic argument. The elections this year in the Soviet Union, the demonstrations this week in Tiananmen Square—all signify not just the survival but the triumph of democracy in its century-long struggle against the totalitarians. For the historian, an exciting time.

June 6

Age. I will be 72 before the year is out. I don't feel (or, I believe, look) a septuagenarian. My memory remains pretty good, though uneven. I forget people whom I have met before—even, what is most astonishing, pretty girls. Climbing stairs and getting into and out of the back seats of automobiles get increasingly irksome. But I still easily walk back from the office every day, in heat and in cold—a mile and a third; about twenty minutes. Cigars? I decided some months ago to smoke up my long treasured hoard of Havanas, and then call it a day for smoking. Why?—because of occasional shortness of breath, which I attribute, perhaps wrongly, to smoking, and because of general doubt about the therapeutic virtues of tobacco. Drink? For many years I have had a dry martini before luncheon every day—a Century martini ($1\frac{3}{4}$) until the last couple of years; in recent times, a generous single. Now I begin to find myself skipping a pre-luncheon drink altogether. Why? For the first time drink begins to make me feel sleepy in the afternoon. But I still have a couple of generous slugs of bourbon before dinner.

My chief known physical disability is a vulnerable back. I did something to it the other day and was obliged for a day or two to hobble around on my father's old malacca cane.

June 15

Last evening Joni Evans of Random House gave a party for Irving Lazar followed by a small dinner at the Four Seasons. Alexandra sat next to Michael Caine at the restaurant; I drew Julie Nixon Eisenhower, who, to my astonishment, turned out to be very pretty and intelligent and filled with charm. Also rather liberal in her views: she favors, for example, the complete abolition of the CIA on the ground that it has become a dangerous source of secret power in our democracy. She also said that the ovation for Goldwater at the last Republican convention almost made her change her registration from Republican to Democratic—though this may be a reflection less of liberal views than of the fact that Goldwater has described her father, to whom she is devoted, as the most dishonest individual he has ever met.

She is easy to talk to, and her friendliness suggests that she has never read anything I have written about Daddy. Or perhaps it is a return for the favorable review I wrote of her husband's book in the *Times*. She said that they had begun reading the review with great apprehension and ended with great relief. It was a good book.

David has put the second volume aside for the moment, and he and Julie are collaborating on a book about 1968 with special focus on the Vietnam War. David, whom I had met before, lacks his wife's grace and gives a somewhat bumbling impression but is cordial, forthcoming, rather definite and decided in his opinions. One thing of interest: in connection with the CIA talk, I made the familiar argument that intelligence agencies in all countries tend to go into business for themselves and said that I did not suppose that President Eisenhower had ordered or authorized the CIA attempts to kill Castro and [Congolese prime minister Patrice] Lumumba. David Eisenhower rather surprisingly demurred. There were still classified Second World War records in the Eisenhower Library, he said, and one file that has not been opened for research is labelled "Clandestine Operations and Assassination" (I may not have the full title right, but the word assassination is part of it). People who had gone through the war, David Eisenhower said, probably did not think about assassination the same way that later generations might. He did not say it outright, but he strongly implied that his grandfather might well have known what was going on. Odd: his father has flatly denied that old Ike would ever have authorized assassination.

August 11

[Isaiah Berlin and I] talked again about the continuing controversy over the Anglo-American failure to save more Jews during the holocaust. Isaiah said that, of course, American Jews might well have harried FDR more to do something; but, had they done so, there was still not much he could have done. Within Germany, bombing the camps or the railroad lines carrying people to the camps would only have killed swiftly men and women who would otherwise have died slowly and miserably. It would not have stopped the Nazis from killing Jews: they were doing that not out of expediency but out of fanatical conviction.

Perhaps more could have been done in Eastern Europe to save Jews through a combination of threats and deals, for there the extermination of Jews resulted more from a desire to propitiate the Nazis than from deep ideological commitment.

Isaiah thinks that there is probably something to the idea that Hitler's first desire was to rid Europe of the Jews, send them to Madagascar or the Dominican Republic or some remote place, and that he turned to extermination only when war closed the avenues of deportation.

I asked Isaiah when he first became aware of the holocaust. He said that, from his vantage point in the British Embassy in Washington, he was not aware of the holocaust until the winter of 1944–45. I have been reading Lady Namier's life of her husband (*Lewis Namier: a Biography,* London 1971) and note that, though Namier was an ardent Zionist and political secretary of the Zionist Organization's Jewish Agency in London, the biography does not mention the holocaust at all in describing Namier's reactions in the war years. I have been trying to remember when, or if, I perceived a moment of decisive break in Nazi policy toward the Jews. Yet I was in the Research and Analysis Branch of OSS surrounded by German Jewish refugees—Franz Neumann, Felix Gilbert, Herbert Marcuse, Otto Kirchheimer—with the most vital interest in the subject. What did OSS know and when did we know it? I have a vague memory of Franz Neumann looking grave one day and saying he had a disquieting report about an intensification of the anti-semitic policy; or do I imagine this?

I note that in Ruth Dudley Edwards's *Victor Gollancz* (London 1987, p. 373), Gollancz was persuaded of the extermination policy by December 1942. In the spring of 1943 he wrote and published *Let My People Go,* calling for a rescue plan. Why was this not published in the United States?

September 1

Evangeline, who is in London, called with the sad though not unexpected news that Joe Alsop had died. Still it is a great blow and sadness.

He was part of Alexandra's life almost from her birth and part of mine for nearly half a century; he was always such a vivid and irrepressible figure in all our lives; and it is hard to accept the fact that he is gone from us.

Of course relations with Joe had their ups and downs. He got very mad at me over Vietnam, blamed Robert Kennedy's defection on me, attacked me in columns and was cold and irritable when we met (Stewart never was). But he forgave me my Vietnam heresy when Alexandra and I joined forces. He gave up his column before he became a stuck whistle, and thereafter friendship mattered far more to him than political agreement. Alexandra and I and all our children rejoiced in Joe's visits and telephone calls and booming laugh and imperious ways and merry companionship. And I greatly admired the uncomplaining gallantry with which he endured his final ordeal.

At Alexander Chancellor's request, I wrote about Joe for the London *Independent*. Although I fear that Joe was mostly known in his last years as the hawk of hawks, the last-ditch defender of the war in Vietnam, the unrelenting Cold Warrior, the scourge of what he used to call with his explosive laugh "liber-*als,*" he actually was at heart a good deal of a liberal himself. He had been an ardent New Dealer; also an early and indispensable New Deal historian. To the end of his life he celebrated FDR's achievements not only in taming business but in ending the WASP monopoly and "including the excluded" in American life. He was a liberal too in his commitment to freedom of speech and expression. Above all, he was a most generous, loving and beloved friend.

Michael Harrington had been dying of lung cancer for some time but confronted death with the same courage that he always confronted life. He was a most attractive man who expended himself without stint in trying to make human and intellectual sense out of socialism. I never knew him as well as I would have liked to do—we were both living too busy lives—but we always met with affection and regard. His mission was to reconcile Marx with Jefferson, socialism with democracy.

Classical socialism envisaged state ownership of the means of production and distribution. How could this be compatible with democracy? For, if the state owns everything, where can opposition to the state find breathing space? where can it find resources? how can it survive? And without opposition how can there be democracy?

It has always seemed to me that democracy has a fundamental structural requirement: the opposition must have a base independent of the state. This means that the state can't own everything and that classical socialism and democracy are incompatible. Democracy, in short, requires diversification of ownership. Mike Harrington's liberal socialism never appeared to me all that different from the mixed-economy-cum-welfare-state devised by FDR half a century ago. Mike, it seemed to me, had a sentimental weakness for Socialism as a word but a practical preference for liberalism as a policy. That is why he collaborated so constructively with the liberal wing of the Democratic party. He was the best company, filled with Irish charm and humor, and no one endured a long dying with more grace and fortitude.

September 11

I heard Boris Yeltsin at the Harriman Institute. He is a stocky, bluff, humorous, robust fellow, fresh after a long hot day; a natural pol and demagogue, earnest and rather naive; a shock of well-combed white hair; ruddy face; likable but not especially impressive; certainly no alternative to Gorbachev.

He said that unless there were substantial improvement in a year there would be revolution from below. Perestroika must be saved, and the U.S. can play a vital role in saving it. He hoped to see the President and make certain proposals to him. "We face a crisis in the economy—a crisis in finance—a crisis in the party—a crisis in the nationalities question. We have to decentralize and demonopolize the whole country."

The people in power, he said, were overconfident about their ability to solve the nationalities question. They did not count on the uneven pace of social development and of the democratization process. There has been a "systematic crushing of national dignity." The only solution is the devolution of power—de facto independence. "If the Baltic republics want to leave the Soviet Union, that is up to them to decide." Political decentralization means the transfer of power from the party to the local soviets.

"I support Gorbachev. I strongly support his strategy for the renovation of Soviet society. But we have differences on tactical issues. He is moving ahead on a broad front. I think it better to concentrate our energies on food, on consumer goods, on housing. Let's neglect other areas for the time being. When a broad front flows through a narrow gorge, it must flow too fast."

A multi-party system? "I think that we should swallow our pride and learn from the American democratic experience. I don't exclude the possibility of a second party, but it is a difficult question. It should be brought into the open. At present, it is a forbidden theme. The party has forbidden any discussion in the mass media."

He handled hostile questions, especially from Trotskyites and Stalinists, with bluff but slightly menacing humor. He finished: "I don't think people will hold back their wrath for another year. I am against a revolution from below, but the only way to prevent it is to supply consumer goods with the cooperation of American business. . . . If revolution comes, five to seven percent of the population will perish."

[As I type these notes in February, I am impressed more than ever by the rapidity of change. In September Boris Yeltsin, the radical, thought talk of a multi-party system almost beyond the pale. Five months later the Central Committee has ended the Communist Party's monopoly on political life and launched the Soviet Union into something approaching democratic politics.]

October 1

We went to Barbara Epstein's for dinner last night with Antonia Fraser and Harold Pinter—the five of us, joined later by Murray Kempton. Harold remains unpredictable, like a time bomb that may or may not explode; a combination of great charm, sardonic humor and sudden rage. He identifies rather dramatically with the oppressed of the world and regards the United States, a country or at least a government he hates, as the main oppressor. This is not in the slightest because he has any pro-Communist leanings, only that he regards communism as feeble and finished. When we were in London recently, I said idly about one of his recent short anti-torture plays that I supposed it took place in Eastern Europe. Harold flared up and said, "Why does everyone think of Eastern Europe? It might be in any country that practices torture. What it is really about is the United States in Central America."

Last night he became rather truculent about the fact that the *New York Review of Books* (of which Barbara is co-editor) no longer publishes Noam Chomsky. He had read Chomsky with care, he said, and admired the precision with which he analyzed the iniquity of American foreign policy. I said that Chomsky fabricated quotations (I had in mind the fake Truman quote I exposed many years ago), that I wouldn't believe the baseball scores in a Chomsky piece (having in mind Paul Douglas's old remark that he didn't believe the baseball scores in the *Chicago Tribune*) and that no serious person in the United States took Chomsky seriously once outside his field of linguistics.

This provoked Harold into an angry all-out assault on American policy in Nicaragua and by implication on the United States as an evil empire. Finally Antonia intervened in a calm, stern, measured and highly effective way, pointing out to Harold that Barbara, Alexandra and I had all opposed the Reagan policy in Nicaragua, so he needn't lecture us. She continued to say that, though she opposed British policy in Northern Ireland, she none the less couldn't help resenting it when young Joe Kennedy came to England and lectured the English on how terrible the policy is; this was, she said, exactly what Harold was doing, and maybe we resented it too.

To change the conversation, I asked Harold what in fact did he think of British policy in Ireland. Antonia said, "I want to hear this. Harold has always been evasive on this question." Harold continued to be evasive. At this point Murray arrived, and we talked of other things. I wondered whether Harold would be angry over Antonia's rebuke, but he accepted it, and, when we all left together, she took his arm and all seemed equable. Partings were amiable all around.

October 16

Nancy Ellis told me this morning about her brother's [George H. W. Bush] relations with the living ex-Presidents. She said that he found Nixon's telephonic counsel very helpful during the Tiananmen Square crisis. "The way to live with Nixon," Bush says, "is to be able to talk to him without seeing him." Ford is useless; all he cares about is making money out of the ex-presidency. Bush likes Carter's seriousness and his continuing concern with foreign affairs, though [James] Baker is a little disturbed by Carter's unilateral interventions in diplomacy—trying to settle the Ethiopian-Somali war, for example. Reagan never calls him; and, when Bush calls Reagan, our latest ex-President has little to offer in the way of suggestion or advice.

Like all presidential sisters, Nancy is fiercely loyal to her brother and boundlessly proud of him. She recalled that this summer in Kennebunkport, when she and a couple of brothers were chatting on a Sunday afternoon, the President strolled into the room, and they all—his sister and brothers—stood up! Yet I suppose we did the same thing when JFK came along; Jerry Wiesner has never let me forget that once when JFK called me in his office I put on my jacket before taking the call. In retrospect, I think that such deference is bad for Presidents. A democracy should not have a royal family.

November 18

The pace of developments in Eastern Europe continues to astonish. So many things have happened in the last year, last month, last week, that I never expected to happen in my lifetime. The collapse of the Berlin Wall is followed by the upheaval in Bulgaria and now by the incipient rescue of Czechoslovakia. How right I have been to argue the inscrutability of history! Once again events defy all our expectations and history outwits all our certitudes.

Schadenfreude is inevitable when one contemplates the fallen prophets. The discomfiture on both left and right yields enormous pleasure. I think of all the people on the left I have known through the years who believed in the superiority, moral and economic, of communism and the infallibility of the Soviet Union, and I think of all the people on the right who have believed that Soviet communism was a static monolith, unchanged, unchanging and unchangeable.

The first class has fallen silent. The second continues to bleat away. Ken Galbraith told me this morning that Richard Pipes had a piece in the *Globe* saying that the Soviet Union is more aggressive and dangerous than ever, instancing threatening Soviet activities in Ethiopia! Last Thursday, the 16th, the Centurion members of the Harvard Class of '38 held their annual dinner. Cappy Weinberger put in an appearance. Over drinks he said to me, "Arthur, let's not get into a debate again. We've done this too many times before the class, so I don't think we have to do it any more." I said sure, supposing that even old Cappy might have recognized that recent events made his theory of the world indefensible. At dinner, however, he began to hold forth about the dangers the Soviet Union still presents, all expounded in his imperturbably smug and certain manner. Very important, he said, to increase defense spending. We could take no chances. How about the budget? someone said. How can we afford to continue spending even at present levels? Easy enough, Cap said; "cut back the social programs." Debate became inevitable. The others present all agreed with me, I think, but as usual were (except for Sinclair Armstrong, an ex-Republican who grows more liberal every year) too diffident or too polite to take on Cappy.

December 2

At yesterday's American Academy luncheon I congratulated George Kennan on his prescience in predicting forty-two years ago that peaceful containment would eventually bring about the break-up or the gradual mellowing of Soviet power. "I believe it would have happened earlier," George said, "if we had not insisted on militarizing the rivalry.

Of course George and Chip [Bohlen] opposed NATO and NSC-68 on the ground that the Soviet Union presented a political threat to be met by political means, not a military threat to be met by military means. When Acheson and Nitze succeeded in imposing the military conception of the Soviet threat and launched American rearmament, the Soviet Union responded in kind. The militarization of the competition, George believes, hardened the rivalry and repressed peaceful forces in Russia that might, if unchallenged, have brought about the mellowing and/or break-up of Soviet power at some earlier point. Is this true? or did not the internal revulsion against the Communist regimes require drastic and indisputable demonstration over a sustained time of the political, economic and moral failure of communism?

December 14

Bill vanden Heuvel told me today that, when he was lunching with Ethel Kennedy at Le Cirque last week, Richard Nixon stopped by the table. Obviously intending to tell Ethel how well she was looking, Nixon said, "You've had a good life, Mrs. Kennedy."

Nixon's maladroitness is formidable. When Bill took Jackie Kennedy to Martin Luther King's funeral, Nixon said to her, "This must bring back many memories, Mrs. Kennedy." And there is of course his statement when he came out of Notre Dame after de Gaulle's funeral: "This is a great day for France."

Bill also said that David Eisenhower had been with Nixon the night in March 1968 when Johnson took himself out of the contest. At Nixon's behest David called his grandfather and asked him whether he would come out for Nixon. Ike refused.

Nixon is irrepressible. He has a piece in this week's *Time* arguing that Gorbachev is out to rejuvenate communism and warning against giving him too much support. I hope this will do something to dent Tricky's reputation as a deep thinker on foreign affairs.

December 21

On Wednesday evening, the 19th, a local television station called to ask me to say something about the reported movement of American troops to Panama. I pooh-poohed the report and declined comment. When I turned on the news the next morning, I discovered to my total astonishment that an invasion was under way.

It is still going on, though no one can find Noriega. I sense the usual quota of military incompetence. And once again, as in the case of Grenada, I am chagrined by the near unanimous applause on the part of my countrymen. Claiborne Pell was almost alone in Congress in questioning the operation. Jimmy Breslin has a fine column in today's *Newsday* denouncing it as lawless; the *Times,* a mealy-mouthed editorial entitled "Why The Invasion Was Justified." Does no one give a damn when an American President goes to war on his own as if American foreign policy were his private property?

As one opposed to presidential wars undertaken without congressional consent, to unilateral U.S. intervention in the hemisphere and to sneak attacks by superpowers on small countries, I am deeply unhappy, but I am very much in the minority (at home at least; abroad the reaction is generally critical). [Manuel] Noriega is such an odious and contemptible figure that most Americans overlook or forgive the transgressions of principle. I continue to believe that a world of law serves U.S. long-term interests a good deal better than the Reagan idea that the U.S. can be a law unto itself. And one cannot escape the feeling that, just as Nixon once proclaimed "I'm not a crook," the message intended to be conveyed by Bush's invasion of Panama is "I'm not a wimp."

If it is all over in a week, Bush will get away with it. If it drags on, and if the puppet government turns out to be incompetent and/or corrupt, Bush will be in trouble.

The case of the Mencken diary. The publication of H. L. Mencken's diary has led to a minor furor over charges of anti-semitism and other forms of racism. A few weeks ago it was written that the National Press Club in Washington was debating whether to withdraw the designation of its library as the Mencken Room. All this seemed to me an overreaction, and I was moved to write a letter not so much in defense of Mencken as in explanation; really, I suppose, in payment of a debt I have felt to Mencken since I first read him (as I tried to explain in a review of the book for the *New Leader*).

I sent the letter to a few fellow writers and asked whether they would care to join in signing it. Results so far: Norman Mailer and Bill Styron, yes, by telephone. Kurt Vonnegut, yes: noting, "A really swell letter, Arthur." Arthur Miller, yes: correcting a typo in the letter. Louis Auchincloss, yes with a proviso: "I am happy to be included, provided you don't think my reputation as 'King of the WASPS' (so described in a vulgar new book on all the discount stands) would hurt. I leave it to you. But it's a *great* letter."

Nays, so far: Phil Hamburger, by telephone: explaining that he had revered Mencken, his doctor uncle had been a great friend; "it wasn't that some of Mencken's best friends were Jews; you could almost say that *all* his best friends were Jews"—and that was why Phil found the diary so upsetting, especially at a time when he was also reading Primo Levi on Auschwitz; "Mencken was a very sick man, and one thing led to the other." John Updike: "Would you be forever offended if I declined to sign your most excellent letter about Mencken? You are of course right that it is silly to get very indignant over what Mencken confided to his diary, especially since the times were much freer about expressing racial and ethnic prejudice. Nevertheless, what I have seen quoted of his remarks (mostly in the introduction to the diary by the editor), taken with his absurd hatred of Roosevelt and remarkably soft spot for the Germans right up to 1940, indicates something more than discourtesy, bordering on pathology. Also, as a non-Jew, I feel a little shy of seeming to tell Jews what they should overreact about. Your letter, already signed by three extremely distinguished intellectual statesmen, would be even stronger if you could get a Jew to sign it." More returns to come.

In the meantime, I record Mencken's diary note of 19 November 1946: "Nine-tenths of the people who call me by telephone I don't want to talk to, and three-fourths of the people I have to take to lunch I don't want to see." He was then 66. That is definitely the way I feel at 72.

1990

January 14

We dined last night at Nicola's with Norman and Norris Mailer, Norman wishing to ruminate on the huge book he is writing about the CIA. The leading character is an Ivy League type inspired by his impressions (not memories) of Jim Angleton, Des FitzGerald and Tracy Barnes, and the action covers the period from 1955 or so to the 1970s. A few real people—Allen Dulles, Howard Hunt—appear. Norman has read the literature and interviewed some remaining operatives (Lucius Conein, for example); and, as he says, the CIA is a subject made for him anyway, given his own predisposition toward conspiratorial interpretations.

"I want to say that Kennedy was the most priapic President since . . . but I don't know how to fill in the blank. Maybe Andrew Jackson?" I said that Jackson was not notably priapic, but how about Harding? Norman thought the Harding comparison demeaning for Kennedy, and he finally settled, at Alexandra's suggestion, on

Cleveland. Cleveland did father an illegitimate child and subsequently married a 21-year-old girl, but I don't know how truly priapic he was.

Alexandra and Norris are believers in reincarnation—a doctrine that makes little sense to me, since, if you cannot remember your past lives, for all practical purposes each life is complete in itself and must be so lived. Norman seems a halfway reincarationist (remember *Ancient Evenings*) and added, to my surprise, that he was compelled by every inner emotion to believe that there was an inherent structure of order in the universe. I declared my own belief that the only structure of order was the one we feebly imposed on the indecipherable chaos surrounding us. "But you don't believe in God, Arthur," Norman said, implying that he did.

Thomas Pynchon's new novel *Vineland* is out this week to generally rave reviews. I have not been able to finish a Pynchon novel—too much showy mystification, self-indulgent absurdism, etc., for my taste—and I asked Norman how he felt. "I haven't been able to finish a Pynchon novel," he said. Somehow the name of [Theodore] Dreiser came up, and Norman, who is a Dreiser enthusiast, said how he wished Dreiser were around to write novels today; much better than Pynchon.

Norman is a man of catholic tastes—appropriate, I imagine, for a novelist with a devouring curiosity about human variations. I never could understand his tolerance of Roy Cohn, who always seemed to me one of the few truly evil men I have ever seen. Of course his tolerance of Henry Kissinger is far easier to understand, but it almost reaches the point of admiration. "A very intelligent man," Norman said; "the kind of man I would go to for intelligent advice."

I first met Norman in the early 1950s at a debate in New York when Mary McCarthy and I represented the 1930s as against Norman Mailer and Norman Podhoretz representing the 1940s. My liking for Norman Mailer and my dislike of Norman Podhoretz were equally spontaneous, and neither feeling has wavered much in the nearly forty years since. Norman is gray now, portly, dressed like a banker, his wilding days long since gone, filled with charm and sardonic humor and, of course, blessed by beautiful Norris, so intelligent, amusing and calming. We always enjoy seeing them.

June 7

On Tuesday, 15 May we flew via Helsinki to Amsterdam, where we soon joined the vanden Heuvels, Tobie [Roosevelt], the Chapins and the rest of the Franklin and Eleanor Roosevelt Institute delegation at the now familiar Hotel Zuiderduin in Westkapelle.

The next morning I gave the keynote talk at a conference in the Roosevelt Study Center in Middelburg on "Franklin D. Roosevelt as seen by his European, Latin American, and Asian Contemporaries."

The Soviet representative was Valentin Berezhkov, who had been Stalin's interpreter at Teheran and Yalta and, before that, Molotov's in the talks with Ribbentrop leading up to the infamous Pact. He is a genial man and a survivor.

Berezhkov shows traces of his Stalinist past; still defending the Pact, for example, on the ground that Chamberlain left Stalin no alternative. I said that some Soviet historians were now condemning the Pact. "Yes," he said. "We have our revisionists too."

His account of Teheran was fascinating. "Stalin," he said, "was determined to make a favorable impression on Roosevelt." He had met Hopkins, Harriman, Hull, but meeting FDR was "something special" for him. The first encounter took place in a small room next to the conference hall. Stalin cased the room, worrying where FDR's wheelchair should be placed and where he himself should sit. His face was covered with smallpox scars, brushed out in the retouched photographs, and he wanted to sit where the light would minimize the pockmarks. He put stays on his heels in order to look taller.

"Stalin had a great desire to have good relations with FDR and with America." Lenin had wanted to combine Soviet spirit with American efficiency. Stalin valued the fact that FDR had established relations with the USSR. When Mikoyan went to America (in the 1930s?), Molotov mentioned that he had a relative there who was a capitalist. Stalin said to Mikoyan, "Cohen is a capitalist. Use him to establish a connection with President Roosevelt." When Mikoyan got to America, he discovered that Cohen only owned a filling station and cabled Stalin, "I don't think that Mr. Cohen is the man to establish relations with President Roosevelt."

Some time ago Gorbachev agreed in principle to accept a Franklin D. Roosevelt Four Freedoms Medal. We had hoped he could come to Hyde Park, but his schedule did not permit. After arduous negotiation, conducted by Bill vanden Heuvel and Verne Newton, the presentation was arranged for the Soviet Embassy at 3 P.M. on Friday, 1 June.

Pamela Harriman provided an excellent luncheon for the out-of-towners (Tobie [Roosevelt], Jean Smith, Trude Lash, George Kennan, Ken, Walter Cronkite, Tom Watson, David Morse and some others), and then we met the rest of the delegation at the Federal City Club—an eminent group of senior statesmen: Mike Mansfield, Bill Brennan, Bill Fulbright, Clark Clifford, Joe Rauh, Herblock, Bob Nathan, etc. Our session was delayed a bit. Gorbachev, we were told, was closeted with Dan Quayle.

Eventually we were escorted into the Embassy and ended up in a small, hot room crowded with Soviet functionaries, cameras, lights and now our group of 25 or so. Soon Gorbachev appeared, looking relatively unperturbed in spite of his troubles at home and of his discussions with Bush, still then in midstream. Anne Roosevelt said a few words, very nicely; I said some more; Bill read the citation; Tobie and Tom Watson adorned Gorbachev with the medal. He then responded in a decent, rather disjointed speech. We all shook hands, and our delegation gave way to a new delegation, headed by Norman Cousins and Jerry Wiesner, presenting him with an Einstein Peace Medal. We were pleased that in a later speech that day Gorbachev referred to and recited the Four Freedoms!

Gorbachev was impressive and charming, giving an impression of contained strength and competence, but was hardly, I would say, magnetic. One did not feel in the presence of an FDR or Churchill or even a de Gaulle. He did not seem under undue strain, but he has had long training in concealing emotions. George Bush has obviously decided to do everything politically feasible to keep him afloat, and the summit, though it left issues like Germany unresolved, was a triumph of sentiment. I thought old Poppy handled himself very well at the press conference on Sunday.

June 15

On Monday the 11th we went to Washington. I spent day and the next day at the Library of Congress, completing research in the papers of Robert H. Jackson. What a perpetual delight manuscript research is! The hours glide by, as I turn over papers from nine to five without a pause for luncheon.

The reason for our visit was the biennial dinner of the Judson C. Welliver Society, the organization of White House speechwriters founded a few years back by Bill Safire. As usual, it was a lot of fun. The Bush speechwriters appeared—candidates for future membership. There are *seven* of them, each with his or her own researcher. Ted Sorensen and I could not believe it. In our day he and I (Ted mostly) turned out drafts for JFK (with considerable help from Dick Goodwin for the first year) without researchers and while we (Ted especially) had many other things to do.

Bill asked me to say a few words. I ruminated on the implications of the semantic shift from "ghostwriter," the term applied in my youth, to "speechwriter," the term invariably used today. Ghostwriters were so called because they were supposed to be invisible. Now no sooner is a speech given than the press reports who wrote it and, often, interviews the writer. I said that I thought this deplorable and continue to believe that accountability for the speech belongs to the person who delivers it, not to the person who drafts it.

I also noted that the use of a segregated unit devoted to nothing but speechwriting has meant the divorce of speechwriting from policy-making. This I thought unfortunate, since involvement in policy arguments is more likely to give depth and substance to speeches. Bill Gavin, a Nixon writer, came up to me afterward and made the interesting point that one reason for the divorce may be the fact that very few policy-makers these days are capable of writing speeches.

August 23

Steve [Smith] died Sunday morning.

On Friday we had called the Smiths in the country. No answer, which was disturbing. Jean has never been terribly communicative about the exact state of Steve's illness, probably shielding herself as well as her friends. We were worried, and on Saturday morning I called Willy from whom, as a doctor, I thought I could get a better reading. Willy said that it did not appear that his father could last for very long—a week at the most.

On Monday, vigil was kept at Frank E. Campbell's funeral home in New York City—my dear Steve in an open casket, friends by him around the clock. The service was held Tuesday at St. Thomas More's Church on 89th Street—lovely music; remembrances by Willy [Smith], Ted [Kennedy] and me. Afterward a cortege of cars headed for Easthampton and the internment. We were with Betty Bacall, Betty Comden and the [Adolph] Greens—an interlude of reminiscence, tears and laughter.

After the interment, we went to the Bridgehampton house for luncheon. I could not but think how many such sorrowing Kennedy times I have been through. Jackie was at the gravesite, her face a tragic mask. Ethel too. Jean has been pale, composed, alert. We stayed Tuesday night, and Alexandra is still there today.

Steve has been such a central part of our lives for the last twenty-plus years that it is hard to think that he has gone forever. The only person I have known to match his vitality, exuberant wit, ability to change the temperature of a room by entering it, capacity for generous and concerned friendship was Phil Graham, who adored Steve as a fellow spirit.

I cannot help but think of the damage wrought by the cigarette in this century. Among my own friends: Steve, Mary McCarthy, Joe Alsop, Jimmy Wechsler, Humphrey Bogart, Yul Brynner, Alan Lerner, John Huston, Ed Murrow, John Bartlow Martin, Dick Dougherty and probably a dozen others. I fear that Lennie Bernstein will be next. Steve tried hard to lick the addiction, resorting to substitutes, hypnosis, accupuncture. But he always fell off the wagon. So many good people might still be alive had they never succumbed. My Lady Nicotine indeed.

September 21

My forebodings about the Gulf multiply. We seem to be drifting toward a war that we will fight more or less alone in a remote and uncongenial terrain over exaggerated threats to our national security. Something had to be done of course when Saddam Hussein invaded and annexed Kuwait, and I thought that Bush began masterfully in organizing a coalition against him. But what started as a multilateral effort aimed at setting standards is getting more unilateral every day and seems to be aimed at war.

The first great mistake in my judgment was the despatch of something like 140,000 American troops to Saudi Arabia. Air and naval power can enter and exit risky situations quickly. Ground forces cannot fold their tents and silently steal away. Would Saddam have invaded Saudi Arabia if we had not made the ground force commitment? I put this question to General Beckett, the British military attaché, at a small luncheon on Wednesday. He said that he knew of no indication that the Iraqis contemplated an attack on Saudi Arabia. He seems to regard the invasion of Kuwait as a brutal attempt at the rectification of long-standing local grievances rather than as part of a larger plan.

At any rate, our troops are there. Withdrawal short of attaining our declared objectives will appear a political defeat. More and more, one senses anticipations of war. Some actively favor it, rejecting any solution that would leave Saddam in power and his nuclear and chemical production facilities intact.

December 8

The Gulf crisis, I think, is over. Saddam Hussein appears to have thrown in his hand, as indicated by the release of the hostages, and my guess is that the fix is in. Bush is keeping up the pressure; but [James] Baker will go to Baghdad, Iraq will withdraw "unconditionally" from Kuwait, and in due course and with appropriate camouflage will receive control over the disputed oil field and access to the sea. Such at any rate is my (current) prediction.

Last Tuesday, the 4th, I testified before the Senate Foreign Relations Committee on the first day of hearings on the Gulf. Bob McNamara, Judith Kipper of the Brookings Institution and a lobbyist for the Kuwait government and former U.S. ambassador to Bahrain (Sakim?) were the other witnesses. Bob was passionate and powerful. It was nice to be on the same side this war. Judith Kipper was intelligent and incisive. The pro-administration fellow was fluent and fatuous. (Enough of alliteration; the speechwriter's curse.)

The committee—Claiborne Pell, Joe Biden, Paul Simon, Pat Moynihan, Paul Sarbanes, Chris Dodd were in attendance and, on the Republican side, only Larry Pressler—was sympathetic. My own remarks were, I think, well received. Bob scribbled a note: "Arthur your statement was eloquent & elegant." C-Span carried the hearings that evening, and in the days since I have received phone calls and letters from all over the country. An especially nice card from Kurt Vonnegut: "Rarely have honor and eloquence served the American people better than in your testimony before Congress about a war with Iraq. I am so glad you exist."

Bob was the most effective witness, but still shows curious abilities of ingenuousness. [Paul] Sarbanes pressed him on the question [of] whether the President has the constitutional authority to send troops to war without congressional authorization. Bob refused to answer the constitutional question, saying "I am not a lawyer." But he had been Secretary of Defense for eight years, and one would have thought that he might have bothered to find out the answer. Claiborne asked him whether there was not a distinction between a "national security" concern and something that was only a matter of "national interest." I suppose he was asking Bob to distinguish between vital and peripheral interests, but again Bob expressed bafflement at the question. Still, he is a fine, honest, honorable, passionate man, and he was the star of the hearing.

Later: Jackie Onassis, who, when I saw her a few days ago, was not sure what she thought about the Gulf, called (on the 13th) to say how much she liked my testimony. Thinking to reinforce my position, I said that McNamara had given eloquent testimony along the same lines. Jackie said, "I love Bob; but on matters like this he is still working out his guilt over Vietnam."

1991

January 18

The most unnecessary war in American history began on the 16th. We heard the news just before going to Henry and Nancy Kissinger's for dinner: an appropriate time and place, I guess, considering the exchanges Henry and I have had about the Gulf. The occasion was the celebration of the 30th wedding anniversary of Irving and Mary Lazar.

The company clustered around the television to hear George Bush's address at 9 P.M. There was sharp but muted division in the ranks. Why are the British so warlike? Lawrence of Arabia, or memories of the RAF success in subduing rebels in Mesopotamia in the 1920s? Anyway, those two inveterate enemies, both present, Rupert Murdoch and Harry Evans, agreed in supporting the war (though this did not bring them together socially). Art Buchwald, to my surprise, wants, only half ironically, to bomb the Iraqis back to the stone age. Israel, I suppose. Jean and Walter Kerr, on the other hand, are passionately against the war. John

Gutfreund thinks it ridiculous. So does Cy Coleman. As you can see, it was a pleasantly variegated party, and would have been more fun (though Jean Kerr gave a witty toast) had one not been so depressed by the war.

Scotty Reston called early the next morning to express his rage over what he called the greatest scandal in American history and to wonder whether there could not be a Blue Book of some sort—a documentary publication of the papers leading up to the decision. After we talked about the war for a few moments, Scotty said, "Well, all we are doing is depressing each other further," and said goodbye. He is particularly disappointed because he was a good friend of President Bush and had high hopes for George.

The war, thank heavens, is going well. The shorter the war, the more nutty it will prove the premise to be. If Saddam Hussein crumbles in a week or two, he is hardly the contemporary Hitler, the great threat to the United States, the terror of the world, that Bush and the hawks have claimed him to be.

January 26

The euphoria of the first 24 hours is over, and the country is settling down to a long, nasty war. Most people simply accept the fact we are in the Gulf, support the troops fervently and no longer wonder why we are there.

There is considerable confusion about what is going on. The flow of information is far more tightly controlled than in any American war in my lifetime: very little independent reporting, no participation by newspapermen in missions, no interviews with the troops except in the presence of an information officer, strict censorship of despatches.

The Pentagon, convinced that honest reporting turned the country against the Vietnam War, is taking no chances this time. What they gain in control they will begin to lose in credibility. People are already beginning to express skepticism about official communiques in the absence of independent verification.

February 1

On Sunday the 27th we had a lively dinner party: Mercia Harrison, Jules and Jenny Feiffer, Dick and Danielle Gardner, Bill Walton. Much discussion of the Gulf—the Feiffers and the Schlesingers on one side; Dick Gardner and (surprisingly) Bill Walton on the other. One interesting thing about the Gulf debate is that, thus far, it seems to be conducted with considerable civility. People are polite to each other, partly perhaps because of nagging inner doubt about the correctness of any position, partly too because of the way the war has cut across old political divisions and created new and incongrous alliances: Dick Gardner signing the *Times* advertisement with Richard Perle and Jeane Kirkpatrick; I reading Pat Buchanan with approval.

On Monday morning I left for Athens, Ohio. John Lewis Gaddis, whom I like very much, met me at the Columbus airport. On Monday night I lectured on the situation, saying that I still regarded this as the most unnecessary war in American history but now that we are in it and by constitutional process I hoped we would win it as soon as possible and with a minimum loss of life. I then offered some reflections on George Bush's New World Order. The audience was sympathetic; my doubts about the war were applauded; and I received a standing ovation. The questions were courteous; no hyperpatriotic harangues. The mood in this midwestern college community seemed one of perplexity as to why we were at war combined with hope that we will get out soon and fear that we won't.

On Wednesday, the 30th, FDR's birthday, we went to the Capitol for a commemoration in Statuary Hall of FDR's 1941 State of the Union, the speech in which he set forth the Four Freedoms. I adore the Capitol. The lovely proportions of the rooms, the weighty 19th century decor, the statues of forgotten politicians make the atmosphere redolent with American history. We gathered in the Speaker's apartment, where the President soon joined us.

He was unexpectedly cordial, hailing me almost as soon as I entered the room—"Arthur, it's been so long since I've seen you"—all this to the astonishment of John Sununu, who was viewing me with a markedly dour and suspicious expression. GB must know what I have written about his war, but he gave no sign of anything but pleasure at seeing an old friend (or, more precisely, acquaintance). There was no point in having a serious talk, so we chatted about the military situation. I said I hoped that they would not rush into a ground war: give the sanctions and the bombs time to weaken the enemy. GB said that he had no intention of rushing into a ground war.

He was charming, and in consequence I found myself being much easier on him at the University of Pennsylvania on Thursday than I had been at Ohio University on Monday. And he looked well—like a man who was at peace with himself about the fateful decisions he had taken.

His remarks at the ceremony were really quite fitting. I feared that he might claim to be carrying the Four Freedoms to Iraq, but his references to the Gulf were brief and muted.

February 25

Despite wars, clamors and other interruptions, I finished the Whittle book on multiculturalism today—32,000 words, written mostly since my return from Rome on 8 February. It is odd: I have spent most of my life in education, but I have always avoided writing about education, lecturing on education or even thinking much about education. Now I find myself writing a book—a short one, it is true—about education. I suppose outrage over the way the cult of ethnicity leads to flagrant abuse of history is why I am involved. Or it may be simply the folly of old age.

It all began with my column on 23 April last in the *Journal* about the ethnic pressures on the universities, the view of history as social and psychological therapy and the implications the cult of ethnicity may have for the national sense of identity. This led to a joint statement with Diane Ravitch and the formation of the Committee of Scholars in Defense of History; and that led to my association with a panel established by New York's Commissioner of Education, a weak reed named Thomas

Sobol, to revise the state's history curriculum—and all that led to the Whittle book, for which I was well paid and as a result of which I will no doubt be in great trouble. However, I have been there before (when I wrote the *Life* piece on the CPUSA in 1946; when I opposed Joe Mc-Carthy in the 1950s; when I opposed the Vietnam War in the 1960s) and doubtless will survive.

Opposing the war in the Gulf is comparatively easy—partly because it all has taken place so fast, but even more because nearly everyone one knows is against the war too. That shows the restricted circles in which I move since, according to the polls, 80 percent of Americans favor the war.

For a moment it seemed possible that Saddam Hussein would withdraw from Kuwait without war, and that could have happened if the administration preferred peace. But George Bush, I guess, could not accept an outcome that would allow Saddam Hussein to stay in power and retain some of his military machine. So he imposed a 24-hour deadline and then launched the ground war last Saturday. But Iraq is pretty badly battered already; and, if Bush had real faith in his New World Order, he would have called upon international institutions to develop the capacities for deterrence, inspection, arms embargoes, etc., that could contain Saddam Hussein in the future.

All appears to be going well in the ground war, and I hope it will be over soonest. If the Iraqi forces keep on collapsing and surrendering, Bush will become politically unassailable, at least for a while, and the Democrats will have to dig themselves out of their (entirely laudable) opposition to the war. Alas.

February 28

The war is over, and George Bush has good reason to be well satisfied with the result—though the Iraqi collapse rather undermines the thesis that Saddam Hussein was a great military threat.

March 31

My computer has broken down (the hard drive, whatever that may be, must be replaced), and I am forced back to the typewriter, the companion of my youth and middle age. Reversion is difficult. The ease of composition on the word processor and more especially the ease of revision leave the typewriter far behind. I shudder, looking back across a long writing life, to think of the number of times I have had to type and retype the same page. On the other hand, the typewriter retains one signal advantage: it works. High technology is less reliable. Not only is my computer *hors de combat,* but my fax machine, while it still receives, no longer transmits, and our telephone answering machine has only recently begun to work again. The further problem is that once one of these machines fades out it is damned difficult to get them repaired.

At any rate, I have finished *The Disuniting of America;* it is already in proof and will apparently be out in April. Fast work. The book will probably get me into a certain amount of trouble, but it is coming out at a propitious time and should have some impact. If one can believe despatches from the campuses, faculties and particularly English departments seem to be in a condition of derangement, and pressure groups—ethnic, racial, "gender"—are having a field day. A sort of reverse McCarthyism is let loose under the banner of "political correctness." English departments appear to be the foci of this nonsense. Historians, who continue to believe that there is a reality beyond deconstruction, are mostly OK.

April 6

Another Kennedy family crisis. Last Monday, the first of April, we went to Jean's Very Special Arts benefit (*Miss Saigon*—a long, lachrymose and overstuffed show). Jean seemed distracted and remote. The next day's paper reported an alleged rape at the Kennedy place in Palm Beach. I went to South Dakota and gave a lecture at South Dakota State in Brookings. When I got back Thursday night, Alexandra said that Jean had asked us to Bridgehampton for the weekend and that she sounded "chipper," and hopeful about a quick disposal of the case. By now newspaper speculation had begun to settle on Willie [William Kennedy Smith] as the chief suspect. Today's *Daily News* has the headline: IT WAS WILLIE.

Poor Willie. I have known him practically since birth. He is a gentle, humorous, considerate young man, modest and funny, who used to spend his summers working on Indian reservations or with refugees and who will make an excellent doctor. It is all too sad.

April 9

We went out to East Hampton on Saturday afternoon to stay with Phyllis Green; Adolph was detained in New York writing new lyrics for *The Will Rogers Follies,* which opens on 1 May. Much talk, of course, about the Palm Beach affair and much concern about Jean.

The Palm Beach story grows more tangled and obscure. We came back to New York Sunday in time for the annual cocktail party before the judging of the Robert Kennedy Book Award. The turnout of Kennedys was impressive—as if to show the flag. Ethel said she had not been able to reach Jean; she is not taking calls. Bobby Jr. told Alexandra that the woman involved stole some objects from the house—a report not carried in the papers till Monday.

April 23

Blair Clark arranged a breakfast this morning for George McGovern at the Regency; Dick Wade, Ann Martindell and Julie Adler also present (Felix Rohatyn and Wyche Fowler at the next table). The idea was to dissuade George from running for the Democratic nomination. George was in excellent form—candid, humorous, dispassionate. It was all most enjoyable.

George said that he and Nixon were on the same shuttle to Washington the other day. After the plane took off, Nixon came over and sat with him, and they chatted all the way to Washington. They first talked about the Soviet Union, from which Nixon has recently returned. "I've made many visits to Russia," Nixon said, "many visit to China. But the only conclusion I have come to is that I don't know what is really going on in either of those countries."

The conversation turned to the question whether George should run or not. Nixon said, "First you have to decide whether you have something to say—something that no one else will be saying. Then you have to decide whether you will be heard—whether people will listen to you over the ridicule and noise and general claptrap of politics. Then you have to decide whether the effort will enhance or diminish your stature." Nixon does have a certain crude authority in such political calculations. He went on to denounce the press: "You can never trust those fellows. If you give them a chance, they will tear your ass off."

George gave us both sides of the case—for and against running. Eleanor, he said, is dead set against it. Even if he were to be nominated and elected, she has told him, she would not want to spend four years in the White House—and of course he would not be nominated and elected. She asked him why he was thinking about running at all. George said frankly that he could not deny a desire for vindication of some sort after the disaster of 1972.

We talked about other liberal prospects. George said he had spoken to three people about running: Cuomo, Bob Kerrey, Bill Clinton. He thinks Cuomo would be the strongest candidate (Nixon agrees). When they talked, Cuomo at first said he had no desire to run, then said maybe they should talk about it again in late spring and early summer, then said, "I would like very much to have your views on whom I should back." George said, "I came away from the conversation with no idea at all of what he was saying." Mario remains a master of mystification.

Bob Kerrey said he was thinking about it but did not feel he was quite ready. Bill Clinton said he was thinking seriously about it; George believes that he is getting close to announcing. Dale Bumpers, who is advising Bill, argues that, even if he loses in 1992, he would be well positioned for 1996. George regards Al Gore as too opportunistic. Jesse Jackson, accompanied by a team of photographers and TV cameramen, called on George when he was in the hospital recently after a prostate operation and said defiantly that the press was premature in writing him out of the 1992 competition; "I got 7 million votes in 1988; if I can get 10 million next time, I will be nominated."

The Middle Eastern mess deepens. Having urged on the Kurds, George Bush is finding it difficult not to help them. I think he is right to oppose military intervention in Iraq—though on that same principle he should not have gone military in the first place. A few weeks ago he pronounced the "Vietnam syndrome" dead; now he is explicitly invoking it as a reason for not getting involved in a civil war in Iraq. And, having disdained economic sanctions last autumn as a way of getting Iraq out of Kuwait, he is now relying on them to get rid of Saddam Hussein.

I can't think that those who opposed the war will need to feel apologetic in another three months.

May 17

Harry Evans and Tina Brown gave a dinner last night for Clark Clifford and the fine book he has done with Dick Holbrooke, *Counsel to the President*. It is sad to see Clark's distinguished career move toward an ignoble end in a bank scandal; nor do I understand how he got into this mess except through octogenarian negligence and reposing undue confidence in a young lawyer in his firm—possibly the son that Clark never had. The ordeal has aged him a great deal in recent months. But last night he was in splendid form, told stories with great gusto and delighted everybody.

I sat at a table for six between Jackie Onassis and Victoria Newhouse. Clark sat on the other side of Jackie with Tina next to him and Phil Habib on her left. I had not had a chance to talk with Habib before and found him frank, intelligent and likable. He had been against going to war in the Gulf and asked Clark what he thought of the war. Clark replied, "An abomination." Habib talked interestingly about his efforts in Nicaragua. He said that he was well on his way to settling the civil war but that Elliott Abrams, Colonel [Oliver] North and others were determined on victory and sabotaged every try at a negotiated solution.

Jackie remains a glowing beauty. She concentrated her charm, as always, and at one point generously informed me that she would rather sit next to me than any person in New York. This would be more convincing if she ever invited us to dinner. But I adore her.

May 23

The Kennedy affair continues to gather momentum. *People* this week has a despicable piece describing Steve and Jean's marriage as one in which the couple "started living apart, and before long . . . were completely estranged," etc. Ted Kennedy and Bill Barry are under attack (at least in the press) as obstructors of justice. One so-called historian, Thomas Reeves, dredges up the sexual stuff on JFK in a new book, *A Question of Character,* and Michael Beschloss, who knows better, appears to be exploiting the same lode in another new book. Jean continues her wry riding out the storm, but it is obviously very hard on her. The sadness is that Ted's many virtues as a public man are being subverted and destroyed by his many frailties as a private man.

May 30

Much talk all weekend about Democratic prospects for 1992. Everyone acknowledges the discussion to be boring; but no one can stay off it. Pam seems rather excited about Jay Rockefeller, who has evidently decided to run. She dismisses previous favorites of hers—Al Gore ("hasn't grown in four years; can't connect with people"); Bill Clinton ("too vulnerable in his private life"); Cuomo ("too elusive, too difficult"). Rockefeller is clean, attractive, a practical but not an ideological liberal, recognizable name, plenty of money, no enemies. Bob Squires says that there are only two serious possibilities for 1992: Rockefeller and Cuomo.

On the whole, the Washington talk ignores Cuomo. When I bring up his name, people grudgingly acknowledge his qualities but are fed up with his game-playing. Should Cuomo ever decide to run, this impatience with his quirks and foibles will vanish, but in this warm-up period people are weary of him.

Vernon Jordan to my astonishment is an eloquent advocate of Governor [Douglas] Wilder of Virginia. My first thought was that Vernon might be hawking Wilder as a way of escaping from Jesse Jackson; but after a moment his enthusiasm for Wilder—"charismatic, highly intelligent," etc.—seemed authentic. They were law school classmates, and Vernon has therefore known him a long time. I said that I had the impression that Wilder was quite conservative. "He's only a fiscal conservative," Vernon said. Pamela told me *sotto voce* that she regards Wilder as hard, ambitious, devious and mean. Apparently he has turned on people like Governor [Gerald] Baliles who helped him on his way up.

Vernon also ventured the prediction that George Bush would not run in 1992. "At this very moment in Kennebunkport," he said, "Barbara is saying to George, 'I don't want you to kill yourself in this job. You've had a successful first term. You've won two wars. You will never be more popular. Remember what happened to Reagan in his second term. Let's get out while the going is still good.'" I doubt that this will happen—people enjoy being President too much—but I wouldn't entirely exclude it.

June 27

The Disuniting of America is out now. Thus far the mail, mostly from historians, has been favorable, including a surprisingly friendly letter from Henry Louis Gates Jr., the black literary theorist. In fact all the mail on both the book and the report has been OK so far, but I expect denunciations to show up soon.

July 2

The multicultural argument continues, spurred on by the imminence of the Fourth of July and by the absence of other national arguments. *Time* has a "Whose America?" cover story this week with a page by me entitled "The Cult of Ethnicity, Good and Bad." My mail continues favorable; I can't remember having received one denunciatory letter so far. No doubt that will soon change.

Last weekend we went to Bridgehampton and stayed with Jean. Willie was there, and we played a lot of tennis. Willie was rueful and sad. He said to me, "I can't wait for this to be over." We all had an interesting discussion one night. Stephen [Smith Jr.], citing Bob Coles, said that the Democratic party had lost touch with the American people, that the party seemed indifferent or hostile to the symbols that moved Americans—flag, church, family—and that it appeared to many Americans as simply the party of the minorities. I suppose there is something to this, even if the Republican exploitation of the symbols is opportunistic and cynical. Reagan, for example—the great patriot who never went to war, the great religionist who never went to church, the great family man who never saw his children.

July 20

I still have not received a single hostile letter in response to my campaign against overzealous multiculturalism. Vann Woodward had a marvelous review of *Disuniting* in the *New Republic* and a powerful piece on "Freedom & the Universities" in the *New York Review of Books*. When I sent Vann a note of congratulations saying that this would help rally the great silent majority of academics against the prevalent nonsense, he replied: "Letters—all negative—have been pouring into the editor of the *New York Review*. Far from 'rallying those who should be with us,' I seemed to have rallied those against us."

Why the differential reaction? Perhaps because those who oppose the Woodward-Schlesinger line have already decided that I am a villain and are consequently not surprised by my villainy, while they (properly) regard Vann as a kinder, gentler and nobler figure and therefore feel that he has betrayed them.

What I find really disconcerting is applause on the right. I don't mind a nice column by George Will, whom I like and who is a good affirmative-government conservative, but approval by Jeffrey Hart, reactionary members of the Harvard Class of '38 and others is a little much. I suppose I may even have to endure favorable words from Charles Krauthammer.

August 15

We returned from Newfoundland yesterday afternoon, and I found a message from Frances FitzGerald asking me to call her. When we finally made contact, she told me that Marietta was in the hospital and that the end was near. She called this morning to say that her mother had died at 3:30 this morning.

It is hard to believe that we met 43 years ago—in the summer of 1948 at the Bruces' apartment in Paris. I still remember her coming into the room in a smashing red dress, walking in beauty and radiating life and delight as she walked. I fell in love with her the first second I saw her. She has been near the center of my life ever since—my best and dearest friend.

Marietta was filled with curiosity as well as charm. She had a passion to learn new things. Life was, in the New England style, an unending quest for education. She also always wanted to help less fortunate people. But, underneath her kind and impeccable manners, she was very sharp and funny and never missed a trick. She once said that her ideal was to be a combination of Carole Lombard and Eleanor Roosevelt. She realized that ideal. I still can't believe that this vital, radiant, sparkling girl has gone.

December 14

George Bush, for all his self-confidence in foreign policy, seems baffled, dispirited, disoriented and totally ineffectual in domestic affairs.

As attention has shifted to our own problems, he has slumped precipitously in the polls; and since the recession shows no sign of ending, he is approaching the condition of free fall. At this point, unless Bush is rescued once more by international crisis, the presidency appears ripe for plucking.

December 23

Mario Cuomo has come and gone. Up to the last moment, it seemed as if he might run. He had gone too far, it appeared, to pull back. Even my son Stephen, who has long been a skeptic, told us on Thursday that he would do it. Even Mario's son Andrew believed on Friday that his father was about to take the plunge. A plane was waiting at the Albany airport to bring Cuomo to New Hampshire in time to file his papers. Then he called a press conference and said no.

Much speculation. Some take him at his word and say that he could not honorably run when he had not yet discharged his duty to the people of New York by working out a budget with the Republicans; or at least that he would be right to regard the New York budget problem as an insuperable political vulnerability if he went ahead. Some cling to a Machiavellian view: he will enter later if none of the present contenders spring out of the pack. I have deeper and darker forebodings: I am afraid that Cuomo, for all his intelligence and cockiness, is basically insecure and provincial and that he is afraid of the presidency. Here was a campaign made to order for him. The recession had brought forward *his* issues. He is the one candidate who would really rattle George Bush. He has explained repeatedly how he would run a campaign against Bush. Yet, in the end, he chickened out. As a writer in yesterday's *News* put it, "He leaves the subject of the presidency as the tough guy at the bar who knows how to talk a good fight."

1992

January 5

On Friday the 3rd we went to a party at the Colony Club in celebration of the marriage on New Year's Day of George Plimpton and Sarah Dudley. I first met George in the late 1950s when Josiah (Mickey) Child, his college roommate, had a house party near Boston for a group of elegant New Yorkers—George, my dear Pidie Gimbel (as she was then; Pidie Bailey had gone to Milton with RFK; later was Dick Goodwin's girl in the 1960s; now married to Sidney Lumet), Bea Dabney (then George's great love; now married to Charlie Adams). George was also an old friend of Alexandra's; and we have been seeing him fairly regularly over the last twenty years.

George is the best company—witty, joyous, considerate, intelligent, thoughtful, generous, a marvelous raconteur. He is also cool, remote, elusive and therefore not the best of husbands. I liked his first wife Freddy (daughter of Willard Espy, whom I see often at the long table in the Century, a courtly word fancier complete with elaborate mustachios), but I suppose that George's elusiveness may have hastened her resort to drugs, from which she successfully pulled out after their divorce.

January 28

My return [from a trip to Cuba] has witnessed the decline and, I fear, the fall of Bill Clinton. When I got back, I found a message to call Harold Ickes, who is running his campaign in New York. Harold wondered whether I might be ready to endorse Clinton when he held a New York press conference on Monday the 20th. I was rather inclined to do so. He seems to me the most substantial of the contenders, and Harold Ickes assures me that, despite the DLC, Bill remains the liberal I used to know. However, Joe Rauh's counsel and my own intuition held me back.

The weekend before the press conference rumors of Bill's skirt-chasing suddenly rose to the surface. These rumors have been around for some time and were thought to be the cause of his decision not to run in 1988. I supposed that his entry into the race this year meant that he had worked out ways to deal with the problem. Now the rumors acquired new momentum when a disreputable supermarket tabloid called the *Star* dug up an Arkansas woman named [Gennifer] Flowers who claims to have been Bill's lover for a dozen years.

We went to a party for Bill on Monday afternoon, the 20th. He seemed composed and handled himself well. But pressure began to build as television and the tabloid press started to play up the *Star* story. His standing in the polls plunged, and he finally decided to go on *60 Minutes* with his wife on Sunday night, the 26th. A smug and odious interviewer named Steve Kroft, mingling sanctimoniousness and prurience, demanded that the Clintons answer the most personal and prying questions. They answered calmly, but it was a wretched affair; and, seeing it with an incredulous Edna O'Brien, who had just arrived from London, I felt ashamed for our country. Today I wrote an intemperate piece for the *Journal* denouncing the adultery test and those super-moralists who try to apply it.

Most voters, according to new polls, reject the adultery test and feel that the Clintons have gone as far as they need go in self-revelation. My guess is that Bill will benefit in New Hampshire from a surge of sympathy. But I fear he may be mortally wounded all the same. One of the strong arguments for him has been his electability. But people may begin to worry that he will be caught lying about Ms. Flowers, or that new ladies will pop up and conclude that running him will be too great a risk. (Dick Wade told me today the current joke in the Kerrey camp: Let a thousand flowers bloom.)

February 6

My *Wall Street Journal* column on Clinton's *60 Minutes* appearance produced screams of rage from Don Hewitt, the producer. Don says that Clinton had asked to appear on the show and wanted the questions to be as tough as possible and that his only motive was to give Clinton a chance to put the rumors at rest. That may be, but it does not alter my point: that *60 Minutes* lifted the story out of the supermarket and into respectability. Also Clinton made a big mistake in not insisting on going on live. Bobby Handman, Harold Ickes's mother-in-law, told me the other night that thirty or forty minutes had been cut and that the best bits were on the cutting room floor.

It looks as if Bill will win New Hampshire out of a backlash of disgust against this kind of journalism, and he will certainly go on to carry most southern states on 10 March (SuperTuesday). If he wins Illinois the next week, it will be hard to deny him the nomination. And if 10 percent of the electorate votes against him because he is an adulterer, he will lose the general election, and I will spend four more of my declining years under a Republican President. One problem is that Ms. Flowers is such an obvious floozy. As Brooke Astor said to Pamela Harriman, "Why couldn't Mr. Clinton have stayed with girls of his own class?"

February 17

On Sunday the 9th, at Fred Papert's request, I spoke at a dinner given by the Municipal Art Society honoring Pat Moynihan. On Monday the 10th we went to Alan Brinkley's for dinner with Peter and Nikki Hall, whom I like, Joe Lelyveld of the *Times* and his wife, also likable, and Frank Rich and his wife Alex Wichel, not likable at all.

On Tuesday the 11th we took Pamela Harriman and Bill Walton to see *A Little Hotel on the Side,* the Feydeau farce which was funnier when Bert Lahr played in it under the title *Hotel Paradiso,* but is still pretty funny with Tony Randall and Lynn Redgrave.

In the course of the week I received a call from Phil Klone, who is organizing a write-in movement for Mario Cuomo in New Hampshire. He asked me to speak at a Cuomo rally on Sunday. After five minutes' thought, I said I would. Clinton may get the nomination, but I doubt that he can win in November. The election will be close, and I fear that enough people will vote against him because they think he is a philanderer or a draft-dodger to insure defeat. There is no strong alternative to Clinton among the other declared contenders; so the one hope, it seems to me, is to drag Cuomo into the race. Stephen thinks that is what he has been maneuvering toward anyway.

Also, like an old firehorse, I respond to the ringing of the campaign bell. Politics is the greatest fun, and I have missed it in recent years. So I flew north to Manchester on Sunday the 16th, accompanied by Blair Clark, another old firehorse who had read in the *Times* that I was going. It was a fine springish day. The streets of Concord were filled with young people waving Cuomo or Clinton or [Bob] Kerrey or [Paul] Tsongas or [Tom] Harkin placards. Kathy drove up from Cambridge; I was hoping that Robert might make it from Middlebury, but apparently his ride collapsed.

The rally at Notre Dame College, Manchester, in the late afternoon was a splendid bit of old-time politics. The hall was crowded, enthusiastic and responsive. Also there were a lot of reporters, TV cameras, etc., though much of the press had to leave before I came on (there were too many speakers) because of the candidates' debate in the evening. I praised Clinton and the others except Tsongas, who, I said, was running in the wrong primary. I went on to explain why a vote for Tsongas would be a vote against what FDR, Truman and JFK stood for. The audience seemed a little taken aback as if they had not focussed on Tsongas's views before, but not resistant.

February 26

The Democratic situation remains confused. Tsongas won in New Hampshire, with Clinton a strong second. The draft-Cuomo movement was a flop; I guess that most of those who wrote in Cuomo on their ballots came to the Manchester rally. Fred Barnes in the *New Republic* this week quotes my comment on Tsongas's anti-government crack: "Can you imagine Franklin Roosevelt or Harry Truman or John Kennedy making such a cheap sneer about the role of government in American democracy?" When asked about this, Barnes writes, "Tsongas was indignant. 'I find that so utterly presumptuous,' he said. Maybe so, Paul, but you'd better get used to it."

This week Bob Kerrey won the South Dakota primary with Tom Harkin second. Clinton is still the favorite, but he has not yet won a primary. His test will come in the South, the part of the country that cares most about military service.

March 12

We are past SuperTuesday. Clinton beat Tsongas decisively in Florida; and, if Clinton wins in Illinois and Michigan next week, he cannot be stopped, short of some new and damning revelation. Then the Republicans will Willy Hortonize him all autumn, and I will spend my declining years under the feeble Presidency of George Bush.

March 18

Bill Clinton took Illinois and Michigan yesterday and is well on the way to the nomination. Tsongas and [Jerry] Brown will hang around in the hope that the next scandal will knock Bill out of the race. I trust that that particular cornucopia is exhausted—and fear that, if there is more to come, the Republicans will withhold it till after the convention.

Who would have supposed two months ago that Tsongas and Brown would be, along with Clinton, the survivors? Everyone expected Kerrey and Harkin. At an earlier George Ball luncheon, George McGovern and Ted Sorensen, both experienced enough in politics, confidently declared the contest was down to Clinton and Kerrey. This is why politics is so endlessly fascinating.

We had another Ball luncheon on Monday—general acquiescence in the inevitability of Clinton. There was some talk about the need to press foreign policy and good words about Tony Lake, who is reputedly Bill's chief foreign policy adviser. No one, including Sorensen, knew who his chief advisers on domestic policy are. We old veterans are certainly out of the picture.

March 27

The New York primary: Clinton under incessant attack, a scandal a day, like Chinese water torture; Jerry Brown, a whirling dervish unbounded in his demagoguery; voters turned off by both. Feeling that Clinton is basically a decent fellow and is getting something of a bum rap, I volunteered to help form an Arts and Letters for Clinton Committee. Norman Mailer said he would be co-chairman. I drafted a statement; Norman amended it slightly.

May 2

The acquittal Thursday of the Los Angeles cops who beat up Rodney King has outraged most of the country. Los Angeles was in flames

Thursday night, and, though New York has remained largely peaceful, rumors of violence swept the city yesterday, and many stores and offices closed down and sent their employees home. Things seem quiet today. Rodney King himself has helped by pleading in anguished tones for the violence to stop. The more I see of life, the more deeply I fear racism is ingrained in everyone. Perhaps it is the Original Sin.

Politically things have quieted down. Bill Clinton has the nomination all but wrapped up. Scandal talk has subsided. His recent success in the Pennsylvania primary shows that he is back in stride; and John Chancellor, who has been covering him on the road, told me at lunch yesterday that he thinks Bill may be out of the woods. The big political development, the Los Angeles riots apart, has been the rise of Ross Perot as a probable contender. Third party candidates always look better in May than in November; but Perot enjoys one signal advantage over his predecessors—that is, $100 million. And a lot of voters don't like either Bush or Clinton.

On the 20th we dined with Douglas and Vera Fairbanks. Doug, in good form, told a couple of memorable stories. After his father, Charlie Chaplin and Mary Pickford founded United Artists, Mary and Charlie had a fight and stopped speaking to each other. Some years later, Doug, making a film in England, saw Chaplin a few times and, in the hope of bringing the two old friends together, said how much Mary missed him and how fondly she spoke of him. Chaplin responded agreeably. Back in Hollywood, Doug took the same tack with Mary Pickford. Chaplin speaks often of you, he said, and sends his affections to you. Mary Pickford asked to hear more of this. Doug obliged. Mary finally said, "I still think he's a son of a bitch."

After Doug came back from the war, he was invited to a big Hollywood party. He was still in naval uniform, had been away for half a dozen years, and, as he entered a large room, his former wife Joan Crawford spotted him, screamed "Douglas" and swept magnificently across the room to embrace him. Her first words: "Douglas, you may not have heard, I have left MGM and have gone to Warners."

July 21

The convention is over, Bill Clinton and Al Gore, Hillary and Tipper, have been on a triumphant bus cavalcade from Madison Square Garden to St. Louis, and westward the land is bright.

The weeks before the convention were dominated by harsh exchanges between the Bush and Perot camps. Obviously the two principals have intense personal dislike for each other. The Republicans painted Perot as a petty autocrat with contempt for the Constitution and for individual privacy. The Perot people painted Bush as an empty incompetent. Both were probably right. Meanwhile Clinton soldiered on, soberly addressing issues. The media did not pay much attention, but Clinton gained a bit as Bush and Perot defamed each other. Lunching one day with John Chancellor and a couple of other reporters, I got the impression that newspapermen have come to like Clinton, are impressed by his substantive seriousness and, feeling vaguely guilty about the zeal with which they pursued his sexual vagaries last winter, await the opportunity to redress the balance.

The question of the vice presidential choice remained. Pamela assured me early in the week of 6 July that it would be Al Gore, and she was right. The choice was widely applauded. With Perot in the contest, the South became competitive for the Democrats, and Gore would strengthen a southern strategy. And he also has national appeal. He is the environmentalists' hero; his military record offsets Clinton's lack of one and exposes Quayle's; and he is a transparently honest and decent, if rather stiff, man.

On Friday the 10th we went out to Arthur Ross's in East Hampton. Kitty Hart and David Hannay, the British ambassador to the UN, were the other guests. On Saturday afternoon Al Gore called from Carthage, Tennessee, and asked whether I would help on his acceptance speech. I said of course and asked what he had in mind saying. He spoke for quite a time about global environmental problems, "family values," the "spirit of caring" and the need for "connections." He talked with passion about the rescue of the planet—"the central organizing principle for the 21st century." (All this is from notes taken at the time.)

He went on to attack the "hubristic" assumption that we are sufficient unto ourselves and wandered off into a long disquisition about gnosticism, Maimonides, Thomas Aquinas, Descartes. Starting 373 years ago, he said (what happened in 1619?), there began the seduction of Western thought into the gnostic belief that we should pour intellectual energy into gaining rational mastery over nature. People are now questioning the assumption that individuals are separate units unconnected to natural world and to society. We are coming to understand the importance of interrelationships—our duty to the environment, to our families, to our communities, etc. Unusual talk from a politician. We agreed to meet in New York the next day.

Of course, like an old firehorse responding to the bell, I was delighted by the invitation. I also had forebodings. Speechwriting is a young man's game, and you have to be in the thick of things to do it right. My mind flashed back to the moment in the 1952 campaign when Adlai said exultantly that Bob Sherwood and Sam Rosenman had agreed to do a couple of speeches. I too was thrilled by the thought of speeches from the grand old FDR team. Adlai sent me to New York to pick up the drafts. I had an uproarious lunch with Bob and Sam and, clutching a manila envelope containing the speeches, I boarded the plane back to Illinois. I began reading the texts, and my heart sank. They were really not much good. Sherwood and Rosenman had been out of things too long. So have I.

But I would not forego the chance to see the candidate and get a glance at the action. We returned to New York on Sunday in time for an entertaining buffet luncheon given by Stephen and Judy. Gore called in the afternoon, and we agreed to meet at the Intercontinental Hotel at 8:30 that evening. We went to a party at the *Times* and then to an RFK party at Gracie Mansion, where Mario Cuomo gave one of his eloquent extemporaneous speeches. (He did, however, say that Jack Newfield's was the best book written about RFK. We were listening to the speech via loudspeaker in another room, and Jules Feiffer said to me, "Jack must be sitting right in front of the podium.")

At 8:30 I presented myself at the Intercontinental. After various security checks, I was ushered into the Gore suite. Al greeted me warmly, and Tipper kissed me. Al said, "I want you to say hello to an old friend" and took me in to see his father and mother. The elder Gores could not have looked happier. Al then said, "I have to talk to Arthur. He can visit with you later," and we went into the suite's drawing room. Here we were joined by Bruce Reed, an intelligent young man, former Rhodes Scholar, courteous but confident, rather as Ted Sorensen and I were forty years ago, and by Al's daughter Karenna, a bright and pretty girl, a Harvard sophomore concentrating in history and lit. She spoke little but everything she said was to the point.

Al then began in a rambling, free-association way to continue his account of themes he proposed to touch on in the acceptance speech. He was slow-spoken but articulate, even voluble. He first registered his concern about the falling-away from the political process, as expressed in the Perot phenomenon and in the country's fervent anti-political mood. "People are giving up on the process, and self-government itself is at risk. . . . There is an erosion of public confidence in our capacity to govern ourselves. If this continues, self-government will be completely adrift. For the first time we might even lose our democracy." He added that George Bush ought to be blamed for the revulsion against politics.

He then mused for a while about the generational aspect. "The baby-boomers are coming of governing age—and everything is declining as we take over the reins." The world is changing, he said, and the shift calls for "a redefinition of our relationship to reality. We are going through the greatest change in world view since the scientific revolution." He spoke about the potentialities of high technology—supercomputers, fiber optic cables, information highways and other esoterica. (This seems to me one of the strongest arguments for the ticket. These kids grew up with the electronic revolution; George Bush and I are still baffled by supermarket check-out systems.)

He then discoursed about "values" and returned to his insistence of the day before on the urgent need for individuals to locate themselves as part of larger wholes, getting in touch with nature and with society. "Our duty is not just to what helps us as individuals but to what is good beyond ourselves. . . . People living unto themselves feel that their lives have no meaning. We must work to reestablish the balance of nature, and we must work to reestablish the balance of society. As the false assumption that we are not connected to our natural environment creates the ecological crisis, so the false assumption that we are not connected to the larger community creates the social crisis. We must restore the connections. . . . We are in a spiritual crisis. The problem is how to define our place in the universe."

All this had become urgently clear to him, he said, as a result of his son's accident. When the little boy was struck by an automobile and nearly killed, "it forced me to think again about life and to focus on what is really important and vital." He went on about regaining authenticity in living by getting back in touch with nature, his discourse had a holistic, even mystical, fervor. I began to wonder what this sort of talk reminded me of. Suddenly the name swam into consciousness: Henry Wallace.

After a time Bill Clinton came into the room, accompanied by his daughter Chelsea (what odd names they give their daughters). Chelsea is a shy, unspoiled, charming 12-year-old. We chatted about the campaign for another hour or so. My impression is that Clinton and Gore had not known each other especially well, and they seemed to be getting along fine. Clinton, who is swifter and more incisive in his talk than Gore, was clearly the dominant partner, but it seemed a genuine partnership.

Before I left, I asked whether they had any material that might be of use and was much entertained when Bruce Reed handed me drafts of Clinton's acceptance speech by Ted Sorensen and Dick Neustadt and some notes from Dick Goodwin. I am not the only old war-horse summoned by bells.

I spent Monday [July 13] turning out a draft for Gore, completed by the end of the day. Then we went to a party for Tom Foley at the

Metropolitan and to Dick and Danielle Gardner's party at Barbetta, where I handed the draft to Gore. Later that evening we went to the crowded and enthusiastic party for George McGovern at Tatou. The party machine, however, treats George as a non-person. Mondale and Dukakis were introduced, spotlights picking them out in the stands, but not McGovern. He was sitting not far from us during Clinton's acceptance speech, his face indescribably sad.

[Tuesday] we went to Madison Square Garden, sitting in the Kennedy box. They showed a touching film about RFK, after which Ted Kennedy gave a fine and fighting liberal speech. Jerry Brown demagogued for a while. Then Mario Cuomo came on with a virtuoso performance in a brilliantly written and brilliantly delivered nominating speech for Clinton—the best nominating speech I have ever heard. After all his cracks and innuendos, Mario went all out, and it was a roaring success. We then left for a party in Ted Kennedy's suite at the Riga Royal Hotel.

[Wednesday] we went to the Garden for the acceptance speeches. As I had rather anticipated, my draft suffered the Sherwood-Rosenman fate. A few lines survived here and there, and a refrain I had picked up from Dick Goodwin's notes ("It is time for them to go") was enlarged and put to excellent use. I am bound to say that the speech as delivered was better than the draft they had received from me. Then Clinton came on and was very effective for about half an hour in building emotion. But, as he continued, one began to sense the emotion dissipating. The speech lacked structure, became repetitious and was twenty minutes too long—the Humphrey effect. But it contained some strong points and excellent lines and must be judged a success.

Then the band played, brightly colored balloons floated down from the ceiling in a wonderful display, and happy Democrats dispersed into the night. We ran into Vernon Jordan, filled with optimism, even saying that the blacks would come out and that Clinton would do well in the South.

We spent the weekend with Jean in Bridgehampton. On Saturday afternoon Al Gore called me from the bus as it moved down the New

Jersey Turnpike. A well brought up young man, he thanked me for my help on the speech. I told him that the end product was considerably better than my draft. He politely said that my draft provided the stimulus that made the end product possible.

The new *Time* magazine has just arrived. Hugh Sidey describes me as "among the convention patriarchs" and as a "sturdy old Democrat"! I guess I am getting there. I recall how impressed I was twenty years ago by Walter Lippmann's half century+ career. Now I have lasted nearly as long. *Orestes A. Brownson* came out 53 years ago.

August 3

Clinton maintains what everyone agrees to be a swollen lead—but still a lead so big as to be almost insurmountable (or so Fred Israel tells me the Gallup people believe). Meanwhile George Bush, who has been threatening to get tough but only after his convention, now is getting meaner every day. Clinton, unlike Dukakis four years ago, counterpunches every time. Bush seems desperate, and his campaign in frantic disarray. Everyone is waiting for Jim Baker. Will he come?

Henry Kissinger says yes; definitely. Given Henry's relations with Larry Eagleburger, I assume he is right. Last weekend Dominique Nabokov invited us (plus Andy, Peter and Natalie) to the house in Connecticut that Alex Liberman has loaned her this summer; and on Saturday night we went to John Richardson's for dinner. The Kissingers were there.

Henry has little use for Bush—"a very petty man," he said—but prefers him to Clinton on the ground of superior "experience" in foreign affairs. (I offered my usual pitch about foreign affairs as not all that arcane and experience in doing things badly as not all desirable, but it made no impression.) Henry then said he couldn't understand why Quayle had such a bad press; he found him well-informed and intelligent. (I take this to mean two things: that Quayle listens reverently to Henry and that Henry thinks Quayle may be President some day.) Henry also said that Jack Kemp was the source of the leak quoting Jim

Baker as making a crack about the Jews—"they never vote for us anyway."

We had a drink with Jack Hemingway and his new wife. Our old friend Margaux was there, very sweet and now living the clean life in the woods after too many drinks, drugs and dunderheads in her previous life. Much talk about Woody Allen, Mia Farrow and their break-up.

I find it all too sad. We do not know Woody and Mia well, but met them on occasion, and they seemed rather adorable together, her warmth making up for his skittishness. Mia's accusation that Woody molested the 7-year-old girl seems hard to believe, and hiring Alan Dershowitz as her lawyer does not improve credibility. But Woody's confessed interest in the 20-year-old Korean stepdaughter gives a darker dimension to his movies. We will never be able to see them in the same way again.

"You know, Woody was in love with Mariel when they made *Manhattan*," Jack said. Woody even came out to visit the Hemingways in Sun Valley. Jack liked him and took him for walks through the mountains. Returning from a hike, Woody said, "Nature and I are as two."

September 12

On Thursday the 10th I lunched with George McGovern. George remains hopeful about Clinton, though the Clinton people, except for John Holum, have ignored him. He would rather like, he said, to be ambassador to the UN, though he thinks the chances of such an appointment are infinitesimal. He also said that Ron Brown had written him saying he was "horrified" by the snub administered to George at the convention; they had not known he was in the hall.

The campaign has settled down to a contest between "change" and "risk." Change of course always involves risk; and from now on the Republicans will do their best to frighten the country by emphasizing the risk in elevating to the presidency the young, inexperienced governor of a poor, rural southern state, someone who is in addition a draft-dodger and a philanderer, at a time when the republic faces momentous problems in a dangerous world. George Bush may not be too inspiring a figure, but he is steady, competent, etc., and you will know what you are getting. That will be the line. And Bush will use to the hilt the powers of incumbency—including the targeted distribution of federal largesse (while denouncing the Congress for pork-barrel legislation).

George and I recalled that the same strategy almost succeeded in 1960. JFK had a comfortable lead till toward the end of October. Then, in the last week before the election, one began to feel the lead ebbing away. Voters were suddenly frightened by the adventure of Kennedy— by the supposed risk of electing a 43-year-old senator with no executive experience in preference to a man who as Vice President had been intimately involved in great affairs for eight years. Had the election been a week later (George and I agreed) Nixon would probably have won. And, though Clinton has put on an excellent campaign, he is a more vulnerable candidate than JFK.

George had recently accompanied Rose Styron on a visit to Mia Farrow. He expected, he said, to find a chaotic, noisy household running over with the children Mia obsessively adopts; instead, he found a warm, harmonious, loving household in which everyone helped and appeared to adore everyone else. Mia gave Rose and George a copy of the video in which the seven-year-old girl describes how Woody molested her; George said that, though there were one or two bits in which it seemed that the child might have been coached, 90 percent seemed totally authentic. He said that Woody had shown these tendencies before and had sought psychiatric assistance. In general George is quite persuaded that Mia is in the right.

September 29

The polls continue to hold up, but Bush is campaigning with more edge and ruthlessness, and I still anticipate some success in frightening voters away from the risk of Clinton. Better the devil you know. . . . Yet it is very difficult to find even any Republicans who show any enthusiasm for Bush.

On Thursday the 24th after an amusing luncheon with my old friend Eric Hobsbawm who is making his annual fall visit to the New School, I strolled over to Bryant Park for a Clinton rally. He was an hour and a half late, but most of the crowd waited in a brilliant, crisp autumn day—perfect political weather—and went wild when he arrived. He responded well, gave an effective stump speech and will carry New York City with 75 percent of the vote.

On Friday the 25th I was driven to Mt. Airy in the Poconos for a panel on multiculturalism sponsored by East Stroudsburg University. The other participants were Cornel West of Princeton and Molefi Kete Asante of Temple. West, who wrote an excellent book on pragmatism, *The American Evasion of Philosophy,* is basically a reasonable man torn, like other black intellectuals, between his own moderation and the militant pressures and expectations of the black intellectual community. When he and I were on the Charlie Rose show together a few weeks back, he was thoughtful and dispassionate. However, before an audience with a large black representation including a claque Asante brought from Temple, West was transformed into a vigorous platform performer with broad gestures, rising and falling intonations, jokes, declamations. Perhaps he was putting on this act to conceal or to render more palatable his essential moderation. Asante, the godfather of Afrocentrism, though friendly personally, shouted away intemperately on the platform; my presentation provoked occasional derisive laughter and some boos; and West deftly hovered somewhere between us.

In the course of the discussion I became rather discouraged about the possibility of reaching blacks so understandably persuaded of their own systematic oppression and victimization. But when it was over, a number, some in African costume from Temple, came up, shook my hand and warmly congratulated me. Politeness? good sportsmanship? recognition that divisiveness could go too far?

Back to politics: Ross Perot is tap-dancing back into the limelight. It looks as if he will reenter. If so, he will hurt Bush in the South, Clinton in the North; but my guess is that, after a temporary splurge, he will end up 5–6 percent in the election.

October 12

I caught most of [the first debate] later on the C-Span replay. Bush was cooler and more effective than usual, Clinton was cautious and careful, and Perot stole the show with a brisk array of one-liners. The general verdict is that Clinton did best. As Jackie Onassis said to Bill vanden Heuvel, "Clinton won by not losing." Perot showed what a strong candidate he might have been had he not dropped out in July, but it is probably too late for him to come back as a significant factor. He delighted the public, but I doubt that many people will in the end throw away their votes on a candidate who cannot possibly win. Contrary to my expectations, Clinton maintains a strong lead in the polls.

October 16

If one has to become 75, this is the way to do it. My resourceful and warm-hearted friend Bill vanden Heuvel not only organized the birthday party at the Century but raised half a million dollars for research grants at the Roosevelt and Kennedy Libraries. I had Mary Bingham on my right, Jackie on my left.

I mentioned to Jackie Stephen Spender's concern that Doubleday might plan to publish the scurrilous new English biography of him. Jackie said she had heard nothing about it and would look into it but that Stephen should not be too distressed over a single book. Then she said, "I guess that it is easy to say if there are a lot of books intruding into your life. It is harder when it is the only book." She then reminisced about the last weeks in the White House before the Texas trip. I have never heard her say anything about JFK that was not fond and affectionate.

October 29

Alas, my forebodings are coming true. Gallup gives Clinton only two points over Bush this morning. I think that Clinton retains a commanding lead in the electoral college, but the popular vote, as I feared, will be close. 1992 promises to be, in short, 1960 all over again—a flight of voters fearing the adventure of Clinton in the last week of the campaign, a very close popular vote, a strong margin in the electoral college.

And if Bush wins? Among the minor casualties will be my first piece for the *New Yorker*. For years I aspired to write for the *New Yorker*. When I served on the jury at the Cannes film festival, I came to see [William] Shawn one day to ask whether he would be interested in my writing something about the experience. He said politely but tepidly that he would be glad to take a look. When I sent him the piece, he politely rejected it. Later *Harper's* published it. I continued to hope for a while that the *New Yorker* might at least ask me to write a book review. Nothing ever happened. Finally I concluded that the people over there had decided, no doubt correctly, that, for better or worse, I just was not a *New Yorker* writer.

Then last week Tina Brown, who took over the editorship a few weeks ago, asked me to write an end-of-an-era piece on the election. (Oddly, she had never asked me to write for *Vanity Fair*.) I wrote the piece over the weekend. It goes to press tomorrow and will be on the newsstands next Monday—the day before the election. The piece ends up with an account of the election as a vindication of my father's cyclical thesis. If Clinton loses, we will all look silly—and go down in history with H. V. Kaltenborn and the November 1948 *Chicago Tribune*.

November 3

Tina Brown called on Friday morning to say that she thought publication should be postponed for a week. I figure that she did not want to run the risk at the start of her new career, and certainly, if by any chance Bush should win, the *schadenfreude* would be merciless, toward her perhaps even more than toward me. I told her that I was much relieved by the decision.

No sooner had we decided on this, however, than Bush's upward surge stopped, and Clinton's lead began to widen. I went to Ohio on Saturday the 31st (to Columbus, my birthplace, to receive the Ohioana

Career Medal) and to Kansas the next day (to lecture in Hutchinson) and was told that both states—even Kansas—might go to Clinton. My guess for tonight is: Clinton, 49%; Bush, 43%; Perot, 8%, with Clinton having a much larger margin in the electoral college.*

I have a good feeling about Clinton, just as I had a bad feeling about Carter in 1976. Clinton may have had his Democratic Leadership Council interlude, and he talks a lot about a new Democratic party and is pursued by characters like Alvin From and Ben Wattenberg, but essentially, I think, he believes in government, which Carter did not, and I am hopeful about a Clinton presidency.

Flying back from Kansas last night, I found myself sitting next to Larry Pressler, the Republican senator from South Dakota. We had met a few times before; he is a former Rhodes Scholar and a member of the Century, and he likes the eastern establishment. He seems ready to adjust to a Democratic victory and was very critical of the Bush campaign, especially for the surrender to the religious right at Houston and for Bush's subsequent reliance on public relations people like Mary Matalin and neglect of elected officials ("Matalin didn't even know who I was when she came with Bush to South Dakota"). Larry says that he expects to be for Jack Kemp in the night of the long knives after Bush's defeat.

November 25

Nigel Hamilton's book is out. He sent me a copy with a typically and nauseatingly sucking-up inscription. But on the Charlie Rose show the other night he attacked me for creating a waxwork image of JFK. He also said that at the behest of the Kennedy family I had written a letter protesting the recent PBS show on the Kennedys. This is a fabrication. I did write—at my own behest—a letter to Alan Brinkley and Geoffrey Ward, the two historical consultants, objecting to the mythologizing aspects of the production and regretting that I had taken part in it; but it

---

* The result: Clinton 43%, Bush 38%, Perot 19%.

never occurred to me even to mention the letter to Jean or any other Kennedy, and they certainly did not ask me to do it.

Hamilton came to see me when he started work on the book. His [Field Marshal Bernard] Montgomery biography was well reviewed, and at first I encouraged him and tried to open doors for him. The more I saw of him, however, the less I liked him. He is a diligent researcher and a sufficiently lively writer; but he is overingratiating, manipulative, obsessed with sex and somewhat paranoid. He sees himself—and portrays himself—as a victim. People, organized by the Kennedys, are forever closing doors to him, throwing him off conference programs, defaming him, etc.

I have not read the book and don't suppose I will. I find it hard to read books about people or events I witnessed at first hand. Even with the best intentions, authors always get things slightly wrong—a commentary on the validity of history—and one always feels both irritated and frustrated. However, I do of course consult the index ("Hi, Norman!" as Bill Buckley famously inscribed next to Mailer's name before he sent Norman a copy of one of his books). On page 771 Hamilton claims that I "obstinately refused to promise Jack support" when he ran for Congress in 1946. His source is Tony Galluccio, with whom I went to Peabody School in the 1920s.

Can this be? I don't think I was even in Cambridge in November 1946. At least Christina was born in Washington on 19 November of that year, and we must still have been living there. My recollection is that I began teaching in 1947. On checking *Who's Who,* however, I note that my Harvard appointment is listed as beginning in 1946. My FBI records, obtained under the Freedom of Information Act, contain a correct listing of my various addresses, but I can't unearth them at the moment in the chaos of my office.

1993

January 22

Wednesday was a crisp, bright, sparkling day. Andy and Robert came by to pick up tickets, kindly provided by Pam's indispensable Janet Howard, and we made our way to the Hill. The crowd was vast and in great good humor. The cops, the ushers, the security people were all exceptionally polite and helpful. A certain sweetness of atmosphere pervaded the proceedings.

We had been sitting in the cold air (not nearly so cold as 1961, however) for more than an hour when the ceremony finally began promptly at 11:30. Billy Graham's prayer was mercifully a good deal shorter than Cardinal Cushing's interminable plea to the Almighty 32 years ago.

The inaugural address was also much shorter than expected, greatly to the relief of the shivering crowd. I thought the speech very good and creditable with some fine phrases though deficient in structure, and agree with Bill Safire's rating of B+ the next day. Wednesday night Jeff Greenfield in a witty commentary for ABC television displayed the several echoes of JFK in Clinton's words and mannerisms. After the address, Maya Angelou read what seemed to me a poor, pretentious, spuriously Whitmanesque poem, Marilyn Horne sang beautifully, and the Age of Clinton began.

The mystery of the transition has been the way the Clinton team, after conducting the campaign with great efficiency and despatch, has been so strangely slow in forming a government. In Defense, for example, 44 out of 45 subcabinet appointments have yet to be made. The explanation seems to be threefold: Clinton's own difficulty in making personnel decisions; the desire to avoid what the Clinton people think was Jimmy Carter's mistake in allowing cabinet members to make their own appointments and thereby allegedly acquiring subcabinet officials who were disloyal to the President; and, above all, the desire to propitiate various minorities—women, blacks, Latinos—by giving them what JFK used to call "visual reassurance."

I don't quite understand the Carter point. It is true that Carter came to feel that Joe Califano and Mike Blumenthal, to my mind two of his best appointments, were disloyal; but these were cabinet members, not subcabinet officials. The most important reason has evidently been the quest for "diversity." Hence Zoe Baird, for example; hence Madeleine Albright for the UN, though she is far less qualified for the job than Ted Sorensen or Dick Gardner or Bill vanden Heuvel, all of whom would have liked it. Ted, Dick and Bill all suffer from the same defect: they are white males. The phrase for such casualties, I was told, is that they were "diversified out." I applaud the zeal for wide representation but not at the expense of quality.

There is also, I think, the inevitable self-sufficiency of a new political generation. They look on survivors from the Kennedy era thirty years ago much as we looked in 1961 on survivors from the Roosevelt era thirty years before that—as fine old figures who did great things in their time but are no longer relevant to a new age.

January 26

The appointment agony is stretched out as never before, and many people are left on the rack. Dick Gardner is understandably bitter over the choice of Madeleine Albright as ambassador to the UN. Dick, who had spent his life preparing for the job, says, "I wouldn't have minded if someone like Fritz Mondale had been appointed. But Madeleine Albright!—a third-rate woman, and not a nice one either; and all because they needed a woman. When Al Gore called to warn me she was to be appointed, he began by saying, "'Have you considered a sex change?'"

February 3

Clinton still hasn't formed a government. He has a Republican running the Department of Justice; many assistant secretaryships are unfilled; resentments grow as the process stretches out. I asked Pamela today what the trouble was. She mentioned the diversity test, which is certainly part of it. I said, "I wonder whether the bottleneck might not be Clinton himself. Do you suppose Bill and Hillary can be worrying personally over every single appointment?" After a second, Pam said with heartfelt emphasis, "Yes."

And of course Clinton has other things on his mind. I have found nothing more puzzling for a long while than the question of what should—and can—be done to stop the slaughter in Bosnia. Cy Vance and David Owen have come up with a proposal that, they assert, will at least end the fighting. The administration apparently opposes the partition idea on the ground that it would reward [Slobodan] Milosevic's aggression and that he can't be relied on in any case to honor the settlement. I see merit in each argument.

But, if the Vance-Owen proposal is rejected, what then? No one wants to send in ground troops. There is general skepticism about the usefulness of air attacks on Serbian objectives. The European countries seem to take the defeatist attitude that the Balkans are after all the

Balkans, now free to doing what comes naturally, and there is not much that can be done about it. They expect the U.S. to take the lead in tackling what is initially at least a European problem, and the American response is that the U.S. cannot solve Europe's problems for it. A mess.

February 4

Last night we dined at the Bundys'. Jackie was also there. I asked her about Hillary Clinton. She could not have been more enthusiastic—so intelligent, so pretty, so cozy, what a good sense of humor. This last item surprised me. I was ready to concede the first two adjectives and even the third, but I supposed her to be somewhat on the stern and humorless side.

February 20

Ted Kennedy called on Sunday the 14th. He seems quite pleased with Bill Clinton and described a meeting Clinton held with senators to discuss the ban on homosexuals in the armed forces. Bob Byrd gave one of his florid disquisitions adorned with classical references, including Tiberius and the Middle East with some mention of Mt. Sinai, all designed to illustrate the perils of sexual decadence. Clinton said, "Well, Senator, Moses went to Mt. Sinai, and the Lord gave him the Ten Commandments, but not one of the 'thou shalt nots' refers to homosexuality."

On Monday the 15th Ted Sorensen and I went to Washington for a meeting of Bill Safire's Judson C. Welliver Society. Our gathering of presidential speechwriters had, as usual, a lavish dinner at Bill's house, preceded by an entertaining cocktail hour. I ran into Pat Buchanan. "I guess you didn't like my Houston speech too much," Pat said. "On the contrary," I said, "I liked it very much. I think it elected Clinton." He laughed affably. I do like old Pat, reprehensible as his views generally are.

At 9 we all saw Clinton's television speech setting forth the elements of his economic program. This was presumably the most qualified audience to pass on the merits of the speech, and, when Clinton finished, Bill went around the room soliciting comments. I gave it an A-. Ted thought less well of it. Ray Price, a Nixon speechwriter whom I used to meet at Bill Paley's and who always seemed to me a gentlemanly type, arose and, to everyone's surprise, vehemently denounced Clinton as a liar. Ben Wattenberg thought the speech too partisan. Etc.

Then George Stephanopoulos arrived. He is a calmly articulate young fellow, who looks about 14 years old, and he responded to technical speechwriters' questions about the composition of the speech. 80 per cent of the time, Stephanapoulos said, Clinton uses no text at all. This time there was no "hard draft" till three days before, but Clinton likes to keep worrying and revising, and the draft did not finally go to the teleprompter till 8:40—twenty minutes before delivery.

I spent the next morning at the Library of Congress looking at Bob LaFollette's papers. Pamela, with whom Ted and I were staying, had persuaded Tom and Heather Foley to give a luncheon at a private room off the House dining room. The Foleys had summoned a small group of liberal congressmen—Barney Frank, Nancy Pelosi, Chuck Schumer, George Miller, Sam Gejdenson—and we had a most entertaining time.

I was especially struck by two things: their enthusiasm for Clinton and their hostility to the media. They all love their new President and are enormously gratified by his command of facts and of issues, his fluency ("he speaks in complete sentences"), his friendliness and goodwill, his determination to move ahead and his courtship of them. And they all feel that the press decided to tear Clinton down even before he became President and has been relentlessly unfair ever since. I do agree that the press probably began to feel that it had been too pro-Clinton in the last stages of the election and hopes to recover a reputation for objectivity by harrying him now that he is in the White House.

Still, listening to the complaints, I finally said that the same number of newspapermen gathered around a table would feel equally persecuted; after all, they would say, every time a politician wants to win applause from a crowd, all he has to do is to attack the press. The legislators rejected the comparison.

Pamela is going to be ambassador to Paris, which is fine. She also said that an ambassador has been chosen for London but she was sworn to secrecy as to who it was. Bill vanden Heuvel and Angie Duke had been campaigning for me, and at one point they were given to understand that I was on the short list. Though I regarded the whole effort as an exercise in fantasy, I must confess that it is the one government job I would like, and I immodestly feel I would have been damned good at it. However, I did not take my prospects seriously enough to be stricken by the result. And had it been offered, it would have wrecked the FDR book and maybe my memoirs too.

Eileen Finletter gave one of her Saturday buffet Knickerbocker Club lunches today. Norman Mailer has been in Minsk in the interests of a book he plans to write about Lee Harvey Oswald's Russian interlude. He says that conditions in Russia are grim and depressing, and that the longer he stays there and sees how rickety and unpopular the system was, the angrier he gets about the Cold War. As for the book, he is playing around with the idea that on his return to America Oswald was recruited by the FBI to penetrate radical groups. He is going to interview Marina Oswald in the near future.

ENEMIES. I reflected the other day on the people who go out of their way to attack me, dragging my name into irrelevant contexts in order to make what they regard as devastating insults. One of course is Gore Vidal, who has been tossing cracks my way ever since Jackie asked me to remove him from a White House party in 1962. Actually when Gore and I meet, we converse amiably, but, pen in hand, he can't resist the dirty aside. I rather like Gore's historical novels, and I am delighted by his recent little book on the movies, *Screening History*. And at least he knows me, which in a way legitimizes his right to attack me.

The others are people I have hardly met. I debated Conor Cruise O'Brien once in the 1960s when he had the Schweitzer chair at New York University. He was then arguing for revolutionary violence as the only means by which Third World countries could liberate themselves from capitalist imperialism. I thought this romantic nonsense for the old and dangerous nonsense for the young, and said so. Later O'Brien became a minister in the Irish government, saw the consequences of IRA direct action and turned righteously against violence. But he has obviously never forgiven or forgotten that one encounter and every once in a while hauls me in while writing about something else. I must say that I find his writings pretentious and unreadable, but Isaiah has a better opinion of him.

Some one once brought Christopher Hitchens to our house during a cocktail party, and that was our one personal encounter. But we had a long and spirited series of exchanges in the letter columns of the *Times Literary Supplement*. It began when he blamed Kennedy for the CIA's recruitment of gangsters to murder Castro. I pointed out that this had happened under Eisenhower, not under Kennedy. This did little to deflect his assault on Kennedy, whom he hates, and he undertook a vigorous whitewash of the CIA, saying that it never did anything without presidential approval. I won that battle easily. Ever since then, Hitchens has interpolated scathing personal comments about me in his pieces in the *Nation* and elsewhere. Too bad; like Vidal, he is a bright and engaging writer.

The attacks by Joan Didion and her husband John Gregory Dunne also derive basically from their hatred of Kennedy. This dreadful couple has moved to New York, and we run into them from time to time. She is a viperish, whispering little creature, and, in my view, a breathy, faux-sensitive writer. He is a sour Irish drunk. Like O'Brien and Hitchens, they manage to find ways of insult in wholly irrelevant contexts.

This exhausts my list of enemies. I wish they were more distinguished.

March 6

On the 19th [of February] Bill Clinton visited Hyde Park. I, alas, was committed to giving a lecture at Messiah College near Harrisburg and had to miss the occasion. Interesting: Clinton can't wait to identify himself with FDR while Jimmy Carter would not even send a message of greeting to the New Deal March 4 reunions. On the 21st Hillary

Clinton spoke at a benefit designed to raise money for an Eleanor Roosevelt statue in Riverside Park. She spoke faultlessly for ten minutes without a note and with considerable charm and humor.

May 8

Though I had a number of other urgent things to do, such as revise my multiculturalism lecture for a German audience, write a piece about Wilson and the new world order for the *Times Literary Supplement* and do a draft for a talk I have to give at the Academy of Arts and Letters ceremonial directly after we get back from Germany, I felt obliged to have my say on Bosnia. The result was published in the *Wall Street Journal* on Monday 3 May.

Al Gore told me later in the week that the column had an immediate effect in the White House. Clinton, he said, had it xeroxed and circulated, saying it was the best argument against intervention he had seen and telling Al that, if they went ahead with "your" policy (Al is evidently pro-intervention), any statement would have to deal with the contentions made in my piece. John Warner told Alexandra at Kay Graham's dinner for Pamela later in the week that the senatorial delegation to Moscow, led by Sam Nunn and Richard Lugar, passed the piece around and discussed it on the way back from Moscow; John gave Alexandra a note to give me: "Your article on Bosnia was on target!" Henry Kissinger sent a note saying, "If I don't tell anyone, can I tell you how much I liked your letter on Bosnia, which reflects my views exactly," and followed it up with a phone call.

But it looks as if we are moving toward intervention nevertheless. Al Gore says that, whatever the European leaders are saying publicly, privately they expressed to him on his recent European visit a fervent desire that the U.S. take the leadership in stopping the Serbs. It may be that, if the Belgrade Serbs are really disowning the Bosnian Serbs, limited air strikes might persuade the Bosnian Serbs to accept Vance-Owen. But if limited air strikes fail, what comes next? I fear that one step leads to the next. The quagmire beckons.

I lunched with Dick Gardner on Wednesday the 5th: like everyone else, he has heard nothing about his future. The next day I flew west—Chicago, Cedar Rapids, Iowa City. I arrived too late for nostalgic returns to the old Capitol and to South Johnson Street, but gave the multiculturalism lecture that night, arose at 5 the next morning, caught a plane to Chicago and thence to Washington, arriving in time for Ethel Kennedy's RFK Book Award luncheon at Hickory Hill. It was there, and again later in the day at the actual ceremony, that I had talks with Al Gore about Bosnia.

Albert Sr. and Pauline also came. The old senator is as bright and lively as ever at 85, and his wife is of course an intelligent and charming lady. She said to me that she was getting awfully tired of hearing young Al described as "wooden." I m/cd the award ceremony; so, after Al gave an effective speech, I said I had been puzzled over the application of the word to the Vice President, "But now I begin to understand what they mean. They mean that he is as graceful as a willow, as handsome as a birchtree and as sturdy as an oak." Great success: Albert Gore Sr. even rose to his feet in applause.

On Wednesday morning the 12th we flew to Berlin, where I had not been since the Wall came down and where Alexandra had never been. Carl-Ludwig Holtfrerich of the Freie Universitat met us at the airport and took us to the Hotel Steglitz International, several steps down from our Heidelberg accommodations. On the way we stopped at the Brandenburg Gate and saw fragments of the Wall, that obscenity that used to disfigure the city as it straggled crazily across Berlin.

May 23

On Friday the 14th we went first to an exhibit of 20th Century American Art at the Gropius Museum [in Berlin]. I suppose it reveals my philistinism (again), but Warhol, Barnett Newman, Roy Lichtenstein, Julian Schnabel, Richard Serra, etc., seem such transparent fakes and con men, and it is almost shaming to see American hype hung and captioned with such reverence abroad. Then we went to an exhibit on the site of the old Gestapo headquarters nearby. The subject was "The Topography of Terror," and it was a grim and graphic introduction to the brutalities of a police state.

In the afternoon Carl Holtfrerich drove us to Potsdam. We arrived too late to see the inside of Sans Souci, but we admired its elegant exterior and paid our respects to the tomb of Frederick the Great. All of a sudden I began to remember how pro-German I had been as a small boy. Frederick the Great was one of my heroes, and I regularly went to see the UFA films shown in Boston at George Kraska's Fine Arts Theater near Symphony Hall. I adored Lilian Harvey, not only *Der Kongress Tanzt* but her lighter musicals like *Die Drei von der Tankstelle*. I learned German at Exeter (during this trip fragments of the language have bobbed up out of the depths of memory). Hitler aborted my pro-German sympathies, and they have never revived.

[Back in New York], Alexandra and I caught the shuttle to Washington [on Wednesday the 19th]. We taxied to Pamela Harriman's, bathed and dressed and then went with Pam and Carter Brown to the White House for a dinner in her honor.

The guests—about 35–40—gathered in the Blue Room. They included George Mitchell and his sister, Tom and Heather Foley and the John Dingells from the Hill; Les Aspin with Melody Miller from Ted Kennedy's office; Peter and Mathea Tarnoff from State; Sandy and Susan Berger from the NSC; George and Liz Stevens, the Vernon Jordans, the Bob Strausses, the George McEntees (president of the State, County and Municipal Employees union) and others who have presently faded from memory.

After a time the Clintons joined us. Then we went upstairs to dinner. FDR's old oval office was set up as a dining room with three or four tables. I made the happy discovery that I was seated on Hillary Clinton's left; Tom Foley on her right. I found Hillary altogether charming— cool, composed, amusing and extremely sympathetic. Her public appearances yield an impression of bluestocking severity; but, as Jackie told me at the Academy luncheon earlier in the day, she has an excellent sense of humor and is great fun. Jackie is right.

Hillary talked about a recent visit by Nixon. Things he had said about her in the campaign had led her to believe that he was unforgiving for her work on the impeachment committee staff, so she was dubious about receiving him. But he was, she said, very agreeable, talked nicely to Chelsea, etc.

The President, who is just back from a trip to California, looks pink and fit. Alexandra, who sat at his table, found him more likable than she expected. I had some small talk with him before dinner. I said that Bob Dole really had given the administration a permanent alibi in case the recession continues to falter and reemployment to lag: all the Republicans' fault because they had blocked the economic stimulus package. The real trouble with the package, I added, was not that it was too large, but that it was too small. Clinton said, "I agree."

After dinner the President invited us all out on President Truman's balcony. It was a misty night, and the lights around the Washington Monument and the Jefferson Memorial twinkled in the distance. Clinton told me that he had marked up my *Wall Street Journal* column on Bosnia, circulated it to his staff and to congressional leaders and said that these were the questions the proponents of intervention had to answer. This is what Al Gore had told me earlier; and, in the course of the White House evening, George Mitchell, Tom Foley and Sandy Berger all (separately) told me the same thing. The administration has now ended up in pretty much the position I recommended, and I have the strong impression that this is where the President wants to be.

Nearly everyone one encounters is against unilateral intervention. Jim Hoge, now the editor of *Foreign Affairs,* with whom I lunched on Thursday, is a dove. Mac Bundy, with whom I spoke on the phone, describes himself as a "raving dove." Henry Kissinger had a powerful dove column this week. Last night Ralph Buultjens invited us to dinner with Eve Curie and Wassily and Estelle Leontieff—doves all. Tony Lewis continues to denounce anti-interventionists as cowardly and immoral, but he seems increasingly isolated as people examine the practicalities of intervention. Still Sidney Gruson called today and asked me to fax my column, adding: "I won't agree with it. I'm an interventionist."

We stayed at Pam's, and she said later that Clinton had told her that he had offered the Supreme Court vacancy to Cuomo. She said, "A clear offer?" and he said that he had called Cuomo to make the offer but Cuomo had preempted him by withdrawing his name. Stephen tells me that Cuomo claims that, had Clinton asked him directly to come on the Court, he would have done so. Stephen says, "I'm afraid that they are doomed to misunderstand each other."

May 28

Since our visit, Clinton has had a rocky week. The dinner took place on the same day that he had a $200 haircut while tying up traffic at the Los Angeles airport for an hour. It was also the day when someone at the White House fired the staff of the travel office and then, when questions were raised, called in the FBI to justify the action; subsequently most of them have been reinstated, or at least put on leave.

The haircut in particular will give television comics fodder for weeks to come, and both incidents weakened Bill just before the crucial House vote on his tax program. He won that vote last night in a squeaker, but commentators are still writing (foolishly) about a "failed presidency." How can they forget so quickly the volatility of polls and the limited attention span of the electorate?

Still there is no doubt that Clinton has to get his act together. One obvious trouble is a weak White House staff—bright fellows but inexperienced and cocky; they do not know how little they know. We were cocky enough thirty years ago, but we had a measure of experience and self-knowledge. Though we failed JFK on the Bay of Pigs, we did not commit the elementary blunders and gratuitous alienations that mark the style of Stephanopoulos & company.

August 3

I suppose I should say a word about Joe McGinniss, now that he threatened (last night on the Charlie Rose show) to write a biography of me.

McGinniss apparently once wrote a pretty good book, not read by me—*The Selling of a President,* about Nixon in 1968. Since then, he has specialized in sensational books. He has now written *The Last Brother* about Ted Kennedy. It is a perfectly terrible book.

Last night McGinniss did his act on the Rose show. Charlie Rose is an intelligent and upwardly mobile fellow from North Carolina who used to run a classy interview show on Channel 13 here in New York. The program was such a success locally that PBS made it national, where it seems somehow less effective. For a time Charlie was having a big affair with my dear friend Amanda Burden, Bill Paley's daughter; but one day, the story goes, a young woman appeared in Amanda's office with tapes of phone calls from Charlie Rose saying that he was rushing to see her as soon as he could elude Amanda. Thus ended the affair. Ba, who is so beautiful and smart, has bad luck with her men.

McGinniss went on in his smug and unctuous way about the nobility of his motives, his sympathy for Ted Kennedy, the persecution he was suffering from the well-organized Kennedy crowd, etc. Charlie Rose mentioned my name. McGinniss said (lightly, I assume) that he would like to do a biography of me to show how an eminent historian had lost his integrity in order to curry favor with the Kennedys. At the end of the interview, Rose brought up the Schlesinger biography again. McGinniss reiterated his wish.

If anyone asks me what I think about this, I shall tell them to ask McGinniss, since he pretends to know every thought that passes through the minds of people he has never met.

September 10

This morning David Gergen called from the White House at the request, he said, of President Clinton. The President, it appears, plans to make a statement Monday on the remarkable negotiations between Israel and the PLO, and he will also speak before the UN General Assembly in a couple of weeks, and he wants suggestions about a larger framework for American foreign policy. There has been criticism recently of the administration's case-by-case, ad hoc approach to international affairs. This is the lawyerly way that Warren Christopher goes about his business, but there is obvious need for larger strategic conceptions and for basic rethinking of the U.S. role in the post–Cold War world. I doubt that I have any miracle cures, and I imagine that the same message has gone out from Gergen to a dozen people. But I will try to come up with something.

September 24

Clinton seems to be at last on the upswing. His statesmanlike management of the Rabin-Arafat meeting, followed by his excellent health-care speech Wednesday night, is beginning to make the President seem "presidential" again. Last night Felix and Liz Rohatyn invited us to their box at the opening of Carnegie Hall. In the entr'acte, a pretty young woman came up, reintroduced herself as Julie Eisenhower, and we talked for a while. She said that her father had been impressed by Clinton's speech—"very strong," she said old Tricky said. I like Julie and David, and they seem to harbor no grudges over my views on their ancestors. They are presently collaborating on a book on 1968.

I forgot to note that I asked Bill Styron at the Willie Morris party about his walk in the woods on the Vineyard with Hillary Clinton. He said it wasn't a walk in the woods but along the beach. Hillary had the death of Vincent Foster very much on her mind, Bill said, and wanted to find out about clinical depression and whether his friends should have recognized the symptoms of ultimate despair. Bill liked her very much. Jules Feiffer told Alexandra the other day, "People on the Vineyard were less impressed by Clinton than they expected and more impressed by Hillary than they expected."

Hillary is emerging now as a sort of heroine. No longer Madame Nhu or the wicked witch of the west, she is regarded as highly intelligent, flexible and endearing. She received two standing ovations from Congress during the President's speech. One congressman said he likes her so much he always wants "to squeeze her."

September 27

Footnote on Nixon and Clinton: someone whom I told about Julie Nixon Eisenhower and her father's praise of Clinton's health speech observed: "That figures. After all, that was the speech in which Clinton praised Nixon [for his interest in health care]."

I talked with Mac Bundy about Dick Reeves's new book *President Kennedy*. We both agreed that Reeves's JFK was not at all the one we had known. I said that I was much disappointed by the book and thought there was a certain meanness in it. Mac rather disagreed on the second point. "The trouble with the book," he said, "is overdependence on the paper trail. It shows how misled the historian can be if he relies only on documents."

October 24

One odd addition to my life: Bianca Jagger. German *Vogue* has been running a series of improbable conversations (Norman Mailer and Taki, for example), and, when they asked Bianca Jagger whom she would like to talk to, she nominated me. I am not sure why; our previous encounters had been casual and fleeting. We met for a couple of hours on the 27th, again that evening at Tina Brown's big party for Dick Avedon, then on 14 October for a photo session (Albert Watson) in a cold gray day along the Hudson River. I like her very much. On the 27th she had just come from meeting Bosnian orphans; she has already made a number of trips to Bosnia. As a Nicaraguan, she is much in earnest about the Third World and occasionally lapses into leftist jargon ("isn't the UN," she would ask, "engaged in neo-colonial interventions as in Somalia?"). But she is intelligent, open-minded, good-hearted and altogether charming.

Peculiarly, her current boy friend appears to be Congressman Robert Torricelli of New Jersey, the author of the recent terrible piece of legislation intensifying the Cuban embargo and seeking to punish foreign countries and companies that trade with Cuba. Bianca asked me what I thought about this policy. I said I thought it was wrong: the best way to do in Castro would be to relax the embargo and flood Cuba with American tourists and American consumer goods. She said she agreed with me.

October 24

On the 12th, back in New York [after a short lecture tour], I lunched with Mac Bundy, Douglas Dillon, Bill Walton and Bill Draper in preparation for an evening, "JFK Remembered," to be held the next week at the Century. The talk turned to Dick Reeves's book. "I read it the usual way," Doug Dillon said, meaning that he had looked up his own name in the index, "and found it full of errors. He had me at meetings that never took place, involved in decisions I knew nothing about and so on." The book evidently portrays JFK as a rigid Cold Warrior and denies that he grew or changed very much during his presidency—all of which could not be more wrong. Mac, by the way, said that on reflection he did not think that JFK would ever have sent U.S. ground forces into the Vietnam War.

Ted Kennedy rang up on Sunday. His reelection prospects look pretty good. Governor [William] Weld has decided not to run against him, and at present the Republicans have no candidate. We communed over Bill Clinton's manifold foreign policy troubles. Ted said, "He is still far the best candidate we could have in '96."

November 26

The 30th anniversary of Dallas attracted far more attention than the 25th. This is partly, because of the cyclical effect and Clinton's revival (exploitation?) of memories of JFK; partly too because JFK is the last President whom people trusted. When he was in the White House, over 70 percent of Americans, according to polls, felt that the national government would do what is right most of the time. Today, after Johnson and Vietnam, Nixon and Watergate, Reagan and quadrupling the national debt, only 29 percent say they have much confidence in the national government.

December 5

Clinton ends the session with a pretty good record and is on the up-swing again. But dissatisfaction is growing with his foreign policy team. Warren Christopher is a decent, cautious, case-by-case lawyer without a strategic mind or much capacity for public education and persuasion. He is ineffectual as a shaper and spokesman for the administration's foreign policy. But Clinton seems trapped by Christopher as Kennedy was by Rusk: he can't get rid of him without impeaching his own judgment in appointing him. (Still, Reagan did get rid of Al Haig fairly early.) In addition, Clinton apparently has warm personal regard for Christopher as a wise man and a "mentor," as people tiresomely say these days.

December 9

Another theatrical party on Tuesday—Betty Bacall for Harold Pinter and Antonia Fraser. Harold was surprisingly well-behaved and controlled his basic anti-Americanism. Apparently at one point early on he started in to say how wicked and hopeless he believes Clinton to be, but Betty said, "None of that tonight, Harold," and he stopped. Probably Antonia had spoken to him. When Harold is not off on that particular tangent, he is charming and funny, as he was at Betty's.

Arthur Miller and John Guare were there; also Edna O'Brien; and Kate Nelligan and other theatrical types. Arthur and Edna were both much irritated over Kate's refusal of one of the three principal roles in Arthur's new play *Broken Glass*. She had asked, Arthur told me, $12,500 a week—which, if extended to all three roles, would mean nearly $40,000 a week for three actors, far more than any producer will pay. Kate insists that she cannot afford less; she has just had a baby and needs money, so she will make movies instead. Shortsighted, one feels; Kate is not a top movie star, and a big Broadway role would probably help her film career. Edna blames it all on her new husband who is, she says, a parasite.

Contemplating these two evenings, I wonder why I have always liked theatrical people so much. I believe Alexandra and I were the only non-professional couple present either time. My delight with the theater goes back to my undergraduate days when my fleeting ambition was to become a drama critic and I would send sample reviews to George Jean Nathan. What other categories of company do I enjoy? I like writers. I like politicians. I like musicians, even though I know little about music. I like historians, economists and predeconstruction professors of literature; not so high on other academics. I get along pretty well with lawyers. When I lived in Cambridge, I used to associate with architects, but not much since, though I like I. M. Pei and Ed Barnes very much. For some reason, I have never had close friends among painters, except those to whom I am related. I have few businessmen friends. I do not care for the company of psychiatrists.

Yesterday they held a party at the Graduate Center to mark my retirement. A former student, Louise Mayo, spoke—Louise portraying me, I fear overgenerously, as a teacher noted for his solicitude toward his students. In fact, I have always felt guiltily that I was not doing nearly enough.

CUNY and the three presidents of the Graduate School—Mina Rees, Hal Proshansky, Frances Horowitz—have been wonderfully tolerant of my diverse requirements and activities. However, I do not regret for a moment that the teaching days are over. Free at last, free at last! I have been a conscientious teacher and probably a pretty good one, but teaching has never fulfilled an organic need; indeed, I have always felt to be something of an impostor, about to be found out and exposed. Real teachers, like Henry Commager, could not bear to stop teaching. I am only puzzled why I waited so long. (Answer: I could not figure out any other way to retain an office, a secretary and room for a thousand or more books. The invention of the word processor reduces the need for a secretary; I do all my serious work at home anyway; but the book problem remains.)

1994

January 7

On Thursday afternoon, the 6th, Betty Bacall invited some Lazar friends to come by (at roughly the time of the Lazar memorial service in Los Angeles) and reminisce about old Swifty. There were about a dozen people and much recollection, mostly in tones of mingled affection and exasperation.

Betty B. concluded [the stories] by recalling an entertainment that Moss Hart had organized in New York for Irving's 50th birthday—"Fifty for Swifty." They wrote skits and songs; everything was carefully rehearsed; and as Irving sat through the evening and listened to the tributes and the expressions of love, he was visibly moved. The time came for his response. He rose to his feet, his voice choked with emotion, was silent for a moment, then surveyed the room, left to right, and said slowly, "Well, I made you—and I can break you."

January 21

My heart had sunk when Bill Clinton announced the appointment of Bobby Ray Inman as Secretary of Defense, and it leaped at the news this week that he had turned down the job. I rejoiced even more to watch Inman self-destruct at a paranoid press conference in which he wailed about criticism from the press (meaning one tough column by Bill Safire and a couple of cavils by Ellen Goodman and Tony Lewis) and then went on to claim that a conspiracy between Safire and Bob Dole was driving him out of public life. Can there be something in the Texas drinking water that induces paranoid fantasy? Inman even began to look a bit like Ross Perot. What is more troubling is to think that this conspiracy-obsessed fellow was for a time deputy director of the CIA— and that he succeeded in taking in so many members of Congress and of the press. I became sufficiently fired up about it to fax in an Op Ed column to the *Times,* which they obligingly ran today.

January 27

Tuesday evening Clinton gave his State of the Union message, a strong speech, ably delivered. The commentary tried to make an issue between "traditional" and "new" Democrats, arguing that Clinton was abandoning the liberals and moving toward the right. It seemed a good, ringing New Deal speech to me. Clinton is plainly of the FDR-Truman-Kennedy-Johnson school and regards government as a key means of promoting the general welfare. The role of government is the dividing line between the Roosevelt and Reagan Democrats. But there aren't many Reagan Democrats any more, even in the Democratic Leadership Council, and the split in the party seems to me largely a fabrication by the press.

February 4

Bill vanden Heuvel reminisced the other day about a talk with Alice Longworth. He had asked her how her father had received word that he was President. When McKinley was shot, she said, TR had gone at once to Buffalo but, told that McKinley was rallying and would pull through, he joined his family mountain-climbing in the Adirondacks. Then a messenger arrived with the news that McKinley was dead.

Bill said, "That must have been a moment of terrible sadness." Mrs. Longworth said, "Are you kidding?"

February 12

A few days ago Margaret Truman called. She said that she is writing a book on "First Ladies" (I hate the term—"Presidents' wives" is much better) and hopes to be able to interview all those still living. Knowing that I was a friend of Jackie's, did I think Jackie would be inclined to grant an interview?

I said I would sound Jackie out, but put it off because I knew Jackie's distaste for interviews and also because I had asked her for a dinner we are giving next Monday for Roy Jenkins, and someone had called on her behalf to decline. One never quite knows how one stands with Jackie. On Thursday I went to the Council on Foreign Relations to hear Tom Pickering on Russia. As we were leaving, Maurice Tempelsman offered me a lift downtown. I asked about Jackie; he said that she was having her troubles and gave that flutter of the fingers gesture indicating that she was in middling shape. I told him about Margaret Truman and said I would call Jackie that afternoon. When I did, she was out.

The next morning I left early because I had to give a talk at a luncheon in Washington and the second large snowstorm of the week had closed La Guardia, so I had to catch an 8 A.M. train. When I opened the *Times,* there was a story that Jackie had lymphoma. After I left the house, the phone rang; Alexandra answered; it was Jackie; and Alexandra, not having seen the morning paper, asked innocently, "How are you?" Jackie replied, "Well, as a matter of fact, I have lymphoma. But it will be all right."

I called her this morning; the line was busy, but before I had a chance to try her again, she called me. She sounded fine but said, "It's a real case of hubris. I have been so proud of being so fit. I have been doing my push-ups every day; I walk every day; I never smoke; I take excellent care of myself; I have been so pleased with my good health—and now this has happened—hubris. But it is not too bad. It was diagnosed early. Dr. Nicholas tells me that many athletes get it and recover—hockey players have had it who are now back at the rink and so on. The chemotherapy isn't too bad. I sit there reading a book while they administer it. No pain, and I can walk a bit and ride a bit. . . . It broke my heart not to be able to go the dinner for Roy, but I just can't do things like that yet."

She said she couldn't talk to Margaret Truman. "I know she's a lovely person, and Jack admired her father so much. After the election, the reporters asked who my model would be among earlier Presidents' wives. They all expected me to say Mrs. Roosevelt. But I wasn't planning to spend my time going down coal mines when I had children in the White House; so I said Mrs. Truman. I thought she had done such a fine job in bringing Margaret up in the midst of that glare of White House publicity."

February 24

It is odd about the Whitewater business. Of course Presidents should be held strictly accountable for all acts committed as President. But I can't remember a President being harried for acts committed a dozen years before he became President. If this standard had been applied to Lyndon Johnson, who served in Congress for a quarter of a century and became a millionaire, one shudders to imagine what might have been unearthed. The *New York Times* really created this as a major issue through Howell Raines's forceful and righteous editorials; Jim Leach, the most liberal Republican in the House, took it up, perhaps to reclaim his Republican franchise; now Robert Fiske has been appointed independent prosecutor. Heaven knows where it will end.

April 5

The fate of an aging liberal. I had sent a note to Barry Goldwater congratulating him on his remarks last week on Whitewater (to the general effect of—Get off Clinton's back and let him do his job). I received a prompt answer: "Dear Arthur: Thanks for taking the time to write. It was good of you to give me this support." I am glad the letter was dated 1994, not 1964. And then a fax today from Gary McDowell: "Lady Thatcher has asked if you would be free to visit with her during your visit here in May. She is quite an admirer of yours." What next?

April 8

Clinton has a third-rate White House staff composed partly of old pals from Arkansas without government experience and partly of young smart-ass kids from the campaign without government experience. The first types are shy and baffled; the second are aggressive but do not know how little they know. If Clinton had had a better staff, he would not have fallen so deep into Whitewater.

April 18

Jackie went to the hospital on Friday when a hemorrhaging ulcer required immediate surgery. I talked to Nancy Tuckerman yesterday. She said that doctors think the chemotherapy she has undergone in order to deal with the lymphoma may have caused the ulcer. This would suggest that they must cut back on the treatment. Nancy said that the doctors were figuring out over the weekend what to do. She had seen Jackie on Saturday and found her weak but cheerful. "You know, Arthur, during this whole business she has not once complained."

April 26

The nation has been having an orgy of grief (real? phoney?) and panegyric over the death of Richard Nixon. What is especially shaming is to see old friends like Murray Kempton and Tom Wicker indulging in this sentimental slop. If you live long enough, I suppose, all is forgiven. As Emerson should have said, every bore becomes a hero at last. But to regard this most paranoid of Presidents as a great statesman, as an inspiration to the young, as a hero of the century is really too much. Jimmy Breslin, Russell Baker and Sam Donaldson have been honorable exceptions to the prevailing worshipfulness.

One curious omission in the slop is the fact that Nixon could have ended U.S. participation in the Vietnam War in 1969 on the same terms that he did when election approached in 1972—that is, dropping the insistence on the concurrent withdrawal of U.S. and North Vietnamese forces. Every American family that lost a member in Vietnam in 1969, 1970, 1971 and 1972 should be sore as hell at Nixon.

Numbers of newspapers and television programs have asked for comment. I have refrained, feeling that what I have to say would be inappropriate in the hours after someone's death. I recall Thomas Hart Benton's comment on the death of John C. Calhoun, whom he detested. "When the Almighty lays his hand on a man's shoulder," Benton said, "Tom Benton takes his hand off." I also recall William Cullen Bryant's comment on the death of Nicholas Biddle. His end came, Bryant said, "at his country seat, where he had passed the last of his days in elegant retirement, which, if justice had taken place, would have been spent in the penitentiary."

May 5

To Washington yesterday for luncheon with the Vice President. I arrived in the midst of torrential rains and ran into John Kennedy at the airport. He was bound for the White House too to attend a bill-signing ceremony, so we shared a cab. The bill provides training for high school graduates who are not bound for college. What an attractive young man John is! He combines the best of his father's and mother's facial features, has impeccable manners and talks crisply and intelligently. I take it that he still has his playboy moments (but I do like beautiful and funny Darryl Hannah the couple of times I have met her); but, if he ever goes into politics, he will be very effective. I asked about his mother. He had seen her the day before with Caroline and her three children, and she had seemed cheerful and regaining strength.

When I arrived in the West Wing, I ran into Paul Nitze, now 87 years old and recently remarried. I told him that his example inspired all us young fellows. After a short wait I was ushered into Gore's office, where I waited a short while more until he appeared, having been trapped on the podium at a luncheon somewhere. We were then provided a terrible luncheon from the White House mess. The quality of the food has sadly declined in the last thirty years.

I like Al Gore, though there is still a certain stiffness about him and, though he is not without humor, humor is not his first reaction. He has been invited to give the commencement address at Harvard this year, and he wanted to discuss what he should talk about. I said he should not talk about ecology; his concern for the earth was already notorious. He agreed.

I then said that he might consider giving a defense of public service, taking off from John Buchan's line, so beloved by Kennedy: politics as "the greatest and most honorable adventure." (He did not seem to have heard of John Buchan. I identified him as the author of *The 39 Steps,* which rang a bell.) The three Harvard Presidents of this century—TR, FDR, JFK—I said, were all notable for the ability to attract young people into government and politics. If democracy is to succeed, we must renew that spirit. The VP was afraid that, in the present climate (Whitewater, Paula Jones), a defense of politics might sound too defensive.

He said he wanted to use this speech as a personal breakthrough. Speeches—he instanced one he had given after the accident in which his young son was nearly killed—sometimes forced him to look into himself, to learn new things and thereby to transcend the day-to-day routine. That is the kind of speech he wanted to give. Of course, he said, the only Harvard commencement speech anyone remembers was [George] Marshall's in 1947, and they remember it because he announced a specific program. (He couldn't recall who had spoken at his own commencement—nor can I recall who spoke at mine.) His relations with the President were such that he probably would be able to announce some new program, but he would rather use the occasion to educate himself and to stimulate thought on the audience.

I listened intently as he tried to explain what he wanted to say about history. By now the mystical, Henry Wallace side that I had noticed before was bursting forth, and I really couldn't understand what he was getting at. I finally said that the lessons of history were ambiguous, people mostly used history to justify policies they wanted to pursue for other reasons, history in any case, as [the Dutch historian Pieter] Geyl said, was "an argument without end," etc.

He had hoped I might help with the speech; but I had already explained that I would be out of the country most of the next month. I promised him a memorandum on the public-service theme.

At the end, we had a brief chat about foreign policy issues. I asked where the OAS was on Haiti. He said that the OAS still has a thing on intervention and would not endorse multilateral action. I also said that we should lift the embargo on Cuba and not let [anti-Castro activist] Jorge Mas Canosa dictate our Cuban policy. He seemed mildly surprised.

His great teacher and friend at Harvard is Dick Neustadt, and he described a weekend retreat of the President and the cabinet at which Neustadt and Ernie May gave a historical account of that frustrating relationship. This is one of several White House meetings of historians and political scientists that Clinton has convened. I begin to wonder why I have not been invited. Can it be because he remembers my ill-judged excursion into New Hampshire on behalf of Mario Cuomo just before the 1992 primary? I must ask Vernon Jordan some day. The VP has not talked to Neustadt about the speech, and I urged him to do so. Al Gore is a fine, upstanding, sober young man.

May 14

Pamela came for dinner on her way back to Paris. I said that, after seeing Al Gore, I had felt a certain undefinable sadness, gloom, in the Washington air. She said that she thought the atmosphere was terrible—everyone distracted by Whitewater and the new sex allegations (Paula Jones and her lawsuit) and buffeted by Bosnia and Haiti; no one sure how to deal with any of these problems.

May 25

On Wednesday the 18th we flew to London.

[Thursday] This was the day of the famous luncheon with Lady Thatcher. I went with some trepidation, fearing that I would get involved in unpleasant arguments about intervention in Bosnia, a subject on which she has been speaking and writing with considerable force in recent months. Gary McDowell picked us up, and we went to her headquarters, a fine old house at 35 Chesham Place. She greeted us cordially, introduced us to Sir Denis and offered drinks. When she asked what I wanted, I said, "As a matter of fact, a martini would be fine." Sir Denis gave me a congratulatory wink, and said he wanted one too.

Lady T., looking pink and cheerful, began by saying how much she admired my book *The Dismantling [sic] of the American Dream*. (Gary McDowell had told me that, when he first called on her, *The Disuniting of America* was on the table in the drawing room.) Then she said she had invited us to come before the other guests so that we could have a chance to talk. At this point she then held forth solo for about twenty minutes on the lack of will in the West, the lack of resolution, the lack of leadership, the failure to do anything about Bosnia, the failure to have gone on to Baghdad during the Gulf War, etc.

I interjected that she could have told George Bush, as she had told him at the start of the crisis, "Don't wobble, George." She said, "I wasn't there to tell him—and he wobbled." She spoke in a friendly but rather patronizing way about Bush.

We lunched at a round table. I was on Lady T.'s right. We talked for a bit about Anglo-American relations. She recalled how outraged she had been when Reagan, without telling her, invaded Grenada. "I sent word that it was a violation of British sovereignty. Also, I said, how can we object to what the Russians are doing in Afghanistan if we do the same things ourselves in the Caribbean?"

At the same time, she kept reiterating her belief that the United States as the greatest and best of powers must take the lead in the world and reaffirming her commitment to the Anglo-American connection. In this belief, she said, she had written a couple of letters to President Clinton but had received no acknowledgment. "I don't take that personally," she said. "I can understand that. I am sure it is a commentary on disorganization in the White House."

She is a most articulate and opinionated woman, speaking in clear, definite, non-stop sentences. But, contrary to my forebodings, I found myself liking her. She is, oddly, rather delightful with some of the grace and much of the magnetism and lordly manner of an accomplished actress. I kept being reminded of somebody, and then of all a sudden I remembered who: Fidel Castro. Both are notable performers of high intelligence and considerable charm; both are great talkers; both listen when one interjects, and both respond in their own various ways; both are imperious, dogmatic and impervious.

As Alexandra and I walked back to Grosvenor Square, the *Evening Standard* was on the street, and we were suddenly transfixed by the headline: JACKIE ONASSIS GOES HOME TO DIE. I couldn't believe it. By the time we got to the hotel, the phone was ringing with requests for interviews. When I went at 6 P.M. to the University of London for my Institute of American Studies talk for Democrats Abroad (on "Reflections on the Clinton Administration"), TV crews were already in place.

We woke the next morning—Friday the 20th—to hear that Jackie had died over the night. Could not take it in.

The funeral took place [in New York] at St. Ignatius Loyola at 10 A.M. on Monday the 23rd. It was a sunny but coolish day. We decided to walk and soon were joined by Pamela Turnure Timmins, who had been Jackie's press secretary thirty years ago. Park Avenue in front of the church was full of quiet sorrowing people. Inside the church were so many familiar faces, too many looking old, all looking somber. The service itself was lovely. Ted Kennedy spoke with eloquence. Maurice Tempelsman read a poem and added a few graceful words himself. The children did scriptural readings and acquitted themselves admirably. Afterward, feeling cosiderably shaken, we went to Mortimer's for lunch with George Stevens, Dick Goodwin, the vanden Heuvels and Milt Gwirtzman and his friend.

I have not seen all that much of Jackie in the last few years, but we spoke from time to time on the phone. Whenever I called, she always returned the call promptly; and, when we met, she was always cordial and affectionate; but I don't think we have been in her apartment for quite a while. But one felt she was always there, and now one feels that a great light has gone out in all our lives.

July 26

I had lunch with [Pamela Harriman] at the Knickerbocker Club. She finds Washington very depressing, and we talked a bit about what has gone wrong with an administration that began with such radiant hope and high expectation. Part of it is bad luck; part unforeseen external troubles; part a cynical opposition digging as never before into a President's pre–White House past; but a good part too is Clinton himself. He is bright, well-informed, in command of issues, pointing the country in the right direction; but he lacks the instinct for decision, goes in too much for government-by-bull-session, caves in too quickly and somehow lacks the *dignitas* that can be such a useful presidential weapon—those awful jogging photographs and so on. Much of the disorganization, it would seem, spills down from the top.

Last Saturday, Alexandra, Peter and I went to see *Angels in America,* the lavishly praised, Pulitzer Prize–winning play. It seemed a pile of pretentious crap to me, and I left after the first act. The homosexual culture assumes too much—it is understandable that it should, but it can become a bore. The crime that dare not speak its name now won't shut up.

August 3

Pamela had told me that she was going to see Clinton; so, by pre-arrangement, I called her in Middleburg at 11 P.M. She was even more depressed. She had been "very blunt" with him, she said, in saying how much trouble he was in; "but it's very difficult to know how much it really penetrates. He feels so terribly hurt and frustrated and belea-guered and sees himself as the object of persecution by the press. Every time you say something he rams it back at you. 'I've accomplished more than most Presidents in my first year, but no one gives me any credit. You say how successful my European trip was, but why the hell does no one write this? I went to Italy: great success, zero stories. To France: great success, zero stories. You know the press. Why can't you talk to them and get them to write about our achievements?' Etc., etc." I asked whether Hillary was any help. Pam said, "No. She is worse."

Presidents are congenitally angry at the press and never feel they are getting the credit due them. But Clinton seems to lack both tempera-mental detachment and historical perspective. JFK, though he would blow up (briefly) at the press, was saved by an ironic slant on life and an objectivity about himself.

September 10

This has been a month of disaster. A few moments before six, on Saturday 6 August, five weeks ago today, Alexandra and I set out for the movies. We went to see *Barcelona,* the new film by Whit Stillman, son of my old friends John and Meg Stillman. About twenty minutes into the film, Peter suddenly appeared, accompanied by an usher, and in a most urgent tone said, "You must leave at once." When we were outside the theater, he said, "The house is on fire." (He later explained that he had not wanted to cry fire in a crowded theater—the only joke to emerge from this lamentable episode.)

We rushed to the house. The fire engines had come with admirable promptitude, and by the time we arrived the fire was under control. It had begun in the stairwell on the garden floor and flamed up through the house, the stairwell serving as a chimney. But the fire brigade arrested the flames before they reached my study. Had the materials for my memoirs been consumed, I don't know what I would or could have done—cut my throat, perhaps.

My heart sank as Alexandra and I stood on 64th Street watching our house burn, and I fell into a depression that I have not yet quite shaken off. I am *never* depressed; I am buoyant by temperament and not a worrier; but I still cannot enter our house—which looks today like a London house bombed by the *Luftwaffe*—without feeling an impulse to cry. Of course it could have been so much worse. After all, no one was hurt; vital papers were saved. The irreplaceable losses are the Lily Cushing paintings in the drawing room, and some other paintings and photographs. In the only intelligent financial decision I have ever made, I have what seems to be a capacious fire insurance policy that would seem to cover almost everything.

But my books have all been removed for an ozone treatment designed to deal with smoke damage. Except for a number that I hastily segregated as essential for the memoirs, the books will not be available until the house is restored, which will not be for another eight to ten months. I know that I will constantly need one or another unavailable book, and in twenty-five years I have not solved the library problem in New York—one reason why I accumulated over 10,000 books in the house. Also where will I write? I have lost two of my four rooms at the University, and I will hereafter share my large office with Dick Wade, who is also retiring. I could not have a more companionable sharer than Dick; but sharing does not help writing, and in any case I have never been able to do serious writing in my office.

Even more serious is the setback to the memoirs. I was writing away and enjoying it; now the momentum is stopped, and I don't know when

I will be able to resume. My faculties still seem OK, except for the usual difficulties in memory retrieval, but I will begin to slow up soon; and I can't afford to lose two or three months at this stage in my life. Cleaning up after the fire did unearth some useful materials, such as a file box containing correspondence from the 1930s and early 1940s; much as cleaning up my office and sending files off to the Kennedy Library uncovered materials I did not know I had. But this does not outweigh the diversion of time and energy, the worry, the useless railing against fate. When I begin to feel too sorry for myself, I think of Rwanda and Bosnia.

Henry Kissinger called, anxiously inquiring about my papers. The *News* had run a story saying that papers had been preserved in a fireproof vault in the basement. Alas, there was no fireproof vault; but Henry said he was fireproofing his basement. Fire is a scholar's nightmare.

In the meantime, we have entered a new and unsuspected world of insurance adjusters, furniture and painting restorers, architects, contractors and so on. I feel hopelessly beyond my depth, resent the time I must give to all this and sink ever more deeply into depression. Alexandra is far more effective and indeed has been generally magnificent, with one fatal exception. She says she does not want to move back into the house. She will be forever fearful of fires. She wants to live in an apartment. And she hates my books and insists that I must get rid of most of them. She does not understand that a historian lives and dies by accessible books. She would like to sell the house at once. I do not think that Robert and Peter will go along with this. 171 East 64th Street is the only home they have, and I believe they want to keep it.

I agreed to appear on a couple of panels at the convention of the American Political Science Association, meeting in New York: one on "*The Imperial Presidency Revisited*" and one on "Stephen Skowronek's *The Politics Presidents Make.*" Both passed agreeably.

David Broder, the self-appointed mediator between journalism and political science, was, as usual haunting the corridors of the Hilton, where the convention was held, and he attended both of my sessions. A few days later, he quoted, quite legitimately, off-the-cuff remarks I had made about the Clinton administration. Schlesinger, he wrote, "described Mr Clinton's free-form White House as 'government by bull session.' He said the President, "suffering from the delusion that he can carry Florida in 1996, has given Cuban-Americans more control over foreign policy than any domestic group has exercised 'since the China lobby in the 1950s.' The role of the Congressional Black Caucus in shaping Haiti policy is an equally 'ominous development,' he said."

These are not comments calculated to win us another dinner invitation to the White House. The foreign policy remarks were part of an argument that the end of the Cold War had created a vacuum in the definition of foreign policy that lobbies were rushing to fill. But in fact I am really fed up with Clinton on Cuba. How shaming to call Jorge Mas Canosa in for advice on how to deal with Castro! Even the *Wall Street Journal* is in favor of lifting the embargo, and so are many leading members of Congress. I am less clear as to what I would have done about Haiti; but I think any course of action that leaves us no alternative but invasion is ill-judged, and that is the situation in which Clinton now finds himself. If in the end he does not invade, it will be one more humiliating Clinton flip-flop.

October 28

The fact that I have made no entry for seven weeks is a measure of the depression into which this damned fire has plunged me. I am by nature buoyant, and I have not been so depressed since the murders of JFK and RFK. It would have been far worse, of course, if anyone had been hurt or if the fire had consumed my papers. But this disruption of life is the last thing I need in my 78th year with a book to write.

September has pretty much vanished into the mists of memory. On the 21st I had a piece in the *Wall Street Journal* entitled "Houdini in the White House," stressing Clinton's capacities as an escape artist. The next day I flew to Indiana to speak at the state university in Terre Haute. On arrival, I checked the voice mail at my office and discovered that Clinton was trying to get hold of me. I called the White House and, after a short delay, was put through to him. He said he had read the *Journal* column and wondered whether I could develop some of the thoughts about foreign policy for the speech he was to give at the UN the following Monday. "People don't understand what we are trying to do," he said. "We need to spell out the framework." I said I would do my best to send something.

Then he digressed into his general situation and went into a rambling attack on the media. No President, he said, had received less accurate coverage. He was the only President never to have been given a honeymoon by the media. The chief reason for the national cynicism was the press. He had never been credited with the legislation he had passed or with the commitments he had kept. "No President has ever been in this position before. . . . It's maddening—a bigger gap than ever existed in modern history." I said that FDR had 90 percent of the press against him. "Yes," Clinton said, "but he had the working press with him." A fair point. "We've got to find a way to get information on what we are doing directly to the people. It is all very frustrating." He went on in this vein for fifteen or twenty minutes.

Certainly the media have been unwontedly tough on Clinton, especially when compared to the indulgence granted Reagan. One reason, I think, is that reporters feel that during the 1992 campaign they were misled by the Clinton people about Whitewater, etc.; and they are determined not to be taken in again. But the air of incipient paranoia in Clinton's wail of exasperation is a little disquieting.

October 30

The sourness of the national mood is a mystery. I have been through angry times before—the isolationist-interventionist debate of 1940–41, the bitterest time of all; the McCarthy period; civil rights; Vietnam—but in all those times something was at stake. Now nothing is at stake. The economy is doing well, unemployment is falling, inflation remains low, foreign policy is non-threatening. Yet the voters are mad, and Clinton is the scapegoat. There must be some more basic sense of insecurity to account for the popular anger.

November 25

During the luncheon at the 20th Century Fund on 16 November there was much discussion of the election. Someone asked Hodding Carter why southern white males hated Clinton so much. He replied, "They look back with longing at the good old days—the days when abortion was in the back alley, gays were in the closet, women were in the kitchen, blacks were in the back of the bus and condoms were under the counter."

The main speech at the Fund dinner the next night was given by Bill Bradley. He is a dull speaker anyway, and this time his talk was pretentious and interminable—the deep thoughts of a bright sophomore.

1995

January 5

Marella Agnelli called Monday afternoon to say that she and Gianni
were in town for a couple of days and asked us to dinner on Tuesday.
Henry Kissinger was there; also Bob Silvers and the painter Sandro
Chia, very rightwing, now shacked up with Marella's niece. Henry was
much concerned about the fate of [Silvio] Berlusconi who has just resigned. He was no admirer of Berlusconi, Henry said, but the alternative would be "the Communists," and that would be far worse. Marella
and I scoffed, wondering what it meant to be a Communist any more.
Communism, I said, was recognized even by old-time Communists as a
total flop. Henry said that Communists would still want to establish an
authoritarian state; how could anyone trust even so apparently civilized
a man as [Giorgio] Napolitano—who had been a faithful Communist
all his life. And why should we accept an alleged change of heart
for Communists when we would not grant the same exemption to
former Fascists like [Gianfranco] Fini? Henry, so intelligent in so

many ways, seems still mesmerized by the Communist threat. It reminded me of the times twenty years ago when he regarded Euro-communism as the great menace, about to take over Portugal and probably Italy too.

I asked Gianni what Berlusconi's future would be. He said crisply, "Berlusconi is finished."

This morning's *Herald Tribune* (the newspaper we are forced to take to find out what is going on politically in Europe, the *Times* having abandoned hard news in favor of soft and generally boring feature stories) carried a dispatch from the *Washington Post* saying that Clinton was seeking advice from various experts, including "presidential historians." This confirmed my feeling that I was now definitely on the shelf, a political has-been, which I guess is what I am.

However, no sooner did I have this feeling than Carey Parker called me from Ted Kennedy's office to say that he and Bob Shrum had written a speech for Ted to give at the National Press Club next Wednesday and that Ted wanted me to take a look at it. Soon a 14-page draft arrived on the fax machine. Then Henry Kissinger's office called saying that Henry wanted to schedule a luncheon.

And then another fax arrived from Donald Baer, "Director of Speechwriting" at the White House, "writing on behalf of the President to solicit your views about the upcoming State of the Union Address. . . . Last year, you made an enormously important contribution to his Address to Congress when you provided written advice on what you then believed his speech should contain. I was hoping that you would be willing to do so again." I have no recollection of having made any such contribution, and I suppose the same fax went to a score of people. But I might as well let them know what I think. At any rate, I felt less neglected at the end of the day than I had felt at the beginning.

January 10

I responded to the White House request by sending a letter of sagacious counsel that will probably finish any Clintonian connection.

However, since in any case my advice has been rarely sought and our social presence only when Pamela Harriman put us on her list, the relationship can hardly be reduced. So, with little to lose, I decided that I might as well say bluntly what I really believed.

Last night, Bill Buckley and I appeared on the Charlie Rose show. Our performances must have disappointed all those who looked forward to a slam-bang, no-holds-barred fight. Indeed, as I saw the show myself (it was taped at 6 P.M. and shown at 11), I thought that here were a couple of old gladiators who in their genial decline were substituting jollity for combat.

Thirty years ago Bill Buckley and I went on occasion from city to city like a couple of professional wrestlers. We really disliked each other then, and no holds were barred. Once, out of my own sense of mischief, I entered a *National Review* contest of some sort and won a prize. Buckley, out of his bolder sense of mischief, awarded me a live donkey, which lived in our backyard on Irving Street for a couple of days until I hired someone to take it away. Our relationship in those times was one of incessant—and heartfelt—reciprocal insult.

Then I came to New York. I liked Pat Buckley. Bill liked Alexandra. Alistair Horne, Bill's old friend and my new friend, took it on as his mission to bring us together. Bill's views moderated; today he would no longer defend Joe McCarthy, as he did forty years ago. My attitudes mellowed with age. I developed a regard for Bill's wit, his passion for the harpsichord, his human decency, even for his compulsion to epater the liberals (which is about all that remains from the wrathful conservatism of his youth). So now we are friends—and go easy on each other.

At New Year's, feeling an obligation to show something to Houghton Mifflin (I was supposed to have half the book finished by the end of 1994), I sent Joe Kanon the first four chapters of the memoir. Yesterday I received a fax beginning: "The book is wonderful. The tone seems to me just right—the Xenia sections were particularly evocative—and makes one greedy for more," etc. This cheered me immensely.

January 19

I lunched today with Caroline Kennedy, also at the Century. When George Weidenfeld was here last month, he asked what I would think of Antonia Fraser's writing a biography of Jackie. I said that it sounded like a fine idea to me, and subsequently Antonia sent me a couple of letters about it. Caroline was less enthusiastic. Jackie of course did not much like Antonia. She admired her diligence as a writer but thought (correctly) that she had treated Hugh badly and really did not much like seeing her.

Caroline rather recoils from the idea of any biography at this time. I said that she could use Antonia as a way of fending off other biographers, but she did not see why it was necessary for her to cooperate with any biographer. Neither she nor John, she said, would be available for interviews; and the papers won't be put in order for a year or so. I guess I will have to tell Antonia that immediate prospects are not too favorable.

Caroline looked exceedingly pretty, and we had a jolly luncheon. She is intelligent and very definite in the female (and male) Kennedy style.

January 28

I have been reading Bob McNamara's new book *In Retrospect: The Tragedy and Lessons of Vietnam*. I cannot remember a public official making such a frank and forthright confession of error. The book is a careful and considered explanation of why he and the country got things so wrong. It seems to me an honest and honorable work, though the right will no doubt attack him for sending thousands of young Americans to their death in a war that he now dismisses as mistaken and futile.

February 22

The National Arts Club in Gramercy Park presented its literary award to Bill Styron. Bill had asked me to speak, which I was of course pleased to do. Art Buchwald was in his best form as master of ceremonies. "I know what acute depression is like," he said. "I have been through it too—at the same time Bill was going through his. But Bill is the only depressed person I know who made a million dollars out of his depression." The other speakers were Peter Matthiessen, Bob Loomis, Bill's publisher, and the obnoxious Joan Didion, who detests me as I detest her. Inevitably we were seated next to each other and made forced polite conversation through the evening. Apart from la Didion, it was a genial party.

On Monday we went to Washington for the first of a series of three dinners given by the Vice President to discuss race relations. Alexandra and I were part of a small group of token whites, along with Dick Goodwin, Larry Fuchs and Marty Peretz, the last of whom has shaved his beard. (Dick Goodwin said to me, "Peretz used to look like a Jewish psychoanalyst. Now he looks like a Jewish used car salesman.") Top black intellectuals and politicos were there—John Hope Franklin and William Julius Wilson made opening statements, and Skip Gates, Jesse Jackson, John Lewis, Stanley Crouch, Lani Guinier, Shelby Steele and others were part of the cast. Some, black and white, talked. I kept my peace. I cannot say that I learned much new, but the talk was interesting, and we were both glad we went. Al Gore presided intelligently and with more easy humor than usual. Tipper was as usual charming.

In an effort to save time and still respect my father's injunction that most letters deserve an answer, I have adapted a formula that Charles Beard suggested to my father c. 1928:

> Arthur Schlesinger Jr. has read your recent communication with attention, thanks you for it and begs forgiveness for failing to respond personally. But, having retired from teaching, I no longer have a secretary, and, in my 78th year, I no longer have time for much else than writing books I should have written long ago. I regret the necessity of resorting to this rather formal mode of reply but find it the only alternative to spending two or three days every week writing letters.

April 22

The 50th anniversary of FDR's death is approaching. On the 5th and 6th I moderated (with Robert Batscha) a couple of panels at the Museum of Television and Radio—the first on "Roosevelt: The Great Communicator" with Bob Nathan, Doris Kearns, Geoff Ward and Dick Hottelet; the second on "The Roosevelt Legacy" with Alan Brinkley, Doug Brinkley, Bill vanden Heuvel and David Gergen. Both panels were excellent, and a full house listened with rapt attention. The FDR magic is still alive. Fifty years after TR's death was 1969, fifty years after Wilson's death was 1974: on neither occasion could a general audience have been assembled of this size and with the same intensity of personal connection.

On Saturday the 8th we left for Warm Springs and the FDR commemoration. That evening Wyche Fowler and Jack Watson staged a Georgia hoe-down with excellent barbecued ribs. In the course of the evening Wyche, who had worked briefly in the Johnson White House before moving on to Congress (he was narrowly defeated last year for reelection to the Senate), told a splendid LBJ story.

Apparently LBJ had a program under consideration for people with dental troubles to be called Dentacare. He decided to give a speech on the subject and brusquely rejected the draft provided by his speech staff. Decending in person upon them, he mimicked a toothless man trying to speak and said, "That draft of yours is is no good. It doesn't have any— what is that intellectual word?—*empathy. Empathy*—that's what I want. When I give that speech, I want you to make that l'l old lady in the front row—the one without a tooth in her mouth—feel my hand under her skirt."

We had invited the President to the ceremony on Wednesday, but he had apparently decided against it when suddenly on Sunday word arrived that he was coming after all. On Monday I phoned Bob Boorstin at the White House asking whether they wanted some thoughts about the speech. Soon I got a return call from Don Baer, the person in charge of the Warm Springs draft. I suggested that they might want to seize the occasion to recall FDR's Economic Bill of Rights of 1944 in his 1944 State of the Union address. "What's that?" Baer said. "I don't think I know about it. Is it the same thing as the GI Bill of Rights?" I was a little taken aback by this historical lacuna but described FDR's list of economic rights. Baer said, "That sounds as if it would fit in quite nicely."

Wednesday, was the big day. The Four Freedoms Awards went to Jimmy Carter, Mary McGrory, Lane Kirkland, Elliot Richardson and Andy Young. The laureates and the other speakers gathered in the Little White House before the ceremony began. Despite past differences, Carter greeted me civilly. As conversation faltered, I asked him about Sudan. He said, "My son Chip is over there, holding things together. Chip is a real politician. . . . I have two politicians in my family—Chip and Rosalynn. I don't like politics. I don't like politics at all." Then looking at me, rather accusingly: "I know that *you* like politics."

Clinton, arriving a little later, went at once over to Carter, shook his hand and inquired with cordiality: "How are you?" Carter said, "Fine." End of conversation; frost in the air. Clinton after a moment moved on and greeted the rest of us.

The ceremony began. I made some brief remarks designed to stimulate Clinton to fight for FDR's legacy. Anna Roosevelt, Jimmy's daughter, then gave a strong talk along the same lines, concluding by reading aloud the Economic Bill of Rights. When she returned to her seat, Clinton, who was sitting next to her, evidently whispered to her good-naturedly, "You've taken half of my speech." But he rallied with equanimity and gave a largely extemporized talk that caught the spirit of FDR pretty well. He made a couple of friendly allusions to my remarks and later asked me to send him a copy. When the ceremony adjourned and he was working the crowd, he spotted Alexandra at a distance and called to her: "Hi, Alexandra!"

The awards were presented. Carter, in accepting his, told how much FDR had meant to him and how he had wept on hearing of his death. Remembering his refusal to send even a message to the New Deal reunions when he was President, I listened with some skepticism.

[On Sunday the 16th] I saw the Warm Springs ceremony and Clinton's speech on C-Span and wrote a letter to accompany the copy of my remarks. Then Kathy Sloane called Alexandra and told her that an interview Ken Galbraith and I had given John Harris of the *Washington Post* had upset the White House. I called Harris, and he faxed me a copy of his piece. Ken was quoted as saying: "FDR enjoyed his enemies. I'd like to see Bill Clinton enjoy them more." My remark: "I think Clinton sees himself in the FDR tradition, all things being equal. Yet FDR loved a good fight; Clinton seems by temperament an accommodator. Accommodation has its uses but it can too easily become appeasement."

Then the next day Judy Woodruff had pressed Clinton in a CNN interview, quoting me and asking whether it was an accurate perception. Clinton replied, "No, I like to fight," and went on to defend his record. She persisted: "You've got people out there like Arthur Schlesinger saying he thinks you're an accommodator." Clinton: "Well, let me ask all those people, then, if that's so true, why did I break the back of trickle-down economics?" And so on.

Meanwhile a new controversy has been swirling up. I can't recall whether I recorded that some months ago Bob McNamara sent me the draft of a book on Vietnam. I read it and made some suggestions. So did a number of other people. I thought the book a fine and courageous job. I cannot remember a public official making a comparable confession of error, and I am sure that the book will survive as a valuable contribution to the history of the times.

Now *In Retrospect* is out, and it is causing heated controversy. I had feared adverse reactions. I expected that rightwingers would denounce Bob for sending American boys to their deaths and then saying sorry, it was all for nothing. But I did not expect the virulence of the attack, coming from left as well as right. The *Times* had an especially hysterical editorial. The implication is that Bob should never have written the book. The head of the American Legion thinks he should be tried for treason.

I called him on Tuesday the 18th, and he seemed undaunted and in a fighting mood. He came to New York on Thursday, and I presided over his meeting at the Council on Foreign Relations. The Kennedy people in the audience were all pulling for him, but he did not do well. I have known for a long time that underneath that disciplined exterior McNamara is a man filled with tense and pent-up emotion. He gives the impression now of a man so wound up that he is almost out of control. He talks in his usual logical, forceful, clearcut way, but he can't stop talking. I finally had to cut his remarks off, and he then overanswered every question.

The questions were courteous but surprisingly tough. One man who had served two years in Vietnam said that, when he came back, he felt he had a moral obligation to speak out against the war; "Why, Mr. Secretary, did you not feel the same obligation?" Bob's answer is pathetic. He draws a phoney distinction between the obligations of a cabinet officer in a parliamentary system, where, as elected officials, their obligation is to their constituents, and in a presidential system, where, as appointed officials, their obligation is to the President. He also invokes the phoney aid-and-comfort-to-the-enemy argument as another excuse for silence. Knowing Bob, the quintessential organization man, I can understand why it has taken so long for him to speak out. He does not help himself by advancing these unconvincing rationalizations.

I could see the faces of Mac Bundy, Ted Sorensen, Ros Gilpatric and others fall as Bob rambled militantly and emotionally along. At the end, he started to read a letter sent him by the widow of a Quaker who had doused himself with gasoline and burned himself to death in front of the Pentagon twenty years ago. The letter pleaded for reconciliation and healing. Bob was about to break into tears, could not go on and gave the letter to me to read. Then he left (and with Joan Braden).

Bill vanden Heuvel said to me, "You did very well in presiding over that therapy session." Ted was very critical. Mac Bundy called the next morning and asked what I thought. When I told him, he said that he entirely agreed but wanted to be sure he had got it right. It was a sad performance by a man we all respect and love.

June 7

I received a fax from Tina Brown inviting me to do a comment for the *New Yorker* on the so-called Camelot Documents—Teddy White's notes on the Hyannis Port interview with Jackie that created the Camelot-Kennedy equation. Of course no one had identified JFK's Washington with Camelot when he was alive, nor did those of us around him see ourselves as Knights of any one's Round Table. Had we proposed this, no one would have been more derisive than JFK.

Teddy had stipulated that the Hyannis Port notes be withheld until a year after Jackie's death. It developed that the release would take place on the 26th, the day I was scheduled to leave the hospital [after an operation]; so, doubting that the notes would add much to the account in Teddy's memoir *In Search of History,* I wrote a quick draft before I went into Lenox Hill. Tina pronounced it "gorgeous," and it ran in the 5 June issue.

On Wednesday the 31st I lunched with Carl Anthony, a young, open-faced writer who has made himself a specialist on Presidents' wives and is now doing a book on Jackie. He said *inter alia* that, when Jackie made her first trip to Europe in 1948, she insisted on going to Dachau and that the last film she saw was *Schindler's List.*

June 26

On Thursday the 8th our neighbor across the street, Joan Rivers, invited us to a dinner for Nancy Reagan. Alexandra had left for Rome the day before; so I went alone to the opulent apartment that in other days had belonged to J. P. Morgan. The transition from banker to celebrity shows the change from old to new New York. I am not altogether clear where Joan Rivers's celebrity came from—I gather that she has been a television personality and latterly has been on the stage. She is in a somewhat incongruous alliance with Orin Lehman and works hard these days at being ladylike.

I had my usual brief and perfunctory exchange with Mrs. Reagan, who is wiry-thin (as against frail-thin) but looks pretty good for her age.

I don't think she ever knows who I am and, if she recognizes me as an ardent critic of her beloved husband, she must be puzzled as to why I am invited to affairs in her honor.

July 14

My exchange of letters with Bill Clinton* resulted in an invitation to Ken, Ted Sorensen, Bill vanden Heuvel, Joe Califano and me to luncheon at the White House on Friday the 7th. The luncheon took place in the so-called family dining room on the first floor of the White House. We were only offered fruit juices before lunch, but two wines were served at the table. The food was pretentious—the kind that seemed to be devised more to be looked at than to be eaten. The President was accompanied by Leon Panetta, whom I had not met before and found intelligent and wryly amusing, Harold Ickes and Carol Rasco, who is apparently head of the Domestic Policy Council.

Bill looked chipper, was his usual articulate self and showed his usual mastery of the details of all issues. On occasion he took notes. I was relieved that there was almost none of the Nixon-style paranoia about the "media" he has displayed on other occasions. It was apparent that he supposed the session would concentrate on domestic policy—his first question was, "What do you fellows think about Dick Gephardt's tax proposal?"—and he raised no questions about foreign policy. When others, especially Bill vanden Heuvel, did, however, he responded knowledgeably and carefully.

On domestic affairs he said he planned to use the veto much more than in the past. We pointed out how useful the veto could be both in

---

* President Clinton wrote Schlesinger a note on April 20, protesting his remarks in the *Washington Post* characterizing Clinton as "an accommodator." In his reply, Schlesinger suggested that Clinton might benefit from the advice of "liberals who have been through the mill," adding that "any time you would like to hear out Ken [Galbraith], Ted Sorensen, Bill vanden Heuvel, Joe Califano and me, you have only to say the word."

dramatizing issues and in defining the position and character of Presidents. He readily agreed. "The Republicans will accuse me of shutting the government down when I veto appropriations bills," he said, "but I think I can explain to the people what is going on."

He engaged in a particular colloquy with Joe Califano about health care and drugs. Someone mentioned that the *National Review* had come out for the legalization of drugs (or perhaps just of marijuana). Clinton said he was against legalization. "We are all prisoners of our experience, and I know that, if drugs had been legalized, my brother would be a dead man today."

I think all of us were both impressed and disarmed by Clinton's intelligence, vitality and charm. I also think we all felt that, if he acts the way he talked, things would improve—but we still wonder about the "if." Anyway the luncheon was thoroughly enjoyable. It lasted from about 12:30 to 2.

August 1

Friday the 28th: luncheon with Bianca Jagger, just back from a trip to Guatemala with Jennifer Harbury, whose husband, a Guatemalan guerrilla, was evidently tortured and murdered by a Guatemalan officer on the CIA payroll. Both the CIA and the State Department apparently withheld, and are still withholding, information about the affair. Bob Torricelli exposed the scandal some weeks ago, bringing down on his head the wrath of Newt Gingrich for allegedly violating the rules of the House Intelligence Committee—a charge of which Torricelli has since been cleared.

Bianca and Torricelli have broken up. She says he is impossible to live with—too cold and self-absorbed. He reminds her of Mick in certain ways, she said, but Mick had much more humor and gaiety about him. She and Bob are still on friendly terms, she said; she and Mick too. I like Bianca. She is of course very attractive and also articulate, perceptive, concerned, occasionally funny and very good company.

September 23

On Thursday the 14th, Bill vanden Heuvel carried on the George Ball luncheons at the Century. JFK Jr. came and talked about *George,* his new magazine. He was intelligent, straightforward and humorous and made a distinctly good impression on a case-hardened but, I suppose, Kennedy-vulnerable crowd. The magazine is a big, glossy job, *Vanity Fair* applied to politics. Young John's sponsorship has gained it much publicity and many advertisements, but I doubt that *George* is destined for a long life.

October 22

We attended a dinner for [Yitzhak] Rabin of Israel. My only meeting with Rabin had been at Lally [Weymouth]'s in the midst of the 1972 campaign when Rabin was Israeli ambassador to Washington. His pro-Nixon remarks and his attack on Ken Galbraith so irritated me that I denounced his intervention in American presidential elections, and we had an argument so unbridled that George Weidenfeld, who was there, mentions it not once but twice in his recent memoirs. But I felt that the world now owes Rabin a debt for following Shimon Peres's lead and thereby making the deal with the Palestinians more politically acceptable in Israel; so we decided to go. I did not have a chance to renew my acquaintance with Rabin.

October 23

Today I went to a luncheon at the Council [on Foreign Relations] for Fidel Castro. He greeted me with cordiality when I arrived and gave me an *abrazo* when I departed, which shows how enmities perish through the years. Oddly there was no anti-Castro demonstration. Les Gelb told me that he had taken out extra insurance for the occasion and had boarded up the Council's windows in preparation for angry protests; but nothing happened.

Fidel began by a mild confession of fallibility. Introducing him, Les Gelb had recalled his last appearance at the Council, in April 1959. "Back in 1959," Fidel said, "I had just come down from the Sierra Maestra, and I didn't know anything about anything; so I take no responsibility for anything I might have said thirty-six years ago. Now that I've had more experience, I am more careful as to what I say."

He went on to say he could not understand why, with the Cold War over, the Russian connection finished, Cuban troops out of Africa, good Cuban relations with the other governments of the hemisphere—the conditions laid down in earlier years for rapprochement—the U.S. persisted in its enmity. With China, Vietnam, even North Korea forgiven, "Why has the U.S. chosen us as the last adversary? We aren't trying to change your system. I know you're not worried about that. But why are you trying to change our system?" Of course, he knows the answer: domestic politics; but he made an effective case.

It was predominantly a business crowd, and questions dealt with compensation for nationalized properties and the like. No one (including me) raised the question of political prisoners and the treatment of human rights activists and other dissidents. (In my case, I have been over that with him before and know what his answer will be, and I guess I didn't want to put him in a bad light before business leaders who rather favor lifting the embargo—which in my view is the measure that will be of greatest help to the dissidents.)

He was dressed in a sober dark blue suit; not in his military fatigues. His remarks were, as usual, fluent, eloquent, laced with statistics and with humor; but there was an intangible sadness about it all, accentuated by his pleading eyes.

November 7

On Wednesday the 25th Alexandra and I went to Washington for a commemoration of the 50th anniversary of the founding of the Truman Library. We went to a black-tie Truman dinner at the Public Buildings Museum, a handsome structure hitherto unknown to me. I took Robert up to meet Clinton and made the mistake of essaying what turned out to be a bad joke. A few days ago Clinton had told a Texas audience that he now believed the administration bill had raised taxes too much. This infuriated Democrats in Congress who had put their own political lives on the line by voting for the bill. Trying to repair the damage, Clinton said, "My mother told me I should never make a speech when I am tired." I now said to Clinton, who was to speak at the dinner, "Don't forget what your mother told you." This seemed to irritate him greatly, and he went into an annoyed and defensive account of how he had been misrepresented, etc. I tried to move on (we were in a receiving line), but he held me by the arm and continued an angry and largely incomprehensible explanation. I seem to have a knack for getting off on the wrong foot with Bill.

A few days later Clinton called, of all people, that jerk Ben Wattenberg, talked with him for an hour and said, in effect, that he had been too liberal in his first two years and was now going to reform and take the Democratic Leadership Council line. This of course delighted Wattenberg, who promptly wrote a column about it. The rest of the press wondered what Clinton stands for, if anything. This second gaffe on top of the first reinforces one's fear that Clinton is not a learner. Kennedy made mistakes but generally learned from them. Clinton generally repeats his mistakes.

1996

May 2

This long interval is the consequence of the hopeless overcrowdedness of my life. Let me recapitulate. On Tuesday the 2nd [of April], after lunching with the Galbraiths at the Carlyle, we took off for Madrid. Dick Gardner is our ambassador in Spain, and he and Danielle persuaded Alexandra that we should join them in Seville for *semana santa*—Holy Week. I protested feebly, but Carlos Fuentes, who was to be a member of the party, told me, when I said that I could not abide religious ceremonies, "Don't be foolish. Holy Week in Seville is a great pagan festival."

We had a most amiable party, Bill and Rose Styron, Tom Wicker and Pamela Hill, John and Mary Ellen Brademas—and Tipper Gore and her daughter Karenna.

[One] evening we dined at the house of Eduardo Osborne. There, or on some other social occasion, I had a political conversation with Tipper Gore. I asked her whether we had a chance in Tennessee. She was doubtful. "If Al and I could do what we used to do—visit every county in the state—we might be able to pull it off," she said, "but we won't be able to do that, and the Republicans are strong in the state—the governor and both senators." Then she said, "We were talking the other day about what Al should do in the unlikely case that we lose the election." I suggested that maybe he should run for the Senate again. She said, "No, we'd like to avoid that. We wondered what other ways Al might find to keep his name before the public." I said that the role of "titular leader" of the party seems to have disappeared. Adlai Stevenson was able to use it in 1953–56, but neither McGovern nor Carter, Mondale or Dukakis, succeeded in reviving the role. Perhaps he might give speeches, write books, etc. Obviously the Gores are setting their sights on 2000.

I like Tipper. In discussing the vice presidential role, she emphasized how close Clinton and her husband had become—"like two fingers," she said, holding up her hand with two fingers close together. This may well be the case. My only cavil came when she talked about her own tasks as "Second Lady." First Lady is a reprehensible enough term; Second Lady is surely going too far in a democracy.

Monday night, 29 April [back in New York], I received the Society of American Historians' Bruce Catton award, including a much-needed $5,000, for lifetime achievement in writing American history. I don't think I deserve it, but I did not complain. Tom Wicker was sufficiently taken with my response to suggest to the *Times* that they run it as an Op Ed piece. They called, I faxed them a copy, and a condensed version appeared on Friday, 3 May. One oddity: my script said that popular excitement over the use and abuse of history was an involuntary tribute to the significance of history for which historians should be duly grateful. "It would be far worse if no one gave a damn what we said or did." The edited version cut this sentence. I asked that it be restored. Howard Goldberg, who does most of the line editing for the Op Ed page, said there was a problem: Howell Raines, the editor of the editorial page, has forbidden the use of the word "damn." I pointed out that even the Legion of Decency in 1939 had permitted Clark Gable to say to

Vivien Leigh, "Frankly, my dear, I don't give a damn." This did not avail, and we finally settled for a much feebler "It would be far worse if no one cared what we said or did." I don't know Raines, but his is an asinine ban.

August 21

On Friday 2 August I lunched, at Bill vanden Heuvel's suggestion, with W. D. Rubinstein, a historian, American by birth who has been teaching in Australia and is now a professor at Aberystwyth. He has completed an impressive manuscript called *The Myth of Rescue: Why the Democracies Could Not Have Saved More Jews During the Nazi Holocaust.* After a rigorous analysis of the rescue schemes proposed at the time, he concludes that very few Jews who perished in the holocaust could have been saved by any action the allies could have taken.

The rescue question was generally ignored in the years after the war. Then in the late 1960s Arthur Morse's *While Six Million Died* and David Wyman's *Paper Walls: America and the Refugee Crisis, 1938–1941,* both published in 1968, initiated the literature of accusation. Wyman, driven by an intense form of Protestant guilt, began a long crusade of blame. Many Jews followed him to the point of turning against FDR, the President previously most revered in American Jewish circles. Some Jewish scholars—Lucy Dawidowicz, Henry Feingold, Richard Breitman—remain thoughtful and objective, but other Jewish writers, especially publicists (Sidney Zion of the *Daily News,* for example) seem to rejoice in the role of victims and condemn Roosevelt with relish.

Some time ago Bill vanden Heuvel became interested in the controversy and decided that FDR was getting a bum rap. One result was the conference at Hyde Park that led to the publication this year of *FDR and the Holocaust.* Another was Bill's successful campaign to persuade the Holocaust Museum to revise a most tendentious account of the failure to bomb Auschwitz. I believe that Rubinstein's book with its meticulous analysis of plans and possibilities may do something to bring this understandably emotional controversy to an end.

At some point in the week Norris Mailer called from Provincetown. The tabloids had been having a field day with the story of Carol Mallory, who was Norman's mistress for several years in the 1980s. Norris called to ask whether we had kept a copy of the *New York Post* with an especially sensational story (we had thrown it away), but she really wanted to discuss the whole business.

I remember a few years back that Norris, whom I adore, was, as she conceded at the time, withdrawn and depressed, but gave no hint why. Carol Mallory was the reason. "I was so angry when I learned about her," she said. "I lost thirty pounds. I could't believe it. I do everything for Norman. I've taken charge of his life. . . . I told him that, if he ever does anything like this again, I will leave him at once and forever." Norman is crazy to risk his marriage with this glorious girl, but the besetting problem of his life is that he cannot resist risks. Apparently, however, he has been behaving (Norris thinks) ever since her demarche.

Clinton has announced that he will sign the Republican welfare bill. This announcement both infuriated and depressed me, more than I would have expected, and I resolved to stop defending Clinton in the future. Defederalization will send welfare to the states. The more humane a program an individual state offers, the more it will attract poor people from other states; so that states will be under constant pressure to lower standards, and we will end with a race to the bottom.

But it will take time for the consequences of defederalization to become palpable. Even if Clinton wins in November and brings in a Democratic Congress, a proposal to refederalize welfare will be generally opposed on the ground that the states must be given a fair chance to do the job. It may take a decade before the failure of the states will be unmistakable. In the meantime, poor people will be hurt. Maybe some of them will become angry. The rich in this country seem to think that they can oppress the poor indefinitely, not recognizing that welfare is one price society pays for social peace.

August 21

[On Sunday] afternoon I took Robert to Bill Clinton's 50th birthday celebration. Barry Landau, a public relations man with Democratic connections, had come up with a couple of tickets.

We went first to a reception at the Sheraton. A lot of people were milling around. I knew few of them. Landau must have got word to the President that I was there because, when Clinton appeared, he began his remarks by saying that he understood that Governor [Hugh] Carey and Caroline McCarthy and (to my astonishment) Arthur Schlesinger were in the crowd. After he finished, a White House aide tracked us down and said that the Clintons wanted to see me. She began to take Robert and me backstage, but even Don Fowler, the executive chairman of the Democratic National Committee, could not persuade the Secret Service man to let us pass through the ropes.

Meanwhile Bill, Hillary and Chelsea were going through the crowd shaking hands. Hillary spotted me, kissed me and waved Robert and me through the Secret Service line. We waited for a few minutes backstage. Hillary, Chelsea and a friend of Chelsea's appeared. We had a nice talk, mostly about Chelsea's choice of college.

Soon the President appeared, greeting us with cordiality. When I started to introduce Robert, he said, "I remember Robert. He represented your family at the Roosevelt dinner." We talked a bit about the Dole-Kemp convention bounce. Clinton, who looked tanned and well after their week in Jackson Hole, said he was not worried. "The Republicans hid their platform and their congressional leadership in San Diego," he said, "but they can't keep them hidden forever. . . . Also I think your turn of the cycle is coming. A new poll shows that 70 percent of the people are favorable to government. I believe that the country is moving to the left."

"To the left"—his words. I refrained from asking why he did not act on that belief, with regard to the welfare bill, for example. The circumstances were not propitious for discussion, and Robert had warned me against a wrangle of the sort I had with Clinton in the receiving line at the White House. He soon hastened on to the Radio City Music Hall for the performance.

How to interpret his words? Presidents often, Bill Clinton especially, say things that they suppose the person with whom they are talking wants to hear. Does he really believe the country is moving to the left? Anyway his talk of the Schlesinger cycles, his personal magnetism and his official power worked their insidious charm, and I am almost prepared to start defending Clinton again.

In his remarks at the Sheraton, and later after the performance at the Music Hall (where he handled pro-welfare hecklers gently and effectively), he said he had plans to change the worst features of the bill. He can make marginal improvements—better treatment of the children of immigrants, for example—but he can't easily repair the basic structural change.

Someone named Dan Pink called from Al Gore's office saying that the Vice President would like any thoughts I might have about his acceptance speech next week. I have sent along a few thoughts, largely in order to have a means of reviving Robert's search for a job in the Gore campaign. I understand that Gore, along with Dick Morris, urged Clinton to sign the awful welfare bill. Leon Panetta and Harold Ickes argued against—and lost.

September 8

I worked all weekend writing three pages for Al Gore's acceptance speech. Dole, in his acceptance address in San Diego, had talked about building a bridge to the tranquility of the past; and I suggested that Gore should reject nostalgia as the basis for policy and define the contest as one between the past and the future, between (citing Emerson) the party of memory and the party of hope.

The Democratic convention began Monday evening. In spite of the decay of conventions as political institutions, the parties outside the hall are still great fun. I wish that someone had asked me to go to Chicago (and was quite envious when Ted Sorensen appeared on TV later in the week commenting on the acceptance speeches).

The first night featured poignant talks by Christopher Reeve, who recently broke his neck in a riding accident, and Sarah Brady, whose husband Jim had been shot when Hinckley tried to kill Reagan. Both speeches were moving, but what they have to do with politics and the presidential election I cannot fathom. Later I participated (by telephone) in a discussion with Bob Shrum, Elaine Kamarck and Jack Beatty on Chris Lydon's PBS talk show.

I dined with Schuyler Chapin on Tuesday night and with Mimi Gilpatric and Tobie Roosevelt on Wednesday. I hurried home from that to catch Al Gore's acceptance speech, wondering whether any thoughts of mine had survived. Not many; though Al did say that, unlike Dole, he and Bill would be a bridge to the future and then used the Emerson quote. However, this passage was rather buried in the speech. It would have had more impact as a peroration. (Later I got a handwritten letter from Dan Pink: "Your discussion of nostalgia—and your wonderful quotation from Emerson—left a deep imprint on the final version of the speech." A nice note; but I could hardly have been alone in proposing the past v. future line.)

Clinton's acceptance was pedestrian. The best convention speeches were those of Ted Kennedy, Jesse Jackson and Mario Cuomo—none of them on prime time, however. The last day was made memorable by the exposure and downfall of Dick Morris—an event that caused much rejoicing in the circles in which I move.

On Tuesday 3 September we bombed Iraq. I suppose we had to do something to show disapproval of Saddam Hussein's latest villainy— his incursion into Kurdish territory, even if on the invitation of one Kurdish faction—but I wish that it had not been a unilateral U.S. action. Nor do we get much outside support from friends abroad, really only from the British. And no American, so far as I have noticed, has asked by what constitutional authority Clinton launched the attack.

Despite the efforts of historians, the war-making power seems to have moved so successfully from Congress, where the Constitution lodged it, to the White House that no one questions presidential war-making any more. Maybe two bombing raids are not considered to amount to war.

September 22

[On Monday the 16th] I heard the distressing and entirely unexpected news (from a *Times* obit writer) that Mac Bundy had died. I found myself considerably shaken by this.

[On Friday the 20th] I attended a memorial service for Jack Chancellor at the Century Club. In the drinking after, David Halberstam denounced me, genially but sternly, for having told the *Times* obituary writer that Mac Bundy was "a man of notable brilliance, integrity and patriotic purpose." As our exchanges continued, David's sternness overpowered his geniality. He remains impassioned and unforgiving about Vietnam, detesting Mac and Bob McNamara as much as ever in spite of their confessions of error, which he considers criminally belated.

On Saturday the 21st we flew to Boston for Mac's funeral. It was a beautiful day. The church—St. John's in Beverly Farms—was filled.

A reception followed at the Bundy house in Manchester (no hard liquor, alas; one needed a drink). Mary was wonderfully composed. Surprisingly few people were there from Harvard, a cold community, or from the Kennedy administration (but there will be a memorial service in New York later).

Mac had told me last spring that he was working on a book about Vietnam in which he would argue, among other things, that JFK would never have enlarged the war. I had a talk at the reception with Mac's collaborator, a young political scientist (Gordon Goldstein). He said that Mac had written about a hundred pages and had outlined the rest of the argument and that the manuscript was rescuable. I hope so. But Mary Acheson Bundy, Bill's wife, told me that Bill and Mac had disagreements about the book, presumably about what Kennedy would have done. I hope that Mac's essay will not end up unpublished, like Bill's own unfinished account of the evolution of Vietnam policy (which he kindly showed me twenty years ago when I was writing the RFK book).

John Kennedy Jr. had left a message on my voice mail begging me to do a piece on Mac for *George*. This I shall do, so I will hold further remarks for that. I remain much shaken by Mac's death.

October 22

On Saturday afternoon (the 19th) I was supposed to be driven to White Plains and fly from there to Lewisburg, Pennsylvania, and Bucknell University—all this to take part in one of Bill Buckley's *Firing Lines,* this one on the election. The Republican team consisted of Buckley, Henry Kissinger, Newt Gingrich, and Senator Kay Bailey Hutchison; the Democrats were George McGovern, Bob Shrum, Robert Andrews, a young congressman from New Jersey (and a Bucknell graduate), and me.

The rains came, airports closed, and my limousine was directed to take me directly to Bucknell. My driver had never been to Pennsylvania, and we drove for four hours through the blinding storm, arriving fifteen minutes late. Since the program was live on television, it had already started. However, it went on for two hours, so there was plenty of opportunity for participation. The discussion was animated and good-tempered. The Republicans hardly mentioned Bob Dole.

Henry Kissinger and I were matched with foreign policy as our subject. He began by noting that we had been friends for forty years. We had an exchange about the enlargement of NATO, which (I think) he did not necessarily win. When Henry criticized Clinton's Kurdish policy, I forebore from mentioning his own abandonment of the Kurds twenty years ago. Senator Hutchison was charming. Bill Buckley seemed incomprehensible and irrelevant; can he be losing his marbles? George was thoughtful and excellent, Bob Shrum tough and sardonic, and young Andrews held his own in this generally fast company.

Gingrich was the sharpest debater on the Republican side. His fault, as usual, was talking all the time. I brought down the house by interjecting, "Now we all know why Mr. Gingrich is called the Speaker." He grinned across the table and shouted, "Touche!" We talked for a moment afterward. *The Age of Jackson,* he said, had had a profound effect on him, and he identified with Jackson in his fight against the establishment. He also praised *The Vital Center* and *The Disuniting of America.* Naturally I liked him much better than I had expected to do. He reminded me of a puppy frisking about hoping to be patted. The Republicans should have nominated him. It would have been a much more interesting campaign, and he could hardly have done worse in the election.

November 6

We dined at Oscar de la Renta's on election night. It was a mostly Republican crowd, already accustomed if not reconciled to the idea of losing the presidency. The dinner was for the Agnellis, who are pro-Clinton. I sat on Marella's left with Gaby van Zuylen on my right. Gianni, who had spent the day with doctors, did not look as well as he had in Torino. Marella, I was told, has Parkinson's, but she remains her lovely self. Henry Kissinger asked me, "Do you know where I was 36 years ago tonight? ... At your house in Cambridge watching JFK win the election."

It was clear from the start that Clinton would win, and suspense involved only the Congress. In the end, the Republicans kept their control, which means a couple of years of investigations and gridlock, unless Clinton can nurture a liberal Republican revival. It was an undistinguished election, and it looks like an undistinguished four years ahead. But at least the Supreme Court has been saved.

November 22

The President said on election night, "Tonight we proclaim that the vital American center is alive and well." He continued to talk about the vital center for a couple of days until Bill Safire pointed out in a column where the phrase came from. Since then Clinton seems to have dropped the term.

The revival, after forty-seven years, is odd but not displeasing. Newt Gingrich of all people quoted approvingly from *The Vital Center* in an interview with Johnny Apple of the *Times* in June. Earlier in the year Irving Louis Horowitz of Rutgers said that his Transaction press would like to bring out a new edition. After negotiations with and through Houghton Mifflin, I recovered the rights and am today sending Transaction a new foreword. I remember how impressed I was in 1963 to be lunching with Walter Lippmann and recollecting that his *Preface to Politics* had come out half a century before. Now I am approaching that record myself.

The next morning we all attended Mac Bundy's memorial service at St. James's. Stephen Bundy gave a moving tribute to his father, touching delicately and in a veiled way on the family conference that led him to give up drinking (not that Mac ever drank heavily, but one or two drinks of bourbon were often too much). Recalling Mac's self-description as a "confirmed but unconvinced-Episcopalian," I wondered what he would have made of the service. Louis Auchincloss and I discussed Mac's agnosticism at the reception after the service. Louis recalled a Groton reunion luncheon where Mac was called upon to speak and held forth on the importance of religious faith. Louis said to him later, "I didn't know you cared. What was all that about?" Mac said, "Too many martinis."

On Monday night we had a really good dinner party—Carlos Fuentes (whose 68th birthday it was) and Sylvia, Edna O'Brien, Murray Kempton and Barbara Epstein, Aubrey (Abba) and Susie Eban, Eric Hobsbawm, Brian and Sidney Urquhart, Ronald and Betsy Dworkin. It was a tremendous success. Much general conversation: Eban on Israel and the Palestinians, "There is a tunnel at the end of the light"; Edna said that applied to Ireland too and explained why; Carlos talked with eloquence about Mexico and the conflict between the rising middle class and the old, arbitrary and corrupt political machinery; Ron Dworkin defending the Court and also advocating adoption of the parliamentary system; Eric describing the three breakdowns of the 20th century, 1918, 1945 and 1989, of which, he claimed, the last was the worst. His measure seemed to be industrial output which, he said, recovered much faster after the two world wars than it is recovering today. I said that 1918 seemed worse in its psychological shocks—the end of European self-confidence, the rising doubts about democracy, the emergence of fascism and communism. Eric still insisted that 1989 was the worst. Murray Kempton whispered to me, "the last Stalinist." True in a way, though I remain fond of Eric.

1997

January 7

In the afternoon, I received a call from the Vice President. After an exchange of political pleasantries (Jim Leach had just come out against the reelection of Newt Gingrich as speaker) and an expression of gratitude for the Emerson quote and the related theme I had contributed to his acceptance speech, Gore launched into the reason for his call. He is of course a computer freak who has long been going down the information superhighway, and he is now interested in the creation of a digital data base for the study of history. The computer's capacity to bring disparate facts together and to display them, he thinks, can yield productive insights for comparative historical analysis, revealing relationships and patterns not perceivable through other means. As an example, he said that Eric the Red and the Norsemen were exploring Greenland about the same time that the Maya civilization was disintegrating. Could the warming spells that encouraged Viking exploration have been a cause of the Maya decline and fall?

He wants names of historians who might be interested in meeting with cyberneticians and discussing the potentialities of the new technologies. I mentioned Bill McNeill and Jim Billington and later thought of David Hackett Fischer and Sam Huntington—all broad stroke men. I will forward him names in due course. It is interesting—Al Gore may be the first 21st century man.

January 30

[On January 9] the Century Club celebrated its one hundred and fiftieth anniversary. Those who had been members for fifty years or more were named and saluted. I just made this group, having been elected in 1947. I had planned to stay and hear the sesquicentennial oration by Brendan Gill (elected in 1946), but the intermediate speeches were so arch and unbearable, and my impatience with ceremonial is so acute, that I could take it no longer and stole away. Too bad: I heard later that Brendan was at his witty best.

Monday the 20th was inauguration. Clinton's address received generally bad notices. It didn't seem so bad to me. It was too obviously a committee-written product, but he spoke effectively in a couple of areas: race and government. He lost me in his rhapsodic utopianism about the 21st century—when "the laughter of children will once again be heard on our streets," etc.

The fact is that people always expect too much from inaugural addresses. But the inauguration is a ceremony of healing, of reunion after the electoral battle, of bringing people together: "We are all Republicans, we are all Federalists." Inaugural speeches are generally bland and banal. They are not vehicles for new policies or programs. People remember only five inaugural addresses in the whole stretch of American history: Jefferson's First, Lincoln's Second, FDR's First and Second, Kennedy's.

February 5

[On Sunday February 2] I called Pam in Paris and left a message on her voice mail. She called back that evening, but we were out (we still have her voice on our voice mail). Monday morning about 9:30 she called again; it was 3:30 P.M. in Paris. We had a long, chatty talk. She spoke about her weekend in London presiding over the christening of her new greatgranddaughter. I kidded her about being a greatgrandmother. She sounded spirited and cheerful, looking forward to returning to Washington and regaining control of her life, adding that she thought she had found a flat in Paris she could use as a *pied-à-terre*.

The next morning, as I was doing back exercises in front of a television set, I heard that she had suffered a massive brain hemorrhage at the Ritz health club (to which she must have gone soon after our conversation). We called Nicole Salinger in Paris, who provided further gloomy detail—"one chance in a hundred of surviving, and, if she should, the brain damage would be hopelessly disabling." Later that day they removed the life support system and she died without ever recovering consciousness.

In retrospect, I suppose there is consolation in the fact that she died at the height of her career and did so without pain and suffering, for she lost consciousness instantaneously. But Alexandra and I really couldn't—still can't—believe that she is gone. She was such a dear and generous friend and so vital a part of our lives. Marietta, Evangeline, Jackie, now Pamela—the glittering ladies are falling away.

March 29

On Wednesday the 12th the Council on Foreign Relations gave a book launch for a new *Encyclopedia of U.S. Foreign Relations*. They asked me to say a few words, presumably because I had contributed a couple of articles (on JFK and RFK). The event was billed in the invitation as a cocktail party. Then to my chagrin only white wine appeared. The theory that white wine is what one needs at the end of a long day seems to me one more evidence of the decadence of the younger generation. Citing the invitation, I asked for a real drink. Nick Rizopoulos succeeded in bringing out the hard stuff, to the gratification of others besides me. Dean Acheson, one man told me, had once agreed to speak at the Brookings Institution. When he discovered that only white wine was to be had, he said, "No martini—no speech." (He got the martini.)

April 13

On Friday the 4th I decided that, if Alexandra could go to Morocco, I could go to Washington and, persuaded by Liz Stevens, flew down in the late afternoon to attend a joint birthday party for George [Stevens] and Kati Marton, formerly married to Peter Jennings, now married to Dick Holbrooke. I always have a hard time finding the Stevens house on Avon Place in Georgetown. The taxi driver had no idea where it is, but I managed to steer him to Avon Place. Then, as usual, I could not find the driveway to the house. The taxi had evidently overshot on a one-way street, so I got out with my bag (I was staying with the Stevenses) and made my way by foot, finally spotting the house.

The door was open for arriving waiters, so I walked in and soon found Liz talking to a couple of people, whom she introduced as Secret Service. I then understood that the Clintons were coming and thought to myself how easy it would have been for assassins to enter the house as I had just done.

After washing up, I went downstairs to the library and found the Holbrookes, Dick, to my surprise, on crutches. He had torn his ligaments slipping on the ice in Telluride, it turned out, and has been laid up for a couple of weeks. Soon the Clintons arrived, Bill on crutches (after his recent fall in Florida). Dick has old-fashioned crutches fitting in the armpits; Bill has new crutches that you grip in your hands; so they went into a specialized discussion on the merits of the respective types.

Soon the room began to fill up—many familiar faces. I had a fairly long talk with the President, who looked as if he hadn't a care in the world, despite the disgusting revelations about fundraising in the White House. He wanted to talk about foreign policy—ironical, in view of his early preference for domestic policy; but foreign affairs are traditionally the escape hatch for Presidents blocked and frustrated at home. He praised Yeltsin at Helsinki—"Yeltsin looked a little pale and pasty, he has lost weight, but his mind was sharp, and he was in command." He also, to my surprise, had nice things to say about John Major, though not in an anti–Tony Blair sense. He was much impressed by the prime minister of Portugal, Antonio Guterres, with whom he said he had spent a couple of hours. He was also much impressed by my shirt, remarking on it twice.

I had a nice talk too with Hillary, who kissed me and reported charmingly on her trip to Africa. The Clintons had declined invitations for dinner but were obviously having a good time at the cocktail hour (not that either drank; both had soda water) and showed no desire to go home. Liz, fearful of the fate of the dinner, kept asking them to stay for dinner until they finally took the hint and departed. At dinner I sat between Madeleine Albright and Brooke Talbott, Strobe's wife. It was a splendid evening, and I was very glad that I had made the trip.

A word about the political situation. Since the election there has been a steady trickle of disclosures about the desperate methods Clinton endorsed and his people used to raise money for the 1996 campaign. Desperation is understandable in view of the need to match the Republicans (which they failed to do). But the methods were deplorable, especially the use of the White House—the people's house—as an instrument for fundraising. This may have been legal, but it is aesthetically displeasing and historically disgusting.

Clinton is rescued by the general cynicism these days about politicians. People think that he is something of a rogue, but a likable rogue and generally on their side. Voters feel they know the worst about him, and it is hard to imagine anything he could do—short of the Edwin Edwards eventuality of being caught in bed with a dead girl or a live boy—that would disillusion them any more than they are already disillusioned about all politicians.

The big loser is Al Gore. He was the Eagle Scout, Mr. Integrity, and his involvement in dubious fundraising is genuinely disillusioning, especially after his disastrous press conference where he shifted blame to his counsel and invoked, seven times, "controlling legal authority." That and the Buddhist temple will be chains around his neck, making it hard for him to call people in the future to raise funds for 2000.

May 30

On Wednesday the Leo Baeck Institute staged a luncheon at the Harvard Club. The question for discussion was "FDR and the Holocaust," and the cast consisted of Fritz Stern of Columbia, Henry Feingold, a CUNY historian, Bill vanden Heuvel, Sidney Zion, an inflammatory columnist for the *Daily News,* and me.

It is interesting the way responsibility for the holocaust has recently emerged as a dominating theme in discussions of the Second World War. More primary questions—like "how did we win the war?"—now recede into the background. Why after half a century has there been this sudden eruption of concern and recrimination? One result has been to excite Jewish resentment against FDR, for so many years a hero for American Jews. Bill vanden Heuvel and I have been engaged for some time in a running defense, or explanation, of FDR against hit-and-run critics.

Sidney Zion is a blatant example of the FDR-hating Jew, and he put on his usual act at this luncheon. He and other critics of FDR draw much of their indictment from books by David Wyman, an Amherst historian driven perhaps by an agonized Puritan conscience to condemn the Roosevelt administration for its supposed betrayal of the refugees. Fritz Stern was judicious and said that, if it had not been for FDR and the admission of Jewish refugees, he would not be there today. Henry Feingold wobbled all over the place, arguing for the importance of context and saying, in effect, that his heart belonged to Zion but his head was with the rest of us.

[On Thursday the 15th] Alice Mason gave one of her overcrowded parties, this time for Norman Mailer. We used to be invited to her parties twenty years ago until one evening when, having had too much to drink in the overlong cocktail hour, I complained loudly about her food (curry) and walked out with Alexandra before dinner was over. This was reprehensible behavior on my part, and she quite naturally struck us from the list. This was more than OK by me since I did not enjoy her parties, especially now that she had become Jimmy Carter's favorite New York hostess. We were invited this time only because it was a party for Norman, and he had put our names on the list.

July 20

On Monday the 16th we went to Washington for Kay Graham's 80th birthday. Princess Di was there. I headed over for closer inspection when I ran into Kitty Galbraith. I had talked to Ken, who is still convalescing, earlier in the day, and he asked me to look out for Kitty at the party, since she would not know many people. So I sacrificed Di to Kitty. But Di looked stunning at a distance. At dinner she was seated between Warren Buffett and Barry Diller. Ben Bradlee, who was at my table, and I agreed that she would have had a much better time sitting between us. Toasts after dinner were confined to the family and were mostly banal, except for Stevie Graham whose remarks were witty, ironical and hilarious.

August 22

On Wednesday the 13th Ted Kennedy called, saying that Caroline Kennedy Schlossberg was giving a small dinner for the Clintons on 20 August in Jackie's house on the Vineyard. She could only have twelve people. There would probably be six Kennedys (Caroline and Ed; John Jr. and Carolyn; Ted and Vicky) plus two Clintons. They wanted to invite us, and they thought they would invite Mike Nichols and Diane Sawyer. Remembering that Mike has just finished the film of Joe Klein's *Primary Colors* and had warned Kay Graham not to ask him to any affairs with the Clintons, I passed this message along to Ted. Thinking of the expenses involved in flying to the Vineyard, I said that we would not be able to come either. He asked for other suggestions. I mentioned the Cronkites, the Mailers, the Goodwins, but none seemed quite right.

Jean was in Bridgehampton. When I told her about the invitation, she upbraided me, asking how could I as an American historian pass up a chance to spend a relaxed evening with the President of the United States. On reflection, I decided that she was right. I called Ted in Hyannis Port and said that, if the quota had not been filled, we would love to come. He said fine.

We left on Wednesday morning, the 20th, flying first to Boston and then to the Vineyard.

The two guests besides the Kennedys, Clintons and ourselves turned out to be Ken Burns, the documentary film producer, and Jane Alexander, the actress and head of the embattled National Endowment for the Arts, both intelligent and attractive people. After a moment, the Clintons appeared. They had been cruising with the Kennedys on Ted's boat (it was a sullen and chilly day). Bill was casually dressed—a T shirt and dark pants. He had lost weight, 15–20 pounds, since his accident, and looked trim. Hillary wore an ankle-length peasant-type skirt.

Drinks were served before dinner, but very slowly. The Clintons had Perrier. Ted, Alexandra and I were the only ones to have spirits. No bourbon was available, but I polished off a Scotch on the rocks rather quickly and waited for the butler to offer to refill my glass. No offer was forthcoming. I was about to ask Ed Schlossberg for another drink when dinner was announced.

In the meantime, there was general conversation, mostly about environmental problems. Both Clintons displayed consuming interest and impressive knowledge—much talk about "aquifers," and the malign impact of jet fuel on the water table, as around the Otis Air Force base. At dinner I sat between Carolyn Kennedy, John's wife, and Vicky Kennedy. Unfortunately it was a rectangular rather than a round table, so general conversation was difficult. Ted, who was in splendid form, did his best to open up the talk. The President spoke about his campaign for voluntary national standards in schools and the bizarre arguments the campaign was encountering. There was also talk about a skeleton recently unearthed in the Northwest and identified as Caucasian of a vintage to suggest that Caucasians had lived on the North American continent before Indians had arrived from Asia. This apparently upsets the Indians. Once again both Clintons displayed impressive technical control of the subjects under discussion.

After dinner I had a private talk with the President. I brought up Cuba. He said that of course he had no intention of signing the Helms-Burton act, but, when Castro shot down the two planes, this left him no alternative. "I don't understand why Castro did this," he said. "We had been in backstairs communication. He knew where we stood and where we were heading. We had negotiated several agreements, and he kept them meticulously. Then all of a sudden he did this, undermining everything we had been doing." I said that maybe Castro understood that the embargo gave him an all purpose alibi and protected his power and his revolution. Clinton said that he would continue to do what he could within his legal authority to suspend the more burdensome provisions of Helms-Burton.

"Another question I want to do something about," he said, "is incarceration. We have more people in prison than any other democracy. This may not be altogether bad. The decline in violent crime may be due in part to the fact that so many violent people are now behind bars. But there are too many things wrong with our prisons."

Apparently, when the Clintons had visited Jackie on their last Vineyard vacation, they had much enjoyed playing a certain game and had expressed a wish to play it again. The game is based on *Bartlett's Familiar Quotations*. One person picks out a quotation from *Bartlett's* and gives the author's name and dates to the other players. Then each player must invent a quotation to be plausibly ascribed to the author. The leader then reads the invented quotations mixing in the authentic quotation; and the group votes on which of the quotations is the real one. The game gives ample scope to individual creativity and turned out to be considerable fun. We all made up plausible quotes from Strindberg and Peter Ustinov as well as from some of *Bartlett's* unknowns.

We had asked the taxi to come at ten, supposing that the Clintons would have been tired by the afternoon cruise. But at eleven they showed no signs of wishing to depart. Nevertheless we felt we could not ask the taxi driver (a young woman) to wait any longer. This, I fear, broke up the party; but Ken Burns assured us the next morning that everyone felt it was time to go anyway. It was an immensely pleasant, even cozy, evening. The Clintons could not have been more relaxed and friendly. Alexandra, who has been quite hostile to Bill, was considerably disarmed by him. They both no doubt have their darksides, but they also both have great intelligence and charm and a certain infectious joie de vivre.

October 4

[On] Thursday the 11th [of September] we left for London. My mission was to give the James Bryce Lecture under the sponsorship of the Institute of United States Studies (Gary McDowell) at the University of London. The lecture took place at 6:30 in the Great Hall in Lincoln's Inn. Lady Thatcher, who had inaugurated the lectureship the year before, was in the chair. She presented me to the audience with a marvelously generous introduction (which she probably regretted later). I then gave the talk—"Has Democracy a Future?" It went over, I thought well, though I feared that my remarks on the dangers of unbridled capitalism would irritate Lady T. When I finished, Ray Seitz, the former ambassador, proposed, with elegance and eloquence, a resolution of thanks. Naturally I changed my mind at once about Seitz, of whom for some reason (I think his quick attack on the Clinton administration when he was not extended in London) I did not have a high opinion.

Lady T. was only mildly reproachful to me. "There is no such thing as unbridled capitalism," she said. "The free market cannot work without rules, especially the rule of law and the sanctity of contract." I said, "That of course is true, but rules change. The 20th century market is different from—and more humane than—the 19th century market because the state has established new rules. 'Unbridled capitalism' is a relative term, and I only meant to emphasize the changes in the rules of the marketplace."

She did not seem to hold my heresies against me. Indeed, she clasped my arm, and then my hand, as we made our way across the courtyard to the Old Hall where the dinner was held. I sat at Lady T.'s left; on my other side was Antonia. They spoke to each other politely but warily. It was a good evening—indeed, I felt, as I rarely do, that my performance was a triumph.

The next day as Alexandra and I were strolling down Bond Street we ran into Nico Henderson who remarked that he had never seen Lady T. so "benign." I mentioned this in a letter I sent Ray Seitz thanking him for his remarks. He replied re my talk, "Gary has told me of the exceptionally high demand for copies. It was stimulating, challenging and a tribute to both you and the audience. The Good Lady T., however, was steaming about your remarks on capitalism, and afterwards, she threw me against a stone wall and began lashing me as the first available American. This doesn't quite fit with Nico's description of Lady T. as 'benign,' but he was probably using the term relatively."

October 30

I am now subsiding, more or less cheerfully, into octogenarianism after a week of giddy celebration of the implacable 80th birthday. You can't fight chronology. But I detect no marked diminution in energy or celerity. My hearing is declining a bit, and I must consult a doctor about that. The chief irritation is the decay of short-term memory. I go into another room to find something and then forget for a moment what I went into the room to do. Also my manual dexterity, always lamentable, has decreased; I keep dropping things or placing them out of balance so they fall on the floor, where to retrieve them I must go down on hands and knees; I can't bend over without straining my back.

But the routine of life remains unchanged. I still awake between 5:30 and 6, ride five miles on a stationary bicycle in my bathroom, reading the while, then go through the morning papers (*Times* and *Herald*

Tribune), make myself breakfast (ordinarily a glass of grapefruit and cranberry juice, vanilla yogurt and one piece of toast) and cross the courtyard to work. We ordinarily go to bed between 11 and 12.

[On Wednesday the 22nd] we went to a party for Sally Quinn and her new book. Betsy Cronkite was there and told me the following story. She was sitting next to Ted Kennedy at my birthday dinner, and a waiter accidentally spilled some red wine on her dress. Ted rose to the situation magnificently, she said, produced napkins, water, white wine, and did everything possible to limit the damage. The next day she told her friends how gallant Ted had been. A few days later she ran into somebody who said, "I hear that Ted Kennedy was very drunk at the Schlesinger party and spilled red wine all over your dress."

November 14

It has been a busy fortnight—grievous (Isaiah's [Berlin] death) and combative (Seymour Hersh's book).

I had a long conversation [at a one-year anniversary party for JFK Jr.'s magazine *George*] with Walter Isaacson, the editor of *Time,* about the Seymour Hersh's book, *The Dark Side of Camelot,* which he had read and which will be *Time*'s cover story in the next issue. Though Time Warner owns Little, Brown, the publisher, Walter, who thinks it a terrible book, has asked Alan Brinkley to review it. The book has been distributed under seal to the bookstores, the seal not to be broken until next Monday.

I received a call from ABC asking whether I would appear on their news discussing the Hersh book. I said that I could not comment on a book I had not read. They agreed to send over the book. I read it that night. On Sunday morning a TV crew appeared and I was interviewed for forty minutes or so. That evening ABC News allotted me fourteen seconds, followed by several minutes of Hersh. I should have realized that ABC has a heavy investment in Hersh (they are planning a Peter Jennings special on the book) and would not be inclined to give time to those capable of discrediting him.

This was an exceptionally busy four days. But rather to my surprise I was elated by the various pressures and deadlines. It reminded me of the old days at the White House. And the excitement continued. On Monday NBC called and asked whether I would appear with Hersh on the *Today* Show. He had appeared that morning and was due to appear again on Tuesday. I said of course I would appear with him and asked them to fax the transcript of his remarks (an invaluable invention, the fax machine).

The transcript soon appeared. I noted the following with interest: "I had Arthur Schlesinger described to me, saying publicly that the election [1960] couldn't have been stolen in Illinois because core corruption unions are controlled by Mayor Daley, not by the mob, and I want to recommend a book to him. It's called 'An Enemy Within' by Robert Kennedy, published in 1961 or '62 that describes mob influence in the election." Of course *The Enemy Within* came out in February 1960, months before JFK was nominated and more months before the election. Apart from the incoherence of his remarks, the truth is simply not in Hersh.

As I was getting ready to deal with Hersh, NBC called again, this time to say that they would not need me; Hersh would appear on Tuesday by himself. I watched him the next morning. He touched on me again, saying that I knew about JFK and girls and adding darkly that he knew that I knew that he knew. In the meantime, CBS called and asked whether I would appear with Hersh. The same thing happened: a few hours later they called to say that they had decided to have Hersh appear by himself. Obviously he is afraid to appear with me. But why should NBC and CBS seek to promote an ABC project? One would think that they would welcome the opportunity to discredit Hersh.

December 4

On Saturday the 16th we dined at Mortimer's with Elizabeth Drew, David Webster and my new friend Joan Didion. John Gregory Dunne was in the hospital, rather to my relief because, if he had come, we would certainly have a wrangle about the Sy Hersh book, Dunne having a black-Irish-envy hatred of the Kennedys. Joan Didion seems to have forgiven all my heresies and now kisses when we meet. Naturally I think much better of her.

ABC had asked me whether I would appear face-to-face with Hersh on *Good Morning America* on Thursday—the day when ABC will show a two-hour Peter Jennings special based on Hersh's book. I said I would, though I was skeptical that Hersh would agree, since he had declined to go on with me when it had been proposed by NBC and CBS. This time he consented. We were kept apart on Thursday morning, like boxers before a big fight, in separate dressing rooms. We shook hands when we met under the lights and shook hands more coldly at the end. He is a fluent, impassive, unstoppable talker and hogged too much of the very short time. I managed to insert some points but fumbled others. Our eight minutes of joy passed like a flash and left both of us, or at least me, deeply unsatisfied.

I also made the mistake of accepting make up (a powdered face). Alexandra recorded the exchange, and I was appalled to see how pale, wan and aged I looked. But I must look old, even though I don't feel it at all. Young women now stand up in buses and offer me their seats— dangerous evidence of apparent debility.

December 10

Monday, the 8th, was a typical wasted day at a time in life when I have too few days to waste: in the morning, I attended a meeting of the executive committee of the Franklin and Eleanor Roosevelt Institute; in the afternoon, I spoke at a memorial service for Mina Rees, the first president of the CUNY Graduate School; in the early evening, we gave a cocktail party to launch Hugh [Thomas]'s new book, *The Slave Trade*.

I was enraged by Simon & Schuster's refusal to pay for this party; even more enraged when, after refusing, they tried to put their name on the invitation as one of the inviters and also to add a dozen S&S employees to the invitation list. I said to Michael Korda, who had the impertinence to come to the party his firm declined to subsidize, "*The Slave Trade* is a distinguished book. It is probably the only book that S&S publishes this year that will still be read a decade from now. Yet you people are so cheap that you won't come up with a few hundred bucks to give the author a party." He said feebly, "I have no control over these decisions. I am only the editor-in-chief." Actually it was only a fair party; somehow it did not jell. Hugh and I are sharing the costs ($350 each).

[On December 9] the Greens gave a dinner for Betty Bacall who was honored last weekend at the Kennedy Center. Earlier in the day I received a message from Bill Richardson's office inviting Alexandra and me to a reception for the President at ten o'clock.

I went off to see the wizard shortly after ten; Alexandra and Betty came along later, arriving just as the Richardson party was breaking up. I was struck by the absence of security. There were plenty of Secret Service people around, but Barbara Walters, whom I ran into in the Waldorf lobby, and I took the elevator up to the 42nd floor and entered the Richardson apartment without anyone checking our names against a list or indeed showing any visible interest.

There were perhaps fifty people milling about. The ones I knew were mostly newspaper and TV journalists (Dan Rather, Pete Hamill, Roone Arledge, Mort Zuckerman, Ed Bradley, John Gregory Dunne, etc.) plus writers like Ed Doctorow and Joan Didion.

The President was his usual ebullient self, still relatively slim, ruddy in face, overflowing with detailed accounts of the way the mayors of New Orleans and Houston had reduced juvenile delinquency by curfews, soccer teams, swimming matches, etc. He was especially eloquent on the subject of Bob Lanier in Houston—a rich Texan, "the last man you would think a Democrat," but a very effective liberal mayor, under whose leadership the voters of Houston (70 percent white) rejected a referendum abolishing affirmative action and elected Houston's first black mayor. He rejoices in talking about problems and solutions. There was one flash of the bitterness against the press so dominant in his first term. Recollecting the incident when he allegedly shut down a runway at the Los Angeles airport while getting a $200 haircut, he said, "Of course it was a damned lie. But did anyone print a correction? Not that you would notice it. NBC finally said something about it a year later."

I had a nice talk with Hillary, who looked very pretty. Someone mentioned the National Endowment for the Arts. I said, "I wonder when Jane Alexander's successor will be appointed." Hillary said dryly, "We have someone in mind, but first we have to check his record in the Merchant Marine"—a nice reference to the unfortunate W. Larry Lawrence, who falsely claimed Merchant Marine service on the Murmansk run during the war and, on the basis of that claim, was buried in Arlington cemetery (from which he will soon be disinterred).

Planning for the millennium is much on Hillary's mind. I hope I will be around to see the results. As we left, Clinton collared us and said, "Have you played Bartlett's recently," referring to the game we played at Caroline's house this summer. Then he collared Pete Hamill and described the game with great relish. He is a character.

December 27

On Wednesday, JFK Jr. phoned about something. Then he expressed his perplexity over the popularity of the Hersh book. "Is there a real backlash against Daddy? Or is it just a perennial interest in anything about the Kennedys?"

1998

❖

January 23

The political picture has changed with startling rapidity, and we may now be seeing the downfall of the Clinton presidency. Bill has been riding high recently. He has never stood better in the polls. Even before the State of the Union message next week, he seemed to have seized the legislative initiative. The Republicans are in notable disarray. Paula Jones lingered on the horizon, but she did not appear an immediate threat. One felt that the voters had grown accustomed to the image of Clinton as a skirt-chaser and accepted him as President none the less.

Now a former White House intern, Monica Lewinsky, emerges. In tapes made by a ci-devant friend, she claims an affair with Clinton and claims further that the President and Vernon Jordan instructed her, in case word of the affair got out, to swear under oath that it never took place—which she subsequently has done. Clinton and Jordan promptly denied both the affair and the suborning of a witness. This might well expose them to charges of perjury and obstruction of justice.

If Lewinsky's tapes hold up, Clinton will be in real trouble. It is even suggested that Clinton distinguishes between oral sex and intercourse; only the second, in his view (it is said), would constitute a sexual relationship. Clinton's Houdini-like skill as an escape artist can never be underrated.

If Clinton is forced to resign, it will be because of self-inflicted wounds. In the meantime, his authority in foreign affairs will be seriously weakened. [Benjamin] Netanyahu and Saddam Hussein must be overjoyed.

January 24

The uproar continues. Monica Lewinsky's lawyer appears to be offering Kenneth Starr an account of her claimed affair with Clinton in exchange for immunity from prosecution for denying it; but Starr wants her to go farther and accuse Clinton and Vernon Jordan of telling her to commit perjury. Clinton is retreating into legalisms, and the White House staff is reportedly sinking into demoralization.

A piece in the 26 January *U.S. News & World Report* entitled "Learning from Big Jumbo: Why Clinton scrutinizes presidents obscure and legendary" describes Bill's interest in presidential history. It also prompts me to think about my own puzzling relations with him. He is always cordial when we meet; Hillary even more so. But I cannot help feeling that for some reason the President is suspicious of me.

He holds periodic White House dinners with historians and political scientists to discuss presidential problems. Despite practical experience in the White House, academic expertise on the presidency and a long relationship with the Democratic party, I am never invited. It can't be just my advanced age. My dear friend Sam Beer, who is 88, was asked to the most recent session three weeks ago. Nor have Alexandra and I ever in six years been invited to a White House dinner except for the farewell dinner when Pam Harriman went to Paris, and then she put our names on the list.

Why should this be? Because I traveled to New Hampshire before the 1992 primary to promote the candidacy of Mario Cuomo? Or because of my contempt for the Democratic Leadership Council crowd? Or simply because he just doesn't like, or trust, me? Anyway it is all very peculiar.

Back to Clinton's predicament. I do not think that the Republicans will agitate for impeachment. If they are sensible, they will prefer to have a wounded and discredited Clinton in the White House than a fresh, clean Gore who would have two years to establish himself as President and would therefore be much harder to beat in 2000. If Clinton stays, Gore in 2000 can be portrayed as the heir and defender of a tarnished administration.

June 22

47 years ago today Adolf Hitler attacked Joseph Stalin. I still remember sitting breathlessly around the radio listening to Churchill's magnificent response. Things are far less exciting in 1998. Kenneth Starr attacks Bill Clinton; not quite the same. No one knows what Monica Lewinsky will do next. Not many care. These are drab tales and drab times.

August 5

Monica Lewinsky has made a deal with Kenneth Starr. In exchange for transactional immunity for herself and her mother, she will tell all about her relationship with the President (and produce all, including the famous semen-stained dress, which seems to exist after all, and her collection of notes and telephone tapes). Republican judges have stripped Clinton of privacy protections available to most Americans: his White House lawyers, his political advisers and Secret Service personnel are now compelled to testify. Clinton himself was about to be subpoenaed when he agreed to testify (at a distance) before the grand jury. Democratic pols are advising him to confess, tell the truth, apologize and ask forgiveness.

The White House continues to insist that the President has told the truth and will keep on denying that he had sexual relations with Lewinsky. I wonder whether there is not some ambiguity in the term "sexual relations." Oral sex can leave a woman's virginity intact; penetration is a completed sexual relationship. Norman Mailer says that there is an old Arkansas saying: "It ain't a sin if you don't stick it in." Newt Gingrich told a mistress that he preferred a blow job because then he could truthfully say that he had not slept with her. The President may well mean one thing by "sexual relations"; the special prosecutor another.

September 19

Life has been busy since my last entry—busy for me, and far busier for Bill Clinton. I no longer know what to expect. I am less sure than I have been that he will not face impeachment. Practical-minded Republicans don't want to jump-start Gore into the White House, but zealots are out for blood, and, once initiated, an impeachment campaign may develop a life and momentum of its own. I don't think Clinton will resign, unless, like Nixon, he is faced with certain conviction by the Senate. Resignation would seem to Clinton a vindication of Starr, whom he hates (understandably; so do most Americans). My guess would still be a resolution of censure somewhere down the road.

There is an evident disjunction between the media people, who are obsessed with the scandals and many of whom manifest deep dislike for Clinton, and the ordinary people, who may gulp in the endless flow of stories but still like Clinton, want him to stay on as President and wish the scandals would go away. His approval rating for presidential performance remains high, even as his character and morals seem to be heading toward a free fall. Blacks are especially united and vehement in his support.

Starr's report lived up to anticipations. It is indeed the most salacious public document in the history of the republic. Next Monday the tapes of Clinton's grand jury testimony will be released, complete, I suppose, with a nasty parade of anatomical detail. This will certainly rebound against Starr, who is already exposed as the nation's number one pornographer, but it may excite a wave of popular revulsion against Clinton too.

November 2

The journal gap is inexcusable, but it is evidence of the hopeless busyness of my life, not in the least reduced by octogenarianism.

We left Saturday night, the 19th [of September], for Rome, arriving Sunday morning to be met by George McGovern's car. George is now our ambassador to the Food and Agricultural Organization and lives in a charming rustic mansion in a park on the outskirts of Rome.

On Monday we inspected the Baths of Caracalla, which is within walking distance of George's house. As we walked, we reminisced. George said that he doubted that RFK, if he had lived, would have won the nomination in 1968. The administration simply had too many delegates locked up for Hubert. Even in New York, without a winner-take-all rule, a large bloc would have been pledged for Humphrey. As for McCarthy, George recalled his 75th birthday luncheon where Bob Dole spoke and where Gene was accidentally lunching in the same restaurant. George asked Gene whether he would say a few words. As he walked away, he overheard Gene whispering to his luncheon companion, "Do I really want to say a few words to celebrate the birthday of the man who destroyed American liberalism?"

We also talked about the incident some years ago on the MacNeil-Lehrer show when John McCain harshly questioned McGovern's patriotism, saying something to the effect that he would still be in a Viet Cong prison camp if George had been elected in 1972. George started to reply that, if he had had his way, McCain would never have gone to Vietnam and was preparing to mention his own record as a decorated bomber pilot in the Second World War when Robin MacNeil interrupted and brought the interview to an end.

McCain is a loose cannon. He has commendably defied his party on campaign finance, but he is also capable of bizarre behavior. Recently, speaking at a Republican dinner, he told the following so-called joke: why is Chelsea Clinton so ugly? because she is the illegitimate child of Hillary Clinton and Janet Reno. This plus his reputedly wayward sex life will surely destroy his evident presidential aspirations.

[Back in New York] Sean Wilentz, a bright and lively historian at Princeton, had been talking to me during the week of the 12th [of October] about the constitutional implications of lowering the bar to impeachment. We decided that this is a point that might well be made publicly by a group of historians. Sean drafted a statement along these lines; I revised it a bit; we called the group Historians in Defense of the Constitution and added Vann Woodward to the team of sponsors. Then we circulated the statement during the week of the 19th. The response was astonishing, as if historians had been waiting the chance to express their outrage over Kenneth Starr. In a few days, aided by E-mail and the Internet, over 400 historians were on board.

On Wednesday the 28th I went to Washington to join with Sean and Vann in a press conference. I thought it went well, though David Broder wrote in Sunday's *Washington Post* that I sounded "at times like James Carville in cap and gown," and Bill Safire writes in today's *Times* that "my long-time pal Arthur Schlesinger" is heading a group of "Lefty Historians to Save Clinton." One result has been an invitation to appear as a witness at the first impeachment hearing of the House Judiciary Committee next Monday. After the press conference, Robert joined us for luncheon. Vann and I returned to New York and appeared that evening with Sean Wilentz in Washington to good effect (I think) on the Charlie Rose show.

This is election day. There are indications of a backlash against Starr & Co., but there are even stronger indications of widespread and generalized indifference and disgust, which would mean a large stay-at-home vote. My guess is that the Republicans will not gain more than ten seats in the House and three in the Senate. This result would be accounted a Democratic victory and would probably end the impeachment drive. In the meantime, I discover that I am expected to file my prepared statement with the House Judiciary Committee by Thursday at 5 P.M. (in 100 copies). To work: fortunately the NY Society Library had copies of Raoul Berger and Charles Black on impeachment, and I have them now.

November 7

I forgot to note in the preceding despatch that Greg Craig called the day after the *Times* ran the historians' ad to say how delighted the Clintons were. I hope they remember who helped in their time of adversity. The DLC crowd and the cowardly-Liebermans ran for cover. It has been the liberals—Ted Kennedy, Barney Frank, etc.—who have manned the gates.

As for politics, the backlash came through. Tuesday night was an eminently satisfactory time, as surprising and as enjoyable as the Truman victory just fifty years ago. The Democrats gained five seats in the House (Dick Morris had predicted a Republican gain of forty), and the Republicans gained none in the Senate. New York was finally liberated from the egregious [Alfonse] D'Amato (whose concession speech was the most likable thing he has done). We rejoiced at dinner and thereafter at the vanden Heuvels with Lauren Bacall, Jean Smith, Carlos and Sylvia Fuentes and Liz Stevens, later to be joined by Bernard and Pat Williams and Cyrus and Caroline Ghani.

The next morning I struggled to write my testimony to be delivered next Monday before the House Judiciary Committee. Sean Wilentz arranged a conference call with two other witnesses: Larry Tribe of the Harvard Law School and Jack Rakove of Stanford. This was helpful. Larry persuaded me to modify my rejection of censure. "I agree with you entirely on principle," he said, "but the Republicans need a face-saving way out, and this may be the practical means of getting it all behind us." I circulated my testimony that afternoon. Tribe, faxing me his testimony the next day, added a note: "I like your statement a lot, Arthur. It makes mine seem fussy by comparison, but I guess both styles are needed." Historians v. lawyers.

Thursday the 5th was the day of the endowment medals [in Washington, D.C.]. The medallists were all put up at the Hay-Adams, a hotel, alas, in decline. We found plenty of pals: among those receiving the National Humanities Medal: Ed Doctorow, Skip Gates, Vartan

Gregorian, Steve Ambrose, Garry Wills (and among new people, Diana Eck of Harvard, a bright and charming historian of religion; also, with her female partner, the co-masters—co-mistresses?—of Lowell House; when I reflect that sixty years ago Kenneth Murdock had to resign as master of Leverett House because of his divorce, the appointment of lesbians as house masters does represent a considerable change in mores). Among the National Medal of Arts recipients were Philip Roth, Gregory Peck, Roberta Peters and Gwen Verdon. Much speculation as to why Doctorow made the Humanities list and Roth the Arts list since they are both in the same line of work.

The medallists were transported by bus from the Hay-Adams to the White House. With one delay after another, including being "canined" by drug- or bomb-sniffing dogs, it took an hour and a half before we were admitted. We could have crawled across Lafayette Square on hands and knees rather more quickly.

Once inside, we were grouped alphabetically according to families while Bill and Hillary made the rounds. All five of my children were there; Peter unfortunately had commitments in Los Angeles. With my dislike of ceremonial occasions, I stupidly had not thought that the kids would be interested in coming; but indignation, communicated through Alexandra, opened my eyes, and Joy Evans of the Endowment for the Humanities was most helpful in putting them belatedly on the list. The Clintons were cordial when they reached us, obviously exhilarated by the election.

We adjourned to a tent on the White House lawn. Hillary introduced her husband. The arts, she said, had brought them together. An early date was to see Rothko paintings and Henry Moore sculptures at a Yale museum. When they arrived, they found that the employees were on strike and the museum was closed. But Bill routed out someone inside the museum and talked their way in. "After that," Hillary said, "I began to understand that he could persuade anybody of anything." She then presented her husband, who began by saying: "Just my luck that Hillary recalls my crossing a picket line when the president of the AFL-CIO is in the audience."

The citations were felicitous. Skip Gates told me that those of the five historians were written by a Harvard history PhD named Widmer now working at the White House. The ceremonies ended a little after noon. Alexandra and I joined the children who had meanwhile picked up Greg Craig, Christina's old friend. Greg walked with us to the Corcoran Gallery, where we were to lunch. I asked him, "Has Starr shot his wad?" Greg said that he expected a couple of more indictments in the next day or so. (None has been announced as of today.) Luncheon at the Corcoran was somewhat wearisome except for witty remarks by Garrison Keillor, as master of ceremonies.

In the evening the Clintons put on a formal dinner for the medallists at the White House. I was seated on Hillary's left; Garry Wills on her right. Greg Peck sat opposite Hillary across the round table. I said to her, "You have no idea what you have done for the morale of scholarship by surrounding yourself with a couple of historians when you could have had Gregory Peck." Hillary said, "But now I can spend the dinner looking at Gregory Peck."

Hillary is a woman of incisive intelligence, formidable articulateness, impressive coolness and great charm; also very easy to talk to. I observed that Howell Raines, the editor of the editorial page of the *New York Times,* was almost as obsessed with the Starr prosecution as Starr himself and wondered why this should be so. Was there some obscure southern grudge at work? She said, "I think it may be a class thing. Someone recently told me of a conversation in which Raines was holding forth on the President's various sins. Her informant, knowing that Raines is a great huntin' fishin' southerner, said, 'But Bill Clinton likes hunting too.' Raines replied scornfully, 'Clinton's hunting is not the real thing,' " implying that Clinton was just an Arkansas redneck.

I made the point that the liberals had stood by Clinton while the DLC people had deserted him and described the miserable [Joe] Lieberman as a "sanctimonious prick." Hillary said, "Well, he is certainly sanctimonious," but showed no eagerness to pursue this line of thought.

After dinner we moved back to the tent where an orchestra played the "Rhapsody in Blue" and Aaron Copland's "Variations on a Shaker

Melody." We sat directly behind the Clintons. Greg Peck, I was glad to see, sat next to Hillary. Greg is a very nice man, a real gent, and I had several agreeable talks with him during the diverse festivities.

November 12

On Monday Alexandra and I caught the 6:30 A.M. shuttle to Washington. We proceeded in due course to Room 2141 in the Rayburn Building, where the hearing before the Judiciary Committee's Subcommittee on the Constitution on "The Background and History of Impeachment" began rather promptly at 9:30. The Republican majority had ten witnesses; the Democratic minority had eight; one witness (Michael Gerhardt of William & Mary) was neutral. Most of the witnesses were lawyers; Forrest McDonald of the University of Alabama (pro-impeachment), Jack Rakove of Stanford (anti) and I were the historians.

The hearing began with statements by members of the subcommittee, all of whom took firm and emphatic positions pro or anti. Since they had already made up their minds, it was not clear why they had summoned us except to hear arguments that would be reassuring and reinforcing. Each member, I believe, could say that he or she "came out by the same door as in I went."

I was (luckily) in the morning panel and the seventh to testify. The witnesses were each allotted ten minutes. Our prepared statements are to be part of the hearing record. After the members of the subcommittee and the ten morning witnesses had performed, it was 12:30, and the committee adjourned for half an hour. Alexandra and I snatched a bite at a government cafeteria.

The hearing resumed at 1 P.M. with questions by the subcommittee to the witnesses. Much of this was done politely, but I fell afoul of a self-righteous congressman from South Carolina named Bob Inglis. I had made the flip statement that "most people have lied about their sex lives at one time or another. . . . Gentlemen always lie about their sex lives," etc.

With elaborate sarcasm, Inglis said, "That is typical of these sophisticated people. It is Schlesinger's view that you can lie as you choose because it just doesn't matter. Lie, lie, lie—that is what Schlesinger advocates. Lie if you're the President. Lie in a case involving sex. Lie, lie, lie! After all, he says, gentlemen do that, and you'd just not be with it if you didn't lie about sex. . . . But we simple, unsophisticated people down in South Carolina believe in telling the truth." I said, "May I comment?" Inglis said, "In a moment"; but he had no intention of letting me reply and continued talking until his time was up.

Charles T. Canady of Florida, the chairman of the subcommittee, though very definitely pro-impeachment, conducted the proceedings fairly, and when I asked again to comment, he let me speak. I said that Inglis had given "a highly sophisticated misrepresentation of my position," which was that lying, while "highly reprehensible," was not necessarily in itself an impeachable offense. Had I known that Inglis was the man whom Fritz Hollings had just beaten for senator (as Barney Frank told me after the hearing), I would have praised the judgment of the voters of South Carolina.

Inglis in his prolonged rant said at one point that Schlesinger has "a great deal of sophistication, but very little common sense." Maxine Waters of California, who came on next, began by addressing me: "It is only someone who has no sense who would accuse you of having no common sense." Afterward several members of the subcommittee came up and semi-apologized for Inglis's performance.

The Republicans on the committee, from Henry Hyde and Canady down, seem determined to press for impeachment—a determination quite unaffected by the election. They seem to have lost touch with reality.

The *Times* made the hearing its lead story the next morning (Tuesday the 10th)—a very good story by Linda Greenhouse. C-Span and CNN had carried the hearings, and for a few hours I became a local hero. People stopped me on the streets, and I was almost applauded when I entered the Century Club.

November 23

My recent exploits provoke attacks from all sides. It seems like old times.

On the left, Christopher Hitchens: "The most eminent 'signer' of this declaration [of Historians in Defense of the Constitution] was Arthur Schlesinger, Jr., who was not known to me before as a historian of any kind, but who presumably squeezed in as a composer of profiles in Democratic opportunism. No sooner was the election a thing of the past— history, you might say—than Schlesinger appeared in full fig at the White House, along with the more energetic and deserving Fats Domino, to receive the National Humanities Medal" (*Nation,* 30 November).

On the right, Taki: "that arch pseud and fraud Arthur Schlesinger, Jr. . . . up in front of the judiciary committee this week raving that everyone lies about sex. In this he is right. But everyone is not President" (*Spectator,* 14 November).

Then a long, sarcastic and nasty piece in the *Financial Times* of 21–22 November by someone named Michael Steinberger, the thesis of which can be summarized by the headlines: "LOYAL KEEPER OF THE KENNEDY FLAME. Arthur Schlesinger has defended Kennedy's reputation at no little cost of his own. . . . He has been denounced as a 'servant,' a 'poodle,' and one of the US's 'more purchasable intellectuals.' " This is the general line, though a nice quote is included from Sean Wilentz: "He is the great liberal Democratic intellectual of our time."

And Stuart Taylor Jr. in the 11 November *National Journal*: "The celebrated historian Arthur Schlesinger Jr. . . . distilled the essence of his scholarly advice into one short sentence: 'Gentlemen always lie about their sex lives.' Always. Even when ordered by a judge to answer a sexual harassment plaintiff's questions under oath. Even to a criminal grand jury," etc. I guess flippancy is a great mistake.

I have not enjoyed such a fusillade for a third of a century. It makes me feel young again.

2000

January 22

I have plowed steadily ahead on [my memoirs,] and now have two, or possibly three, chapters to go. I must finish by early February for the book to be published this year, or so Houghton Mifflin tells me. My preferred title is *Innocent Beginnings,* but my literary consultant, Edna O'Brien, doesn't think much of that and proposes *In the Beginning*. This has too much of a religious inflection for my taste. The subtitle will be *A Life in the Twentieth Century*, and vol ii will be called *Unfinished Business*.

On the 31st we went to Washington to see the new millennium in, arriving in time for luncheon with Robert. I had been surprised to receive the invitation for New Year's Eve at the White House. In the Clinton years we have never been asked to a state dinner. We have dined twice at the White House—once at a farewell dinner for Pamela Harriman on her way to Paris (Pam put our names on the guest list) and once at a dinner for Arts and Humanities medallists (as a medallist, I had to be invited). Both times, though, I was seated next to Hillary.

Alexandra thinks, probably correctly, that we owe our invitation this time to George Stevens, who is co-producing the millennial entertainment with Quincy Jones.

We stayed at the Hay-Adams and made our way to the White House around six o'clock. A reporter asked me how I would sum up the last millennium. I said, "I'm glad it's over." A long cocktail hour followed, during which we were astonished by how few of the other guests we even recognized. I suppose most were big contributors. We talked to Chris Dodd and his charming new wife, Ted and Vicky and Jean Kennedy, the Fred Duttons, the Bob Shrums, a few others.

At dinner Alexandra, sitting between Alan Greenspan, chairman of the Federal Reserve, and Jim Wolfinson, president of the World Bank, held for a moment the financial future of the world in her hands. Greenspan, whom I have known slightly for years, has been much humanized by his marriage to Andrea Mitchell. He came over and talked cordially to me for some minutes, and Alexandra found him an engaging dinner partner.

Bill Clinton was seated between Sophia Loren and Elizabeth Taylor. Liz Taylor was rather pathetic. She needs two men, one on each side, to support her when she walks, and she spent much of the time in a wheelchair.

Around ten o'clock we were summoned to buses that took us to the Mall in front of the Lincoln Memorial. Fortunately the temperature was in the forties; had it been really cold, the evening would have been unbearable. As one who detests country music and rock-and-roll, I found it pretty unbearable anyway. The Spielberg film was perfunctory, and Clinton's speech, just before midnight, was prosaic at a moment that demanded poetry. I said later to George Stevens that they should have got a Democratic Peggy Noonan to write it. He said, "Bob Shrum did a fine draft, but the people at the White House wanted a programmatic speech." At a time when the world was ready for wisdom, the speech sounded like a trailer for a State of the Union message. The fireworks at midnight, however, were superior, and the flashes of light cascading up the Washington Monument were smashing.

Buses took us back to the White House, where several hundred additional post-dinner guests appeared. We returned to the Hay-Adams about 3:30 A.M.

The presidential contests are returning to normal. The media, having built up Bradley and McCain in their quest for a story, are now tearing them down. Both insurgencies have stalled. It looks now as if Gore and Bush will have nominations in hand by the ides of March. The country will then be in for seven more months of boring politics.

August 15

This is my first entry since 22 January last. On 23 January it occurred to me that, if volume one (*Innocent Beginnings*) of *A Life in the Twentieth Century* was to be published in the year 2000, I would have to cast everything else aside and concentrate on finishing The Book. "Everything else" did not include foreign travel; but it included correspondence, filing, journal-keeping and other routine time-consuming occupations.

I am laboring away at the book. I think the thing I most enjoy in my old age is writing. I like solving problems of structure. I like the ease of revision made possible by the word processor. I like the search for the right word to delineate the right shade of meaning. My eternal struggle is to find time to write.

Politics. By the end of January Bush and Gore had repelled their challengers (McCain and Bradley). The last remaining suspense came from the choice of running mates. Bush confined his search to Richard Cheney, who, after interviewing the other candidates, proceeded to choose himself. Cheney is a disarming but deeply conservative fellow— we ran into him exiting from an elevator in the Waldorf Towers sometime in the winter and had a friendly, non-political talk. This was before he was anointed. After the Republican convention he was given a $20,000,000 farewell present by the oil company (Halliburton) he has been serving for the last half-dozen years. This has provoked mighty little criticism, but it seems to me a pretty large bribe.

Cheney's wife Lynne was Reagan's director of the National Endowment for the Humanities. She was a great admirer of *The Disuniting of America* until she met me, and I fear I swiftly disillusioned her. She was holding forth on the great threat of multiculturalism. I said that even a greater threat, to my mind, was monoculturalism, especially as propounded by born-again zealots and imposed on small-town school and library boards (see pp. 163–166 in the revised edition of *Disuniting*). Lynne did not agree. She could be a liability for the Republican ticket, but thus far she has been muzzled. She does, however, show much irritation when questioned about her lesbian daughter.

The Republicans held their convention in Philadelphia. The Bush people did an effective job in putting a human face on their retrograde party. The diehard right was banished; the religious right was subdued; and the stage, though not the auditorium, was crowded with minorities. Young Bush gave a creditable acceptance address moving the party toward the middle of the road. Sixty percent of his words might have been spoken by Al Gore.

Gore had meanwhile confined his vice presidential search to Warren Christopher, who, unlike Cheney, did not end by choosing himself. On 13 July I faxed Chris a letter making the case for George Mitchell. He replied almost at once, describing himself as "a longtime George Mitchell fan" and calling him "not only a fine man but a first-rate speaker." This gave me hope.

I had concluded my letter by wondering why Chris Dodd was not mentioned for VP—"a far better man than his sanctimonious colleague from Connecticut." But Christopher, according to the press, recommended to Gore that same sanctimonous colleague, which shows how much influence I have.

On Monday 7 August Gore announced his vice presidential choice: Senator Joseph Lieberman of Connecticut. I was so outraged that for a moment I thought I would not be able to support the ticket. In this mood I wrote a protest statement, which wiser heads (Robert, Bill vanden Heuvel) prevailed on me to cancel the next day.

But I was still outraged. Lieberman is not only sanctimonious but a hypocrite—the "conscience of the Senate" got there by defeating a fine liberal Lowell Weicker in one of the nastiest campaigns in recent history. Lieberman is also president of the Democratic Leadership Council, the Republican wing of the Democratic party, and even more conservative than Gore, who is himself too conservative for my taste (or for his father's, who whispered to me at a Democratic banquet in Washington seven or eight years ago, after I said to him how proud he must be of young Albert, "Yes, I am very proud—but I wish he were a little more liberal").

I began to feel like the old Gold Democrat Senator David B Hill, who, asked how he viewed Bryan's nomination in 1896, replied, "I am still a Democrat—very still." For a moment I even wished I could vote for Ralph Nader. I had heard part of his acceptance speech at the Green Party convention one morning when I was doing my exercises, and I was rather taken by the thoughtfulness of his remarks. He spoke about leadership, for example, and said that the real task of leadership was to produce, not followers, but leaders. I liked too his argument that the corporations have taken over both major parties. But I disagree with his trade policy, and his statement that he would have voted for Clinton's impeachment and conviction shows a totally inadequate understanding of the constitutional standards for impeachment.

Nearly everyone to whom I talked—Bill vanden Heuvel, Sean Wilentz, John Morton Blum, George McGovern, Arthur Ross—was equally concerned about Lieberman. Andrew Wylie told me Philip Roth's reaction. After receiving a number of press calls asking what he thought of Lieberman, Philip said, "I am considering issuing a statement: 'Mr. Roth is not available for interviews. He has gone to the hospital to have his foreskin sewed back on.'"

About 12:50 this morning I received a call from Al Gore. He was calling, he said, from Rachel Carson's study in Springdale, Pennsylvania.

After an exchange of civilities, I said that I was not terribly happy about his vice presidential choice. He asked why. I said that there is little more insufferable than self-appointed guardians of the public morals.

"I don't know Lieberman. But he strikes me as the most sanctimonious member of the Senate. And I remember his dirty campaign against Lowell Weicker."

Gore said, "Lieberman was fourth on my list. I came very close to naming John Edwards, though he has only been in politics for 17 months. But then something happened last weekend when I was in the Hamptons. Someone came up to me and whispered urgently, 'You can't pick Joe Lieberman.' I asked why. He said after a moment, 'Well, because of his Clinton speech.' But I felt that there was a gap between the urgency of his whispered advice and the reason he offered. I felt that there was something behind it coming from some dark, formless place." He implied a lurking anti-semitism.

I asked, "Was the whisperer a Jew?" thinking that many Jews are unhappy about Lieberman, fearing a resurgence of anti-semitism. Gore said, "No. He was an African-American. . . . The incident stayed with me when I approached the final decision. I discovered that I was unconsciously weighing Lieberman's negatives unduly—more than I was doing with the others. Then I began to think that the choice of Lieberman might make the country feel better about itself. It would be a leap of faith, but it was a bet I would like to place on the fundamental decency of the American people."

I said, "Well, it's done now. But I hope you will get him to stop invoking God all the time." Al said, "I've talked to Joe about that, and he understands. But I know how he felt. When I was named Vice President, I began the press conference with a prayer."

He then told the following story. While he was in one room making the final decision, his staff were in another room trying to guess how it would come out. They decided to spin the bottle—and four times the bottler named Lieberman. Then they tried flipping a coin—and four times the coin named Lieberman. I can't believe this story and fear it is one more of Al's exaggerations.

Then he said, "The reason I'm calling you is that I need your help. I need language for my acceptance address saying that our history shows that when we do the right thing, however unpopular it might be, we will be the better off for it. I am turning to you because you know our history and our traditions."

I said, "Wouldn't remarks along that line seem unduly defensive? After all, the choice of Lieberman has been a political success thus far. And you can't equate, say, the choice of Lieberman with Lincoln's Emancipation Proclamation." He laughed at this and denied defensiveness. "I was wrong to have begun by saying that the American people have a chance to make history by voting for the ticket. But the selection of Lieberman was a great learning experience. The reaction was that it was a bold choice, a gutsy choice. It made me feel proud of our country. It seemed to break through shapeless fears. There is a sense of exhilaration at this historic opportunity, at this levelling of barriers. It goes far beyond Jews—to women, to African-Americans, to ecology. And I believe that commitment creates its own possibilities and brings unforeseen benefits." He mentioned a quote from the introduction to *Earth in the Balance*. "I want to say something about this, but I am having difficulty in finding words to express what is in my mind. We can do the right thing, and we will be better for it. I am looking for ways to rekindle the American spirit."

The Vice President signed off about 1:25. He has good phrases, but he also has a tendency toward mysticism. I weakly agreed to try my hand at something, but I really don't understand what he wants or what he was talking about. I think he is making a mistake if he goes out of his way to defend the Lieberman choice. As I said in response to one of his vague generalities. "There are two separable problems. One is the levelling of barriers to whole categories of citizens. The other is the question of the individual beneficiary of such levelling."

The Democrats convened in Los Angeles. On Monday the 14th Bill Clinton made his farewell address and knocked the ball out of the park. The American people have come to terms with Clinton. They regard him as a rogue, but an endearing rogue and a pretty good President. If he were eligible to run for a third term, he would be easily reelected.

Tuesday was Liberal Night—Ted Kennedy, Caroline, Jesse Jackson, Bill Bradley. Ted was not at his best, too constrained by his assignment, which was to talk about health care. Jesse was his usual rousing self, and Bradley, to my astonishment, gave a stirring, vigorous liberal address—if he had talked that way during the primaries, he would have done a good deal better.

Wednesday was Lieberman, self-satisfied, unctuous, with feeble jokes. Mr. Integrity is discarding all his views that conflict with Gore and the party platform. The rightwing, which applauded his designation, is now denouncing him as an opportunist.

Thursday was Gore himself. He did surprisingly well. He looked classy and speeded up his delivery, thereby avoiding the slow, measured, condescending tone that has marred so many of his speeches. Delegates left greatly encouraged, though Bush is still ahead in the polls. It will be a more interesting election than I expected.

August 28

Joe Lieberman, though he refrained in his acceptance speech from attributing his nomination to the personal intervention of the Almighty, cannot keep his wretched sanctimony out of the campaign. On 27 August (I am writing this now on the 29th) he gave a speech in Detroit declaring that belief in God is the basis of morality and of the American republic. One wonders why the Founding Fathers did not bother to mention God in the Constitution. "As a people," Holy Joe opined, "we need to reaffirm our faith and renew the dedication of our nation and ourselves to God and God's purpose." Lincoln had it better when he reminded the nation in his second inaugural, "The Almighty has his own purposes." The Lieberman rule would brand all agnostics and atheists as incapable of morality and of American citizenship. In spite of all this, the Lieberman nomination continues to work politically. And his Jewish faith still protects him from criticism.

I have not yet started volume 2 and am worried about finding time to do it. Though we spent a month abroad earlier this year and will leave next Sunday for another fortnight, it seems never enough for Alexandra.

Being so much younger, she does not understand the finitude of time. It is the one major contention in an otherwise cheerful marriage. She thinks I don't respect her preferences, but she seems oblivious to my problem, which is the imminence of death.

September 2

I note that in recalling high and low points in the months when the journal was suspended I neglected to mention one very surprising development: a letter from Neil Rudenstine informing me that the Harvard Corporation had voted to confer an honorary degree on me in 2001!

I know that my name has been proposed through the years, most recently by Bob Reischauer and Doris Kearns Goodwin. I know also that it has been regularly rejected. I assume, without knowing, that I had been vetoed by the Harvard American historians, the Handlin gang, or that Republicans among the overseers and the Corporation felt that, if any member of the class of '38 should be honored, it should be Cappie Weinberger. Perhaps unworthy suspicions, both of them.

Why did I forget to record the honorary degree? I suppose that, while I am delighted to get it, my life would not be deeply marred if I never got it. Honors are sometime things based on external considerations. I know better than the bestowers whether I deserve them or not.

October 1

On Monday the 18th I was invited to a dinner given by Ambassador Sharma, the Indian ambassador to the UN, for the Indian foreign minister Jaswant Singh. The other guests were Kofi and Nan Annan, Henry and Nancy Kissinger, Dick and Kati Holbrooke, Bill and Wendy Luers, Frank and Christine Wisner, Nicky and Sheila Platt, Fareed Zakaria and Ismail Merchant—a classy crowd.

Kati Marton told me that she and Dick had given a dinner for George Bush (the elder) and Barbara when they were in New York a few months ago. She sat next to Poppy and asked, "What do you suppose your son will do if he loses the election?" GB answered, "Well, I have another son, Jeb, and I think he will be ripe for national politics." He continued in this vein, Kati told me, for several minutes. This seems to confirm the widespread suspicion that the Bush parents always expected Jeb to be the main contender in the next generation.

Meanwhile the campaigns roll on.

I can't understand why Gore is not a dozen points ahead. Here is a time of unexampled prosperity, no great demand for a change, general approve of the national direction. If Clinton could run again, he would be triumphantly reelected. Yet Bush, after a post-convention relapse, is rising again in the polls. Why? Because Bush makes voters feel comfortable while Gore makes them feel uncomfortable?

October 4

Last night—the First Debate. It was boring. I doubt that it changed many votes. I think that Bush's performance reassured his followers, and that Gore's performance somewhat disappointed his followers. Gore's make-up gave him the appearance of a fugitive from Madame Tussaud, and too often we saw his charmless, know-it-all side. Also he kept repeating various mantras (Bush did too), and in his artificial quest for humanization Gore named various individuals allegedly in the audience (we never saw them) as examples of the injustices he promises to remedy. Bush maintained his poise and avoided syntactical fumbles but did not score as often or heavily as Gore.

We saw the debate at Norman Mailer's. "I despise them both," Norman said, "—the groaner and the whiner. I'm going to vote for Ralph Nader. . . . But I think Bush will probably gain a point or two in the polls." The people at the Mailer's were all pro-Gore, but their candidate's repeated anecdotal invocations of people in the audience produced increasing hilarity.

October 17

Sean Wilentz, my anti-impeachment co-conspirator, had talked me into giving a paper at a conference at Princeton on "The Progressive Tradition: Politics, Culture and History." President Clinton was somehow persuaded to give the keynote address on Thursday 5 October.

I had a few moments' chat with Clinton before he spoke. He mentioned that he had seen CNN's recent replay of the first Kennedy-Nixon debate. We had seen it too, and I said that I hoped Al Gore had also seen it. "He should take a look at Kennedy's expression when Nixon was talking," I said, "—courteous and impassive, with occasional faint flickers of an ironic smile. Much better than the Vice President's groans and sighs and grimaces." Clinton said, "I couldn't agree with you more."

When Clinton entered the Helm auditorium in McCosh Hall, the audience erupted in a standing ovation with wild shouts of applause. I could not help thinking that a year ago Clinton was fighting impeachment—and now he was getting this uproarious reception on a rather conservative campus. If it were not for the 22nd Amendment, he would be trumphantly reelected. The American people, it seems to me, have come to terms with the Clinton phenomenon. They see him as a rogue, but as an endearing rogue and as a pretty good president; also they have grown accustomed to his face.

We went to dinner at Al and Louise Hirshfeld's to hear the second debate.

This time Gore overreacted to criticisms of his performance in the first debate. Instead of being condescending and know-it-all, he kept agreeing with Bush and quite failed to take advantage of Bush's weak points and errors. By the end, I felt a certain pathos about Gore. I felt that he knew he was losing and could not understand why. Bush, on the other hand, became almost smug at the end. He has what his father used to call the "big mo." He gives the impression of knowing who he is. Al Gore does not seem to know who he is.

I received yesterday a letter in that once so familiar handwriting— the first in a number of years. I had written Nancy Bush Ellis after the

Republican convention saying how proud she must be about her nephew and praising his acceptance speech and his success in putting a human face on his retrograde party. She writes, "I'm confident that we have the better man—very himself, honorable and *disciplined*—and such a touch with people. Better campaigner really than his father if not quite as noble a person." I wonder at "disciplined"—on the other hand, he does seem to remember his briefings.

October 18

Yesterday morning Hillary spoke at the Council on Foreign Relations. Big turnout. Ted Sorensen gave a witty introduction. Hillary's prepared remarks were perhaps a little long and, for this audience, a little weighted on the feminist side, but they went over well and the question period was a triumph. Oz Elliott exclaimed to me, "Wasn't she fantastic!"

Can she win? Lazio is so complete a twerp—but so many people hate Hillary. I don't understand why educated and professional women like Alexandra and like Sidney Urquhart, otherwise intelligent and tolerant, are so unreasonably possessed by Hillary-hatred. It has become impossible to talk to Alexandra about her. But I cannot extract a clear statement of why they all detest her.

The third debate took place in the evening. Gore was at his best, and he won by a technical KO, or so it seemed to me. Bush was like a battered fighter clinging to that ropes. He answered questions by repeating that he was a leader and could bring people together, but was vacuous about all substantive questions. Yet some polls report that it was a draw or even that Bush won! Robert thought it was a draw.

November 4

The first returns on *Innocent Beginnings* are coming in. *Kirkus Reviews*, *Booklist* and *Publishers Weekly* all printed semi-raves, and the *Economist,* breaking the publication date, has a wonderful review in the

28 October issue. It was apparently written by a Washington lawyer named Dan Davidson, and it could hardly have been better. It concludes by comparing the book to *The Education of Henry Adams*— which, of course, is the comparison I have always had secretly in mind. The actual publication date is 14 November.

Now for the election. The level of debate does not improve. Bush, after all his self-serving talk about restoring dignity and honor to the White House, has been caught suppressing the story of his own arrest thirty years ago for drunken driving and then (apparently) lying about it to a Dallas newspaperman. What is even worse is his statement on 2 November: his plan for social security, Bush said, "frightens some in Washington. Because they want the federal government controlling the social security like it's some kind of federal program. We understand differently." Bush's ignorance about social security ought to have the same impact that Gerald Ford's liberation of Eastern Europe from communism had on the 1976 election.

The trouble is that the alternative to ignorant Bush is strident Gore, so often depicted on television shouting at the top of his voice, "I want to work for you. I will fight for you," etc. Not a happy choice, though one I have no personal difficulty about making. But what will the electorate do?

November 11

My pre-election predictions were highly uncertain, varying according to mood. Two weeks before the election I thought Bush would win. Then one became aware of a Gore surge, especially after Bush amazingly denied that social security was a federal program. My last prediction the day of the election was that Bush would win the popular vote and Gore the electoral vote. Of course precisely the reverse may have happened.

I lunched with Stephen on election day. He has been a consistent optimist, resting his case on the state of the economy, but he was less optimistic today. All hands agree that Gore has not been a good campaigner, that he has not exploited the economic issue as he should have done, that he has not used Clinton intelligently, that he shouts too much and comes over as strident and hectoring, etc., etc.

We heard the early results at Dick and Danielle Gardner's apartment. Ted Sorensen was there, and we reflected on the elections we had been through over the last forty years. We were immensely cheered by the news that Gore was leading in Florida, Pennsylvania and Michigan. The first exit polls seemed to point to a Gore victory.

Alexandra had a cold and was feeling poorly, so we left around 11 P.M., missing Tina Brown's party at Elaine's. When we went to bed, Gore seemed still in the lead. But I awoke Wednesday morning to discover not only that the networks were proclaiming the election "too close to call" but that Gore had conceded in the night and then had retracted his concession, memorably remarking, when Bush protested, "You don't have to get snippy about it."

Who in the world could have advised Gore to offer this premature concession? The result has been to make it easy for the Republicans to paint him as a sore loser who knew that Bush had won but decided not to do the noble thing and admit it.

On Thursday afternoon Katharine Graham gave a splendid party for the book. It was filled with old friends, and we had a fine time. Much talk about Florida, Jack Valenti said, "If a scriptwriter had outlined this as a plot for a movie, he would have been laughed out of the studio." At one point, Kay called for order, quieted the noisy multitude and gave a wonderful endorsement of the book—a far better review, it seems to the author, than the moderately snide notice contributed by Jonathan Yardley in Sunday's *Washington Post*. Yardley's review was less of the book than of the author, whom he indicts as a name dropper, social climber, celebrity hound, Kennedy toady, etc., etc.

We had been invited that evening both to Tina Brown's party at the British Embassy for Simon Schama's new book and to a presidential dinner celebrating the 200th anniversary of the White House, and had regretted both in view of Kay's party. Then Kay, informed that the White House dinner would be a historic occasion, arranged that the three of us could come late.

We arrived at the White House after the guests had been seated in the East Room and in time for the procession of ex-Presidents plus the soon-to-be ex-President and their wives toward the dais. It was, I guess, a historic occasion. Never before had three ex-Presidents and their wives dined at the White House together. After dessert the ex-Presidents spoke. To my astonishment, Ford was the best—funny, modest, honest, touching. Clinton came in second. Bush began promisingly, thanking "our hosts—President Clinton and Senator Clinton" and wasn't too bad. Carter, who seemed to be the only speaker without a text, relied on inspiration, and inspiration failed him. Both Ford and Carter, opponents in 1976, stressed the depth of their friendship today. During the proceedings Barbara Bush and Hillary Clinton several times had whispered exchanges of what appeared to be cordial comments. Also to my surprise.

I shook hands with Bush and with Carter and had a few moments of conversation with Clinton about Florida after dinner. In 1996, Bill said, he received 45 percent of the overseas absentee ballots in Florida, and he was confident that Gore would do better; so he had advised Gore to "hang in there." Bill looked well and ran things with his usual brio.

November 17

The Florida roller-coaster rushes on. Very odd succession of sensations: in the morning, Bush is winning; in the late afternoon, Gore is granted a reprieve and is still in there. I suppose Bush will win in the end. But if he wins when votes are still uncounted, it will be a regarded as a steal.

November 28

On Sunday the 26th the *Times Book Review* came out with my face on the cover, surrounded by dignitaries of the past (Lippmann, Alsop, De Voto, Frankfurter, Bundy, Bohlen, MacLeish), all under the title "The Age of Schlesinger." Inside was a long review by Max Frankel, generally positive though with enough digs along the way to establish objectivity. Louis Auchincloss recalled Gore Vidal's advice to authors:

"Don't read reviews. Measure them." By this criterion Max's review is very helpful.

[Monday afternoon] Bill vanden Heuval organized a party for the book at the Century Association. It was a grand affair and great fun. Afterward Jean [Smith] invited twenty or so people to her flat for a buffet supper. We heard Gore give a brief statement of his determination to keep on fighting for a full count of the Florida vote. He was dignified and effective, especially as compared to Bush's speech the day before claiming victory; Bush looked like a frightened ventriloquist's dummy.

INDEX

ABOUT THE EDITORS

Andrew Schlesinger is the author of *Veritas: Harvard College and the American Experience* (2005). After his graduation from Harvard in 1970, he taught high school in Santa Fe, then worked as a staff reporter for the *Nashville Tennessean* and the *Rocky Mountain News*. In 1980 he joined ABC News in their documentary division, where his film scripts won two Emmy Awards and a Writers Guild Award. His documentary work has appeared on PBS, HBO, CNN and A&E. He lives in Cambridge, Massachusetts.

Stephen Schlesinger is the former Director of the World Policy Institute at the New School. In the early 1970s, he edited and published *The New Democrat Magazine* and later spent four years as a staff writer at *Time* magazine. For twelve years, he served as New York State Governor Mario Cuomo's speechwriter and foreign policy advisor. He is the author of three books, including *Act of Creation: The Founding of The United Nations,* for which he won the 2004 Harry S. Truman Book

Award; *Bitter Fruit: The Story of the U.S. Coup in Guatemala* (with Stephen Kinzer), a *New York Times* notable book; and *The New Reformers*. He is a frequent contributor to magazines and newspapers, including the *Washington Post,* the *Los Angeles Times, The Nation,* and *The New York Observer*. He lives in New York City.